CANADIAN TAXATION OF LIFE INSURANCE

by

Tax, Retirement and Estate Planning Services
Manulife Financial

7th Edition

Editors

Florence Marino, B.A., LL.B., TEP
Assistant Vice President, Tax, Retirement and Estate Planning Services, Kitchener
John Natale, B.COMM, LL.B.
Assistant Vice President, Tax, Retirement and Estate Planning Services and Advanced Sales Concepts, Kitchener

CARSWELL®

ISBN 978-0-7798-6074-6

A cataloguing record for this publication is available from Library and Archives Canada.

Printed in the United States by Thomson Reuters.

THOMSON REUTERS

CARSWELL, A DIVISION OF THOMSON REUTERS CANADA LIMITED

One Corporate Plaza
2075 Kennedy Road
Toronto, Ontario
M1T 3V4

Customer Relations
Toronto 1-416-609-3800
Elsewhere in Canada/U.S. 1-800-387-5164
Fax 1-416-298-5082
www.carswell.com
Contact www.carswell.com/contact

PREFACE TO THE SEVENTH EDITION

Life Insurance is considered a crucial component of many estate plans, providing for such traditional needs as dependant support, estate equalization, buy-sell needs, and funding estate liabilities. Modern insurance products can satisfy these traditional needs as well as a number of more innovative estate planning strategies. Insurance products have evolved into sophisticated, and complex, financial instruments combining elements of protection and investment. As insurance products have evolved, so, too, has their tax treatment. Insurance products are subject to a specialized tax regime which affords many insurance products a unique tax status. Terms of art such as "exempt life insurance" and "prescribed annuity contract" hint at the privileged tax status of certain of these insurance products. Accordingly, an understanding of the taxation of life insurance products is critical to many estate plans.

Significant changes are on the horizon for exempt life insurance, prescribed annuity contracts and many of the policyholder tax rules governing them. Draft legislation was released on August 23, 2013 to modernize the rules governing exempt life insurance policies and prescribed annuity contracts. Also, some specific measures were announced in the 2013 federal budget to eliminate the tax benefits of two particular leveraged life insurance arrangements — 10/8 plans and leveraged insured annuities.

It is hoped that this text will provide the reader with useful information pertaining to insurance products, the tax treatment of life insurance, and some of the estate planning strategies involving insurance. The reader is, of course, cautioned that the information contained herein is of a general nature and one should retain expert professional advice before engaging in any particular transaction.

This seventh edition of the text is current to August 31, 2013 including numerous recent technical interpretations from the CRA, relevant Court decisions, and enacted and proposed legislative changes to that date.

The editors would like to thank colleagues in Manulife Financial's Tax, Retirement and Estate Planning Services who devoted long hours to preparing this text. Thank you to:

Hemal Balsara
Joël Campagna
Barbara Cook
Nick Fabiano
Dianna Flannery
Gordon Giacomin
Jason Giuricich
Diane Hamel

Jon Hreljac
Jennifer Janeczko
Serge Lessard
Ian Taylor
Dereka Thibault

The editors would also like to thank Stephen Krupicz, AVP Actuarial and Underwriting Consultants for his assistance regarding Chapter 1 and 2, Caroline McKay, Associate Counsel, Advanced Markets of John Hancock Life Insurance Company (U.S.A.) for her assistance regarding United States estate and gift taxes, and Rita Levato of McKellar Structured Settlements for reviewing Chapter 18 "Taxation of Structured Settlements".

TABLE OF CONTENTS

Chapter 3: — TAXATION OF LIFE INSURANCE POLICIES, DISPOSITIONS, AND SELECTED VALUATION ISSUES

Chapter 12: — INSURANCE AND CHARITABLE GIVING

Chapter 14: — TAXATION OF ANNUITY CONTRACTS

Chapter 15: — DEFERRED ANNUITIES

1 — The History of Life Insurance Policy Taxation and Current Legislative Proposals

Updated by Florence Marino, B.A., LL.B., TEP and Stephen Krupicz, F.S.A., F.C.I.A.

1.1 — Introduction

The definition of a life insurance policy found in Provincial Insurance Acts is: a contract between the policyholder and an insurer under which premiums are paid and as a result the insurer agrees to pay a certain sum to a designated beneficiary at a future time or when a specific contingency dependent on human life occurs (e.g., the death of the person whose life is insured under the policy). Life insurance generally provides for the financial security of the deceased's dependants or indemnifies financial obligations or losses arising from death. Provincial Insurance Acts also include annuities in the definition of "life insurance". For income tax purposes, life insurance includes annuity contracts as well as segregated fund policies. This chapter will deal with what is conventionally viewed as life insurance.

In order to attain a reasonable understanding of the system of taxation of life insurance policies and policyholders, it is important to analyze life insurance from a historical perspective and also to examine the *Income Tax Act* and its evolution. In order to appreciate where we are today, we must look at where we've come from.

Developing a fair tax system for life insurance policyholders has proven to be a significant challenge. There are many issues peculiar to life insurance policies and the life insurance industry in general, including:

- the contingent and long-term nature of a life insurance policy;
- the question of whether there should be taxation of mortality gains;
- the issue of how income earned from investment of policy reserves should be taxed;
- the question of who should be responsible for paying tax in respect of the policy, namely the policyholder or the insurer.

Before 1968, life insurance policies and policyholders were exempt from tax. No attempt was made to tax the mortality gain on the death of the person whose life was insured under a policy nor any investment gain arising on death or during life. There was no tax on a disposition of the policy, such as by way of a surrender, nor was tax payable on any other termination of the life insurance policy. A key date or turning point came with the Carter Commission and the subsequent federal budget of 1968.

1.2 — Pre-1968 History

Subsection 3(1) of the *Income War Tax Act* of 1917 provided an explicit exemption from taxation for policyholders in respect of "the proceeds of life insurance policies paid upon the death of the person insured, or payments made or credited to the insured on life insurance endowment or annuity contracts upon the maturity of the term mentioned in the contract or upon the surrender of the contract."

In 1948 this explicit exemption was removed. However, it was made clear by the Minister of Finance, Douglas C. Abbott, that gains realized on death, maturity or surrender of life insurance policies were not to be subject to tax. This approach remained unquestioned until the Carter Commission released its report on February 24, 1967.

1.3 — The Carter Commission Report

The Carter Commission, a royal commission on taxation, was appointed to investigate and make recommendations for reform of the tax system. It recommended far reaching changes to the system affecting all sectors. Its recommendations for the taxation of life insurance considered the perspectives of both the insurer and the policyholder. In summary, dealing with policyholder taxation, the Commission recommended:

- That life insurance policy premiums should not ordinarily be deductible in computing the policyholder's income;
- That the investment income accumulated for the benefit of the policyholder should be included in the policyholder's income in the year in which it is accumulated. However, as an alternative, it was suggested that a form of withholding tax could be used under which insurers would pay tax in respect of investment income on policy reserves;
- That policy dividends should be included in the income of the policyholder;
- That, after a transition period, mortality gains and losses should be included in the income of policyholders. It was thought that the introduction of this change should be postponed because the other measures recommended by the Commission would in themselves involve a substantial change in the tax treatment of life insurance and that a transitional period should be allowed.

1.4 — The 1968 Federal Budget

Following the Carter Commission report, the 1968 federal budget was brought down on October 22, 1968 by Finance Minister Edgar Benson. The proposals set out a defined structure for the taxation of life insurance but did not go as far as the recommendations made by the Carter Commission. Notwithstanding this, the proposals put forth in the 1968 budget represented a very significant change from the tax treatment prior to that time. Mr. Benson stated in his budget speech as follows:

> It is essential...in terms of equity between those who save in the form of insurance policies and those who save in other forms, to levy some tax on the investment income which policyholders receive through the insurance companies, either in the form of policy dividends or otherwise. The Royal Commission proposed valuing these elements of investment income each year — whether or not received directly by the policyholder — and taxing them directly to him. We have worked out a much simpler and more practical method which should achieve substantially similar equity.[1]

A. — Taxation of policy gains on disposition

These proposals were eventually finalized in 1969 by R.S.C. 1968-1969 c. 44. The legislation introduced the concept of a "disposition" of a life insurance policy and brought about a realization of the accumulated investment income in respect of the policy on such a disposition. Paragraph 79D(1)(c) of the Act, as it then read, included the following events as dispositions of a policy: a surrender or termination, a disposition by operation of law only or the maturity of the policy. It excluded termination of the policy due to the individual life insured's death, a collateral assignment of a policy or a lapse with a subsequent reinstatement within 60 days and for 1973 and subsequent taxation years termination by reason of total and permanent disability (added by R.S.C. 1973-1974, c. 30). Also, subsection 79D(2) of the Act deemed a disposition to occur upon the policyholder becoming entitled to a policy dividend.

Where a life insurance policy is annuitized (i.e. proceeds are made payable in the form of an annuity contract before the death of the individual life insured), subsection 79D(7) of the Act deemed the annuity contract or payments not to be proceeds of disposition of an interest in a policy, the payments to be regarded as payments under an annuity contract and the purchase price of the annuity to be the "adjusted cost basis" ("ACB") of the contract immediately before the first payment. Thus annuitizations were not taxable events. The "proceeds of disposition" in excess of the "ACB" of the policy upon such dispositions were required by subsection 79D(1)(a) of the Act to be included in the policyholder's income in the year.

The "proceeds of disposition" in respect of dividends received were deemed to be the amount of dividends to which the policyholder was entitled. (This was later amended by the 1992 Technical Bill, C92 which received Royal Assent June 10, 1993, for policy dividends received or receivable in taxation years that begin after December 20, 1991 to deal with the case where part of the dividend is automatically applied to pay a premium or repay a policy loan in accordance with the terms of the policy. This amendment ensured that such internal policy transactions do not attract double taxation.) For certain types of dispositions (gifts, distributions from a corporation or by operation of law only to a person not dealing at arm's length with

---

[1]Debates, House of Commons Canada, 1st Session 28th Parliament Vol. II, pp. 1686-1687.

the policyholder) the proceeds of disposition were deemed to be the "value" of the interest (subsection 79D(8) of the Act). "Value" was defined in paragraph 79D(10)(h) as cash surrender value or, if there is no cash surrender value associated with a policy, nil.

The "ACB" of an interest in a policy was defined in paragraph 79D(10)(a) as the aggregate of the cost to the policyholder of acquiring all of the policyholder's interests in the policy and all amounts paid on account of premiums under the policy in excess of all proceeds of disposition before that time except to the extent that the proceeds were required to be included in income prior to that time.

B. — Relief for existing policies

Relieving provisions were included in subsection 79D(9) of the Act for policies held on October 22, 1968. For such policies, the new rules applied to dispositions made after January 1, 1970 (for individual policyholders) or in the 1970 taxation year (for corporate policyholders). In order to avoid retroactive taxation on these policies, an alternative calculation of the ACB of such policies was provided so long as these policies were not disposed of prior to the second anniversary date after October 22, 1968 (defined as the policy's "tax anniversary date" under paragraph 79D(10)(f) of the Act). For such policies, the tax anniversary date was the starting point from which taxable policy gains are determined.

For such policies, if the cash surrender value of the policy exceeded the ACB of the policy as determined under the new rules on the tax anniversary date, the policyholder was deemed to have acquired an interest in the policy at that time at a cost equal to the cash surrender value. In determining the cash surrender value and the ACB at that time, any premium due on that date was ignored. Policy dividends payable on that date were taken into account. Where the ACB exceeded the cash surrender value, the policyholder of such a policy was entitled to use the ACB as calculated under the new rules.

1.5 — A New Act

With R.S.C. 1970-71-72 c. 63, the Act was renumbered. Section 148 of the new Act corresponded to section 79D of the old Act.

1.6 — The 1977 Federal Budget

On March 31, 1977 the Honourable Donald S. Macdonald, Minister of Finance, brought down the 1977 federal budget. This budget (reflected in the legislation-Bill C-56, tabled in the House of Commons by Mr. Macdonald on June 15, 1977) proposed to tax the investment income realized by a policyholder on the death of the individual life insured. An exemption for the first $10,000 of gain on death was provided where the taxpayer was the deceased or the deceased's spouse. In addition, the proposals extended the tax net for amounts falling into taxable income by including policy loans in the definition of "disposition." A new tax anniversary date was also proposed.

The attempt to tax a portion of the death benefit proceeds (commonly referred to as the "widows and orphans tax") was met with considerable opposition by both the insurance industry and the public in general. As a result, in a statement made in the House of Commons on October 20, 1977 the Honourable Jean Chretien, then Minister of Finance, announced that the government would not be proceeding with this measure pending further study. The remaining provisions announced in the budget as originally proposed were implemented by Bill C-11, dated November 2, 1977, which received Royal Assent on December 15, 1977.

A. — Policy loans as a disposition

A "policy loan" made after March 31, 1978, was treated as a disposition of an interest in a life insurance policy under subparagraph 148(9)(c)(iv) of the Act. A policy loan was defined in paragraph 148(9)(e) of the Act as an amount advanced by the insurer to a policyholder in accordance with the terms and conditions of the life insurance policy. Therefore, if a policy loan exceeded the ACB of a policy, a taxable policy gain would arise.

The definition of ACB in paragraph 148(9)(a) of the Act was amended to reflect the inclusion of the portion of a policy loan which has been included in income so that the policy gain on a policy loan transaction is not taxed on a later disposition of the policy. While a repayment of a policy loan would not entitle the taxpayer to a refund of tax paid, the amount of the repayment was added to the ACB of the policy (except if the repayment was deductible for income tax purposes pursuant to paragraph 20(1)(hh) of the Act — repayments of inducements or reimbursements). Any interest paid on policy loans (paid after 1977, added by R.S.C. 1977-78, c.32) was considered a "premium" defined in paragraph 148(9)(e.1) of the Act and therefore added to the ACB of the policy. This was so whether or not the interest was deductible for income tax purposes.

B. — New tax anniversary date

Income that accrued within a policy and which was reflected in the cash surrender value of the policy running from the first policy anniversary after March 31, 1977 would become taxable for dispositions after March 31, 1978. A bump up of the ACB of such policies was provided for the amount by which the cash surrender value exceeded the ACB of the policy as defined on the first anniversary date after March 31, 1977. Until the first anniversary date after March 31, 1977, the old rules would apply to any dispositions.

1.7 — The 1981 Federal Budget

On November 12, 1981, the Honourable Allan MacEachen, Deputy Prime Minister and Minister of Finance, presented the 1981 federal budget and a Notice of Ways and Means Motion to Amend the *Income Tax Act*. In relation to life insurance policy taxation there were several significant changes originally proposed. First, it was proposed that policies issued after November 12, 1981 be subject to triennial tax reporting to individual policyholders (and annual tax reporting to corporate policyholders) of investment income accrued within such policies. Second, any remaining untaxed investment income in respect of such policies was to be taxed upon the death of the individual insured under the policy. Third, in respect of a partial disposition of a policy after November 12, 1981, there was to be included in the policyholder's income the amount in excess of the portion of the adjusted cost basis of the policy to which the proceeds relate (resulting in a blended payment of taxable proceeds and ACB as opposed to being able to extract the ACB first). Fourth, in respect of any disposition of a policy after November 12, 1981, the ACB of the policy was to exclude that portion of any premium not attributable to the savings element within the policy (i.e. the mortality costs in relation to the policy).

These proposals were met with a great deal of opposition. Not only were the proposals purporting to tax at least a portion of death benefits under a life insurance policy, something which had been suggested in the Carter Commission Report and tried in 1977, but the measures relating to dispositions after the budget date were to have retroactive application to existing policyholders. The first step in an about face on some of the proposals came by way of a document entitled "Notes on Transitional Arrangements and Adjustments Relating to Tax Measures Announced November 12, 1981" tabled by Mr. MacEachen in the House of Commons on December 18, 1981. In this document the proposal to reduce the ACB of a policy by the mortality costs was confined only to policies issued after November 12, 1981.

Over the course of the next six months, the life insurance industry engaged in extensive consultation with the Minister of Finance regarding these proposals. At the time of the June 28, 1982 federal budget, Mr. MacEachen issued a press release relating specifically to the proposals dealing with the taxation of life insurance. This release carried forward most of the proposals from the 1981 budget but changed the effective date to June 29, 1982. The Minister stated that all pre-June 29, 1982 policies would be unaffected by the proposals, preserving their then current tax status. He also set out the broad outlines of the new rules relating to policies issued after June 28, 1982. He stated that accrual tax reporting would apply to policies which do not qualify as "exempt" policies, that the ACB of the policy would be reduced by mortality costs for policy years commencing on or after June 1, 1985 and that upon a partial withdrawal of the cash value or a policy loan against the cash value, the policyholder would be taxed on the portion of the accumulated income in the policy attributable to the loan or partial surrender. The press release also contained the original proposals relating to the elimination of the capital dividend account for life insurance proceeds which stated that corporations would be allowed to continue to receive life insurance death benefits on a tax-free basis but that for policies purchased after June 28, 1982 these amounts would no longer be permitted to be paid out tax-free to shareholders by way of the capital dividend account.

1.8 — The December 1, 1982 Notice of Ways and Means Motion and December 7, 1982 Bill C-139

After further extensive consultations with the life insurance industry, the final proposals were presented by way of a Notice of Ways and Means Motion to Amend the *Income Tax Act* on December 1, 1982. These were contained in Bill C-139, An Act to Amend the Statute Law Relating to Income Tax (No.2) tabled in the House of Commons on December 7, 1982. At the same time, the Department of Finance released draft *Income Tax Regulations* on the taxation of life insurance policies. Bill C-139 received Royal Assent March 30, 1983 and the associated regulations, were gazetted on November 24, 1983.

This legislation brought about, for the most part, the tax regime governing life insurance policies applicable today. It introduced the concept of an "exempt policy," the extension of accrual taxation to the growth in the accumulating fund of non-exempt policies, the annual reduction in the ACB of such policies by the "net cost of pure insurance" (NCPI), the prorating of the ACB for certain dispositions of a policy, the exclusion of premiums for certain riders and ancillary benefits from ACB, and the expansion of the definition of disposition to include annuitizations for most policies. Policies last acquired prior to December 2, 1982, referred to as "grandfathered policies," are not subject to this regime and therefore retain certain additional tax advantages not available to post-December 1, 1982 policies. However, grandfathered policies may lose their grandfathered status if certain events occur and may become subject to the post December 1, 1982 regime. The final amendments passed into law effective December 2, 1982 are summarized below.

A. — New rules — post-December 1, 1982 policies

i. — Accrual taxation

For non-exempt policies last acquired after December 1, 1982, individual policyholders were required by then subsection 12.2(3) of the Act to include in income on the third anniversary date of the policy, the excess of the accumulating fund over the ACB at that time. Regulation 307(1)(b) generally defines the accumulating fund of a policy as the Maximum Tax Actuarial Reserve ("MTAR") that the insurer may hold for this policy (as defined in Regulation 1401(1)(c)). In general, MTAR is the maximum policy reserve that an insurer can deduct from its income for income tax purposes.

The rules relating to taxation of accrued income (now found at subsection 12.2(1) of the Act) were changed in 1989 to provide for individual policyholder accrual taxation on an annual basis effective for non-exempt life insurance policies last acquired after 1989. The legislation containing these provisions, Bill C-28, received Royal Assent on October 23, 1990. These measures were subsequently amended (by Draft Amendments to the Act introduced on July 13, 1990, included in Bill C-92 which ultimately received Royal Assent on June 10, 1993), to clarify certain items one of which was to modify the definition of "anniversary day" to mean policy anniversary and not calendar year end.

For corporate policyholders of post-December 1, 1982 non-exempt policies, accrual reporting was required annually.

In addition to bringing into income any untaxed amounts which had accrued between the last accrual reporting date and the date of death, non-exempt policies last acquired after December 1, 1982 are deemed to have been disposed of under paragraph 148(2)(b) of the Act for proceeds equal to the accumulating fund. Since the ACB is adjusted on such policies to reflect income reported as a result of accrual taxation, this requires only the investment income earned between the last accrual reporting date and the date of death to be reported and does not include mortality gains.

ii. — "Exempt policies"

The concept of an "exempt policy" was introduced as a compromise to ensure that an exemption from accrual taxation be provided for policies which were seen as having been acquired primarily for insurance protection as opposed to policies acquired for investment accumulation. The test to determine whether a policy qualifies as an exempt policy is performed by comparing the actual policy with a theoretical benchmark "exempt test policy" defined in *Income Tax Regulations* 306 and 307. If the accumulating fund within the actual policy exceeds that of the exempt test policy, the policy will not be considered to be an exempt policy and would be viewed as primarily an investment or savings vehicle subject to accrual taxation. As a result, the exempt test limits the rate at which insurance coverage is funded by limiting the level of tax- sheltered investment earnings relative to the overall death benefit in respect of the policy.

Exempt testing is performed on every policy anniversary. To pass, it must be determined that the policy's accumulating fund has not exceeded, does not exceed and will not exceed the accumulating fund of the benchmark policy. That is, the policy must not only pass the test on each policy anniversary but also on a prospective basis at each anniversary until the individual insured attains age 85, assuming the terms and conditions of the policy do not change. Subsection 306(2) of the Regulations deems a policy that passes the test on its first policy anniversary to have been an exempt policy from issue until that anniversary.

Paragraph 306(3)(d) of the Regulations generally defines the exempt test policy to be an endowment at age 85 policy with a 20 year premium payment period. The accumulating fund of the exempt test policy as set out in Regulation 307 may be summarized as the value of a sinking fund growing at an assumed interest rate minus the cost of insurance that would be required to equal the face amount of the policy at age 85. The accumulating fund value of the exempt test policy is based on the interest rates and mortality rates used by the insurer in designing the actual policy.

To ensure that one cannot defeat the purpose of the exempt test rules, increases in death benefit after issue (either by paid-up additions or by other adjustments, for example, indexing) are subject to certain limitations. Regulation 306(3)(c) provides that increases in death benefit exceeding 8 percent in a policy year result in the deemed issue of a separate exempt test policy for the coverage in excess of 8 percent. The separate exempt test policy would have its own accumulating fund calculated in the same manner as any other exempt test policy. This therefore requires that the accumulating fund be built up gradually in respect of this separate coverage (just as is the case with respect to the original policy) and prevents funding increases in death benefit by a large lump sum payment. In technical interpretation 2001-007922, dated November 2, 2001, the CRA confirmed that all elements of the policy that can be paid out as a death benefit should be included in the calculation of the 8 percent test, including the policy's cash values where the death benefit is composed of the face amount plus any account or fund value.

Another provision, (Regulation 306(4)(b)) prevents large lump- sum deposits to a policy after its seventh anniversary date. This rule provides that if on the tenth or subsequent policy anniversary, the accumulating fund of the policy exceeds 250 percent of the accumulating fund on the third preceding anniversary, then each exempt test policy is deemed to have been issued on the later of the third preceding anniversary and the deemed date of issue of a separate exempt test policy (described above). The end result of this rule is to limit the rate of growth of the accumulating fund of a policy after its seventh policy anniversary.

In July of 1990, the Canadian Life and Health Insurance Association ("CLHIA") became aware that some insurers were interpreting Regulation 306 in such a way as to permit "single premium" universal life policies to be considered exempt policies and as a result recommended wording changes to Regulation 306. Regulation 306 was interpreted by these insurers as permitting an exempt test policy with an increasing death benefit of 8 percent per year, matching the actual policy's death benefit pattern. This permitted larger accumulations of cash value on an exempt basis under such policies than if this interpretation were not taken, and hence the ability to fund a policy with a single lump sum amount.

Regulation 306 was amended in accordance with the CLHIA recommendations which clarified that each exempt test policy is to have a level death benefit based on the current coverage in force at the time the exempt test is performed. That is, increases in coverage after the date of the test would be ignored for purposes of the exempt test. This change was made effective for policies issued after March 26, 1992, effectively grandfathering those policies which had been issued prior to that date pursuant to this interpretation.

If a policy fails the exempt test, Regulations 306(1)(c) and (d) provide that it will always be non-exempt. The one main exception to this rule is provided in Regulation 306(4)(d). This regulation provides that if a life insurance policy ceases to be exempt on a policy anniversary, the policy may be retested 60 days thereafter, giving the policy owner 60 days grace to restore the policy's exempt status.

The onus is generally not placed upon the policyholder to monitor and maintain the exempt status of the policy. Many insurers contractually commit to take steps to keep their policies exempt. This may be done by taking actions up front to ensure exempt status is preserved. For example, the insurer may not allow the deposits into the plan to exceed certain maximum amounts. Alternatively, exempt status could be preserved by taking actions after the fact. For example, such actions may include the following: increasing the death benefit in accordance with the terms and conditions of the policy and the limits prescribed by the regulations described above; reversing premiums paid in the same policy year by forcing any excess premiums into a separate side account (subject to annual accrual taxation) until they can be deposited into the policy; and causing a withdrawal from the cash value of the policy (which may result in taxable policy gains being included in the income of the policyholder). Note, however, in technical interpretation 2006-0181641E5, dated November 5, 2007, the CRA indicated that "a 'premium reversal' appears to result in a partial disposition of the policy under section 148 of the Act." For further discussion refer to section 3.2.B.

iii. — Reduction of ACB by NCPI and the treatment of premiums for certain riders

The ACB of a policy is an important concept when dealing with dispositions of the policy. On a disposition of a policy, the ACB portion attributable to the disposition is received by the policyholder on a tax- free basis. The reduction of the ACB for the NCPI and not adding premiums to the ACB relating to certain riders was a significant development in that it greatly reduced the shelter provided by the ACB on a disposition of the policy.

The definition of ACB in subsection 148(9) (as it then read in clause L at paragraph (a)) provides that the ACB is to be reduced by the NCPI of the policy calculated immediately before the end of each calendar year. The first reduction for NCPI was to be made for the calendar year ending in a taxation year that begins after May 31, 1985. Therefore, for individual policyholders the effective date for excluding the NCPI from ACB was for the calendar year beginning January 1, 1986. For corporate policyholders, the effective date was the same if the corporate year end was December 31.

NCPI is calculated by multiplying the "net amount at risk" under the policy by the probability of death for the year. The 1969–1975 Canadian Institute of Actuaries Select and Ultimate Mortality Tables are used in order to determine the probability of death in respect of the insured under the policy. To determine the net amount at risk under the policy for the year, Regulation 308 provides that either the accumulating fund (determined without regard to any policy loan) or the cash surrender value determined as of the end of the year (whichever is the method regularly followed by the insurer) be subtracted from the death benefit (excluding accidental death benefits but including term insurance riders).

The probability of death increases with age. NCPI therefore will increase with age. The NCPI may become greater than the actual premium paid under a policy resulting in an erosion if not elimination of the ACB of the policy. The ACB of a policy may be reduced to zero. However, no taxable gain would result upon the ACB being reduced to zero unless there is a disposition of the policy.

Premiums paid after May 31, 1985 on post-December 1, 1982 policies for most types of riders and ancillary benefits are excluded from the ACB by virtue of paragraph (c) of the definition of premium at subsection 148(9). For example, premiums paid for the following would not be included in the ACB of the policy: accidental death benefits; disability benefits; sub-standard ratings; cost of converting a term policy to another type of policy; settlement options; and guaranteed insurability benefits. Therefore, only premiums paid in respect of the basic policy, any term insurance riders and paid-up additions would be included in the ACB of post-December 1, 1982 policies.

iv. — Prorating ACB for partial dispositions (withdrawals)

On a partial disposition (i.e. a withdrawal or partial surrender of a policy's cash value) of a post-December 1, 1982 policy subsection 148(4) of the Act requires the ACB to be prorated in accordance with the ratio that the withdrawal is to the accumulating fund of the policy. Prior to the introduction of this rule, all of the ACB was permitted to be withdrawn before taxation was levied on the investment portion of the policy. This is still permitted in respect of policy loans.

v. — Annuitization as a disposition

The annuitization (except at a time when the insured is totally and permanently disabled) of a post-December 1, 1982 policy is a disposition of the policy under paragraph 148(2)(d) of the Act and Regulation 306(1). Subsection 148(6), as it read prior to the new rules, provided that an annuitization did not bring about a disposition of a policy. This subsection was amended to apply only to "grandfathered policies."

B. — Old rules — pre-December 2, 1982 policies ("grandfathered policies")

i. — The tax rules

Grandfathered policies are those which were acquired prior to December 2, 1982. Paragraph 148(10) (c) of the Act provides that the acquisition date of a life insurance policy held continuously since its issue is the later of the day the policy came into force and the day the application was filed with the insurer. Unlike contracts acquired on or after December 2, 1982, grandfathered contracts are not subject to exempt testing (unless the policy has had a prescribed premium as defined in Regulation 309) and as a result there is no accrual tax reporting for grandfathered contracts. It is therefore possible to accumulate larger cash values within a grandfathered policy than under post-December 1, 1982 policies without risk of current taxation on the growth.

Policy gains are only taxed on a disposition of a grandfathered policy. Grandfathered policies have more favourable treatment than post-December 1, 1982 policies in that there is no prorating of the ACB on a partial disposition of the policy, allowing the entire ACB to be extracted from the policy before taxation is levied on the investment portion of the policy. Also, for grandfathered policies, the full amount of premiums paid, including those for riders and ancillary benefits under the policy, are included in calculating the ACB of the policy and there is no reduction to the ACB made for NCPI. A higher ACB provides a greater tax shelter to the policy owner on a disposition of the policy. However, a higher ACB is a negative attribute if the policy is not disposed of and has a corporate beneficiary.

The higher ACB of the policy would reduce any capital dividend account credit permitted.

Subsection 148(6) of the Act provides that the conversion of a grandfathered policy to an annuity pursuant to a right to do so under the contract does not trigger a disposition of the policy. Also, the annuity would not be subject to annual accrual taxation resulting in any policy gain being spread evenly over the lifetime of the annuity payments. Also, the exercise of a reduced paid-up option under a grandfathered policy would not result in the disposition of the policy.

ii. — The effect of changes made to grandfathered policies

Certain changes to grandfathered policies will cause the loss of this status. Preservation of grandfathered status is generally desirable and for this reason, changes to such policies and replacement of them with newly issued policies should be examined carefully before such actions are taken. If an action is undertaken which would cause the loss of grandfathered status, the policy would become subject to exempt testing. If the policy fails the test, it will be considered a non-exempt policy and will be subject to accrual taxation. If the policy passes the exempt test, policy gains will only be taxable upon a disposition of the policy. However, the ACB would be calculated in accordance with the post- December 1, 1982 regime resulting in reductions for NCPI commencing as of the end of the year in which the action causing the loss of grand-fathered status occurs. At the time of the first premium payment after the change in status, premiums paid for riders and ancillary benefits would be excluded from the ACB. On any subsequent partial disposition of the policy, the ACB would be prorated.

In order to preserve grandfathered status, such policies must remain in force as originally contracted or only be altered in conformity with permitted changes outlined by the Regulations. This is so provided that none of the following occur: there is a "prescribed premium" paid and a "prescribed increase" in death benefit; a prescribed premium is paid and the policy does not pass the exempt test; there are changes in ownership other than those permitted by the Act and the Regulations discussed below.

Regulation 309(1) defines a prescribed premium. It is basically an unscheduled increase in a premium or premiums paid after December 1, 1982. Specifically, a premium paid after December 1, 1982 is a prescribed premium if it exceeds the amount of the premium that was to be paid at that time and that was fixed and determined on or before December 1, 1982. A premium increase is not considered to be a prescribed premium if the increase arose from:

- a change in underwriting class;
- a change in frequency of premium payments;
- an addition or deletion of waiver of premium, disability income, accidental death, or guaranteed insurance option benefits;
- the use of dividends to provide term insurance and paid-up additions;
- adjustments required by the terms of a policy whose death benefit is linked to the consumer price index or adjustments made as a result of interest, mortality

or expense considerations where such adjustments are made pursuant to the terms of the contract on a class basis;

- the correction of incorrect information in the application;
- the re-dating of lapsed policies provided that reinstatement occurs within 60 days after the calendar year of lapse;
- the late payment or early payment of a premium (no more than 30 days before the premium due date as established on or before December 1, 1982);
- or the payment of policy loan interest after 1977 that has not been deducted as an interest expense under paragraphs 20(1)(c) or (d) of the Act.

Once there has been a prescribed increase in premiums, the policy must be exempt tested. If the policy passes the exempt test, then grandfathered status is preserved except that the policy would be subject to the life insurance capital dividend account rules (discussed in section 1.8.B.iii) until they were repealed in 1985. If this policy is later annuitized, there would be no disposition upon annuitization but if the annuity does not qualify as a prescribed annuity under Regulation 304 it will be taxed on an accrual basis resulting in all post-1981 income accrued in the life insurance policy being taxable on the first accrual reporting date. Under Regulation 305(3), the pre-1982 income will be taxed over the period that the annuity is paid out (as unallocated income accrued before 1982). However, if it fails the exempt test, it loses grandfathered status and becomes subject to the post-December 1, 1982 tax regime. At the next accrual reporting date after the policy anniversary which exposed the non-exempt nature of the policy, the policy will be taxed on the accumulating fund less the ACB with accrual tax reporting continuing thereafter. If the policy is subsequently annuitized, there would be a disposition of the policy resulting in any accrued income being reported at that time. The taxation of the annuity contract thereafter would depend upon whether it is prescribed or non-prescribed.

A "prescribed increase" in death benefit is defined in Regulation 309(2) as an increase in death benefit over that which was fixed and determined under the policy prior to December 2, 1982. If an increase was predetermined in the policy before December 2, 1982 to take place at some specific time in the future, this would not result in a prescribed increase in death benefit. An increase in death benefit is not considered to be a prescribed increase if it results from:

- dividends being used to provide paid-up additions;
- adjustments required by the terms of a policy whose death benefit is linked to the consumer price index or adjustments made as a result of interest, mortality or expense considerations where such adjustments are made pursuant to the terms of the (pre-December 2, 1982) contract on a class basis;
- the prepayment of premiums (so long as such premiums are not "prescribed premiums") under the policy and provided that the increase does not exceed the total of all premiums that otherwise would have been paid;
- the death benefit being a mathematical factor of the policy's cash surrender value and that function has not changed;

- or a gratuitous increase made on a class basis without consideration that was not granted under any term of the contract.

Where there is both a prescribed premium and a prescribed increase in death benefit, grandfathered status is lost causing the policy to become subject to the post-December 1982 tax regime. Where there is a prescribed increase in death benefit with no prescribed premium, grandfathered status is preserved. However, the policy would lose grandfathered status for purposes of the capital dividend account and would have become subject to the life insurance capital dividend account rules until they were later repealed.

The types of events that give rise to a prescribed premium and a prescribed increase in death benefit are limited by subsection 12.2(10) of the Act (which was repealed in 1989 but continues to apply to pre- December 2, 1982 policies with a new subsection substituted applicable to riders issued after 1989 for post-1990 policies). The addition of a term insurance rider or the exercise of a guaranteed insurance option after December 1, 1982 is deemed by subsection 12.2(10) as it then read to be a separately issued policy and overrides the general rule which would have resulted in such events causing a prescribed premium and a prescribed increase in death benefit. This allows the rider to be treated as a post-December 1, 1982 policy and the original policy to retain its grandfathered status.

In addition to those mentioned above, some of the more common policy changes which can be made without affecting grandfathered status would include: a collateral assignment of the policy; beneficiary changes; a change in dividend options; conversion at attained age of a level term policy if the new policy is exempt and there is no increase in amount (e.g., a level term conversion to whole life or level death benefit universal life); a change to reduced paid-up; change to a less expensive policy if the policy is exempt and no increase is made in the premium (e.g., a change of policy from endowment to whole life or universal life with corresponding increase in face amount for the same premium); cancellation of any additional benefits; the renewal of a term insurance policy at the end of the renewal period under the terms of a pre-December 2, 1982 policy, provided that there is no prescribed increase in death benefit; or a reduction in the amount of insurance.

In addition to those mentioned above, some of the more common policy changes which would cause the loss of grandfathered status would include: conversion of a level term policy to a new policy with an increase in death benefit; conversion of a level term policy to a new policy with no increase in death benefit, but the new policy fails the exempt test; change of a policy to a non-exempt policy together with the payment of a prescribed premium (e.g., whole life to endowment at age 65 policy); or re-dating of a lapsed policy where reinstatement occurs more than 60 days after the calendar year of lapse.

Under paragraph 148(10)(e) of the Act, certain non-arm's length transfers of grandfathered policies would not affect grandfathered status. The following represents those transactions in respect of which grandfathered status will be retained: a transfer for no consideration from a parent or grandparent to a child or grandchild where child or grandchild is the life insured under the policy; a transfer from a parent to a child where the parent is the life insured; a transfer from a spouse for no consideration to a spouse where the new owner is also the life insured; a transfer from a supporting spouse to a dependent spouse as part of a divorce settlement where the supporting spouse is the life insured; a transfer from an individual or related individuals to their controlled corporation; a transfer from a controlled corporation to an individual or related individuals who control the corporation; or a transfer from a related corporation to a related corporation (i.e. parent to subsidiary or vice versa). It should be noted that notwithstanding that grandfathered status is preserved some of these transfers would result in a disposition of the policy and may result in taxable policy gains being reported to the transferor (paragraphs 148(10)(d) and (e)).

iii. — Life insurance capital dividend account

Bill C-139 also contained legislation which implemented the proposals in the June 28, 1982 press release relating to the capital dividend account ("CDA"), although significantly watered down. As a result of Bill C-139, where a private corporation becomes the beneficiary under a life insurance policy after June 28, 1982, the gain on that policy will no longer be included in the corporation's CDA. However, to recognize that a portion of the life insurance proceeds should be permitted to be transferred to shareholders on a tax-free basis, paragraph 89(1)(b.2) was added to the Act to establish a life insurance capital dividend account ("LICDA"). Dividends received out of the LICDA of another corporation plus life insurance proceeds received by a corporation (which became a beneficiary under the policy after June 28, 1982) on the death of a person were added to this account to the extent that they exceeded the ACB of the policy. Provided an election was made under subsection 83(2.1) of the Act as it then read, tax-free dividends were permitted to be paid out of the LICDA. However, under paragraph 53(2)(r) of the Act as it then read, the capital dividend paid out of the LICDA would reduce the ACB of the shares on which the capital dividend was paid where the shares or shares for which they were substituted, were acquired by an estate, heirs or beneficiaries as a consequence of the death of the shareholder and the dividend is considered to be paid as, on account of or in lieu of proceeds for the disposition of the shares. This essentially eliminated the tax deferral resulting from the use of corporate-owned insurance to redeem the shares of a deceased shareholder but did not affect other forms of buy/sell arrangements which paid tax-free capital dividends to surviving shareholders to enable the purchase of the deceased shareholder's shares.

As alluded to above in the discussion relating to grandfathering of pre-December 2, 1982 policies, the loss of grandfathered status could also have an effect on the application of the rules governing the CDA and LICDA on the policy in question. A corporate beneficiary under a policy on June 28, 1982 would not be considered to be a beneficiary on that date (and would therefore "become" a beneficiary after that date) if a prescribed increase in death benefit occurs or a prescribed premium is paid under the policy after December 1, 1982. In such circumstances, the policy was to be treated as a new policy for purposes of section 89 and therefore, proceeds payable would be included in the LICDA of the corporation rather than the corporation's CDA.

The LICDA rules were repealed two years later under the 1985 Budget introduced by Minister of Finance the Honourable Michael H. Wilson on May 23, 1985 (Bill C-84, dated November 26, 1985). While no explanation was given for their repeal, it was widely understood that these rules were quite difficult to administer. In addition, perhaps the argument relating to undue tax-deferral on death lost some steam with the introduction of the then $500,000 capital gains exemption which occurred at the same time as the repeal of the LICDA rules.

1.9 — Proposed Changes to the Exempt Test

A. — Background

The significant changes in 1982 established the framework of taxation for life insurance policies. With the passage of time, product design has evolved and many of the modern product features that exist today had not been specifically contemplated in many of the sections of the Act and Regulations that formed the basis for this framework. The need for "modernization" of the regime of taxation for life insurance policies has been recognized by the Department of Finance and the insurance industry for many years.

The first substantial recommendation for modernization was made in an August 1998 submission to the Department of Finance by the CLHIA, which provided recommendations regarding modifications to the exempt test and accumulating fund calculation for life insurance policies in Canada. The main recommendations in this submission were intended to address several larger developments in product design — the advent of universal life products generally; addressing joint and multi-life policies; and dealing with substandard risks and non-life benefits under life insurance policies. The submission primarily dealt with the underlying actuarial assumptions and made proposals that would address these developments within the existing exempt test framework.

A confidential draft discussion paper was released by the Department of Finance on July 30, 1999 to the life insurance industry. This paper outlined the current exempt test rules and specific areas of concern that the Department thought needed to be addressed in relation to universal life insurance policies. The list included:

- Determining the appropriate accumulating fund of universal life insurance policies because such policies did not have specified premiums that could be used in computing a "modified net premium reserve";
- Addressing the taxation of "disability capital benefits" made out of a universal life insurance policy;
- Properly dealing with death benefits comprised of the policy's cash values payable under a joint or multi-life policy on first death;
- Dealing with ancillary risks such as disability, critical illness or long term care costs and benefits within a universal life insurance policy.

Also, other more general tax issues relating to life insurance policy taxation were discussed in the 1999 Paper. These more general issues included:

- The appropriate endowment period;
- What reserve concepts should be used to value a policy's accumulating fund;
- More generally dealing with the exempt test as it applies to joint and multi-life policies;
- Modernizing mortality assumptions in the exempt test framework;
- Determining how the NCPI for over age 70 should be done;
- Addressing anomalies that may exist for the taxation of internal policy transactions;
- Considering the appropriate taxation of collateral assignments of life insurance policies.

The CLHIA responded to the 1999 discussion paper in December of 1999. Many of the areas that were the subject of prior recommendations in the 1998 paper were reiterated in this response.

In the following several years, Department of Finance officials would attend both CLHIA Tax Officers Conferences and CALU Annual General Meetings to state that modernization of the exempt test is on the agenda. However, no formal proposals were released.

In 2004, CLHIA and CALU submitted a joint discussion paper to the Department of Finance, which in some part addressed the tax regime relating to the provision of critical illness and long term care benefits under life insurance policies. The main focus of the paper was to clarify the current tax rules relating to critical illness and long term care insurance provided on a "stand-alone" basis. However, the submission requested that the same tax treatment apply where such benefits are paid under or in combination with life insurance policies. No formal response from the Department of Finance was received by the industry.

Early in 2006, some informal questions from the Department of Finance relating to the determination of NCPI and the appropriate table to use based on more current mortality assumptions were received by the industry. The industry informally expressed that although this is an area that appears easy to "modernize", fixing the table is only one piece of the exempt test puzzle and urged looking at the test holistically and in a more principled manner.

In mid-2007, the Department of Finance indicated to the industry that it was interested in commencing informal technical discussions relating to the exempt test. Initially, the Department was seeking confirmation that the 1998 and 2004 papers still represented the views of the industry. Informal questions and alternative approaches to a regime of taxation for life insurance policies were raised with the industry over the ensuing years.

In the spring of 2010, an informal consultation paper was released to the industry that appeared to be the Department's starting position for a continuing informal technical consultation period ending in the fall of 2011. In the course of this process, the industry formally withdrew its 1998 submission and put in numerous alternative and supplementary submissions to address the specific questions posed by the Department.

B. — The 2012 federal budget

Through the consultation process, the industry was obviously aware that the Department of Finance was interested in working towards a new regime and accompanying draft legislation to make changes to life insurance policy taxation. However, at that time, the industry was not aware that the Department intended to publicly announce in the context of a federal budget that it intended to change the rules.

Finance Minister Jim Flaherty delivered the federal budget on March 29, 2012. The budget included an outline of changes to the exempt test. In general, the changes were within the range of what the insurance industry expected based on the consultation to that point. The outlined changes did not bring about a wholesale, fundamental reform of the exempt test rules and appeared to maintain the basic framework of the exempt test with updates to underlying assumptions and methods within it. However, the updates that were outlined would be significant and would generally negatively impact the level of tax-deferred growth permitted within exempt life insurance policies, both participating and non-participating alike.

The announced changes were not of a detailed nature. From the details provided at that time, the general impact could be described as likely to be:

- A reduction in the maximum premiums and/or deposits permitted in an exempt policy;
- A lengthening of the "quick-pay" period possible under any given set of assumptions in a life insurance policy illustration; and
- Lower permissible maximum cash value accumulations inside exempt insurance policies.

The announced changes included modifications to both the benchmark policy and the determination of the savings component of the actual policy. The current benchmark policy is generally described as a 20-pay endowment at age 85 policy where the savings component is determined using the mortality and interest rate assumptions that were used in determining the premiums of the actual policy (for non-participating policies) or that were used in setting the cash values of the policy (for participating policies). The 2012 budget would change the benchmark policy to an 8-pay endowment at age 90 measured using a 3.5 percent interest rate and the Canadian Institute of Actuaries ("CIA") 86–92 mortality table. This would have the following impact:

- Shortening the assumed payment duration to eight years would increase the savings component of the benchmark policy, thereby increasing the maximum deposit permitted to an exempt policy in the early years of that policy.

- Lengthening the assumed endowment age to 90 would decrease the savings component of the benchmark policy, thereby reducing the maximum deposit permitted to an exempt insurance policy.
- Changing the mortality and interest assumptions that are used in determining the premium or cash value of the actual policy to the newly prescribed assumptions would have a varying effect depending on the levels of the assumptions that are currently in use relative to the newly prescribed assumptions. Although there would likely be a wide variation between products and between companies across the Canadian insurance industry, it is expected that the average effect of these changes would be to lower the savings component of the benchmark policy, thereby lowering permitted maximum deposits.

The current measurement of the savings component of the actual policy uses the greater of the cash value of the policy (i.e. after deducting surrender charges) and a reserve calculated using premium or cash value assumptions as appropriate for the policy (i.e. participating or non-participating, respectively, as noted above).

The 2012 budget announced that surrender charges would no longer be deducted in determining the cash value of the policy, that the reserve would be calculated using the same 3.5 percent interest assumption and CIA 86–92 mortality table as would be prescribed for the benchmark policy, and that a different method for determining the reserve would be prescribed. The impact of these changes would be as follows:

- Disallowing the deduction of surrender charges would increase the value of the actual policy, thereby reducing the permissible maximum deposit to an exempt policy.
- Changing the mortality and interest assumptions that are used in determining the premium or cash value of the actual policy to the newly prescribed assumptions would have a varying effect depending on the levels of these current assumptions relative to the newly prescribed assumptions.
- The new reserve method, referred to as "net premium reserve" in the 2012 budget, was only described in very generic terms. As such, the exact impact of this change was not possible to state definitively at that time. However, from the generic terms used, the new reserve method would generally produce a higher value for the policy than the reserve method used in the current exempt test, thereby reducing the permissible maximum deposit to an exempt policy.

The 2012 federal budget specifically noted that these changes would not take effect until after 2013 and would not apply to policies issued before 2014. No transitional rules were provided at that time, so it was unclear if there were to be limitations placed on existing policies to remain "grandfathered" from the changes.

In Budget 2012, the government committed to consult with the industry on these changes. In late May 2012, a formal consultation paper was released by the Department of Finance to the CLHIA and CALU. The consultation process continued throughout the period following the 2012 federal budget, ending in November of 2012. After the close of this consultation period, it was widely expected that draft legislation would follow.

C. — August 23, 2013 draft legislation

On August 23, 2013, the exempt test draft legislation was released. This draft legislation was focused on implementing changes to the Act and Regulations for the exempt test, the calculation of ACB for policies, and the definition of dispositions as described below. Some of the industry's recommendations and suggestions from the 2012 consultation process were reflected in the draft legislation. However, some areas that the industry expected would be addressed in the draft legislation involving related policyholder tax issues and considerations were not in the draft legislation. In this category are items such as, the tax rules dealing with the taxation of life insurance policies on transfers to and from corporations related to the policyholder and clarification of the capital dividend account credit in respect of a life insurance policy where the corporation who receives the life insurance proceeds does not own the policy.

Two specific arrangements — 10/8 plans and leveraged insured annuities — were the subject of targeted measures announced in the March 21, 2013 federal budget. Therefore, the draft legislation released on August 23, 2013 did not include these targeted measures. (Please see sections 4.3.E and 17.6, respectively, for a full discussion of the 10/8 plan and leveraged insured annuity proposals.)

The draft legislation and regulations were released with explanatory notes and provided a stated formal consultation period ending on November 6, 2013. As these measures are extremely complex, it is expected that there will be some technical modifications to the rules to ensure the impact of the measures is in accordance with the intent of the measures as expressed in explanatory notes or through the consultation process. At the time of writing, industry committees were already in the process of providing feedback and formal submissions to the Department of Finance relating to these measures.

One general measure contained in the draft legislation will provide an enforcement tool to the CRA in applying the exempt test rules. A specific "anti-avoidance" provision applicable to post-2015 life insurance policies is contained in the draft legislation. Its scope is broad and allows discretion for the CRA to apply the rule. Further clarification is required to understand its intended application. As drafted, it could apply to a policy if:

- a transaction or an arrangement is undertaken to decrease the accumulating fund of the life insurance policy or increase the accumulating fund of the benchmark policy — that is, to increase the available funding room under the policy;
- the Minister identifies the transaction; and
- the policy would be non-exempt in the absence of the transaction.

The effective date expressed in the draft legislation for the measures is January 1, 2016 with policies issued prior to that date generally being "grandfathered" from the proposed rules and remaining subject to the current exempt test rules. The one exception is that some of the changes specified for the 250 percent test will apply retroactively to all policies last acquired after December 1982 (see section 1.9.C.v below). Each of the areas of change and the parameters for grandfathering are discussed below. For the purposes of this discussion, the current legislation will be described as applying to pre-2016 policies and the draft legislation will be described as applying to post-2015 policies. For greater certainty, this terminology is not totally accurate as grandfathered, pre-2016 policies could lose their grandfathered status and become subject to the post-2015 provisions.

What follows is an overview of the main changes proposed in the draft legislation.

i. — Changes to actuarial assumptions and reserve methods

As announced in the 2012 federal budget, the draft legislation proposes that new methods and assumptions are to be employed to determine the accumulating funds of policies and exempt test policies for post-2015 policies. While these calculations are to continue to be performed for pre-2016 policies using assumptions set by insurance companies, the draft legislation mandates the use of a 3.5 percent interest rate and the mortality rates specified in the Canadian Institute of Actuaries 1986–1992 (i.e. CIA 86–92) mortality table for post-2015 policies. The draft legislation changes the reserve calculation for the accumulating fund of exempt test policies from a "20-pay, endowment at age 85" general basis for pre-2016 policies to an "8-pay, endowment at age 90" general basis for post-2015 policies. The accumulating fund of post-2015 policies is to be calculated as the greater of cash value, determined without regard to surrender charges, and a "net premium reserve" calculation that is defined in the draft legislation instead of the explicit recognition of surrender charges and the use of a "1.5 year preliminary term" reserve calculation that will continue to apply to pre-2016 policies.

These proposed changes to assumptions and reserve methods for post-2015 policies will have the most significant impact on Universal Life policies (see section 2.8). The proposal to ignore surrender charges will cause an immediate reduction in the maximum deposits permitted to Universal Life policies. The proposed net premium reserve will cause a material increase in the accumulating fund of the policy and therefore a reduction in the maximum deposits permitted to Universal Life policies, particularly for Level COI (see section 2.8.D.i.b) and limited-duration level COI (see section 2.8.D.i.d) cost of insurance structures.

The impact of these changes will vary between types of insurance products and between insurance companies because the current rules rely upon assumptions that are independently set by each insurance company. However, in general, the impact is expected to be a lessening of the difference between the accumulating fund of the exempt test policy and the accumulating fund of the policy and therefore a reduction in the maximum premiums and/or deposits permitted in an exempt policy.

ii. — Changes to NCPI calculation

The draft legislation proposes to change the NCPI for post-2015 policies. The mortality rates to be used in this calculation are to be those specified in the CIA 86–92 mortality table (i.e. the same mortality table specified for reserve calculations). In addition, the net amount at risk for post-2015 policies is to be determined by comparing the death benefit of the policy to the new accumulating fund that is defined for the policy.

Both of these changes will generally act to lower the NCPI for policies relative to the current legislation. Since NCPI reduces the ACB of a policy each year, lower NCPI values will generally result in a higher ACB for policies. A higher ACB will result in lower taxable income to the policyholder from any dispositions that occur while the ACB is positive. A higher ACB will generally result in reducing the credit to the capital dividend account of a private company by a higher amount than a policy governed under the current rules if a death benefit becomes payable while that ACB is positive.

In addition, the draft legislation proposes that for post-2015 insurance coverages that are issued on a rated basis (i.e. insuring a substandard risk and thus charging a higher premium), the NCPI is to be calculated by applying the rating for that insurance coverage to the prescribed CIA 86–92 mortality rates. This change will result in a higher NCPI and a correspondingly smaller ACB for rated post-2015 policies.

It should be noted that NCPI is also relevant to the collateral insurance deduction. For standard risks, these changes will mean a lower NCPI for these purposes.

iii. — Changes to the capital portion of annuity payments from prescribed annuity contracts ("PACs")

The draft legislation proposes the use of a more modern mortality table, the *Annuity 2000 Basic Mortality Tabl*e instead of the *1971 Individual Annuity Mortality Table* that is currently prescribed as well as recognition of substandard risks for PACs issued after 2015. The proposed change to the mortality table would have the effect of increasing the taxable portion of each annuity payment. The proposed recognition of substandard risks would have the effect of reducing the taxable portion of each annuity payment. For a more detailed discussion of these measures see section 13.5.

iv. — Changes to the 8 percent test

Under the current legislation the 8 percent test applies to the total death benefit of a life insurance policy. Under the draft legislation it is proposed that post-2015 policies are to apply this rule separately to each insurance coverage under the policy.

This change is primarily intended to ensure that the legislation appropriately addresses the modularity and flexibility of Universal Life policies. For example, it will lessen the increase in the maximum premiums and/or deposits that occur when a new insurance coverage is added to an existing life insurance policy (see grandfathering below) but will not otherwise have a significant effect on the results of the exempt test.

v. — Changes to the 250 percent test

Under the proposed draft legislation, the general structure of the 250 percent test is preserved. Pre-2016 policies continue to apply the 250 percent test starting on the tenth anniversary of the policy. For post-2015 policies, this test is to start at the eighth anniversary of a policy. The general nature of the test, comparing the current accumulating fund of the policy to 250 percent of the accumulating fund of the policy three years previous is maintained.

The draft legislation proposes expanded relief provisions in the event that the accumulating fund of the policy grows to more than 250 percent of its value from three years prior. These expanded relief provisions would apply retroactively to all policies that are subject to the exempt test.

The first relief provision allows the accumulating fund of the policy to grow by more than this 250 percent limit over the three-year period of the test provided the growth in the accumulating fund of the policy is less than the growth in the accumulating fund of the exempt test policy(s) over the three-year period. This relief provision addresses situations where the accumulating fund of a policy was very low. For example, a policy that had an accumulating fund of $0 three years prior to the test is not allowed any growth in the absence of this relief provision as 250 percent of $0 is still $0.

The second relief provision applies when the 250 percent test is failed and as a consequence of this failure the exempt test policies of a policy are re-dated to be no more than three years old. The draft legislation specifies that when such re-dating of the exempt test policies occurs, the 250 percent test is not to be applied again until seven years have elapsed for pre-2016 policies or five years have elapsed for post-2015 policies. Essentially, the 250 percent test is only to be applied on or after the policy anniversary at which the duration of the oldest exempt test policy associated with a policy is ten years for pre-2016 policies or eight years for post-2015 policies. In the absence of this relief provision the re-dating of exempt test policies in response to a failure of the 250 percent test was often required to take place in consecutive policy years.

vi. — Changes to address joint policies

The current legislation does not specifically contemplate joint policies. The draft legislation proposes rules and guidance for joint policies relating to the establishment and structure of exempt test policies, NCPI calculations, the reserve calculation for the accumulating fund of the policy and several of the definitions contained in the draft legislation. These changes should ensure that joint policies are treated more consistently across product types and insurance carriers for all post-2015 policies.

vii. — Changes to the calculation of the ACB of a policy

The draft legislation proposes several changes to the definition of the ACB for post-2015 policies, as follows:

- All premiums or deposits paid to post-2015 policies are to be added to the ACB of the policy as they are paid.
- The premium or costs of insurance charged in respect of any benefits other than death benefits are to be deducted from the ACB of post-2015 policies as they are paid or are charged.

- A reduction to the ACB of a multi-life policy will be made in respect of a death benefit paid on a coverage that has terminated but the policy continues in force (for example, a multi-life policy that insures four people and one of the lives insured dies.) This ACB reduction addresses a problem that arises in respect of such policies held by a corporation. The problem that exists today is that there is no reduction to the ACB for previous death benefits paid, therefore on successive deaths, the unreduced ACB unduly reduces the CDA credit.
- Any portion of cash values or fund values paid on disability or on death without a resultant termination of an insurance coverage (i.e. amounts that are commonly referred to a "disability capital benefits" and "accumulated value on first death benefits") are to be deducted from the ACB of post-2015 policies as they are paid. For a discussion of these types of benefits see sections 3.2.C.iii and i.
- For post-2015 policies with rated insurance coverages, the NCPI in respect of such coverages is to be determined by applying the rating to the mortality rates in the prescribed CIA 86–92 mortality table.
- In certain circumstances, the repayment of a policy loan that was immediately applied to pay a premium will increase the ACB.

viii. — Changes to dispositions

Proceeds of the disposition on policy surrender or maturity for pre-2016 policies are reduced by outstanding policy loans. For post-2015 policies, it is proposed that this reduction in the proceeds of the disposition on maturity or surrender be restricted to policy loans that were immediately applied to pay a premium under the policy.

The draft legislation proposes that certain transactions give rise to proceeds of the disposition for post-2015 policies that provide coverage to more than one life insured (i.e. for multi-life policies). To the extent that the fund value that is paid as a death benefit in respect of an insurance coverage exceeds the fund value that is allocated to that coverage under the exempt test policies associated with that insurance coverage, that excess will be deemed to be proceeds of disposition. Where the fund value death benefit paid is higher than the amount which could have been paid in respect of that coverage had it been a separate policy, the excess would represent proceeds of disposition and may therefore result in some tax payable on the payment of such a death benefit.

It is proposed that dispositions that do not arise from the termination or maturity of a post-2015 policy (i.e. partial surrenders) be deemed to have a proportionate ACB based on the ratio of the ACB of the policy to the net cash value of the policy (i.e. cash value less policy loans). For pre-2016 policies, this proportionate ACB for such dispositions is based on the ratio of the ACB of the policy to the accumulating fund of the policy. The proceeds of the disposition in excess of this proportionate ACB are considered taxable income to the owner of the policy. Since the accumulating fund of the policy is equal to or greater than the net cash value of a policy, the result of this change is that such partial dispositions will result in the same or lower taxable income to the owner of a post-2015 policy than would be the case for a pre-2016 policy.

ix. — Grandfathering

The draft legislation proposes that pre-2016 policies that were last acquired after December 2, 1982 be generally grandfathered with respect to the proposed changes (other than the retroactive changes noted above for the changes in the 250 percent test). It is proposed that this grandfathered status be lost (i.e. the policy would be fully subject to the post-2015 rules) if additional amounts of life insurance (e.g. a rider or new coverage) is underwritten and added to the policy.

As a consequence, policyholders who are contemplating increasing coverage on a pre-2016 policy after the new rules come into effect, should understand the impact the new rules would have. Generally, the application of the new rules would reduce the maximum premiums and/or deposits of that pre-2016 policy from current levels. As a result, it may be advisable to purchase the new coverage as a separate policy.

Policies that were last acquired before December 2, 1982 (i.e. policies that are currently grandfathered policies) remain grandfathered under the pre-1982 rules. However, it is proposed that policy changes or transactions that cause current grandfathered status to be lost, be tested against the post-2015 exempt test rules.

1.10 — Conclusion

A historical review of life insurance policy taxation reveals significant changes to policyholder taxation over time. Certain basic truths, however, have prevailed. Life insurance policy death benefits remain nontaxable, notwithstanding that a portion of these amounts may represent investment gains. Investment growth within policies is not subject to tax in the policyholder's hands until disposition of the policy provided that the policy is either "grandfathered" or qualifies as an "exempt policy." Non-exempt policies are subject to accrual taxation.

The basic truths that prevail today are essentially a result of significant changes that occurred in 1982 establishing the framework of taxation for life insurance policies. With the passage of time, product design has evolved and many of the modern product features that exist today had not been specifically contemplated in many of the sections of the Act that formed the basis of this framework. "Modernization" of the regime of taxation for life insurance policies has been an agenda item for the insurance industry since submitting a consultation paper to the Department of Finance in 1998 for this purpose. Although this may not have been at the top of the Department of Finance's agenda to this point, the time has come and the process of change is underway.

2 — Life Insurance Products

Updated by Stephen Krupicz, F.S.A., F.C.I.A.

2.1 — Introduction

This chapter will deal with those factors and assumptions that determine how a life insurance policy is priced. It will also consider the differences between various types of life insurance products and the attributes thereof.

2.2 — An Overview of Pricing

A. — The elements of premium calculations

To price a life insurance product, the insurer makes a large number of assumptions regarding all of the factors which go into determining the anticipated benefits the product will provide and the costs of providing those benefits. These assumptions include such things as the cost of underwriting and issuing policies, the ongoing expense of administering the policies once they are issued, the likelihood of policy lapsation or surrender and the probable surrender benefits to be paid, the level of compensation to be paid to the selling agent and other distribution costs, the likelihood of death and the likely death benefits to be paid, the probable investment earnings that the life insurance company will realize on the premiums that will be paid for the product and the amount of interest the company is likely to credit to those who purchase the product. All of these, and many more assumptions are combined through mathematical computer models to arrive at the price the company will charge for its product.

Even though there are many assumptions that go into calculating premium amounts (the price of the product) the following section will look at four important assumptions in more detail. These assumptions are; mortality, expenses, lapse and investment income.

i. — Mortality

Mortality is an important assumption that is used to determine the price of a life insurance product. Basically, mortality is the number of deaths that occur in a population over a period of time. It is normally represented in rate form. Insurance companies can either use published industry mortality rates or rates based on their own mortality experience to price a product. Large insurance companies normally develop their own mortality rates and in all cases these rates are recorded in mortality tables. Companies may have access to a number of different mortality tables but normally use a specific table to determine the price of a particular product.

Mortality tables separate mortality rates by age, gender and preferred underwriting status. The newest type of underwriting assesses specific factors regarding the individual's health and lifestyle to provide a more accurate estimate of life expectancy. This "preferred underwriting" method examines the individual's tobacco use, blood pressure, cholesterol, diabetes risk, cancer risk, other illness risk, family medical history, weight and height for health measures. As well, the individual's lifestyle including motor vehicle record, alcohol/drug abuse, travel, hazardous sports and aviation is examined. The life insurance company uses these underwriting factors to better classify the individual's mortality risk and has a separate mortality table for each classification. This means there are separate tables for males and females and for each of the preferred underwriting statuses. These separate tables reflect past mortality experience showing that, on average, women outlive men of the same age and that those in better health and lifestyle are expected to live longer. By creating different tables, companies are able to charge lower prices to individuals they expect to live longer.

Life expectancy is a value that can be derived from a mortality table. Mathematically, life expectancy is an integration (in the calculus sense of that term) of the probability of survival for any given attained age. It is approximately equal to the time period over which a person of that age has a 50 percent chance of dying. Life expectancy is a value that is commonly used in financial planning as the point in time that the death benefit of a life insurance policy is expected to be paid.

ii. — Expenses

Expenses to the insurance company are its cost of doing business. Typical expenses include advertising and promotion, underwriting expenses, overhead costs, agent commissions, employee salaries and benefits. The insurance company looks at all of the different expenses and factors them into the cost of the product. The amount included in the price of the product assumes that each policy makes a contribution towards these expenses.

Insurance companies may recoup expenses in various ways. This may be done through load charges, policy fees, administration fees, or surrender charges.

A load charge is a charge applied to deposits made to the policy. The charge is set at a specified rate and may or may not be guaranteed under the contract.

A policy fee is a flat fee charged on an ongoing basis. It may be a monthly fee or an annual fee. Policy fees are normally guaranteed never to change. They can vary in term from a specified duration (e.g., the first 10 years a policy is in force) to as long as the policy is in effect.

Administration fees are flat fees that may be charged on an ongoing basis or charged when a certain event occurs. For example, an insurance company may charge a monthly or annual fee based on the number of lives insured under the contract. The insurer may also charge a fee to process a specific transaction (for example, charging a $25 fee to make a withdrawal of funds from the policy).

Finally, insurance companies may spread the cost of setting up and administering policies over a number of years. If companies do this they often apply a surrender charge to a policyholder who cancels a policy before the company can recoup all of these costs. The charge represents a lump sum amount kept by the company intended to approximate the costs not yet recouped.

iii. — Lapse

Another key pricing assumption is the assumed lapse rates. A lapse occurs when premium obligations are not met and the life insurance coverage terminates or when the policyholder surrenders the policy for its cash surrender value. A lapse rate is the percentage of policies that terminate in a year compared to the number in force at the beginning of the year. Lapse rates help the insurance company to project the number of policies on which it will receive premiums and on which it will have to pay a benefit. This information can then be used to help determine what premium the company should charge for the product.

iv. — Investment income

An insurance company will make assumptions regarding investment income in pricing its products. These assumptions have a significant impact on price. If the company assumes a high rate of return on premiums invested and it assumes passing this high return back to the policyholder the price will be lower. For example, the price of a $500,000 policy based on an 8 percent interest rate assumption will be lower than the price for the same policy using a 5 percent interest rate assumption.

B. — Impact of assumptions

The assumptions made by insurance companies when pricing products are based on actuarial studies that look at past experience and projected future events that may have an impact on the product. If the assumptions made in pricing the product are wrong the future costs and benefits of the policy may be significantly affected. The nature of the impact will depend on the type of policy and the guarantees provided by the policy.

If the features of the policy are fully guaranteed, policyholders will be protected from this risk. As actual experience deviates from the assumptions made in the pricing of the product, the cost of the policy and the benefits provided by the policy will not change. Instead, the insurance company will experience a different level of profit than it anticipated in the design and pricing of the insurance product.

If the features of the product are not fully guaranteed, policyholders will share in the risk that actual experience will differ from the assumptions made in the pricing of the insurance product. If actual experience is worse than these assumptions, the insurance company may have the option to increase charges associated with the product or decrease the rate of interest it credits to the policy or to reduce the amount of policy dividend that it pays to participating policies. Conversely, if actual experience is better than these assumptions, the insurance company may decrease charges, or increase the rate of interest it credits to the policy or increase the policy dividend.

2.3 — Differences Between Life Insurance Products

A. — Term vs. permanent

Life insurance products can generally be divided into two categories: term insurance and permanent insurance.

i. — Term insurance

Term insurance provides temporary life insurance coverage for a specified period of time. Term insurance will be used either to satisfy a temporary life insurance need (for example, mortgage insurance) or to satisfy a permanent need temporarily. Term insurance typically covers life insurance needs that diminish or expire over time, since, by definition, term insurance will expire. On the other hand, permanent insurance, assuming it remains in force, will not expire and will provide life insurance protection on death whenever death occurs.

ii. — Permanent insurance

a. — Participating vs. non-participating policies

One method of classifying policies is by whether they are participating or non-participating. Typically, this distinction is only material for permanent life insurance policies as term insurance plans are predominantly non-participating. There have been some instances of insurers issuing participating term policies in the past. Participating term policies are largely a matter of historic interest, especially in relation to demutualization (see section 2.13).

Participating policies share or participate in the experience or profits of the insurance company that issued the policy. This participation or sharing is via a periodic credit or payment to the policy known as a policy dividend. If the insurance company is a mutual company, its participating policyholders are nominally the owners of the company although such ownership is primarily academic in nature as the ownership rights are not fungible unless that company demutualizes.

The nature and degree of the sharing or participation will vary by the type and terms of permanent product. Participating traditional whole life policies share in all aspects of the company's experience relative to that group of policies. The policy is designed with the expectation that annual policy dividends will be returned to policyholders. These dividends are increased or decreased as the insurer's experience on this portion of their business is more or less favourable than assumed in the design of the policy. The experience factors that can influence the policy dividend include investment return, claims rates, insurer expenses, and policy persistency/lapse rates.

Other types of policies can also be designed to be participating. As an example, the Canadian insurance market has seen participating Universal Life policies wherein the monthly administrative fee charged by the policy is raised or lowered to reflect changes in the insurer's costs of administering those policies (i.e. the policy dividend takes the form of a reduction in the monthly administrative fee). Participating limited-pay whole life policies exist where the policy dividend is credited annually as a reduction in the premium due on the policy (i.e. the sole option for policy dividends is "premium reduction").

Non-participating policies may also share in the experience of the insurance company. As the term "policy dividend" is generally associated with participating policies, such non-participating policies have chosen different nomenclature or methods for their experience sharing. Non-participating traditional whole life policies have adopted the different nomenclature approach. These policies pay an annual "performance credit" in lieu of the policy dividend of a participating traditional whole life policy. These "performance credits" allow policyholders to fully share in the investment experience of the insurer but flow variations from expected claims rates, expenses, and persistency/lapse rates to the company's shareholders (i.e. positive or negative deviations in these latter factors increase or decrease the insurer's profitability).

Many non-participating universal life policies provide that policyholders will share in changing expense experience by altering the deposit loads in the policy to reflect changes in provincial premium tax rates. Some of the older universal life policies sold in Canada provide that cost of insurance rates will be changed in line with changes in the expected claims rates, lowering cost of insurance rates if mortality experience is favourable and increasing them if mortality experience is poor.

Many non-participating adjustable whole life products were issued in Canada in the 1980s and early 1990s. These policies provided that premium rates and/or policy death benefits or cash values would be periodically re-determined by the insurance company to reflect changes in investment returns, expense levels, or claims experience. 2013 saw the re-introduction of adjustable non-participating whole life policies to the Canadian marketplace. At the time of writing, these policies are not receiving wide acceptance in the insurance market.

Both participating and non-participating policies can allow the policyholder to share in some or all aspects of the insurer's experience relative to that block of business. Participating policies typically share more fully in more aspects of the insurer's experience. Participating policies typically leave the timing and degree of such sharing to the discretion of the insurance company under the general obligations imposed by the company's written Dividend Policy and the requirements of the federal *Insurance Companies Act* that such discretion be exercised in a manner that is fair and equitable in the opinion of the "actuary of the company" and board of directors of the company. Non-participating policies that share in the experience of the company generally share in fewer aspects of company experience and do so under a timing and degree that is set out in the terms and conditions of the policy with much less discretion left for insurance company management.

b. — Pricing permanent policies — the level premium system

Under a "pure" insurance system each individual pays premiums based upon the mortality costs for that individual's age. This creates a system of premium payments that increases dramatically with age (as is the case with term insurance). This might encourage cancellation of the insurance at older ages as the cost increases dramatically. However, at older ages the need for insurance is often at its greatest.

To address this issue, the level premium system has been developed to provide permanent insurance that is both affordable at the age of issue and is level throughout life.

The level premium system has often erroneously been described as a payment of a premium for mortality plus a savings element that will be used later to offset the increasing cost of mortality. Under this description the "savings" element becomes the cash value. For policies with a cash surrender value, this type of description can lead to some unfortunate and inaccurate conclusions that create misunderstandings concerning how the level premium system is affected by the various elements of premium calculation.

Instead, the level premium system and any resulting cash values is more accurately regarded as the following:

1. A system that allows an individual to purchase insurance for an entire lifetime by paying a level premium, and

2. The funding of such a policy appropriately creates a reserve, a portion of which, for certain policies, could be paid to a policyholder should the policyholder wish to cancel the insurance prior to maturity as a death benefit (i.e. the cash surrender value).

Table 1 illustrates how the level premium system works. It assumes an insurance company will insure one thousand males, all age 40, for $1,000 each. Each column represents one step in the process. Columns 1 to 5 illustrate how the premium is calculated. Columns 6 to 8 illustrate how the reserve is determined.

Table 1

Year	Mortality rate per 1,000	Survivors from original 1,000	Claims for the year	PV of claims 3%	PV of $1 per survivor 3%	Total premiums for the year	Total reserves	Reserve per policy
1	0.68	999.32	680	660.19	1,000.00	14,729.49	14,491.37	14.50
2	0.79	998.53	789	744.14	970.21	14,719.47	29,297.70	29.34
3	0.92	997.61	919	840.69	941.21	14,707.84	44,407.06	44.51
4	1.06	996.55	1,057	939.55	912.96	14,694.31	59,816.94	60.02
5	1.22	995.34	1,216	1,048.76	885.43	14,678.73	75,514.75	75.87
6	1.41	993.94	1,403	1,175.35	858.59	14,660.83	91,477.42	92.04
7	1.63	992.32	1,620	1,317.30	832.41	14,640.15	107,680.99	108.51
8	1.90	990.43	1,885	1,488.35	806.84	14,616.29	124,080.80	125.28
9	2.17	988.28	2,149	1,647.21	781.85	14,588.52	140,680.16	142.35
10	2.45	985.86	2,421	1,801.67	757.43	14,556.86	157,472.85	159.73
11	2.74	983.16	2,701	1,951.44	733.57	14,521.20	174,452.62	177.44
12	3.08	980.13	3,028	2,123.87	710.25	14,481.41	191,573.92	195.46
13	3.51	976.69	3,440	2,342.65	687.44	14,436.81	208,750.80	213.73
14	4.03	972.75	3,936	2,602.20	665.08	14,386.13	225,894.98	232.22
15	4.62	968.26	4,494	2,884.61	643.10	14,328.16	242,935.71	250.90
16	5.52	962.91	5,345	3,330.70	621.49	14,261.96	259,568.81	269.57
17	6.19	956.95	5,960	3,606.16	600.06	14,183.24	276,004.17	288.42
18	6.90	950.35	6,603	3,878.56	578.97	14,095.44	292,199.62	307.46
19	7.65	943.08	7,270	4,146.09	558.23	13,998.18	308,113.55	326.71
20	8.49	935.07	8,007	4,433.15	537.83	13,891.10	323,658.03	346.13
21	9.48	926.21	8,865	4,765.11	517.73	13,773.16	338,689.62	365.67
22	10.66	916.34	9,873	5,152.85	497.88	13,642.59	353,028.78	385.26
23	12.09	905.26	11,079	5,613.39	478.23	13,497.16	366,443.22	404.79
24	13.75	892.81	12,447	6,123.24	458.69	13,333.98	378,723.22	424.19
25	15.58	878.90	13,910	6,643.49	439.20	13,150.64	389,720.09	443.42
26	17.50	863.52	15,381	7,131.98	419.77	12,945.75	399,365.06	462.49
27	19.54	846.65	16,873	7,596.12	400.41	12,719.20	407,573.61	481.40
28	21.68	828.29	18,355	8,022.67	381.15	12,470.67	414,290.31	500.17
29	23.99	808.42	19,871	8,432.06	362.03	12,200.30	419,414.63	518.81
30	26.58	786.93	21,488	8,852.70	343.05	11,907.62	422,774.10	537.24
31	29.55	763.68	23,254	9,301.25	324.21	11,591.11	424,142.31	555.39

Table 1 (continued)

Year	Mortality rate per 1,000	Survivors from original 1,000	Claims for the year	PV of claims 3%	PV of $1 per survivor 3%	Total premiums for the year	Total reserves	Reserve per policy
32	32.88	738.57	25,110	9,751.05	305.46	11,248.60	423,342.87	573.19
33	36.50	711.61	26,958	10,163.79	286.81	10,878.74	420,290.49	590.62
34	40.35	682.90	28,714	10,510.44	268.30	10,481.67	414,981.80	607.68
35	44.37	652.60	30,300	10,768.18	249.97	10,058.73	407,491.58	624.41
36	48.41	621.01	31,592	10,900.35	231.92	9,612.43	398,024.87	640.94
37	52.72	588.27	32,739	10,967.14	214.27	9,147.09	386,647.72	657.27
38	57.59	554.39	33,878	11,018.09	197.06	8,664.86	373,293.71	673.34
39	63.16	519.37	35,015	11,056.15	180.30	8,165.85	357,888.21	689.08
40	69.41	483.32	36,050	11,051.27	163.99	7,650.09	340,454.80	704.40
41	76.39	446.40	36,921	10,988.74	148.17	7,119.10	321,080.07	719.26
42	84.17	408.83	37,574	10,857.25	132.86	6,575.27	299,911.35	733.59
43	92.86	370.86	37,964	10,650.47	118.13	6,021.83	277,147.39	747.30
44	102.65	332.80	38,069	10,368.99	104.04	5,462.64	253,019.09	760.28
45	113.28	295.10	37,699	9,969.08	90.64	4,901.90	227,959.58	772.49
46	124.59	258.33	36,766	9,439.18	78.03	4,346.62	202,509.34	783.92
47	136.37	223.10	35,228	8,781.01	66.32	3,805.07	177,275.36	794.59
48	148.52	189.97	33,135	8,018.65	55.61	3,286.17	152,843.32	804.58
49	160.58	159.46	30,505	7,167.12	45.97	2,798.11	129,805.83	814.02
50	172.79	131.91	27,553	6,285.13	37.47	2,348.79	108,565.86	823.04
51	185.13	107.49	24,420	5,408.17	30.09	1,942.94	89,403.87	831.76
52	197.60	86.25	21,240	4,566.80	23.80	1,583.25	72,477.06	840.33
53	210.45	68.10	18,151	3,789.03	18.54	1,270.40	57,808.88	848.91
54	223.86	52.85	15,244	3,089.57	14.22	1,003.04	45,331.97	857.70
55	238.98	40.22	12,631	2,485.34	10.71	778.50	34,862.93	866.76
56	256.86	29.89	10,332	1,973.69	7.91	592.45	26,187.53	876.11
57	278.43	21.57	8,323	1,543.59	5.71	440.28	19,104.14	885.75
58	305.62	14.98	6,592	1,186.97	4.00	317.69	13,412.77	895.58
59	340.26	9.88	5,096	890.90	2.70	220.60	8,946.43	905.45
60	384.44	6.08	3,799	644.74	1.73	145.54	5,566.20	915.17
61	440.51	3.40	2,679	441.51	1.03	89.59	3,146.21	924.57
62	511.10	1.66	1,739	278.26	0.56	50.12	1,553.00	933.47
63	599.08	0.67	997	154.81	0.27	24.51	628.16	941.76
64	707.58	0.20	472	71.17	0.10	9.82	185.16	949.33
65	840.00	0.03	164	23.99	0.03	2.87	29.84	956.14
66	1,000.00	—	31	4.44	0.00	0.46	0.00	1000.00

c. — Level premium calculation

Column 1. — Mortality Rate per 1,000

As a first step in determining the pricing for a level premium, an appropriate mortality table is chosen. For purposes of this example, in Table 1 we have chosen to use the 1969–1971 mortality tables of the Canadian Institute of Actuaries as published in Volume XVI of the Proceedings of the Canadian Institute of Actuaries. It is worth noting that these tables are currently used by the *Income Tax Act* as the basis for determining the net cost of pure insurance for tax purposes. (Based on draft legislation released on August 23, 2013, a newer table will be used for this purpose for policies issued after 2015. See section 1.9.C.ii for a detailed discussion.) It should also be noted that this is a "Select and Ultimate" table. That is, it assumes each individual has been subjected to a medical exam and less healthy individuals have been rejected or assessed an extra cost for poor medical health. In the years closest to issue the insured population experiences better mortality than the average population (Select mortality). The effect of this examination will reduce over time; in this case it is assumed to take 15 years. At the end of this time the experience is the same as for the general population (the Ultimate rates).

Column 2. — Survivors from the Original 1,000

Column 2 shows the number of survivors from the original 1,000 individuals. In order to project the premium payments expected to be received by the insurer it is necessary to know how many of its original individuals will be surviving, each year, after the expected deaths have been taken into account.

Column 3. — Claims for the Year

Column 3 calculates the expected death claims that will be paid each year. In the example this is simply the number of deaths per thousand for the year multiplied by the number of people alive at the beginning of the year multiplied by the $1,000 of coverage.

Column 4. — Present Value ("PV") of Claims at 3 percent

As noted above, the collection of premiums is not the only element in a premium calculation. Those premiums will be invested and a conservative rate of return of 3 percent has been assumed. This conservative approach is necessary as the obligations are long range.

Column 4 illustrates the present value of each year of future claims at the time the policies will be issued. In other words this is the amount that must be available at the beginning, invested at 3 percent, so that there will be sufficient funds available to pay the claims in the respective year. The calculation has been simplified. Claims are payable throughout the year and it is usually assumed that on average only half a year of earnings would be available. This is usually included in the calculations. To simplify the example it is assumed that claims are only paid at the end of the year. The total of all of the present values is $335,862.52. The total of all claims actually paid will be $1,000,000.

Column 5. — Present Value of $1 per Survivor at 3 percent

Column 5 calculates the present value of $1 paid by each survivor. It reflects the decreasing premium-paying consumer base as time goes by plus the loss of investment earnings on premiums that are to be received on an annual basis rather than as a single premium. The total of this column is $22,802.05.

By dividing the Present Value of the Future Claims ($335,862.52) by the Present Value of $1 of premium per Survivor ($22,802.05) the level annual premium for each policy is calculated. The level annual premium per policy is $14.73.

Added to the above calculation would be an allowance to cover the expenses involved in administering the policies in order to arrive at a final level annual premium.

d. — The reserve calculation

Column 6. — Total Premiums for the Year

Column 6 is simply the level premium multiplied by the number of survivors at the beginning of the year. At the beginning of year one there are one thousand premium payers.

Column 7. — Total Reserves

Column 7 shows total reserves. Having collected premiums the funds will be invested until the end of the year with an assumed rate of return of 3 percent. After the first year both the reserve from the previous year and the new premiums will be invested for the year.

In this simplified example, claims are paid at the end of the year. Premiums plus the reserve from the previous year plus interest minus claims result in the reserve for the entire "block" of insurance.

When the process is calculated for each year it can be seen that the total reserve for the total block of insurance will increase and then will decrease. Thus the reserve is an integral part of the death benefit. The reserve builds up in the early years because the level premium is greater than the costs. In the later years mortality costs exceed these level premiums and the reserve is used to pay the deficiency. So, the reserve is essentially a prepayment of the death benefit rather than a savings element.

Column 8. — Reserve per Policy

Column 8 shows the per policy reserve. The total reserve for the block of insurance divided by the number of individuals surviving provides a calculation of the reserve for each policy.

Unlike the reserve for the total block of insurance which increases for a while and then decreases, the reserve for each policy continues to grow throughout the period of time. The number of survivors each year decreases faster than the decrease in the total reserves for the block.

For permanent life insurance policies, a portion of the reserve may be available to the policyholder through the policy's cash surrender value. The existence of the cash surrender value allows for a number of ancillary benefits which can be provided by the life insurance policy to the policyholder.

The tables and premium calculations provided above are intended to provide a simple explanation of how the level premium system works. In reality, the actual calculations and assumptions required to price or determine reserves for a policy are extremely complex.

2.4 — Term Insurance

A. — General attributes

Term insurance is the purest form of life insurance. Its function is to provide temporary life insurance protection in the event of the death of the life insured during a specified period of time. For example, the specified period of time may be a 10-year term, 20-year term or term coverage to the age of 65, 70 or 75 years.

Term insurance plans are easily understood. They provide temporary life insurance protection, with little or no cash values, for a wide variety of financial needs. It is for these reasons that term insurance can be an inexpensive insurance solution. Depending on the type of term insurance the insurance premium can be a fixed level amount, an amount that begins level and then at a specified date in the future changes (renews) to a higher amount or the premium can renew on a yearly basis. At renewal there will be an increase in the premium amount payable since the renewal premium will be based on the age of the insured at that time.

B. — Conversion features

Many term insurance policies offer a feature known as convertibility. This feature allows the policyholder to convert the term coverage into one of the permanent plans offered by the insurance company at that time without having to provide evidence of the insurability of the life insured. When this feature is available in a term policy it is called convertible term. This feature is attractive to individuals who need large amounts of insurance protection but also currently have a limited budget. It also provides security to the policyholder in the event that a temporary insurance need becomes a permanent insurance need at a time when the insured can no longer qualify for insurance protection. For a discussion of the tax consequences of conversions, see section 3.2.B.

i. — Attained age conversion

Typically, there are two types of conversion options available to a term policyholder. The first is an "attained age" conversion. Under this conversion option the insurance rate for the new permanent policy is calculated at the insurance age of the life insured at the time of conversion. There is no credit given for premiums previously paid for the term policy although there may be a refund of any unused portion of the most recent premium paid for the term coverage. This is the more common form of conversion right.

ii. — Original age conversion

The second conversion option available is "original age" conversion. Under this option the insurance rate for the new permanent policy is calculated using the age of the life insured at the point in time when the term policy was originally issued. Full credit is normally given for all premiums paid under the original term policy but all arrears (the difference between (i) the premium for the permanent policy; and (ii) the term insurance premium which was actually paid) must be paid. An interest charge may also apply in determining the amount in arrears. Original age conversions are typically restricted to a shorter time period (e.g., only allowed in the first five years of the term policy) as the cost of paying the arrears can become prohibitive.

C. — Joint coverages

Many term insurance plans are offered on a joint coverage basis insuring the lives of two or more individuals jointly under the same policy contract. There are two joint options commonly found in term insurance policies: joint last-to-die coverage and joint first-to-die coverage.

i. — Joint last-to-die

Under joint last-to-die coverage, two lives are insured jointly. The death benefit is not paid at the time the first insured dies but instead is payable when the last insured dies. Such coverage is desirable in situations where the two lives insured share a common liability which will only arise in the event of the death of the survivor (for example capital gains tax payable upon the ultimate deemed disposition of capital property owned by spouses). Joint last-to-die insurance will be less expensive than single life insurance coverage on either of the lives insured.

ii. — Joint first-to-die

Under joint first-to-die coverage two lives are insured jointly and the death benefit is payable when either of the two lives insured dies. Such coverage is desirable in situations where the two lives insured share a common liability which will arise upon the death of one of the insureds (for example in a business situation where a surviving party is to buy out a deceased party's interest in the business immediately following the death of that party). Joint first-to-die insurance will be more expensive than single life coverage on either of the lives insured, but often less expensive than an equal amount of coverage on both of the lives insured.

D. — Forms of term insurance

An overview of some of the more popular forms of term insurance coverage follows.

i. — Annual renewable term

Annual renewable term insurance provides temporary coverage which terminates on the policy anniversary date when the life insured reaches a specified age. Under annual renewable term insurance the contract will renew annually and the basic rate of insurance will increase annually based on the then current age of the insured.

ii. — 10- and 20-year renewable term insurance

A 10- or 20-year renewable term insurance policy provides temporary coverage and is designed to terminate on the policy anniversary date when the life insured reaches a specific age. The insurance company may use age 70, age 75, or some other age as the age for determining when the term policy terminates. Under a 10-year renewable term policy the contract is renewable every ten years meaning that the basic rate of insurance is level for the first 10 years of the policy but will increase at each such renewal date based on the then current age of the insured at the time of renewal. The basic rate of insurance remains level for each subsequent 10-year period. The same applies to 20-year renewable term except that the contract is renewable every twenty years and the basic rate of insurance remains level for each 20-year period.

iii. — Level term insurance

Level term insurance provides temporary coverage to the policy anniversary date when the life insured reaches a specified age. The insurance company may use age 60, 65, 70 or some other age as the age for determining when the term coverage expires. Under level term insurance the basic premium is guaranteed never to change until the policy expires.

2.5 — Term-to-100

Term-to-100 is a form of permanent life insurance with premiums payable to age 100. Generally, term-to-100 insurance will stay in force after the life insured reaches age 100 with the premium payment obligation ceasing at that point. For most policies, all of the benefits and costs associated with this type of policy are guaranteed for the life of the contract. This means that premiums are guaranteed not to change. Generally, as long as the premium requirements are met, the insurance amount will be paid by the life insurance company when death occurs.

Term-to-100 policies can vary in design by company. A traditional term-to-100 policy is one that provides a level death benefit amount with level premiums payable for life. These policies provide pure insurance protection with no cash surrender value. The insurance company only pays a benefit at the time of death.

Quite arguably, term-to-100 policies are not term insurance policies as they do not typically expire at a specified date or age but provide life insurance for the whole lifetime of the person insured. The "term" classification of this type of policy is more due to the fact that, like term policies, this type of policy typically provides no cash values. The dividing line between term-to-100 and permanent is admittedly a rather arbitrary distinction, especially as the insurance industry in Canada has introduced cash values and/or different premium durations to their term-to-100 offerings. These product variations are sufficient to warrant a classification of their own, "Limited Pay Whole Life."

2.6 — Limited-Pay Whole Life

Limited-pay whole life policies are permanent life insurance policies. These policies provide a fixed amount of life insurance coverage for the entire life of the insured person(s). A fixed premium rate is payable for a fixed duration, such as 10, 15, or 20 years, or until a specified age, such as age 60 or 65 of the life insured. Failure to pay or fund these premiums as they fall due is an act of forfeiture, causing whatever non-forfeiture options that are provided by the policy to come into play (see section 2.10). However once this premium duration has been satisfied, the insurance coverage provided by this policy is fully funded and will continue for the remaining lifetime of the life(s) insured without any further cost to the policyholder.

Limited-pay whole life policies typically provide guaranteed cash values. These cash values typically commence once a policy is 3 to 10 years old and continue for the lifetime of the policy. Typically these cash values "endow" or grow to equal the face amount of the coverage at age 100 or some other similarly advanced contractually-specified age (e.g., age 99 or age 105).

Limited-pay whole life plans are typically non-participating with fully guaranteed premium rates, premium durations, death benefits, and cash values. The guaranteed limited-pay nature of this policy makes it an ideal consideration for individuals who have a permanent insurance need but seek to fund that need over a limited period such as during their employment years when disposable income is greater than it may be in retirement.

Some versions of these policies include optional non-guaranteed features. One such example is the option to deposit additional funds to the policy to be invested in a range of investment accounts, similar to the investment options offered in universal life policies. The value to which these additional funds accrue is not guaranteed but is dependent upon the performance of the various investment accounts and the policyholder's allocation of funds between these accounts. The accrued value of these additional funds is paid out in addition to the guaranteed face amount of the base policy at the time of death or in addition to the guaranteed cash values at the time of policy surrender. The accrued value of any such additional funds deposited to the policy in early policy durations can be used by the policyholder to fund the required premiums due in later policy years, thereby effectively shortening the premium duration below that specified in the policy.

2.7 — Traditional Whole Life

Traditional whole life is permanent life insurance that provides guaranteed minimum cash surrender values. This type of policy provides for a fixed level premium that is usually higher than for other types of insurance. The level premium may be required for life or for a specified limited duration such as 15 or 20 years. The premium for this policy funds not just the face amount of the policy and the guaranteed cash values but also an expected stream of annual credits to the policy. These expected annual credits are generally designed to increase annually as the policy ages. The expected level of credits set by the insurer is known collectively as the company's "scale" (i.e. "dividend scale" if the policy is participating or "performance credit scale" if the policy is non-participating).

If the traditional whole life policy is participating (see section 2.3.A.ii.a), the annual credit to the policy is known as a policy dividend and the schedule of expected annual credits is known as the "dividend scale". The insurer will periodically increase or decrease its dividend scale to reflect positive or negative deviations of actual experience from those expected when the original scale was set or last modified. Participating traditional whole life policies typically consider all aspects of experience: investment return, claims rates, expenses, and persistency/lapse rates.

If the traditional whole life policy is non-participating (see section 2.3.A.ii.a), the annual credit to the policy is known as a performance credit, and the schedule of expected annual credits is known as the "performance credit scale". The insurer will periodically increase or decrease its performance credit scale to reflect increases or decreases in investment return.

The *Income Tax Act* specifically addresses the policy dividends that are paid in participating versions of this product. However, the performance credit paid annually in the non-participating version of this product is not specifically mentioned in the *Income Tax Act*. Accordingly, these performance credits are taxed similarly to the investment or persistency bonuses that are often included in universal life plans.

A. — Credit options

Traditional whole life policies provide policyholders with a number of options as to how to use the annual credits paid to their policy (i.e. their policy dividends or performance credits depending on whether the policy is participating or non-participating). The annual credit may or may not be taxable to the policyholder, depending upon the credit option selected.

i. — Cash

Under this credit option the annual credit is paid directly to the policyholder by cheque. See section 3.2.G.iv for a discussion of the taxation of cash policy dividends. Performance credits taken in cash are taxed as policy withdrawals (see section 3.2.G.ii.)

ii. — Reduce premiums

Under this credit option, the annual credit is used to reduce the premium amount payable. The policyholder is required to pay the remaining balance outstanding. If the annual credit becomes larger than the premium due, the premium will be paid in full. The remaining balance will be left to accumulate at interest in the policy or may be applied under another credit option. Policy dividends in participating traditional whole life policies that are applied to reduce premiums may, in some instances, create deemed dispositions and, hence, taxable income for the policyholder. See section 3.2.G.iv for details. This does not occur in non-participating traditional whole life policies. For both participating and non-participation forms of this policy, if the annual credit is more than sufficient to pay the premium for the policy, any residual annual credit will be taxed in accordance with how those excess amounts are deployed within the policy.

iii. — Accumulate at interest

Under this credit option annual credits are left with the insurance company to accumulate and earn interest much like a savings account at a bank. The annual statement or premium notice to the policyholder will show the amount accumulated as well as the current annual credit. Generally, credits left to accumulate can be withdrawn at any time.

Traditionally, the account in which these credits accumulate was treated as a separate accumulation account by insurers, affiliated with the traditional life insurance policy but a separate account for purposes of the exempt test. As such, interest earned in this account is taxable interest income and is reported annually to the policyholder on a T5 income tax form.

Newer versions of traditional whole life policies, most notably the non-participating version of this policy, have structured this accumulation account as an integral option of the insurance contract. As such, interest earned in this newer version is investment income inside an exempt life insurance policy and the crediting of such interest is not subject to annual tax reporting.

iv. — Purchase paid-up additions

Under this credit option the annual credit each year is used to purchase a single premium insurance amount. The amount of additional insurance coverage will depend on the amount of annual credit, the age, sex, and smoking status of the individual and the type of base permanent policy. The policyholder will be informed of the amount of credit each year and the amount of paid up insurance purchased through the annual statement or the premium notice.

The single premium insurance amount purchased will have a gradually increasing cash value and will itself generate annual credits. The subsequent annual credits will be used in a similar manner creating increasing insurance and cash values in addition to the base policy. The cash value of the paid up insurance is generally available to the policyholder at any time. If this value is withdrawn in cash, the corresponding amount of additional paid up insurance is surrendered. If all of the paid up insurance is surrendered, only the base coverage will remain.

The application of annual credits to purchase paid-up additions under this credit option are not deemed dispositions of the policy and do not create taxable income for the policyholder under either the participating or the non-participating versions of the traditional whole life policy.

v. — Term insurance enhancements

a. — One-year term to insure cash value

Under this credit option the annual credit is used to purchase one-year term insurance for an amount equal to the lesser of:

a) the amount of insurance that the credit can purchase, and;

b) the amount equal to the guaranteed cash value of the policy at the end of the following policy year.

If the annual credit is in excess of what is needed to fund the one-year term insurance amount the remaining portion of the credit can normally be used to accumulate at interest, purchase paid up insurance or be used to reduce premium. The amount of the one-year term insurance enhancement will depend on the amount of credit and the age, sex and smoking status of the individual. Generally, the cost of the term insurance enhancement will be tied to the yearly renewable term insurance rates of the insurance company and quite often the term insurance amount can be converted by the policyholder to one of the permanent insurance policies offered by the insurance company.

b. — Enhancement options

Under this credit option the annual credit is used to purchase a layer of insurance coverage at policy issue providing supplemental coverage to the base permanent plan. This "enhancement" coverage is funded by the annual credits paid to the policy. Normally, the cost of this coverage is based on the insurance company's yearly renewable term rates and the amount provided is dependent on the amount of credit, and the age, sex, and smoking status of the individual. The annual credit is also used to purchase a small amount of paid-up additions each year. These paid-up amounts will be used to reduce the amount of the enhancement that is composed of term insurance in future years so that, in time, the paid up insurance amounts may totally substitute for the term insurance within this enhancement. If this happens the enhancement then comprises only permanent paid-up additions coverage.

The application of annual credits to purchase either form of term insurance enhancement under this credit option are not deemed dispositions of the policy and do not create taxable income for the policyholder under either the participating or the non-participating versions of the traditional whole life policy.

vi. — Premium offset

Premium offset (sometimes referred to as "vanishing premiums") is a method of using the current year's credit to pay the policy's annual premium. Technically, this is not a credit option, but a method of using credits that have generated paid-up additions. The earliest premium offset date is that point in time where the sum of all future credits (after paying for any additional term protection) is projected to be enough to pay for all future premiums. If the insurer's scale of credits goes down in the future, the premium offset date could be pushed out later or the client may be required to resume premium payments if the policy is already in premium offset. The term "vanishing premium" has become less popular because it suggests that the premiums actually disappear, while in fact, the premiums always continue, they are simply paid for by policy values.

The taxation of premium offset is similar to that for the premium reduction credit option. The application of policy dividends in participating traditional whole life policies to pay premiums may, in some instances, create deemed dispositions and, hence, taxable income for the policyholder. See section 3.2.G.iv for details. Non-participating traditional whole life policies do not face this issue; premiums paid via performance credits are not deemed dispositions.

A number of class action suits were launched in the United States and to a lesser degree in Canada in respect of policyholders whose premiums did not "vanish." See, for example, *Dabbs v. Sun Life Assurance Co. of Canada*, [1998] I.L.R. I-3575 (Ont. Gen. Div.); appeal quashed (1998), [1999] I.L.R. I-3629 (Ont. C.A.); leave to appeal refused (1998), 235 N.R. 390 (note) (S.C.C.).

These suits alleged that the premium offset dates and projected values and benefits within the policies were misrepresented to the policyholders to be contractually guaranteed. Most of these suits have been settled in Canada. The tax implications of any such settlement would vary from case to case.

B. — Coverage options

Coverage options for traditional whole life policies include single life coverage, joint first-to-die and joint last-to-die. See section 2.9 for further details on these options.

2.8 — Universal Life

A. — General attributes

Universal life is a permanent insurance plan which first made its appearance in Canada in the early 1980s. Like traditional whole life, it is designed as a long-term financial planning vehicle, combining both cash accumulation and insurance protection. Unlike traditional whole life, universal life policies are usually interest-sensitive, although a number of insurance companies offer universal life policies with minimum interest rate guarantees. Universal life policies are normally very transparent in design and flexible in their use.

All life insurance is priced using a number of assumptions. Three main assumptions include: the risk the insurance company takes for paying a death benefit; the administrative and other expenses the company incurs in issuing and maintaining the policy contract; and the expected return on contributions to the plan. Because of the open design of universal life, these three elements are readily apparent. The policyholder can see: (i) how much is being charged for the life insurance protection, (ii) how much is being charged for expenses and (iii) the interest the policy is earning. It is for these reasons that universal life insurance is commonly referred to as an "unbundled" policy.

Product flexibility is one of the key reasons for universal life's appeal in the insurance marketplace. Policyholders can decide (within certain limits) how much money to deposit into the policy. They have the flexibility to change that amount at any time and in certain situations may decide to discontinue making deposits altogether. This deposit flexibility is possible as long as there are sufficient funds within the policy to cover the costs of keeping the policy in force.

Universal life policies also have protection flexibility. This includes the flexibility to change coverage amounts where necessary. Insurance coverage under the plan can be increased or decreased as the policyholder's needs change, although increases in coverage are normally dependent on the insured being able to provide satisfactory evidence of insurability.

Protection flexibility also means the following:

- persons to be insured on a single policy can be added or deleted,
- choices of coverage including single life, joint-first and joint-last,
- types of death benefits (level or increasing, for example),
- types of coverage riders or other benefits including:
  - additional layers of protection for accidental death or critical illness,
  - riders covering premiums in case of disability,
  - disability benefits linked to the policy cash values (for a discussion of tax treatment see section 3.2.C.iii),
  - term insurance riders,
  - guaranteeing availability of additional protection without the need for underwriting information,
  - riders which automatically increase coverage in order to maximize tax sheltered room in the policy,
  - riders to keep pace with a growing protection need and/or inflation,
  - riders to maximize the capital dividend account credit to a private corporation, or
  - riders to provide cost recovery (e.g. return of premiums) to the owner/beneficiary,
- coverage for a number of lives,
- flexible deposits (amount, timing, etc.),
- types of cost structure (yearly renewable term or level cost of insurance).

B. — Investment options available

Premium payment patterns and coverage amounts are not the only design features that provide tremendous flexibility to the universal life policyholder. Universal life policies also provide the policyholder with a wide variety of investment options. Investment choices may include daily interest accounts, fixed-term investments with simple or compound interest options, equity index accounts where the rate of return reflects the performance of an outside index (e.g., the S&P/TSX 60 Index, the S&P 500 Index, the NASDAQ 100 Index, the Nikkei 225 Index, various global indices and various bond indices), managed accounts where the rate of return reflects the performance of an outside actively managed retail mutual fund, or portfolio average accounts where the rate of return reflects a specified segment of the bond market.

It is worth noting that in January, 2002, the Office of the Superintendent of Financial Institutions ("OSFI") issued a letter to the Canadian Life and Health Insurance Association ("CLHIA") confirming that it had obtained an opinion on the status under the federal *Insurance Companies Act* of certain index-linked insurance products. Essentially, the opinion letter indicated that "where the liabilities in respect of the investment component of these policies are linked either to some specific evidence of indebtedness, some market index, or the performance of a specified segregated fund or mutual fund, the policies are not policies described in section 450." Policies described in section 450 must comply with reserve requirements established for segregated fund policies. Those that are not described in section 450 are general fund policies and must comply with the statutory reserves required to cover the liabilities of the insurer's general fund.

In technical interpretation 2002-0147535, dated December 4, 2002 the CRA confirmed that index-linked life insurance policies will only be considered segregated fund policies for purposes of the *Income Tax Act* if the insurer's reserves vary depending on the performance of a specified group of properties. The CRA stated that "this determination must be based on review of the valuation methodologies for determining its liabilities in respect of the policy." Given that the valuation methodologies for determining an insurer's liabilities are based on the characterization of assets and liabilities as "general fund" versus "segregated fund", this interpretation has provided insurers with comfort that the tax treatment of universal life policies with these types of accounts flows from the regulatory treatment of these policies.

Given OSFI's and CRA's positions and the general practice of most insurers not to allow direct investing in the underlying fund, the exempt status of universal life policies structured in this manner appears to have been settled.

Investment decisions within the universal life policy should be dependent on the policyholder's tolerance of risk and return preferences. Different investment options provide different levels of risk with the highest risk options providing the potential for the greatest return. For example equity index accounts can provide high rates of return but depending on the circumstances the policyholder could lose all the funds invested in this type of account. Conversely investing in a fixed term simple interest account may provide the policyholder with a guaranteed rate of return of 2 or 3 percent for example, but potential return may only be modestly higher than the minimum guaranteed rate. It is therefore very important for the policyholder to strike a balance between risk and return.

C. — Bonuses

A feature that is common to universal life policies is bonus interest payments. These bonus payments are designed to reward long-standing policyholders. These bonuses vary widely by insurance company. For example, a bonus may take effect at the fifth policy anniversary date and every policy anniversary thereafter. Bonuses are typically based on a formula and may be fully guaranteed or may be subject to one or more conditions.

A guaranteed bonus means that the insurance company is contractually obligated to pay a bonus at specified dates. Under a conditional guarantee the policyholder or economic factors are required to satisfy certain conditions in order for a bonus payment to occur. One example of a policyholder condition might be that the policyholder accumulate a certain amount within the policy by a specified date. If this amount has not been accumulated, the life insurance company would not be required to make the bonus payment. An example of an economic condition might be that a bonus would only be payable if the investment return realized within the policy was to exceed a specified limit (for example, 5 percent).

Insurance companies use different formulae in determining a bonus payment. Some bonus payments are determined by taking a percentage of the total interest earned by the policyholder in the bonus period, whereas others are determined by taking a percentage of the policy's average investment balance over a specified period of time.

Recently, a number of insurance companies have made changes to the structure of bonuses under their policies. Some companies now offer bonuses that take effect immediately with bonus payments made at the first policy anniversary date and every policy anniversary thereafter. Conversely, a number of insurance companies have provided policyholders with the option of removing their bonuses and in return, policyholders are given access to investment accounts with lower management expense ratios (MERs). The determination of which option is appropriate is dependent on the policyholder's time horizon and investment preferences. When comparing these available options it is important that any differences in MERs or other aspects of the policy are incorporated into the comparison.

D. — Expenses

Insurance companies will charge a policyholder different expenses for keeping the contract in force. These expense charges generally include the cost of insurance, surrender charges, a deposit load, an administration fee and policy transaction fees. It is important to note that each insurance company has its own specific expense structure and that some of the expense charges described will only apply to certain universal life policies.

i. — Cost of insurance

The cost of insurance (COI) for a life insurance policy is the charge for insuring the person(s) insured under the policy. The COI rates that apply to any insurance coverage under the policy are based on the portion of the death benefit that represents the "net amount at risk." The net amount at risk under a level death benefit policy is equal to the death benefit provided by the insurance coverage, less the investment balance (accumulated value) amount of the policy. There are several types of cost of insurance structures available for insurance coverages under a universal life policy as detailed below.

a. — Yearly renewable COI

Yearly renewable COI (also referred to as yearly increasing COI) is normally derived from a mortality table of the insurance company that reflects the company's expected mortality experience. The amount is expressed as a unit cost per $1,000 of net amount at risk and varies by age, sex, and smoking status of the life insured. Under this option the cost of insurance renews each year based on the insured's current insurance age. The cost of insurance under this option increases each year.

b. — Level COI

Level COI will also be derived from the same mortality table as yearly renewable COI and is expressed as a unit cost per $1,000 of net amount of risk. Level COI rates vary by issue age, sex and smoking status of the life insured but once the insurance policy is in force the insurance rates do not change as the life insured ages. They remain level for the life of the policy.

c. — Limited-duration yearly renewable COI

These costs of insurance rates are similarly derived from the same mortality table as the yearly renewable COI and Level COI described above. The rates vary by issue age, sex, and smoking status of the life insured(s). These limited-duration yearly renewable rates increase annually similar to yearly renewable COI. However, these limited duration COI rates cease at some specified point in time. The most common such options are Yearly Renewable to 85 under which the COI rates cease at attained age 85 and 20-Year Yearly Renewable under which the COI rates cease after 20 years. Under these COI options, the insurance coverage runs for the lifetime of the insured person(s) with only the period that COI rates are assessed being abbreviated. Since the COI rates in these limited-duration options run for a shorter period than the yearly renewable COI, the rates for these options are higher than for the yearly renewable COI rates.

d. — Limited-duration level COI

These costs of insurance rates are similarly derived from the same mortality table as the COI options described above. The rates vary by issue age, sex, and smoking status of the life insured(s). These limited-duration level rates do not change as the insured person(s) ages, similar to level COI. However, these limited duration level COI rates cease at some specified point in time. The most common such options are 10-year, 15-year, and 20-year options under which the COI rates cease at after 10, 15, and 20 years, respectively. The insurance coverage runs for the lifetime of the insured person(s) with only the period that COI rates are assessed being abbreviated. Since the COI rates in these limited-duration level COI options run for a shorter period than the level COI option, the rates for these options are higher than for level COI.

Some limited-duration Level COI options also provide policyholders with guaranteed cash values within the insurance coverage. Effectively, these COI options are the same as embedding a Limited Pay Whole Life option (see section 2.6) within a universal life policy.

Generically, the insurance company sets the levels for all four of these cost of insurance options such that they expect to collect, on average, the same present value of COI from all four options when insuring the same risk (although this principle would not apply when one option provides guaranteed cash values and the other does not). The insurer is therefore generally indifferent between which COI option a policyholder elects to use to pay for the insurance coverage selected. The choice of which option to select is therefore typically based on the needs and circumstances of the policyholder and insured life(s).

Cost of insurance rates may or may not be guaranteed under a universal life insurance contract. If COI rates are guaranteed the rates are fixed and do not change for the life of the insurance coverage. This provides the policyholder with protection should the life insurance company experience poor mortality results. Poor mortality experience could force the insurance company to increase its COI rates for all new policyholders but this increase will not be applicable to existing policyholders where their rates are guaranteed in the contract. Conversely, if COI rates are not guaranteed, the insurance company can apply the increased insurance rates to existing universal life policyholders. Where COI rates are not guaranteed, the insurance company may also, however, reduce COI rates on existing universal life policies should the insurer experience favourable mortality results (see section 2.3.A.ii.a).

ii. — Surrender charges

The fee structure of a universal life policy is designed to spread the cost of administering and setting up the policy over a number of years. The insurance company may charge a surrender fee to recoup some of these costs should a policyholder cancel the policy within a certain period of time. The surrender fee results in a reduction in the amount of funds available to the policyholder upon surrender of the contract. The surrender fee is normally outlined in a schedule within the policy contract and is guaranteed not to change. Surrender fees normally decrease over time to a point where they disappear completely. Some insurance companies offer universal life policies with no surrender charges.

While surrender charges reduce the amount of funds available to policyholders upon surrender of the policy, they also serve to increase the amount of funds that can be deposited into an exempt policy. (See section 1.8.A.ii for a discussion of exempt policies.) Therefore, if a policyholder is interested in funding the policy to the greatest extent possible, a policy with very high surrender charges may be preferable. The August 23, 2013 draft legislation proposes that the determination of the accumulating fund of post-2015 policies be calculated without regard to surrender charges. This means that for post-2015 policies, surrender charges will not allow increased room. See section 1.9.C.i for a more detailed discussion.

While surrender charges, where they exist, always apply upon the surrender of a universal life policy, there is considerable variation between universal life policies regarding other circumstances in which such charges may apply. Some universal life policies consider reductions in the amount of insurance provided by the policy or withdrawals of some of the cash that has accumulated in the policy to be impacted by surrender charges. Such policies may apply the surrender charges of the contract on a pro-rata basis to reductions in insurance coverage (i.e. if 25 percent of the coverage is removed from the policy then 25 percent of the surrender charge is assessed as a non-refundable fee against the value that has accrued inside the policy) or on a pro-rata basis to withdrawals from the policy (i.e. if 10 percent of the cash value is withdrawn from the policy then 10 percent of the surrender charge is assessed as a non-refundable fee against the value that has accrued inside the policy), or both. Clients should be aware of the potential fees that may apply to withdrawals or reductions in the amount of coverage to understand the impact these could have. It is important to review the life insurance contract to determine if such fees would apply.

iii. — Deposit loads

A deposit load is an amount deducted from the deposit paid into the universal life policy. Normally it is represented as a percentage amount (e.g., 2 percent). In general, the main expense covered by this amount is provincial premium taxes charged to the insurer. The deposit load may or may not be guaranteed. If guaranteed it will remain the same for the life of the contract. If not guaranteed the insurance company has the contractual right to change the rate at any point in time in the future. Many universal life policies offer a form of hybrid guarantee. A hybrid guarantee may state for example that the deposit load is guaranteed not to change unless there is a change in premium taxes affecting the policy.

iv. — Administration fees

An administration fee is a set dollar amount charged to the policy on a monthly basis. The fee may be one amount or broken down into separate components forming the total administration fee (e.g., a policy fee or a life fee).

v. — Policy transaction fees

Insurance companies may or may not charge the policyholder a fee to make a policy withdrawal, to transfer funds from one investment option to another, or to substitute a life. These fees are normally based on a specified dollar amount and are charged each time the specific transaction is made (for example, a $25 fee each time funds are withdrawn from the policy). Some policies may offer a limited number of free transactions.

vi. — Market value adjustments

Most universal life policies reserve the right for the insurer to charge a market value adjustment fee when funds are withdrawn or transferred out of fixed-interest accounts. The fee is typically based on the term to maturity for the account and the spread between the interest rate that is being credited to the account (e.g., the interest rate that a 5-year GIC-type account picked up when the account was established or renewed) and then-prevailing rates for similar accounts. The fee applies when then-prevailing rates are higher than the rate being credited to the account. The purpose of the fee is to approximately cover the capital losses that the insurer would incur in unwinding any fixed-interest investments it may have purchased to hedge the fixed-interest account within the universal life policy.

E. — Death benefit types

Universal life policies offer a wide variety of death benefit types that are designed to give the policyholder the flexibility to design a plan to meet a wide range of business or personal protection needs. The more common death benefit types include, level face, face plus accumulated value, accumulated value on first death, and accumulated value on last death (the latter two death benefit options generally apply to multi-life policies but may also be available under certain joint last-to-die policies).

The level face policy provides a fixed, level amount of insurance coverage. It is cost-effective because the net amount at risk reduces as the policy's accumulated value grows. This results in a decrease in the cost of insurance. A face plus accumulated value policy can satisfy a policyholder's need for increasing life insurance protection. The face plus accumulated value death benefit equals the base coverage face amount plus any accumulated value in the policy. This results in the total death benefit increasing with increases in the policy's accumulated value.

The accumulated value on first death benefit option under a multi- life policy has the accumulated value of the policy paid out in whole or in part in addition to the insurance coverage when one of the insureds under the policy dies. For a discussion of the tax treatment of this option see section 3.2.C.i. The accumulated value on last death benefit option under a multi-life policy has the accumulated balance paid out in its entirety upon the death of the last insured under the policy in addition to the face amount of the insurance coverage on that last person to die.

Where accumulated value on first death benefit option is offered under a joint-last-to-die policy, the CRA has confirmed that such a payment would qualify for the exclusion from the definition of disposition afforded to death benefits (subsection 148(9) definition of disposition at paragraph (j)). See section 3.2.C.i for a full discussion.

2.9 — Coverage Options

Life insurance policies may offer a number of different coverage options. Although the range of options that is available was initially offered only within universal life policies, these options are increasingly being offered on all of the different types of insurance plans: term, limited-pay whole life, and traditional whole life.

A. — Single life and joint

Life insurance policies may offer single life coverage, joint coverage, or multiple coverages (commonly referred to as a multi-life policy). Single life coverage means that only one life is insured under the policy. The policy may also be issued jointly on a joint first-to-die or joint last-to-die basis. Joint policies insure more than one individual and, depending on the option chosen, pay out a death benefit when the first insured person dies or when the last surviving insured person dies. Commonly, two spouses may be insured jointly. However, joint coverage may be issued in respect of more than two different persons.

B. — Multi-life

Under a multi-life policy more than one life is insured under one contract (for example one life may be insured for $100,000 under the policy and a second life may be insured for $250,000 under the same policy). Multi-life coverages differ from a joint coverage in that a multi-life policy provides a death benefit for each life insured or each joint-life combination under the policy. Effectively, a multi-life policy is an aggregation of several single life and/or joint-life coverages into a single policy.

i. — Multi-life in private corporation situations

A multi-life policy is often used, for example, to solve a business-related insurance need. In most cases, the corporation is both the owner and beneficiary of the policy. This may be because the direct interests of the business are being protected (for example key employee coverage, or buy/sell insurance) or because it is more tax effective to have the deposits made with corporate dollars. In circumstances where there are multiple lives to be insured and the owner is a private corporation the use of a multi-life policy must be given proper consideration. This is because the adjusted cost basis (ACB) of a life insurance policy is determined at a policy level. When a death benefit is paid to a private corporation, the corporation will receive a credit to its capital dividend account (CDA) equal to the death benefit paid less the ACB (as defined in subsection 148(9) of the Act) of the policy to the corporation. If the policy in question is a multi-life policy, currently the ACB will reflect the total premiums paid for all of the lives or joint-lives insured under that policy. This would result in the ACB being greater for a multi-life policy than it would have been had a separate policy been purchased on each life, and a greater reduction in the credit to the CDA when a death occurs. Furthermore, currently the ACB of a policy is not altered by the payment of death benefits. This can have a material impact on the successive CDA credits that would be available upon successive death claims from a multi-life policy relative to those that would be available from separate single life policies. The August 23, 2013 draft legislation proposes relief for this problem for policies issued after 2015. See section 1.9.C.vii for a detailed discussion.

Consider as an example a situation involving two identical lives with identical universal life insurance coverage and identical facts (i.e. male, 50, nonsmokers):

- Face amount = $500,000
- Premiums paid = $125,000 (in 5 annual installments of $25,000 each)
- Cumulative Net Cost of Pure Insurance (NCPI)
  - = $45,000 over 15 policy years
  - = $99,000 over 20 policy years.

If these are two separate single life policies, the ACB of each policy would be $80,000 after policy year 15 (i.e. 125,000 - 45,000) and $26,000 after policy year 20 (i.e. 125,000 - 99,000). Should the two lives insured die at the end of years 15 and 20 respectively, the successive CDA credits, ignoring any accumulated cash value that would be payable at each death would be:

- ACB at Year 15 = 125,000 - 45,000 = $80,000
- CDA Credit at year 15 = 500,000 - 80,000 = $420,000
- ACB at Year 20 = 125,000 - 99,000 = $26,000
- CDA Credit at year 20 = 500,000 - 26,000 = $474,000

If instead these two coverages are combined in a single multi-life policy with successive deaths occurring after 15 and 20 years, we would have the following (ignoring any death benefit paid from accumulated cash values):

- ACB at year 15 = 125,000 + 125,000 - 45,000 - 45,000 = $160,000
- CDA Credit at year 15 = 500,000 - 160,000 = $340,000
- ACB at year 20 = 125,000 + 125,000 - 45,000 - 99,000 = $106,000
- CDA Credit at year 20 = 500,000 - 106,000 = $394,000

ii. — Splitting a multi-life policy

Some multi-life policy contracts allow for splitting of the contract into separate policies on occurrences such as marriage breakdown or change in business relationship of the lives insured. The splitting of a policy into two separate policies would appear to result in a disposition of the original policy. In relation to the original policy, there would be a decrease in coverage (i.e. a partial surrender) and the issuance of a new policy in the amount of the coverage which was reduced on the original policy.

The tax consequences of policy splitting have not been directly commented on by the CRA. Technical interpretations 2001-0096125, dated December 3, 2001 and 2002-0127505, dated May 7, 2001 considered the substitution of lives insured under a policy. Technical interpretation 2000-0021175, dated January 26, 2001 considered switching the form of coverage from two single to one joint coverage. Technical interpretation 2005-016071E5, dated May 4, 2006 considered where a clause in the policy contract permits a conversion of all or a part of a joint first-to-die coverage into a joint last-to-die coverage. In each of these, the CRA expressed that it is a question of fact whether a disposition occurs and that the language of the policy contract must be examined. These technical interpretations provide some guidelines as to how the CRA would determine whether there would be a disposition. These comments center on whether the change is viewed as "fundamental", and whether the policy contract language provides "sufficient detail . . . such that no negotiation or renegotiation of the terms and conditions of the policy would be required". The contract language would have to be examined to determine if an argument could be made that there is not a taxable disposition on splitting multi-life coverages into separate policies. For more in-depth discussion of this issue see section 3.2.B.

2.10 — Non-Forfeiture Options

In the event the policyholder discontinues premium payments at a time when there is cash value in the policy, many policies offer options to the policyholder to use this value in a variety of ways. These options are primarily available in permanent policies. Not all of the non-forfeiture options discussed below will be available for every policy. The policy contract will indicate what options are available.

A. — Cash value

Most permanent forms of life insurance policies provide a cash value. Typically, the policyholder can access this cash value in one of two ways: by withdrawing it in the form of cash or by policy loan. Accessing the policy cash value, through either of these options will affect the total insurance provided. Generally, term or Term-to-100 policies do not have cash values.

B. — Reduced paid-up values

This option provides the policyholder with insurance coverage that continues for the lifetime of the insured(s) for a reduced amount of coverage without a requirement for further premium payments (i.e. the coverage is "Paid Up" but for a reduced amount). Actuarially it is quite possible to calculate and design life insurance coverage that is purchased via a one-time, single premium. This non-forfeiture option simply applies some or all of the cash value of the policy to purchase as much of such single-premium, paid-up insurance as it can. If the policy in question is a traditional whole life policy that already contains Paid-Up Additions that have been purchased through the operation of the policy (see section 2.7.A.iv), these existing Paid-Up Additions are typically left intact and only that portion of policy cash value that is not associated with these Paid-Up Additions is used to purchase Reduced Paid-Up coverage.

In isolation, the *Income Tax Act* generally considers such single-premium Paid-Up insurance coverage to be non-exempt. Fortunately, the exempt test applies to policies at an aggregate level, with due consideration to the history of the policy. This aggregate application of the exempt test permits Paid-Up Additions that would be non-exempt on a stand alone basis to exist within an exempt life insurance contract provided the remainder of the policy has a sufficiently low value that the combination is within the limits set by the exempt test. The fact that the exempt test considers the history of the policy permits a Reduced Paid-Up coverage to be exempt provided the policy is of sufficient age when this option is elected. For example, selecting a Reduced Paid-Up option at the twentieth anniversary of a policy is not considered by the exempt test to be a new policy but rather the election of a lower total amount of coverage in a policy that is 20 years old. Although the mechanism for calculating the amount of Reduced Paid-Up coverage is a single premium mechanism, the exempt test recognizes the policy to have the actual duration of the original contract, not the duration of one that would apply to a new policy.

A consequence of the exempt test is that electing a Reduced Paid-Up option on a relatively young policy (i.e. a policy that has been in force for a relatively short duration) may result in that policy being classified as non-exempt. Generally, the tax consequences of such a non-exempt classification are quite undesirable. Consequently, many insurers restrict the ability of policyholders to elect this non-forfeiture option if such an election would cause the policy to become non-exempt. Insurers that take this approach generally require a policy to be in force for 15 to 20 years before the Reduced Paid-Up non-forfeiture option is available under current legislation. The August 23, 2013 draft legislation proposes changes to the exempt test regime that may allow a reduced paid-up option to be elected sooner for post-2015 policies than under the current legislation. Section 1.9.C discusses the main changes proposed in the draft legislation.

C. — Extended term values

Alternatively, the policyholder may want the same amount of coverage to continue for as long as possible. This non-forfeiture option uses the cash value of the policy as a single premium to purchase the same amount of insurance for as long a period as possible. Under this non-forfeiture option the policyholder assumes the risk that the life insured may outlive the period of coverage.

D. — Automatic premium loan

An automatic premium loan is not strictly a non-forfeiture option. However, it is frequently the automatic alternative should the policyholder fail to pay premiums and not provide specific instructions to elect one of the alternative options.

Under an automatic premium loan, each premium is paid via a loan against the cash value of the policy. Such policy loans can be repaid, with interest, at any time. Should the interest at the end of each policy year not be paid the interest will be capitalized on the loan. The policy will continue as if the premium had been paid but with this loan owing against the policy. Should death occur or if the policy is surrendered for cash, the accumulated loan will be deducted from the death benefit or cash surrender value payable. If the loan grows to exceed the cash value of the policy, the policyholder will need to pay the excess amount or the policy will terminate without value.

2.11 — Advanced Death Benefits from Life Insurance Policies

Most insurers offer terminally ill policyholders access, by way of collateral loan, to a portion of the death benefit that would be payable under a life insurance policy. A fewer number of insurers provide advanced death benefits by virtue of defining terminal illness as a "disability payment". During 1989 and 1990, in response to the emergence of AIDS and HIV infection, the CRA confirmed their position regarding the tax treatment of advanced death benefits. The CRA position was contained in three technical interpretations (58266, dated November 24, 1989, 59125, dated February 7, 1990 and 900718, dated July 11, 1990). These provided that such amounts would be viewed as tax-free receipts by the terminally ill policyholder. In letter 900718 in the context of disability payment style advanced death benefits, terminal illness was confined by the CRA to a life expectancy of less than 12 months.

Since that time, the Financial Services Commission of Ontario (FSCO) has adopted a recommendation that life insurers should provide funds to terminally ill policyholders who have a life expectancy of less than 24 months. In technical interpretation 2002-013889, dated February 25, 2003 the CRA confirmed that collateral loan payments by insurers who implement the recommendation by FSCO would not be viewed as dispositions of the policy. This letter also confirmed that such payments must be made extra-contractually (i.e. "not under the terms and conditions of the life insurance policy") or they would be viewed as policy loans. A policy loan is a disposition of a policy under paragraph (b) of the definition of "disposition" in subsection 148(9) of the Act.

At the time of death, the insurer would first use the proceeds to repay the collateral loan principal and interest (if any). The remainder of the death benefit would be paid to the beneficiary(ies) under the policy.

Advance death benefits are an alternative that a terminally ill policyholder should consider. This alternative allows for the policy to remain in force so that any remaining death benefit could still meet the objectives for which the policy was purchased. Most insurers have limits in relation to the amount which may be received by a policyholder in such circumstances but will generally make these payments available in respect of any type of policy — term or permanent.

Where this activity is legal, another alternative to a terminally ill policyholder is a "viatical" settlement. A viatical settlement involves a terminally ill person transferring ownership of the policy and thus giving up all rights to a life insurance policy in exchange for a cash payment from a third party. This transfer for consideration would be a disposition of the policy for tax purposes. The third party then owns the policy and must continue to make premium payments to receive the policy's death benefit. The cash payment made by the third party would represent a percentage of the policy's face amount. To the third party purchaser, if the insured person lives a short period of time, the "investment return" can be substantial. If the insured person lives beyond estimates of his or her life expectancy, the purchaser may realize a "loss". A CRA technical interpretation (2000-005561B) dated December 5, 2001 deals with the tax consequences to the purchaser of a life insurance policy in such circumstances.

Viatical settlements are not prohibited under the *Insurance Act* in some provinces (Nova Scotia, New Brunswick, Quebec, Saskatchewan). However, the Canadian Life and Health Insurance Association (CLHIA) has confirmed that Saskatchewan is committed to considering inserting an anti-trafficking provision the next time it reviews its *Insurance Act*. Also, the draft harmonized *Insurance Act* for the Atlantic provinces now includes anti-trafficking provisions which New Brunswick and Nova Scotia intend to adopt. Ontario proposed the legalization of viatical settlements but has never passed Regulations that would have brought the provisions into force. The last version of draft regulations in Ontario were released on July 13, 2001 by FSCO and these proposals have not been enacted. In all other provinces there is a prohibition in the provincial *Insurance Act* against "trafficking" in life insurance policies. Although viatical settlements are not prohibited in all provinces, some insurers prohibit advisors in any province from engaging in investor-owned life insurance programs, stranger-owned life insurance programs, and life policy re-marketing or trafficking programs.

There has been some litigation concerning the opportunity to invest in US life insurance policies provided by US viatical settlement and life settlement companies operating in Ontario. Ontario's Superintendent of Financial Services pursued a cease and desist order against Universal Settlements Inc. (USI) which engaged in this practice. In January 2002, the Ontario Financial Services Tribunal found that the part of the Insurance Act which includes the anti-trafficking provision only applies to insurance undertaken in Ontario so it could not enforce a cease and desist order in this case. However, the Ontario Securities Commission pursued the matter and issued an order on September 29, 2006 that the interests in death benefits of life insurance policies from insured persons offered by USI are securities within the meaning of the Ontario *Securities Act*. It found USI not in compliance with its obligations under the *Securities Act* including its obligations to issue a prospectus before offering the securities for sale. The Commission ordered USI to cease trading unless it met the relevant requirements under securities law and to refund prior moneys to investors for the period it operated while not in compliance with securities law.

2.12 — Variable Life Insurance Policies — General Attributes

Variable life insurance policies have not gained a great deal of popularity in Canada. Their basic design is simply a combination of a reducing amount of insurance and a savings component that is invested in the segregated fund of the insurance company. There are no particular tax advantages to using this form of policy rather than owning the two elements, insurance and investment, separately. Specifically, investment returns on the segregated fund portion of the contract are not exempt but subject to taxation as in any segregated fund contract. (See Chapter 19.)

Part of the premium for variable life policies is allocated to pay the costs of insurance. The insurance company calculates the cost of this insurance as it would in the course of designing any other insurance policy. The costs may be modified as the insurance element is of a reducing nature and may expire at some point in time.

The balance of the premium payment is invested in a segregated fund of the insurance company. The amount of the reduction in the insurance coverage may be integrated with the amount being invested in the segregated fund portion of the policy. For example, the insurance reduces by exactly the amount that is allocated to the segregated fund portion of the policy.

At death the total death benefit is a combination of the stated death benefit plus all or a portion of the fund value. As an example, a policy may provide a guaranteed return of the deposits made to the segregated fund (even if the fund had lost value) plus an amount of insurance that had reduced by the amount of the fund investments made to date plus the growth, if any on the fund values. With a reasonable expectation of growth on the fund portion the result would be a death benefit that increased over time.

Often these policies provide a point in time when they mature. At maturity the insurance ends and the fund values are paid out. There is a minimum guaranteed amount to be paid. The policy may provide that the total values received at maturity will be equal to no less than the total premiums paid including the insurance premiums. This ensures a growth factor on the fund values. However, with the past experience of the increase in fund values over significant lengths of time this guarantee appears not to be significant to many potential consumers who are interested in investing in funds since they expect the funds to outperform this guarantee.

Subsection 148(3) of the *Income Tax Act* sets out special rules for the taxation of the income from these policies.

2.13 — Special Considerations for Certain Participating Policyholders

Participating policies represent a significant proportion of in-force policies in the Canadian marketplace. Participating policies issued by mutual companies entitle the policyholder to ownership rights in the mutual company. The largest mutual companies operating in Canada carried out the process of "demutualization" in the late 1990s. A brief discussion of demutualization from the policyholder's perspective follows.

A. — What is demutualization?

Demutualization is the process of converting from a mutual company to a shareholder owned company. A mutual company is owned by its participating policyholders who have ownership rights in the company. However, these ownership rights are not tradable or exchangeable and expire when the underlying policies terminate. Under the process of demutualization, common shares, cash or other benefits are given in exchange for these ownership rights, and eligible policyholders, who are entitled to receive common shares have the opportunity to keep or sell these shares. Demutualizing companies may offer cash in lieu of shares or a combination of cash and shares. As well companies may offer enhanced policy benefits.

Neither the process of demutualization, nor an eligible policyholder's decision to take cash, shares or other benefits will alter the terms of the insurance contract owned by the policyholder. That is the benefits and protections under the policy contract will not be adversely affected in any way by demutualization. Appropriate reserves will continue to protect policies. Participating policyholders will continue to receive dividends on their policies as declared. Policyholders will also be required to continue paying their policy premiums in accordance with the contract.

B. — Policyholder tax regime for demutualization benefits

On August 27, 1998, the consultation paper on the proposed regulatory regime relating to the process by which large mutual life insurance companies convert to stock companies was released. It contained a brief outline of the proposed income tax rules that would apply to policyholders. On December 15, 1998, draft income tax legislation was released and on January 14, 1999, some modifications to these draft proposals were announced. The final proposals are contained in legislation tabled on December 7, 1999 and later contained in the 1999 budget bill (C-25) which received Royal Assent on June 29, 2000. What follows is a summary of the basic tax regime relating to policyholders receiving demutualization benefits (referred to as "conversion benefits").

The disposition, alteration or dilution of the policyholder's ownership rights in the mutual company undergoing demutualization is deemed not to give rise to any gain or loss. Where the policyholder gives up ownership rights in the mutual company undergoing demutualization as consideration for shares of a new stock company, the cost of the shares is deemed to be nil. Therefore, there will be no immediate tax consequences to the policyholder in receipt of the shares. However, on any subsequent disposition of the shares the entire proceeds will represent a capital gain.

A "taxable conversion benefit" is a conversion benefit other than shares (e.g. cash, although not limited to cash). When a taxable conversion benefit is received, the corporation that conferred the benefit is deemed to have paid a dividend and the policyholder is deemed to have received a dividend equal to the fair market value of the benefit. This dividend is deemed to be a dividend from a taxable Canadian corporation, thus allowing an individual resident in Canada who receives a dividend to claim a dividend tax credit in respect of the benefit. Nonresidents in receipt of taxable conversion benefits would be subject to non-resident withholding tax in respect of such benefits.

Other taxable conversion benefits include "specified insurance benefits." These are defined as an enhancement of benefits under an insurance policy, an issuance of an insurance policy, an undertaking of an obligation to pay a policy dividend or a reduction in the amount of premiums that would otherwise be payable under the policy. In the latter case, the present value at the time of demutualization of the additional premiums that would have been payable if the premiums had not been reduced, would represent the value received by the policyholder. A policy premium is deemed to have been paid in respect of the value of "specified insurance benefits." This bumps up the adjusted cost basis of the policy and ensures that the policyholder will not be double taxed upon a subsequent disposition of the policy.

Clarification is provided relating to the timing of receipt of benefits, particularly in situations where an undertaking is made to provide a future payment. The value of the benefit is normally its fair market value at the time of receipt of the benefit. It is the policyholder who receives the benefit notwithstanding that the actual recipient of the benefit may be another person.

2.14 — Impact of Legislation and Accounting Standards Governing Insurance Companies

A. — Disclosure in respect of participating and adjustable life insurance policies

Bill C-57, which received Royal Assent on November 25, 2005, resulted in amendments to the federal *Insurance Companies Act*. The amendments cover a variety of items including governance provisions for policyholders, clarifying the role of company directors, provisions governing shareholders, company securities, e-commerce provisions, certain types of company transactions, and other general amendments.

With respect to governance provisions for policyholders, the amendments require insurance companies to have: an established policy respecting the management of participating accounts, and established criteria for making changes to adjustable policies (i.e. changes to premiums, insurance charges, amounts of insurance or surrender values, for policies where these changes may be made at the discretion of the insurance company). Ongoing internal monitoring is required to ensure that the actual dividends credited to participating policies, and changes made to adjustable policies, are consistent with the established policies and criteria and are fair to policyholders. Regulations to complete this legislation were enacted in November of 2010 with an effective date of June 2011. Owners of policies governed by these regulations can request a copy of the criteria and policies established by their insurance company for making changes to adjustable products and managing participating policies.

B. — Accounting standards for recognition and measurement of financial assets of insurers

The Canadian Institute of Chartered Accountants Handbook Section 3855 ("S. 3855") provides for the reporting of financial results of insurance companies in fiscal years beginning on or after October 1, 2006. Prior to the introduction of S. 3855, financial assets were held on the balance sheet at amortized cost, and gains and losses (both realized and unrealized) were amortized into income over a number of years. This resulted in a smoothing of gains and losses on the income statements of insurance companies and stability on the balance sheet.

S. 3855 changed how gains and losses are recognized on the income statement and balance sheet. Bonds and publicly traded equities experienced the biggest change. Most insurers have chosen to treat bonds and publicly traded equities under the Fair Value Option, which means that gains and losses will be immediately recognized into income and the assets will be held at their fair market value on the balance sheet. If interest rates rise in a quarter then the fair value of the bond will decrease and that decrease will be immediately recognized in income for the quarter. If the equity markets surge upward in a quarter then all of that gain will be recognized in income for the quarter, rather than being smoothed out over a number of quarters. Mortgages and private debt are classified as "Loans". While these assets will continue to be held at amortized cost on the balance sheet, realized gains on sales will come immediately into income. The changes under S. 3855 will lead to increased volatility in investment income that will be off-set in liabilities.

The annual credits paid to traditional whole life policies, policy dividends in participating versions, and performance credits in non-participating versions, reflect the investment performance earned by the insurer on the assets held in the separate accounts that they maintain for these policies. If an insurer determines these annual credits based on the statutory yield of the respective accounts then the same kind of increased volatility would be passed on to owners of traditional whole life policies through their participating policy dividends or non-participating performance credits. To address this issue, many insurers have chosen to adopt smoothed yields for their tracking of investment performance in these separate accounts (very similar to the yields before S. 3855 came into effect) for the purposes of determining policy dividends and performance credits. For these insurers, the adoption of S. 3855 has had little impact on the volatility of the annual credits they pay to their traditional whole life policies.

For fiscal years beginning on or after January 1, 2011, "publicly accountable enterprises" were required to report using International Financial Reporting Standards (IFRS) rather than Canadian accounting standards. As a result, Canadian insurers began accounting for financial assets based on IFRS in 2011. Discussions are underway regarding applying IFRS to insurance contract liabilities. The Canadian insurance industry has raised material objections to an Exposure Draft published by the International Accounting Standards Board leading to reconsideration of these proposals. The outcome of these discussions and the timing for implementing the ultimate standards is not known at this time.

2.15 — Conclusion

Over the past 20 years, the Canadian insurance marketplace has changed dramatically. The types of insurance products have expanded as have the attributes of the policies. Today's consumer has a broad range of insurance products to choose from and an array of policy features to consider. Whether the insurance need is temporary or permanent, fixed, increasing or decreasing, an appropriate policy can fill the need providing insurance protection and, where desired, tax-effective investment options.

3 — Taxation of Life Insurance Policies, Dispositions, and Selected Valuation Issues

Updated by Jennifer Janeczko, MTax

3.1 — Introduction

This chapter will introduce the income tax rules relating to the taxation of exempt life insurance policies (including dispositions such as surrenders, transfers of ownership, and policy loans) and review selected valuation issues impacting insurance policies, particularly corporate-owned insurance policies.

3.2 — Taxation of Exempt Life Insurance Policies

Section 148 in Division G, "Deferred and Other Special Income Arrangements," of the *Income Tax Act* contains many of the rules related to the taxation of exempt life insurance policies. For a discussion of "exempt" policies see section 1.8.A.ii. Also, proposed changes that will impact exempt policies after 2015 were released in August 23, 2013 draft legislation. These are discussed in detail in section 1.9.C. Where these measures would represent a change to the discussions in the chapter, these areas will be indicated.

Section 148 and the related Regulations include many defined terms, calculations, exceptions and special cases. The CRA provides little guidance as to its administrative views regarding the taxation of life insurance policies. However, archived Interpretation Bulletin IT-87R2, "Policyholders' Income from Life Insurance Policies," dated February 15, 1996, does provide guidance on certain of the rules contained in section 148.

Most practitioners rely on the life insurance company to provide accurate tax reporting for transactions involving a life insurance policy. This is usually appropriate once the transaction has occurred. However, having a general understanding of the life insurance taxation rules will enhance the effectiveness of planning recommendations made by practitioners to clients who currently own life insurance policies or who need to purchase additional life insurance.

A. — General rules and terminology for dispositions

An exempt life insurance policy is not subject to income taxation unless there is an actual or deemed disposition of an interest in the policy.

When a policyholder disposes of an interest in an exempt life insurance policy, the rules in paragraph 56(1)(j) and subsection 148(1) apply. The term "interest in a life insurance policy" is not defined by the Act. Clearly, it includes absolute ownership of a policy. It would also include a co-ownership interest or a split-dollar interest where, for example, one party owns and pays for the policy account value and the other party owns and pays for the face amount of coverage. For a detailed discussion of split-dollar life insurance see Chapter 8.

Paragraph 56(1)(j) of the Act requires a policyholder to include income from the disposition of an interest in an exempt life insurance policy in their taxable income for the year in which the disposition occurs. The income inclusion, or "policy gain", is the amount, if any, by which the "proceeds of the disposition" of the policyholder's interest in the policy exceeds the "adjusted cost basis" to the policyholder pursuant to subsection 148(1) of the Act. The definitions of "proceeds of the disposition" and "adjusted cost basis" are both set out at subsection 148(9).

The disposition of an interest in a life insurance policy cannot result in a loss for tax purposes. The words "if any" ensure that while policy gains are taxable, a taxpayer cannot deduct a policy "loss" from their taxable income.

Policy gains are considered income from property, and are fully included in taxable income. They are specifically excluded from the definition of "capital gains" under subparagraph 39(1)(a)(iii). Some have argued that because policy gains are included in income under subdivision d of Division B of the Act "Other Sources of Income", as opposed to subdivision b "Income or Loss from a Business or Property", policy gains should not be considered income from property.

The CRA has considered the taxation of policy gains in technical interpretations 2006-0174111C6, dated May 9, 2006, 9622725, dated October 16, 1996, and 5-901540, dated January 14, 1991. CRA's view is that income from a corporate-owned life insurance policy, included pursuant to subsection 56(1)(j), is "income from a source that is a property for purposes of paragraph b of the definition of 'aggregate investment income' in subsection 129(4)." As a result of being income from property, taxable policy gains reported would be:

- subject to the attribution rules under 74.1,
- subject to refundable tax under section 207.5 where the policy is held by an RCA trust,
- viewed as "investment income" for purposes of section 110.6 in calculating "cumulative net investment loss", and
- viewed as investment income earned by a corporation with respect to calculating the corporation's refundable dividend tax on hand.

It is always the policyholder who is taxed on a disposition of an interest in a life insurance policy. For example, in the case of a collaterally assigned insurance policy that is surrendered, the proceeds may be payable to the collateral assignee but the policy gain, if any, is reported to the policyholder.

B. — What is a disposition of an interest in a life insurance policy?

Understanding the various terms in the calculation of the income inclusion under subsection 148(1) is essential to avoid unexpected tax consequences arising from transactions involving life insurance policies.

A disposition of an interest in a life insurance policy under subsection 148(1) generally refers to any transaction in which the interest is transferred to another party. This may include an absolute assignment of the interest, whether by way of gift or sale, and includes a transfer of the interest in a policy that insures a third party that may occur upon the death of the policyholder. Note that at death, where the policyholder is not the life insured, and the policy passes through the estate (i.e. is transferred to another person via the Will as opposed to a successor owner designation), there will technically be two transfers: a transfer to the estate at death resulting in a disposition by the deceased, and a second transfer from the estate to the beneficiary (unless there is a rollover to a spouse under subsection 148(8.2)).

The definition of "disposition" in subsection 148(9) is not exhaustive. "Disposition" is defined under subsection 148(9) to include:

- a surrender of the interest, including a partial surrender of the interest;
- a policy loan made after March 31, 1978, including automatic premium loans and capitalization of unpaid loan interest;
- the dissolution of the interest by virtue of the maturity of the policy (e.g., an endowment policy at the time of maturity); and,
- a disposition of the interest by operation of law only (such as a transfer to a successor owner or by right of survivorship in joint tenancy).

Certain actions taken by insurers at the policy anniversary to maintain a policy's exempt status can result in a disposition of the policy. For example, withdrawing amounts from the policy's cash value and placing these amounts into a separate side account (which is subject to annual accrual taxation) until the amounts can be deposited into the policy, would be a partial surrender of an interest in a policy. Another method that may be used by insurers to maintain a policy's exempt status is to reverse any excess premiums, refunding the policyholder for these amounts. In technical interpretation 2006-0181641E5, dated November 5, 2007, the CRA considered whether the reversal of premiums in a universal life policy constitutes a disposition under section 148 of the Act. The CRA indicated that a premium reversal appears to result in a partial disposition of the policy under section 148 and that there is no legal basis to reverse transactions that have previously occurred. For more information relating to exempt testing and administration of exempt policies see section 1.8.A.ii.

In several technical interpretations the CRA has considered the payment of a refund of premiums upon the expiry of a life insurance policy. The CRA considers the dissolution of an interest in a policy due to the expiry of the policy as a disposition and the return of premium amount as the proceeds of the disposition. (See technical interpretations: 2011-0404941E5, dated May 24, 2011; 2008-0269941M4, dated April 21, 2008; 2007-0233631E5, dated January 26, 2009; 2007-0257601E5, dated November 6, 2007; 2007-0230321E5, dated May 1, 2007; 2006-0209431E5, dated

October 26, 2006; 2004-0089921E5, dated October 14, 2004 and 2003-0060381E5, dated March 1, 2004.) This position has been confirmed in *Brosseau v. The Queen*, 2006 TCC 646, 2006 CarswellNat 6151, and *White v. The Queen*, 2008 TCC 414, 2008 CarswellNat 2543, [2009] 1 C.T.C. 2477, 2008 D.T.C. 4428.

A number of technical interpretations have dealt with changes made to policies and discussed the criteria applied by the CRA in determining whether a disposition of the policy was considered to occur. Technical interpretations 2001-00696125, dated December 3, 2001 and 2002-0127505, dated May 7, 2002 considered the substitution of lives insured under a policy. Technical interpretation 2000-0021175, dated January 26, 2001 considered switching the form of coverage from two single life coverages to one joint coverage. As well, technical interpretation 2005-0160761E5, dated May 4, 2006 considered a contractual right in the policy that allowed a conversion of all or part of a joint first-to-die coverage into a joint last-to-die coverage without providing additional evidence of insurability.

These technical interpretations express similar points of view. The comments in technical interpretation 2002-0127505 are basically representative of the CRA point of view and suggest the following test: "It would be necessary to determine whether the alteration of the agreement constitutes a variation of the existing agreement such that the original agreement survives, or whether the alteration is so fundamental that it results in the creation of a new contract between the parties and the extinguishment of the original agreement."

Complicating these interpretations is the potential application of paragraph 148(10)(d). That paragraph states that for purposes of section 148, "except as otherwise provided, a policyholder shall be deemed not to have disposed of or acquired an interest in a life insurance policy (other than an annuity contract) as a result only of the exercise of any provision (other than a conversion into an annuity contract) of the policy". CRA's comment in respect of the potential application of this paragraph in 2002-0127505 is as follows: ". . .paragraph 148(10)(d) of the Act was never intended, nor do we believe provides, for the non-disposition of an insurance policy by simply recognizing that the policy may be materially changed." In relation to policy contract language which permits alterations for substitution of lives, the CRA further stated: "If sufficient detail was provided in the policy such that no negotiation or renegotiation of the terms and conditions of the policy would be required in connection with the substitution, the exercise of the right of substitution provision may not result in a disposition."

In technical interpretation 2005-0160761E5, the CRA discussed the meaning of paragraph 148(10)(d) as follows:

> In order to give meaning to the word 'only' it is our view that it is necessary to determine whether the changes that are made to the terms of the policy, including but not limited to the premium structure, are so fundamental as to go to the root of the policy. If this were the result, there would be a disposition of the policy and the acquisition of a new policy.

The exercise of conversion rights was the subject of two CRA comments, 2005-0164711C6, dated May 26, 2005 (Question 9 from the 2005 CLHIA Roundtable) and 2007-0229771C6, dated June 21, 2007 (Question 4, 2007 CLHIA Roundtable).

The first of these confirmed that in the context of either a merger between two insurers or an acquisition of one insurer by another, conversions from a prior insurer's term policies to whole life policies issued by the successor insurer or acquirer insurer would not be a disposition where all other terms of the original conversion rights are respected.

The latter technical interpretation dealt with several conversion scenarios — a full conversion of a term policy to a permanent policy, a full conversion with the addition of new coverage to the converted policy with evidence of insurability, and a partial conversion where a portion of the term coverage is converted and the remaining term coverage is retained. The CRA reiterated their previous comments and added the following in respect of the partial conversion scenario:

> We can confirm that there is nothing in the Act that provides for an allocation of the adjusted cost basis of a life insurance policy where the policy is "split" into two separate policies. . . . It is a question of fact whether in such circumstances a disposition would result on the conversion. In our view, the fact that the legislation does not contemplate this type of situation suggests that paragraph 148(10)(d) was never intended to provide for a non-disposition of the policy in such circumstances.

In addition to the definition of "disposition" in subsection 148(9), subsection 148(2) may apply to deem the policyholder to have disposed of a part of an interest in a life insurance policy when a policyholder who owns a participating whole life insurance policy is entitled to receive a policy dividend, unless the policy dividend qualifies under the internal policy transactions rules in paragraph 148(2)(a).

There are several exceptions to the general rule governing income inclusion under subsection 148(1) and there are several transactions affecting life insurance policies which are specifically excluded from the definition of "disposition" in subsection 148(9).

C. — What is not a disposition of an interest in a life insurance policy?

The following transactions are specifically excluded under the definition of "disposition" in subsection 148(9) and therefore do not trigger taxation:

- a payment under the policy in consequence of the death of any person whose life was insured under the policy (i.e. death benefits paid from the policy are tax-free; see section 2.8.E for a discussion of the types of death benefits available);
- any transaction or event by which an individual becomes entitled to receive, under the terms of an exempt policy, all of the proceeds payable under the policy in the form of an annuity contract or annuity payments if the individual whose life is insured under the policy is totally and permanently disabled;
- a payment under the policy as an accidental death benefit or as a disability benefit;
- an assignment of all or part of an interest in the policy as security for debts or loans other than policy loans (a collateral assignment of the policy); and
- a lapse and then reinstatement of the policy during the calendar year of the lapse or within 60 days thereafter.

While life insurance premiums are generally not deductible for income tax purposes (see section 6.4), the fact that benefits paid under the policy in the event of death and in the case of total disability are tax-free, represents a significant advantage of the use of exempt life insurance policies in planning for liquidity needs. Any clarification and commentary relating to these exclusions is discussed in turn.

i — Accumulated value paid on first death

Where accumulated value on first death benefit option is offered under a joint-last-to-die policy, the CRA has considered whether such a payment would qualify for the exclusion from the definition of disposition afforded to death benefits (subsection 148(9) definition of disposition at paragraph (j)).

The wording considered in the earlier commentary focused on whether the first to die under a joint-last-to-die policy could be considered "any person whose life was insured under the policy". The CRA's first response (technical interpretation 1999-0006975, dated April 11, 2000 and also at 2000 CALU Annual General Meeting CRA Roundtable, May 9, 2000) was that although the words "are very broad and might be interpreted as including the payment which may be made at the time the first person dies" it concluded that "the only life actually insured under the policy is that of the person that is the last to die." In coming to this conclusion, the CRA reasoned "it appears that the insurer is not at risk with respect to the amount payable on the death of the first person since the actual death benefit is paid upon the death of the last person covered under the policy and there is no mortality risk assumed by the insurer in respect of any benefit that may be paid on the death of the first of the two lives covered under the policy." As a result, the CRA considered the amount paid to be either a policy loan or a partial surrender — both dispositions under the definition.

Later, in technical interpretation 2000-0033885, dated September 11, 2000 the CRA reversed this position. The CRA stated that the wording in question does not expressly require "the insurer to be at risk for all or a portion of the benefit payable." As a result, the CRA stated that "subject to the terms and conditions of the policy, the relevant words could be interpreted to include the payment made as a consequence of the first to die under a joint last to die policy with the result that the payment of the benefit would not constitute a disposition."

The CRA further considered specific joint-last-to-die policy contract wording offering this feature. Technical interpretation 2003-0042861E5, dated June 25, 2004 did not focus on the question of whether the first to die is an insured person. Rather, the issue related to the nature of the feature under certain policy language. It is apparent from the response that if the payment of the amount on the first death involves "policyholder discretion as to whether a death benefit will be paid" the CRA suggests that this would not be a payment made "in consequence of death" and, therefore, the payment would not be excluded from the definition of disposition under the relevant paragraph.

The August 23, 2013 draft legislation proposes a change for post-2015 policies that would introduce the possibility of taxation of some portion of the death benefit paid on accumulated value paid on first death. See section 1.9.C.viii for a more detailed discussion.

ii. — Annuitization where the life insured is totally and permanently disabled

The term "totally or permanently disabled" is not defined in the Act. A CRA technical interpretation (2009-0308411E5, dated February 13, 2009) sought guidance relating to what constitutes total and permanent disability for this purpose. In particular, the question related to a situation where the policyholder surrendered their policy and chose to receive the proceeds of the policy as an annuity (which was one of several payment options described under the terms of the policy). At the time of surrender of the policy, the individual, whose life is insured, was receiving disability benefits under the *Canada Pension Plan Act* (the CPP Act).

The CRA expressed the view that the definition of "disposition" in subsection 148(9) does not require that the insurance policy contemplate the policy surrender and use of the full proceeds to purchase an annuity contract as a result of the disability of the life insured. They also stated that whether the individual, whose life is insured, was totally and permanently disabled for the purposes of the exclusion of such a payment from the definition of "disposition" in subsection 148(9) is a question of fact that must be determined based on the nature, severity, and expected duration of the individual's mental or physical impairment and is independent of the disability determination required pursuant to the CPP Act. Although it is clear from these comments that the CRA will not use the CPP definition of disability for the purposes of this section of the ITA, there is no clarification of what the CRA will view as total and permanent disability.

iii. — Disability benefits

In another technical interpretation (2007-0257591E5, dated December 15, 2008), the CRA was asked to consider whether the amount of all or a part of the account value of a universal life insurance policy paid where the insured became disabled would be viewed as a "disability benefit". In the arrangement described, the amount of the payment actually made would be at the discretion of the insured.

The CRA indicated as follows:

> It is not clear to us that a payment that is linked to a return to the policyholder of investment income earned in the policy would necessarily constitute a "disability benefit" even though the payment may be triggered by an event of disability, particularly where the policyholder has discretion over the amount of the benefit paid. The purpose of a disability policy is to replace income lost due to the disablement of the insured. Therefore, payments under such policies should not be capped to the amount of the account value of the policy.

One could make the case that the CRA may be reading in what it would like the requirements of the term "disability benefit" to be. There is nothing in the Act that requires that there be any particular level of risk exposure to constitute a "disability benefit". Since the term is not defined in the *Income Tax Act*, the general rule of statutory interpretation is to look at the literal or ordinary meaning of the words in the context that they are used. The CRA admitted that it would be a payment on disablement, and it is difficult to imagine how such a payment would not be a "benefit". As a result, it is unclear how it is possible to conclude that such a payment is not a "disability benefit".

On April 1, 2009 CALU wrote to the CRA asking it to reconsider this position. In June of 2009, CALU received an "informal" reply that will not be released publicly. CALU has reported that the CRA re-affirmed this position.

The August 23, 2013 draft legislation proposes an adjustment be made to the ACB of a post-2015 policy for disability payments. These amounts still would represent an exclusion from the definition of disposition and would be received tax-free. For a more detailed discussion of the draft legislation see section 1.9.C.vii.

D. — Proceeds of the disposition

The term "proceeds of the disposition" is defined in subsection 148(9) to be the amount of the proceeds that the policyholder is entitled to receive on the disposition of the interest in the policy. In the case of a surrender or maturity, the amount of the proceeds will equal the cash surrender value of the interest in the policy, adjusted for outstanding policy loans and unpaid premiums under the policy. In the case of a policy loan, the amount of the proceeds generally equals the amount of the loan less any portion of the loan applied to pay a premium under the policy.

The August 23, 2013 draft legislation proposes technical changes relating to the adjustments made for policy loans in calculating "proceeds of the disposition" for post-2015 policies. See section 1.9.C.viii for a more detailed discussion.

E. — Cash surrender value

The term "cash surrender value" is also defined in subsection 148(9). In most cases, "cash surrender value" simply means the cash surrender value of the life insurance policy reported by the insurer, without regard to any policy loans made under the policy and, in the case of participating insurance policies, excluding dividends left on deposit and interest thereon.

F. — Adjusted cost basis (ACB)

The adjusted cost basis represents the cost amount of a policyholder's interest in a life insurance policy. This is the base value from which policy gains are calculated.

The adjusted cost basis of a policyholder's interest in a life insurance policy is computed by reference to a complex formula set out at the definition of "adjusted cost basis" in subsection 148(9). The formula indicates that the adjusted cost basis will change with transactions affecting the life insurance policy. Certain factors increase the adjusted cost basis while other factors decrease the adjusted cost basis. The August 23, 2013 draft legislation proposes changes to several components of the definition of ACB for post-2015 policies. In general these include: recognition of premium ratings for substandard risks; changes to NCPI; reductions for payments of death benefits in certain situations; and reductions for disability payments.

See section 1.9.C.vii for a full discussion. The formula is cumulative and cannot result in a negative amount pursuant to section 257 of the Act.

Factors that increase the adjusted cost basis include:

- the cost of an interest in the policy acquired by the policyholder (e.g., the amount paid for an interest in an existing policy);
- premiums paid by or on behalf of the policyholder ("premium" is defined under subsection 148(9); for policies acquired prior to December 2, 1982, premiums include all premiums paid under the policy; for policies acquired after December 1, 1982 and premiums paid subsequent to May 31, 1985, premiums include premiums for the basic policy and term insurance riders only and exclude premiums for accidental death benefits, disability benefits, premium ratings for substandard lives, the cost of a conversion right, guaranteed insurability benefits, and any other ancillary benefits);
- policy dividends on a participating policy applied to purchase paid- up additions or enhancement coverage;
- interest paid after 1977 on a policy loan, other than interest that is deductible under paragraph 20(1)(c) or (d);
- policy gains required to be included in the policyholder's income from the disposition of an interest in the policy; and,
- policy loan repayments after March 31, 1978 in excess of the deduction permitted in paragraph 60(s) of the Act.

Factors that decrease the adjusted cost basis include:

- proceeds of disposition of an interest in the policy, including policy loans taken after March 31, 1978; and,
- in the case of a policy last acquired after December 1, 1982 by the policyholder, the cumulative total of all amounts each of which is the "net cost of pure insurance" (NCPI) as defined by Regulation 308 (under the 1982 transition rules, the deduction for NCPI is effective for calendar years subsequent to May 31, 1985).

The formula provided under the definition of "adjusted cost basis" in subsection 148(9) is quite extensive and includes various other factors that apply to non-exempt life insurance policies and annuity contracts.

Typically, the key factors that determine the adjusted cost basis of an exempt life insurance policy are the cumulative premiums for the basic plan (and any term insurance riders) less the cumulative NCPI. This assumes the policy was originally issued to the current policyholder and that no dispositions have taken place.

The NCPI, as the name suggests, represents the pure mortality costs under the policy each year. The NCPI is calculated in accordance with the rules contained in Regulation 308 and is based on mortality factors obtained from the Canadian Institute of Actuaries (CIA) 1969–1975 Select and Ultimate Mortality Tables applied to the net amount at risk. The net amount at risk is the difference between the death benefit and the accumulating fund, determined without reference to any policy loan outstanding, or the cash surrender value of the policy (depending on the method regularly followed by the insurer in calculating NCPI). The accumulating fund is defined in Regulation 307. The August 23, 2013 draft legislation proposes a more recent table, reflection of substandard ratings and changes to the calculation of the net amount at risk for post-2015 policies. See section 1.9.C.ii for a detailed discussion.

The apparent logic behind deducting the NCPI from the adjusted cost basis of the policy is that the NCPI represents the portion of the premium related to the cost of insurance whereas the adjusted cost basis is intended to measure the cost amount of the investment portion of the policy.

The NCPI increases each year after a policy is issued, primarily because of the increase in mortality factors as the life insured ages. The cumulative NCPI has a profound effect on the calculation of the adjusted cost basis of the policy. Simply put, if premium deposits exceed the NCPI in a given year, the adjusted cost basis will generally increase; if the NCPI exceeds the premium deposits in a given year, the adjusted cost basis will generally decrease. The higher the adjusted cost basis, the lower the policy gain in the event a disposition of an interest in the policy occurs.

The appropriate calculation of the NCPI of a policy where the life insured is older than age 70 was the subject of CRA comment (2005-0114801, dated May 12, 2005). The prescribed table ends at age 70. The CRA suggested that "where the table does not prescribe a particular rate of mortality due to the age of the life insured, it will be necessary to extrapolate from the information set out in the tables. . .using a method that is considered by the company's actuary(ies) to be reflective of accepted actuarial practices and provided that the method is employed consistently across all the company's policies of the particular class for which such extrapolation is necessary."

Following are two examples showing the adjusted cost basis calculated for each year. Both examples use hypothetical exempt universal life insurance plans and assume the life insured is a healthy 45-year-old male nonsmoker.

Example 1 assumes minimum level deposits of $4,000 are made into the insurance policy for life. The cash values are minimal. The illustration indicates the adjusted cost basis of the policy will initially increase each year, reach a maximum in about 15 years, and then decrease each year thereafter. In the example, the adjusted cost basis reduces to nil after about 23 years. At this time, the cumulative NCPI fully offsets the cumulative premium deposits.

Example 2 assumes the policyholder pays level maximum deposits of $17,000 into the insurance policy for a 20-year period. This has the effect of dramatically increasing the cash values, the total death benefit, and the adjusted cost basis relative to Example 1.

Example 1:
Male, age 45, non-smoker

$500,000 insurance need
Universal life policy
Face Plus coverage option
6% product rate
Minimum deposits of $4,000 paid for life

Year	Annual Deposit	Cumulative Deposits	NCPI	Cumulative NCPI	ACB	Cash Value	Death Benefit
1	4,000	4,000	520	520	3,480	0	500,144
2	4,000	8,000	615	1,136	6,864	0	500,297
3	4,000	12,000	726	1,861	10,139	0	500,459
4	4,000	16,000	846	2,707	13,293	0	500,630
5	4,000	20,000	982	3,689	16,311	0	500,812
6	4,000	24,000	1,122	4,811	19,189	0	501,005
7	4,000	28,000	1,293	6,104	21,896	0	501,210
8	4,000	32,000	1,499	7,603	24,397	0	501,426
9	4,000	36,000	1,751	9,354	26,646	0	501,656
10	4,000	40,000	2,048	11,403	28,597	0	502,071
11	4,000	44,000	2,371	13,774	30,226	0	502,339
12	4,000	48,000	2,714	16,488	31,512	0	502,623
13	4,000	52,000	3,076	19,564	32,436	1,099	502,925
14	4,000	56,000	3,456	23,020	32,980	2,331	503,244
15	4,000	60,000	3,885	26,905	33,095	3,827	503,827
16	4,000	64,000	4,740	31,645	32,355	4,201	504,201
17	4,000	68,000	5,330	36,975	31,025	4,597	504,597
18	4,000	72,000	6,045	43,020	28,980	5,017	505,017
19	4,000	76,000	6,875	49,895	26,105	5,462	505,462
20	4,000	80,000	7,790	57,685	22,315	6,452	506,452
21	4,000	84,000	8,750	66,435	17,565	6,983	506,983
22	4,000	88,000	9,770	76,205	11,795	7,547	507,547
23	4,000	92,000	10,840	87,045	4,955	8,143	508,143
24	4,000	96,000	11,995	99,040	0	8,776	508,776
25	4,000	100,000	13,290	112,330	0	10,193	510,193
:	:	:	:	:	:	:	:
:	:	:	:	:	:	:	:

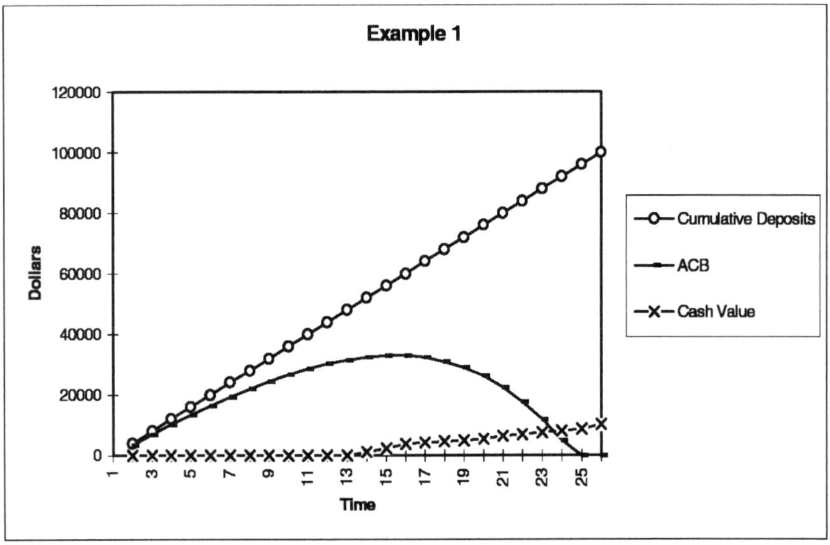
Example 1
120000
100000
80000
60000
40000
20000
0
Dollars
1
3
5
7
9
11
13
15
17
19
21
23
25
Time
Cumulative Deposits
ACB
Cash Value

Example 2:				**$500,000 insurance need**			
Male, age 45, non-smoker				**Universal life policy**			
				Face Plus coverage option			
				6% product rate			
				Maximum level deposits of $17,000 paid for 20 years			

Year	Annual Deposit	Cumulative Deposits	NCPI	Cumulative NCPI	ACB	Cash Value	Death Benefit
1	17,000	17,000	527	527	16,473	6,525	513,373
2	17,000	34,000	632	1,159	32,841	13,853	527,548
3	17,000	51,000	745	1,904	49,096	28,879	542,574
4	17,000	68,000	868	2,772	65,228	44,806	558,501
5	17,000	85,000	998	3,770	81,230	66,254	575,384
6	17,000	102,000	1,138	4,908	97,092	85,063	593,280
7	17,000	119,000	1,309	6,217	112,783	104,946	612,250
8	17,000	136,000	1,514	7,731	128,269	125,967	632,358
9	17,000	153,000	1,764	9,495	143,505	148,194	653,672
10	17,000	170,000	2,059	11,554	158,446	178,274	682,839
11	17,000	187,000	2,377	13,931	173,069	203,530	707,182
12	17,000	204,000	2,715	16,646	187,354	230,247	732,986
13	17,000	221,000	3,076	19,722	201,278	258,512	760,338
14	17,000	238,000	3,456	23,178	214,822	288,418	789,331
15	17,000	255,000	3,885	27,063	227,937	332,859	832,859
16	17,000	272,000	4,740	31,803	240,197	366,203	866,203
17	17,000	289,000	5,330	37,133	251,867	401,548	901,548
18	17,000	306,000	6,045	43,178	262,822	439,014	939,014
19	17,000	323,000	6,875	50,053	272,947	478,728	978,728
20	17,000	340,000	7,790	57,843	282,157	553,047	1,053,047
21	0	340,000	8,750	66,593	273,407	582,304	1,082,304
22	0	340,000	9,770	76,363	263,637	613,316	1,113,316
23	0	340,000	10,840	87,203	252,797	646,188	1,146,188
24	0	340,000	11,995	99,198	240,802	681,033	1,181,033
25	0	340,000	13,290	112,488	227,512	765,229	1,265,229
26	0	340,000	14,775	127,263	212,737	807,217	1,307,217
27	0	340,000	16,440	143,703	196,297	851,724	1,351,724
28	0	340,000	18,250	161,953	178,047	898,901	1,398,901
29	0	340,000	20,175	182,128	157,872	948,908	1,448,908
30	0	340,000	22,185	204,313	135,687	1,067,606	1,567,606
31	0	340,000	24,205	228,518	111,482	1,127,737	1,627,737
32	0	340,000	26,360	254,878	85,122	1,191,474	1,691,475
33	0	340,000	28,795	283,673	56,327	1,259,037	1,759,037
34	0	340,000	31,580	315,253	24,747	1,330,653	1,830,653
35	0	340,000	34,705	349,958	0	1,498,519	1,998,519
:	:	:	:	:	:	:	:
:	:	:	:	:	:	:	:

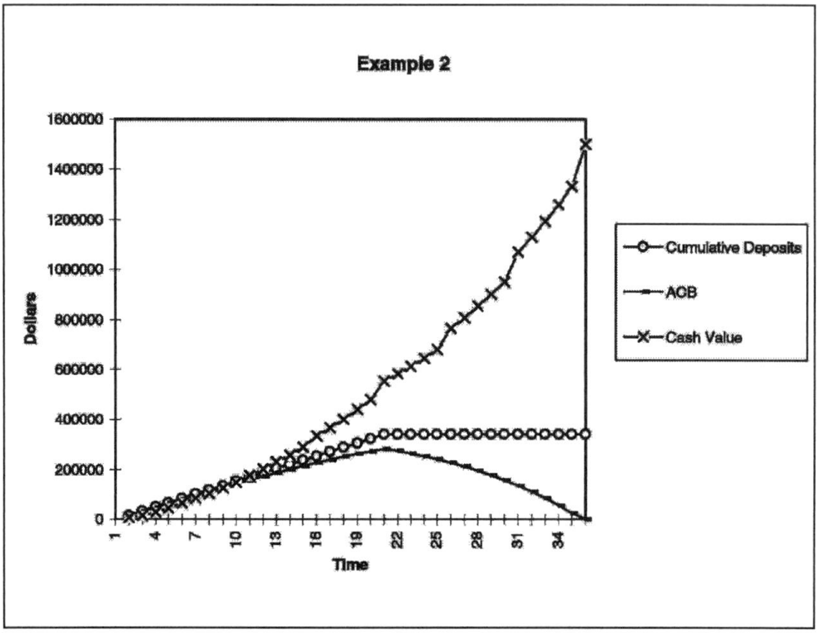

G. — Disposing of an interest in a life insurance policy

The following examples will help explain the income tax rules related to common transactions involving life insurance policies. In certain of the cases, reference will be made to the illustration previously used in Example 2 in the computation of the adjusted cost basis.

i. — Full surrender of the policy

The policyholder may choose to surrender the insurance policy in full. This might occur, for example, because the insurance coverage is no longer required, the policy has been replaced or the policy has been collaterally assigned and the third party lender has called the loan. At the time of the surrender, the policyholder is contractually entitled to an amount equal to the cash surrender value of the contract less policy loans and unpaid premiums (and, of course, amounts payable to a collateral assignee).

As noted previously, a surrender is a disposition of an interest in the policy pursuant to the definition of "disposition" under subsection 148(9). The policy gain under subsection 148(1) is calculated as the excess of the proceeds of the disposition (cash surrender value less outstanding policy loans and unpaid premiums) over the adjusted cost basis immediately before the disposition.

For example, using the illustration in Example 2 in the computation of the adjusted cost basis, above, the tax implications of a full surrender of the policy at selected intervals follow:

Policy surrendered in year	Cumulative deposits	CSV	ACB	Policy gain s. 148(1)	After tax proceeds
					[50% tax rate]
5	85,000	66,254	81,230	0	66,254
10	170,000	178,274	158,446	19,828	168,360
15	255,000	332,859	227,937	104,922	280,398
20	340,000	553,047	282,157	270,890	417,602
25	340,000	765,229	227,512	537,717	496,370
30	340,000	1,067,606	135,687	931,919	601,646
35	340,000	1,498,519	0	1,498,519	749,259

Initially, the adjusted cost basis exceeds the cash surrender value and no policy gain results. Over the years, the cash surrender value increases as deposits are made into the policy. The adjusted cost basis initially increases, reaches a maximum, and then declines to nil in year 35 in this example. Therefore, starting in year 35, the full cash surrender value is subject to taxation in the event the policy is surrendered.

While this result may, at first glance, seem unfair, it simply reflects the fact that the cumulative deposits made into the insurance policy have been fully ground down by the NCPI, and therefore the full cash surrender value represents the tax-sheltered investment earnings in the policy — earnings that have not previously been subject to policyholder taxation.

ii. — Partial surrender of the policy

The policyholder may choose to surrender a portion of the insurance policy. This might occur in order to fund a living buyout of a business owner's interest in a business, to provide supplementary retirement income, to meet emergency cash needs and so forth.

A partial surrender is a disposition of an interest in the policy pursuant to the definition of "disposition" under subsection 148(9). The policy gain under subsection 148(1) is calculated as the excess of the proceeds of the disposition (i.e. the amount withdrawn) over the proportionate adjusted cost basis immediately before the disposition. Subsection 148(4) provides that for policies acquired after December 1, 1982 the adjusted cost basis must be prorated between the amount of the partial surrender and the remainder of the policy at the time of the partial surrender. Specifically, the ACB of the partial interest is the proportion of the ACB of the policyholder's entire interest that the "proceeds of the disposition" are of the accumulating fund of the policy immediately before the withdrawal. The August 23, 2013 draft legislation proposes changes to the basis of the calculation for the pro-ration of the ACB on partial dispositions for post-2015 policies. See section 1.9.C.viii for a full discussion. The accumulating fund is defined in Regulation 307 as the greater of (i) the cash surrender value of the policy and (ii) the insurer's maximum reserve (present value of future benefits minus the present value of imputed future premiums) for the policy. Generally, for most products, the accumulating fund equals the cash surrender value of the policy, depending on the method regularly followed by the insurer. However for some policies the "greater of" amount may be the insurer's maximum reserve. This could be so where this reserve reflects not only the cash surrender value but any pre-funded portion of the cost of insurance. Since it is the "greater of" CSV and the insurer's maximum reserve that is used in the proportion required by subsection 148(4), a smaller proportion of the ACB is available to shelter the partial surrender from taxation where the reserve as opposed to CSV, is used.

Technical interpretation 2005-0145821E5, dated March 28, 2006 sought to confirm whether it is possible to determine the insurer's maximum reserve for a universal life insurance policy. In particular, it considered whether a "modified net premium" (the term used in Regulations 307 and 1401 to calculate the present value of imputed future premiums) could be determined for a universal life policy. Universal life policies generally do not require an insurer-determined premium to be paid and, while deposits to the policy are actually premiums paid, they are not determined by the insurer and are not fixed in advance. In the context of determining an insurer's investment income tax liability, the CRA confirmed that "in the event that the insurer can support its position that no reasonable amount in respect of its universal life insurance policies can be computed. . .it is our view that it would be acceptable to consider the amount determined. . .based on the CSV of the universal life insurance policies." The August 23, 2013 draft legislation proposes a prescribed basis for the calculation of the accumulating fund for Universal Life insurance policies issued after 2015. See section 1.9.C.i for a full discussion.

Using the illustration in Example 2 in the computation of the adjusted cost basis, above, the tax implications of a partial surrender, representing 10 percent of the accumulating fund, where the accumulating fund equals the cash surrender value of the policy, at selected intervals follows:

Policy surrend-ered in year	Total CSV	ACB	Surrender proceeds	Prorated ACB	Policy gain s. 148(1)	After tax proceeds
						[50% tax rate]
5	66,254	81,230	6,625	8,123	0	6,625
10	178,274	158,446	17,827	15,845	1,982	16,836
15	332,859	227,937	33,286	22,794	10,492	28,040
20	553,047	282,157	55,305	28,216	27,089	41,760
25	765,229	227,512	76,523	22,751	53,772	49,637
30	1,067,606	135,687	106,761	13,569	93,192	60,165
35	1,498,519	0	149,852	0	149,852	74,926

In this example, the tax implications of a partial surrender mirror the tax implications of a full surrender, but the amount reported as a policy gain is a prorated portion of the total accrued policy gain. As noted above, where the accumulating fund is the insurer's reserve, a smaller portion of the ACB will be available and thus a higher taxable policy gain would be reported.

A partial surrender also impacts the calculation of the adjusted cost basis of the policy. The adjusted cost basis is reduced by the proceeds of the disposition and is increased by the policy gain reported on the partial disposition. For instance, if the partial surrender in the preceding example occurs in year 15, the adjusted cost basis would decrease by the proceeds of the disposition ($33,286) and would be increased by the policy gain ($10,492), a net reduction of $22,794.

iii. — Policy loans, policy loan repayments, and policy loan interest

The policyholder may choose to access the policy values in the form of a policy loan under the insurance policy. This might occur to meet emergency cash needs, to provide funds for investment purposes, to provide supplementary retirement income and so forth.

Many cash value insurance policies provide the policyholder with the right to a policy loan. The amount of outstanding loans cannot exceed the cash surrender value of the insurance policy.

A policy loan is defined in subsection 148(9) as an amount advanced by an insurer to a policyholder in accordance with the terms and conditions of the life insurance policy.

These advances are typically referred to as policy loans in the life insurance policy. However, these advances are not true loans in the common commercial sense. They are advance payments of the policyholder's entitlement under the policy and the insurer cannot force the repayment of these advances. This view is confirmed in CRA technical interpretation RCT A-0579, dated December 12, 1984.

A policy loan taken after March 31, 1978 constitutes a disposition for tax purposes, pursuant to the definition of "disposition" under subsection 148(9) of the Act. The proceeds of the disposition will be the lesser of (i) the amount of the policy loan (other than the part of the loan which is used to pay a premium for the basic policy and any term insurance riders) and (ii) the excess of the cash surrender value of the policy over the balance outstanding from previous policy loans. This limits the proceeds of the disposition to the amount of the cash surrender value of the policy.

A policy gain will be reported under subsection 148(1) to the extent the policy loan proceeds exceed the full (not the prorated) adjusted cost basis of the policy. This means the policyholder may obtain a policy loan up to a maximum of the adjusted cost basis on a tax-free basis but that further advances will be taxable.

As mentioned previously, the adjusted cost basis of a life insurance policy is reduced by the policy loan proceeds and is increased by the amount of the policy gain calculated under subsection 148(1). The tracking of the cost amount in this manner ensures that amounts previously subject to taxation are not subject to double tax in the hands of the policyholder. The computation of the adjusted cost basis is also impacted by policy loan repayments and, in certain circumstances, by policy loan interest.

If a policy loan is repaid in whole or in part, paragraph 60(s) of the Act permits the policyholder to deduct from income the lesser of (i) the amount of the repayment and (ii) the amounts previously included in income as a policy gain under subsection 148(1) of the Act minus repayments made in a preceding year that were deductible under paragraph 60(s). This essentially ensures that, if a policy loan results in taxation under subsection 148(1), an offsetting deduction will be allowed as the policy loan is repaid. Any amount of the repayment in excess of the amount deductible under paragraph 60(s) is added to the adjusted cost basis of the policy. The August 23, 2013 draft legislation proposes changes to the calculation of the adjustment to ACB for repayments of policy loans for post-2015 policies. See section 1.9.C.viii for a detailed discussion.

If the life insured under a policy dies and a policy loan is outstanding on the policy, the death benefit paid is reduced by the amount of the policy loan. The CRA takes the view that no deduction under paragraph 60(s) is available where the policyholder/life insured previously included a policy gain in income in respect of the policy loan. It is the CRA's view (2009-0327091C6, dated October 9, 2009, Question 14 APFF and 9909075, dated June 17, 1999) that the person who had the income inclusion as a result of obtaining a policy loan (the policyholder) is different from the person who constructively repays the policy loan by way of a reduced death benefit from the policy (the policy beneficiary).

If interest on the policy loan is paid after 1977 and is not deductible from income under paragraph 20(1)(c) or (d), it is considered a "premium" under the definition of the term in subsection 148(9). The amount of the interest payment is added to the adjusted cost basis of the policy.

Similarly, if the policy loan interest is capitalized and is not deductible from income under paragraph 20(1)(c) or (d), it is also considered a premium and the capitalized amount is added to the adjusted cost basis of the policy. However, capitalized interest represents a further policy loan advance. The addition to the adjusted cost basis is, therefore, offset by a reduction to the adjusted cost basis and, accordingly, the adjusted cost basis is left unchanged when policy loan interest is capitalized (confirmed in 2008-0264301E5, dated March 2, 2009).

The preceding rules do not apply if the policyholder deducts the policy loan interest from income under paragraph 20(1)(c) or (d).

There are several requirements that must be met under paragraph 20(1)(c) or (d) in order for interest to be deductible, including, the interest must be paid or payable in the particular year (depending on the method regularly followed by the taxpayer), there must be a legal obligation to pay, and the borrowed funds must, generally, be used for the purpose of earning income from a business or property (other than property that produces exempt income or an interest in a life insurance policy).

In order for policy loan interest to be deductible, the requirements of paragraph 20(1)(c) or (d) must be met. There is a further requirement under subsection 20(2.1) that the policy loan interest must be verified by the insurer in prescribed form (CRA Form T2210: Verification of policy loan interest by the insurer). The insurer must verify that the interest is paid in the year on that policy loan (capitalized loan interest is considered to be paid at the time it is added to the policy loan for this purpose) and that the amount of the interest has not been added to the adjusted cost basis of the policy. This is discussed in detail in archived Interpretation Bulletin IT-355R2 "Interest on Loans to Buy Life Insurance Policies and Annuity Contracts, and Interest on Policy Loans," dated August 26, 1994. When interest is deductible under paragraph 20(1)(c) or (d), the payment of interest against the policy loan is not considered to be a premium and the amount is not added to the adjusted cost basis of the policy.

If deductible interest is capitalized, the capitalization is considered a new policy loan. However, unlike non-deductible interest, the proceeds of disposition for a policy loan generated by the capitalization of deductible interest is not reduced by the interest capitalized since the interest is not considered an eligible premium. Therefore, the proceeds of disposition in this case will equal the capitalized interest and a taxable policy gain will result if the capitalized interest is greater than the ACB of the policy (subject to the CSV ceiling). This is confirmed in 2009-0319451E5, dated January 28, 2010.

If policy loans related to capitalized interest that was deductible are repaid, then the portion of the repayment (not greater than the policy gain previously included in income) is deductible by the policyholder under paragraph 60(s) of the Act. The portion of the repayment in excess of the deductible amount would be added to the ACB of the policy (unless the CSV ceiling came into play when the interest was capitalized).

To summarize, consider the following example, again using the illustration in Example 2 in the computation of the adjusted cost basis (see section 3.2.F), the tax implications related to a $150,000 policy loan taken at the end of year 30 and repaid over the next three years:

Year	Loan Amount	Total ACB	Income s. 148(1)	Loan repayment	Deduction s. 60(s)	Impact on ACB
30	150,000	135,687	14,313			-135,687
31				- 50,000	- 14,313	+35,687
32				- 50,000		+50,000
33				- 50,000		+50,000

In the year the policy loan is taken, the $14,313 excess of the loan proceeds over the adjusted cost basis of the policy is included in the policyholder's income. Assuming equal repayments over the next three years, the first $14,313 repaid will be deductible under paragraph 60(s). Excess loan repayments over this amount ($35,687 in the first year and $50,000 each year thereafter) increase the adjusted cost basis of the policy. The actual adjusted cost basis in each of the years 31 through 33 will, of course, be affected by other factors as well, including cumulative premiums and the cumulative NCPI reductions.

There are certain advantages of taking a policy loan versus a partial surrender of an interest in the policy. For one, the proceeds are only taxable to the extent they exceed the full adjusted cost basis of the policy whereas a partial surrender results in proportional recognition of accrued policy gains because the adjusted cost basis is prorated. For a given amount of funds accessed from the insurance policy, the taxation of a policy loan will often be less than a partial surrender as long as the adjusted cost basis exceeds nil at the time of the transaction. Secondly, a policy loan may be repaid at any time, and a deduction taken for the amount of the policy gain previously included in income. A partial surrender represents a permanent withdrawal from the insurance policy.

iv. — Policy dividends on participating insurance policies

Policy dividends are generally declared by the life insurer annually and are paid or credited to participating policyholders on their policy year anniversary date. They are not to be confused with "taxable dividends" as defined in subsection 89(1). Policy dividends are often referred to as a refund of excess premiums paid on participating insurance plans. Perhaps a more accurate description is that a policy dividend represents the policyholder's share of the operating success of the participating fund of the insurer (see sections 2.3.A.ii.a and 2.7).

Policy dividends trigger a deemed disposition of an interest in the insurance policy under paragraph 148(2)(a).

The proceeds of the disposition for a policy dividend are deemed to be the amount of the policy dividend less any amount used to pay a premium under the basic policy or for any term insurance riders, or to repay a policy loan.

If the proceeds of the disposition under paragraph 148(2)(a) are less than the adjusted cost basis of the interest in the policy immediately before that time, the proceeds simply reduce the adjusted cost basis and the policy dividend does not result in a policy gain. However, if the proceeds of the disposition exceed the adjusted cost basis of the interest in the policy, the excess results in a policy gain under subsection 148(1) reported to the policyholder. In this case, the computation of "adjusted cost basis" under the definition provided under subsection 148(9) indicates the adjusted cost basis is reduced by the proceeds of the disposition and is increased by the policy gain reported to the policyowner.

The result of these rules is that generally policy dividends used in internal policy transactions (for example, to pay premiums, to purchase paid-up additions or term insurance added to the basic coverage, or to repay policy loans) will have zero proceeds under the deemed disposition rule in paragraph 148(2)(a). In these cases, the policy dividend has no impact on the adjusted cost basis because there are no proceeds and there is no policy gain. Note, however, that a policy gain may arise where some of the "premiums" paid are not included in the term "premium" for tax purposes. The definition of "premium" in subsection 148(9) excludes premiums for accidental death benefits, disability benefits, premium ratings for substandard lives, the cost of conversion rights, guaranteed insurability, and any other ancillary benefits. (See section 1.8.A.iii for further discussion of the definition of "premium".)

v. — Transfer of ownership (absolute assignment)

The policyholder may choose to transfer ownership of the interest in the insurance policy to another person. This might occur, for example, because (i) the insurance coverage was purchased by a parent (or grandparent) on the life of a child (or grandchild) and the policy is to be transferred to the life insured child (or grandchild) after they reach a certain age, (ii) the policy is corporate-owned insurance on the life of the owner-manager who, following retirement, requires the insurance to meet ongoing estate planning needs, or (iii) two shareholders who had previously purchased insurance on each other to fund a buy/sell agreement in the event of death are selling the business and wish to go their separate ways, and so forth.

A transfer of ownership of an interest in a life insurance policy represents a disposition for tax purposes. The taxation of a transfer of ownership of an interest in a life insurance policy depends on the relationship between the transferor and the transferee, whether the general rules in subsection 148(1) or the specific rules in subsection 148(7) apply, and whether an exception is to be found under subsection 148(8), (8.1) or (8.2).

a. — The general rule

A transfer of ownership of an interest in a life insurance policy is a disposition for tax purposes. The policy gain under subsection 148(1) is equal to the excess of the proceeds of the disposition, usually the transfer price, over the adjusted cost basis of the interest immediately before that time. The policy gain is included in the transferor's income and taxed accordingly. In accordance with the formula definition of "adjusted cost basis" in subsection 148(9), the initial adjusted cost basis to the transferee is the transfer price.

b. — Gifts, corporate distributions, non-arm's length transfers, etc.

Notwithstanding the general rule, specific rules are provided in subsection 148(7) relating to certain transactions. The provision applies where an interest in an insurance policy is disposed of by the owner, whether for consideration or not, in one of four circumstances:

a. it is transferred by way of gift or bequest;

b. it is distributed from a corporation;

c. it is disposed of by way of operation of law only (such as a transfer to successor owner or joint tenant); or

d. it is disposed of to any non-arm's length person

unless paragraph 148(2)(b) applied to the disposition.

The provision will not apply to an arm's length sale of a life insurance policy. The specific rules in subsection 148(7) override the general rules noted above. Subsection 148(7) deems the proceeds of the disposition to the transferor to be equal to the "value" of the interest at the time of the disposition, and the transferee is deemed to acquire the interest at a cost equal to that "value."

The term "value" at a particular time of an interest in a life insurance policy is defined in subsection 148(9) to be the amount that the holder of the policy would be entitled to receive if the policy were surrendered (essentially the cash surrender value net of policy loans) if the policy has cash value, otherwise the value is nil.

Subsection 148(7) covers quite a range of possible situations involving the transfer of an interest in a policy, particularly gifts, transfers from a corporation, and transfers between persons not at arm's length.

The purpose of the rules in subsection 148(7) is to ensure that the calculation of the policy gain is based on the cash surrender value, if any, and not a higher or lower amount. For example, if the fair market value of the policy exceeds the cash surrender value, subsection 148(7) ensures the computation of the policy gain to the transferor is based on the cash surrender value and not the fair market value. Alternatively, if the interest is transferred for proceeds less than the cash surrender value, for example, between parties not dealing at arm's length, subsection 148(7) ensures the policy gain to the transferor is based on at least the cash surrender value.

The tax implications related to corporate distributions and non-arm's length transfers involving corporate-owned insurance are canvassed in more detail below (see section 3.3.I.).

c. — Tax-free rollovers

Subsections 148(8) to (8.2) provide automatic rollovers on the transfer of an interest in a life insurance policy to a child, spouse or common-law partner, or former spouse or common-law partner of the policyholder in specific situations. Where a rollover applies, the transferor will be deemed to have disposed of the interest in the policy for proceeds of the disposition equal to the adjusted cost basis of that interest, and the transferee will be deemed to have acquired the interest in the policy at a cost equal to those proceeds.

Effectively, these rules permit a tax-free rollover in specific situations. The limited circumstances in which these rules apply are outlined below.

I. — Generation transfers and intergeneration transfers

Subsection 148(8) provides an automatic tax-free rollover where an interest in a life insurance policy has been transferred to the policyholder's child for no consideration and a child of the policyholder or a child of the transferee is the life insured under the policy. Any policy gain on a subsequent disposition of the policy would be taxed in the hands of the transferee provided the transferee is 18 years of age or older. A rollover is not allowed if the policy is transferred to the owner's child and the owner is the life insured under the policy (2001-0098185, dated October 17, 2001).

For the purposes of subsection 148(8), the term "child" is defined in subsection 148(9) and, indirectly, subsection 252(1) and subsection 70(10). The definition of "child" is very broad. Subsection 148(9) of the Act defines the term "child" to include the definition found in subsection 70(10) of the Act. This provision extends the definition to grandchildren, great-grandchildren and persons under the age of 19 who are wholly dependent and in the custody and control of the taxpayer. The extended definition of "child" for all purposes of the Act is found in subsection 252(1) of the Act. Depending on the facts, any one of these provisions may be considered.

The definition of "child" may include a step-child or step-grandchild. For example, consider a grandparent with a child who has a step-child. A step-child is considered a child of the step-parent under subsection 252(1)(c) of the Act, which states that a child includes a child of the taxpayer's (step-parent's) spouse or common-law partner. A step-grandchild is considered a child of the grandparent under subsection 70(10) of the Act, which states that a child includes a child of the taxpayer's (grandparent's) child. Since the step-child is a child of the step-parent, the step-child is considered a child of the grandparent. However, in order for a tax-free rollover to occur, the definition of "child" under paragraph 252(1)(c) of the Act must be met at the time of the transfer. In technical interpretation 2005-0114721E5, the CRA discussed whether the step-parent continued to be related to the adult step-child after the death of the parent of the step-child. In this case, the adult step-child no longer qualified as a child of the step-parent as the step-child was at no time wholly dependent on the step-parent and was not adopted in law or fact by the step-parent. This is consistent with the position that the step-child and step-parent would no longer be considered to be related to each other by marriage as the marriage is considered to be dissolved by the death of the parent. As the definition of child is no longer met, a tax-free rollover would not be available. Similarly, where the marriage breaks down prior to the transfer occurring, the tax-free roll-over may not be available.

The definition of "child" in subsection 70(10) of the Act may also include a person (for example, a nephew or niece) where the person was wholly dependent and under the custody and control of the taxpayer at any time before the person attained the age of 19 years.

Meeting the definition of "child" in these cases may be dependent on meeting or having met the definition of "wholly dependent" prior to age 19 and will be fact specific. Where this definition has been met, a transfer can occur at any time afterwards, and need not be met at the time of the transfer.

The transferee child does not have to be the same person as the child whose life is insured. For example, a life insurance policy on the life of the policyholder's child may be transferred under subsection 148(8) to the policyholder's grandchild.

In order to take advantage of the tax-free rollover under subsection 148(8) it is necessary to comply strictly with the requirements of the provision. In technical interpretation 9433865, dated February 15, 1995, the CRA expressed the view that the rollover would not be available where the policyholder transferred the interest in the policy to the child under provisions in the policyholder's Will. The CRA noted that the policy in this case would first be transferred to the deceased policyholder's estate and then to the child rather than directly from the deceased to the child, so the requirements in subsection 148(8) would not be met. In this case the deceased policyholder has a disposition of the policy, and any policy gain would be taxable in the terminal return. Note that administrative practice among insurance carriers may differ, and T5s may sometimes be issued to the estate in these circumstances.

In technical interpretation 9618075, dated September 3, 1996, the CRA confirmed that the rollover would apply where the policy is transferred to the child on the death of the policyholder by virtue of a successor owner designation made under, for example, subsection 199(1) of the *Insurance Act* (Ontario).

The CRA in technical interpretation 9826715, dated January 19, 1999 has also commented that "it is not possible for a policyholder to transfer their interest in a life insurance policy (that otherwise meets the conditions of subsection 148(8) of the Act) to any type of trust under subsection 148(8) of the Act. This is the case even if a policyholder transferred his/her interest in a life insurance policy (that otherwise met all the other conditions of subsection 148(8) of the Act) to a trust established solely for the benefit of his/her minor child since the transfer would not have been made to the child of the policyholder as required by subsection 148(8) of the Act." In the case where a transfer of a policy to which 148(8) would otherwise apply, is made to a guardian of a child's property, the CRA confirmed in technical interpretation 2008-0270431C6 (Question 7 CALU CRA Roundtable dated April 29, 2008) that the rollover applies because "a guardian of property is appointed to manage the financial affairs of a minor or a person who is mentally incapable of doing so for himself or herself" and this "will not affect the ownership of the interest since the guardian of property only act on the incapable person's behalf. The property (the interest in the life insurance policy) is still belonging to the minor or the incapable."

Other structures that have attempted to qualify for this rollover include the use of substitute life or multi-life insurance policies. With a substitute life policy, the original insured would be the parent but the child would become the substituted life prior to the transfer of the policy to the child. In a multi-life policy, the parent and the child would be insured under one policy contract. Technical interpretation 2004-0065441C6, dated May 4, 2004 confirmed that a rollover under subsection 148(8) would not apply to a transfer of a life insurance policy under which more than one person is insured regardless of whether all of the lives insured meet the definition of child under this provision.

The purpose of these structures is to take advantage of the higher premium deposits permitted under the exemption test rules for an adult compared to the premium deposits permitted for a minor child. The higher the premium deposits, the greater the ability to shelter the investment growth within the insurance policy.

The CRA has indicated in at least two technical interpretations that in order for the tax-free rollover to apply, the child must be the only life insured under the policy, and it is arguable that this narrow view applies to both substitute life and multi-life insurance policies (technical interpretations AU91_285.286, dated August 1, 1991, and 5-8204, dated July 11, 1989). However, in interpretation 2005-0116681, dated May 3, 2005 the application of a rollover was considered in relation to a joint last-to-die policy insuring the lives of a parent and a child. The child would be the successor owner on the parent's death. The CRA agreed that there would be only one life insured remaining on the policy at death and if all the other conditions for a rollover were met, subsection 148(8) would apply and allow the policy to be transferred to the child on a rollover basis. (Similar conclusions were found in technical interpretations 2005-0125391E5, dated August 29, 2005 and 2005-0137151E5, dated December 12, 2005).

Subsection 148(8) effectively permits a parent (or grandparent) to transfer on a tax-free basis a life insurance policy, purchased by the parent on the life of the child, to the child. There is no time limit as to when the transfer must take place, allowing parents to maintain control of the policy until such time as they deem the child capable of taking ownership of the policy.

For example, a parent (or grandparent) could purchase a life insurance policy on the life of a child (or grandchild). The purpose of the policy would be to ensure the child has lifetime protection and to accumulate funds on a tax-sheltered basis for future use by the child. At some time in the future, the policy may be transferred to the life insured child on a tax-free rollover basis under subsection 148(8). Any policy gains arising from any disposition of the interest in the policy subsequent to the transfer will be taxed in the child's hands. Typically, the transfer will take place after the child attains age 18 in order to avoid the attribution rules under subsection 74.1(2).

In the case of a grandparent purchasing a life insurance policy on the life of a grandchild, it would be necessary to plan for the possibility of the death of the grandparent prior to the grandchild attaining age 18. This could be accomplished by designating the grandparent's spouse or common-law partner, or a child of the grandparent (who is a parent of the insured grandchild) as a successor owner of the life insurance policy. The successor owner would receive the policy on a rollover basis pursuant to either 148(8.2) or 148(8). The policy could then be transferred to the grandchild under subsection 148(8) by the successor owner after the grandchild attains age 18.

II. — *Inter vivos* transfer to spouse or common-law partner

Subsection 148(8.1) applies to transfers during life to the policyholder's spouse or common-law partner, or a former spouse or common-law partner in settlement of rights arising out of their marriage. There is no requirement that the life insured be the policyholder's spouse or common- law partner in order for subsection 148(8.1) to apply. However, both the policyholder and the transferee must be resident in Canada at the time of the transfer.

If subsection 148(8.1) applies, the interest is deemed to have been disposed of by the policyholder for proceeds of disposition equal to the adjusted cost basis of the interest immediately before the transfer and to have been acquired by the transferee at a cost equal to those proceeds.

Subsection 148(8.1) is an automatic provision which is intended to mirror, in many respects, the spousal rollover provisions in subsection 73(1) and elsewhere in the Act. The policyholder can elect out of the automatic rollover by filing an election in the policyholder's income tax return for the year of the transfer. There is no prescribed form so a letter providing the relevant details and stating the fact that the policyholder wishes to elect out of the automatic rollover under subsection 148(8.1) would be appropriate.

If the policyholder elects out of the rollover available under subsection 148(8.1), subsection 148(7) applies to the transfer. This is confirmed in CRA technical interpretation 9232987, dated December 10, 1992.

Because life insurance is considered "property" for income tax purposes, the spousal attribution rules under section 74.1 must be considered. If the policyholder transfers an interest in a life insurance policy to a spouse or common-law partner under the automatic rollover provisions in subsection 148(8.1) and the transferee spouse or common- law partner subsequently disposes of the interest in the policy, any resulting policy gain, and income and capital gains generated from substituted property, will be taxable to the original policyholder (i.e. the transferor).

III. — Transfer to spouse or common-law partner at death

Subsection 148(8.2) is also an automatic rollover provision. This provision applies to a transfer of an interest in a life insurance policy to the policyholder's spouse or common-law partner as a consequence of the death of the policyholder. There is no requirement that the life insured be the policyholder's spouse or common-law partner in order for subsection 148(8.2) to apply. However, in order to qualify for the rollover provision, both the deceased policyholder and the surviving spouse or common-law partner must be resident in Canada immediately before the policyholder's death.

If subsection 148(8.2) applies, the interest is deemed to have been disposed of by the policyholder for proceeds of disposition equal to the adjusted cost basis of the interest immediately before the transfer and to have been acquired by the transferee at a cost equal to those proceeds.

Subsection 148(8.2) is an automatic provision. The deceased's personal representative may elect out of the automatic rollover by filing an election in the policyholder's terminal income tax return. There is no prescribed form so a letter providing the relevant details and stating the fact that the policyholder wishes to elect out of the automatic rollover under subsection 148(8.2) would be appropriate.

As above, if the deceased's personal representative elects out of the rollover available under 148(8.2), subsection 148(7) applies to the transfer. This is confirmed in CRA technical interpretation 9232987, dated December 10, 1992.

It should be noted that the provisions of subsections 148(8.1) and 148(8.2) do not apply to the transfer of a policy to a spousal trust. Such a transfer would give rise to proceeds of disposition equal to cash surrender value.

Estate planning often contemplates joint ownership arrangements. Owning property jointly may result from a relationship with another individual or for convenience to assist an elderly person in managing assets. While a full discussion on the various types of ownership and the issues associated with such arrangements is beyond the scope of this chapter, a brief discussion follows of transfers and joint tenancy arrangements involving life insurance.

Life insurance may be owned by way of a joint tenancy arrangement or as tenants in common. Joint tenants have one and the same interest. There is a right of survivorship in the interest by the other owner. This differs from a tenancy in common relationship where on death the interest is severed and reverts back to the estate of the deceased individual and would then pass by way of the deceased's Will.

When property is transferred into joint tenancy from single ownership or out of joint tenancy (on death or otherwise), the CRA generally takes the position that a disposition of a 50 percent interest in the property would occur for tax purposes (technical interpretation 2005-0152011E5, dated July 6, 2006).

Where a joint tenancy arrangement exists in respect of a life insurance policy, whereby A and B are joint tenants, on the death of A, the policy will pass to the survivor, B, but may also trigger a taxable disposition of the policy unless a rollover provision applies (see 3.2.G.v.c above in relation to rollover provisions). It will, however, not be subject to probate fees and is therefore attractive for estate planning purposes.

When a policy is transferred into joint ownership from single ownership, for example, from A, to A and B jointly, according to the CRA general position, a disposition of a 50 percent interest in the policy at the time of the transfer would occur unless a rollover provision applies (as previously discussed at section 3.2.G.v.c). Where a rollover provision does not apply, the transfer into joint ownership should be considered carefully as a taxable policy gain (T5 income) may result where the cash value exceeds the adjusted cost basis of the policy.

3.3 — Selected Valuation Issues

Life insurance creates and preserves wealth. At the same time, the income tax rules relating to the taxation of life insurance permit substantial wealth accumulation within the insurance policy, subject to the exempt test limits. As a result, an interest in a life insurance policy is a valuable asset. This is an advantage when it comes to designing insurance strategies. However, it can also create certain issues that need to be addressed in the planning process.

This section outlines certain of the valuation issues that should be considered when designing life insurance strategies, particularly in the case of corporate-owned life insurance. Chapters 6 and 7 cover specific business insurance needs.

A. — Valuation of an interest in a life insurance policy

The CRA has set out business valuation procedures in Information Circular IC 89-3 "Policy Statement on Business Equity Valuations," dated August 25, 1989. The information circular outlines the valuation principles, practices and policies that the CRA generally considers and follows in the valuation of securities and intangible property of closely held corporations for income tax purposes. The information circular also provides a list of factors that the CRA would consider when determining the fair market value of corporate-owned life insurance (see paragraphs 40 and 41 of IC 89-3).

Determining the value of shares in a private corporation requires the consideration of a number of fundamental factors, including the nature of the business, the outlook for the company and the industry, the company's balance sheet, financial condition, earnings record, goodwill, etc. There are also numerous factors and issues relevant to the valuation of specific shareholdings, including the existence of options, buy/sell agreements, special rights or privileges attached to certain classes of shares, controlling interests versus minority shareholdings, and the existence of corporate-owned life insurance.

While IC 89-3 generally applies to the valuation of shares in private corporations, the CRA has indicated that the list of factors used for determining the value of corporate-owned life insurance will also be used to determine the fair market value of any interest in a life insurance policy.

There are a number of circumstances when a valuation involving a life insurance policy is required under the *Income Tax Act*. When a specific income tax provision applies, the valuation for tax purposes is determined under the specific provision. For example, subsection 70(5.3) of the Act deems the value of corporate-owned life insurance on a deceased shareholder's life to be the cash surrender value when determining the fair market value of the deceased's shares immediately before death for purposes of the deemed disposition rules under subsection 70(5). However, when a specific income tax provision does not apply, the CRA will use normal valuation approaches to determine the value of a corporate-owned life insurance policy.

Paragraph 40 of IC 89-3 lists the factors that would be considered in determining the value of corporate-owned life insurance:

a) the cash surrender value of the policy;

b) the policy's loan value;

c) the face value of the policy;

d) the state of health of the insured and his/her life expectancy;

e) conversion privileges under the policy;

f) other policy terms, such as term riders, double indemnity provisions; and,

g) the replacement value of the policy.

The application of normal valuation approaches to an interest in a life insurance policy can produce a fair market value which is materially different than the cash surrender value of the insurance policy. For example, if the death of the life insured is considered imminent and the normal valuation approaches apply, the fair market value of the interest in the insurance policy may well exceed the policy's cash surrender value, and may actually approach the total death benefit in extreme cases.

In the Saskatchewan decision of *Paterson v. Remedios* (1999), 29 E.T.R. (2d) 279 (Sask. Q.B.) the Court of Queen's Bench assigned a significant value to a term insurance policy that had no cash surrender value. Although the decision is not a tax case, the reasoning of the decision is pertinent. The case concerned the valuation of family property in the context of a marital breakdown for purposes of the *Matrimonial Property Act* (Saskatchewan). The life insured changed the beneficiary designation on a term life insurance policy after being informed that he had a terminal illness. The prior beneficiary was the life insured's former spouse. A few months later the life insured died. The issue before the court was whether the policy had any "value" for family law purposes. The court noted that normally the value of a term insurance policy would be nominal. However, the determination of value differs where the life insured is ill. The court considered the ability of an insured person to obtain living benefits in respect of a life insurance policy and concluded that for purposes of the *Matrimonial Property Act* the policy actually had a value of nearly 50 percent of its face amount.

Determining the fair market value of an interest in an insurance policy is not an exact science. Fair market value is a question of fact. However, some basic truths exist. The fair market value of a life insurance policy will generally not be lower than the cash surrender value, if any, of the policy but can be significantly higher than the cash surrender value, if any, based on normal valuation principles. Because fair market value is a question of fact, it is important that taxpayers who are asserting a particular point of view relating to fair market value appropriately establish the basis for their view. As in any other matter of valuation, it is appropriate to seek the opinion(s) of a valuation professional(s).

The CRA noted in the 2008 APFF CRA Roundtable, Question 17 (technical interpretation 2008-028615, dated October 10, 2008), that it will examine taxpayer requests concerning complex appraisal topics. The CRA stated, "the purpose of the service is to assist taxpayers by answering their questions regarding the methods or approaches used. However, we do not issue opinions on the value of a property or on estimates or statements proposed by a taxpayer, nor do we discuss the specific elements entering into the determination of the FMV of a specific property. The comments provided do not constitute an advance ruling and are not binding on the CRA. Moreover, we limit our comments when the information provided is incomplete or inadequate. Once the transaction is completed, it may be audited by us, just as if no request for an opinion had been submitted."

B. — Valuation and the type of insurance product

Term insurance policies and term-to-100 permanent insurance policies typically do not have cash values. Permanent whole life policies and universal life policies usually have cash values.

If a specific provision under the *Income Tax Act* applies to a particular transaction involving an interest in a life insurance policy, the income tax rules are based on the specific provision. However, in the absence of a specific provision, the normal valuation approaches for life insurance policies may have to be considered.

C. — Valuation of shares for the deemed disposition upon death under subsection 70(5)

i. — Corporate-owned life insurance on deceased shareholder, related parties and other shareholders or employees

Subsection 70(5) of the Act provides the general rule that a deceased taxpayer is deemed to have disposed of each capital property (including private corporation shares) for proceeds equal to the fair market value of the property immediately before death. As a result, any accrued capital gain/loss will be realized for income tax purposes on the deceased's final income tax return (unless a specific relieving provision applies, for example, subsection 70(6) under which the property may be transferred on a tax-free rollover to a surviving spouse or common- law partner, or qualifying spouse trust).

In the case of private corporation shares, the guidelines provided in IC 89-3 are useful in determining the fair market value of the shares for purposes of the deemed disposition rule under subsection 70(5). The question arises as to how a corporate-owned insurance policy will impact the valuation of the deceased's shares immediately before death.

If a buy/sell agreement exists and the parties are dealing at arm's length, then the buy/sell agreement will generally be determinative of value as long as the agreement meets the following requirements (see paragraph 28 of IC 89-3):

(a) the agreement must obligate the estate to sell the shares at death either under a mandatory sales and purchase agreement or at the option of a designated purchaser;

(b) the agreement must restrict the shareholder's right to dispose of his/her shares at any price during his/her lifetime;

(c) the agreement must fix a price for the shares or set out a method for determining the price on a current basis; and

(d) the agreement must represent a *bona fide* business arrangement and not a device to pass the decedent's shares to his/her heirs for less than an adequate and full consideration.

If the above qualifications are satisfied the valuation of the shares will be made in accordance with the provisions of the buy/sell agreement, and corporate-owned insurance will not create any special valuation concerns. See section 7.4 for a discussion of various insurance funded buy/sell strategies.

If a buy/sell agreement exists but the parties are not dealing at arm's length, then the buy/sell agreement may still be determinative of value as long as the agreement meets certain additional requirements (see paragraph 29 of IC 89-3):

(a) it is a *bona fide* business arrangement;

(b) the stipulated price or formula price in the agreement provides full and adequate consideration, and represents the fair market value of shares (which may include the cash surrender value of a life insurance contract) determined without reference to the agreement at the time it is executed; and

(c) it is a legal and binding contract.

In this case, the valuation of the shares will again be made in accordance with the provisions of the buy/sell agreement, and corporate-owned insurance will not create any special valuation concerns.

However, if there is no buy/sell agreement or the buy/sell agreement is not determinative of value, normal valuation approaches will be used in determining the fair market value of the shares. This will necessitate determining the fair market value of the underlying assets of the corporation, including corporate-owned life insurance.

Formerly, the CRA took the position that the death benefit paid under a corporate-owned life insurance policy on the life of the deceased shareholder could increase the value of the corporation's shares for purposes of the deemed disposition rules under subsection 70(5), using normal valuation approaches. This position could have had a significant impact on the capital gains tax liability on private corporation shares held by the deceased. However, the CRA's position was successfully challenged in *Mastronardi v. The Queen*, [1977] C.T.C. 355 (F.C.A.).

In the *Mastronardi* case, the deceased taxpayer owned shares in a private corporation. At the time of his death in 1973, the corporation owned a $500,000 term insurance policy on the deceased taxpayer's life. The insurance policy paid a $500,000 tax-free death benefit to the corporation following the death of the taxpayer.

Under subsection 70(5) the deceased's shares were deemed to have been disposed of "immediately before death" for proceeds equal to their fair market value at that time. The Minister assessed the deceased on a deemed capital gain based on the premise that "immediately before death" meant the instant of death so that the insurance proceeds would have become receivable. Based on the facts presented in the case, the deceased taxpayer's shares in the corporation would have had a value of $323.58 each if the insurance proceeds were disregarded and $778.59 each if those proceeds were taken into account in determining the value of his shares. The inclusion of the insurance proceeds significantly increased the taxable capital gain on the deceased's terminal return. The court held that the words "immediately before death" in subsection 70(5) should not be construed as meaning at the instant of death and, therefore, the life insurance policy proceeds should not be considered in determining the fair market value of the deceased's shares. Subsection 70(5.3) was subsequently introduced to reflect the *Mastronardi* decision.

For purposes of the deemed disposition rule at subsection 70(5) where subsection 70(5.3) applies, in determining the fair market value of shares owned by the deceased shareholder the fair market value of a corporate-owned life insurance policy is deemed to be its cash surrender value immediately before death.

Subsection 70(5.3) provides specific rules for determining the value of a corporate-owned life insurance policy on the life of the deceased shareholder. However, subsection 70(5.3) only applies to corporate-owned life insurance policies held on the life of the deceased shareholder and other individuals not dealing at arm's length with the deceased shareholder. The CRA has indicated in IC 89-3 that it will value corporate-owned life insurance policies on other lives at fair market value, determined in accordance with the factors noted previously.

Therefore, the valuation of a corporate-owned life insurance policy on the life of the deceased shareholder and non-arm's length individuals will be based on the cash surrender value of the policy pursuant to subsection 70(5.3), but corporate-owned life insurance on any other lives (e.g., the surviving shareholders if dealing at arm's length with the deceased) will be valued using normal valuation approaches.

Based on a strict reading of former subsection 70(5.3), the provision did not apply to joint life or multi-life insurance policies. In these cases, the normal valuation approaches listed in Information Circular 89-3 applied. The reason subsection 70(5.3) did not apply is found in the words "of any life insurance policy under which the taxpayer was the person whose life was insured." The CRA is of the view that the words "the taxpayer" and "the person" limited the application of former subsection 70(5.3) to an interest in an insurance policy on the life of the deceased shareholder only.[1]

This issue was called to the Department of Finance's attention at the 1998 APFF Congress. Their response (Roundtable 9M 18520, question 41, dated October 9, 1998) was that from a tax policy standpoint it would be appropriate to apply the same cash surrender value rule. They indicated that they would examine the ques-

---

[1]The CRA has taken a restrictive view of similar language contained at subsection 148(8) concerning intergenerational rollovers (discussed *supra* at section 3.2.G.v.c.I of this chapter). In technical interpretation 5-8204, dated July 11, 1989, the CRA indicated that the rollover only applies where the taxpayer is "the" life insured and thus multi-life policies do not qualify for the rollover.

tion when there is more than one person insured under a single life insurance policy. No amendment in this regard was included in the December 17, 1999 draft legislation and it appeared that the Department of Finance had decided the wording should stand. However, the June 5, 2000 Notice of Ways and Means Motion expanded the application of the subsection to any policy under which the deceased was "a person" whose life was insured under the policy. This provision applies to dispositions that occur after October 1, 1996. Further, the Notice of Ways and Means Motion extended the application of the subsection to any policy under which an insured person was not dealing at arm's length with the deceased shareholder at that time or at the time the policy was issued.

The CRA's assessing practices with respect to the valuation of insurance policies on other lives in the corporation have not been challenged in the courts to date. The issue would only be a significant concern if the application of normal valuation approaches results in a valuation which exceeds the actual amount received by the estate for the shares, and the resulting increase in the deceased's capital gain cannot otherwise be offset by the increased capital loss in the deceased's estate under subsection 164(6) of the Act.

ii. — Life insurance shares

In some cases, it might be possible to utilize "life insurance shares" to direct insurance proceeds to a specific individual. Life insurance shares are generally shares that entitle the holder to the death benefit proceeds from a corporate-owned life insurance policy, but otherwise have no control or value. Typically this is done by creating shares that are non-voting, non-participating, and redeemable for $1 at the discretion of the corporation, and entitling the holder to receive a dividend equal to the proceeds of the life insurance received by the corporation when the life insured dies. The shares would also provide that the dividend would be paid as a non-taxable capital dividend to the extent of the CDA credit arising from the life insurance policy.

The following are examples of situations where life insurance shares could be used. Life insurance shares may be used to stream corporate-owned life insurance proceeds to specific beneficiaries who may not otherwise be shareholders of the corporation (for example life insurance shares could be used to equalize family members not active in the business). This type of planning may avoid probate by not having the corporate-owned life insurance proceeds flow through the deceased's estate. Life insurance shares may also assist in structuring post mortem planning and may provide tax efficiencies.

Life insurance shares can also be used to resolve the conflict of interest issue with respect to the executor's role as director of the corporation to act in the best interests of the company and as executor of the estate to act in the best interests of the beneficiaries. If it is intended that a shareholder's estate benefit from the life insurance proceeds (for example to provide funding for capital gains tax liabilities arising on death), life insurance shares can be issued to the shareholder before the purchase of the policy by the corporation. When the shareholder dies, these shares enable the executor to force redemption of these shares and the use of the CDA as a right created by the attributes of the shares. Because the executor does not need to cause the corporation to redeem the shares and use the CDA balance (as a director of the corporation), the conflict is avoided.

The main tax issue with such shares is whether the $1 purchase price represents a reasonable value for the shares. This issue has been the subject of CRA commentary at the 2005 and 2008 APFF Conferences. Several questions were dealt with in 2005 but it appears that only two scenarios were assigned a technical interpretation number (2005-0138361C6, dated October 7, 2005, perhaps erroneously referring to these scenarios being Question 12, which, in the APFF Conference report, is referred to as Question 13).

2005-0138361C6 involved the following two questions: Scenario "A" involved the purchase of a life insurance share for $1 (non-voting, non-participating, redeemable for $1 at the discretion of the corporation, entitling the holder to receive a dividend equal to the proceeds of the life insurance received by the corporation when the 100 percent common shareholder dies) by the adult child of the 100 percent common shareholder. After the purchase of the share the corporation acquires at Term-to-100 policy with no cash value. The question asked whether the fair market value of the share was $1. The CRA would not express an opinion on fair market value without "an exhaustive review of the property to be valued at a given time."

Scenario "B" involved shares with the same attributes, however, the 100 percent common shareholder acquires the special share for $1. The life insurance subsequently issued to the corporation has a cash surrender value by the time death occurs. The question was whether the cash surrender value would be taken into account in valuing the deceased's common shares or his special share. The CRA stated as follows:

> Generally, we are of the opinion that it would be reasonable to distribute the cash surrender value of the life insurance policy between the different categories of shares based on the rights and conditions attached to them, in the same manner as the overall value of a business is distributed between the different categories of shares in circulation. To be able to answer the question definitively, it would be necessary to obtain a description of all the rights and conditions attached to the different categories of shares of the corporation. Subject to obtaining additional information, it appears that the overall value of the corporation that would be attributed to the special share immediately before the death would be nominal. Accordingly, the value of the common shares immediately before death would take into account almost the entire cash surrender value of the life insurance policy.

The more interesting scenario was published in the APFF Conference report as Question 12 (and referred to herein as such) and was not assigned a technical interpretation number. APFF Conference Question 12 specifically dealt with the valuation of shares of a company, including life insurance shares, for the purposes of the deemed disposition at death and a specific fact pattern with specific share attributes was commented on.

These are outlined as follows: The taxpayer is the sole shareholder of all of the common shares of a company. The company wants to purchase a life insurance policy on the life of the taxpayer of which it will be the beneficiary. A class of shares is added to the company's authorized capital (the life insurance shares) which are: non-voting; entitle the holder to a dividend in the amount corresponding to the death benefit payable under the policy to be declared only after the death of the taxpayer; callable at any time after death by the corporation for an amount corresponding to the death benefit less any dividend declared on the shares; callable by the holder prior to death for an amount corresponding to the cash surrender value (CSV) of the policy at the time with payment of the CSV deferred until the company receives the death benefit; and entitle the holder to CSV upon a winding-up of the company. The taxpayer's adult child purchases 1 life insurance share for $1. The company then purchases the life insurance policy and at the time of purchase, the policy's CSV is nil.

The CRA confirmed that for purposes of 70(5.3) the CSV of the policy is allocated to the life insurance shares and not to the common shares held by the deceased taxpayer. After stating something similar to the general comments outlined above in respect of Scenario "B", the CRA commented as follows (unofficial translation):

> In this situation, the insurance class of shares issued to the son is callable by the holder immediately prior to the insured's death, at an amount equal to the cash surrender value of the policy. Furthermore, according to the facts presented in this case, it would not be unreasonable to allocate the amount of the policy's cash surrender value to the insurance shares, immediately prior to death. Therefore the value of the common shares held by the taxpayer in the situation, would not take into account the cash surrender value of the life insurance policy on the taxpayer's life.

These comments suggest that life insurance shares can be an effective mechanism for streaming life insurance proceeds from corporate-owned insurance policies to a particular person in a tax effective manner.

APFF Question 17 at the 2008 APFF Conference (2008-0286151C6, dated October 10, 2008) also dealt with the valuation of shares of a company, including life insurance shares, for the purposes of the deemed disposition at death and a different fact pattern with some share attributes was commented on.

These are outlined as follows: The taxpayer is the sole shareholder of all of the common shares of a company. The company wants to purchase a term life insurance policy with no cash surrender value on the life of the taxpayer of which it will be the beneficiary. A class of shares is added to the company's authorized capital (the life insurance shares) which are non-voting, non-participating, and redeemable at the option of the holder before death, at its issue price of $1 and after death, at its issue price plus the proceeds of the life insurance policy.

Subsequently, the shareholder acquires one special share for $1. At the time of his death, the taxpayer owns all the common shares and one special share.

The CRA was asked to confirm for the purposes of subsection 70(5) that the fair market value of the special share would be equal to its issue value of $1, because of the provisions under subsection 70(5.3) which specify that only the cash surrender value of a life insurance policy subscribed on the life of the deceased shareholder is to be considered in the valuation of his shares.

The CRA stated that it could not express an opinion on FMV without an exhaustive review of the property to be valued at a given time. Consequently, the CRA could not definitively conclude that the fair market value of the special share will always be the issue price. Subsection 70(5.3) gives some details for valuing an asset such as the life insurance policy but does not specify how to value the various classes of shares.

D. — Valuation of shares held by certain trusts

If shares of a corporation are held by an alter ego trust, spouse trust or joint partner trust, the shares will be deemed to be disposed of at the end of the day on which the settlor, surviving spouse or common-law partner (as the case may be) dies pursuant to subsection 104(4). The fair market value of the shares must be determined at that time. The corporation may have purchased life insurance to provide estate liquidity upon the death of the surviving spouse or common-law partner. Valuation of the shares at the end of the day on which the settlor, surviving spouse or common-law partner (as the case may be) dies will include the value of the insurance policy. The question is whether subsection 70(5.3) applies for this purpose. Former subsection 70(5.3) only applied for purposes of subsection 70(5); not subsection 104(4). However, subsection 70(5.3) now provides that the subsection applies for the purposes of subsections 104(4) for deaths after October 1, 1996. With this amendment, a corporate-owned life insurance policy will be valued at cash surrender value for purposes of determining the fair market value of shares owned by an alter ego trust, a spouse trust or joint partner trust at the end of the day on which the settlor, surviving spouse or common-law partner (as the case may be) dies. CRA technical interpretation 2010-0390911E5, dated July 26, 2011 confirms this. Subsection 70(5.3) applies for purposes of the taxpayer migration rules at section 128.1 as well.

E. — Valuation of other properties deemed disposed of

Subsection 70(5.3) also applies in determining the value of any property deemed to have been disposed of as a consequence of a particular individual's death (under subsections 70(5) or 104(4)) or as a consequence of the particular person becoming or ceasing to be a resident in Canada (under section 128.1). Like the discussion above relating to valuation of shares, property such as partnership interests or interests in a trust where the partnership or trust holds life insurance on the individual or persons related to the individual, will be valued at the policy's cash surrender value immediately before death or change in residence of the individual. This provision applies for such dispositions after October 1, 1996.

Again, it should be noted that life insurance on any other arm's length individuals will be valued using normal valuation approaches.

F. — The lifetime capital gains exemption

Capital gains arising from the disposition of shares of a private corporation owned by an individual may qualify for the lifetime capital gains exemption under section 110.6 of the Act. The federal budget of March 21, 2013 increased the capital gains exemption from $750,000 to $800,000 for the 2014 taxation year, with indexation for inflation applicable for taxation years after 2014. With the inclusion rate for capital gains and capital losses at 50 percent, the capital gains deduction limit was increased from $375,000 (50 percent of $750,000) to $400,000 (50 percent of $800,000).

To be eligible for the capital gains exemption, the disposition triggering the capital gain must be attributable to a qualified small business corporation ("QSBC") share, a qualified farm property or, after May 1, 2006, qualified fishing property. These terms are defined in subsection 110.6(1). In order for shares to qualify as QSBC shares, there are several complex tests that must be met with respect to the type of assets owned by the corporation and the length of time during which the shares are held by the taxpayer.

A corporate-owned life insurance policy is an asset of the corporation and therefore may impact whether or not shares of the corporation qualify as shares of a QSBC. Consideration must be given as to whether a corporate-owned life insurance policy held while the life insured is alive is used in an active business carried on in Canada, and whether the death benefit proceeds from a life insurance policy are considered to be used in an active business. Further, the "value" of the policy must be determined for purposes of the asset tests.

In Question 32 at the 1988 Canadian Tax Foundation annual Roundtable, the CRA indicated that a life insurance policy would normally be considered to be a passive asset, that is, an asset not used in carrying on an active business by the corporation. This position was clarified in an answer to Question 12 posed at the 1993 Annual CALU Conference (technical interpretations 9310100, dated May 17, 1993 and 9310105, dated May 23, 1993). In the responses, the CRA indicated that a life insurance policy with cash surrender value is a form of long-term investment and would not, therefore, qualify as an asset used in an active business prior to the death of the life insured. In an answer to a further question posed at the same conference, the CRA indicated that where a term insurance policy without cash value is held by a corporation in a situation where the policy is considered to have value prior to the death of the life insured, it would be a question of fact whether or not the policy would be considered to be an asset used in an active business.

With respect to the death benefit proceeds from a life insurance policy, this issue was also discussed in the questions posed at the 1993 Annual CALU Conference. The CRA indicated that the proceeds from a life insurance policy would not normally be considered an asset used in an active business where the life insurance proceeds are to be distributed by the corporation as a dividend or used to fund a buy/sell agreement. However, the insurance proceeds would likely constitute an active business asset where the proceeds are used to recruit, hire and train new management personnel and also used to overcome short- term financial difficulties arising on the death of a key employee. The determination would be a question of fact in every case.

Once determination of the type of asset (passive or active) is made, the measurement of the fair market value of the life insurance policy must be determined. Paragraph 110.6(15)(a) applies to provide a special rule applicable for the purpose of the definition of QSBC share. This rule applies where a shareholder of the corporation (or a corporation connected with the particular corporation) is the life insured under the corporate-owned life insurance policy. Subparagraph 110.6(15)(a)(i) provides that the fair market value of the life insurance policy at any time before the death of the life insured will be equal to its cash surrender value (as defined in subsection 148(9)). The definition of cash surrender value in subsection 148(9) is computed without reference to any policy loans made under the policy. CRA technical interpretation 2013-047298, dated March 14, 2013 confirmed the application of 110.6(15) in the context of a terminally ill shareholder/life insured.

If a person other than a shareholder (for example an employee) is the life insured, the fair market value would be determined in accordance with normal valuation practices. This was confirmed by the CRA in an answer to Question 12 at the 1993 Annual CALU Conference (technical interpretations 9310100 and 9310105). The CRA stated that the policy would be valued in accordance with the position stated in Information Circular 89-3.

Subparagraph 110.6(15)(a)(ii) provides that the cash surrender value (as defined in subsection 148(9)) immediately prior to death will be considered to be the fair market value of the death benefit proceeds if the proceeds are used within 24 months after death to redeem, acquire or cancel shares owned by the life insured immediately before death. This rule applies to the death benefit proceeds from the life insurance policy and any assets attributable to those proceeds. A written application can be made to the CRA for an extension of the 24-month period. The special valuation rule applies until the redemption, acquisition or cancellation of the shares or the day that is 60 days after payment of the proceeds, whichever is later.

If the death benefit proceeds are not used directly or indirectly to redeem, acquire or cancel the shares owned by the life insured, or if a shareholder is not the life insured (for example if an employee is the life insured), the fair market value would be determined in accordance with normal valuation practices, taking into consideration all relevant factors. Generally, the fair market value of the death benefit proceeds would be equal to the amount received or receivable.

In summary, when determining if the shares of a corporation will meet the tests in the definition of QSBC shares, the impact of a corporate-owned life insurance policy must be contemplated. A determination of the type of asset (passive or active) and the value of the life insurance policy must be made to determine eligibility.

G. — Valuation and the corporate attribution rules

Where an individual has transferred or loaned property, either directly or indirectly, to a corporation and one of the main purposes of the transfer or loan may reasonably be considered to be to reduce the income of the individual and to benefit a person who is a "designated person" (generally a spouse or common-law partner, or minor child) in respect of the individual, subsection 74.4(2) may deem an amount to be included as interest in computing the income of the individual in respect of the property.

The corporate attribution rules do not apply if the corporation qualifies as a small business corporation. There are certain asset tests that must be met in order to qualify as a small business corporation. A small business corporation is defined in subsection 248(1) to include a Canadian controlled private corporation all or substantially all of the fair market value of the assets of which are attributable to assets that were used principally in an active business carried on primarily in Canada. The phrase "all or substantially all" generally means 90 percent or more; therefore, when a corporation has more than 10 percent of the fair market value of its assets in passive investments, or used in other non-qualifying activities, it may not qualify as a "small business corporation." Corporate-owned life insurance is generally considered a non-active asset for purposes of this test. Subsection 110.6(15) which provides that the fair market value of a life insurance policy at any time before death of the life insured will be equal to its CSV applies for purposes of determining if a corporation meets the definition of small business corporation in 248(1). Technical interpretation 2013-0473981E5 confirms this in a situation where the shareholder is terminally ill and whether the shareholder holds all of the shares directly, a percentage of the shares directly, has preferred shares without voting rights or holds preferred shares of a corporation that is connected to the corporation. Because qualifying as a small business corporation is relevant to whether the corporate attribution rules apply, it is important to consider the impact corporate-owned life insurance will have on meeting this definition. Indeed, the impact of corporate-owned life insurance must be considered in any case where the status of a corporation as a small business corporation is at issue.

H. — Disposition of shares under the promissory note method

Under the promissory note buy/sell method, the deceased's estate will sell the shares of the corporation to the surviving shareholders in return for a demand promissory note. The surviving shareholders will then cause the corporation to declare a tax-free capital dividend, funded by corporate-owned life insurance, to themselves. The funds received are then used to repay the promissory note. See section 7.4.D.ii for a discussion of the promissory note method.

If a mandatory buy/sell agreement exists between the shareholders of a corporation and a death occurs, the deceased shareholder will be deemed to have disposed of shares in the corporation at fair market value immediately before death. Under subsection 70(5.3) the fair market value of corporate-owned insurance on the life of the deceased shareholder is deemed to be the cash surrender value of the policy.

The CRA has consistently stated that, on the sale of shares by the estate to a purchaser with whom it does not deal at arm's length, an adjustment might occur under section 69 of the Act to include the value of the life insurance proceeds in the proceeds received by the estate, thereby increasing the capital gains tax liability to the estate. This view was expressed, for example, in response to Question 13 at the 1993 CALU Annual Meeting (technical interpretation 9310110, dated May 17, 1993). However, the CRA also stated in this interpretation letter that if the disposition of shares by the estate is governed by a *bona fide* buy-sell agreement among shareholders, its provisions should be determinative of value as stated in paragraphs 28 to 31 of Information Circular IC 89-3. If the agreement is not *bona fide* then valuation would be a question of fact.

I. — Transfer of insurance policies involving corporations and a shareholder or employee

A transfer of ownership of a life insurance policy is considered a disposition for income tax purposes. Subsection 148(7) provides the specific rules which may apply when a corporate-owned life insurance policy is transferred to or from a shareholder or an employee. In such a circumstance, subsection 148(7) may apply either because the corporation and shareholder or employee are not dealing at arm's length or the transfer is considered to be a "distribution from a corporation".

In question 5, at the 2003 CALU Annual Meeting (2003-0004285), the CRA indicated that a sale for fair market value consideration of a policy to an arms' length shareholder or employee would not constitute a "distribution" from a corporation, and as a result, subsection 148(7) would not apply. Whether or not a shareholder or an employee is dealing at arm's length with a corporation, such that it becomes relevant whether the transfer of a policy would be a "distribution" from the corporation is a question of fact.

Subsection 148(7) will always apply when the transfer is made to (or from) a shareholder or employee who is not dealing at arms' length with the corporation whether for consideration or not. In general, related persons do not deal at arm's length. A corporation and a person who controls the corporation or a person who is a member of a related group that controls the corporation are related; as are any two corporations if they are controlled by the same person or group of persons. The examples that follow in this section are confined to situations involving non-arm's length parties.

Subsection 148(7) deems the proceeds of disposition to the transferor and the new adjusted cost basis to the transferee to be equal to the "value" of the policy. The term "value" is defined in subsection 148(9) of the Act to be the amount that the holder of the policy would be entitled to receive if the policy were surrendered (essentially the cash surrender value net of policy loans).

At the Canadian Life and Health Insurance Association Tax Officers Conference Roundtable on May 1, 2009 (2009-0316671C6), the CRA considered the tax consequences of a scenario involving two individuals (A and B) with a desire to transfer a policy owned by A to individual B (and vice versa) for no consideration. A took a policy loan for the cash surrender value of the policy and reported a policy gain. A transferred the policy to B for no consideration. Subsequent to the transfer, A repaid the policy loan and claimed a deduction under 60(s) to offset the policy gain previously reported. The CRA confirmed that in these circumstances the policy loan is a disposition of the policy and a taxable policy gain would be reported to A. The CRA also confirmed that 148(7) would apply so that the transfer would occur at "value". Since "value" is defined as cash surrender value net of policy loans, the transfer would occur at zero proceeds of disposition and the ACB to the new owner would also be zero. Finally, the CRA confirmed that the deduction under 60(s) of the Act would be permitted on the repayment of the policy loan for which a taxable policy gain was reported. It also confirmed that this would have no impact on the ACB of the policy. However, CRA's closing comments were as follows:

> The transactions described above are intended to provide for the transfer of insurance policies in circumstances to which subsection 148(7) of the Act applies, without tax arising on tax deferred surpluses that have accumulated within the policies. We have discussed this situation with the Department of Finance which is reviewing the policy implications of this and other tax-motivated or tax-planned transactions involving life insurance policies. The possible application of section 245 of the Act should also be considered.

Subsection 148(7) does not eliminate the potential taxable benefit conferred on the shareholder or the employee as a result of a transfer from a corporation. The CRA has consistently stated that a shareholder benefit under subsection 15(1) or an employee benefit under paragraph 6(1)(a) will be taxed in the hands of the transferee to the extent the fair market value of the insurance policy, using the normal valuation factors listed in Information Circular 89-3, exceeds the amount of the consideration paid by the shareholder or employee. See, for example, technical interpretation 9327305, dated January 13, 1994.

The potential taxable benefit issues must be considered when contemplating a transfer of a corporate-owned insurance policy to a shareholder or employee if the fair market value of the policy is greater than the amount of consideration paid by the shareholder or employee.

The implications of these rules are provided through a series of examples, which follow.

i. — Example 1: Corporate-owned insurance transferred to shareholder (or employee)

The facts

A corporation owns an exempt life insurance policy on a shareholder who is also a key executive. The shareholder does not deal at arm's length with the corporation. The shareholder retires. The corporation decides to transfer the life insurance policy to the shareholder. The insurance policy has a cash surrender value (CSV) of $125,000 and an adjusted cost basis (ACB) of $50,000.

Income tax implications

The corporation is transferring ownership of the insurance policy, therefore there is a disposition for tax purposes. The transfer is made to a non-arm's length party, accordingly subsection 148(7) of the Act will apply. This subsection will deem the proceeds of the disposition for the company to be the value of the policy. Value is defined in subsection 148(9) essentially to be the CSV of the policy. The corporation will have a policy gain under subsection 148(1) to include in income.

Subsection 148(7) will also apply to deem the shareholder's new ACB to be the value of the policy. As discussed above, value is defined in subsection 148(9) essentially to be the CSV of the policy.

Under subsection 15(1) of the Act, the shareholder will have a taxable benefit to include in income equal to the excess of the fair market value of the life insurance policy over the consideration paid to the corporation. The fair market value of the life insurance policy would be determined in accordance with CRA guidelines discussed in Information Circular 89-3.

A number of scenarios might result, depending on whether the shareholder pays an amount to acquire the interest in the insurance policy. For example, assuming the fair market value equals the cash surrender value at the time of the transfer:

Situation 1: Corporation transfers the life insurance policy to the shareholder for no consideration

Situation 2: Shareholder pays the corporation an amount equal to the ACB of the policy ($50,000)

Situation 3: Shareholder pays the corporation an amount equal to the CSV of the policy ($125,000)

	Transferor: Corporation			**Transferee: Shareholder**		
	Deemed Proceeds [148(7)]	**ACB**	**Policy Gain [148(1)]**	**Amount Paid**	**Taxable Benefit [15(1)]**	**New ACB [148(7)]**
Situation 1	125,000	50,000	75,000	0	125,000	125,000
Situation 2	125,000	50,000	75,000	50,000	75,000	125,000
Situation 3	125,000	50,000	75,000	125,000	0	125,000

Observations

If subsection 148(7) applies, the tax implications to the transferor are consistent, regardless of whether the policy is transferred for no consideration or the transferee pays for the policy. For the transferee, the tax implications depend on whether a payment is made for the policy. To the extent the fair market value exceeds the amount paid by the transferee, a taxable benefit will arise under subsection 15(1), in the case of a shareholder, or paragraph 6(1)(a), in the case of an employee.

Based on earlier CRA technical interpretations (see, for example, 9327305, dated January 13, 1994), the amount of the taxable benefit should be added to the adjusted cost basis of the interest acquired by the transferee. A strict reading of the definition of "adjusted cost basis" in subsection 148(9) together with the CRA's technical interpretations result in an adjusted cost basis which may actually exceed the cash surrender value of the policy. In technical interpretation 9705125, dated April 16, 1997, the CRA indicated these results appear to be inappropriate, and that their views on the calculation of the adjusted cost basis to the transferee may need to be reviewed.

There appears to be significant confusion in the calculation of the adjusted cost basis of the policy to the transferee when subsection 148(7) applies.

At the 2003 CALU conference (Question 4, 2003-0004275), the CRA was asked to confirm, that in the above example under Situation 1, the new ACB to the transferee would be $250,000. The CRA disagreed, and indicated that in a transaction where:

(a) subsection 148(7) applied

(b) fair market value (FMV) of the policy exceeded CSV and

(c) transferee was required to include an amount in income under subsection 15(1)

then only the excess of the FMV of the policy over the CSV is allowed to be added to the ACB of the transferee.

As part of its response to the above question, the CRA confirmed that if the benefit were conferred to the individual in the capacity as employee rather than shareholder, the corporation would be entitled to a deduction equal to the fair market value of the policy.

Since, on the one hand, the CRA's longstanding position is that shareholder benefits are not deductible by the corporation for tax purposes and on the other, both employee benefits under paragraph 6(1)(a) and shareholder benefits under subsection 15(1) are taxable at the taxpayer's marginal tax rate, the transfer to an individual who is both an employee and a shareholder should be structured to provide an employee benefit.

It therefore appears that the ACB to the shareholder in the above three situations would be $125,000.

Based on this commentary, if the fair market value exceeds the cash surrender value, the tax implications can change quite dramatically. In the preceding example, if the FMV of the insurance policy, as determined under the normal valuation approaches in IC 89-3, were $250,000, the following would be the results:

Situation 1: Corporation transfers the life insurance policy to the shareholder for no consideration

Situation 2: Shareholder pays the corporation an amount equal to the ACB of the policy ($50,000)

Situation 3: Shareholder pays the corporation an amount equal to the CSV of the policy ($125,000)

Situation 4: Shareholder pays the corporation an amount equal to the fair market value of the policy ($250,000)[2]

---

[2]The conclusions for situation 4 appear to be anomalous but the results are consistent with the specific language of the legislation.

	Transferor: Corporation			Transferee: Shareholder		
	Deemed Proceeds [148(7)]	ACB	Policy Gain [148(1)]	Amount Paid	Taxable Benefit [15(1)]	New ACB [148(7)]
Situation 1	125,000	50,000	75,000	0	250,000	250,000
Situation 2	125,000	50,000	75,000	50,000	200,000	250,000
Situation 3	125,000	50,000	75,000	125,000	125,000	250,000
Situation 4	125,000	50,000	75,000	250,000	0	125,000

In this example, the shareholder is in a better position by having the distribution taxed as a benefit rather than actually paying the corporation, which appears to be inappropriate from a policy perspective.

ii. — Example 2: Transfer between related corporations (sister companies)

The facts

An individual is the sole shareholder of two corporations: Corporation A and Corporation B. Corporation A owns an exempt life insurance policy on the shareholder. Corporation A is to be sold. Prior to the sale, Corporation A transfers the life insurance policy to Corporation B. The insurance policy has a cash surrender value (CSV) of $125,000 and an adjusted cost basis (ACB) of $50,000.

Income tax implications

Corporation A is transferring ownership of the insurance policy therefore there is a disposition for tax purposes. The transfer is a non-arm's length transfer from the corporation and, accordingly, subsection 148(7) of the Act would apply. This subsection will deem the proceeds of the disposition for the company to be the value of the policy. Value is defined in subsection 148(9) essentially to be the CSV of the policy.

Subsection 148(7) will also apply to deem Corporation B's new ACB to be the value of the policy. As discussed above, value is defined in subsection 148(9) essentially to be the CSV of the policy. The consideration paid by Corporation B and the fair market value of the policy will not have an impact on the deemed proceeds of the disposition or the cost of acquisition.

Situation 1: Corporation A transfers the life insurance policy to Corporation B for no consideration

Situation 2: Corporation B pays Corporation A an amount equal to the ACB of the policy ($50,000)

Situation 3: Corporation B pays Corporation A an amount equal to the CSV of the policy ($125,000)

Situation 4: Corporation B pays Corporation A an amount equal to the fair market of the policy ($250,000)

	Transferor: Corporation A			Transferee: Corporation B		
	Deemed Proceeds [148(7)]	**ACB**	**Policy Gain [148(1)]**	**Amount Paid**	**Taxable Benefit[3]**	**New ACB [148(7)]**
Situation 1	125,000	50,000	75,000	0	n/a	125,000
Situation 2	125,000	50,000	75,000	50,000	n/a	125,000
Situation 3	125,000	50,000	75,000	125,000	n/a	125,000
Situation 4	125,000	50,000	75,000	250,000	n/a	125,000

Observations

If subsection 148(7) applies, the tax implications to the transferor are consistent, regardless of whether the policy is transferred for no consideration or the transferee pays for the policy. In the case of intercorporate transfers where the transferee is not a shareholder of the transferor, no taxable benefit should arise under section 15 of the Act. However, at the 2006 APFF Conference (Question 13, 2006-0197211C6, dated October 6, 2006), the CRA was asked to confirm the tax implications of the above transaction. In its response the CRA stated:

> We are of the opinion that section 148(7) would apply to the situation that you described because it is a situation where a policyholder's interest in a life insurance policy is disposed of to a person with whom the policyholder is not dealing at arm's length.
>
> Furthermore, it is possible that the assigning corporation would be impoverished as a result of the aforementioned transaction. In such a case, provided that it is demonstrated under the terms of the transaction that the assigning corporation is conferring a benefit on the sole shareholder, section 15(1) would apply in such a manner as to require the individual to include the value of the benefit conferred in computing his income.

The CRA appears to be implying a two-part test in shareholder benefit analysis: that the transferor corporation is impoverished and the sole shareholder is enriched. This notion of impoverishment appears to be derived from *Del Grande v. The Queen* (1992), [1993] 1 C.T.C. 2096, 93 D.T.C. 133, Bowman J. (T.C.C.) which

[3]Although there is no taxable benefit to Corporation B, there may be a taxable benefit to the individual shareholder(s). See Observations section for a full discussion.

provided that: "Paragraph 15(1)(c) (as it then read) contemplates the conferral of a genuine economic benefit upon the shareholder. The word 'confer' implies the bestowal of bounty or largess, to the economic benefit of the conferee and a corresponding economic detriment to the corporation." The CRA has not indicated what criteria it would use to determine whether a corporation has been impoverished, therefore, practitioners should be mindful of this commentary when structuring such transactions. If subsection 15(1) does apply to include the value of a benefit in the shareholder's income, there would be no increase in the ACB of the transferee's interest in the insurance policy, as no amount was required to be included in the income of the transferee — being Corporation B in the example described above.

The transfer between sister corporations could be deemed an indirect payment and be subject to tax under subsection 56(2) or section 246. The shareholder could then be assessed a taxable benefit equal to the FMV of the policy in excess of the consideration paid, if any.

Based on CRA commentary, where some form of benefit to the sole shareholder is seen to occur, whether by virtue of subsections 15(1), 56(2), or section 246, it appears that the income tax result to the transferor (Corporation A) is not impacted by the amount paid by Corporation B or by the fair market value of the interest in the insurance policy due to the operation of subsection 148(7). Also, for this reason, the adjusted cost basis to the transferee (Corporation B) on the acquisition of the insurance policy would appear to be limited to the cash surrender value of the interest.

iii. — Example 3: Transfer between related corporations (intercompany shareholdings)

The facts

The shareholder owns Corporation B which owns Corporation A which in turn owns an exempt life insurance policy on the life of the shareholder. For business and estate planning reasons, Corporation A wishes to transfer the life insurance policy to Corporation B. The insurance policy has a cash surrender value (CSV) of $125,000 and an adjusted cost basis (ACB) of $50,000. The fair market value (FMV) is also $125,000.

Income tax implications

Corporation A is transferring ownership of the insurance policy therefore there is a disposition for tax purposes. The transfer is a non-arm's length transfer from the corporation and accordingly subsection 148(7) of the Act applies. This subsection will deem the proceeds of disposition for the company to be the value of the policy. Value is defined in subsection 148(9) essentially to be the CSV of the policy.

Subsection 148(7) will also apply to deem Corporation B's new ACB to be the value of the policy. As discussed above, value is defined in subsection 148(9) to be the CSV of the policy. Under subsection 15(1) of the Act, Corporation B will have a taxable benefit to include in income for the excess of the fair market value of the life insurance policy over the consideration paid to Corporation A. This scenario is contemplated in CRA technical interpretation 9204375, dated March 12, 1992.

Situation 1: Corporation A transfers the life insurance policy to Corporation B for no consideration

Situation 2: Corporation B pays Corporation A an amount equal to the ACB of the policy ($50,000)

Situation 3: Corporation B pays Corporation A an amount equal to the CSV of the policy ($125,000)

	Transferor: Corporation A			Transferee: Corporation B		
	Deemed Proceeds [148(7)]	**ACB**	**Policy Gain [148(1)]**	**Amount Paid**	**Taxable Benefit**	**New ACB [148(7)]**
Situation 1	125,000	50,000	75,000	0	125,000	125,000
Situation 2	125,000	50,000	75,000	50,000	75,000	125,000
Situation 3	125,000	50,000	75,000	125,000	0	125,000

Observations

If subsection 148(7) applies, the tax implications to the transferor are consistent, regardless of whether the policy is transferred for no consideration or the transferee pays for the policy. In the case of intercorporate transfers where the transferee is a shareholder of the transferor, a taxable benefit will arise under subsection 15(1).

Based on the views of the CRA discussed above (2003-0004275), the ACB to the transferee will be consistent, regardless of the amount of the taxable benefit.

If the fair market value exceeds the cash surrender value, the tax implications can change quite dramatically. In the preceding example, if the fair market value of the insurance policy, as determined under the normal valuation approaches in IC 89-3, were $250,000, the following would be the results:

Situation 1: Corporation A transfers the life insurance policy to Corporation B for no consideration

Situation 2: Corporation B pays Corporation A an amount equal to the ACB of the policy ($50,000)

Situation 3: Corporation B pays Corporation A an amount equal to the CSV of the policy ($125,000)

Situation 4: Corporation B pays Corporation A an amount equal to the fair market value of the policy ($250,000)

	Transferor: Corporation A			Transferee: Corporation B		
	Deemed Proceeds [148(7)]	ACB	Policy Gain [148(1)]	Amount Paid	Taxable Benefit	New ACB [148(7)]
Situation 1	125,000	50,000	75,000	0	250,000	250,000
Situation 2	125,000	50,000	75,000	50,000	200,000	250,000
Situation 3	125,000	50,000	75,000	125,000	125,000	250,000
Situation 4	125,000	50,000	75,000	250,000	0	125,000

Alternatively, the taxable benefit under subsection 15(1) may be eliminated by having Corporation A transfer the insurance policy as a dividend in kind. In this case, the value of the dividend will equal the fair market value of the interest in the insurance policy but will be treated as an intercompany dividend which should be deductible under subsection 112(1), and subsection 15(1) will not apply. This alternative could be considered for any intercompany transfer from a subsidiary corporation to a parent corporation, whether the fair market value exceeds the cash surrender value or not.

Situation 1: Corporation A declares a dividend to Corporation B in an amount equal to the fair market value of the life insurance policy (assume fair market value = CSV = $125,000)

Situation 2: Corporation A declares a dividend to Corporation B in an amount equal to the fair market value of the life insurance policy (assume fair market value = 250,000)

	Transferor: Corporation A			Transferee: Corporation B		
	Deemed Proceeds [148(7)]	ACB	Policy Gain [148(1)]	Taxable Dividend	Taxable Benefit	New ACB [148(7)]
Situation 1	125,000	50,000	75,000	125,000	n/a	125,000
Situation 2	125,000	50,000	75,000	250,000	n/a	125,000

Paying a dividend in kind is discussed in archived Interpretation Bulletin IT-67R3 "Taxable Dividends from Corporations Resident in Canada," dated May 15, 1992. Paragraph 6 of IT-67R3 states that the value to be placed on a dividend paid by a corporation in assets other than cash is the fair market value of such assets at the date of transfer to the shareholders. The amount of the dividend paid by Corporation A to Corporation B is therefore equal to the fair market value of the life insurance policy even though the proceeds of disposition and the new adjusted cost basis is the cash value. Corporation A is controlled by Corporation B, therefore the intercorporate dividend is deductible by Corporation B under subsection 112(1) of the Act. The excess of the dividend over the cash surrender value in Situation 2 will not be added to the new adjusted cost basis. A shareholder benefit under subsection 15(1) does not apply to dividends. This was confirmed by the CRA in technical interpretation 2000-0056205, dated April 10, 2001. It should be noted, however, that if the dividend is paid in contemplation of a sale of Corporation A, subsection 55(2) could apply to recharacterize the dividend as a capital gain.

iv. — Example 4: Transfer insurance policy from a shareholder to a corporation

The facts

A shareholder owns an exempt life insurance policy on a personal basis. For business and estate planning reasons, the shareholder wishes to transfer the life insurance policy to the corporation. The insurance policy has a cash surrender value (CSV) of $125,000 and an adjusted cost basis (ACB) of $50,000.

Income tax implications

The shareholder is transferring ownership of the insurance policy therefore there is a disposition for tax purposes. The transfer is presumably between parties not at arm's length and accordingly subsection 148(7) of the Act applies. This subsection will deem the proceeds of disposition for the shareholder to be the value of the policy. Value is defined in subsection 148(9) essentially to be the CSV of the policy.

Subsection 148(7) will also apply to deem the corporation's ACB to be the value of the policy. As discussed above, value is defined in subsection 148(9) essentially to be the CSV of the policy. It should be noted that a life insurance policy is not "eligible property" within the meaning of subsection 85(1.1) and therefore does not qualify for the section 85 rollover. A submission made by CALU to the Department of Finance in February of 2009 seeks a technical amendment which would include an interest of a policyholder in a life insurance policy in the definition of "eligible property" under subsection 85(1.1). No response from the Department has been provided at the time of writing.

A number of scenarios might result, depending on what amount the corporation pays to acquire the interest in the insurance policy. For example, assuming the fair market value equals the cash surrender value at the time of the transfer:

> Situation 1: Shareholder transfers the life insurance policy to the corporation for no consideration
>
> Situation 2: The corporation pays the shareholder an amount equal to the ACB of the policy ($50,000)
>
> Situation 3: The corporation pays the shareholder an amount equal to the CSV of the policy ($125,000)

	Transferor: Shareholder			Transferee: Corporation		
	Deemed Proceeds [148(7)]	**ACB**	**Policy Gain [148(1)]**	**Amount Paid**	**Taxable Benefit**	**New ACB [148(7)]**
Situation 1	125,000	50,000	75,000	0	n/a	125,000
Situation 2	125,000	50,000	75,000	50,000	n/a	125,000
Situation 3	125,000	50,000	75,000	125,000	n/a	125,000

Observations

If subsection 148(7) applies, the tax implications to the transferor are consistent, regardless of whether the policy is transferred for no consideration or the transferee pays for the policy. For the transferee, the tax implications are not, in this case, dependent on whether a payment is made. Therefore, the corporation should generally pay an amount at least equal to the cash surrender value of the interest in the insurance policy. This will not impact the tax implications to either party.

If the fair market value exceeds the cash surrender value the tax implications do not change, but there may be an opportunity for the shareholder to withdraw an amount from the corporation equal to the fair market value without attracting additional taxation in the hands of the transferor shareholder.

In the preceding example, if the fair market value of the insurance policy, as determined under the normal valuation approaches in IC 89-3, were $250,000, the following would be the result:

> Situation 1: Shareholder transfers the life insurance policy to the corporation for no consideration
>
> Situation 2: The corporation pays the shareholder an amount equal to the ACB of the policy ($50,000)
>
> Situation 3: The corporation pays the shareholder an amount equal to the CSV of the policy ($125,000)
>
> Situation 4: The corporation pays the shareholder an amount equal to the fair market value of the policy ($250,000)

	Transferor: Shareholder			Transferee: Corporation		
	Deemed Proceeds [148(7)]	**ACB**	**Policy Gain [148(1)]**	**Amount Paid**	**Taxable Benefit**	**New ACB [148(7)]**
Situation 1	125,000	50,000	75,000	0	n/a	125,000
Situation 2	125,000	50,000	75,000	50,000	n/a	125,000
Situation 3	125,000	50,000	75,000	125,000	n/a	125,000
Situation 4	125,000	50,000	75,000	250,000	n/a	125,000

In this case, the shareholder could receive up to the fair market value of the interest in the insurance policy and the tax implications would not change. However, the new adjusted cost basis to the corporation would be limited to the cash surrender value, which would impact future policy gains, but could also be an advantage in terms of the credit to the capital dividend account of the corporation under subsection 89(1) in the event of death.

At the 2002 CALU conference (2002-0127455), a similar scenario was provided to the CRA for its comments. The CRA agreed that the *Income Tax Act* resulted in the above. However they added the following comments:

> The result of this transaction is that the shareholder is effectively receiving a distribution from the corporation on a tax-free basis. Notwithstanding that the corporation will have a reduced adjusted cost basis in the policy it is not clear that the above result is intended in terms of tax policy. We previously brought this situation to the attention of the Department of Finance and have been advised that it will be given consideration in the course of their review of policyholder taxation.

The CRA reconfirmed the above tax results, its concerns and the Department of Finance's review in technical interpretations: 2003-0040145, dated October 6, 2003 and 2008-0303971E5, dated May 27, 2009.

Note that it would generally be prudent to obtain an independent valuation of the policy to substantiate the fair market value before undertaking such a transaction.

Although this may be an attractive strategy for extracting funds from a corporation, before proceeding with such a transaction, consideration should be given to other longer term implications of the strategy including the following:

- A corporate-owned policy is exposed to the creditors of the corporation.
- To avoid shareholder benefit tax issues, the corporation will generally be the beneficiary of the policy. Given this fact, consideration should be given to whether there is an appropriate and tax-efficient method of getting the death benefit to the ultimate intended beneficiary.

- Undesirable tax consequences (e.g., shareholder benefits) may arise if there is a need to transfer the policy prior to death (for example if the corporation is sold).
- The cash surrender value of the policy is a passive asset to the corporation that will affect the value of the shares of the corporation at death or on emigration of the shareholder and could impact eligibility of the shares for the enhanced capital gains exemption.
- Potential impact of the stop-loss rules on the taxation of the shares at death.

v. — Miscellaneous transfers

The previous examples dealt with the more common situations involving transfers to and from corporations and in each case the application of subsection 148(7) was, arguably, clear.

There are, however, other situations involving the transfer of a corporate-owned life insurance policy where the application of subsection 148(7) would seemingly contradict other applicable provisions of the Act, notably in the case of amalgamations and wind-ups of corporations.

a. — Amalgamations

Generally speaking, when two or more corporations (the predecessor corporations) are merged to form a single new corporation, the tax consequences of the merger will be determined pursuant to section 87 of the Act. (This section may also apply in the case of the wind-up of a wholly-owned subsidiary, as defined therein). The rules basically ensure that there are no immediate tax liabilities for either the predecessor or new corporations as a result of the amalgamation.

Paragraph 87(2)(j.4) states that for the purposes of the definition of "adjusted cost basis" of a life insurance policy at subsection 148(9), the new corporation is deemed to be the same as and a continuation of the predecessor corporations. Thus, the ACB of the policy will not be affected by the amalgamation. There remains some question, though, of whether a predecessor corporation will nonetheless have disposed of its interest in the policy at the time of the merger.

This issue was addressed at CALU in 1992 (9211260, dated May 11, 1992). In addition to paragraph 87(2)(j.4), the CRA referred to case law (*R. v. Black & Decker Manufacturing Co.* (1974), [1975] 1 S.C.R. 411, and *Canada v. Guaranty Properties Ltd.*, [1990] 2 C.T.C. 94 (F.C.A.) to suggest that the predecessor corporations did not cease to exist following an amalgamation. The CRA thus inferred that since the new company was the same as the merged companies and that the predecessor corporations did not cease to exist, there was no parting of property or passing over of control from one person to another, hence, no disposition for tax purposes. Coming to this conclusion, then, there was no need to consider and indeed no reference in the commentary to subsection 148(7) or its possible application.

b. — Wind-ups

Subsection 88(1) applies to the wind-up of a subsidiary where the parent corporation owns not less than 90 percent of the issued shares of each class of the capital stock of the subsidiary. Generally speaking, the subsidiary will be deemed to have disposed of each of its properties transferred to the parent, for proceeds of disposition equal to its cost amount of the property and the parent company will be deemed to have acquired the property at a cost equal to the subsidiary's deemed proceeds of disposition. Under these rules, a life insurance policy owned by the subsidiary and transferred to the parent in the course of the winding-up would be rolled over without any tax consequences to either party. In the same 1992 technical interpretation discussed above, the CRA confirmed that this would be the correct result. Again, there was no reference to subsection 148(7).

The application of subsection 148(7) in the case of a wind-up to which subsection 88(1) applies was raised at CALU 2005 (2005-0116631C6, dated May 3, 2005). The CRA stated that the specific rules for windings-up in subsection 88(1) would be applicable and would override the rules of subsection 148(7). The CRA also confirmed that the ACB of the policy to the parent would be equal to the ACB of the subsidiary.

The CALU 2005 commentary also dealt with which provision of the Act would be applicable where subsection 88(2) applies and one of the properties disposed of is a life insurance policy. This subsection will apply to a winding-up of a corporation where subsection 88(1) does not apply. Where subsection 88(2) applies, subsection 69(5) deems the corporation being wound-up to dispose of its property for proceeds equal to FMV and the person to whom the property is transferred to acquire it at that FMV. The CRA was asked which of the two subsections, 69(5) or 148(7), would apply where the property transferred by the corporation being wound-up was a life insurance policy. The CRA responded that where two provisions of a statute conflict, it is the more specific provision that should take precedence. Though the CRA was inclined to the view that subsection 69(5) would apply in such a situation, it tempered its response by adding that it "...would want to review the facts of the particular case to ensure that this provides a reasonable result."

3.4 — Conclusion

Income tax rules relating to dispositions of exempt life insurance policies are relevant in understanding the attributes of a tax-exempt policy. Some specific valuation issues arise, particularly in the context of corporate-owned policies.

4 — Leveraged Life Insurance — Borrowing Against a Policy

Updated by Nick Fabiano, C.P.A., C.A.

4.1 — Introduction

A policyholder may wish to access the tax deferred cash surrender value growth within an exempt life insurance policy. Life insurance companies may provide access to the cash surrender value in a variety of ways. Policyholders may gain direct access by withdrawing the cash surrender value by partially or fully surrendering their life insurance contract. There are alternative methods that the policyholder may use without actually withdrawing cash surrender value or surrendering the policy. One alternative is for the policyholder to request a policy loan from the life insurance company. The tax implications of accessing the cash surrender value using this traditional method are discussed in section 3.2.G.

Another method of accessing the accumulated cash surrender value in an exempt life insurance contract, without surrendering or disposing of the policy, is for the policyholder to use the life insurance policy as collateral security for a bank loan. This method provides liquidity to the policyholder, allows the policy to continue to accumulate tax-deferred income and generate tax-free proceeds on death.

4.2 — Overview of Conventional Leveraged Life Insurance Programs

In general, the steps to structure a leveraged life insurance program are the following:

1. The value within an exempt life insurance policy accumulates on a tax-deferred basis to create the asset which will be leveraged.
2. When funds are required, the policyholder applies for a loan from a financial institution. The loan is secured with a collateral assignment of the policy.
3. The loan can be arranged with interest or interest and principal paid on a regular basis, or the lender may agree to capitalize the interest and add the sum to the outstanding loan amount. Most financial institutions that participate in leveraged life insurance strategies require that the loan balance not exceed a specified percentage of the policy's cash surrender value.
4. If the loan remains in good standing, it may be structured so that principal repayment does not occur until death. Upon the death of the life insured the proceeds from the life insurance policy will repay the outstanding loan.

This concept has numerous applications, each with the potential for significant benefits. However, each application also has associated financial and tax risks. The financial risks that may be applicable are:

- values suggested in life insurance illustrations may not be realized;
- the life insurance product may not perform as projected;
- loan interest rate risk;
- leveraging of indexed accounts may be subject to a reduced leveraging percentage;
- life expectancy may differ from projection assumptions.

Section 4.3 provides several examples of leveraged life insurance applications and the associated risks. As will be quickly apparent, many of these leveraging strategies are structured in order to allow the deduction of interest expense for tax purposes. The following outlines some of the general areas of concern relating to interest deductibility that would have to be considered in respect of any leveraged life insurance strategy.

A. — General areas of concern relating to interest deductibility and leveraged life insurance

The courts have traditionally considered interest and financing charges to be a non-deductible expenditure for tax purposes since they are on account of capital. Consequently, such costs are only deductible if they meet the conditions of paragraph 20(1)(c) and related provisions.

i. — Simple interest

Under paragraph 20(1)(c), a reasonable amount of interest is deductible when it is paid or payable in respect of the year (depending upon the method regularly followed by the taxpayer) pursuant to a legal obligation and the borrowed money is used for the purpose of earning income from a business or property, or to acquire property for the purpose of gaining or producing income thereon, or for the purpose of gaining or producing income from a business. Interest on borrowed money used to earn exempt income or to acquire a life insurance policy is not deductible. Interest on money borrowed to acquire a prescribed annuity contract is not deductible, whereas interest on money borrowed to acquire a non-prescribed annuity is deductible with certain limitations.

Singleton v. The Queen, [2002] 1 C.T.C. 121, 2001 D.T.C. 5333 (S.C.C.) upheld the ability of the taxpayer to structure his affairs (when purchasing a home) to obtain interest deductibility by using cash (from a capital interest in a partnership) to buy a house and borrowing money to infuse capital back into the partnership. The Supreme Court of Canada held in favour of the taxpayer and upheld the specific legal form of the transactions.

Paragraph 13 of archived Interpretation Bulletin IT-533, "Interest Deductibility and Related Issues," dated October 31, 2003, states that it is the direct use of the borrowed funds that generally determines whether interest will be deductible. The paragraph quotes the Singleton case as support for that conclusion.

If interest is to be deductible in the context of leveraged life insurance strategies, it is important that the direct use of the borrowed funds is for the purpose of gaining or producing income and not to acquire the life insurance policy.

ii. — Compound interest

Generally compound interest (i.e. interest on interest) will be deductible under paragraph 20(1)(d) if it is paid in the year, and the related simple interest meets the conditions in paragraph 20(1)(c). Note that unlike simple interest which is deductible when it is paid or payable (i.e. accrued), compound interest is only deductible when it is physically paid. It will not be deductible in the year it arises if it is capitalized by simply adding the interest to the outstanding loan balance.

In the context of leveraged life insurance strategies, this means that if interest is capitalized, then interest arising on that interest (i.e. compound interest) will only be deductible when it is paid. Since many loans in leveraged life insurance arrangements are intended to be outstanding until the death of the insured, this would mean that compound interest will only be paid, and therefore deductible, at death.

A strategy to ensure the annual deductibility of what would otherwise be compound interest is to pay all interest annually with cash or with the proceeds from the sale of assets which generate income and then arrange a new loan each year for an amount equal to the interest paid. Provided that the new loan is used to produce income, interest on the new loan should be deductible. One way to accomplish this is to sell investments that generate income and use the proceeds from the sale to pay the interest on the original loan. Then a new loan for the same amount is taken out, and the investments previously sold are repurchased with the borrowed funds. Since the new loan is used to purchase an income earning property, interest on the loan should be deductible. The same series of steps will apply to all compound interest. Therefore, obtaining a deduction for what would otherwise be "compound interest" requires careful and extensive planning.

Several CRA technical interpretations have created some uncertainty as to what will be considered to be compound interest. (See technical interpretation 2004-0070341E5 dated December 16, 2004 and Q5 CALU CRA Roundtable dated May 3, 2005 (2005-0116661C6)). These considered whether interest on a loan used to pay simple interest is deductible. The CRA responded that interest paid during the year or payable for the year (depending on the method normally used by the taxpayer in computing his income) on the second loan will be deductible when computing income from a business or property under paragraph 20(1)(c) of the Act if the interest on the first loan is deductible under this same section. In other words, where a taxpayer obtains a loan to pay the interest on an earlier loan, the interest on the second loan will be deductible.

This CRA position is surprising for two reasons at least. The first is that the interest on the second loan could be viewed as compound interest and thus should only be deductible when it is paid as stipulated under paragraph 20(1)(d) of the Act, rather than when payable. The second reason is that the second loan does not appear to be used for an eligible purpose. It is used to pay interest and not to earn income from a business or property as required under paragraph 20(1)(c) of the Act.

Based on this interpretation, the borrower no longer has to pay the interest and then re-borrow. The borrower can simply take a new loan equal to the interest on the initial loan and save a step in the process while preserving interest deductibility.

However, the CRA was subsequently asked to consider the deductibility of interest with respect to the following three loan structures, assuming in each case that the taxpayer takes out a loan for the purpose of producing income from a business or property, and that the amount of interest is reasonable:

- Interest on a line of credit is payable annually at the end of each year. At the end of each year, the taxpayer takes an additional advance on the line of credit to pay the loan interest owing, pursuant to the line of credit agreement.
- Pursuant to the line of credit agreement, interest on the line of credit is added to the loan balance (i.e. is capitalized) each year.
- Instead of a single line of credit, the loan has two separate accounts. Each year, the taxpayer takes a loan advance from account A and arranges for interest on the loan to be charged to account B. Then the taxpayer takes an additional advance from account A to pay the interest that was charged to account B.

In each circumstance, the CRA was asked to clarify whether the interest on the advance to pay the interest each year would be deductible as simple interest or, alternatively, whether it is compound interest and consequently deductible only when paid.

The CRA's response in technical interpretation 2006-0188621E5 dated March 30, 2007 provided little commentary; it merely stated:

> As you indicated, at the 2005 CALU Conference (2005-0116661C6) and in 2004-007034, we considered situations where a taxpayer used borrowed money to pay interest on an earlier loan. In our view, the situations you describe are not the same as or similar to those considered in those documents. Accordingly, we would not consider our general views in 2005-0116661C6 or 2004-007034, as applicable hereto. Furthermore, where a series of transactions is entered into merely to derive the benefit of an interest deduction, the general anti-avoidance rule may be relevant.

Further, the CRA states that matters of interest deductibility are a question of fact and it would only deal conclusively with this question in the context of an advanced income tax ruling. While the CRA did not provide a substantive response to the questions posed, borrowers should take note of this commentary because, whether the CRA's rationale is correct or not, borrowing to pay interest more than in an isolated incident appears not to be looked upon favourably.

iii. — Proposed legislation

On October 31, 2003, the Department of Finance released draft legislation concerning the deductibility of interest and other expenses.

The draft amendments propose a new section of the Act (section 3.1) that would introduce the following concept: a loss generated from a source that is business or property will only be deductible in a particular year if it is reasonable to assume that the taxpayer will realize a cumulative profit from the business or property during the time the taxpayer has carried on or held, or can be reasonably be expected to carry on or hold, the business or property. Subsection 9(3) of the Act would be modified to explicitly exclude any capital gain or capital loss from the determination of profit under proposed subsection 3.1(2) of the Act.

Essentially, this means there must be a cumulative "reasonable expectation of profit" (i.e. that income will eventually exceed expenses from that source) and that a taxpayer must evaluate this expectation each year. In a given year, if the profit is not expected to be positive on a cumulative basis (projected out over the lifespan of the business or property), any loss will not be considered to be "from a source" and will not be deductible by the taxpayer in that year. Deductions for losses taken in prior years would be unaffected by a subsequent determination that there is no reasonable expectation of profit.

As drafted, these proposed amendments have quite a broad application. Not only will the taxpayer have to prove that the cumulative profit test will be met, but there would now be a direct link between an expense, say interest on borrowed money or the collateral insurance deduction, and the income from business or property generated by the expenditure, i.e. the borrowed funds. Should the cumulative profit test not be met, any expense in excess of the income would not be deductible against any other source of income. Nor does it appear that the non-deductible loss could be carried over.

This last point is significant because many of the leveraged life insurance strategies depend on interest deductibility to be financially effective. The potential inability of a taxpayer to earn income in excess of the cost of borrowing could seriously undermine the viability of several of the following strategies, particularly those of the "immediate" type.

These amendments were intended to take effect for taxation years beginning after 2004, but as of this writing no revised or final amendments have been published, nor have the proposals been withdrawn. The Department of Finance sought comments on the proposed legislation. The CRA indicated in technical interpretation 2006-0182181M4, dated June 21, 2006 that the Department of Finance intends to address the concerns raised by such comments prior to the legislation being enacted. Given the time that has passed since the proposal, it seems unlikely the amendments would be passed in the original form.

On the same date as the release of the proposed amendments above, the CRA released Interpretation Bulletin IT-533, "Interest Deductibility and Related Issues" (now archived). Focusing on interest expense, it outlines the CRA's current administrative policy on the deductibility of interest expense. Though it emphasizes the requirement that borrowed money must be used to earn income from a business or property for interest to be deductible, it does not refer to a cumulative profit test. In fact, the IT relies on the Supreme Court of Canada's decision in *Ludco Enterprises Ltd. v. Canada*, [2001] 2 S.C.R. 1082, and its comment that the plain meaning of "income" in the Act is not an equivalent of "profit". The IT does not take into account the proposed amendments. Reference will be made in the following analysis to CRA's current administrative practice as set out in IT-533.

Pending the release of definitive legislation affecting the deductibility of interest, interested parties should consider the impact of the proposed modifications when evaluating the applicability of leveraged life insurance to their own situation.

iv. — Special rules in Quebec

Residents of Quebec have to consider that province's separate income tax legislation in addition to the federal income tax rules. As far as the deductibility of interest is concerned, the rules are clearer for Quebec resident individuals and trusts. Quebec's 2004-2005 budget, tabled on March 30, 2004, included new rules limiting the deductibility of investment expenses to investment income. Investment expenses include interest on money borrowed to earn income from a business or property, and investment income includes interest, taxable dividends, and taxable capital gains. Any non-deductible expenses in a given year may be carried back to any of the three previous years or carried forward indefinitely. This treatment is analogous to that afforded net capital losses. In addition, the calculation is done on a portfolio basis; there is no requirement to link a particular expense to a specific source.

These special Quebec rules do not apply to corporations or to expenses incurred by an individual or a trust to earn income from a business or a rental property.

v. — Application of the general anti-avoidance rule

It is possible that the CRA could seek to apply the general anti-avoidance rule (GAAR) under subsection 245(2) of the Act in respect of interest-deductibility and leveraged insurance arrangements. As noted by the Supreme Court of Canada in *Canada Trustco Mortgage Co. v. Canada*, [2005] 5 C.T.C. 215, 2005 D.T.C. 5523, 2005 CarswellNat 3212, in order for GAAR to apply three conditions must be satisfied. First, it must be determined whether the taxpayer received a tax benefit. Second, it must be determined if there has been an avoidance transaction. Finally, it must be determined if the avoidance transaction results in a misuse of a specific provision of the Act or an abuse of the Act read as a whole. If GAAR applies to an avoidance transaction, then the tax consequences of the transaction "shall be determined as is reasonable in the circumstances in order to deny a[n intended] tax benefit". The income tax consequences of a transaction that is recharacterized are determined based on the facts and circumstances in each case.

The term "tax benefit" is defined at subsection 245(1) as a reduction, avoidance or deferral of tax or other amount payable under the Act or an increase in a refund of tax or other amount owing under the Act. An "avoidance transaction" is defined at subsection 245(3) as a transaction, (or part of a series of transactions) that results in a tax benefit unless the transaction could reasonably be considered to have been undertaken primarily for *bona fide* purposes other than to obtain the tax benefit.

GAAR was introduced in 1988. The provision represented a marked departure from the traditional tax planning perspective established by the House of Lords in *Duke of Westminster v. Commissioners*, [1936] A.C. 1 and echoed by the Supreme Court of Canada in *Stubart Investments Ltd. v. R.*, [1984] C.T.C. 294. The traditional perspective recognized that "tax avoidance" is permissible and that taxpayers are entitled to structure their affairs in a tax effective manner. In the immediate aftermath of its introduction, the potential scope of GAAR generated a certain degree of tax planning "chill". That is, there was initially a fair degree of uncertainty as to how broadly GAAR might apply.

In recent years, more and more GAAR cases have reached the courts and, finally, GAAR cases have reached the level of the Supreme Court of Canada. With the growing volume of GAAR jurisprudence, the scope of the rule is becoming more clearly defined. Case law to date suggests that, generally speaking, the threshold for determining if there has been a tax benefit or an avoidance transaction is relatively low. The main focus of a GAAR inquiry will be whether there has been a misuse or abuse of the Act. Consideration of the misuse or abuse issue in the context of leveraged life insurance is discussed in more detail below.

Notwithstanding that a taxpayer may have structured their affairs to meet the specific requirements of paragraph 20(1)(c) or (d), it is possible that the CRA may apply GAAR to a series of transactions designed to achieve interest deductions. The CRA attempted to use the GAAR to deny interest deductibility in *Lipson v. The Queen*, 2009 SCC 1, [2009] 1 C.T.C. 314, 2009 D.T.C. 5528.

In this case, a husband and wife (Mr. and Mrs. Lipson) entered into a series of transactions designed to make interest on the mortgage of their home deductible. Briefly, the facts of the case were as follows: Mrs. Lipson borrowed funds to purchase the shares of a corporation from Mr. Lipson using a demand loan. Mr. Lipson used the proceeds from the sale of the shares to purchase a home. Mr. And Mrs. Lipson then mortgaged the home to repay the original loan. Since the mortgage on the home provided financing in substitution for the demand loan used to acquire the shares, the interest on the mortgage would normally qualify for deductibility under subsection 20(3) of the Act. There was no gain on the sale of the shares to Mrs. Lipson due to the application of a rollover provision (subsection 73(1)). Because of the rollover, the attribution rule in subsection 74.1(1) applied so that the income (i.e. dividends) and expenses (i.e. the loan interest) related to the share investment were attributed back to Mr. Lipson. As a result, the interest expense was claimed as a deduction by Mr. Lipson rather than by Mrs. Lipson.

At the Tax Court level (*Lipson v. The Queen*, [2006] 3 C.T.C. 2494, 2006 D.T.C. 2687), it was held that GAAR applied to the series of transactions as they constituted a misuse of the provisions of the Act. According to the trial judge, the money was borrowed to, in the end, buy a residential property and therefore the interest should not be deductible. The Lipsons appealed to the Federal Court of Appeal (*Lipson v. The Queen*, [2007] 3 C.T.C. 110, 2007 D.T.C. 5172). The Federal Court was deferential to the trial judge and accepted his finding that "these transactions formed part of a series, the purpose of which was to make interest payable on the mortgage deductible." On this basis, the interest deduction was denied in its entirety.

In October of 2007, the *Lipson* case was granted leave to appeal to the Supreme Court of Canada. The case was heard in April of 2008 and on January 8, 2009, the Supreme Court of Canada released its decision in the case. The Court, in a narrow 4-3 majority decision, found the general anti-avoidance rule (GAAR) applied to the series of transactions entered into by Mr. and Mrs. Lipson, but the reasoning of the Supreme Court differed substantially from that of the lower courts.

Both parties conceded that the transactions gave rise to tax benefits and that there was an avoidance transaction.

With regard to whether there was a misuse or abuse, the majority of the Court held that the Minister had not established that 20(1)(c) (interest deductibility) and 20(3) (substitute borrowing) were misused and abused, but rather concluded that the spousal attribution provisions were misused and abused. In particular, the majority stated:

> Mr. Lipson sold his shares to his wife and bought the residence with the proceeds of that sale. . . . In the result, Mrs. Lipson financed the purchase of income-producing property with debt, whereas Mr. Lipson financed the purchase of the residence with equity. To this point, the transactions were unimpeachable. They became problematic when the parties took further steps in their series of transactions. The problem arose when Mr. Lipson and his wife turned to ss. 73(1) and 74.1(1) in order to obtain the result contemplated in the design of the series of transactions, namely to have Mr. Lipson apply his wife's interest deduction to his own income. This was contrary to the purpose of s. 74.1(1).

As a result, the court denied the interest deductions claimed by Mr. Lipson. However, interestingly, the dividend income was still included in Mr. Lipson's income, and Mrs. Lipson was allowed to claim the interest deductions. Allowing the deductions to Mrs. Lipson was in sharp contrast to the denial of the interest deduction entirely by the lower courts.

A few observations can be made as a result of the *Lipson* decision. The Supreme Court rejected the "overall purpose" approach used in the lower courts and indicated that it saw no abuse of the provisions related to the interest deduction [20(1)(c) and 20(3)]. The Court affirmed basic "*Singleton*-type" organizing of one's affairs to obtain interest deductibility. However, it concluded that the attribution rules that resulted in Mr. Lipson being able to claim the interest deduction (as opposed to Mrs. Lipson) were abused.

Because of the division of the court, it may take further cases to clarify the point at which abusive tax avoidance starts and legitimate tax planning ends.

Unfortunately, the case failed to contribute analysis that would provide more certainty around the application of GAAR in the future. As noted earlier, all three decisions (the majority and the two dissenting) concluded that the steps taken to allow Mrs. Lipson to rely on paragraph 20(1)(c) to deduct the interest incurred on the mortgage loan did not, on their own, constitute a misuse or abuse of the Act and that GAAR should not apply to Singleton-type transactions. Similarly, in leveraged life insurance arrangements, rearranging one's affairs so that cash is used to make deposits to an exempt life insurance policy, and then using a loan against the cash value of the policy, should be a valid way to structure one's affairs to achieve interest deductibility.

However, it would appear that the decision opens the door for the CRA to attempt a GAAR attack if other provisions are used in conjunction with interest deductions. As a result, care must be taken when undertaking any leveraged transaction that involves more than just a reorganization of one's affairs to meet the direct use test required by 20(1)(c).

B. — General areas of concern relating to GAAR and leveraged life insurance

When considering any leveraged life insurance strategy, the possible application of GAAR to matters other than interest deductibility may also be a concern.

If the CRA did seek to apply GAAR one possible result would be to recharacterize a collateral loan as a policy loan. Different tax consequences are specifically contemplated in the Act for both a collateral loan and a policy loan. The tax consequence of classification as a policy loan is a disposition which may result in a taxable policy gain. A policy loan is defined in subsection 148(9) of the Act to be "an amount advanced by an insurer to a policyholder in accordance with the terms and conditions of the life insurance policy." In order to meet the definition of policy loan, the amount must be advanced by an insurer. In contrast, the assignment of all or any part of an interest in a life insurance policy for the purpose of securing a debt or loan is specifically excluded in paragraph (f) from the definition of disposition in subsection 148(9). CRA commentary has pointed to the definition of "policy loan" itself to view certain collateral loans as policy loans under the Act and also the possible application of GAAR to bring about this result.

In response to a question about the income tax treatment where a loan would be made from an insurance company to its policyholder under a separate loan agreement similar to a loan agreement used by any bank, the CRA issued technical interpretation JL91_037.038 dated July 3, 1991. The CRA's view was that the policyholder received an advance from the insurer in accordance with the terms and conditions of the life insurance policy. Although the legal form was separate agreements, the two agreements appeared to be interdependent to form a single transaction. Accordingly, the CRA interpreted that the separate loan agreement from the insurer would be considered a policy loan.

A similar question asked for the CRA's position at the 1992 CALU Annual meeting (technical interpretation 9210680 dated May 11, 1992). The question was in respect to an advance by an insurer to a policyholder where the loan is made under a separate contract collaterally secured by the policy and not governed by the terms and conditions of the policy. The CRA's position was that, in general, it should be possible for an insurer to make a loan under a separate contract to a policyholder that is not a policy loan. The loan must reflect commercial terms, be capable of standing on its own and be permitted under the relevant governing statute. However, the CRA was of the opinion that if funds were advanced by the insurer to the policyholder with no obligation to repay the principal or interest until the death of the insured, the arrangement would likely be viewed as a policy loan.

In technical interpretation 9606425 dated April 9,1996, the CRA replied to a series of hypothetical questions involving leveraged life insurance arrangements where the lender involved is a corporation related to the insurer. The CRA indicated that the pledge or assignment of a life insurance policy as collateral security for a loan from the insurer or a corporation related to the insurer would not, by itself, cause the CRA to conclude that a policy loan had been made. The conclusion could only be made after a review of the terms and conditions governing the policy. With respect to the possible application of GAAR, the CRA indicated that all the facts, circumstances and documentation surrounding a specific situation would need to be reviewed in order to determine if GAAR would apply.

In CRA technical interpretation 2006-0175401I7 dealt with a situation where a shareholder borrows from the issuer of the policy using the corporation's policy as security. It considered the question of whether this would be considered to be a "policy loan", and thereby a disposition of the policy, or could GAAR apply to bring about this result? Like earlier commentary, the CRA stated:

> In general, assigning a life insurance policy as collateral security for a loan granted by the issuer of the policy or a related person does not allow, in itself, a conclusion to the effect that a policy loan has been granted.

However, as had been suggested in the CALU Roundtable in 1992 (in the context of loans advanced by an insurer under a separate contract from the insurance policy) and 1996 (in the context of a leveraged corporate insured annuity), the CRA in the 2006 commentary stated:

> There might be an argument for applying the general anti-avoidance provision... when financial products are interconnected and interdependent (for example, a life insurance policy and a loan) and more particularly when there is no obligation to repay the loan in question and corresponding interest prior to death. In such a case, the tax consequences could be recharacterized.

While the potential application of GAAR will always depend on the specific facts of each individual case, based on language of the Act, existing GAAR case law and the views from the CRA, it is arguable that GAAR should not apply to standard leveraged insurance arrangements involving collateral loans from a financial institution other than the insurer or even if made by the insurer, if the collateral loan is commercially independent of the policy. First, the funds would be borrowed from a separate financial institution, not the life insurance company. The insurer would therefore not be advancing the funds to the policyholder as a condition of the contract and accordingly the loan would not meet the definition of policy loan set out in the Act. Second, the financial institution has the right to demand payment of the loan in full recourse if the loan does not remain in good standing. This differs from a policy loan where the insurer cannot force the policyholder to repay the advance payments of the policyholder's entitlement under the contract. Third, it is an established principle of tax law that an individual is entitled to structure his or her affairs in a tax efficient manner and in general, GAAR case law has reaffirmed that general principle. Fourth, the arrangement should not be considered to result directly or indirectly in a misuse of the provisions of the Act or an abuse having regard to the provisions of the Act as a whole.

The Act itself, in subsection 148(9), distinguishes between a policy loan and a collateral assignment and the applicable tax treatment. Unlike a policy loan, the collateral assignment of a life insurance policy is specifically excluded from the definition of "disposition" in relation to an interest in a life insurance policy at subsection 148(1). The distinct tax treatment of collateral loans acknowledges that a policy loan is a prepayment of policy benefits and the insurer's obligation to the policyholder is thus reduced, whereas a collateral assignment of a life insurance policy as security does not impact the obligations of the insurer to the policyholder and is simply a normal commercial transaction. For all of these reasons and in light of the views expressed by the CRA, it is arguable that GAAR should not apply and a collateral loan should not be recharacterized as a policy loan.

C. — Aggressive tax planning

In its 2010 budget tabled on March 4, 2010, the federal government declared its intention to release proposals for consultation requiring taxpayers to report aggressive tax planning transactions to the CRA. A backgrounder and further details about the proposed reporting regime were released on May 7, 2010. Draft legislation, in the form of new section 237.3 of the Act was released on August 10, 2010 and Explanatory Notes were released on September 10, 2010. Bill C-48, which received Royal Assent on June 26, 2013, implemented many previously proposed amendments to the Act including those related to the reporting of aggressive tax planning transactions.

A detailed analysis of these amendments are beyond the scope of this book. In essence, the reporting regime will apply where an avoidance transaction, as defined at 245(3) of the Act, or a series of transactions which include the avoidance transaction, meets the definition of "reportable transaction". A reportable transaction will be one which features two of three of the following "hallmarks":

- "fees" to the "promoter" or "advisor" in respect of the transaction that are contingent, in any way, on obtaining a tax benefit, on the amount of a tax benefit or attributable to the number of taxpayers who participate;
- the promoter or advisor requires "confidential protection" about the transaction; and
- the taxpayer or person who enters the transaction obtains "contractual protection" against the failure of the transaction resulting in the tax benefit sought, reimbursement of expenses relating to disputing the tax benefit or an undertaking to provide assistance in respect of such a dispute (otherwise than as a result of a fee described in the first hallmark).

Failure to file an information return in respect of a reportable transaction would result in a redetermination of the tax consequences of the transaction or series containing the transaction as if GAAR applied and a penalty being imposed potentially equal to any fee received or receivable by an advisor or promoter. Advisors acting diligently to prevent the failure to file would have a "due diligence" defense and, if successful, would not be subject to this penalty.

Several submissions were received by the Department of Finance relating to these measures. CALU made a submission on July 26, 2010 which pointed out concern that the rules are drafted so broadly that they could apply to "normal" insurance sales where, subsequent to purchase, insurance is integrated into some form of tax planning that may ultimately be found to be an avoidance transaction. In verbal discussions of several fact patterns with the Department of Finance relating to its submission, insurance commissions were not considered to be "fees" for purposes of this legislation. This particular viewpoint was not reflected in the Explanatory Notes released on September 10, 2010, but CALU did seek written confirmation from the Department of Finance on this point. Unfortunately, no changes to the definition of "fee" were made in the legislation tabled on October 24, 2012; however, slight modifications to the explanatory notes involving this definition were made. The notes express clarification that for purposes of these rules, "a fee based solely on the value of the services provided in respect of a transaction or series of transactions, determined without reference to the tax results of the transaction or series, would not be a fee . . ."

These measures apply to transactions completed after 2010. Transactions to which these reporting obligations already apply would need to have information returns filed within 120 days of Royal Assent of the current legislation. Taxpayers, promoters and advisors may be subject to penalties for failing to report relevant transactions.

These measures are along the same lines but do not go as far as the Quebec government has gone with its Aggressive Tax Planning measures introduced in 2009. While this preemptive self-identification is not necessarily an admission of abusive tax avoidance, it will assist the CRA in identifying those transactions that may be subject to GAAR application.

Whether these reporting requirements could apply to transactions involving life insurance including leveraged life insurance strategies, will need to be considered. Where planning involves significant tax benefits, there must be an understanding reached between the various advisors, promoters, and taxpayers as to whether a filing is necessary and, if so, who is going to make the filing. Many of the leveraged life insurance strategies discussed in this chapter are already quite well known in the marketplace. To the extent that no confidentiality agreement is required by the advisor or promoter and no form of guarantee of tax benefits offered to the client, it may be doubtful that these strategies meet the definition of a reportable transaction. It is unclear whether the effect of these rules will be that care is taken to ensure the "hallmarks" do not exist resulting in few filings or whether, out of an abundance of caution, many filings will result.

4.3 — Application and Associated Risks of Leveraged Life Insurance Programs

The following section will describe several of the leveraged life insurance applications and discuss the associated risks.

A. — Example 1: Individual retirement application

The facts

Mr. A is a 44-year-old businessman. He is in the highest marginal tax bracket, maximizes his contributions to his RRSP and TFSA, and has eliminated his non-deductible debt. He has a $500,000 need for life insurance for family protection coverage. He is looking for a tax efficient investment vehicle that can provide him with additional cash flow at retirement.

The structure

Mr. A acquires an exempt life insurance policy insuring his life with a face amount of $500,000. Deposits are made to the policy throughout the 16 years prior to his retirement at age 60. The cash surrender value in the policy accumulates on a tax-deferred basis.

Upon Mr. A's retirement, he borrows the additional funds (lump sum or in a series of annual borrowings) that he requires for personal living expenses from a financial institution. Under the terms of the loan, the life insurance policy is assigned as collateral security. The loan is structured so that interest is capitalized and added to the outstanding principal.

At Mr. A's death, the life insurance death benefit proceeds will be used to fund the repayment of the outstanding bank loan. Any proceeds remaining after the repayment will be paid tax-free to the named beneficiaries under the policy. It is important to note that the loan amount plus the capitalized interest will reduce the amount of the death benefit payable to the beneficiaries of the policy upon the death of the life insured. The death benefit pattern should be structured to ensure that there is at least a sufficient death benefit to repay the bank loan as well as cover the original need for insurance.

The analysis

Financial risks

Use of illustrations

Generally, the benefits of leveraged insurance arrangements are demonstrated through the use of numerical spreadsheet illustrations. These illustrations calculate future bank loan advances that may be available based on the life insurance proposal, which is a projection of the future values of the life insurance product. The illustrations may demonstrate the projected impact of capitalizing loan interest and may illustrate interest deductibility, if it is applicable. The illustrations are based on a number of assumptions and there is a risk that the actual performance of the arrangement will differ if the assumptions are not realized.

Performance of the life insurance product

During the accumulation phase where the cash surrender value is growing tax-deferred within the exempt life insurance policy, the risks are similar to any insurance purchase. The risks concern the performance of the life insurance product and whether the assumptions on mortality, expense charges and investment return will be realized. The life insurance proposal projects the future values of the life insurance product based on an assumed investment return (whether an interest rate, a performance credit scale, or a dividend scale). If actual experience does not conform to the assumptions made in the preparation of the product proposal, the product values illustrated may or may not be achieved. For further information on life insurance product performance refer to Chapter 2.

During the access phase when the policy is pledged as collateral security and bank loan advances are made, if the product values illustrated are not achieved, the illustrated loan advances will also not be achievable. Conversely, if the investment return and resulting product values exceed the illustration, additional loan advances may be available. The risk is that the projected values will not be realized if actual results differ from the assumptions made in the illustrations.

Interest rate risk

The terms and conditions of the loan will vary depending on the financial institution used, although many of the features and terms of loans secured with life insurance as collateral are similar. Generally, the interest rate charged on the loan advances will be a floating rate based upon the prime rate plus a margin. If the loan rate increases due to unforeseen economic conditions, the outstanding loan may grow very rapidly particularly if the loan is structured with capitalized interest. Generally, the financial institution will require that the outstanding loan balance not exceed a specified percentage of the life insurance policy's cash surrender value to remain in good standing. If the interest rate charged on the loan is higher than expected and/or the investment return in the life insurance product is the same or lower than projected, the outstanding loan balance may exceed the acceptable limits detailed in the loan agreement. The financial institution will then require that measures be taken to bring the value of the collateral security back in accordance with the terms of the loan agreement. The financial institution could require current servicing of the loan interest (i.e. demand that loan interest be paid and not added to the outstanding loan amount), the repayment of principal, additional security provided as collateral for the loan, or a surrender of the life insurance policy as provided for under the terms of the collateral security agreement.

In the worst case scenario, if the life insurance policy is surrendered, the financial institution would receive the proceeds of the policy to satisfy the amount of the outstanding loan and any remainder would be returned to the policyholder. The owner of the policy would have a disposition for income tax purposes which may result in a substantial taxable policy gain. The owner may not have sufficient funds available from the remainder that was returned to pay the resulting tax liability owing on the disposition of the policy. As well, the insurance protection that was provided by the policy would be lost.

Banking risks

In addition to the interest rate risks there may be banking risks. For example, the terms of the loan will be negotiated at some point in the future. The financial institution's lending policies 15 or 20 years hence may differ from current lending practices. Such lending practices may relate to the percentage of the cash value against which the financial institution will lend, the ability to capitalize interest and even whether the financial institution will lend against life insurance cash values at all.

Leveraging indexed accounts

Another lending issue to consider is the procedure of some financial institutions to reduce the leveraging percentage if the accumulation in a universal life policy is allocated to accounts that link the investment return to an equity index or fund. In these cases, the loan advances available at the time of borrowing may be less than originally illustrated. It is important to note that reducing the leveraging percentage is not the procedure of all financial institutions issuing collateral life insurance loans.

Life expectancy

Illustrations of the leveraged concept make an assumption regarding the life expectancy of the individual insured under the policy. The illustration generally will show the maximum loan advances available so that at life expectancy the maximum acceptable collateral security limit will be reached. At this point, the outstanding loan balance will reach the maximum percentage of the cash surrender value in the life insurance policy. If the life insured lives beyond the assumed age of life expectancy the outstanding loan may exceed the acceptable margin and the financial institution may demand any one of the measures discussed above to bring the value of the collateral security back in accordance with the terms of the loan agreement.

Tax risks

Application of the general anti-avoidance rule

It might be argued that the GAAR may be applicable in this situation, possibly to recharacterize the collateral loan as a policy loan. It will be necessary for the client's tax advisor to review this scenario as set out above considering the general discussion of the GAAR as discussed in section 4.2.B.

Interest deductibility

In the individual retirement application the borrowed funds would be used for personal living expenses. The requirements under paragraph 20(1)(c) would not be met as the borrowed funds are not used for the purpose of gaining or producing income. Accordingly, interest on the bank loan would not be deductible for income tax purposes.

B. — Example 2: Corporate application using leveraged life insurance for retirement redemption

The facts

A successful operating company is owned equally by two brothers (B & C). Each of the brothers have frozen the value of their shares and have now introduced other family members into the corporate holdings.

The brothers each exchanged their common shares for preferred shares redeemable at $1,000,000. The adult children of the brothers have subscribed for new common shares. Brother B intends to retire in 10 years and, pursuant to the terms of their new shareholders' agreement, the company will redeem his preferred shares over 10 years. If B dies before all the shares are redeemed, the shareholders' agreement provides that the company will redeem the remaining outstanding shares from his estate.

The structure

The company acquires and is the beneficiary of an exempt life insurance policy insuring brother B's life with a face amount of $1,000,000. This amount of coverage provides the insurance that is required if B dies prior to the scheduled redemption. Deposits are made to the policy throughout the 10 years prior to B's retirement. The cash surrender value in the policy accumulates on a tax-deferred basis.

Upon brother B's retirement, the company borrows an annual series of bank loans to fund the scheduled redemption of the preferred shares. The life insurance policy is used as collateral security for the loan. Some or all of the loan interest may be deductible to the company under paragraph 20(1)(c) of the Act, as the funds are being used to redeem shares. The loan is structured so that the lender agrees to make additional loans to the company equal to the after-tax cost of interest on the outstanding balance. The funds from these loans must be used to generate income from business or property. These additional loans are added to the outstanding principal and secured by the assignment of the policy. By capitalizing the after-tax cost of the interest, there is no impact on the company's cash flow.

At brother B's death, the life insurance death benefit proceeds will be received by the company tax-free and will be used to fund the repayment of the outstanding bank loan. If B dies prior to having all of the shares redeemed, the company will use a portion of the death benefit to redeem the remaining shares from B's estate.

The analysis

In addition to the tax and financial issues described above, the following are issues of concern in the retirement redemption application not previously discussed:

- interest deductibility
- availability of the credit to the capital dividend account

Tax Risks

Interest deductibility

When a corporation purchases an insurance policy and subsequently uses the cash surrender value of the policy as collateral security for a loan, the interest on the borrowed funds may be deductible if the criteria set out in paragraphs 20(1)(c) and (d) are met.

Although borrowed money used to redeem shares or pay dividends to a shareholder does not meet the direct use (for an income producing purpose) test under paragraph 20(1)(c) of the Act, the CRA's current administrative practice (outlined in paragraph 23 of IT-533) accepts that the borrowed money is used to "fill the hole" created by removing the capital on the distribution. The CRA will accept that the purpose is to produce income from business or property provided that the capital was being used for purposes that would have qualified for interest deductibility had the capital been borrowed money. Capital for this purpose includes the contributed capital and accumulated profits. It does not include the cash surrender value of a life insurance policy. In situations where only a portion of shares is being redeemed, only the capital of those shares computed on a pro- rata basis would be replaced with borrowed money. This general practice was confirmed in the context of a wholly-owned subsidiary borrowing to pay a dividend to its parent company (2009-0344721E5 dated July 12, 2010). However, other aspects of the taxpayer's proposed structure led the CRA to suggest that GAAR could apply to the series of transactions. See Section 17.5.C.ii for further discussion.

The description of the arrangement indicates that the loan is structured so that the lender makes additional loans to the company equal to the after-tax cost of interest on the outstanding balance, and the funds from these loans are used to generate income from business or property. In order to avoid these loans being characterized as compound interest that would only be deductible when repaid with the death benefit, care must be taken. As noted earlier, one way to accomplish this is to sell investments that generate income and use the proceeds from the sale to pay the interest on the original loan. Then a new loan for the same amount is taken out, and the investments previously sold are repurchased with the borrowed funds. Since the new loan is used to purchase an income earning property, interest on the loan should be deductible. Any tax savings resulting from the deduction of the interest expense could then be used to reduce the loan balance. The same series of steps needs to be undertaken each year.

Leveraged insurance and the capital dividend account

Subsection 89(1) provides for a credit to a private corporation's capital dividend account (CDA) for the excess of the proceeds of a life insurance policy received by the corporation on the death of the life insured over the adjusted cost basis of the policy to the corporation. The CDA can be used by the corporation to pay a tax-free capital dividend to a shareholder.

Archived Interpretation Bulletin IT-430R3 "Life Insurance Proceeds Received by a Private Corporation or a Partnership as a Consequence of Death", released on January 7, 2003 sets out the position of the CRA regarding a CDA credit where a life insurance policy is used as security for indebtedness. Paragraph 6 provides:

> . . .when a life insurance policy has been assigned as collateral for securing indebtedness (as opposed to an absolute assignment of the policy) or is the subject of a hypothecary claim by a creditor, and the debtor remains the beneficiary or policyholder, the proceeds in excess of the adjusted cost basis of the policy would be included in the capital dividend account of the debtor. This is so because, in such cases, the proceeds of the insurance policy would be constructively received by the debtor in its capacity as beneficiary or policyholder, even though paid directly to the creditor in accordance with the assignment or hypothec.

Until this clarification was made there was a great deal of confusion regarding this point. To retrace the issue the following documents would be relevant: original Interpretation Bulletin IT-430R2 dated May 17, 1991; revisions contained in Interpretation Bulletin IT-430R3, dated February 10, 1997; reversal of revision for common law provinces in technical interpretation 970718 dated April 18, 1997 and Income Tax Technical News Number 10, dated July 11, 1997; the issue respecting the Quebec Civil Code is exposed in technical interpretation 9833605F dated March 17, 1999; the Civil Code issue is resolved in technical interpretation 2002-0122944F dated July 8, 2002. For a full account of these issues and their history see the discussion at section 6.2.C.ii.

C. — Example 3: Corporate application using leveraged life insurance to pay a bonus

The facts

D is the sole shareholder and president of a successful operating company. If D were to die, the loss of the keyperson may make it difficult for the company to continue operating after her death. D would like the company to purchase keyperson insurance coverage on her to ensure that the company would have the funds to continue in the event of her death to meet the demands of the customers and creditors. She would also like the corporation to have the opportunity to use the policy's cash surrender value as a potential source of liquidity to fund future corporate expenses which could include salary payments, although no promises to do so have been made.

The structure

The company acquires and is the beneficiary of a tax exempt life insurance policy insuring D's life. Deposits are made to the policy throughout 10 years. The cash surrender value in the policy accumulates on a tax-deferred basis.

After cash surrender value has accumulated in the policy, D may wish to pay herself a bonus without impacting the company's cash flow. The company could borrow the funds required for the bonus using the life insurance policy as collateral security for the loan. The loan interest may be deductible to the company under paragraph 20(1)(c) of the Act, as the funds are being used to earn income from business. The loan is structured so that the lender agrees to make additional annual loans to the company equal to the after-tax cost of interest on the outstanding balance. The funds from these loans must be used to generate income from business or property. These additional loans are added to the outstanding principal and secured by the assignment of the policy. By capitalizing the after-tax cost of the interest, there is no impact of servicing the debt on the company's cash flow.

At D's death, the life insurance death benefit proceeds will be received by the company tax-free and will be used to fund the repayment of the outstanding bank loan.

The analysis

In addition to the issues discussed above, in the leveraged life insurance used to pay a bonus concept the applicability of the Retirement Compensation Arrangement (RCA) rules is an issue of concern which must be addressed:

Tax Risks

Applicability of the RCA rules

Subsection 207.6(2) of the Act deems the RCA rules to apply to situations where, generally:

1. the employer has a legal obligation to provide benefits that are to be received or enjoyed by any person, on, after, or in contemplation of any substantial change in services rendered by, the retirement or loss of an office or employment of, a taxpayer;
2. the employer acquires an interest in a life insurance policy, and
3. it is reasonable to consider that the life insurance was purchased, in whole or in part, to fund the obligation.

Question 10 at the 2012 CALU CRA Roundtable (technical interpretation 2012-0435771C6) explored the meaning of the phrase "may reasonably be considered to be acquired to fund, in whole or in part." The CRA listed the following factors it would consider in determining whether subsection 207.6(2) of the Act would apply to deem a life insurance policy held in connection with an employee retirement plan to be the subject property of an RCA:

- the identity of the employees whose lives are insured as compared to those to be provided benefits under the plan;
- the timing of the acquisition of the insurance and the setting up of the plan;
- the extent of the monetary coverage under the insurance as contrasted with the value of the benefits under the plan; and
- reasons (other than the existence of the plan) for the employer's purchase of insurance. For example, we have previously opined that the RCA deeming rule may not necessarily apply to: (i) 'key man' insurance acquired as coverage for losses or damages the employer might suffer on the death of an employee; and (ii) life insurance policies acquired solely to pay benefits in the event of the death of an employee.

The test is not only applied at the time of acquisition of a policy. The CRA states that "the RCA deeming rule can apply even where the life insurance policy is acquired before the retirement benefits become provided." The context of the question was where a life insurance policy is acquired at a particular time and at a subsequent time the employer becomes legally obligated to pay retirement benefits to an employee (Question 10 – 2012 CALU CRA Roundtable).

Ultimately, it is a question of fact in each circumstance. The CRA has stated that the policy and all relevant documentation would have to be reviewed to determine if that interest may reasonably be considered to be acquired to fund retirement benefits.

If the corporate leveraged life insurance arrangement is deemed to be a RCA, the company that acquired the interest in the policy will be deemed to be the custodian of the RCA plan and the interest in the policy would be considered property of the RCA trust. The company would not only have to pay the insurance deposit, but also a refundable tax to the CRA equal to the amount of the deposit. For example, assuming the corporation deposits $12,000 to the life insurance policy that is deemed to be a RCA, the refundable tax payable to the CRA would be an equal amount of $12,000.

If the corporate leveraged life insurance arrangement is deemed to be a RCA the following summarized rules with respect to a RCA investing in and owning a life insurance policy would apply (for detailed information on RCA plans funded with life insurance refer to section 7.7):

1. Where the property of a RCA trust is an exempt life insurance policy, there is no refundable tax liability in respect of the internal accumulation within the exempt policy.

2. A disposition of an interest in an exempt policy may give rise to a policy gain and may be subject to the 50 percent refundable tax. However, in technical interpretation 2000-001706 the CRA suggests that there would be no refundable tax in respect of amounts received as a result of a policy withdrawal in the context of a deemed RCA under subsection 207.6(2).

3. The life insurance death benefit proceeds are received by the RCA trust tax-free.

4. Any payment out of the RCA trust is taxable to the recipient. Accordingly, the death benefit proceeds under the insurance policy can only be flowed out of the RCA trust on a taxable basis. Further, where a private corporation receives or is deemed to receive the proceeds through the RCA trust, the corporation will not receive a credit to its capital dividend account in respect of any death benefit proceeds.

5. The refundable tax will be returned to the RCA trust as benefits are paid out of the plan, to the extent that there is a balance in the refundable tax account. One dollar is refunded for every $2 in payments made.

The application of these rules would significantly impact the benefits and costs of the leveraged life insurance used to pay a bonus concept.

The first test in the RCA deeming provision is that a legal obligation by the employer to provide benefits to an employee must exist. In shareholder owner/manager situations it can be argued that no obligation to provide the benefits would exist. That is, a controlling shareholder would likely not enter into a legal obligation with a controlled corporation to provide any benefits whether they be future bonuses or death benefits. The shareholder in his capacity to make decisions on behalf of the company could cause the company to pledge the life insurance policy as collateral security at any time. The shareholder acting in his capacity to direct the company could also cause the corporation to make a bonus payment. Accordingly, the first test of the RCA deeming rules would fail and the arrangement would not be deemed a RCA.

Particular consideration should be given to whether the RCA deeming provisions would apply to situations where the person receiving the bonus is a minority shareholder. It may be questionable in this case whether a minority shareholder has the power to direct the decisions of the company. The facts of the situation would need to be reviewed to determine if a legal obligation by the company to provide post retirement benefits has been established. Consideration should also be given to situations where the employee receiving the bonus is not a shareholder. Again the facts of the case would determine if a legal obligation to provide post retirement benefits has been established and if it is reasonable to consider that the life insurance was purchased to fund the obligation.

Careful consideration should be given to whether the RCA deeming provisions would apply where an obligation is established in the future after the purchase of the life insurance policy.

D. — Example 4: Corporate application using leveraged life insurance for a living buyout

The facts

Mr. E and Ms. F each own 50 percent of a company. Mr. E is a number of years older than Ms. F and has expressed his desire to be bought out by her when he retires. The buyout would take place over a number of years. If he dies prior to retirement he would like his estate to receive full consideration for his shares. Mr. E has not taken advantage of the capital gains exemption and he wishes to structure the buyout in a manner that would facilitate its use. Ms. F is concerned about having sufficient funding to buyout Mr. E's shares. Ms. F would prefer to use corporate, rather than personal cash flow, to provide the funding for the buyout.

The structure

The company acquires and is the beneficiary of an exempt joint first-to-die life insurance policy insuring Mr. E and Ms. F. Deposits are made to the policy annually until Mr. E's retirement. The cash surrender value in the policy accumulates on a tax-deferred basis.

When Mr. E retires, Ms. F will purchase his shares at fair market value for consideration of a promissory note payable over a number of years. Mr. E would have a disposition and capital gain on the sale. He would use his capital gains exemption to shelter a portion of the gain.

Ms. F would personally borrow the funds required to make the annual payments on the promissory note. These personal loans would be secured by the pledge of the corporate-owned life insurance policy. She would deduct the loan interest from taxable income under paragraph 20(1)(c) of the Act on the assumption that as a common shareholder she will receive dividends. The loan is structured so that the lender agrees to make additional annual loans to Ms. F equal to the after-tax cost of interest on the outstanding balance. The funds from these loans must be used to generate income from business or property. These additional loans are added to the outstanding principal and secured by the assignment of the policy. By capitalizing the after-tax cost of the interest, there is no impact for servicing the debt on Ms. F's cash flow.

If Mr. E is the first to die, Ms. F would replace the security provided by the life insurance policy with other collateral allowing the financial institution to release the collateral security on the life insurance policy. The death benefit proceeds will then be directly received by the company tax-free. The company will receive a credit to its CDA equal to the proceeds from the life insurance policy less the adjusted cost basis of the policy. The company will use the CDA credit to pay a tax-free capital dividend to Ms. F. Ms. F will use these funds for repayment of the outstanding bank loan and any balance outstanding on the promissory note to Mr. E.

If Ms. F is the first to die, Ms. F's estate would replace the security provided by the life insurance policy with other collateral allowing the financial institution to release the collateral security on the life insurance policy. The death benefit proceeds will then be directly received by the company tax-free. The company will receive a credit to its CDA equal to the proceeds from the life insurance policy less the adjusted cost basis of the policy. The company will use the CDA to pay a tax-free capital dividend to the estate of Ms. F. The estate will use the funds for repayment of the outstanding bank loan and the repayment of any balance outstanding on the promissory note to Mr. E. Ms. F's estate could then wind-up the company and distribute the net assets or could sell the shares to another interested party.

The analysis

A personal loan to the shareholder has the advantage of allowing the borrower to use the total amount of principal. If a corporation borrows an identical amount, the distribution to a shareholder will normally be taxable, either as a dividend or as a salary, depending on the circumstances. The individual then, has only an after-tax amount available for their use.

There are, however, other tax consequences to consider when a corporate-owned life insurance policy is used as security for a personal loan to the shareholder. The approach to be taken will depend on the facts and circumstances of the parties involved at the time of borrowing. All of these potential tax consequences should be considered in arriving at a final decision as to whether a particular leveraged arrangement should be structured with corporate borrowing or shareholder borrowing.

In addition to the issues discussed above, in the living buyout concept the possible assessment of a shareholder benefit is an issue of concern which must be addressed. As well, consideration should be given to the impact of shareholder borrowing on valuation of the shares and use of the capital dividend account.

Tax Risks

Shareholder benefit issue

Subsection 15(1) of the Act provides for the inclusion in the taxable income of a shareholder the amount or value of a benefit that has been conferred on a shareholder by a corporation. In the living buyout situation, the corporation has pledged its assets as security to the financial institution in respect of the personal loan made to the shareholder. The question arises as to whether a shareholder benefit would be assessed to the shareholder. There are two times during the course of the living buyout situation which could give rise to a taxable shareholder benefit.

For the most recent commentary from the CRA regarding this issue in the context of corporate-owned insurance with shareholder borrowing see 2006-0174011C6 Question 14 2006 CALU dated May 9, 2006 and technical interpretation 2001-011288 dated January 10, 2002. This commentary, however, is quite general in nature and refers to many of the previously stated positions set out below.

While loan is outstanding

The first time that a benefit may be assessed is during the time the loan is outstanding. A benefit may be received if a more favourable interest rate is obtained or if the terms of the loan are more favourable because of the corporate security supporting the loan.

The CRA addressed the issue of whether a corporation's guarantee of a bank loan made to a shareholder gives rise to a taxable benefit in Question 62 at the 1986 Canadian Tax Foundation annual Roundtable. The CRA stated that in theory a benefit likely does arise as a result of a corporation guaranteeing a bank loan of a shareholder or an employee. The CRA indicated that the value of the benefit would be the difference in interest rates charged with and without the corporation's guarantee or the amount a third party would charge for the provision of a similar guarantee. However, the CRA indicated that it is unlikely that it would attempt to assess such a benefit unless there is some evidence from the outset that the shareholder would not be able to repay the loan. A benefit would be assessed if the corporation is actually called upon to honour the guarantee.

The CRA was asked a similar question at the 1991 Canadian Tax Foundation annual Roundtable (Question 24). It responded that it is a question of fact whether or not there is a benefit conferred. The answer contemplated that one way to determine the value of the benefit would be to examine the difference between the interest rates charged with and without the collateral security provided by the corporation.

The CRA was asked (at a panel discussion held in July 1992) to clarify whether the response to this 1991 Roundtable question represented a change in the position indicated at the 1986 Roundtable. The reply was that there had not been a change in position because the underlying facts of the question were different. The answer to the 1986 Roundtable question referred to a situation where the recipient of the guarantee was a minority shareholder or employee. The answer to the 1991 Roundtable question referred to a situation involving any shareholder. The CRA summarized its administrative practice to be that where the shareholder or employee is dealing at arm's length with the corporation a benefit will generally not be assessed unless there is evidence that the shareholder or employee was unable to repay the loan at the time the guarantee was granted. In any other case, where the shareholder is not dealing at arm's length, the determination of whether or not a benefit has been conferred and the amount of such benefit can only be made following a review of all of the circumstances of the particular situation.

At the 1992 Manitoba CBA/CICA Roundtable (technical interpretation 9206080 dated February 24, 1992), the CRA was asked whether the granting of a mortgage on property owned by a corporation to secure a shareholder loan would give rise to a taxable benefit. The CRA indicated that the facts in each case would determine whether a benefit is received by the shareholder. The CRA commented that the benefit could be determined as the difference in interest rates charged with and without the pledge of the corporate security or as the amount that the borrower would have to pay to a third party to provide similar security for the loan.

This issue was again considered in technical interpretation 9206635 dated March 18, 1992. The CRA's response was that whether a guarantee by a corporation of a shareholder loan resulted in a taxable benefit and the value of the benefit were both questions of fact.

In summary, it appears that during the period when the loan is outstanding, the CRA's general position is to assess a benefit where the shareholder does not deal at arm's length with the corporation. The taxable benefit may be measured as the difference in interest rates charged with and without the pledge of the corporate security or as the amount that the borrower would have to pay to a third party to provide similar security for the loan.

At the time of repayment

The second time that a benefit may be assessed is at the time of repayment of the bank loan. If the loan is repaid directly by the proceeds of the life insurance policy, there will be a taxable benefit assessed to the shareholder. This is because funds that the corporation is entitled to are used to pay personal shareholder expenses. Direct repayment of the outstanding loan could happen if the loan does not remain in good standing with the financial institution and the financial institution causes the life insurance policy to be surrendered prior to death. Direct repayment may also happen on death if the life insurance death benefit proceeds are paid directly to the bank pursuant to the collateral assignment of the policy. In both of these situations, if the insurance proceeds directly repay the loan, a taxable benefit would be assessed to the shareholder, which could cause severe hardship. (If the direct payment is made following the death of the shareholder, it is the shareholder's estate that will be assessed the taxable benefit and incur the related tax liability.) In the event of surrender of the policy there would also be a taxable disposition of the policy which could result in a policy gain reported to the corporate policyholder.

At the time repayment occurs, the transactions should be structured to ensure that no direct payment from the policy is made. This would involve the release of the collateral security by the financial institution in order to allow the funds to be paid to the corporation. The bank would require the borrower or her estate to provide alternative security to replace the security provided by the life insurance policy. The funds would then be paid directly to the corporation. If the repayment is a result of death, the corporation would receive a credit to the CDA equal to the proceeds of the policy less the adjusted cost basis of the policy. The corporation would use the CDA credit to pay a tax- free capital dividend to the estate. This would allow the estate to repay the shareholder's personal borrowing.

If for any reason the bank fails to release its security (for example, if adequate alternate security is not provided) and requires repayment directly from the insurance proceeds, a taxable benefit will result at that time. The amount of the benefit will be equal to the amount of the proceeds used to repay the shareholder's personal borrowing and could result in a significant tax liability. It is therefore extremely important that all parties to the arrangement understand the intended structure.

Valuation of shares

A corporate-owned life insurance policy on the life of a deceased shareholder contributes to the fair market value of the shares of the deceased shareholder immediately before death. Subsection 70(5.3) provides that the cash surrender value of the policy immediately before death would be used. (See the discussion at section 3.3.C.i for greater detail). Where the CSV of the policy has guaranteed a personal loan, there will be no offsetting reduction in the FMV of the shares by the amount of the loan outstanding at the time of death. Essentially, the personal loan outstanding becomes a capital gain to the deceased shareholder, taxable at the deceased shareholder's marginal tax rate (the lifetime capital gains exemption, if available/applicable could mitigate the impact of the capital gain).

Use of the capital dividend account

The use of the CDA to distribute life insurance proceeds at least equal to the loan outstanding at death, to avoid the potential of a shareholder benefit to the estate, penalizes the surviving shareholders of the corporation. Current tax rates on dividends (eligible or not) are higher than those on capital gains. If instead, the corporation is the borrower, there is no need to use the CDA to repay the loan. The CDA will therefore remain available for future use by the surviving shareholders.

E. — Examples 5, 6, and 7: Immediate borrowing application

The following examples are similar to the previous examples with two significant differences. The first is that the loans are made immediately following deposits into the policy or soon thereafter. There is no time for cash values to accumulate tax-deferred before borrowing commences. The second important difference, discussed in examples 6 and 7, is the offer of guaranteed insurance policy rates of return and loan interest rates (or guaranteed spread between the two). Example 6 illustrates immediate borrowing where the insurer lends money pursuant to a collateral assignment of the life insurance policy. Example 7 illustrates immediate borrowing using a policy loan. Both example 6 and 7 are commonly referred to as "10/8 Loan Arrangements", since, at the time these arrangements first appeared in the marketplace, the loan interest rate (whether by way of a collateral assignment of the policy or policy loan) was typically set at 10 percent at issue and the policy interest rate was set at 8 percent. Since then, some arrangements have used lower rates for both the loan and the policy, for example 9 percent for the loan and 7 percent for the policy, while maintaining the 2 percent spread between the two. In the discussion that follows, the "10/8" moniker will continue to be used. The discussion points raised in respect of "10/8 arrangements" would equally apply to "9/7 arrangements".

In its 2013 budget tabled on March 21, 2013, the federal government proposed to eliminate the "unintended tax benefits" under 10/8 arrangements — both 10/8 collateral loan (example 6) and policy loan (example 7) versions. Leveraged life insurance strategies where the policy and the loan are not linked (example 5) were not impacted by the proposed measures.

While the 2013 budget proposals will deny the tax benefits for 10/8 policies, examples 6 and 7 are included for historical reference and to illustrate the types of structures that were possible under these arrangements. Also, notwithstanding the 2013 budget proposals, existing 10/8 arrangements may still be subject to audit by the CRA with respect to the tax benefits, particularly the reasonableness of amounts deducted as interest, for years prior to 2014 and the potential application of GAAR.

The CRA originally expressed its concern regarding the type of immediate borrowing application dealt with in example 7 in technical interpretation 2004-0065531E5 dated December 6, 2004. The facts dealt with a policy loan for which the insurer sought to maintain a 2 percent spread between the "collateral account" and the loan interest rate. If the commercial borrowing rate was 5 percent then the collateral account would yield 3 percent. The CRA was then asked its views if the 2 percent spread were maintained but the loan interest rate charged was 10 percent and the collateral account credited 8 percent. The CRA recognized that the policyholder would benefit from a stepped up deduction for interest and an increased return under the insurance policy. The CRA specifically questioned the reasonableness of the loan interest rate (see below), and generally the concept as a whole by concluding:

> . . .as it would seem that this type of arrangement is not in accord with the purpose and spirit of the provisions of the Act related to exempt insurance policies we have referred this matter to the Department of Finance for their consideration.

Starting in November of 2008, the CRA also began to indicate an intention to audit 10/8 loan arrangements. Both the CLHIA and CALU were advised that, starting in 2009, audits of policyholder tax activities relating to 10/8 loan arrangements would commence. It was indicated by the CRA that life insurers' tax reporting and documentation would be examined, which it expected would result in policyholder audits and the potential application of GAAR. These intentions were also raised by the CRA at the Canadian Tax Foundation Annual Conference in November 2008, a CTF Conference following the *Lipson* decision in February of 2009, and at the STEP conference in June of 2009. It is interesting to note that the CRA's comments post-*Lipson* continued to focus on GAAR as an avenue of attack. It is unclear if the focus of the CRA was on the collateral loan version (example 6) or the policy loan version (example 7) of 10/8 loan arrangements or both. What is clear was an intention to closely examine these arrangements and possibly use GAAR to call the tax results generated by them into question. In response to a question at the CTF Annual Conference in November 2010, the CRA confirmed that their examination of these arrangements was ongoing.

At the same time, the CRA was seeking information concerning policyholders of 10/8 plans from insurers that issued these plans through *ex parte* orders pursuant to subsection 231.2(3) of the Act. The CRA was prevented from obtaining client lists from insurance carriers offering 10/8 plans in *Minister of National Revenue v. RBC Life Insurance Co.*, 2013 FCA 50, [2013] 3 C.T.C. 126. This subsection has now been amended by Bill C-60, *Economic Action Plan 2013 Act, No. 1*, which received Royal Assent on June 26, 2013 to require that notice to the third party be given when the CRA seeks a court order from a judge of the Federal Court.

As indicted above, the 2013 budget tabled on March 21, 2013 proposed to eliminate the "unintended tax benefits" under 10/8 arrangements — both 10/8 collateral loan and policy loan versions. Annex 2 — Tax Measures: Supplementary Information and Notice of Ways and Means Motions (hereinafter referred to as the NWMM) at section 40 proposed amending subsection 248(1) of the Act to define a "10/8 policy" as a life insurance policy (other than an annuity) where an amount is or may become payable under a policy loan or under the terms of a borrowing where the policy or an investment account of the policy has been assigned and either the rate credited in the investment account is tied to the interest on the borrowing or the maximum amount of the investment account is determined by reference to the amount of the borrowing or policy loan.

The following tax benefits are denied for 10/8 policies:

- Deductibility of loan interest paid or payable after 2013 (NWMM subsection 36(3) proposed subsection 20(2.01) of the Act);
- Collateral insurance deduction after 2013 (NWMM subsection 36(2) proposed subparagraph 20(1)(e.2)(ii) of the Act); and
- The increase in the capital dividend account by the amount of the death benefit payable after 2013 under the policy that is related to the borrowing (NWMM subsection 38(1) adding subparagraph (iv) to paragraph (d) of the definition of "capital dividend account" in subsection 89(1) of the Act).

Where a taxpayer repays a borrowing in respect of a 10/8 policy by withdrawing funds from the policy, the NWMM (subsection 39(1) adding paragraph (5) to subsection 148 of the Act) contains a relief measure which would alleviate the income tax consequences of a withdrawal if it was made on or after March 21, 2013 and before January 1, 2014. This measure provides a deduction to a policyholder for the least of the amount reported to the policyholder as a policy gain, the amount that reduced the borrowing and the amount the policyholder is entitled to receive as a result of the disposition. The first of these would generally be the least amount. This essentially gives rise to taxpayer self-identification that they have a 10/8 policy.

Related to this, it is unclear whether these measures will halt CRA audit activity for taxation years before 2014. The budget materials made the following statement: "The Government is challenging 10/8 arrangements under existing income tax provisions. Since these challenges are both time-consuming and costly, the Government is also acting now to introduce legislative measures to prevent 10/8 arrangements from being used in the future." In verbal remarks at the CLHIA Tax Officers Conference in May of 2013, it was indicated that it would continue to apply the current law while the budget proposals are pending and will review its approach to auditing 10/8 arrangements once the budget proposals receive legislative approval. As noted above, the main areas of concern expressed in prior CRA statements relating to 10/8 plans involved reasonableness of loan interest and the potential application of GAAR.

Both CLHIA and CALU have made submissions to the Department of Finance seeking clarification of the 2013 budget measures and advocating for an extended timeframe for transitional relief. At the time of writing, only the proposals as outlined in the NWMM had been released by the Department of Finance. Further, we are not aware of responses from the Department of Finance to either the CLHIA or CALU submissions.

It should also be noted that the budget materials stated as follows: "The Government will monitor developments in this area and, if structures or transactions emerge that undermine the effectiveness of the measure, evaluate whether further action is warranted, with possible retroactive application." Any strategies developed after these measures that closely resemble 10/8 plans would need to consider this warning. Will taxpayers seek rulings from the CRA or comfort letters from the Department of Finance relating to any such developments?

i. — Example 5: Immediate borrowing application — collateral loan

The facts

Ms. G owns several income producing real estate rental properties. On her death she is expected to have a capital gain resulting from the deemed disposition rules in subsection 70(5) of the Act. The income tax liability on the capital gain and recaptured depreciation, if she were to die currently, is estimated to be approximately $1,500,000. She is considering purchasing life insurance to cover the tax liability on death but she is having difficulty finding the cash flow required to pay the annual deposits to the life insurance policy.

The structure

The immediate borrowing concept is suitable for the taxpayer who is at ease with undertaking complex income tax planning.

Ms. G purchases an exempt life insurance policy insuring her life with a face amount of $1,500,000. She uses the cash flow from her rental properties to make the annual deposits to the policy. The cash surrender value in the policy accumulates on a tax-deferred basis.

Ms. G borrows the funds needed to replace the cash flow taken from the rental properties from a bank. Under the terms of the loan, the life insurance policy and the rental properties are assigned as collateral security. The loan is structured so that after-tax interest is effectively capitalized and added to the outstanding principal.

At Ms. G's death, the life insurance will be used to fund the repayment of the outstanding bank loan. The remaining proceeds will be used to pay the income tax liability resulting from the deemed disposition at death.

The analysis

The distinguishing feature between the immediate borrowing concept and the other life insurance leveraging concepts is the timing of the bank loan. In immediate borrowing situations the timing of the loan is either imminent or expected in the short term (i.e. within the first five years of the policy's existence). Common situations in which the timing of the loan is either imminent or expected in the short term include: where the client lacks the cash flow required to fund a life insurance policy but has other assets available which could be used as collateral for a loan; or where the client has sufficient cash flow but prefers to borrow because of a reluctance to invest current cash flow into a life insurance policy because of a perception that a greater return would be derived if the cash were invested into an existing investment or business opportunity.

In addition to issues relating to interest deductibility and GAAR discussed at 4.2.A and B, the following issues would also be relevant to immediate borrowing application — collateral loan structures.

Interest deductibility

Prior to the Supreme Court of Canada decision in the *Lipson* case, there was a greater concern in immediate borrowing situations than in respect of the conventional leveraged insurance situations that the interest deduction on the borrowed funds would be denied using GAAR. The risk was that the CRA would deny the deduction for interest taking the position that the overall purpose of the loans was to purchase a life insurance policy. Interest on funds borrowed to purchase life insurance is not deductible under subparagraph 20(1)(c)(i).

In this example, as long as cash from rental revenues is used to acquire the life insurance policy and the borrowed money is used to pay expenses, the interest on the bank loan should be deductible. The *Lipson* decision confirmed the ability of taxpayers to organize their affairs so that the direct use of funds was to gain or produce income from a business or property without fear that GAAR would apply to deny interest deductibility.

Collateral insurance deduction

Where a life insurance policy is used as collateral security for a loan, a portion of the premium may be deductible for tax purposes if certain criteria are met. In general, the assignment of the policy must be required by the lender, the lender must be a restricted financial institution, and the interest payable on the money borrowed must, generally, be deductible in computing the taxpayer's income. Due to this latter requirement, if the interest on the borrowed money is denied, the collateral insurance deduction will also be denied. For further discussion of the collateral insurance deduction, refer to section 6.4.E.

Financial risk

In the early years of the leveraged life insurance with immediate borrowing concept, the funds borrowed generally exceed the leveraging limits allowed by financial institutions under the terms of the loan agreement. Other assets may be pledged in addition to the life insurance to support the loan advances. Therefore, if the policyholder experiences financial difficulties, there is not only the risk that the bank will cause the surrender of the life insurance policy but the assets pledged in addition are in jeopardy of being seized to satisfy the outstanding loan balance. The surrender of the life insurance policy may result in a taxable policy gain for the policyholder to include in income. The disposition of the other assets may result in a capital gain for the policyholder to include in income. The result may be additional tax liabilities that must be satisfied and the policyholder may not have sufficient funds.

ii. — Example 6: Immediate borrowing application — 10/8 collateral loan tied to policy — prior to 2013 federal budget

The facts

Mr. I is a 45-year-old non-smoker. He is an accountant with a high level of disposable income. He is married and has three young children. He operates his profession through a professional partnership with two other accountants. The partnership generates significant cash flows. Mr. I wants to purchase $2,000,000 of life insurance to provide protection for his family to replace his income if something should happen to him. His advisor has suggested an insurance solution that will provide this protection while at the same time provide him with deductions which will reduce his taxable income and therefore increase his return on his partnership investment.

The structure

Mr. I purchases a tax exempt universal life insurance policy insuring his life with a face amount of $2,000,000. Mr. I uses withdrawals from his professional partnership to make deposits to the policy in excess of what is needed to fund the policy charges. The cash surrender value in the policy accumulates on a tax-deferred basis.

Mr. I assigns the policy as collateral security for a loan from the insurer to recover the amount of the deposits in excess of the policy charges. The borrowed funds are reinvested back into the partnership. Under the terms of the collateral loan, the interest rate is set at 10 percent for a term of 10 years and an amount equal to the loan is transferred from the regular policy investment accounts to a special investment account. The special investment account earns a guaranteed rate equal to the loan rate less 2 percent. Since the loan interest rate is 10 percent, the special investment account earns 8 percent. Mr. I is out of pocket for the policy fees and cost of insurance charges as well as 2 percent of the loan interest annually. Mr. I also claims an interest deduction on his tax return for the loan interest since the loan was used to invest in his partnership. The loan balance must always equal the balance in the special investment account. At Mr. I's death, the life insurance will be used to fund the repayment of the outstanding loan from the insurer. The remaining proceeds will be distributed to Mr. I's beneficiaries as a death benefit.

The analysis

A fundamental distinguishing feature between the immediate borrowing strategy in Example 5 and this Example is that the insurance contract specifies that, to the extent the policy owner has borrowed money via a collateral loan from the insurer, the return on the leveraged portion of the policy's account value will be the loan rate less 2 percent. This ensures that there is no interest rate risk or product performance risk.

In addition to the issues relating to interest deductibility and GAAR generally discussed above at section 4.2.A and B, the following issues would also be relevant to immediate borrowing application - 10/8 collateral loan strategies.

Applicability of GAAR

It is arguable that GAAR may be even more applicable in this situation than previously discussed in section 4.2.B. The ability to invest policy funds in the special investment account (earning 8 percent) in the policy is contingent upon taking out the loan (at 10 percent), and vice versa. Thus, the policy and the loan facility are inextricably linked and both provided by the insurance company. It seems more possible that such a linked loan might be considered a "policy loan", or that it might fall within the intent of that provision of the Act, and therefore be considered an abuse of the definitions of "disposition" and "policy loan" in subsection 148(9).

In light of the CRA's expressed intention to audit 10/8 loan arrangements and its persistent references to the possible application of GAAR, it will be necessary for the client's tax advisor to review this scenario considering the general discussion of GAAR in section 4.2.B and the specific comments relating to 10/8 loan arrangements by the CRA discussed in section 4.3.E above.

Interest deductibility

As in Example 5, based on the Lipson decision, as long as taxpayers structure their affairs so that the direct use of borrowed funds is to gain or produce income, the CRA should not be successful in applying GAAR to deny interest deductibility.

In the 10/8 collateral loan structure there is a concern that because the loan interest rate is tied to the product, it may not be an "arm's length" rate of interest and, therefore, may be susceptible to attack by the CRA on the issue of reasonability. Paragraph 20(1)(c) limits any interest deduction to a "reasonable amount". Although technical interpretation 2004-0065531E5 (discussed above in section 4.3.E) and in Example 7 (below more fully) was in the context of a 10/8 policy loan, the comments therein may be equally applicable to 10/8 collateral loan structures.

As well, the focus of many CRA statements relating to potential audit activities relating to 10/8 loan arrangements (also discussed in section 4.3.E) mentioned reasonability of the 10 percent loan interest rate.

In addition, in 10/8 collateral loan arrangements, the manner in which the 10 percent loan interest is paid, for example through a combination of cash out of pocket (for 2 percent) and additional loan advances (for 8 percent), may give rise to an issue regarding the timing of any deduction for compound interest expenses. If amounts are considered compound interest, they may only be deductible when the death benefit repays the loan, severely reducing the benefits of the strategy.

Collateral insurance deduction

To the extent that the collateral insurance deduction is claimed in respect of a 10/8 collateral loan arrangement, the same issues would apply as would be the case in the previous Example 5 (at section 4.3.E.i).

Financial risk

A collateral loan cannot be repaid using policy values without triggering a disposition of the life insurance policy. To repay a collateral loan with policy values, a partial or full surrender of the policy is required. The proceeds from the surrender would be paid first to the collateral assignee (in this example, the insurer). The excess, if any, would be paid to the policy owner. However, surrenders can result in taxable policy gains.

As a result, the proceeds received by the policy owner may not be sufficient to cover the tax liability arising as a result of the surrender. In the 10/8 collateral loan situation, as is true for immediate borrowing collateral loans, the only tax-effective way of repaying the loan may be to use other assets and this would be a problem if liquid assets are not available to repay the loan.

iii. — Example 7: Immediate borrowing application — 10/8 policy loan — prior to 2013 federal budget

The facts

Mr. J is a 50-year-old non-smoker. He is owner/manager of his own business, JCorp. His financial advisor has stressed the importance of keyperson insurance on Mr. J's life to ensure the business will continue uninterrupted in the event of his death. Mr. J's advisor has identified an immediate death benefit need of $2,000,000 and shows Mr. J how he can "quick pay" the contract in ten years.

Being the shrewd business man that he is, Mr. J is also looking for a higher after tax return on his investment.

The structure

Mr. J causes JCorp to purchase a tax exempt universal life insurance policy insuring his life with a face amount of $2,000,000. JCorp uses the cash flow from the business to make the deposits to the policy. The cash surrender value in the policy accumulates on a tax -deferred basis. The policy provisions allow for policy loans and guarantee a 2 percent spread between the rate of return on the policy funds and the loan rate.

JCorp borrows the maximum amount from the policy without incurring a taxable policy gain. The borrowed funds are used to replace the cash flow taken from the business. Under the terms of the contract, the policy loan rate is set at 10 percent for the life of the contract and an amount equal to the loan is transferred from the regular policy investment accounts to a special secured account. The secured account earns a guaranteed 8 percent. The loan interest is paid by JCorp annually.

At Mr. J's death, the life insurance will be used to fund the repayment of the outstanding policy loan. The remaining proceeds will be distributed to Mr. J's estate by way of capital dividend and used to pay the income tax liability resulting from the capital gain arising on the deemed disposition on death of the JCorp shares.

The analysis

One distinguishing feature between the immediate borrowing strategy in Example 6 and this example is the type of loan. In Example 6, the insurer issued the loan with the policy as collateral. In this example, although the lender is the insurer as well, the terms of the loan are set out under the policy contract. However, in both examples 6 and 7 sole security for the loan is the cash value of the policy. In contrast, under example 5, a bank may require more than just the life insurance policy to secure the loan and the interest rate on the loan and the policy's performance are not tied or linked.

Because the policy loan rate and the secured account rate in this example are generally guaranteed for the life of the contract, there is no floating loan rate and therefore no interest rate risk.

There is an issue of concern regarding policy loan interest with respect to interest deductibility and payment of the loan interest which must be addressed.

Tax risks

Interest deductibility

In this example, the borrowed funds were used in the business operations and therefore were used for the purpose of earning income from business. Funds required for the life insurance premiums were paid out of excess cash. The policyholder has structured his affairs in a tax efficient manner. Based on the *Lipson* decision, the CRA should not be successful in applying GAAR to deny interest deductibility.

As with collateral loan 10/8 arrangements, another issue to be aware of is that paragraph 20(1)(c) limits the interest deductibility to a "reasonable amount". Where the interest rate is established in an arm's length market, it is generally a reasonable rate. In this example, the rates are guaranteed for the life of the contract which could be until death. With the fluctuation of market rates throughout this period, there is the risk that the interest amount may not be considered reasonable and the amount may not be fully deductible. In technical interpretation 2004-0065531E5, discussed above at section 4.3.E, the CRA emphasized that to be deductible under paragraph 20(1)(c), the interest on the loan had to be reasonable. One of the facts to consider would be the rate charged under a policy loan that did not offer the guaranteed rate in the policy (8 percent in the case at hand) and ". . .the rate of interest that is being charged by other lenders (sic) with similar credit ratings."

In order for policy loan interest to be deductible, the requirements of paragraph 20(1)(c) or (d) must be met. There is a further requirement under subsection 20(2.1) that the policy loan interest must be verified by the policyholder and by the insurer in prescribed form (CRA Form T2210: *Verification of policy loan interest by the insurer*). The policyholder and the insurer must verify that the interest is paid in the year on the policy loan and that the amount of the interest has not been added to the adjusted cost basis of the policy. It is important to note that filing this form is an annual requirement and interest deductibility for a particular year may be denied if the form is not filed.

Policy loan interest

If the annual interest expense is not paid but is added to the outstanding loan balance there is a risk of incurring taxable policy gains from the capitalization of interest. When interest on a policy loan is capitalized the transaction is treated as two transactions; the taking of a policy loan (thereby increasing the outstanding loan amount) and the payment of loan interest due under the contract. Generally, the taking of a policy loan is a disposition of the policy and the payment of loan interest is considered to be a premium payment. For a more detailed discussion of this issue see section 3.2.G.iii.

Compound interest is deductible under paragraph 20(1)(d) of the Act if it is paid in the year and the simple interest meets the conditions in paragraph 20(1)(c). If the interest is capitalized the compound interest will only be considered paid in the year in which the loan is repaid. However, this does not apply where interest on a policy loan is capitalized based on the two part treatment of the transaction; the taking of a policy loan and the payment of loan interest due under the contract. Archived Interpretation Bulletin IT-355R2 "Interest on Loans to Buy Life Insurance Policies and Annuity Contracts, and Interest on Policy Loans", dated August 26, 1994 discusses the treatment of interest on policy loans.

To the extent that loan interest is tax deductible, the payment of the loan is specifically excluded as a premium payment and thus the result is that the capitalization of the loan interest constitutes a disposition and the amount of capitalized loan interest must be subtracted from the ACB. Also if the amount of deductible loan interest is greater than the ACB immediately before the transaction, then the excess must be reported to the policyholder as a taxable policy gain (subject to the CSV ceiling). Refer to section 3.2.G.iii for further details regarding the treatment of policy loans where the loan interest is tax deductible.

Collateral insurance deduction

The collateral insurance deduction is not available in relation to policy loans since policy loans are not true loans in the common commercial sense. They are advance payments of the policyholder's entitlement under the policy and the insurer cannot force the repayment of these advances. A policy loan is a right of the policyholder under the terms of the contract and, therefore, does not require a collateral assignment of the policy. For further discussion of policy loans refer to section 3.2.G.iii.

Financial risks

In the early years of the policy, the ACB of the policy is high. Policy loan amounts up to the policy ACB are tax free. Accordingly, this structure works best if the borrowing is done in the early years. In later years, the ACB is reduced by the net cost of pure insurance, which is deducted each year for purposes of calculating the ACB of the policy. The reduced ACB limits the ability to obtain tax free loan amounts. Loan amounts taken in excess of the ACB result in taxable policy gains.

Should a policyholder experience financial difficulties whereby the interest is capitalized increasing the outstanding loan balance, there is also a risk that the loan balance will exceed the cash value of the policy and cause the policy to lapse.

Where the policy is corporate-owned and the policy loan is repaid out of the death benefit proceeds, the credit to the CDA is net of the outstanding policy loan amount and the ACB of the policy. An example of this result is provided in CRA technical interpretation 2004-008914 dated October 8, 2004 (Question 5 APFF Conference). The corporation would experience lower CDA credits to pay a tax-free capital dividend to the estate compared to some other leveraging strategies.

4.4 — Conclusion

Access to a policy's cash value through leveraging the policy may be an interesting alternative to causing a disposition of a policy. Interest deductibility is integral to many leveraged life insurance strategies. Careful planning is required to realize this key assumption. Also, due to CRA's concern with certain leveraging concepts, policyholders with the help of their professional advisors should exercise due diligence when implementing any leveraged life insurance strategy.

5 — Personal Life Insurance Needs and Applications

Updated by Dianna Flannery, B.A. (Hons.), J.D. and Serge Lessard, LL.B., Fin. Pl., FLMI

5.1 — Introduction

Throughout the lifetime of an individual, his or her situation in life and need for life insurance changes. Life insurance is generally used as a major source of funding in order to meet the needs of a family or estate following an individual's death. In the business insurance context, life insurance is used as a source of funding to provide for the needs of a business following an individual's death. A discussion of business insurance needs and applications is found in Chapters 6 and 7. The focus of this chapter is on life insurance funding for family and estate needs upon an individual's death and during one's lifetime.

5.2 — Funding Needs at Death

In general, one of the greatest benefits of life insurance is that it provides a tax-free lump-sum payment upon the death of the individual who is the life insured. A life insurance policy beneficiary designation enables the proceeds to be paid directly to the party indicated by the policyholder on the death of the individual life insured. In the personal context, life insurance is generally used to provide protection for surviving dependants, to preserve, create or increase the value of an estate or replenish capital by providing funds that will allow for an equitable distribution of an estate. Each of these areas will be dealt with in turn.

A. — Protecting dependants

Life insurance proceeds received on the death of an individual provide funding for the maintenance of the deceased's dependants. The proceeds may be used to replace the deceased's earnings and to pay down debts and other liabilities. The proceeds may be used for the repayment of the home mortgage, education costs and expenses of daily living for dependants.

Normally, death benefits are received in one tax-free lump sum payment. However, insurance carriers may also provide a number of settlement options. The policyholder or the beneficiary may choose to have the insurance proceeds used to purchase an annuity for the beneficiary or beneficiaries. This would allow for the payment of the death benefit in installments over a period of time. (The taxation of annuities is dealt with in Chapter 14.)

Also, to ensure that death benefit proceeds are received at an appropriate time or circumstance the policyholder may designate a trustee as beneficiary of the proceeds. It is advisable to provide the trustee with formal instructions (in a trust document, Will, or as part of the life insurance beneficiary designation) as to the timing of distribution of the proceeds. In Quebec, the trust must be created by a Will or trust deed and cannot be created solely by a beneficiary designation. This is particularly useful in situations where intended beneficiaries are minors, mentally incompetent or incapable of prudently managing their own financial affairs (testamentary insurance trusts are discussed in section 9.5.D).

B. — Estate preservation

Life insurance proceeds may be used to pay down debts, tax liabilities and other estate costs. In this case, estate assets do not have to be eroded, liquidated or borrowed against in order to pay for these expenses. In this context a few areas will be highlighted: funding capital gains tax liabilities, funding tax liabilities associated with registered plans like RRSPs and RRIFs, funding estate tax liabilities and funding estate costs and probate fees in particular.

i. — Funding the tax liability in relation to deemed disposition of capital property at death

Paragraph 70(5)(a) provides that a deceased taxpayer is deemed to have disposed of each capital property owned by him or her, immediately before death, for proceeds equal to the fair market value at that time. Capital property includes depreciable and non-depreciable property. Shares of a corporation, partnership interests, mutual or segregated fund units, cottage properties and land are all examples of non-depreciable capital property. Depreciable capital property includes machinery, buildings and business automobiles.

A capital gain will be realized for tax purposes to the extent that the fair market value exceeds the deceased's adjusted cost base ("ACB") of the property. Paragraph 38(a) includes an amount equal to 50 percent of this gain in the deceased's terminal income tax return.

The deceased may utilize any remaining capital gains exemption if the property consists of "qualified small business corporation shares", "qualified farm property" or "qualified fishing property" (all terms are defined in subsection 110.6(1) of the Act). Any taxable capital gains that are not sheltered by the capital gains exemption will be subject to tax in the deceased's terminal return.

For tax purposes paragraph 70(5)(b) provides that the deceased's estate is deemed to have acquired the property at fair market value and, accordingly, this becomes the estate's ACB of the property.

In addition, for depreciable capital property, the deceased taxpayer may have recapture of capital cost allowance to include in the terminal income tax return (paragraph 70(5)(c) and subsection 13(1) of the Act). Recapture is equal to the amount by which the lesser of capital cost and fair market value immediately before death exceeds the undepreciated capital cost ("UCC") of the property. Such amounts are fully taxable as regular income.

Life insurance may be purchased to provide the funds necessary to pay the tax liability resulting from the capital gains and recaptured depreciation triggered upon the death of the individual. Life insurance will be particularly important as a funding vehicle if the beneficiaries wish to retain the property or if market conditions will not provide the estate with an amount equal to the fair market value of the property.

A rollover may occur if a spouse or common-law partner, or a qualifying spouse trust receives a capital property of the deceased. Under subsection 70(6) of the Act, the property will be deemed to have been transferred at proceeds of disposition equal to the ACB (the capital cost and UCC in the case of depreciable capital property) of the property. As a result no capital gain or loss would be realized by the taxpayer in the year of death. Any capital gains (or recapture of capital cost allowance) is postponed until the property is disposed of, or deemed disposed of, by the spouse or common-law partner, or qualifying spouse trust. A qualifying spouse trust is described in paragraph 70(6)(b) of the Act as a trust where only the surviving spouse or common-law partner is entitled to its income and no one but the spouse or common-law partner may receive or otherwise obtain the use of the income or capital of the trust before the surviving spouse's or common-law partner's death.

Where a rollover is available the tax liability will result on the death of the surviving spouse or common-law partner. Therefore the funding need is postponed until that time. Joint last-to-die life insurance may be used to fund the tax liability resulting from the capital gains and recaptured depreciation triggered upon the death of the survivor spouse or common-law partner.

ii. — Funding tax liabilities in relation to registered plans on death

At death, a taxpayer is deemed to have disposed of registered retirement savings plans (RRSPs) and registered retirement income funds (RRIFs) for proceeds equal to their fair market value pursuant to subsections 146(8.8) and 146.3(6) of the Act, respectively. From a tax perspective "locked-in" registered plans (i.e. arising from a pension plan) such as RLSP, LIRA, LIF, LRIF and RLIF are treated in the same manner as RRSPs and RRIFs. This is included as regular income and is fully taxable in the year of death. A rollover to a spouse's or common-law partner's RRSP or RRIF is permitted by paragraph 60(l) of the Act. Similar to the capital gains tax liability, life insurance may be purchased to fund the tax liability associated with bringing registered funds into income on the first or second (of two spouses') death.

Rollovers of registered funds to a child or grandchild who is financially dependent on the deceased upon the death of the annuitant under an RRSP or RRIF are permitted in paragraph (b) of the definition of "refund of premiums" in subsection 146(1). These beneficiaries are permitted to roll these proceeds into an annuity which must mature by age 18. However, if the dependant is disabled, a rollover to an RRSP is permitted. Also, a rollover of registered funds is permitted from a deceased spouse or parent/grandparent to a Henson-type trust to purchase a life annuity for certain dependents — a mentally infirm spouse or common-law partner or a child or grandchild who was financially dependent on the deceased annuitant because of a mental infirmity. These measures were contained in Bill C-48 and received Royal Assent on June 26, 2013.

iii. — Funding estate taxes

A deceased person may be liable for estate taxes in other jurisdictions. The United States imposes estate taxes, income and gift taxes on its citizens' worldwide assets, no matter where they reside. US residents, no matter what their citizenship, are also subject to income, gift and estate taxes on their worldwide estate. Also, the US generally imposes estate taxes on the US *situs* assets of non-residents. In such circumstances, the purchase of an insurance policy may provide sufficient funds to pay these liabilities. However, Canadian resident US citizens may need to take special care to ensure that any life insurance (and as a result any proceeds under the policy) purchased for the purpose of funding tax liabilities does not increase the value of the estate for US estate tax purposes. Ownership of the policy is generally structured in an irrevocable life insurance trust to prevent this treatment. See section 10.2.B for a more detailed discussion of irrevocable life insurance trusts.

iv. — Probate fees and other estate costs

In recent years, probate costs have become more significant in many provinces. For example, in Ontario, fees are $5 per $1,000 for the first $50,000 of the value of the estate and $15 per $1,000 for the value of the estate in excess of $50,000, with no maximum. Life insurance can provide the necessary funding for estimated probate costs in addition to other estate costs. Other estate costs would include burial and funeral arrangement expenses and estate administration costs like executors fees, legal and accounting fees.

As well, life insurance may be used as a tool in minimizing probate fees. The use of named beneficiary designations in respect of life insurance and annuity contracts can perform this function. For example, subsection 196(1) of the *Insurance Act* (Ontario) provides that where a beneficiary is designated, proceeds payable under the contract are not part of the estate of the insured (owner) and are not subject to the claims of the creditors of the estate. Article 2455 of the *Quebec Civil Code* is equivalent to this section, and articles 2445-2462 generally address beneficiary designations and their effects. Section 171 of the *Insurance Act* (Ontario) defines the "insured" as the person who makes a contract with the insurer and defines a "beneficiary" as a person, other than the insured or his personal representative, to whom or for whose benefit insurance money is made payable in a contract or declaration. Therefore probate fees are not minimized if the estate of the insured (owner) is the beneficiary designated.

As a result, in provinces where probate fees are significant, it may be advantageous to transfer cash or near cash assets into life insurance or annuity contracts and designate a beneficiary to avoid probate fees being levied on the value of these assets in the estate. One may utilize this strategy to build up the tax-exempt accumulation within an exempt policy. Exempt policies are not subject to accrual taxation under section 12.2 of the *Income Tax Act*. The growth in the cash value of an exempt life insurance policy is allowed to accumulate tax-deferred and will not be taxed unless there is a disposition of the policy as defined in subsection 148(9) of the Act. The death of the life insured is not a disposition of an exempt policy. The death benefit is received by the beneficiary tax-free. A discussion of exempt life insurance is found in section 1.8.A.ii.

v. — Collateral insurance

Often, a lender will require that the borrower provide life insurance as collateral security for a loan. The borrower would be the life insured under the policy. Should the borrower die, the lender would be assured of the quick repayment of the debt that is secured by the policy. Where a separate policy is purchased for this purpose a collateral assignment of the policy is required. Such a policy would be owned by the borrower and the borrower would have the right to name a beneficiary. (This should be distinguished from "creditor insurance" which is generally a type of group insurance owned by the creditor with the creditor as beneficiary but where the borrower pays the premiums.) A collateral assignment of a separate policy assures that the death benefit proceeds are used first to repay the creditor and any remaining amount would be paid to the designated beneficiary. In this context, depending upon the use of the funds, all or part of the life insurance premium may be deductible for tax purposes. Collateral insurance is discussed at length in section 6.4.E.

C. — Create, increase or replenish an estate

It may be difficult to accumulate sufficient assets to pass on to beneficiaries. Life insurance is often a cost efficient means to create an estate. The death benefit proceeds received tax-free on death can provide sufficient funds to pass on wealth to the next generations. Also, by "investing" funds that would normally be subject to annual accrual taxation into an exempt policy more funds may be provided to heirs than would have otherwise been the case. As discussed above, the growth in the cash value of an exempt life insurance policy will not be subject to annual accrual taxation and may never be taxed if the policy is held until death without a disposition.

Life insurance is often used to replenish an estate. For example, during life an individual may donate property to a charity. The donor would benefit from the tax credits available in respect of such a donation as discussed in Chapter 12. To ensure that the estate is not depleted by such gifts, life insurance is often purchased to replace the capital which was conveyed to the charity.

Another instance in which capital replacement is the goal is where the individual utilizes the insured annuity concept as discussed in Chapter 17 under which a prescribed annuity contract, as defined in Regulation 304, in combination with a life insurance policy is purchased. This strategy is commonly employed when the individual desires to increase after-tax income during life and preserve capital upon death. A prescribed annuity contract is not subject to annual accrual taxation. Instead paragraphs 56(1)(d) and 60(a) provide that a blended payment of capital and income in the same ratio for the term of the contract is deemed to be received. This averages out the amount subject to tax and results in more favourable current tax treatment due to an element of tax deferral. However, it "uses up" the capital during life. To replace this capital erosion, a life insurance policy would be purchased. Usually, a term-to-100 policy is employed in these circumstances. Term-to-100 policies are permanent policies under which the premium and the face amount are guaranteed. The requirement to pay premiums ceases at age 100 but the coverage continues in force beyond age 100. Commonly, term-to-100 policies do not provide any cash values but may depending upon policy design. For more information on term-to-100 policies see section 2.5.

D. — Estate equalization

Another common use for life insurance is to facilitate the equal or equitable distribution of an estate amongst beneficiaries. A common example is the distribution of shares of a family business to the family members who are active in the business. Often the business represents the major asset of the estate and the value of the remainder that will be divided among the other family members who are not part of the business is significantly reduced. Life insurance may provide a lump sum to non-active family members to ensure an equitable or fair inheritance.

5.3 — Other Benefits of Life Insurance

The discussion above has explored the use of life insurance death benefits. A final note should be made in relation to the use of exempt policy cash values. An overview of this is provided in this chapter with more detailed explanations of the strategies outlined in Chapters 3 and 4.

A. — Creditor protection during life

Traditionally, life insurance policies have been given special protection against the claims of creditors under provincial insurance legislation. The legislation, which is generally consistent across Canada, is intended to protect the rights of the beneficiaries under the contract.

The definition of life insurance in all provinces includes annuity contracts. Note should be taken in the province of Quebec, where annuity contracts are defined under the *Civil Code*. The Supreme Court of Canada in *Bank of Nova Scotia v. Thibault*, [2004] 1 S.C.R. 758, determined that a self-directed RRSP cannot be characterized as an annuity contract within the meaning of the *Civil Code*, when the contract reserves the investor's ownership and control of his or her capital. This is not an alienation of funds, which is essential in defining an annuity contract under the *Code*. Since this decision, a case involving a life insurance RRSP has been heard in Quebec which came to a similar conclusion (*Gervais v. Appel & Cie. inc.* (July 11, 2005), Doc. no. C.S. Longueuil 505-11-004415-019 (Que. S.C.), reported 2005 CarswellQue 7353. The Supreme Court of Canada decision in the *Thibault* case had a significant impact on creditor protection in Quebec. In response, the *Act respecting insurance* and the *Act respecting trust companies and savings companies* were amended in 2005. As of March 1, 2006 all annuity contracts had to comply with the existing definition of annuity found in the *Civil Code of Quebec* and the new legislative provisions. Generally, the insurance industry has amended its contracts to ensure they meet this definition which would enable the potential for creditor protection where a proper beneficiary is named.

Most RRSPs and RRIFs issued by insurance companies take the form of an undertaking to provide an annuity and as such come under the definition of life insurance in provincial insurance legislation.

Creditor protection during the life of the owner can be achieved in two ways: by making an irrevocable beneficiary designation in a life insurance contract, or by designating as beneficiaries certain family members specified in the provincial insurance legislation. In the former case, where a beneficiary is designated irrevocably, the owner, while that beneficiary is living, may not alter or revoke the designation without the consent of the beneficiary and the insurance money is not subject to the control of the owner or of the owner's creditors and does not form part of the owner's estate. See, for example, subsection 191(1) of the *Insurance Act* (Ontario). Further, without the consent of the irrevocable beneficiary, the insured (owner) may not assign, exercise rights under or in respect of the contract. See section 197 of the *Insurance Act* (Ontario). The *Insurance Act* of each common law province is substantively similar and is based on the *Uniform Insurance Act*.

In the case of a beneficiary designation in favour of certain specified family members of the life insured, the provincial insurance legislation prevents creditors of the owner from seizing and surrendering the contract during the lifetime of the life insured. In most provinces, the family member must be a spouse, child, grandchild or parent of the life insured in order for the policy to provide creditor protection. See for example subsection 196(2) of the *Insurance Act* (Ontario). Depending upon the province, common-law spouses and same-sex partners may be included under the definition of spouse in the *Insurance Act*. For instance, under the *Insurance Act* of British Columbia, "spouse" includes any person married to another person or living with another person in a marriage-like relationship. This however is not the case in the province of Alberta where "spouse" is defined under the *Insurance Act* as a husband or wife who are married. In Quebec, spouse is defined for these purposes as a married or civil union spouse.

Ramgotra (Trustee of) v. North American Life Assurance Co., [1996] 1 C.T.C. 356 (S.C.C.), was a case involving the bankruptcy of an individual who owned a life insurance RRIF under which his spouse was designated as beneficiary. The Supreme Court of Canada considered the scope of provincial creditor protection under the *Insurance Act* in light of the federal *Bankruptcy and Insolvency Act*. The *Bankruptcy and Insolvency Act* contains a provision which exempts from seizure in a bankruptcy context assets protected under provincial legislation. The Supreme Court held that the RRIF was exempt from claims of creditors by virtue of being a life insurance policy with a beneficiary designation in favour of a specified family member; namely the individual's spouse.

Amendments to the *Bankruptcy and Insolvency Act* (Bill C-62 proclaimed in force on July 7, 2008), allow for creditor protection of insurance and non-insurance RRSPs and RRIFs, subject to a clawback of contributions made in the 12 months prior to bankruptcy. These amendments leave provincial exemptions intact for life insurance products with appropriate beneficiary designations while introducing creditor protection for all registered products, whether insurance or non-insurance. Some provinces have also enacted provincial legislation which protects registered products from creditors. Currently, the provinces that have such exemptions are, Alberta, British Columbia, Saskatchewan, Manitoba, Prince Edward Island, and Newfoundland and Labrador.

As a result, an insurance RRSP or RRIF can be protected from creditors under the *Bankruptcy and Insolvency Act* or in certain provinces even if an *Insurance Act* exemption would not apply (i.e. named beneficiary is not a certain family member or is not named irrevocably). If the appropriate beneficiary designation is made, creditor protection afforded by the *Insurance Act* also remains intact.

In Quebec, under Article 2457 of the *Civil Code*, the class of specified family members is wider and includes all ascendants and descendants of the owner.

In all provinces except Quebec, the relationship must be between the life insured and the beneficiary. In Quebec, it is between the owner and the beneficiary. (See *Re Malenfant, (*sub nom. *Perron-Malenfant v. Malenfant (Trustee of))* [1999] 3 S.C.R. 375.) The definition of spouse, may include common law spouses or same-sex spouses, depending upon provincial legislation.

Unfortunately, the *Insurance Act* is silent as to whether the family class can be extended to a trustee or trust for those beneficiaries. On a plain reading of the legislation, it is questionable whether protection would be extended to a designation made in favour of an insurance trustee. It seems an unusual result, however, as that effectively means that creditor protection will be extended where a designation is made in favour of children who are of the age of majority (who can receive the proceeds directly) but not for minors. This argument has not yet been tested in court.

Where the beneficiary is a member of the designated family class, the contract is exempt from seizure, even where the appointment of the beneficiary is revocable. In the case of the appointment of a revocable beneficiary other than one in the designated family class, the policy does not qualify for creditor protection under provincial insurance law during the lifetime of the life insured. However, after the death of the life insured, where a beneficiary is designated, the creditors of the owner are prevented from seizing the policy proceeds. (It should be noted here that a designation in a policy of the owner or the owner's estate is not considered a designation of a beneficiary under provincial insurance legislation. See for example subsection 196(1) of the *Insurance Act* (Ontario).) The death benefit is specifically excluded from the estate of the owner as the proceeds flow directly to the beneficiary and are thus exempt from the claims of creditors. Article 2455 of the *Civil Code of Quebec* has the same effect. Note that this would not prevent the creditors of a beneficiary under an insurance policy from attacking the proceeds received by that beneficiary.

Where the owner is the life insured and the owner or the owner's estate is designated, there would be no creditor protection either during lifetime or at death. Creditor protection is less clear in common law provinces, however, where the owner is designated and a third party is the life insured. Consider the following example. Assume the wife owns a policy with the husband as the life insured and there is a designation in favour of the wife. Since the critical relationship is between the life insured (husband) and the "beneficiary" (wife) the requirements for creditor protection appear to be met. The issue is complicated by the fact that the legislation does not contemplate a beneficiary designation in favour of the policyholder. For example, section 171 of the *Insurance Act* (Ontario) defines beneficiary as "a person, *other than the insured (owner) or the insured's personal representative*, to whom or for whose benefit insurance money is made payable in a contract or by a declaration". Interestingly, creditor protection during lifetime does not require that a "beneficiary" be designated; rather, the requirement is that "a designation in favour of [a member of the prescribed class] is in effect" (see subsection 196(2) of the *Insurance Act* (Ontario)). The argument in favour of creditor protection would therefore be that there is a designation (in favour of the spouse) which gives rise to creditor protection even though the wife is not a "beneficiary" within the meaning of the legislation.

While the extension of creditor protection to this scenario is unclear, there is some support for an expansive interpretation in the case law. In *Tennant v. Tennant* (2002), 222 D.L.R. (4th) 51 (Ont. C.A.) Simmons J.A. noted "Although not directly relevant to the outcome of this appeal, it is worth noting that subsection 196(2) does not actually require that *a beneficiary* be designated to trigger the exemption contained in the section. Rather, it requires a designation from amongst a specified class. The significance of this distinction is that the "insured" is not excluded from the class of persons who may be designated under subsection 196(2)." The comment, however, is *obiter*, set out in a footnote to the decision.

Where creditor protection is important, it is advisable to name alternate beneficiaries also within the protected class since the exemption from seizure can be lost if the designated beneficiary dies.

While creditor protection remains available in many instances, despite numerous challenges in recent years, it is important to be aware of the limitations that exist to its application. Creditor protection for insurance products is not absolute. The specific requirements of the *Insurance Act* must be met. Further, even if the formalities of the legislation are satisfied, some competing claims may supercede the protection afforded by the *Insurance Act*. Areas in which other legislation or case law could erode such creditor protection include fraudulent conveyance legislation, dependant relief claims for support, property claims relating to marriage breakdown, other property claims such as constructive trust claims and claims by the CRA.

One final comment of note relates to Article 2378 of the *Civil Code of Quebec*. This provides creditor protection to the capital of an annuity, which is required for the annuitant's support, whether or not there is a beneficiary designated who is in the class of specified family members or an irrevocable beneficiary. The extent of this protection has not been the subject of sufficient case law to enable further comment.

B. — Using the tax-exempt accumulation of a life insurance policy — withdrawals, policy loans and leveraging

A significant amount of cash value is permitted within an exempt life insurance policy. See the discussion of exempt policies in section 1.8.A.ii. Once a significant cash value has been built up within an exempt policy, it may be utilized for any number of purposes including to supplement the owner's retirement income or provide funding for a shortfall experienced during a period of disability.

The cash values within the policy may be accessed directly by way of a withdrawal or policy loan. These transactions would be considered dispositions of the policy and potentially subject to taxation. A discussion of the taxation of dispositions is provided in section 3.2. In respect of withdrawals, the policy's adjusted cost basis (ACB) will be allocated proportionate to the ratio that the withdrawal is of the accumulating fund of the policy. For example, where the accumulating fund is equal to the cash value of the policy, if 1/4 of the cash value is withdrawn, 1/4 of the policy's ACB is available to shelter the withdrawal amount from potential taxation. There may be some circumstances where the accumulating fund may be greater than the cash value. See section 3.2.G.ii for further detail. In respect of policy loans, it is the entire ACB of the policy that is available.

Even where a withdrawal or policy loan is subject to taxation either in whole or in part, there still may be a tax advantage to "investing in" life insurance. It may be possible to accumulate more in an exempt life insurance policy than would have been possible had the same funds been invested in a traditional investment that is subject to annual taxation. The growth on the savings may be increased by moving the savings from a tax-exposed environment to a tax-sheltered environment. When amounts are withdrawn from the policy, the tax liability on the disposition may be less than the total amount of tax that would have been paid over the years on the annual earnings from a traditional investment. It is for this reason that this strategy can make economic sense.

Also, in respect of participating traditional whole life policies, one may choose to receive policy dividends in the most tax efficient manner, switching credit options when the tax efficiency is no longer a factor. For example, if it is desired to make use of a policy's ACB as a protective shelter, one may choose to receive policy dividends from participating traditional whole life policies in the form of cash until the point at which the ACB is diminished and the amounts received would be subject to tax. At this point, the credit option could be switched to using policy dividends to purchase paid-up additions which would not result in a tax liability. See section 2.7.A for a more in depth discussion of these policy transactions.

The collateral assignment of a policy is not a disposition for tax purposes. Leveraging an exempt life insurance policy which has accumulated sufficient cash values is another method of accessing the tax-free growth within the policy. A full discussion of leveraged life insurance strategies is found in Chapter 4.

C. — Intergenerational transfers of life insurance

Certain transfers of a life insurance policy will not be subject to taxation. A life insurance policy, therefore, may be a vehicle for transferring accumulated wealth to the next or succeeding generations on an *inter vivos* basis. Subsection 148(8) of the Act allows for a tax-free transfer of an interest in a life insurance policy to a child under certain conditions. Where this subsection applies the transfer takes place for proceeds equal to the adjusted cost basis (ACB) of the interest in the policy. The transferor will be deemed to have disposed of the interest in the policy at the ACB and the transferee will be deemed to have acquired the interest in the policy at a cost equal to that same ACB. (For a detailed discussion see section 3.2.G.v.c.I.) The steps involved in the use of life insurance for this purpose would be as follows:

1. A parent or grandparent purchases an exempt policy on the life of a child/grandchild.
2. The parent/grandparent funds the policy to the extent permitted under the Act. The cash value within the policy accumulates on a tax- deferred basis within these limits.
3. When the child/grandchild is age 18 or older, the policy is transferred to the child/grandchild. The Act allows for a tax-free rollover if no consideration is received for the transfer and the child/grandchild is the life insured under the policy.
4. When the child/grandchild requires funds (for example, to pay for post-secondary education or for a down payment on a home), the cash value may be accessed by any of the means discussed above in section 5.3.B.
5. Control of the policy may be maintained by the parent/grandparent after the transfer by designating the parent/grandparent as an irrevocable beneficiary of a small percentage of the policy. The designation would have to be made by the new owner (child/grandchild) after the transfer of the policy to him or her. An irrevocable beneficiary is given notice of any transaction in relation to the policy that would affect their interest in the policy. Cash value withdrawals, changes in investment options, a collateral assignment of the policy or a change in the beneficiary are just a few of the transactions in relation to the policy that the irrevocable beneficiary would be given notice of and would be required to consent to in order to carry out.
6. In situations where the grandparent is elderly, consideration should be given to naming a successor owner to whom the policy would pass should the grandparent not survive until the child attains age 18. Frequently, a spouse or common-law partner (the other grandparent) may be chosen who may also be elderly. In the situation where the grandchild is the life insured, the transfer could be made to the parent of that child on a rollover basis. The policy may then be subsequently transferred to the grandchild (after age 18 is attained) by the parent of that child, also on a rollover basis.

To qualify for the rollover, the interest in the policy must be transferred for no consideration to the policyholder's child and a child of the policyholder or a child of the transferee must be the life insured under the policy. For purposes of the rollover, the definition of child includes a grandchild, a great-grandchild, a spouse of a child, a child of the person's spouse or an individual under 19 years of age who is or was wholly dependent on the policyholder for support and is or was in the custody of the policyholder at the relevant time.

In order to qualify for the rollover, the transfer must not be made under the terms of the will of the parent or grandparent. In such a case, the policy would be transferred from the parent or grandparent to the estate and then from the estate to the child or grandchild. Subsection 148(8) does not contemplate a transfer of the policy at death. In technical interpretation 9433865 dated February 15, 1995, the CRA indicates that in order to qualify for the rollover the transfer must be made *inter vivos* or by way of a successor owner designation in order to prevent the policy from passing to the estate and thereby giving rise to a taxable disposition.

Care should be taken if the policy is transferred prior to the child/ grandchild attaining age 18 and the child/grandchild makes a taxable withdrawal, surrenders the policy or takes a taxable policy loan from the policy. The attribution rules will apply and the policy gain associated with the transaction will be taxable in the hands of the parent/grandparent. If the child/grandchild is 18 years of age or older and makes a taxable withdrawal, full surrender or taxable policy withdrawal, the attribution rules will not apply. Any related policy gain would be taxable in the hands of the child/grandchild.

A limitation of this approach is the impact of the exempt test on the accumulation within the life insurance policy. The exempt test under the Act limits the amount of cash value that can be accumulated in an exempt life insurance policy. In general, the maximum permissible under any given policy is a function of the age of the life insured, the amount of coverage on that individual and the duration of the policy. When the life insured is a younger individual and the amount of coverage is low this will result in relatively little room under the exempt test to create significant cash values. This strategy should be considered if there is a longer term outlook in respect of a young member of a high net worth family.

D. — Other personal insurance strategies

Life insurance may be purchased by an *inter vivos* family trust for the benefit of trust beneficiaries. The benefits of having the family trust invest in a life insurance policy include avoidance of the 21-year deemed disposition rule and no annual income to allocate to the beneficiaries. A full discussion of this strategy is found in section 9.5.

Often, "split-dollar" arrangements are used in the personal insurance context to benefit two or more family members. The members jointly purchase a policy and enter into a formal split-dollar legal agreement. One party may have a need for a permanent level amount of insurance to fund a personal need for death benefits; another party may have a need for a tax-efficient investment vehicle, with an accompanying need for a death benefit in this amount with the potential for this amount to continue to grow over time. Each party would pay a portion of the premium for the benefit that they receive. A full discussion of the issues relating to split-dollar arrangements is found in Chapter 8.

5.4 — Conclusion

Life insurance is a versatile financial instrument that can serve many different purposes. Traditional needs for life insurance death benefits include protecting one's dependants, preserving one's estate by paying down debts, tax liabilities and other estate costs, creating, increasing or replenishing an estate and equalizing an estate amongst many different beneficiaries. Combined with these are the added benefits which may be addressed during one's lifetime. Life insurance cash values may be utilized to supplement one's retirement income or lifestyle and may be used to provide for a child's educational or personal needs. Combining various needs of different parties whether for death benefits or living benefits is possible by entering into a split-dollar arrangement.

6 — Business Insurance Needs — Technical Issues

Updated by Diane Hamel, C.P.A., C.G.A., TEP

6.1 — Introduction

In previous chapters, we investigated the history of the taxation of life insurance policies, the various types of life insurance policies available in the marketplace in Canada today, the income tax rules relating to dispositions of life insurance policies, leveraged life insurance strategies and the use of insurance policies in meeting personal insurance needs. In this chapter we introduce the use of insurance policies in meeting business insurance needs.

6.2 — Theory of Integration, Life Insurance and the Capital Dividend Account

A. — Introduction

The principle of tax integration is fundamental to the Canadian tax system. Under this principle, income earned by a private corporation and distributed as a dividend to its shareholders should be subject to approximately the same amount of tax as if the income had been earned by the shareholders directly.

One of the components of tax integration is the ability to flow certain amounts received by a private corporation to its shareholders on a tax-free basis to the extent that those amounts are received tax-free by the corporation and would have been tax-free if received directly by the shareholders.

The capital dividend account is a notional account that is available to private corporations and is one of the methods by which tax integration is achieved.

B. — The capital dividend account (CDA)

The purpose of the CDA is to track certain tax-free surpluses accumulated by a private corporation. These surpluses may be distributed in the form of tax-free capital dividends to the shareholders of the corporation who are resident in Canada for income tax purposes.

Provided that a capital dividend election is prepared and filed in the prescribed manner, a capital dividend can be received on a tax- free basis by a Canadian resident shareholder of a private corporation under subsection 83(2) of the Act. Where capital dividends are received by a corporation, the dividends are not subject to the anti-avoidance rule in subsection 55(2). Capital dividends received directly by non-residents are subject to withholding tax under Part XIII of the Act, and may be subject to tax in the foreign jurisdiction. In technical interpretation 2003-0020695, dated July 17, 2003, the CRA was presented with a situation where a trust received a capital dividend one year and in the following year, made a distribution of an amount equal to the amount of the capital dividend, to its sole beneficiary who is a non-resident of Canada. The CRA stated that subsection 212(11) of the Act applied to characterize the amount paid as income of the trust for purposes of paragraph 212(1)(c) of the Act. Subparagraph 212(1)(c)(ii) of the Act then applied to impose withholding tax to an amount that "can reasonably be considered . . . to be a distribution of, or derived from, an amount received by the estate or trust as . . . a dividend . . . other than a taxable dividend". At the APFF Conference in October 2009, Question 5 (technical interpretation 2009-0327001C6) dealt with a situation where a death benefit from a life insurance policy paid to a corporation is distributed to a Canadian estate by a capital dividend where it is used for the payment of estate taxes. One question was whether the distribution of the remainder of the estate to the non-resident beneficiaries would be excluded from the application of subsection 212(11) and paragraph 212(1)(c) of the Act. The CRA responded that it was a question of fact. To the extent that it is viewed as income subject to withholding, the CRA confirmed that it would be considered estate and not dividend income. This would have relevance to the rate of withholding tax under many treaties.

The capital dividend account is defined at subsection 89(1) of the Act.

Life insurance proceeds constitute a key component of the capital dividend account. The CDA is credited by life insurance proceeds received by the corporation as beneficiary on the death of the life insured in excess of the adjusted cost basis (ACB) of the policy to the corporation immediately prior to death. The ACB is discussed in detail in section 3.2.F. The August 23, 2013 draft legislation concerning the exempt test and the tax regime for policyholders of tax exempt policies proposes changes to the calculation of the net cost of pure insurance (NCPI) for policies issued after 2015. Since the NCPI is one of the components of the ACB of a policy, this will have an impact on the amount credited to the CDA. See section 1.9.C.ii for further details.

In order to obtain a credit to the CDA, the corporation must receive the life insurance proceeds as a consequence of a death of any person. There is no requirement that the beneficiary corporation be the owner of the policy. Where the owner is not the beneficiary of the policy, the credit to the CDA is not reduced for the ACB of the policy because the ACB belongs to the policy owner, not the beneficiary (this issue is discussed in detail in section 6.2.D). On May 2, 2013, CALU made a submission to the Department of Finance recommending that the definition of the CDA be amended so that the policy's ACB would be attributed to the beneficiary of the insurance proceeds no matter who is the owner of the policy.

It should be noted that where there is more than one coverage under one corporate-owned policy (for example, a multi-life policy insuring three individuals), on each death the CDA will be reduced by the ACB of the policy. Since there is no change to the ACB of the policy as a result of the death of a life insured, this has the effect of reducing the CDA credit available as compared to where multiple contracts are utilized. (Refer to section 2.9.B.i for greater detail.) The August 23, 2013 draft legislation proposes a change to the calculation of ACB to adjust for death benefits received under a multi-life policy issued after 2015. See section 1.9.C.vii for a detailed discussion.

Other components of CDA include the tax-free portion of capital gains in excess of capital losses, the tax-free portion of dispositions of eligible capital property and capital dividends received from other companies. It also includes the non-taxable portion of net capital gains and capital dividends received by a trust and distributed to a private corporation. In technical interpretation 2012-0469591E5F, dated May 14, 2013, the CRA confirmed that where a trust receives a capital dividend in a given year and intends to distribute the dividend to a corporate beneficiary, it must do so in the same year in order to preserve the capital dividend treatment to the corporation.

The capital dividend account is reduced, *inter alia*, by any capital dividends paid during the period that the capital dividend account is being determined. Although the individual components of the CDA calculation cannot be negative, because of the cumulative nature of the calculation it is possible to have a negative CDA balance. Consider the following scenario. A Corporation realizes a $1,000,000 capital gain in year one resulting in a $500,000 credit to the CDA. At the end of year one, a capital dividend of $500,000 is declared and paid. The balance of the CDA at the end of year one is zero (+500,000 -500,000). In year two the corporation realizes a capital loss of $400,000. The CDA balance at the end of year two is now negative $200,000 (+500,000 -200,000 -500,000). Although a negative CDA has no immediate tax consequences, it may prevent the distribution of all of the CDA credit arising from the receipt of life insurance by a corporation. Continuing the example above, if in year three the corporation receives a death benefit of $500,000 from a life insurance policy with no ACB, the credit to the CDA will be $500,000, but only $300,000 may be paid out as a capital dividend because the CDA balance is calculated as follows:

Excess of non-taxable portion of capital gains over non-deductible portion of capital losses (+500,000-200,000)	$300,000
Excess of life insurance proceeds over the ACB of the policy	$500,000
Less capital dividends paid by the corporation	*($500,000)*
CDA Balance	*$300,000*

The CRA's views on the CDA and on capital dividends are contained in archived Interpretation Bulletin IT-66R6 "Capital Dividends," dated May 31, 1991. Interpretation Bulletin IT-66R6 also discusses rules relating to the life insurance capital dividend account ("LICDA"). These rules were repealed in 1985 (see section 1.8.B.iii). Any credit which existed in the corporation's LICDA immediately before May 24, 1985 automatically transferred to the corporation's CDA following the 1985 changes.

A corporation may own life insurance for any number of reasons, including funding for a buy-sell agreement, business loan protection, keyperson protection, etc. The credit to the CDA is often a fundamental component of the overall plan, and represents a key advantage of life insurance strategies over alternate strategies that might be considered.

C. — Life insurance proceeds received by a private corporation

As previously noted, a private corporation's CDA as defined in subsection 89(1) is credited by an amount equal to the excess of the proceeds of a life insurance policy received by the corporation following the death of the life insured over the adjusted cost basis (ACB) of the policy to the corporation immediately before death.

Excluded from the death benefit proceeds, and thereby excluded from the capital dividend account, is any interest income from the date of death received by the corporation from the insurer. This can arise in the event of a delay in the death benefit payout.

The reduction of the credit to the CDA for the ACB of the policy is intended to account for the fact that, if amounts had been distributed by the corporation to the shareholders personally to pay for the life insurance, such amounts would have been taxable to the shareholders.

It should also be noted that the 2013 federal budget proposed that life insurance proceeds from certain policies not enable a CDA credit (proposed subparagraph 89(1)(d)(iv) of the definition of "capital dividend account"). A corporation that receives life insurance proceeds from a policy that meets the definition of a "10/8 policy" will be denied an increase after 2013 to the CDA by the amount of the death benefit related to the borrowing in respect of a "10/8 policy". Also, for a life insurance policy that meets the definition of an "LIA (leveraged insured annuity) policy" any death benefit received will be denied a CDA credit. See sections 4.3.E and 17.6 for further details.

i. — Life insurance proceeds received by a trust

Life insurance proceeds received by a trust and distributed to a corporate beneficiary of the trust are not credited to the CDA. In technical interpretation 5-1766, dated July 24, 1986, the CRA indicated that proceeds received by a trust and distributed to a corporation (e.g., where there may be a concern about potential corporate creditors) would not be credited to the corporation's CDA because they would not represent proceeds of a life insurance policy but would represent distributions of property from the trust in satisfaction of an interest in the trust and would not retain their character as life insurance proceeds. A submission made by CALU to the Department of Finance in February of 2009 seeks a technical amendment that would allow a distribution of life insurance proceeds received by a trust and distributed to a private corporation beneficiary of the trust to retain its character as life insurance proceeds and, therefore, create a credit to the corporation's CDA.

The definition of CDA was amended by the 2001 Technical Bill (C-22, June 14, 2001) to include the non-taxable portion of capital gains and capital dividends received by a trust and distributed to a private corporation. Although this change addresses a portion of the disparity in the ability to flow tax-free amounts through to the shareholder, it does not address the situation where a trust receives life insurance proceeds and distributes those proceeds to a private corporation that is a beneficiary of the trust. Presumably this is because the amendments were drafted with the mutual fund trust context in mind.

At the CLHIA CRA Roundtable (Q11 reported as 2011-0399771C6, dated May 20, 2011), the CRA was asked to consider if the concept of "constructive receipt" could be applied to a specific fact pattern involving a trust receiving life insurance proceeds and paying those proceeds to private company beneficiaries of the trust to satisfy the beneficiary company's obligations under a buy-sell agreement. The CRA was not prepared to extend this concept beyond the context of creditor insurance (discussed below at section 6.2.c.ii). For more detail relating to receipt of life insurance proceeds by a trust and a distribution to a private corporation, also see section 9.5.E).

Using a bare trustee to receive insurance proceeds for the administration of a buy-sell agreement will not prevent a private corporation from receiving a CDA credit so long as the bare trustee is truly acting as an agent for the beneficiaries (2012 CALU CRA Roundtable Q6, reported as 2012-0435641C6, dated May 8, 2012). See section 7.4.F.iii for a more detailed discussion.

ii. — Life insurance proceeds received by lenders

Former Interpretation Bulletin IT-430R2 "Life Insurance Proceeds Received by a Private Corporation or a Partnership as a Consequence of Death," dated May 17, 1991, sets out the CRA's previous administrative position when a private corporation was the beneficiary of a life insurance policy that was assigned to a third party as collateral security. The interpretation bulletin indicated that, on the death of the life insured, the corporation received a credit to the CDA equal to the excess of the proceeds over the policy's adjusted cost basis. This applied even where the policy was used to secure indebtedness of the corporation with part or all of the proceeds arising upon the death of the life insured being paid directly to the creditor.

This traditional position was consistent with other comments made by the CRA in various written responses provided to specific taxpayer questions. In a technical interpretation dated May 12, 1987, the CRA stated:

> [W]here a company paid the premiums under a company-owned life insurance policy that was used to secure bank indebtedness of the company and the proceeds arising upon the death of the person whose life was insured, which are paid directly to the bank as beneficiary or assignee for security, reduce the company's indebtedness to the bank by an equivalent amount, it is our view, that the company would be entitled to add to its capital dividend account, pursuant to subparagraph 89(1)(b)(iv) of the Act, the amount by which the proceeds of the life insurance policy exceeds the adjusted cost basis of the policy to the company immediately before that person's death.

On February 10, 1997 the CRA issued Interpretation Bulletin IT-430R3 to replace Interpretation Bulletin IT-430R2. IT-430R3 indicated that where a life insurance policy is used to secure a loan and all or part of the death benefit is paid directly to a creditor as beneficiary of the policy *or* as an assignee for security, the entitlement to the addition to the CDA will belong to the creditor, and not the debtor corporation. This is regardless of whether or not the premium cost is borne directly or indirectly by the debtor.

The CRA indicated that its reasoning for the change was that the debtor corporation does not actually receive (i.e. directly in cash) the life insurance proceeds, as the CRA interpreted was required in the definition of the capital dividend account in subsection 89(1) of the *Income Tax Act*. The change was to be effective for proceeds of a life insurance policy received on or after February 10, 1997 (i.e. the date of the revised Interpretation Bulletin).

On April 8, 1997 the CRA issued a letter indicating that a correction sheet would be issued revising IT-430R3. In this letter the CRA indicated that IT-430R2 and IT-430R3 address two separate situations. The first situation concerns creditor insurance arrangements, and the second concerns the collateral assignment of the policy. With creditor insurance, the creditor is the beneficiary and quite often the policyholder, but the premium costs are borne by the debtor either directly or indirectly. In contrast, in the case of a collateral assignment, the debtor is the policyholder and beneficiary of a policy but the policy is assigned as security against indebtedness.

According to the CRA, in the first situation (creditor insurance) the debtor corporation is not entitled to an addition to its capital dividend account for life insurance proceeds because the debtor does not receive, constructively or otherwise, the life insurance proceeds as required by subparagraph 89(1)(b)(iv) of the definition of "capital dividend account." However, if the creditor is a private corporation it would be entitled to the addition. The CRA went on to note that the change in the bulletin was precipitated by a concern that the interpretation of former IT-430R2 could have resulted in both the creditor and debtor obtaining a credit to the capital dividend account. The CRA noted that it was not intended to deny a CDA credit in circumstances where the policy was only collaterally assigned, in which case the corporate beneficiary would be entitled to the CDA credit on the basis of having constructively received the proceeds.

This revised position was reflected in the CRA's Income Tax Technical News No. 10, dated July 11, 1997.

Revisions to (now archived) IT-403R3 were released on January 7, 2003 to clarify this issue. Paragraph 6 confirms that for creditor insurance, "the entitlement to the addition to the capital dividend account . . .remains with that creditor." It also confirms that in the case of a collateral assignment or securing a hypothecary claim (in Quebec) the debtor would be entitled to the addition to the capital dividend account so long as the debtor remains the beneficiary or policyholder.

In Quebec, the *Civil Code* provision governing the collateral assignment or "hypothecation" of a life insurance policy provides as follows:

> 2462(2) The hypothecation of a right arising out of a contract of insurance confers on the hypothecary creditor only a right to the balance of the debt, interest and accessories and entails revocation of the revocable designation of the beneficiary or the subrogated policyholder only in respect of those amounts.

In technical interpretation 9833605F, dated March 17, 1999, the CRA took the position that because of this provision of the *Civil Code*, a debtor corporation would not receive a CDA credit for proceeds received by the creditor under a collateral assignment of the policy. It was their view that, because of this provision, it was the creditor who is the beneficiary and therefore no CDA credit can accrue to the corporation. This position was reversed in technical interpretation 2002-0122944, dated July 8, 2002 followed by the above change incorporated in IT-430R3.

The CRA's administrative position that a private corporation is not entitled to a credit to its CDA when proceeds of a life insurance policy are paid directly to a creditor as a beneficiary was successfully challenged in the case of *Canadian Motivel Inc. v. The Queen* (Docket #2006-3071(IT)G, dated March 18, 2008). The *Motivel* case was an out-of-court settlement in which the CRA allowed the taxpayer to receive a CDA credit where creditor insurance repaid the corporation's debt to the lender. The lender was the owner and beneficiary of the insurance and the taxpayer paid the insurance premiums. At the APFF conference on October 10, 2008, the CRA was asked to comment on the impact the *Motivel* case has on its existing practice. The CRA stated that the current position is as is stated in IT-430R3. In order for a CDA credit to arise in respect of business loan coverage, the company must be the beneficiary or policyholder under the policy which has been collaterally assigned to the lender. As a result, the CRA was not willing to allow a CDA credit for the constructive receipt of life insurance proceeds where the creditor is the owner and beneficiary of the policy and stated that the settlement arrived at in the *Motivel* case was case specific.

The CRA's position was also successfully challenged in *Innovative Installation Inc. v. The Queen*, 2010 FCA 285, [2011] 2 C.T.C. 73, 2010 D.T.C. 5175. Here, the bank's outstanding loan with the company was secured in part by a creditor life insurance policy on the life of the company's owner, with the bank as the owner and beneficiary of the policy. The company paid the insurance premiums. Upon the death of the insured, the bank received the death benefit as beneficiary of the policy and used the funds to reduce the outstanding loan. The CRA had denied the company a CDA addition. However, the Federal Court of Appeal upheld the earlier Tax Court of Canada decision by ruling the debtor company was entitled to CDA, finding "constructive receipt" of the death benefit by the debtor corporation because its loan balance was reduced. The Federal Court of Appeal further stated the Act "does not require that a corporation receive the proceeds directly from the insurer or that it be named as the beneficiary. . ."

At the Institute of Chartered Accountants of Alberta CRA Roundtable (Q7 reported as 2011-0401431C6, dated May 3, 2011) and subsequently in 2011-0401991E5, dated July 4, 2011, the CRA confirmed that it will be following the decision in the *Innovative Installation* case. The CRA stated:

> The application of this position is effective as of October 27, 2010 (the date of the FCA's decision) and is limited to fact situations that are similar or identical to the Innovative Installation decision. The CRA will not retroactively adjust the CDA of a corporation for a prior year, nor reverse a taxable dividend that was previously assessed. Rather the CDA balance will be adjusted so that the prior year insurance amount would increase the balance of the CDA on or after October 27, 2010.

The CRA has also noted that it will be revising paragraph 6 of IT-430R3 accordingly.

In a technical interpretation (2012-0447171E5, dated March 25, 2013) the CRA confirmed that in respect of creditor insurance the full amount of the death benefit would be added to the debtor's CDA, without a reduction for the adjusted cost basis (ACB). The CRA's rationale for this conclusion was as follows:

> . . . creditor's group life insurance products are generally "pure" insurance products, in that they are generally term and non-participating insurance products with no cash surrender value, typically designed to pay the outstanding balance of a loan upon death of the life insured. Moreover, it is our understanding that premiums payable with respect to a particular debtor for this type of products (sic) are generally calculated to cover the cost of insurance over the term of the certificate, that is, the term of the loan. It is therefore our understanding that if an ACB calculation was effected with respect to each particular certificate holder, the result would generally be a very low figure, if not nil.

A similar response was received to the same question at the 2012 APFF Conference in October of 2012. The CRA also confirmed (APFF Q7) in situations where a debtor names a creditor as an irrevocable beneficiary under an individual insurance policy in addition to making a collateral assignment of the policy to the creditor, the debtor would be permitted an addition to its CDA. (This is a common practice amongst lenders in Quebec because of differences in the law under the *Civil Code*.) An unofficial translation of the response stated as follows:

> . . . we are of the opinion that the same position could reasonably be applied in such circumstances, provided that the debtor corporation is able to demonstrate that the life insurance proceeds paid directly to the lending institution were used to reduce the debt owed by the corporation to the lending institution, as per the contractual relationship between the parties.

The CRA also stated that the CDA credit would be reduced by the debtor's ACB, if any, as owner of the insurance policy. It is clear that CRA comments about not having to reduce the CDA by ACB are confined to creditor insurance products as described.

iii. — Capital Dividend Account where insured or insurer is non-Canadian

A common question is whether a Canadian private corporation can obtain a credit to its capital dividend account when it receives life insurance death benefit proceeds and either the life insured, or the insurer, is a non-resident of Canada. The relevant CDA provisions do not require the life insured or the insurer to be a Canadian resident. Thus, provided the financial instrument constitutes a life insurance policy, a beneficiary that is a private corporation will receive a credit to its CDA even where the life insured, or insurer, is a non-resident of Canada. This interpretation was confirmed by the CRA in document 2005-0132331C6, dated October 7, 2005. Of course, in order to determine the CDA credit, the corporation must calculate the policy's ACB in accordance with the regular rules set out in subsection 148(9), as only the excess of the death benefit proceeds over the ACB immediately before death is credited to the CDA. See also section 10.5 for more information on foreign life insurance policies.

D. — Planning to maximize CDA

In certain circumstances, the insurance policy may be owned by one corporation (e.g., a holding company) and the beneficiary may be another corporation (e.g., an operating company). This structure might be appropriate to meet an insurance need in one company but protect the cash values of the life insurance policy from the creditors of that company. In the event of death, the proceeds are paid to the beneficiary corporation. The credit to the CDA is not reduced for the ACB of the policy because the ACB belongs to the policy owner, not the beneficiary. This would maximize the credit to the CDA.

In the past, the CRA has indicated that if such a structure is undertaken for no reason other than to maximize the CDA credit without an identified business purpose, it could be challenged as an avoidance transaction under the general anti-avoidance rule at section 245 of the Act (see technical interpretations 9824645, dated December 15, 1998, 9908430, dated June 30, 1999 Question 3 CALU CRA Roundtable, and 2004-0065461C6, dated May 4, 2004 Question 8 CALU CRA Roundtable).

An example of a valid business purpose for structuring the policy with the operating company as the beneficiary and the holding company as the policy owner may be to provide the operating company with buy-sell insurance to fulfill its obligations under buy-sell provisions of a shareholder's agreement. The holding company as the policy owner would enable each shareholder to have control over the policy on their life as well as enable the retention of the policies without having to transfer them out of the operating company in the event the operating company is sold in the future. Some shareholders may choose to utilize the tax deferred accumulation afforded by exempt life insurance policies while others may simply insure for the pure risk protection required for the buy-sell. By holding the policy in the holding companies, this would protect the policies from the operating company's creditors until death. However, at death the proceeds required for the buy-sell would flow to the operating company and may, at that time, be subject to the operating company's creditors. (See section 7.4 for a discussion of insurance for buy-sell funding.)

More recently, the CRA has indicated that there may be a shareholder benefit under subsection 15(1), other income inclusions (under section 9 or 12(1)(x)), or a benefit under 246(1) of the Act if the corporate policy owner is not the beneficiary of the policy. These inclusions would be in addition to GAAR issues raised relating to the CDA credit.

At the 2009 APFF Conference Roundtable on October 9, 2009 (2009-0329911C6) and at the 2009 Canadian Tax Foundation Annual Tax Conference (2009-0347291C6), the CRA stated that where a wholly-owned subsidiary owns and pays the premiums for a policy under which the 100 percent shareholder (the parent company) is named as beneficiary, the subsidiary has conferred a shareholder benefit on the parent company pursuant to subsection 15(1) of the Act. This represented a change in position and for existing arrangements the CRA expressed that it would not start assessing shareholder benefits in relation to this structure until the 2011 calendar year. Taxpayers with existing arrangements of this sort may need to review beneficiary designations to ensure this issue does not give rise to negative tax consequences. In this commentary, the CRA also reiterated that GAAR could apply if the holding of insurance was structured to unduly increase the capital dividend account.

The CRA also commented on several different structures in which the corporate owner of a policy designated another company as beneficiary. Two of the structures involved a parent company designating a subsidiary company as beneficiary (see technical interpretation 2007-0257251E5, dated November 19, 2009, Q2 CALU CRA Roundtable reported as 2010-0359421C6, dated May 4, 2010, and Question 9 APFF reported as 2010-0371901C6, dated October 8, 2010).

In one case the beneficiary designation was irrevocable, and the subsidiary reimbursed the parent company for the premium and, in the other case, the beneficiary designation was revocable, and there was no reimbursement of the premium. The CRA suggested that the payment from the subsidiary to the parent company to reimburse the premium might be taxable income from property to the parent company under section 9 or paragraph 12(1)(x) of the Act. Section 9 states that income from a business or property is the profit from that business or property for the year. Paragraph 12(1)(x) generally includes in income any amount received in the year in the course of earning income from a business or property and includes amounts such as refunds, reimbursements, grants, allowances, or subsidies to the cost of a property, an outlay, or expense. No mention was made as to whether an election could be made under subparagraph 12(2.2) of the Act to offset the premiums paid (the "outlay or expense") with the amount reimbursed such that it would be excluded from inclusion under paragraph 12(1)(x) by virtue of subparagraph 12(1)(x)(vii) of the Act. Presumably, the election would not be available because a premium under a policy would be "an outlay or expense in respect of to the cost of property." The CRA also stated that if a reimbursement is not included in the parent company's income, there would be a subsection 15(1) benefit to the parent company. In addition, the CRA stated that there would be no adjustment for the reimbursed premium to the life insurance policy's adjusted cost basis, as the definition of that term in 148(9) of the Act does not contemplate this.

In the situation where there was no reimbursement of the premium, the CRA suggested that subsection 246(1) of the Act could apply to include the premium in the income of the subsidiary. Subsection 246(1) of the Act is a broad provision that includes an amount in the income of the recipient for the amount of a benefit conferred on it by another individual or corporation to the extent that the amount would have otherwise been taxable had the amount of the benefit been a payment made to the subsidiary directly. Generally, a parent company can infuse capital and lend money at no interest to a subsidiary without tax consequences. Although it is generally beneficial to the subsidiary to have the parent company pay the insurance premiums under a policy under which the subsidiary is the beneficiary, it is unclear that the requirements of subsection 246(1) of the Act would be met to bring about an income inclusion. No comment or distinction was made by the CRA in these comments regarding the irrevocable versus revocable nature of the beneficiary designation.

The third structure involved two companies wholly-owned by the same shareholder. One company owned and paid the premiums for a life insurance policy naming the other company as beneficiary. The beneficiary company reimbursed the owner company for the premiums paid. In this case, the CRA again suggested that there could be an income inclusion (under section 9 or 12(1)(x) of the Act) to the owner company for the premiums reimbursed by the beneficiary company.

In all three structures, the CRA continued to reiterate its view that if the ownership and beneficiary designation is structured to maximize the CDA, GAAR would apply to adjust the calculation of the amount to be included in the CDA. Indeed the following comment from the 2010 APFF conference indicates that the CRA will be looking at CDA elections carefully:

> . . . the CRA will review any situation involving a corporate family where life insurance proceeds included in a corporation's CDA are not reduced by the adjusted cost basis of the policy.

In summary, since these comments intertwine benefit issues along with the potential application of GAAR, corporate groups should review their life insurance holdings and address those situations where the owner and beneficiary are different. One of the options includes unifying ownership and beneficiary designation in the same company. This could be done by transferring the ownership of a life insurance policy to the company that is the beneficiary. However, this would be a disposition of the policy and may trigger taxable income (see section 3.3.I for a discussion of such transfers). Changing the beneficiary to the owner company avoids a disposition of the policy, but other planning adjustments may be necessary to accommodate this change. The CRA has confirmed (2011 CLHIA CRA Roundtable Question 5 reported as 2011-0398401C6, dated May 20, 2011) that change in beneficiary or ownership to address these issues would not, in and by itself affect the grandfathered status of the shares for purposes of the stop-loss provision in subsection 112(3) of the Act. (For a more detailed discussion of grandfathering for purposes of the stop-loss rules see section 7.4.E.ii).

Taxpayers may choose to use different corporate owners and beneficiaries particularly where it makes business sense to do so. In such circumstances, given CRA's GAAR comments, taxpayers may wish to consider reducing any CDA credit by the ACB of the policy to avoid a challenge from the CRA. As mentioned previously, CALU made a submission to the Department of Finance dated May 2, 2013 recommending that the definition of the CDA be amended so that the policy's ACB would be attributed to the beneficiary of the insurance proceeds. This would not address the benefit issues raised by the CRA which would also need to be considered.

E. — Payment of a capital dividend

A dividend (including a capital dividend) is declared by the directors of the corporation and is made payable to the shareholders of record as of a certain date. The resolution of the directors declaring the dividend is recorded in the minutes of the corporation.

Typically, dividends paid by a corporation are taxable dividends. However, if a positive balance exists in the CDA prior to the declaration of the dividend and the directors elect in the prescribed manner and form, an otherwise taxable dividend will be a tax-free capital dividend pursuant to subsection 83(2) of the Act.

In order for a dividend to be treated as a capital dividend it must meet the conditions contained in subsection 83(2). Specifically:

- The dividend must be payable by a private corporation. The definition of a private corporation can be found in subsection 89(1) and would include "a corporation that is resident in Canada, is not a public corporation and is not controlled by one or more public corporations. . ."
- The corporation must elect to pay the capital dividend on CRA form T2054 within the prescribed time limits.

As with the payment of any dividend, corporate financial capacity tests may need to be satisfied. Reference should be made to the appropriate corporate law in each jurisdiction.

It should be noted that it is not possible to elect to treat part of a dividend as a capital dividend and the balance as a taxable dividend. The election must be made in respect of the *full amount* of the dividend. However, if the elected amount exceeds the available CDA balance, it is possible to file an election under subsection 184(3) to treat the excess as a separate taxable dividend. But for filing such an election to treat the excess as a separate taxable dividend, the corporation would be liable for tax under Part III of the Act for an amount equal to 3/5 of the excess amount. Prior to the enactment of Bill C-48, which received Royal Assent on June 26, 2013, the penalty tax was equal to 3/4 of the excess amount. The new rate, which simply reflects a general reduction in tax rates, applies to taxation years ending after 1999.

F. — How an election is made

The capital dividend election is made by completing CRA form T2054 as required by Regulation 2101 under the Act. The Regulations require a corporation to file the following forms in order to make a capital dividend election:

- CRA form T2054;
- a certified copy of a director's resolution authorizing the CDA election to be made;
- schedules showing the computation of the capital dividend account immediately prior to the distribution of the capital dividend.

An election to pay a capital dividend should be filed no later than the day on which the dividend becomes payable or the first day on which any part of the dividend is paid, whichever is earlier. A dividend will generally be considered to be payable on the day stipulated by the resolution of the directors declaring the dividend.

Subsection 83(3) of the Act allows for a special deeming rule in certain circumstances where a dividend becomes payable to the shareholders and subsection 83(1) and (2) would have applied to the dividend except that the election was not filed within the prescribed time. Subsection 83(3) deems the election to have been made at the earlier of the time the dividend became payable and the first day in which the dividend was paid provided the following three conditions are met:

- The election is made in the manner prescribed under Regulation 2101;
- An estimate of the applicable late filing penalty is paid at the time the election is filed; and
- The directors of the corporation authorize the election to be made.

The late filing penalty is equal to the lesser of 1/12 of 1 percent of the amount of the dividend and $41.67 multiplied by the number of months and part months between the date that the election was due and the date which the election was actually made.

G. — CDA — miscellaneous issues

Where a taxpayer's shares are being redeemed, a capital dividend can be paid to one shareholder to the exclusion of other shareholders. This was confirmed by the CRA at Question 23 of the 1991 Canadian Tax Foundation annual Roundtable.

This position must be distinguished from the general rule as noted in *Bowater Canadian Ltd. v. R.L. Crain Inc.* (1987), 62 O.R. (2d) 752 (C.A.) that all holders of a particular class of shares must be treated equally. Thus where shareholder A and shareholder B each own 50 percent of the common shares of AB Corp, the corporation cannot declare a dividend and pay capital dividends to A and taxable dividends to B.

The above Roundtable question makes reference to subsection 83(2.1). Subsection 83(2.1) is an anti-avoidance rule which denies capital dividend treatment where, generally, a share was acquired as part of a series of transactions one of the main purposes of which was to receive the dividend. Where subsection 83(2.1) applies the dividend is treated as a taxable dividend.

However, subsection 83(2.3) exempts the distribution of life insurance proceeds from the application of subsection 83(2.1). This suggests it may be possible to acquire shares which are only entitled to capital dividends resulting from the receipt of life insurance proceeds. This issue was addressed at Question 2 at the 2005 Conference for Advanced Life Underwriters' annual Roundtable (technical interpretation 2005-0116621C6). There the CRA considered a situation where a corporation issued a special share to its sole shareholder's adult child for the purpose of streaming life insurance proceeds to that child. The CRA was asked whether the shareholder benefit provisions at subsection 15(1) would apply on the acquisition of the share by the shareholder's child. In its response the CRA indicated that provided that the issue price for the special share reflected the fair market value thereof at the time of issuance, subsection 15(1) would not apply to include a benefit in the child's income as a consequence of the child acquiring the special share. While this response leaves open the issue as to how to determine fair market value of such a share, it does recognize the use of such special shares to stream insurance proceeds to a particular class of shares. For more information on life insurance shares refer to section 3.3.C.ii.

In *Groupe Honco Inc. v. The Queen*, 2012 TCC 305, 2012 CarswellNat 4917 (T.C.C. [General Procedure]); affirmed 2013 FCA 128, 2013 CarswellNat 4181, a capital dividend derived from life insurance proceeds and distributed through a series of companies after an amalgamation was re-characterized as a taxable dividend under subsection 83(2.1) of the Act because the court found that one of the main purposes of acquiring the shares was to receive a capital dividend. Oddly, the exception to the anti-avoidance provision in subsection 83(2.3) that applies where CDA arises from the payment of life insurance proceeds was not argued by the taxpayer at the trial level and was not reconsidered at the appeal court level.

Subsection 112(3) of the Act, contains a "stop-loss" rule that reduces the amount of a loss that would otherwise be claimed by an individual or a corporation on the disposition of shares which are capital property, by the amount of capital dividends received by the individual or corporation. These stop-loss rules apply unless the individual or corporation owned the shares for 365 days or longer before the loss was sustained, and the taxpayer and other non-arm's length parties did not own more than five percent of the shares of any class when the capital dividend was declared. Similar rules for trusts and partnerships can be found in subsections 112(3.1) and (3.2).

These stop-loss rules do not affect either the determination of a corporation's capital dividend account or the ability of a corporation to pay a capital dividend. The rules will, however, affect the ability of individuals and corporations to claim a capital loss on the disposition of shares where a capital dividend has been received on these shares. The stop-loss rules are more fully discussed in section 7.4.E.

6.3 — Shareholder and Employee Benefits

A. — Introduction

Shareholder or employee benefits may arise as a result of certain transactions involving a corporate-owned life insurance policy, or as a result of inappropriate structuring of the life insurance strategy at the time of purchase. Situations which may result in either shareholder or employee benefits are reviewed in this section.

B. — Group life insurance premiums

As described in section 6.4.C, employers typically provide a variety of benefits to employees. Such benefits may include group life insurance. While the premiums paid by an employer for a group life insurance policy are deductible for tax purposes by the employer against business income, employer paid premiums represent a taxable benefit to the employee and are included in the employee's income under subsection 6(4).

Previously, the portion of the premium for group term life insurance premiums on the first $25,000 of insurance coverage was treated as a tax-free benefit in the hands of the employee. This concession was eliminated effective June, 1994.

Group term life insurance premiums paid by an employer are now treated as a taxable benefit.

Employers typically report the amount of the taxable benefit related to group life insurance premiums to their employees on the T4 supplementary tax slip issued to the employees at the end of each year.

A planning strategy which is particularly effective for senior executives within the organization is to consider carving such executives out of the group life insurance plan and providing the executives with individual life insurance funded in part by the employer. This will provide the executives with an opportunity to establish a permanent life insurance program and to build equity within the policy with excess personal cash flow. The after-tax cost to the employer may be designed to be equal to the after-tax cost of providing the group insurance benefits. Depending on the nature of the group insurance plan, this strategy may also reduce the unit cost for the remaining employees.

C. — Premiums paid by a corporation on personally-owned insurance

A corporation may fund the life insurance premiums on a policy where the shareholder or employee is the owner and/or beneficiary of the policy. This structure results in a taxable benefit which will be taxed as (i) a shareholder benefit under subsection 15(1) of the Act if the policyholder or beneficiary is a shareholder of the corporation (or a person related to a shareholder of the corporation), or (ii) an employee benefit under paragraph (6)(1)(a) of the Act if the policyholder or beneficiary is an employee of the corporation (or a person related to the employee).

The distinction between a shareholder benefit and an employee benefit is important because shareholder benefits are not a deductible expense to the corporation whereas employee benefits may be deductible. In *Green Acres Fertilizers Services Ltd. v. The Queen*, [1979] C.T.C. 431 (Fed. T.D.); affirmed [1980] C.T.C. 504 (Fed. C.A.), the corporate taxpayer was denied a deduction for an insurance premium that it paid on behalf of the shareholders who were also employees of the corporation. The payment was held to have been made in their capacity as shareholders and not as employees.

In the case of life insurance premiums which are to be paid on behalf of a shareholder who is also an employee of the corporation, it might be advisable to treat the payment as a lump sum bonus and to gross up the payment for the related income tax withholding. It may also be advisable to provide for this payment and benefit in an employment agreement. In this way the total payment should be deductible to the corporation.

D. — Beneficiary designation under corporate-owned life insurance

Generally, the beneficiary of a corporate-owned life insurance policy should be the corporation. The CRA had previously commented that there would be no shareholder benefit where a wholly-owned subsidiary designates its parent corporation as beneficiary (CRA technical interpretation 9824645, dated January 8, 1999 and Question 8 at the 2004 CALU Roundtable reported as 2004-0065461C6). However, this position has now been reversed by the CRA as detailed at the 2009 APFF and CTF tax conferences (discussed in section 6.2.D).

Williams v. M.N.R., 66 D.T.C. 755 (Tax App. Bd.) considered the shareholder benefit issue in a situation involving an insurance policy on the life of the president and principal shareholder of a group of private corporations. In that case, the insurance premiums were paid by one corporation but the policies were owned by another corporation. The Tax Appeal Board held that the payment structure did not result in a shareholder benefit being conferred on the principal shareholder.

It is not advisable for the estate, the spouse, or other related parties of the life insured shareholder to be the beneficiary of a corporate-owned life insurance policy. In this case, premiums paid by the corporation would be considered to be a shareholder benefit. In technical interpretation 2004-008190, dated June 23, 2004, the CRA confirmed that the shareholder benefit would be based on premiums paid in respect of the policy and not the proceeds paid under the policy. Further, it should be noted that the corporation is not permitted to claim a tax deduction in respect of the shareholder benefit. This is a significant disadvantage and detracts from the benefits generally associated with corporate-owned life insurance. This structure should be avoided.

This tax treatment was confirmed in *Reakes Enterprises Ltd. v. The Queen*, [2006] 4 C.T.C. 2206, 2006 D.T.C. 3161 (T.C.C.) (I.P.). In *Reakes Enterprises*, the corporate taxpayer funded (and sought to deduct for tax purposes) a number of personal expenses of its sole shareholder. Among the personal expenses were premium payments for a life insurance policy owned by the sole shareholder and in respect of which the shareholder's spouse was the beneficiary. Beaubier J. held that the expenses were not deductible by the corporation as they were personal or living expenses within the meaning of paragraph 18(1)(h) and further held that the sole shareholder was in receipt of a taxable shareholder benefit as a result of the corporation funding the personal expense. In *Larue v. The Queen*, 2003 TCC 288, 2003 CarswellNat 5252 (T.C.C.) (I.P.), a case involving similar facts, the court again held there to be a shareholder benefit and further held that the circumstances justified a reassessment beyond the normal reassessment period and imposition of penalties.

If the plan requires the life insurance proceeds to be paid directly to a beneficiary other than the corporation, it is generally advisable that the insurance policy be owned and funded personally by the shareholder. Alternatively, the intended beneficiary can be a shareholder of the company, perhaps holding life insurance shares, with the idea of having the company as owner and beneficiary of the policy and the ultimate death benefit paid to the intended beneficiary via a tax-free capital dividend on those shares. (See section 3.3.C.ii for further discussion of life insurance shares.)

E. — Transfer of ownership of corporate-owned life insurance

There may be circumstances in which a corporate-owned life insurance policy is transferred to the life insured. This may occur, for example, in the case of a life insured shareholder who is contemplating the sale of the corporation and who wishes to retain the insurance policy on a personal basis following the sale, or upon the retirement or termination of a life insured key executive.

A transfer of ownership of a corporate-owned life insurance policy from the corporation to the life insured results in a disposition of the life insurance policy for tax purposes. Subsection 148(7) would generally govern the policyholder tax consequences of this transaction. A taxable benefit may also arise on the transfer to the extent that the fair market value of the insurance policy exceeds the amount paid by the life insured for the interest in the policy. In this case, the taxable benefit may either be a shareholder benefit under subsection 15(1) or an employee benefit under paragraph 6(1)(a) of the Act, depending on the circumstances.

The tax implications related to transfers of ownership are discussed in detail in Chapter 3.

6.4 — Deductibility of Life Insurance Premiums

A. — Introduction

One of the most common questions relating to the taxation of life insurance policies is whether the premiums paid by a policyholder may be deductible for income tax purposes.

As a general rule, premiums paid under a life insurance policy are considered to be capital outlays and not an outlay or expense made or incurred by a taxpayer for the purpose of gaining or producing income from a business or property. Therefore, a deduction is generally prohibited under the general limitation for payments on account of capital in paragraph 18(1)(b).

Notwithstanding the general rule, a deduction for life insurance premiums is permitted in the following limited circumstances:

- *Registered life insurance policy* — a portion of the premiums paid under a life insurance policy which has been registered as a retirement savings plan under section 146 is deductible.
- *Employee benefits* — group insurance premiums paid by an employer or employer paid premiums on a policy owned by an employee are generally deductible.
- *Charitable gift of a life insurance policy* — a deduction is permitted in respect of premiums paid under a life insurance policy that has been donated by a corporation to a registered charity. Note that an individual taxpayer who donates a life insurance policy to a registered charity is entitled to claim a non-refundable tax credit in respect of premiums paid under a life insurance policy that has been donated to a registered charity. See Chapter 12 for more details regarding charitable giving and life insurance.
- *Collateral insurance* — all or a portion of the premiums paid under a life insurance policy that has been collaterally assigned to a restricted financial institution (as defined at subsection 248(1)) may be deductible.

The exceptions to the general rule are described more fully below. The discussion will only briefly cover the first three exceptions and will then focus on the rules for collateral insurance.

Note that premiums paid under life insurance policies used to fund buy-sell arrangements at death or keyperson insurance are not deductible.

B. — Registered life insurance policy

A portion of a premium paid for a life insurance policy that has been registered as a retirement savings plan under section 146 is treated as a contribution to a registered retirement savings plan and is deductible against the income of the contributor subject to the limits set out under section 146.

If an insurance policy is registered in this manner, the amount at risk under the policy (that is, the total death benefit minus the cash surrender value of the policy) is not considered to be part of the registered plan. Therefore, the portion of the premium which is attributable to the amount at risk is not considered to be a contribution to a registered retirement savings plan and is not deductible for tax purposes. For example, a whole life insurance policy is purchased and is registered as a retirement savings plan under section 146. The annual premium is $5,000. The level annual premium for the net amount at risk is $2,000. This represents the equivalent cost of decreasing term insurance coverage because the net amount at risk decreases as the policy reserves increase. Therefore, the contribution to the registered retirement saving plan is $3,000 each year.

Registered policies were once quite popular but are rarely used today because of statutory restrictions, the lack of flexibility and the limited investment choices. Further, registered retirement planning and life insurance planning involve different objectives and therefore may be accomplished more effectively with separate product solutions. For more information regarding life insurance and RRSPs see the CRA's archived Interpretation Bulletin IT-408R "Life Insurance Policies as Investments of Registered Retirement Savings Plans and Deferred Profit Sharing Plans," dated February 15, 1980, which outlines the CRA's position on the eligibility of insurance policies as investments for registered plans.

C. — Employee benefits

Employers often provide a variety of benefits to their employees, including group life insurance, health and dental coverage, and disability income protection. Premiums paid by an employer for a group life insurance policy are deductible for tax purposes by the employer against business income.

Group insurance premiums paid by an employer are a taxable benefit to the employees under subsection 6(4). This is discussed in more detail at section 6.3.B.

Similarly, if an employer pays the premium for a life insurance policy owned by an employee, the employer should be able to deduct the premium as employee remuneration. The premiums would be included in the employee's income as a taxable benefit. (Confirmed in technical interpretation 2009-0312171E5.)

D. — Charitable gift of a life insurance policy

A corporation may donate a life insurance policy to a registered charity. Premiums paid by the corporation in respect of the life insurance policy after it has been donated are considered to be charitable gifts and are deductible to the corporation under paragraph 110.1(1)(a) subject to the limits set out at that paragraph.

An individual taxpayer who donates a life insurance policy to a registered charity is not allowed to deduct subsequent premiums paid under the life insurance policy against taxable income but is permitted to claim a non-refundable tax credit for such premiums subject to certain maximums under subsection 118.1(3).

The rules related to charitable gifts of life insurance policies are discussed in detail in Chapter 12.

E. — Collateral insurance

It is not unusual for a lender to require a life insurance policy to be purchased on the life of a business owner or other key employee and then be collaterally assigned to the lender as security for a loan. Under this arrangement, the policyholder retains ownership rights in the insurance policy, but the policy proceeds must first be used to satisfy the debt owing to the collateral assignee. Any excess proceeds may then be paid to the policyholder or (in the event of death) the beneficiary designated under the insurance policy.

Where a life insurance policy is used as collateral for a loan, a portion of the premium may be deductible for tax purposes if certain criteria are met. The legislative criteria are provided in paragraph 20(1)(e.2) and the CRA's administrative guidelines are outlined in archived Interpretation Bulletin IT-309R2 "Premiums on Life Insurance Used as Collateral," dated February 28, 1995.

The 2013 federal budget proposed the denial of the collateral insurance deduction to certain leveraged insurance arrangements. A life insurance policy that meets the definition of a "10/8 policy" will be denied a collateral insurance deduction after 2013 (proposed subparagraph 20(1)(e.2)(ii) of the Act). For further discussion of these measures see section 4.3.E. Also, a life insurance policy that is considered an "LIA policy" on or after March 21, 2013 will similarly be denied the collateral insurance deduction. It is important to note that unlike 10/8 policies, arrangements in existence which would otherwise meet the definition of an LIA policy are grandfathered and would not face the denial of collateral insurance deductions relating to them. For a more detailed discussion see section 17.6.

The current legislative rules governing paragraph 20(1)(e.2) and their historical context are described below. This discussion assumes that the "10/8 policy" and the "LIA policy" rules do not apply.

i. — Historical perspective

Where the purchase and assignment of a life insurance policy is a condition of a loan and the proceeds of the loan are intended to generate income from business or property, one might naturally conclude that the life insurance premium expense should be deductible for tax purposes as an expense of borrowing. However, prior to the introduction of paragraph 20(1)(e.2) of the Act there was no legislative basis for deducting life insurance premiums incurred pursuant to a loan transaction under which a life insurance policy is purchased and assigned to the lender as collateral for the loan. Rather, a deduction for life insurance premiums was permitted in limited circumstances and only as an administrative concession by the CRA.

The CRA's administrative position was outlined in Interpretation Bulletin IT-309R "Expense of Borrowing Money — Life Insurance Premiums," dated January 10, 1979. This bulletin provided guidance on whether collateral insurance premiums would be considered an expense of borrowing and would, therefore, be deductible for tax purposes.

Amongst the various rules and criteria contained in Interpretation Bulletin IT-309R was the requirement that the life insurance policy be a term insurance policy. Under these rules, premiums for collateral life insurance were deductible, but only if the life insurance policy was for term insurance and not permanent insurance.

The CRA's administrative position was subjected to various court challenges over the years, the most important of which was *Antoine Guertin Ltée v. R.*, [1981] C.T.C. 351 (F.C.T.D.). In that case, a corporate taxpayer collaterally assigned a whole life insurance policy to a lending institution and sought to deduct the equivalent term insurance costs as an expense of borrowing under subparagraph 20(1)(e)(ii). The CRA had challenged the deduction based on its administrative position as outlined in Interpretation Bulletin IT-309R which clearly stated that only term insurance was acceptable when determining whether any amount of premiums would be deductible.

The Federal Court Trial Division in *Antoine Guertin Ltée* found in favour of the taxpayer. However, the decision was reversed in the Federal Court of Appeal as reported in *The Queen v. Antoine Guertin Ltée*, [1988] 1 C.T.C. 360, 88 D.T.C. 6126 (F.C.A.). In overturning the lower court decision, Mr. Justice Marceau relied upon the decision in *Equitable Acceptance Corp. v. M.N.R.*, [1964] C.T.C. 74 (Ex. Ct.) in which it was held that whole life insurance policies are an asset and therefore premiums payable under a whole life insurance policy should not be a deductible expense.

Unfortunately, the Federal Court of Appeal decision in the *Antoine Guertin Ltée* case had more serious implications than simply deciding the issue of whether comparable term insurance costs might be deductible. In rendering his decision, Mr. Justice Marceau questioned whether a deduction for any life insurance premiums should be allowed in collateral insurance situations because a life insurance policy, whether term insurance or permanent insurance, could offer value to the policyholder (that is, the corporation in the present case) after the expiration of the debt for which the policy was used as collateral. Following this reasoning, Mr. Justice Marceau suggested that no premiums paid for collateral insurance should be deductible under subparagraph 20(1)(e)(ii), including term insurance premiums.

The comments by Mr. Justice Marceau created confusion as to whether the CRA would change its administrative position as outlined in Interpretation Bulletin IT-

309R and deny the deduction for term insurance premiums in collateral insurance situations.

In the 1991 technical bill, the collateral insurance issue was resolved with the introduction of new paragraph 20(1)(e.2), effective for premiums payable after 1989. Paragraph 20(1)(e.2) permits a limited deduction in respect of life insurance premiums where the policy has been assigned as collateral for a loan. This amendment counters the decision of the Federal Court of Appeal in the *Antoine Guertin Ltée* case and generally codifies the CRA's administrative practice described in Interpretation Bulletin IT-309R with some modification.

ii. — Paragraph 20(1)(e.2)

Paragraph 20(1)(e.2) of the *Income Tax Act* provides a limited deduction for premiums in respect of a life insurance policy assigned as collateral security for a loan. This paragraph, which was added to the Act in 1991, applies with respect to premiums payable after 1989.

a. — Requirements for deductibility

In order to be eligible for deductibility under paragraph 20(1)(e.2), the assignment of the life insurance policy must be required by the lender, the lender must be a "restricted financial institution" as defined in subsection 248(1), and the interest payable on the money borrowed must, generally, be deductible in computing the taxpayer's income.

A "restricted financial institution" is defined in subsection 248(1) to include a bank, a trust company, a credit union, an insurance corporation, a corporation whose principal business is the lending of money to persons with whom it deals at arm's length (or the purchasing of debt obligations issued by such persons), or a corporation controlled by one or more of the above.

A 2003 technical interpretation from the CRA has added a wrinkle to the collateral insurance deduction by requiring that the lender continue to be the original institution that made the loan. The technical interpretation (2002-0167085, dated January 14, 2003) concluded that where the restricted financial institution has assigned/sold its rights under the loan agreement to a trust or other third party, the borrower would not be permitted a deduction. This assignment of debt, referred to as securitization, means that even though the borrower continues their relationship with the original institution in respect of payments, statements, etc., the actual debt is held by another party.

Where interest deductibility is denied, the collateral insurance deduction will also be denied. However, if the interest deduction is limited (for example, if it is limited to a "reasonable amount"), it is unclear whether the collateral insurance deduction would be available, unavailable, or somehow prorated. At the 2004 APFF Conference, the CRA was asked to comment on the availability of the collateral insurance deduction in a situation where a corporation's interest expense deduction might be limited to the annuity income on a non-prescribed annuity purchased with the borrowed funds (due to subparagraph 20(1)(c)(iv) of the Act) (2004-0085551C6). The

CRA expressed the opinion that in this case the requirement that "the interest payable in respect of the borrowing is . . . deductible" in order to claim the collateral insurance deduction would be satisfied even if only a portion of the interest were deductible. The CRA confirmed this position at the 2005 CALU CRA Roundtable Question 4 (2005-0116651C6) and again in an advance ruling (2005-0143281R3).

b. — Amount deductible

Paragraph 20(1)(e.2) of the Act provides that the amount deductible in respect of a policy for a taxation year is determined as follows:

The portion of the lesser of:

(i) the premiums payable by the taxpayer under the policy (other than an annuity contract) in respect of the year, and

(ii) the net cost of pure insurance ("NCPI") of the policy for the year

as can reasonably be considered to relate to the amount owing from time to time during the year by the taxpayer.

Premiums payable by the taxpayer under the policy in respect of the year — Neither the legislation nor IT-309R2 specifically deal with situations where the premiums on a policy are paid with internal policy values, for example, with policy dividends in a participating whole life insurance policy or from the accumulated investment account in a universal life insurance policy.

The CRA has indicated in technical interpretation (9220255) dated September 23, 1992, that the Act refers to premiums payable under a life insurance policy rather than to premiums paid and that the method by which the premiums are paid is not relevant to their deductibility. Therefore, where premiums are being paid with internal policy values (i.e. with dividends or out of investment accounts), the contract wording is very important. For policies where there is a stipulated premium (e.g., participating whole life policy), arguably the premium payable in respect of the year is the stipulated premium under the contract. For contracts that do not have a stipulated premium (e.g., universal life policies), a contractual obligation does not exist and, therefore, the CRA would not consider the premium "payable".

Where a universal life contract is maximum funded and a premium holiday is taken, there would be no premium payable in respect of the year and therefore it is CRA's view that a deduction would not be available even if the policy is used as collateral security (see technical interpretation 9901875). Question 3 at the 2007 APFF conference (2007-0241911C6) confirmed CRA's position maintaining that the CRA is generally of the opinion that, for universal life policies, the premiums payable correspond to the premiums that the policyholder elects to pay to the insurer under the terms of the policy and the amounts that the insurer withdraws from the accumulation account to cover the cost of insurance and related fees do not constitute premiums. In such circumstances, the borrower may wish to actually pay a premium at least equal to the NCPI on an annual basis to take advantage of the deduction for collateral insurance purposes.

Net Cost of Pure Insurance (NCPI) of the Policy for the Year — NCPI in respect of a policy for purposes of 20(1)(e.2) is defined in Regulation 308 of the Act as the net amount at risk multiplied by a mortality factor. The net amount at risk is equal to the excess of the death benefit over the cash value of the policy. Regulation 308 refers to the 1969-75 mortality tables of the Canadian Institute of Actuaries for purposes of determining the mortality factor in respect of any given policy. For example, assume that a $100,000 policy has a $10,000 cash value and the mortality rate for the attained age is $10 per $1,000 (or a mortality factor of 0.0100). The NCPI of the policy for the year would be $900 [($100,000 - $10,000) × 0.0100].

Where the insured under a policy is rated (i.e. the life insured is a substandard risk based on medical underwriting due, for example, to a health problem), standard mortality tables are generally used for the NCPI calculation for 20(1)(e.2) as well as the calculation of NCPI for purposes of determining the adjusted cost basis of the policy. This may cause an "unfair" result in rated cases because the actual insurance costs may be significantly higher than the NCPI calculated on this basis.

The August 23, 2013 draft legislation proposes a more recent mortality table, reflection of substandard ratings and changes to the calculation of the net amount at risk for policies issued after 2015. See section 1.9.C.ii for a detailed discussion. In general, using a more recent mortality table will mean lower NCPI amounts and hence lower potential collateral insurance deductions. However, the recognition of substandard ratings will allow for higher potential collateral insurance deductions.

For life insurance policies issued prior to December 2, 1982, there is no requirement to deduct the NCPI from the ACB of the policy; however, it is possible that policies issued prior to December 2, 1982 may be assigned as collateral for a loan. Question 7 at the 2008 CALU Annual General Meeting (2008-0270441C6) dealt with this issue and the CRA confirmed that where a pre-December 2, 1982 policy is used as collateral security for a loan, the taxpayer would be permitted a deduction for the lesser of the premium and NCPI and that in calculating the NCPI of the policy, the taxpayer would have to determine this in accordance with Regulation 308.

Where the taxpayer's taxation year does not correspond to the policy year, the premiums payable under the policy and the NCPI should be prorated on a reasonable basis to the taxation year.

Portion of Deductible Amount Reasonably Relating to Amount Owing in the Year — Once the "lesser of" amount is determined in respect of the year, only the portion that may reasonably be considered to relate to the amount owing in the year may be deducted. IT-309R2 provides the following example: Where the life insurance coverage under the assigned policy is $500,000, and the amount owing under the loan throughout the taxation year is $200,000, the amount deductible under paragraph 20(1)(e.2) of the Act is limited to 40 percent of the lesser of the premiums payable and the NCPI of the policy for the year.

Question 1 at the 2006 CALU Annual General Meeting (2006-0174781C6) dealt with determining the portion of the premiums or NCPI that "can reasonably be considered to relate to the amount owing from time to time during the year by the taxpayer" where a life insurance policy has a cash surrender value. The question assumed a policy had a death benefit of $1 million, a cash surrender value of

$300,000, and an amount owing of $500,000. The net amount of risk in this example is $700,000, which is the amount of insurance for which the NCPI is determined. The CRA stated that, regardless of whether the NCPI or the premium is the limiting factor in the "lesser of" calculation, the simple interpretation of this phrase means that the deductible amount of either premium or NCPI is prorated, in this case by 50 percent, "calculated with reference to the death benefit payable under the insurance policy and the outstanding amount of the loan without reference to other collateral or the cash surrender value of the policy."

IT-309R2 indicates that an unused line of credit is not an amount owing in determining the portion that "can reasonably be considered to relate to the amount owing from time to time during the year", even if the unused line of credit is subject to a standby charge or commitment fee.

iii. — Archived Interpretation Bulletin IT-309R2: Premiums on Life Insurance Used as Collateral

Paragraph 20(1)(e.2) partially confirmed the administrative practice of the CRA discussed in Interpretation Bulletin IT-309R in permitting a deduction in respect of life insurance premiums. The legislation changed the rules relating to the requirement that the policy be a term insurance policy. The type of insurance policy is no longer an issue. Also, the previous administrative policy is modified by the codification of the conditions to be met and by the limitations placed on the amount deductible.

Certain other modifications to the CRA's administrative practices were also introduced with the release of Interpretation Bulletin IT-309R2 "Premiums on Life Insurance Used as Collateral," dated February 28, 1995.

Perhaps the most significant change found in Interpretation Bulletin IT-309R2 relates to whether the borrower must also be the policyholder. Under its previous administrative policy, the CRA indicated that the borrower need not be the policyholder. For example, a shareholder could assign a personal term insurance policy as collateral for a corporate debt and the corporation could pay the premiums under the policy and claim the deduction and no taxable benefit would result in the hands of the shareholder. The CRA now takes the view that a deduction under paragraph 20(1)(e.2) will only be permitted if the borrower and the policyholder are the same person. This is confirmed in CRA technical interpretations 9528015, dated November 9, 1995 and 2007-0219601E5, dated March 14, 2007.

A planning strategy to alleviate the impact of this requirement is the use of split-dollar insurance. Under this strategy, the corporation and a shareholder would jointly own a life insurance policy. The corporation would be entitled to and pay for the pure insurance component of permanent insurance and the shareholder would be entitled to and pay for the investment portion of the policy. Split-dollar insurance is described in more detail in Chapter 8.

In Question 2 at the 2006 CALU CRA Roundtable (2006-0175101C6) the CRA commented where a partnership borrowed money from a restricted financial institution with a partner-owned policy used as collateral security. The CRA stated that the partner would not be permitted to deduct the lesser of the premium and NCPI under the policy since the paragraph requires that "the interest on the borrowed money be deductible in computing the income of the taxpayer who paid the premiums. In the example above, the interest is deductible by the partnership in computing partnership income by virtue of subsection 96(1), rather than in computing the income of the partner who is paying the premiums."

Interpretation Bulletin IT-309R2 does eliminate the previous administrative requirement that a valid business reason had to be established for the lender to require that the lives of more than one person be insured in respect of a particular borrowing. Previously, if the borrower could not satisfy this requirement, the premiums on only one policy would be deductible. Interpretation Bulletin IT-309R2 also indicates that each such policy should be treated as if it were the only policy assigned for purposes of paragraph 20(1)(e.2).

Interpretation Bulletin IT-309R2 also grants relief in circumstances where the total collateral (including the life insurance policy) exceeds the outstanding loan. Previously, a deduction for the life insurance premiums would only be deductible if the loan was not fully covered by the other collateral. Under Interpretation Bulletin IT-309R2, the existence of such additional excess collateral will not result in a denial of the deduction for the life insurance premiums under paragraph 20(1)(e.2) so long as the assignment of the insurance policy is reasonable in the circumstances and is not required by the lender merely to accommodate a tax deduction for the borrower. The administrative guidance on this issue confirms the CRA's views as outlined in technical interpretation 9414527, dated September 30, 1994.

iv. — Related matters

Creditors' life insurance — Premiums paid for bank life insurance, known as "creditors' life insurance," are not deductible under paragraph 20(1)(e.2) because the creditor is the owner and the beneficiary under the policy. Since the creditor is the policyholder, the debtor is not in a position to assign the policy as security for the borrowing. This view is confirmed in CRA technical interpretation 9407245, dated April 15, 1994.

Credit to capital dividend account of private corporation — A private corporation that is the beneficiary designated under a life insurance policy is entitled to a credit to its capital dividend account under paragraph (d) of the definition of capital dividend account at subsection 89(1) to the extent the life insurance proceeds exceed the adjusted cost basis of the policy to the corporation immediately before the death of the life insured. The question arises as to whether the credit to the capital dividend account is affected by the collateral assignment of the life insurance policy. The CRA has confirmed in revisions to archived IT-430R3 and technical interpretation 2004-0068141E5 that the calculation of the credit to the capital dividend account is not affected by whether the insurance policy is collaterally assigned to a lending institution. Also, with the expressed intention that it will follow the *Innovative Installation* case, the CRA has confirmed that it will allow a CDA credit in respect of creditors' life insurance under which the creditor is the owner and beneficiary. This issue is discussed in detail in section 6.2.C.ii.

Safe income calculation — For purposes of subsection 55(2) of the Act, the CRA has indicated that non-deductible expenses such as non-deductible life insurance premiums will reduce safe income on hand (see Income Tax Technical News No. 37). However, the CRA has also indicated that to the extent that non-deductible premiums have been reflected in the cash surrender value of the policy, they do not reduce safe income on hand (technical interpretation 2005-0113931I7).

Butterfly transactions — At the 2011 APFF Conference CRA Roundtable held on October 7, 2011 (reported as 2011-0399401C6), the CRA commented on a butterfly transaction where the assets of the company to be divided included life insurance policies. Although the CRA indicated that each situation must be examined on a case-by-case basis, it stated that in the past it has considered the cash surrender value of an insurance policy to be "cash or cash equivalents", while the excess of the policy's fair market value over its cash surrender vale could be classified as "investments" or "business property", depending on the circumstances.

6.5 — Accounting for Life Insurance

A business may own a life insurance policy for any number of reasons including funding the shareholder/partnership agreement, as collateral for a loan or to cover the loss of a key employee. The financial statements of the business must reflect the ownership of the policy.

A. — Authoritative support

For fiscal years beginning on or after January 1, 2011, "publicly accountable enterprises" will be required to report using International Financial Reporting Standards (IFRS). Publicly accountable enterprises are all reporting entities other than private, not-for-profit, and public sector enterprises. Private enterprises (essentially defined as a profit-oriented enterprise that is not publicly traded and is not a bank, credit union, mutual fund, securities broker/dealer, or insurer) will be allowed to choose to adopt IFRS or, alternatively, they may use a new set of standards called "Accounting Standards for Private Enterprises" (ASPE).

Neither IFRS nor ASPE specifically address accounting for life insurance. However, in the United States, the Financial Accounting Standards Board (FASB) has released a statement on the appropriate financial reporting treatment for life insurance. Generally, when IFRS or ASPE guidance is silent on a particular transaction, U.S. accounting standards can be considered persuasive in both IFRS and ASPE. Therefore, the general concepts from IFRS or ASPE and the FASB statement can both be used to determine the appropriate accounting treatment.

B. — Financial reporting

The FASB statement indicates that an asset should be recorded on the financial statements at the amount that could be realized under the insurance contract at the financial statement date. In determining the expense or income to be recognized for the period, the premiums paid are adjusted for the change in the cash surrender value.

Therefore, the cash surrender value of the life insurance contract is recorded as an asset on the balance sheet. Each year the change in the cash surrender value changes the asset on the balance sheet. The difference between the premiums paid in the year and the increase in the cash surrender value is recorded as the net insurance expense on the income statement. In the later years of the policy, the increase in cash surrender value may exceed the premiums paid in the year. The excess is recorded as income on the income statement. Since term insurance does not have a cash surrender value, the entire premiums paid for term life insurance are recorded as an expense on the income statement.

Where a business purchases a policy that is already in force, there may be an argument to record the policy at the purchase amount as opposed to the cash surrender value. If the purchase was not at arm's length, the fair market value should be supported by an actuarial valuation.

Disclosure in the notes to the financial statements should be made if the life insurance policy has been pledged as security for bank indebtedness.

On the death of the life insured, the company or partnership will receive the proceeds of the life insurance policy. The life insurance asset on the balance sheet will be eliminated. The excess of the life insurance proceeds received over the amount recorded as an asset is reported as income on the income statement. This income may be disclosed as a separate item.

The ownership of a cash value life insurance policy affects the balance sheet, income statement, retained earnings and possibly the notes to the financial statements. Since Provincial capital taxes are often calculated based on accounting values, cash value life insurance owned by a corporation can affect its capital tax liability. In addition, Ontario has a corporate minimum tax ("CMT") which is based on financial statement income. A life insurance death benefit received by a corporation may trigger CMT in the year. In addition, many banking agreements have provisions relating to financial statement values and ratios. The impact of corporate-owned life insurance on such items may be important.

6.6 — Conclusion

Pivotal concepts in the context of insurance for business needs involving corporate-owned life insurance are: the capital dividend account, the potential for shareholder or employee benefits and the deductibility of insurance premiums. Each of these areas has intricate components and areas of interpretation and commentary from the CRA. As well, as an asset of the company, a life insurance policy must be reflected on the financial statements of the entity.

7 — Business Insurance Needs — Applications

Updated by Gordon Giacomin, C.P.A., C.A.

7.1 — Introduction

Chapter 6 considered a number of technical issues relating to business insurance needs. This chapter focuses on the application of life insurance in the business context and considers a variety of strategies intended to maximize the benefits associated with business insurance. It discusses business insurance needs and the use of life insurance as a source of funding to provide for the needs of a business following an individual's death.

7.2 — Business Loan Protection

A. — Introduction

Business loan protection involves the use of life insurance to create immediate working capital for a business to repay business debts in the event of the death of the business owner or other key executives.

In many small business situations, adequate debt financing is difficult to obtain. Creditors will often require that a loan be personally guaranteed by the business owner.

The untimely death of the business owner or another key executive may cause creditors to demand immediate repayment of outstanding business debts. This may place an unbearable burden on the business and force the liquidation of key business assets at fire sale prices at a time when the business may already be severely impacted by the death. In addition, if the business owner has personally guaranteed the debts incurred by the business, the business owner or the owner's estate may be liable for any outstanding debts that the business cannot pay.

In the absence of proper planning, the very survival of the business may thus be affected by the death of the business owner or another key executive.

A typical solution involves the purchase of an insurance policy by the business on the life of the business owner or other key executives. Proceeds from the life insurance policy received as a consequence of the death of the life insured are tax-free and may be used to pay down the outstanding business debts.

The insurance policy may or may not be collaterally assigned to a creditor as security for the business debts. The creditor may require the purchase of collateral life insurance to protect the interests of the creditor, particularly in small business situations in which the death of the business owner may impair the value of business assets used to secure the debt. In other cases, the business owner may simply have a desire to have business debts fully repaid in the event of death to minimize financial risks for the heirs and to permit them to continue the business free of debt.

B. — Implementation

Implementation of a life insurance strategy designed to provide business loan protection against the death of the business owner or another key executive might be summarized as follows:

The business owner and/or the accounting advisors list the various business debts currently outstanding, including payables, bank indebtedness, bank loans, and so forth, the current outstanding amount of each debt, repayment terms, security pledged against each debt (including any life insurance pledged as collateral), and any expected changes in the amount of each debt in the near future. This will help to identify potential coverage deficiencies.

The business purchases a life insurance policy on the life of the business owner or other key executives sufficient to fund repayment of the debts, including any expected increases in the amount of debt outstanding in the near future. The business is the owner, premium payer and beneficiary under the policy. The life insurance policy is collaterally assigned to the creditor if this is a condition of the loan. A life insurance policy purchased from a life insurance company may generally provide more flexibility, control and tax benefits than life insurance issued by the creditor.

Upon the death of the life insured, the insurance company pays the tax-free life insurance proceeds to the business, or, if the life insurance policy is collaterally assigned to the creditor, the proceeds are paid directly to the creditor to the extent of the outstanding debt. In either case, the insurance funds are used to pay down the outstanding business debts. Any excess life insurance proceeds may be used for other business purposes, to fund a buy/sell agreement, or to provide additional liquidity in the deceased's estate.

C. — The tax rules

Generally, life insurance premiums paid by the business for business loan protection are not deductible for tax purposes. However, in the case of a life insurance policy which has been collaterally assigned to a restricted financial institution, a portion of the premiums may be deductible under paragraph 20(1)(e.2). Reference should be made to the discussion on deductibility of life insurance premiums in section 6.4.E.

A collateral assignment of a life insurance policy is not a disposition of the policy as provided in paragraph (f) of the definition of "disposition" in relation to an interest in a life insurance policy in subsection 148(9). Section 3.2.C provides further detail regarding what is not considered a disposition of a life insurance policy.

Life insurance proceeds from an exempt policy received as a consequence of death are tax-free. The receipt is tax-free because a payment under an exempt life insurance policy, in consequence of the death of any person whose life is insured under the policy, is not considered a disposition according to paragraph (j) of the definition of "disposition" in subsection 148(9) of the Act.

In the case of a private corporation which receives life insurance proceeds as a consequence of death, the excess of the proceeds over the adjusted cost basis of the policy to the corporation credits (increases) the capital dividend account of the corporation. The calculation of the amount of the credit is provided at paragraph (d) in the definition of "capital dividend account" in subsection 89(1). Under subsection 83(2), tax-free capital dividends may be elected to be paid to the shareholders of the corporation to the extent of any balance in the capital dividend account. The credit to the capital dividend account is not affected by the fact that the insurance policy may have been collaterally assigned to a creditor and the proceeds used to repay the debt. Reference should be made to section 6.2.C.ii for a detailed discussion of these rules.

D. — The benefits associated with this strategy

Business loan protection provides many potential benefits to the business, the business owner and the owner's family.

Life insurance can improve the ability of the business to negotiate loans.

A portion of the life insurance premiums may be deductible under paragraph 20(1)(e.2) if the insurance policy is collaterally assigned to a restricted financial institution and the legislative and administrative criteria for deductibility are met.

Ownership of a permanent life insurance policy provides the opportunity to build equity within the policy and a future source of liquidity to meet cash flow needs.

Business debts can be repaid in the event of death of the business owner or other key executives using tax-free life insurance proceeds.

The business owner or the owner's estate will not be personally liable for the business debts in the event of death.

Life insurance proceeds received by a private corporation in excess of the adjusted cost basis of the policy as a consequence of death result in a credit to the capital dividend account of the corporation and permit the payment of tax-free capital dividends to the extent of any balance in the capital dividend account.

7.3 — Keyperson Insurance Protection

A. — Introduction

Keyperson insurance protection involves the use of life insurance to create immediate working capital for a business to meet immediate cash needs and to find a replacement in the event of the death of the business owner or other key executives.

The death of the business owner or other key executive results in the loss of a key member of the management team and can cause severe financial impact. During the resulting disruption, lenders may curtail credit, creditors may press for immediate payment, debtors may delay making payments, employees and customers may lose confidence, and competitors may take advantage of the situation.

Key executives spend considerable time and effort in acquiring the knowledge, experience, judgment, reputation, relationships and skills that make them valuable to the business.

Large corporations are often in a much better position to prepare for key executive turnover by sheer size and numbers. However, the death of a business owner or another key executive in a small business organization is not resolved as easily. In either case, what is needed is an immediate replacement with qualifications which are equal to those of the deceased.

Unfortunately, finding an immediate replacement is seldom possible in small business situations. In these cases, it is often necessary to look outside of the business to find a replacement, causing delays, disruption and reduced efficiency. The resulting effect on business profits may further weaken the financial stability of the business. In the absence of proper planning, the very survival of the business may be affected by the death of the business owner or another key executive.

A typical solution involves the purchase of an insurance policy by the business on the life of the business owner or other key executives. In the event of death, the life insurance proceeds provide the business with needed working capital to meet immediate cash needs and to provide a source of funds for finding, attracting, hiring, and training a replacement for the deceased executive or, in the case of the death of a business owner, to hire interim management.

Given both time and money, most businesses can replace key executives. Keyperson insurance protection provides cash to buy time and to fund the hiring of a replacement for the deceased executive.

B. — Implementation

Implementation of a life insurance strategy designed to provide keyperson insurance protection against the death of the business owner or another key executive might be summarized as follows:

The business owner identifies those individuals in the organization whose sudden loss would have a severe financial impact on the business.

The business purchases a life insurance policy on the life of the business owner and/or other key executives. The amount of life insurance will depend on the facts and circumstances of the case but should be sufficient to cover the estimated financial loss to the business resulting from the death of the key executive. The business is the owner, premium payer and beneficiary under the policy.

Upon the death of the life insured, the insurance company pays the tax-free life insurance proceeds to the business. The proceeds may be used by the business to meet immediate cash needs and to provide a source of funds for finding a replacement for the deceased or to hire interim management. Any excess life insurance proceeds may be used for other business purposes, to fund a buy/sell agreement, or to provide additional liquidity in the deceased's estate.

C. — The tax rules

Life insurance premiums paid by the business for keyperson insurance protection are not deductible for tax purposes. Reference should be made to the discussion on deductibility of life insurance premiums in section 6.4.A.

Life insurance proceeds from an exempt policy received as a consequence of death are tax-free. The receipt is tax-free because a payment under an exempt life insurance policy, in consequence of the death of any person whose life is insured under the policy, is not considered a disposition according to paragraph (j) of the definition of "disposition" in subsection 148(9) of the Act.

In the case of a private corporation which receives life insurance proceeds as a consequence of death, the excess of the proceeds over the adjusted cost basis of the policy credits (increases) the capital dividend account of the corporation. The calculation of the amount of the credit is provided at paragraph (d) in the definition of "capital dividend account" in subsection 89(1). Under subsection 83(2), tax-free capital dividends may be elected to be paid to the shareholders of the corporation to the extent of any balance in the capital dividend account. Reference should be made to section 6.2 for a detailed discussion of these rules.

A corporate-owned life insurance policy may be deemed to be a retirement compensation arrangement pursuant to subsection 207.6(2) if the employer is obliged to provide retirement benefits to any person and where the interest in the life insurance policy may reasonably be considered to have been acquired to fund, in whole or in part, those benefits. The implications of these rules are discussed in detail in section 7.7.

A transfer of a corporate-owned insurance policy to the life insured business owner or other key employee may have tax implications for both the corporation (transferor) and the shareholder/employee (transferee). Reference should be made to sections 6.3 and 3.3.I for a detailed discussion of these rules.

D. — The benefits associated with this strategy

Keyperson insurance protection provides many potential benefits to the business, the business owner and the owner's family.

Keyperson insurance can improve the ability of the business to attract and retain executive talent.

Creditors and employees of the business are satisfied that the business will continue notwithstanding the death of the keyperson.

The insurance proceeds are paid tax-free to the business.

The life insurance proceeds provide immediate cash at the time of death that contributes to the immediate working capital of the business.

The life insurance proceeds provide cash at the time of death to find, attract, and train a suitable replacement.

The cost of keyperson insurance protection is low in relation to the value to the business in the event of death of the owner-manager or other key executive.

Ownership of a permanent life insurance policy provides the opportunity to build equity within the policy and a future source of liquidity to meet cash flow needs.

Life insurance proceeds in excess of the adjusted cost basis of the policy received by a private corporation as a consequence of death result in a credit to the capital dividend account of the corporation and permit the payment of tax-free capital dividends to the extent of any balance in the capital dividend account.

7.4 — Funding Buy/Sell Arrangements

A. — Introduction

A key part of an integrated financial plan is planning for business succession. The business interest often accounts for a substantial portion of the wealth the business owner has accumulated. Ensuring a plan is in place for the eventual transfer of the business interest will help the business owner realize full value for the business interest and will also help the business, and the remaining owners, survive the transition. This is particularly true in the event of premature death.

Changes in ownership may create financial obligations on the part of the remaining owners and may also have income tax implications for the withdrawing owner and the remaining owners.

An integral part of the succession plan is to ensure financing is in place in the event of death to fund the purchase and sale of the business interest. The succession plan should also provide the business owner with sufficient liquidity to fund the related income taxes and, where possible, take advantage of any tax deferral or tax minimization strategies that may be available.

In the case of closely-held corporations, one of the most important tools for implementing the business succession plan is the shareholders' agreement. Once the business succession plan is developed, a shareholders' agreement can be drafted with buy/sell provisions that reflect the needs and wishes of the various parties.

Life insurance is generally the most efficient means of funding a buy/sell obligation under a buy/sell agreement in the event of the death of a shareholder.

In certain cases, life insurance policies may offer riders that allow the policyowner to increase the coverage without evidence of insurability where there is a proven increase in the value of the shares of the corporation.

There are numerous possible ways of structuring a buyout on death and this section will review the most commonly used arrangements and the life insurance funding implications surrounding the same. In considering the various methods for structuring a buy/sell arrangement at death, it should be borne in mind that there is no "right way" to proceed. Each method has its own "pros" and "cons" and must be considered in light of the circumstances of a given case.

B. — Overview of structures for life insured buy/sell arrangements at death

At a high level there are two basic ways that buy/sell arrangements at death can be structured. Either the surviving shareholders can purchase the deceased's shares, or the corporation can purchase the deceased's shares by redeeming the shares.

If life insurance is used to fund the buy/sell obligation at death, then there must be a life insurance policy (or policies) on the life of each shareholder with a death benefit equal to the value of that shareholder's shares as specified or calculated pursuant to the agreement.

If the agreement provides that the surviving shareholders will purchase the deceased's shares, then the buy/sell obligation may be funded with insurance owned by the shareholders using the "Criss-Cross Purchase" method, or it may be funded with insurance owned by the corporation using the "Promissory Note" method.

If the agreement provides that the corporation will purchase the deceased's shares, then the buy/sell obligation may be funded with insurance owned by the corporation. This structure is often referred to as the "Corporate Redemption" Method.

It is also possible to use a combination of the "Promissory Note" and "Corporate Redemption" Methods (often called the "Hybrid" method). In this case, the shareholders' agreement contemplates that some or all of the deceased's shares will be purchased by the corporation, and some or all of the deceased's shares will be purchased by the surviving shareholders. In this situation, the obligation is funded with insurance owned by the corporation.

Criss-Cross Purchase Method

In this arrangement, the agreement specifies that on the death of a shareholder, the surviving shareholders are obligated to purchase the shares of the deceased shareholder. Each shareholder of the corporation is the owner and the beneficiary of a life insurance policy on every other shareholder. If one of the shareholders dies, then the life insurance proceeds would be paid to the surviving shareholders and they would each use the proceeds to purchase the deceased's shares. Refer to section 7.4.D.i for a detailed example of this method.

Promissory Note Method

When this method is used, just as in the "Criss-Cross Purchase" method, the agreement specifies that on the death of a shareholder the surviving shareholders are obligated to purchase the shares of the deceased shareholder at the value as specified or calculated pursuant to the shareholders' agreement. However in this arrangement, instead of purchasing the shares for cash, the agreement specifies that the surviving shareholders will purchase the shares with a promissory note (payable to the deceased's estate from the survivors). The corporation is the owner and beneficiary of a life insurance policy on the life of each shareholder. After the shares have been purchased, the corporation is required under the agreement to pay the insurance proceeds out to the surviving shareholders as a dividend. (This dividend can be paid tax-free to the shareholders to the extent of the Capital Dividend Account (CDA)). The surviving shareholders are then obligated to use the dividend proceeds to repay the promissory note. Refer to section 7.4.D.ii for a detailed example of this method.

Corporate Redemption Method

In this arrangement, the agreement obligates the corporation to repurchase, or redeem, the shares of a deceased shareholder at the value as specified or calculated pursuant to the shareholders' agreement. The corporation is the owner and beneficiary of a life insurance policy on the life of each shareholder. If one of the shareholders dies, then the life insurance proceeds would be paid to the corporation, and it would use the proceeds to redeem the deceased's shares. Refer to section 7.4.D.iii for a detailed example of this method.

C. — Corporate- vs. personally-owned life insurance

One of the key factors in deciding which buy/sell structure is appropriate in a given situation is whether it is more desirable for the insurance to be owned corporately or personally. The following sections discuss issues to be considered with respect to corporate-owned vs. personally-owned insurance in the context of buy-sell funding.

i. — Tax leverage

Premiums payable in respect of a life insurance contract are generally not deductible for income tax purposes. Therefore, it may be advantageous to have insurance owned at the corporate level in order to have the corporation pay the premiums. Where the corporation is in a lower tax bracket than the individual shareholders, a tax saving may be generated and this factor alone is often decisive in favouring ownership of the insurance at the corporate level. For example, an individual shareholder with a marginal tax rate of 50 percent would require $2,000 of income to pay a $1,000 insurance premium. A corporation paying tax at the small business rate of 20 percent (or less in some provinces) would require only $1,250 of income in order to pay the same premium.

ii. — Policing of policy premiums

Where the insurance policies are individually owned, it may be difficult for one shareholder to be certain that the other shareholders are continuing to make the necessary premium payments. This difficulty is magnified as the number of shareholders increases. A shareholder's failure to pay premiums may only come to light at the death of the "life insured" shareholder, when it is discovered that there are no insurance proceeds to fund the buy/sell arrangement. Furthermore, where a death benefit is received, there is a risk that the beneficiary may ignore his obligations under the agreement and misappropriate the funds.

On the other hand, if the policies are owned by the corporation, each shareholder has access to the corporate records to ensure that the policies are being kept in force. On the death of the shareholder, his or her personal representative may also take steps to ensure that the death benefit paid to the corporation is in fact used to fund the purchase of the estate's shares as set out in the buy/sell provisions of the shareholders' agreement.

iii. — Allocation of cost of premiums

Where one shareholder is significantly older than the others, or is in poor health, personal ownership of the policies places a heavy premium burden on the other shareholders. While it may be argued that this heavy premium burden simply reflects the actuarial realities regarding the life expectancies of the various parties, the unequal financial burden frequently dictates against the use of personally-owned insurance.

In contrast, where corporate-owned insurance is used, the cost will be effectively shared among the shareholders according to their *pro rata* interest in the company. This is often viewed as being more equitable.

iv. — Ease of administration

Where there are several shareholders who are parties to the shareholders' agreement it may become expensive and confusing for each shareholder to own policies on the lives of all the others (for example, five shareholders necessitates the purchase of 20 separate policies). The requirement would be reduced to one policy on the life of each shareholder where corporate-owned insurance is used. This could also lead to lower expense costs and lower aggregate premium costs, as the costs of insurance may decrease as the amount of coverage per policy increases.

v. — Tax complexity

The provisions of the *Income Tax Act* applicable to corporate-owned life insurance create a much greater degree of complexity than those applicable to personally-owned life insurance. In addition, issues such as the stop-loss rules, the availability of the capital gains exemption and the availability of a "general rate income pool" ("GRIP") are further complicating factors which enter into the decision of whether to use corporate- or personally-owned insurance. These issues will be discussed in greater detail below.

vi. — Creditor protection

Where corporate-owned insurance is used to fund a buy/sell arrangement, the proceeds payable to the corporation on the death of one of the shareholders will be subject to the claims of the corporation's creditors. In addition, as a condition of lending funds to a corporation, banks and other creditors may place restrictions on the corporation's ability to pay dividends and/or salaries to shareholders. Finally, the corporate legislation in place in many jurisdictions requires that prior to the payment of dividends (including capital dividends) certain liquidity, net worth or financial capacity tests must be satisfied. All of these restrictions could impair the ability of the corporation and/or the surviving shareholders to fulfill the terms of the buy/sell provisions of their shareholders' agreement in the case of corporate-owned insurance.

Many of the above problems may be avoided by incorporating holding companies to own each shareholder's interest in the operating company. These holding companies could also hold the life insurance on the lives of the other shareholders and be the beneficiary thereof. Provided the holding companies have not guaranteed the obligations of the operating company, the life insurance proceeds would be protected from the creditors of the operating company. Since the holding companies would likely not carry on business in their own right, they are unlikely to have creditors which would attempt to seize the insurance proceeds or otherwise place restrictions on the use of corporate funds.

This would essentially result in a criss-cross buy-sell arrangement between the holding companies and would not enable the use of the corporate redemption, promissory note, or hybrid method of buy-sell. An alternative structure would be to have a holding company in which each shareholder holds a proportionate share, holding the insurance and being the beneficiary thereof. This would enable the creditor protection elements discussed above and the use of corporate redemption, promissory note, or hybrid methods of buy-sell planning.

Other structures using holding companies to own the insurance and naming an operating company as beneficiary are commented on below at section 7.4.C.vii and in greater detail at section 6.2.D.

vii. — Potential transfer of ownership

Where corporate-owned insurance is used to fund a buy/sell arrangement, it is important to consider a potential transfer of ownership of the life insurance policies. This may occur if the shareholders sell their participation in the company. The shareholders will often wish to keep their own policy. The transfer of a life insurance policy to a shareholder will result in a disposition of the policy and a potential taxable benefit to the shareholder to the extent the fair market value of the policy exceeds the amount of the consideration paid by the shareholder. Reference should be made to section 3.3.I for a detailed discussion of these rules.

Where the shareholders' interest in an operating company is held by individual holding companies, the life insurance policies may be held by each holding company with the operating company being designated as beneficiary of the policies. In order to provide for the liquidity to pay the insurance premiums, the operating company can declare a tax-free intercorporate dividend. This strategy would make unnecessary a future transfer of ownership of the policies. Should the operating company be sold, the holding company can simply change the beneficiary designation without triggering a disposition of the policy. Although this would result in a maximization of the CDA, it may result in taxable benefits, other income inclusions, and the potential application of GAAR. Reference should be made to section 6.2.D for a detailed discussion of these rules and CRA's comments on different ownership and beneficiary structures in a corporate group. This strategy will, however, have an effect on the allocation of the cost of the premiums as discussed above in section 7.4.c.iii.

D. — Structuring the buy/sell provisions with life insurance

The shareholders' agreement is a key component of the business succession plan for both the withdrawing shareholder and the remaining shareholders. In the event of the death of a shareholder, the agreement will typically specify the buy/sell methodology as well as the funding mechanism. Generally, life insurance provides the most cost-effective funding mechanism for the following reasons: (i) death is an uncertain event and life insurance provides the funds at the exact time required, (ii) the insurance proceeds are received tax-free, (iii) insurance is usually the least costly alternative, (iv) as a result of certain of the unique tax attributes associated with life insurance, the buy/sell may be structured in a manner to provide significant tax benefits to the deceased shareholder and the survivors.

As noted earlier there are various methods of structuring the buy/sell provisions using life insurance as the funding mechanism in the event of death.

The following relatively simple fact situation will illustrate the various options.

Ms. Smith and Mr. Jones are the owners of all of the outstanding shares of Opco, a Canadian-controlled private corporation carrying on an active business in Canada. The details are set out in Diagram 1.

Diagram 1

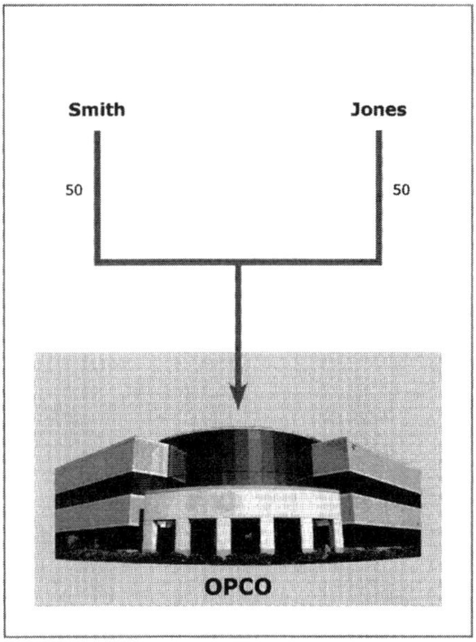

- Each shareholder owns 50% of the common shares of Opco.
- The current fair market value of Opco is $2 million.
- The adjusted cost base of the shares is nominal (assume nil).
- The paid-up capital of the shares is nominal (assume nil).
- Neither shareholder has utilized their capital gains exemption.
- The shares are "qualified small business corporation shares".
- The marginal tax rate for the shareholders is 50%.

There are four basic insurance financed structures available. Each structure has certain advantages and disadvantages. The four insurance financed arrangements are discussed in detail below. In each case, it is assumed Mr. Jones meets an early demise.

i. — Cross-purchase method

The cross-purchase method of structuring a buy/sell agreement is often the simplest method. The buy/sell agreement is between the shareholders or between the shareholders and a trustee but does not directly involve the corporation.

a. — Without use of trustee

Under this structure, the shareholders enter into a shareholders' agreement such that, in the event of death, the surviving shareholder will purchase and the estate of the deceased shareholder will sell the shares formerly held by the deceased shareholder. The purchase price will be funded by personally-owned life insurance. Typically, the insurance is held on a crisscross basis, with Ms. Smith as the policyholder, premium payer and beneficiary of a policy on the life of Mr. Jones, and with Mr. Jones as the owner, premium payer and beneficiary of a policy on Ms. Smith. The structure is summarized in Diagram 2.

Advantages

- This structure is relatively simple.
- The life insurance proceeds provide the survivor with the funds to implement the buy/sell.
- The deceased's estate receives full value for the shares on a timely basis.
- For income tax purposes, this structure will permit the deceased shareholder to take full advantage of the capital gains exemption to the extent it is available.
- The surviving shareholder receives a step-up in the adjusted cost base of her shares.

Disadvantages

- Premiums for the insurance are paid with personal after-tax funds.
- It can become more complex and difficult to manage if there are multiple shareholders.
- There may be a need to negotiate sharing of premiums if the age, health or ownership percentages differ significantly.

Following the purchase and sale, Mr. Jones' net estate value will be $950,000, and Ms. Smith will own 100 percent of the shares of Opco, worth $2 million and with an adjusted cost base of $1 million. Therefore, should Ms. Smith subsequently sell her entire participation in Opco (assuming no growth in the value of Opco), she would receive net proceeds of $1,950,000.

The tax implications of the cross-purchase method:

		With Insurance Funding
The deceased shareholder:		
Deemed proceeds on death (subsection 70(5)	$	1,000,000
Less: adjusted cost base of shares	-	0
Capital gain	$	1,000,000
Taxable capital gain	$	500,000
Capital gains exemption	-	400,000
Net taxable capital gain	$	100,000
Income tax liability	$	50,000
The deceased's estate		
Purchase price paid in cash	$	1,000,000
Income tax liability	-	50,000
Net estate cash	$	950,000
The surviving shareholder		
Fair market value of shares	$	2,000,000
Adjusted cost base of shares		1,000,000
Accrued capital gain	$	1,000,000
Survivor's tax payable on a subsequent sale (assuming no growth in value)		
Taxable capital gain	$	500,000
Capital gains exemption	-	400,000
Net taxable capital gain	$	100,000
Income tax liability	-	50,000
Net proceeds	$	1,950,000

Diagram 2
Insurance Financed Cross-Purchase Method

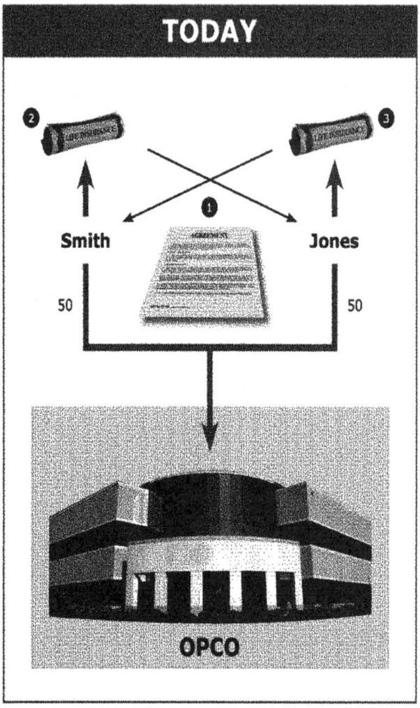

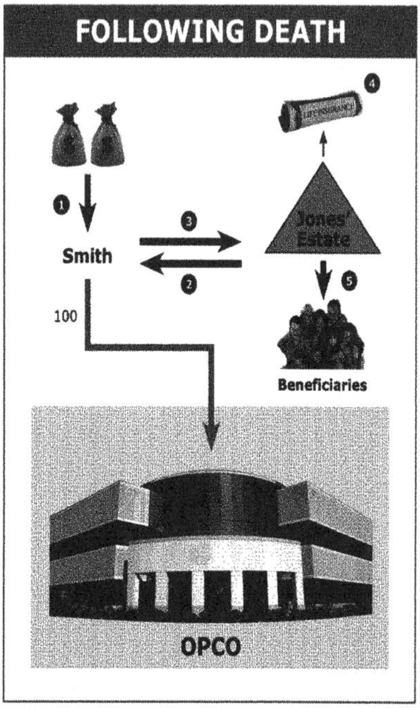

❶ Smith and Jones execute a written shareholders' agreement with buy-sell provisions in the event of death structured under the cross purchase method, funded with personally owned life insurance.

❷ Smith purchases a life insurance policy on Jones, pays the premium with after-tax personal funds, and is the named beneficiary under policy.

❸ Jones purchases a life insurance policy on Smith, pays the premium with after-tax personal funds, and is the named beneficiary under the policy.

❶ In the event of Jones' death, the life insurance proceeds are paid tax-free to Smith as the beneficiary of the policy.

❷ Smith purchases the 50% interest owned by Jones' estate. As a result, Smith now owns 100 shares, representing 100% of the outstanding shares of Opco.

❸ As consideration for the shares, Smith pays Jones' estate the purchase price in cash, funded by the life insurance proceeds.

❹ Jones' estate either surrenders the insurance policy it owns on Smith, or transfers the policy to Smith for fair market value consideration.

❺ Jones' estate distributes the net estate value (after payment of debts, taxes and so forth) to the intended beneficiaries.

b. — Use of a trustee

A trustee is sometimes used in a cross-purchase buy/sell arrangement to simplify the ownership of insurance and the mechanics of the buy/ sell on death. A trustee is most commonly used when there are more than two shareholders. The ownership of insurance policies can become complex when each shareholder purchases policies on the other shareholders in proportion to their buy/sell commitments. With a trustee, a single policy can be purchased on each shareholder with the trustee as owner and beneficiary. For example, if there are four shareholders A, B, C, and D and no trustee involved in the buy/sell agreement, then A must purchase policies on each of B, C, and D covering his/her share of the buy/sell commitment. In turn, B must purchase policies on A, C and D and so on. This would lead to twelve policies being required.

If a trustee is involved in the buy/sell arrangement, then a single policy is purchased on the life of each shareholder covering the purchase of all the individual's shares. As a result, in this example there would only have to be four policies. The insurance premiums would be funded by contributions to the trust by each shareholder in proportion to their obligations under the buy/sell provisions of the shareholders' agreement. The trustee would be the owner and beneficiary of the policies and would have responsibility for collecting the death benefit proceeds in the event of death and using the proceeds to purchase the shares from the deceased shareholder's estate. The shares would then be distributed to the surviving shareholders pursuant to the terms of the shareholders' agreement. For tax purposes, the distribution of the shares would usually be considered a capital distribution from a trust that can be distributed to any Canadian resident beneficiary at cost pursuant to subsection 107(2) of the *Income Tax Act*. Consequently, there should generally be no gain to the trust and the cost base of the shares to the surviving shareholders (i.e. the beneficiaries) will equal the purchase price paid by the trustee.

The use of a trustee also allows for the policing of premium payments as a shareholder can inquire of the trustee if there are any outstanding premium obligations. Without a trustee, the shareholders must rely on each other to ensure that policies are kept in force.

If a trustee is included in the buy/sell provisions of the shareholders' agreement, there should also be a separate trust agreement stating the duties and responsibilities of the trustee.

ii. — Promissory note method

Under this structure, the shareholders and Opco enter into a shareholders' agreement such that, in the event of death, the surviving shareholder will purchase and the estate will sell the shares formerly held by the deceased shareholder, funded by corporate-owned life insurance. Opco would be the policyholder, premium payer and beneficiary of life insurance policies on each of the lives of Ms. Smith and Mr. Jones. The structure is referred to as "promissory note" since the purchaser (Ms. Smith) originally pays for the shares with a note. Once Ms. Smith is the sole shareholder of the corporation, the corporation can distribute the insurance proceeds in excess of the policy's adjusted cost basis by means of a capital dividend. The capital dividend cannot be declared, however, until after the sale of shares by Mr. Jones' estate. Payment of a capital dividend prior to sale would have to be made *pro rata* to both common shareholders. This structure is summarized in Diagram 3.

Advantages

- This structure is relatively simple to set up and administer, particularly where there are multiple shareholders.
- The life insurance proceeds provide the survivor with the funds to implement the buy/sell.
- The deceased's estate receives full value for the shares on a timely basis.
- For income tax purposes, this structure will permit the deceased shareholder to take full advantage of the capital gains exemption to the extent it is available.
- The surviving shareholder receives a step-up in the adjusted cost base of her shares.
- Premiums for the insurance are paid with corporate after-tax funds. The premium commitment is effectively shared on the basis of each shareholder's ownership percentage.
- Premium payments are not a shareholder benefit as long as Opco is the beneficiary of the policy.

Disadvantages

- Insurance proceeds may be subject to the claims of the creditors of the corporation.
- Corporate solvency tests may need to be met in order to make any dividend payment.

Following the purchase and sale, Mr. Jones' net estate value will be $950,000 and Ms. Smith will own 100 percent of the Opco shares, worth $2 million and with an adjusted cost base of $1 million. The numerical example is the same as the example for the cross-purchase method. Therefore, should Ms. Smith subsequently sell her entire participation in Opco (assuming no growth in value of Opco), she would receive net proceeds of $1,950,000.

Diagram 3
Insurance Financed Promissory Note Method

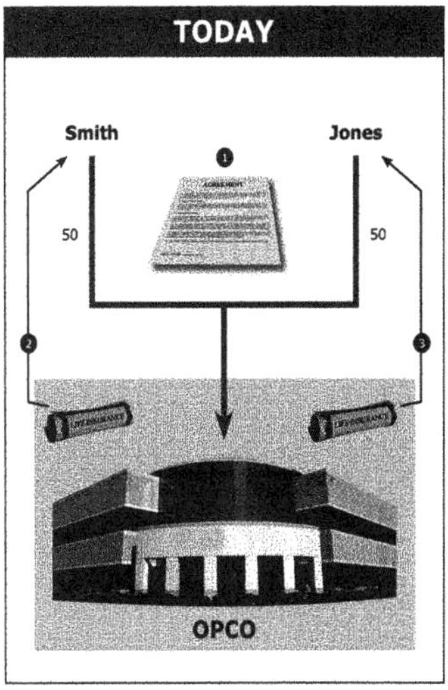

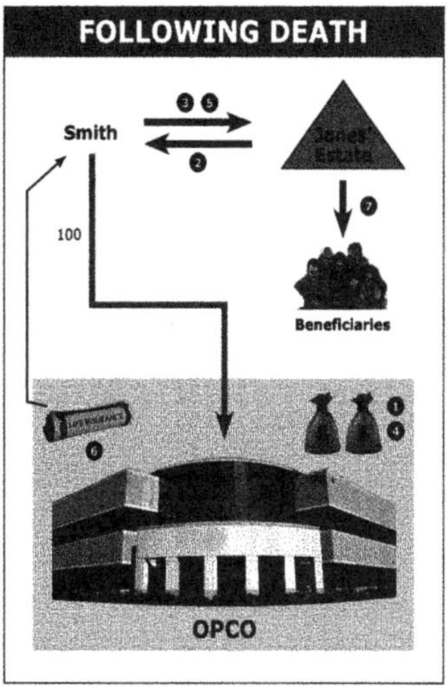

❶ Smith, Jones and Opco execute a written shareholders' agreement with buy-sell provisions in the event of death structured under the promissory note purchase method, funded with corporate owned life insurance.

❷ Opco purchases a life insurance policy on Smith, pays the premium with after-tax corporate funds, and is the named beneficiary under the policy.

❸ Opco purchases a life insurance policy on Jones, pays the premium with after-tax corporate funds, and is the named beneficiary under the policy.

❶ In the event of Jones' death, the tax-free life insurance proceeds are paid to Opco as the beneficiary of the policy. The excess of the proceeds over the adjusted cost basis of the policy at the time of death is credited to Opco's capital dividend account.

❷ Smith purchases the 50% interest owned by Jones' estate. As a result, Smith now owns 100% of the outstanding shares of Opco.

❸ As consideration for the shares, Smith issues a demand promissory note to Jones' estate in an amount equal to the purchase price.

❹ Smith causes Opco to declare and pay a dividend. The dividend is elected to be a tax-free capital dividend to the extent of the balance in the capital dividend account.

❺ Smith uses the proceeds from the dividend to satisfy the demand promissory note.

❻ Opco either surrenders the insurance policy it owns on Smith, retains the policy to cover future insurance needs, or transfers the policy to Smith for fair market value consideration.

❼ Jones' estate distributes the net estate value (after payment of debts, taxes and so forth) to the intended beneficiaries.

iii. — Share redemption method

Under this structure, the shareholders and Opco enter into a shareholders' agreement such that, in the event of death, Opco will purchase (redeem) from the estate of the deceased shareholder the shares formerly held by the deceased shareholder. The redemption would be funded by corporate-owned life insurance. Opco would be the policyholder, premium payer and beneficiary of life insurance policies on the lives of each of Ms. Smith and Mr. Jones. This structure is summarized in Diagram 4.

Advantages

- This structure is relatively simple to set up and administer, particularly where there are multiple shareholders.
- The life insurance proceeds provide Opco with the funds to implement the buy/sell.
- The deceased's estate receives full value for the shares on a timely basis.
- For income tax purposes, this structure may result in the proceeds being entirely tax-free (if the shares are grandfathered shares for purposes of the stop-loss rules in subsection 112(3.2)).
- Premiums for the insurance are paid with corporate after-tax funds. The premium commitment is effectively shared on the basis of each shareholder's ownership percentage.
- Premium payments are not a shareholder benefit as long as Opco is the beneficiary of the policy.

Disadvantages

- Insurance proceeds may be subject to the claims of the creditors of the corporation.
- Corporate solvency tests may need to be met in order to make the dividend payment.
- This structure will not permit the deceased shareholder to take advantage of the capital gains exemption.
- The surviving shareholder doesn't receive a step-up in the adjusted cost base of her shares.
- This structure could result in potential double tax if the stop-loss rules under subsection 112(3.2) of the *Income Tax Act* apply (unless the agreement is properly structured to eliminate or reduce the impact of these rules).

This structure will be impacted by the stop-loss rules under subsection 112(3.2) unless the shares are grandfathered for the purposes of these rules. See section 7.4.E for a full discussion of the stop-loss rules.

Before the implementation of the stop loss rules in 112(3.2), in a typical share redemption agreement, the deemed dividend on the share redemption was elected to be paid from the capital dividend account of Opco to the fullest extent possible.

The portion of the deemed dividend which was elected to be a capital dividend was tax-free to the estate. In addition, the share redemption likely results in a capital loss in the estate. The capital loss could be carried back to offset the capital gain on the deceased's terminal return under subsection 164(6). The combination of the tax-free capital dividend and the ability to offset the capital gain on the deceased's final income tax return with the capital loss in the estate resulted in effectively tax-free proceeds to the estate.

Under the stop-loss rule, the capital loss in the estate will be reduced if capital dividends have been paid on the shares. (The stop-loss provisions for estates, at subsection 112(3.2), do allow for a certain amount of capital dividends to be paid without causing the loss to be "stopped." This strategy, referred to as the "50 percent solution," is discussed in section 7.4.E.iii.b.) However, even if the deceased is denied a capital loss (or if the capital loss is reduced) the surviving shareholder does not receive a step-up in the adjusted cost base of her shares. Hence the potential for double tax exposure.

If the stop-loss rules do not apply (for example, in the case of grandfathered shares) and the share redemption is fully funded with life insurance, this arrangement provides an opportunity to fully defer the income taxes at the time of the first death. In our simple case, Mr. Jones' net estate value would be $1 million and Ms. Smith would own 100 percent of the shares of Opco, worth $2 million and with an adjusted cost base of $ nil. The capital gain is effectively deferred until Ms. Smith eventually disposes of her shares, in which case (assuming no growth in value of Opco) she would receive net proceeds of $1,700,000.

If the stop-loss rules do apply and the share redemption is fully funded with life insurance, this arrangement could result in a double tax exposure. As discussed below, eliminating or minimizing the double tax exposure would require the use of very flexible buy/sell provisions.

The tax implications of the share redemption method (assuming stop-loss rules do not apply):

		With Insurance Funding
The deceased shareholder:		
Deemed proceeds on death (subsection 70(5))	$	1,000,000
Less: adjusted cost base of shares	-	0
Capital gain	$	1,000,000
164(6) loss carryback from estate	-	1,000,000
Capital gain	$	0
Taxable capital gain	$	0
Capital gains exemption		unused
Net taxable capital gains	$	0
Income tax liability	$	0
The deceased's estate		
Purchase price paid in cash	$	1,000,000
Income tax liability on deemed dividend	-	0
Net estate cash	$	1,000,000
The surviving shareholder		
Fair market value of shares	$	2,000,000
Adjusted cost base of shares		0
Accrued capital gain	$	2,000,000
Survivor's tax payable upon subsequent sale (assuming no growth in value of Opco)		
Taxable capital gain	$	1,000,000
Capital gains exemption	-	400,000
Net taxable capital gain	$	600,000
Income tax liability	-	300,000
Net proceeds	$	1,700,000

Diagram 4
Insurance Financed Share Redemption Method

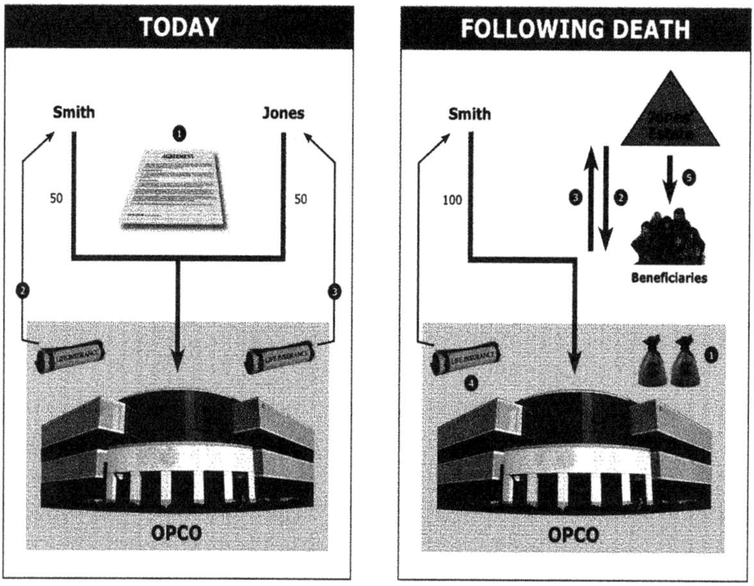

1 Smith, Jones and OPCO excute a written shareholders' agreement with buy-sell provisions in the event of death structured under the share redemption method, funded with corporate owned life insurance.

2 OPCO purchases a life insurance policy on Smith, pays the premium with after-tax corporate funds, and is the named beneficiary under the policy.

1 In the event of Jones' death, the tax-free life insurance proceeds are paid to Opco as the beneficiary of the policy. The excess of the proceeds over the adjusted cost basis of the policy at the time of death is credited to Opco's capital dividend account.

2 Opco redeems the 50% interest owned by Jones' estate. As a result, Smith now owns 100% of the outstanding shares of Opco.

3 OPCO purchases a life insurance policy on Jones, pays the premium with after-tax corporate funds, and is the named beneficiary under the policy.

3 The share redemption results in a deemed dividend to the extent the proceeds of redemption exceed the paid-up capital of the shares. All or a portion of the deemed dividend is elected to be a tax-free capital dividend to the extent of the balance in the capital dividend account.

4 Opco either surrenders the insurance policy it owns on Smith, retains the policy to cover future insurance needs, or transfers the policy to Smith for fair market value consideration.

5 Jones's estate distributes the net estate value (after payment of debts, taxes and so forth) to the intended beneficiaries.

iv. — Hybrid (combination) method

Under this structure, the shareholders and Opco enter into a shareholders' agreement such that, in the event of death, the surviving shareholders will purchase and the estate of the deceased shareholder will sell a specified number of shares formerly held by the deceased shareholder, and Opco will purchase (redeem) the remaining shares from the estate, all funded by corporate-owned life insurance. Opco would be the policyholder, premium payer and beneficiary of life insurance policies on the lives of each of Ms. Smith and Mr. Jones. Typically, the deceased shareholder's estate trustee would advise the surviving shareholder as to the value of shares to be purchased by the survivor. The survivor would purchase such shares using the promissory note structure. The balance would be redeemed by the corporation. In determining the value of shares to be purchased by the survivor, the estate trustee would have regard to the deceased's adjusted cost base immediately before death, any capital loss carryforwards which the deceased may have, the availability of any unused capital gains exemption and so forth. This structure is summarized in Diagram 5.

Advantages

- This structure is relatively simple to set up and administer, particularly where there are multiple shareholders.
- The life insurance proceeds provide Opco with the funds to implement the buy/sell.

- The deceased's estate receives full value for the shares on a timely basis.
- For income tax purposes, this structure may permit the deceased shareholder to take full advantage of the capital gains exemption to the extent it is available.
- For income tax purposes, this structure may result in the proceeds received by the estate on the shares redeemed from the estate being entirely tax-free (if the shares are grandfathered shares for purposes of the capital dividend stop-loss rules in subsection 112(3.2)).
- The surviving shareholder receives a step-up in the adjusted cost base of her shares to the extent she purchases shares from the estate of the deceased shareholder.
- Premiums for the insurance are paid with corporate after-tax funds. The premium commitment is effectively shared on the basis of each shareholder's ownership percentage.
- Premium payments are not a shareholder benefit as long as Opco is the beneficiary of the policy.

Disadvantages

- Insurance proceeds may be subject to the claims of the creditors of the corporation.
- Corporate solvency tests may need to be met in order to make any dividend payment.
- The surviving shareholder doesn't receive a step-up in the adjusted cost base of her shares to the extent the deceased's shares are redeemed by Opco.
- This structure may result in potential double tax if the stop-loss rules apply (unless the agreement is properly structured to eliminate or reduce the impact of these rules).

This structure will be impacted by the stop-loss rules under subsection 112(3.2) of the *Income Tax Act*, unless the shares are grandfathered for purposes of these rules.

If the stop-loss rules do not apply (for example, in the case of grandfathered shares) and the share purchase redemption is fully funded with life insurance, this arrangement provides an opportunity to fully defer the income taxes at the time of death partially through the use of the capital gains exemption and partially by the loss carryback generated as a result of the redemption of shares. In our simple case, Mr. Jones' net estate value would be $1 million and Ms. Smith will own 100 percent of the shares of Opco, worth $2 million and with an adjusted cost base of $800,000. Therefore, should Ms. Smith subsequently sell her entire participation in Opco (assuming no growth in the value of Opco) she would receive net proceeds of $1,900,000.

If the stop-loss rules do apply and the share redemption portion is fully funded with life insurance, this arrangement could result in a double tax exposure. Eliminating or minimizing the double tax exposure would require the use of very flexible buy/sell provisions.

The tax implications of the hybrid method (assuming stop-loss rules do not apply):

		With Insurance Funding
The deceased shareholder:		
Deemed proceeds on death (subsection 70(5))	$	1,000,000
Less: adjusted cost base of shares	-	0
Capital gain	$	1,000,000
164(6) loss carryback from estate	-	200,000
Capital gain	$	800,000
Taxable capital gain	$	400,000
Capital gains exemption	-	400,000
Net taxable capital gain	$	0
Income tax liability	$	0
The deceased's estate		
Purchase price paid in cash	$	1,000,000
Income tax liability	-	0
Net estate cash	$	1,000,000
The surviving shareholder		
Fair market value of shares	$	2,000,000
Adjusted cost base of shares		800,000
Accrued capital gain	$	1,200,000
Survivor's tax payable on subsequent sale (assuming no growth in value of Opco)		
Taxable capital gain	$	600,000
Capital gains exemption	-	400,000
Net taxable capital gain	$	200,000
Income tax liability	-	100,000
Net proceeds	$	1,900,000

Diagram 5
Insurance Financed Hybrid (Combination) Method

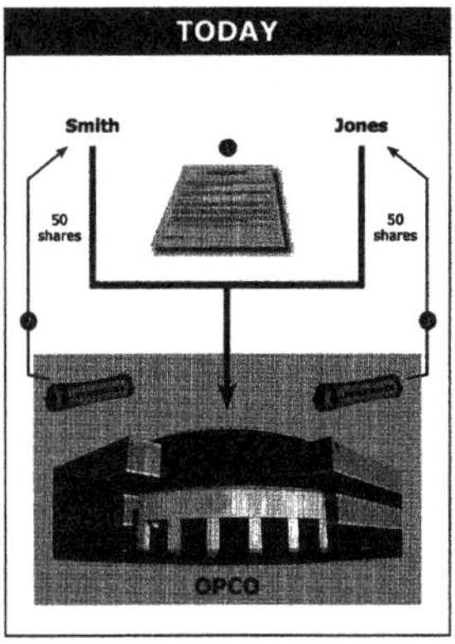

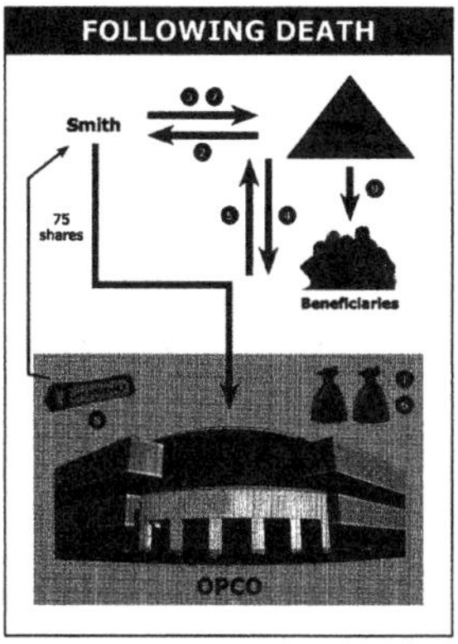

● Smith, Jones and OPCO execute a written shareholders' agreement with buy-sell provisions in the event of death structured under the hybrid (combination) method, funded with corporate owned life insurance.

● OPCO purchases a life insurance policy on Smith, pays the premium with after-tax corporate funds, and is the named beneficiary under the policy.

● OPCO purchases a life insurance policy on Jones, pays the premium with after-tax corporate funds, and is the named beneficiary under the policy.

● In the event of Jones' death, the tax-free life insurance proceeds are paid to Opco as the beneficiary of the policy. The excess of the proceeds over the adjusted cost basis of the policy at the time of death is credited to Opco's capital dividend account.

● Smith purchases sufficient shares (say 40% of the company shares) from the estate for the estate to fully utilize Jones' capital gains exemption. As a result, Smith now owns 90 % of the outstanding shares of Opco.

● As consideration for the shares, Smith issues a demand promissory note to Jones' estate in an amount equal to the purchase price.

● Opco redeems the remaining shares owned by Jones' estate. As a result, Smith owns 100% of the outstanding shares of Opco.

● The share redemption results in a deemed dividend to the extent the proceeds of redemption exceed the paid-up capital of the shares. Assuming the stop-loss rules do not apply, the deemed dividend is elected to be a tax-free capital dividend.

● Smith causes Opco to declare and pay a dividend. the dividend is elected to be a tax-free capital dividend to the extent of the balance in the capital dividend account.

● Smith uses the proceeds from the dividend to pay off the demand promissory note.

● Opco either surrenders the insurance policy it owns on Smith, retains the policy to cover future insurance needs, or transfers the policy to Smith for fair market value consideration.

● Jones' estate distributes the net estate value (after payment of debts, taxes and so forth) to the intended benficiaries.

v. — Optimization clauses

The nature of buy-sell provisions is that they set in place buy-out mechanisms today for events occurring perhaps many years from now. Changes are likely to occur to the shareholders' personal situation as well as with tax rates and legislation. These future uncertainties make it difficult, if not impossible, to draft a buy-sell arrangement today that will always optimize the tax effectiveness of an eventual buy-out.

The hybrid method attempts to deal with these uncertainties by giving representatives of deceased shareholders the option to either have their shares redeemed by the company or purchased by the survivors. This flexibility is helpful in minimizing the disposition tax to the deceased's estate.

Another way to deal with the issue is to allow the survivors the option to restructure the buy-out provided this does not negatively impact the deceased's estate. For example, a hybrid style agreement could require the deceased's estate to submit to the survivors its choice of buy-out method (including the number of shares to be redeemed and the capital dividend account to be utilized), along with a calculation of the amount of tax this would attract. The survivors would then have the option to either accept this arrangement, or alternatively restructure the buy-out in any way, provided the deceased's estate receives the same after-tax retention as their initial choice. This might include changes to the purchase price, the number of shares redeemed and/or the capital dividend account utilized.

E. — Stop-loss rules

i. — Application

The amendments to the stop-loss rules under subsection 112(3.2) of the *Income Tax Act* were initially announced by the Department of Finance in a technical bill dated April 26, 1995. Of particular concern from a business and estate planning perspective was the potential impact of the new stop-loss rules on share redemption strategies funded by corporate-owned life insurance.

Under the stop-loss rules, a loss realized by an estate under a share redemption agreement will be reduced by the amount by which the lesser of

- capital dividends received on the shares, and
- the amount of the loss otherwise determined minus taxable dividends received by the estate on the shares

exceeds 50 percent of the lesser of

- the amount of the loss otherwise determined, and
- the individual's capital gain from the disposition of the shares on his or her final income tax return.

Under a typical corporate share redemption strategy, the share redemption is funded by a corporate-owned life insurance policy. As discussed earlier in this chapter, the excess of the proceeds over the adjusted cost basis of the policy at the time of death is credited to the capital dividend account of the corporation. The deemed dividend arising on the share redemption under subsection 84(3) would normally be elected to be a tax-free capital dividend to the fullest extent possible.

The share redemption would create a capital loss in the estate, which would be carried back by the estate under subsection 164(6) to offset the deemed capital gain on the deceased's final income tax return under subsection 70(5).

For estate planning involving family corporations and for business succession planning involving shareholders in private corporations, this former strategy would result in a significant tax-deferral opportunity. The capital gain on death would generally be fully offset by the carryback of the capital loss in the estate, and the deemed dividend would be a tax-free capital dividend. The net result would be a tax-free payout of the value of the deceased's shares at the time of death. The accrued capital gain is not eliminated but is "transferred" to the surviving shareholders because the value of their shares increases, but there is no corresponding increase in the adjusted cost base or paid-up capital of their shares under a share redemption strategy.

The stop-loss rules could have a significant impact on business and estate planning, particularly where a corporate share redemption strategy is chosen, and where life insurance funding is involved.

In the absence of planning for the stop-loss rules, structuring a share redemption agreement in the manner described above would result in a double tax exposure, assuming the stop-loss rules apply to the disposition of the shares by the estate. The loss in the estate would be effectively reduced by up to 50 percent of the capital dividend, thereby increasing the capital gain taxed on the deceased's final income tax return. However, because the surviving shareholders do not receive any increase in the adjusted cost base of their shares, the same gain is taxed in the hands of the deceased in the year of death and then again to the surviving shareholders when they eventually dispose of their shares.

The stop-loss rules applicable to individuals and trusts apply to dispositions occurring after April 26, 1995 to the extent the grandfathering provisions do not apply.

Notwithstanding the introduction of the stop-loss rules, the use of life insurance to fund a redemption of shares in the event of the death of a shareholder can continue to be an effective strategy. The introduction of the stop-loss rules has reduced the potential benefits in some situations. However, significant benefits may be obtained by either the estate of the deceased shareholder or the surviving shareholders from an insured share redemption strategy if the strategy is properly planned.

In addition to the potential tax benefits, the life insurance proceeds do provide the cash required to fund the agreement, thereby minimizing the financial impact on the corporation and the surviving shareholders, and ensuring a timely purchase of the deceased's shares for full value in the event of death.

ii. — Grandfathering rules

The stop-loss rules contain generous grandfathering provisions for plans or arrangements that existed on April 26, 1995. The stop-loss rules will not apply to a disposition of shares if either of the following criteria are met:

1. *Pre-existing agreement rule:* A disposition that occurs pursuant to an agreement in writing made before April 27, 1995; or,
2. *Pre-existing insurance rule:* The shares were owned by a taxpayer on April 26, 1995, a corporation was the beneficiary of a life insurance policy on April 26, 1995, and it is reasonable to conclude that a main purpose of the policy on April 26, 1995 was to fund a redemption of the shares.

Under both grandfathering rules, the purchase of new or additional life insurance or the replacement or conversion of an existing policy will not impact the grandfathered status of the shares.

An earlier version of the grandfathering rules in respect of the proposed legislation required a completed shareholders' agreement prior to April 1997 in order to fall under the pre-existing insurance rule. However, this requirement was eliminated in Bill C-28, dated June 18, 1998. Of course, completing a shareholders' agreement is still advisable in order to formalize the relationship between the shareholders, for the reasons outlined elsewhere in this chapter.

With respect to the first grandfathering rule, (the pre-existing agreement rule) changes to an agreement that existed on April 26, 1995 may cause the shares to lose their grandfathered status. In archived Income Tax Technical News Number 12, dated February 11, 1998, the CRA indicated that where an existing agreement is altered to such an extent that it would constitute a new agreement, grandfathering relief under this rule would be lost. This would be a question of fact to be determined in each case based on common law principles. The CRA also considered the circumstances where parties to an agreement in writing made before April 27, 1995 choose to revise the terms of their relationship by concluding a separate agreement so that the existing agreement remains unchanged. According to the CRA, where a separate agreement is entered into by the parties to revise the terms of their relationship contained in a grandfathered agreement, the grandfathering based on the agreement made before April 27, 1995 will be lost if the separate agreement is considered to cancel, nullify or replace the original agreement.

Grandfathering will also be extended under the pre-existing insurance rule to shares owned by a trust on April 26, 1995 which are subsequently distributed to an individual who was a beneficiary of the trust on April 26, 1995, and then redeemed by the corporation from the individual, the individual's spouse or common-law partner or a spouse trust. In this case, the existing insurance policy must be on the life of the individual or the individual's spouse or common-law partner, and meet the other criteria for the pre-existing insurance rule.

Clarification of the pre-existing insurance rule is provided in the explanatory notes to the legislation. First, the shares being disposed of do not have to be shares of the corporation that is the beneficiary under the policy. In other words, the shareholder of Holdco would be eligible for grandfathering in respect of a disposition of shares of Holdco, where there is a redemption buy/sell under which Opco is beneficiary of the insurance and a main purpose of the insurance was to fund a redemption of the shares of Holdco, and the intention was to use the proceeds of the policy (which are paid up to Holdco) to acquire the deceased taxpayer's shares.

Secondly, the explanatory notes state:

> The shares need not be acquired with the proceeds of the life insurance policy that was in place on April 26, 1995. Therefore, policies may be renewed, converted or entered into after April 26, 1995 without necessarily eliminating the application of these grandfathering rules.

The pre-existing insurance grandfathering rule can have extremely broad application. For example, if a corporation was a beneficiary on April 26, 1995 of a term insurance policy that provided funding for a buy/sell agreement structured as a redemption of shares, the term insurance policy could be converted to a permanent policy without jeopardizing the application of the grandfathering provision. It also appears that additional life insurance coverage or replacement policies may be purchased subsequent to April 26, 1995 to provide buy/sell funding without eliminating the applicability of the grandfathering provisions. This was confirmed by the CRA in technical interpretation 2005-0124311, dated June 28, 2005.

In order to qualify for grandfathering relief under the pre-existing insurance rule, the policyholder has to satisfy a purpose test. In archived Income Tax Technical News Number 12, the CRA noted that the onus is on the taxpayer claiming grandfathering relief to establish that it is reasonable to conclude that on April 26, 1995 a main purpose of the life insurance policy was to fund, directly or indirectly, in whole or in part, a redemption, acquisition or cancellation of the shares. The CRA noted that that there can be more than one main purpose for the acquisition of a life insurance policy. However, the policyholder must be able to provide evidence to substantiate that the life insurance policy was acquired to fund the share redemption. Satisfactory evidence could consist of documents issued by the insurance company, minutes of the corporation, correspondence from the legal advisors or the accountants or any correspondence relating to the issuance of the life insurance policy.

In addition, grandfathering under the pre-existing insurance rule is preserved for shares acquired in exchange for grandfathered shares in specified tax-deferred rollover transactions, including certain share conversions (section 51), share-for-share exchanges (section 86), amalgamations (section 87) and rollovers (section 85).

Question 3 at the 2011 APFF Conference CRA Roundtable (reported as 2011-0399401C6) asked, in part, whether subsection 112(3) grandfathered shares are still grandfathered shares after a butterfly reorganization. The CRA responded they were unable to make a definitive ruling in this instance. Generally, a butterfly reorganization should not change the grandfathered status of the original shares held where a section 85 election is filed regarding the exchange of the original grandfathered shares for the new shares.

It is important to note that the grandfathering status of shares is to be determined as of April 26th, 1995. There may very well be situations where, at first glance, shares may not seem to meet the conditions under the pre-existing insurance rule (sole shareholder of a holding company for example). However, if there have been numerous reorganizations between April 26th, 1995 and the time at which the grandfathering status is being considered, care should be taken in examining the situation as it existed on April 26th, 1995.

If the shares held by the shareholders are eligible for grandfathering under the stop-loss rules, this represents a significant opportunity to take advantage of the benefits available under an insured corporate share redemption strategy. This can be particularly attractive in the case of family-owned enterprises, where the parents may have frozen the value of their shareholdings. If the freeze shares qualify for grandfathering under the stop-loss rules, the insurance funded share redemption strategy would result in a significant tax deferral opportunity.

iii. — Planning under the stop-loss rules

Since the stop-loss rules were first introduced on April 26, 1995, several planning strategies have been developed to enhance the effectiveness of insurance financed share redemption structures. Several of the strategies are briefly outlined below. Of course, planning strategies often involve elements of risk and reward, and should be evaluated based on the specific facts of the case at hand.

a. — Use of spousal rollover

If the shares of the deceased are transferred to a surviving spouse or common-law partner or a spouse trust on a tax-deferred basis under subsection 70(6) and then redeemed using tax-free capital dividends, the capital gain under 70(5) is deferred (actually, from the surviving spouse's perspective, the tax is effectively eliminated), the deemed dividend is a tax-free capital dividend, and the impact of the stop-loss rules is bypassed. This "roll-and-redeem" strategy can also be considered with children if the company is a qualifying farm or fishing company.

In order to qualify for the rollover under subsection 70(6), the shares must vest indefeasibly in the spouse or common-law partner or the spouse trust. If the shares are the subject of a mandatory buy/sell, this condition will not be satisfied.

Perhaps the best way to avoid the vesting problem is if the shareholders own their shares of the operating company through personal holding companies. At the time of death, the shares of the holding company may be transferred to the surviving spouse, common-law partner or a spouse trust on a tax-free rollover basis and the shares held by the holding company in the operating company may be redeemed by the operating company. The deemed dividend on the redemption of the operating company shares is elected to be a tax-free capital dividend. The holding company may then be wound up using tax-free capital dividends. This is a very effective strategy.

Another possible way to deal with the vesting problem is to permit the transfer to the surviving spouse, common-law partner or a spouse trust under the agreement, and provide the corporation with a "call option" and the spouse, common-law partner or spouse trust with a "put option." In this way, either party can force the purchase of the shares, but the sale does not become mandatory until such time as the option is exercised. This may also be an effective strategy.

CRA technical interpretation 2010-0378451E5, dated March 12, 2012, confirmed that paragraph 8(d) of Archived IT 449R — Meaning of "Vesting Indefeasibly" "in and by itself, is still supportable". This states that where a buy-sell agreement provides for an option to buy or an option to sell and permits the shares to pass by the Will to a shareholder's spouse or a spouse trust on their death, the shares received by the spouse or spouse trust can be seen as "vesting indefeasibly" in the spouse. This is important in planning for "spousal roll and redeem" strategies.

Care should be taken in drafting put and call options. Put and call options were the focus of a case involving a buy-sell arrangement in *Denille Industries Ltd. v. Island Enterprises Inc.*, 2012 ABCA 140, 2012 CarswellAlta 778, 100 B.L.R. (4th) 1. The shareholders had signed a unanimous shareholders' agreement giving a deceased's estate the option to "put" some or all of its shares to the surviving shareholders. A "call" option allowed the survivors to purchase a deceased's shares but only in the event the put was not exercised. Upon the death of a shareholder, his estate cleverly exercised the put option with respect to just one of the 40 shares it held. (Presumably it was to the estate's advantage to remain a shareholder in the company.) A surviving shareholder tried to force the buy-out of the estate's remaining interest by exercising his call option on the deceased's shares. This was unsuccessful as the court found the estate's exercise of its put option, albeit just for the one share, precluded the call option according to the wording of the shareholders' agreement.

Of course, planning techniques involving a spousal rollover are predicated on the spouse or common-law partner surviving the shareholder.

b. — 50 percent solution

Under this technique, the life insurance proceeds received by the corporation are used to redeem the shares held by the deceased shareholder, but the amount of the capital dividend is limited, by some mechanism, to 50 percent of the lesser of the deemed capital gain on the shares (reported on the deceased's final income tax return) and the capital loss realized in the estate. This takes advantage of the provision under the stop-loss calculation that limits the loss reduction to 50 percent of the lesser of the capital gain on the deceased's final income tax return and the capital loss realized in the estate. This has the effect of reducing the effective tax rate on the deemed dividend.

Under subsection 112(3.2), the 50 percent solution is available to a trust where the trust is an individual's estate. Under subsection 112(3.3), the 50 percent solution is also available to a trust that acquires shares as a consequence of subsection 104(4) (i.e. property acquired by the trust following the deemed disposition of property by a spousal trust on the death of the spouse, by an alter ego trust following the death of the settlor, and by a joint partner trust following the last to die of the two partners).

The balance in the capital dividend account is retained for the benefit of the surviving shareholders. The payout of the balance in the capital dividend account will reduce the fair market value of the shares held by the surviving shareholders, effectively eliminating the double tax exposure under the stop-loss rules.

There is a technical difficulty in implementing this technique. The full amount of the deemed dividend on the share redemption must be elected to be a capital dividend, whereas the intent is only to elect on a maximum of 50 percent of the capital dividend. CRA technical interpretation 2009-031060117, dated June 9, 2009, confirmed that the stop-loss calculation will apply to each redemption separately if done in more than one transaction. This results in a reduction of the loss carry back.

The solution may be to file an excessive election for the full amount of the deemed dividend, and then amend the election to treat the excess as a separate taxable dividend. This is rather cumbersome, but appears to be necessary to achieve the desired result. There may be an issue, however, if the company really does have the full amount of the capital dividend available in the capital dividend account at the time the election is made. Typically this would be the case under an insured share redemption agreement.

An alternative which may be "cleaner" may be to simply increase the paid-up capital of the shares of the deceased by 50 percent of the lesser of the capital gain (reported on the deceased's final income tax return) and the capital loss realized in the estate. To implement this structure, the deceased shareholder would have to own shares of a separate class from the surviving shareholders. This technique should achieve the desired result because the increase in the paid-up capital is deemed to be a dividend under subsection 84(1) and could be elected to be a tax-free capital dividend under subsection 83(2). Where the deceased owns 50 percent or more of the shares, an increase in the paid-up capital of all shares prior to the redemption of the deceased's shares can have the same effect and there is no need to have separate classes of shares.

Implementing the 50 percent solution will generally reduce the deceased's tax on a disposition of private company shares from a capital gains tax rate to one-half the dividend tax rate. As dividend tax rates increase the tax rate reduction as between a capital gains tax rate and one-half the dividend tax rate becomes less significant. For example, for 2013 in Ontario at the highest marginal tax rate, the capital gains tax rate is 24.76 percent and the ineligible dividend tax rate is 36.47 percent, making the net tax rate reduction as between capital gains rates and half the ineligible dividend rate just over 6.5 percent. Particularly in family owned companies where tax planning can be carried out at the family rather than individual level, it may be advantageous to let the deceased's capital gains tax rate stand and save the capital dividend account for use where it would provide greater tax savings. Of course, having insurance in place to generate an increase to the capital dividend account allows this type of flexibility.

iv. — Summary

There are numerous planning opportunities that continue to exist for insurance financed corporate share redemption strategies, even after stop-loss.

F. — Other considerations

i. — Use of the capital dividend account

A life insurance funded buy-sell should include clauses dealing with the capital dividend account. It generally makes sense that the deceased's estate would have the right to require the company to elect any redemption dividend be a capital dividend to the extent of the capital dividend account arising from the company's receipt of the life insurance death benefit. However, unless this is specified in the shareholders' agreement, the company is not necessarily obliged to make a capital dividend election.

This was demonstrated in the Ontario Superior Court case of *Ribeiro v. Braun Nursery Ltd.*, 2009 CarswellOnt 171, 45 E.T.R. (3d) 292, 2009 CanLII 1149; additional reasons at 2009 CarswellOnt 1331, 47 E.T.R. (3d) 132 (Ont. S.C.J.). In this case, the trustee of the Ribeiro estate argued the company ought to have drawn on its capital dividend account when it redeemed the deceased's shares. The Ribeiro estate was seeking a judgment of $249,903 representing the amount of tax generated by the absence of a capital dividend election. As the shareholders' agreement was silent on this issue, the Court concluded the company had met its obligations in liquidating the estate's shares, and that the company did not have an obligation to make a capital dividend election.

It is also important that shareholders' agreements which use life insurance to fund a buy-out at death do not require the declaration of a capital dividend equal to the death benefit proceeds from the life insurance policy or equal to the CDA credit arising from the receipt of the life insurance death benefit. A requirement of this type can result in an excessive CDA election which has significant punitive tax consequences. If the full death benefit from a life insurance policy is elected as a capital dividend, an excessive election could occur because a CDA credit is only available to the extent the proceeds exceed the ACB of the policy. An excessive election could also occur if the CDA balance was negative before the addition of the CDA credit arising from the life insurance death benefit. Reference should be made to section 6.2.B for a detailed discussion of these rules.

ii. — Eligible dividend tax regime

With the introduction of the dividend tax regime proposed in the 2006 federal budget, "eligible dividends" are subject to a reduced rate of tax. Since the introduction of these rules, in some provinces the difference in rates between eligible and ineligible dividends is not that significant, while in some provinces there remains a very large difference. The legislation requires a CCPC to determine its "general rate income pool" ("GRIP"). A CCPC can distribute eligible dividends to the extent it has a positive balance in its GRIP at the end of the taxation year in which the dividend is paid. The GRIP balance at the end of any particular year tries to approximate the corporation's undistributed after-tax earnings that were subject to the high general federal corporate tax rate. A CCPC can pay eligible dividends first, depleting its GRIP before paying non-eligible dividends. To the extent that eligible dividends are not distributed and surplus is annually retained by the corporation, the GRIP can increase over time.

In planning for the death of a shareholder, the available GRIP should be considered. In some jurisdictions the resulting tax consequences of a share redemption versus a share purchase may be quite different. In buy-sell situations, the deceased and the surviving shareholders may have very different preferences. Recognizing that there will be adverse interests at death, it is advisable to contemplate whose interests are going to prevail. It is probable that this will make drafting of shareholders' agreements that contemplate the tax attributes of various buy-sell strategies considerably more complex. It may also be advisable for clients with existing shareholder agreements to revisit their current buy-sell methodology in light of these rules. Redemption buy-sell agreements or hybrid agreements using the redemption method for at least a portion of the buy-sell may become more favoured in jurisdictions where eligible dividends are received at lower rates of tax than capital gains.

iii — Use of a bare trustee

A shareholders' agreement may appoint a bare trustee to act as an administrator of the buy-sell provisions. This is done to ease administration of the buy-sell once it has been triggered by the death of a shareholder, appointing a trustee to hold the insurance proceeds while the necessary steps are taken and transactions carried out. Question 6 at the 2012 CALU CRA Roundtable (reported as 2012-0435641C6) confirmed that where an insurance trustee in this context "can reasonably be considered to act as agent for its sole beneficiary Corporation A such that the arrangement is deemed not to be a trust for purposes of the Act, Corporation A may generally be considered to have received insurance proceeds for its capital dividend account . . .". This was true whether the scenario involved either: 1) Corporation A being named as beneficiary under the policy with specific instructions in the shareholders' agreement to pay over the proceeds to the insurance trustee; 2) Corporation A as beneficiary but gives an irrevocable direction to pay insurance proceeds to the insurance trustee; or, 3) insurance trustee is named as beneficiary of the policy as "bare trustee for the Corporation".

7.5 — Life Insurance Used in Family Business Succession Planning

A. — Introduction

Succession of a family business is often a key objective of estate planning. The business interest often accounts for a substantial portion of the wealth the business owner has accumulated. Family members may or may not be active or interested in being active in the business. Issues of equity, fairness, and family dynamics can enter into the planning process. Ensuring a plan is in place for the transfer of the business interest may be more difficult due to these factors than may be the case where planning for the transfer of a business interest is made in an arm's length situation. Even though these factors may make it more difficult, ensuring a plan is in place for the eventual transfer of the business interest can help the business owner accomplish a smooth transition.

Some business owners want to realize full value for their business interest as would be the case in an arm's length situation. Others may wish to simply convey their interest within the family covering the tax liabilities arising on the transfer. Often, estate equalization concerns may arise when planning in these contexts. Planning of this nature will also help the business and the successors survive the transition.

An integral part of this planning should be to ensure that financing is in place in the event of death to facilitate the transfer of the business interest. Life insurance can provide sufficient liquidity to facilitate the business succession plan and can often enhance the tax deferral or tax minimization strategies that may be available.

Life insurance is generally the most efficient means of funding a need for capital at death. Business succession planning in the family business context can result in a need for capital to fund tax liabilities, to carry out a redemption or to facilitate the purchase of a business owner's shares to the extent desired. Many of the same methods are used in the family business succession context as were discussed in the context of funding buy-sell agreements in section 7.4.

B. — The role of life insurance in common family business succession plans

This section will discuss the uses for corporate-owned life insurance in structuring business succession plans and, in particular, where a successor(s) within the family has been identified. Specifically, the role of life insurance in business succession planning to a successor will be discussed where there is:

- a fair market value sale of shares for a promissory note during the business owner's lifetime to a successor;
- the use of an estate freeze to transfer ownership to a successor during life; or
- a transfer at death by way of gift to a successor.

i. — Sale to a successor during life for a promissory note

In situations where a business owner wants to receive the full value of his/her business interest, as in arm's length situations, the buy-sell provisions of a shareholders' agreement is extremely useful in carrying out a related business succession plan. Once the family business succession plan is developed, a shareholders' agreement can be drafted to carry out the desired transfer of the business interest.

If the shares are sold during the business owner's lifetime and the proceeds or a portion are satisfied with a promissory note, the corporation could be the owner and beneficiary of a life insurance policy on the business owner's life. The advantage of the corporation owning the policy (as opposed to the successor personally) is that the premiums can be paid with cheaper corporate dollars. When the business owner dies, the corporation can receive the death benefit tax-free and would also receive an addition to its capital dividend account for the amount by which the death benefit exceeds the policy's adjusted cost basis. As is the case with the promissory note method of buy-sell funding discussed in section 7.4.D.ii, the corporation could then pay a tax-free capital dividend on the shares owned by the successor and the successor could use the funds to repay the promissory note owing to the business owner's estate. The loan repayment received by the estate could then be distributed to the beneficiaries of the estate.

ii. — Use of an estate freeze to transfer ownership to a successor during life

Estate freezes are common planning techniques in the family business succession context. The business owner may freeze all or a portion of the value of the business and therefore also freeze the related tax liability arising upon the deemed disposition of the shares on death. Various techniques may be used over the lifetime of the business owner which may "waste away" the ultimate capital gains tax liability arising on the deemed disposition on death by carrying out serial redemptions of preference shares over the course of the business owner's life.

If the business owner holds preference shares at death, often the estate plan will require the corporation to redeem the remaining preference shares in order to provide cash to pay tax liabilities and make distributions from the estate. Corporate-owned life insurance may be used to provide the full or partial redemption value of shares at the death of the business owner.

Post-mortem planning can be done in order to minimize the overall tax burden. Life insurance can be an integral part of the post-mortem planning that is done in respect of a deceased business owner's preference shares. Corporate-owned life insurance used in conjunction with "pipeline" planning or redemption and loss carryback planning can improve the outcome.

If the stop-loss rules apply, the 50 percent solution (discussed at section 7.4.E.iii.b) can be used. Also, where there is a spouse to whom preference shares may be rolled, the spousal rollover and share redemption strategy may be employed. A discussion of the use of life insurance in this strategy is provided as section 7.4.E.iii.a.

iii. — Transfer at death to a successor

Where conveyance of the interest in a family business as a gift at death is desired, the business owner's Will should reflect the approach to be taken in respect of the transfer of the shares of the business. Life insurance to cover the tax liabilities arising on such a gift either on the death of the business owner or on the second to die of the business owner and their spouse can provide the liquidity to enable a transfer of the shares. Personal or corporate-owned life insurance may be used to accomplish this.

Corporations generally have a lower income tax rate and, therefore, the after-tax cost of the insurance premiums is generally less than personally held insurance. If corporate-owned life insurance is used to fund the tax liability, the corporation would be the owner and beneficiary of a life insurance policy on the life of the business owner or on the lives of the business owner and his or her spouse, payable on the last-to-die. When the business owner (or the last of the business owner and the spouse) dies, the corporation will receive the life insurance proceeds and an addition to its capital dividend account equal to the excess of the death benefit over the adjusted cost basis of the policy. The corporation can then pay a tax-free capital dividend to the estate to fund the tax liability.

It is important that the gift of the shares to the successor does not happen until after the capital dividend is paid, otherwise, there will be no way to assure the money goes to the estate to pay the tax liability. Direction in the business owner's Will and/or a shareholders' agreement regarding the use of the insurance proceeds and related capital dividend account generated by them is important to ensure the executor causes the corporation to carry out the contemplated transactions.

Life insurance also may be an option to provide funds to inactive family members to ensure an equitable distribution of assets. Corporate-owned insurance on the life of the business owner with the corporation as beneficiary may be used to accomplish estate equalization in a number of ways:

- On the business owner's death, the shares of the corporation could be gifted equally to all his or her children. The corporation would receive the life insurance proceeds and an addition to its capital dividend account equal to the death benefit proceeds less the adjusted cost basis of the policy. The corporation could redeem the shares owned by the inactive children, which would result in the child(ren) receiving a deemed dividend equal to the redemption amount less the paid-up capital of the shares. The deemed dividend could be designated as a tax-free capital dividend. This would allow the insurance proceeds to flow to the inactive children tax-free and the active children would be the remaining shareholders of the corporation. Clear direction in the business owner's Will and/or a shareholders' agreement regarding the shares to be redeemed, the use of the insurance proceeds and the related capital dividend account credit is important.
- A similar corporate-owned life insurance planning option would involve the successor purchasing the shares of the company from the inactive shareholders. As above, the business owner gifts the shares equally between all of his or her children on his or her death. The successor purchases the shares from the inactive shareholders for their fair market value using a promissory note. There should not be a gain or loss on the disposition of the shares by the inactive children, since the adjusted cost base of the shares will equal fair market value as a result of the deemed disposition of those shares on the business owner's death. As with the promissory note method of buy-sell funding discussed in section 7.4.D.ii, after the sale, the life insurance proceeds received by the corporation could be used to pay a tax-free capital dividend to the active shareholders to retire the promissory note paid to the inactive shareholders. The end result is that the children who are active in the business are the only shareholders of the company and the children who are not active in the business have received tax-free proceeds for their share of the company's value. Again, the business owner's Will and/or a shareholders' agreement should address the contemplated transactions to ensure a smooth transition.

7.6 — Life Insurance as a Corporate Investment

A. — Introduction

Often, the profits or surplus cash of an operating company or an investment holding company are retained in the corporation and invested in taxable investments instead of being paid out to the shareholder. This may be because the shareholder does not need the income and/or because the distribution will trigger dividend tax. Particularly where these taxable investments or a portion of them are viewed as never needing to be distributed to the shareholder while living, this may not be the most advantageous way for the corporation to invest its retained profits. An efficient alternative is to reposition retained profits into an exempt life insurance policy.

An exempt life insurance policy provides immediate life insurance protection and cash values can accumulate within the policy on a tax-deferred basis. Exempt policies are not subject to accrual taxation and cash values are only subject to tax if there is a disposition of the policy. Where funds to pay insurance premiums are inside a corporation, an income tax savings may result if the corporation pays the premium directly rather than paying dividends or salary to a shareholder so that the shareholder can pay the premium. Life insurance proceeds are received tax-free by a corporate beneficiary. In addition, private corporations are able to pass out some or all of the life insurance proceeds on a tax-free basis to shareholders as a capital dividend. Taking into account the tax cost of distribution out of the corporation, net estate values provided by life insurance can exceed that provided by taxable investments.

B. — Impact of a corporation owning a cash value life insurance policy

When a corporation owns a cash value life insurance policy, this may have implications for the income taxation of the corporation as well as any provincial capital taxes the corporation may be subject to. Most of these implications result from the fact that for corporate income and capital tax purposes, a life insurance policy is considered a passive asset (i.e. not an asset used in an active business). These issues are discussed in section 6.5.B.

Also, for purposes of determining if the shares of the corporation are qualified small business corporation shares eligible for the capital gains exemption, again, cash value life insurance is considered to be a passive asset. This is discussed in section 3.3.F.

A taxpayer is deemed to have disposed of capital property immediately before death for proceeds equal to the fair market value at the time under subsection 70(5) of the Act. Life insurance owned by the corporation is relevant in determining the fair market value of the deceased's shares immediately before death. Subsection 70(5.3) of the Act provides that for purposes of subsection 70(5), the fair market value, immediately before death of a taxpayer, of any share deemed to have been disposed of as a consequence of death, shall be determined as though the fair market value of any life insurance policy under which the taxpayer was a person whose life was insured is equal to its cash surrender value. This is discussed in greater depth at section 3.3.C.i.

C. — Issues to consider in comparing corporate-owned life insurance to taxable investments

In considering corporate-owned life insurance as compared to an alternative taxable investment, there are many financial considerations as well as post-mortem tax considerations to be made.

i. — Financial considerations

In comparing life insurance to an alternative investment, it is helpful to consider the internal rate of return (IRR) of the policy as compared to the alternative investment. This is the rate of return that would have to be earned on the deposits to the policy in order to provide the same lump-sum death benefit (after tax) as is provided by the policy. It is surprising to some investors that life insurance can have a very competitive IRR as compared to alternative investments. This occurs as a result of the combination of the protection element and the tax-sheltered investment component of life insurance which together deliver the estate values. While decreasing tax rates will have an impact, this may just serve to narrow the gap between life insurance and the alternative investment as opposed to switching their positions.

The need for liquidity should be considered when making these comparisons. Life insurance compares most favourably if the amounts set aside are not required during the insured person's lifetime. If liquidity is required, consideration should be given to how policy values might be accessed (withdrawals, policy loans, collateral loans, etc.) and the tax consequences of doing so, and how this compares to an alternative investment.

Today's universal life insurance products offer a wide range of investment options mirroring investment choices in the external tax-exposed environment. It should be understood that the funds invested in a life insurance policy become part of the insurer's general assets. The policy owners themselves are not investing in the underlying index or fund, rather the insurer is crediting a rate of return based on the underlying index or fund.

ii. — Post-mortem tax considerations in comparing alternatives

In comparing the net estate value arising from a corporate-owned life insurance policy to an alternative corporate-owned investment, a simplistic approach is to assume that the corporation pays the death benefit from the life insurance, or the proceeds from the sale of the alternative investment as a dividend to the estate. Under this assumption, since the life insurance death benefit typically generates a large CDA credit to the corporation, most of the life insurance proceeds are received by the estate tax-free. In contrast, the taxable investment may generate some CDA (from untaxed portion of capital gains arising on the taxable investment) but, typically, most of the dividend will be a taxable dividend. As a result, the tax arising on the distribution of the taxable investment will be considerably higher and, therefore, the estate value will be much lower, even if the value of the investment is comparable to the life insurance death benefit.

However, in reality, it is important to remember that taxes also arise on death as a result of the deemed disposition of the shares, and that often post-mortem planning procedures involving a capital loss carryback (under subsection 164(6) of the Act) and/or "pipeline" procedures, are used to minimize the taxes arising on death.

The capital loss carryback procedure envisions the redemption of a deceased shareholder's shares within one year of death. This redemption generally produces a capital loss and a deemed dividend to the estate, and special rules in subsection 164(6) of the Act allow the estate's capital loss to offset the deceased's capital gain. This technique eliminates the double tax issue on company shares essentially by converting the deceased's capital gain tax into a taxable dividend to the estate. Where CDA exists, the opportunity for non-taxable dividends arises (subject to the stop-loss rules).

Where capital gain tax rates are lower than dividend rates, "pipeline" strategies may be preferred. Pipeline refers to post-mortem planning strategies designed to maintain capital gains treatment at death. A typical pipeline strategy allows subsection 70(5) of the Act to operate at death, triggering a fair market value deemed disposition on the company shares and giving the deceased's estate a cost base on these shares equal to this fair market value amount. Planning is done to create a "pipeline" through which assets, equal to the estate's adjusted cost base (ACB), can be extracted from the corporation on a tax-free basis. Usually this is accomplished by the estate transferring the company's shares to a new holding company in exchange for a promissory note from the new company equal to the ACB of the shares transferred. Company assets can then be flowed out to the estate by paying down this promissory note.

One issue is whether structuring a pipeline strategy runs afoul of the anti-avoidance provisions of subsection 84(2) of the Act. Where applicable, these "dividend-strip" provisions deem the original company to have paid a dividend to the estate. Several CRA rulings were previously granted in specific fact situations involving post-mortem pipeline planning structures, and these rulings allowed pipeline strategies to operate without the application of the "dividend-strip" provisions of subsection 84(2). Recent CRA commentary has drawn the use of pipeline strategies in the investment holding company context into question by suggesting subsection 84(2) may apply to these pipeline structures.

In October 2009, at the APFF conference (2009-0326961C6), the fact pattern under consideration involved the death of a 100 percent shareholder of a company ("ACO") holding only cash assets. A pipeline is undertaken. The question tried to clarify if there is a specific time period which must be awaited before the winding-up occurs and if this is relevant to the application of the dividend stripping provisions. If the waiting period is longer than one year and a dividend pursuant to subsection 84(2) of the Act is deemed to occur, the relieving provision of subsection 164(6) of the Act may not be available to eliminate double tax. In the APFF response, the CRA distinguished the facts of this situation from the prior rulings as follows:

> . . . Subsection 84(2) of the ITA requires that funds or property of a particular corporation must have been distributed or otherwise appropriated, in any manner whatever

> to or for the benefit of the shareholders on the winding-up, discontinuance or reorganization of its business or the particular corporation. In advanced rulings F2002-0154223 and F2005-0142111R3, the individual had ceased to be a shareholder of the particular corporation for a period of at least one year, before the receipt of the funds or the property on the winding-up, discontinuance or reorganization of its business of the particular corporation.
>
> In addition, the situation briefly described in the present question appears to us to defer (sic) from those described in the advanced rulings . . . among others, ACO does not appear to be carrying on a business prior to the death of the taxpayer and all of its assets consist of liquid assets. Consequently, and given that the present situation only summarily describes an hypothetical particular situation, we cannot provide any comments on the potential application of subsection 84(2) of the ITA . . .

This train of thought continued at the 2010 and 2011 Canadian Tax Foundation Conferences (2010-0386001C6, dated November 28, 2010 and 2011-0426371C6, dated November 27, 2011). Furthermore, a ruling's request in a similar circumstance was denied (2010-0389551R3). The fact pattern there involved post-mortem pipeline planning for a deceased 100 percent shareholder of a holding company that has "no investment activities" and that is "currently inactive" with "liquid assets (possibly only cash)." However, the CRA seems prepared to rule favourably on pipeline transactions where there is a delay of one year or more before the corporation's business is discontinued, and a further delay before the note is fully paid (see 2011-0401811R3 and 2012-0464501R3).

A further development regarding the surplus-stripping provisions of subsection 84(2) of the Act is the case of *Canada v. MacDonald*, 2013 FCA 110, [2013] 4 C.T.C. 251, 2013 D.T.C. 5091. Here the Federal Court of Appeal reversed a decision of the Tax Court of Canada (2012 TCC 123, [2012] 4 C.T.C. 2099, 2012 D.T.C. 1145) by applying subsection 84(2) to characterize a taxpayer's proceeds of disposition of certain shares as a dividend. At the time of writing, the taxpayer had not sought leave to appeal to the Supreme Court of Canada. The taxpayer's professional corporation was winding down activities and liquidating assets. He sold the company's shares to a related party for a note, realizing a capital gain. The buyer combined the corporation with a newly formed corporation and used the company's assets to satisfy the note to the taxpayer. The CRA applied subsection 84(2), treating the proceeds as a dividend to the taxpayer.

The transactions effected in the *MacDonald* case are similar to those carried out with pipeline post-mortem planning, except that the initial capital gain in *MacDonald* arose from an actual sale transaction instead of a deemed disposition at death. The initial Tax Court of Canada decision noted the similarity of pipeline planning to avoid double taxation in the post-mortem planning context to that undertaken by Mr. MacDonald in finding that subsection 84(2) did not apply. With the reversal by the Federal Court of Appeal, the use of post-mortem pipeline planning may also be in question.

Due to these evolving pipeline strategy issues, tax practitioners may seek rulings in each fact situation to assure proposed pipeline transactions are not questioned as dividend-strips, or plan to withdraw funds over extended periods of time to avoid being part of a "winding-up, discontinuance, or reorganization" of the business.

Where insurance is in place, reliance on pipeline planning is not as crucial since dividends (indeed tax-free capital dividends) are part of the planning.

When determining the net estate value arising from a life insurance death benefit, a complete analysis should consider the taxes arising on the shares (at death) attributable to the life insurance policy. The cash value of a corporate-owned life insurance policy (immediately before death) is generally included in the valuation of the shares for purposes of the deemed disposition at death rules. Arguably, the capital gains tax arising on the value of the shares attributable to the cash value of the life insurance policy should reduce the net estate value said to arise from the policy. However, there also may be post-mortem planning that can be done to reduce the tax burden on the shares, and stop-loss rules that should be taken into account.

When comparing to an alternative investment, the CDA and refundable dividend tax on hand (RDTOH) balances arising from that alternative investment as well as the impact on the capital gain arising on the shares at death, and any post-mortem planning that may be done, should similarly be taken into account.

7.7 — Retirement Compensation Arrangements

A. — Introduction

It is common practice for public corporations and large private corporations to provide retirement benefits to their employees through some form of pension arrangement. However, an executive's pension income expectations may exceed the maximum benefits available under statutory plans, such as registered pension plans, for any number of reasons. For example, an executive's level of earnings may well exceed the statutory limit used to determine maximum contributions into the plan. Alternatively, an executive may make several changes of employment during a career, the result being that the executive's years of service may be less than the number of years required for a full pension at the time of retirement. In these circumstances, it is common for the employer to provide executives with some form of "supplementary executive retirement plan" (SERP).

A SERP is essentially a promise by the employer to provide supplementary retirement benefits designed to bridge the gap between the retirement benefit provided under statutory plans and the expected retirement benefit based on the executive's final average earnings. A SERP is a particularly valuable incentive for high income executives because the provision of SERP benefits will help to ensure the executive's retirement income is reasonable in relation to pre-retirement income.

The employment agreement may call for a reduced SERP entitlement in the event of early retirement. The employment agreement may also call for a graduated entitlement to SERP benefits over a period of years, and may also terminate eligibility for benefits, for example, in the event of a termination with cause. The agreement between the employer and the executive may be designed in such a way as to balance the needs of the employer with the wishes of the executive. This flexibility in design helps to ensure the incentive works for both parties.

A SERP may be funded or unfunded. An unfunded SERP is essentially an unsecured promise of future benefits. There is no immediate financial commitment on the part of the employer. The expectation is that the employer will fulfill the commitment through internal funding following the time of retirement. This poses a risk to the executive and diminishes the value of the SERP as an incentive from the executive's perspective. Future changes in senior management, in the Board of Directors, in the ownership and control of the employer, or the solvency of the employer could jeopardize an unfunded promise.

Alternatively, the SERP may be funded. A funded SERP provides both the executive and the employer with significant benefits, albeit at a current cost to the employer. Typically, a formal trust is established as the custodian of the SERP assets. The employer makes contributions to the trust in accordance with an actuarial report. The trust invests the contributions, files annual trust tax returns, and eventually distributes the funds to the executive as a retirement income in accordance with the employment agreement.

A SERP funded in this manner provides the executive with a much greater level of security, and this has a significant impact on the value the executive places on the SERP benefit. Benefits provided by a fully funded SERP are secure (to the extent that the SERP assets are not reinvested in shares or debt of the employer or a related company) because the assets are held in a trust and do not form part of the employer's general assets.

From the employer's perspective, a funded SERP may be more cost effective than an unfunded plan in the long term. The SERP is funded from current cash flow, thereby matching the funding with the contribution the executive makes to profits. Employers may also find it increasingly difficult to attract and retain key executives unless they offer funded, as opposed to unfunded, SERPs.

For income tax purposes, a SERP that is funded will generally be taxed as a "retirement compensation arrangement."

B. — Retirement compensation arrangement (RCA)

The retirement compensation arrangement (RCA) rules were introduced in 1986 as an anti-avoidance measure. The rules were intended to prevent the use of unregistered retirement funding arrangements to circumvent the limits on tax-assisted retirement saving. The rules were specifically designed to ensure tax-exempt organizations and other nontaxable employers could not set aside essentially pre-tax retirement funds for employees. However, the application of the rules was not limited to tax-exempt organizations, and the result has been to increase the after-tax cost of supplemental funding arrangements for all organizations, whether the employer is taxable or tax-exempt.

In the past, use of RCAs for owner-managers of private companies had gained some popularity. As in a public company or large private company context, funds can be set aside from the general assets of the company in an RCA to provide SERP benefits. In the owner-manager context, however, the tax-disadvantages of the RCA are particularly poignant because the owner-manager can control the mix between remuneration (including benefits) and dividends in a manner not open to employee executives. Since 2007 with recent decreases in corporate tax rates on active business income, RCAs are even more tax-disadvantaged when compared to simply paying tax and retaining corporate profits at the corporate level. As a result, many of the life insurance-funded structural alternatives discussed at section 7.7.E may simply be for historical reference in the owner-manager context. Instead, strategies involving corporate-owned life insurance as an investment may well be considered using after-tax profits retained by the private corporation and, if need be, may be used as an alternative source of dividend income to a shareholder in retirement years. See discussion at section 7.6.

Also, the CRA has undertaken an audit initiative relating to RCAs. Due to the fact that employers must apply for an RCA account number and send in the RCA trust agreement with this application (Form T733), this is relatively easy to carry out. The CRA has been sending audit inquiry letters to both employers and trustees of RCAs beginning in May of 2010. At the 2011 CLHIA Tax Conference (Q1 referenced as 2011-0398351C6, dated May 20, 2011), the CRA gave a status update of this audit initiative as follows: "The refundable tax creates an enormous liability for the government that must be managed. Reviews of these trust arrangements are identifying issues that are of concern to the CRA, including whether a *bona fide* RCA even exists (versus a salary deferral arrangement for example)."

In addition, the 2012 federal budget introduced "prohibited investment" and "advantage" rules, implemented in Bill C-45 which received Royal Assent on December 14, 2012 (new sections 207.61–207.65 and definitions added to subsection 207.5(1) of the Act), based closely on existing rules for RRSPs, RRIFs and TFSAs applicable to RCAs that have a "specified beneficiary". A specified beneficiary is an individual who has a significant interest (more than 10 percent) in the employer or related entity or a person not at arm's length with that employee. The definition therefore includes owner-managers. A discussion is included below in section 7.7.C.

i. — RCA defined

An RCA is defined in subsection 248(1) as a plan or arrangement under which contributions are made by an employer (or former employer) to another person (referred to as the "custodian") in connection with benefits to be received or enjoyed by any person on, after or in contemplation of any substantial change in the services rendered by the taxpayer, the retirement of the taxpayer or the loss of an office or employment of the taxpayer.

There are a number of plans or arrangements which are specifically excluded from the definition of an RCA, including:

a) a registered pension plan,

a.1) a pooled registered pension plan,

b) a disability or income maintenance insurance plan under a policy with an insurance corporation,

c) a deferred profit sharing plan,

d) an employees profit sharing plan,

e) a registered retirement savings plan,

f) an employee trust,

f.1) an employee life and health trust,

g) a group sickness or accident insurance plan,

h) a supplementary unemployment benefit plan,

i) a vacation pay trust,

j) a plan or arrangement established for the purpose of deferring the salary or wages of a professional athlete,

k) a salary deferral arrangement,

l) a plan or arrangement (other than an athlete's plan) that is maintained primarily for the benefit of non-residents in respect of services rendered outside Canada,

m) an insurance policy, or

n) a prescribed plan or arrangement.

While insurance policies and, by definition, annuities are excluded from the definition of an RCA, special rules apply that have the effect of treating insurance policies held by an employer in certain situations as RCAs (see section 7.7.F).

ii. — Salary deferral arrangements

One of the issues which must be considered is whether the arrangement is an RCA or is in fact a salary deferral arrangement (SDA). An SDA is defined in subsection 248(1) as a plan or arrangement under which an employee has a right to receive an amount at a future date where it is reasonable to consider that one of the main purposes for the creation or existence of the right is to defer tax on salary or wages of the taxpayer for services rendered by the taxpayer in the year or a preceding taxation year. This can include a right that is subject to one or more conditions unless there is a substantial risk that a condition will not be satisfied. Where a particular arrangement is an SDA, the employee will be taxed currently on amounts contributed under subparagraph 6(1)(a)(v) and subsection 6(11) of the Act.

In order to avoid the possible application of the SDA rules, it is essential that the funding of the RCA should be accomplished without a corresponding reduction of the executive's regular compensation. See technical interpretation 2005-0132401I7, dated September 16, 2005. The calculation of the RCA contribution should be based on an actuarial valuation of the contributions required to meet the expected SERP benefits.

At the 2005 APFF Conference (Question 13 indexed as technical interpretation 2005-0149161C6, dated October 7, 2005) the CRA made some general comments about the interaction of the RCA and SDA rules. Of note are the following comments:

> The CRA has recently considered arrangements to fund benefits that are to be provided to employees under the provisions of plans that are identified as unregistered pension or supplementary pension plans. CRA has taken the position that these plans

> will generally be RCAs if the arrangements are pension plans and the benefits being provided are reasonable. Where a plan provides benefits that are not reasonable, the CRA is of the view that a salary deferral arrangement will exist.

At the 2008 CALU Roundtable dated April 29, 2008, the CRA was asked to comment if the SERP plan terms must mirror the underlying RPP terms in designing a "top-up" arrangement for an executive. The CRA reiterated that, in its view, if benefits are unreasonable, the arrangement would be characterized as an SDA and not an RCA and stated that supplementary pension benefits will be considered reasonable if the terms are substantially the same as those of the RPP (but for the defined benefit or money purchase limits) that applies to the same beneficiaries whom the SERP applies. The CRA continued as follows:

> We would not view use of multiple years of service or multiple years of salary rather than actual years of service as appropriate. In addition, any vesting schedule that is less than the vesting schedule under the pension plan may also not be appropriate.

Another theme throughout CRA commentary relates to the underlying theory that RCAs are viewed as pension plans, albeit unregistered pension plans, and the notion that the arrangement should not permit actions that would impair the ability to fund a pension benefit (such as using trust assets to secure a debt unrelated to the pension obligation). In such a case, the arrangement may not be viewed as a "valid" RCA and may potentially be viewed as an SDA or employee benefit plan. See technical interpretation 2003-0000797, dated February 6, 2003. In addition, the CRA now has as another tool, the new penalty tax rules on "prohibited investments" and "advantages" to apply in the RCA context.

The CRA has also stated that if "the plan or arrangement was entered into with the intention of paying, or allowing for discretionary payment of benefits before a termination of employment, where there has been no substantial change in services rendered by the employee, the plan or arrangement may not qualify as an RCA . . ." See technical interpretation 2002-0130701E5.

C. — Taxation of RCAs

Contributions to an RCA are subject to a 50 percent refundable tax under paragraph (a) of the definition of "refundable tax" in subsection 207.5(1) of the Act. For example, if the annual funding requirement is $50,000, the total contribution will be $100,000, of which $50,000 will be paid into the RCA trust and $50,000 will be withheld by the employer and remitted to the CRA as a refundable tax. Under paragraph 153(1)(p) of the Act, the refundable tax withheld by the employer must be remitted by the fifteenth day of the month following the month the contribution is made to the RCA trust.

The total contribution, that is, the actual payment made by the employer to the RCA trust plus the amount withheld and remitted as a refundable tax, is deductible by the employer for income tax purposes under paragraph 20(1)(r) of the Act. The deduction is restricted to *bona fide* contributions for the benefit of employees. Contributions must be reasonable in accordance with section 67 and a deduction under paragraph 20(1)(r) of the Act will be denied to the extent that the contribution exceeds a reasonable amount. In technical interpretation 2005-0132401I7, the CRA stated that it is always a question of fact whether a contribution to an RCA is reasonable. It further stated that "Contributions that are clearly supported by either an actuarial valuation or the use of some formula-based calculation may be more justifiable; however reasonability must be weighed taking into account all the relevant factors." At the 1998 CALU CRA Roundtable, the CRA stated in response to Question 1 that reasonableness for these purposes is determined in the same manner as reasonable salaries and bonuses. The deduction will be denied where the contribution is made as part of a series of contributions and refunds. For example, a deduction may be denied where a contribution is made at the year end by an employer that will be refunded in the next year where the contribution is made to obtain a deduction rather than to provide for retirement benefits.

Paragraph 8(1)(m.2) of the Act allows a deduction in respect of qualifying employee contributions made to an RCA where the custodian of the RCA is resident in Canada. Qualifying contributions consist of contributions that the employee is required by the terms of his or her office or employment to make. However, no deduction is available if the employee's contributions to the plan in the year exceed the employer contributions in respect of the employee.

It is important to note that the CRA has specifically commented on the reasonableness of employee contributions as follows, also in technical interpretation 2005-0132401I7:

> The provision (8(1)(m.2)) was not intended to allow the deduction of amounts which were unreasonable in the circumstances and which would be considered unreasonable if paid in full by any employer to the RCA. In other words, it is our opinion that an employer should not be permitted to contribute otherwise unreasonable amounts to an RCA by first paying part of the contribution to an employee and thereafter having the employee pay them to the RCA.

The CRA stated in technical interpretation 9707227, dated April 15, 1997, that where a sole shareholder of a corporation enters into an agreement with his or her particular corporation under which the shareholder is required to contribute to an RCA that has been set up for his or her benefit, contributions made by the shareholder would not be considered to result from the shareholder's terms of employment. Their view is that, generally, a shareholder would be responsible for setting his or her own terms of employment. Consequently, contributions by the shareholder to the RCA would not be deductible under paragraph 8(1)(m.2) of the Act because the conditions for deductibility would generally not be met.

An RCA is exempt from tax under Part I pursuant to paragraph 149(1)(q.1) of the Act. However, the custodian of an RCA trust is liable to pay a special refundable tax under Part XI.3.

An RCA is an *inter vivos* trust for income tax purposes pursuant to subsection 207.5(1) of the Act. Under paragraph (b) of the definition of "refundable tax" in subsection 207.5(1), income earned within an RCA is subject to a 50 percent refundable tax. The income of the trust includes interest income, dividend income (the gross-up and tax credit mechanisms do not apply to an RCA trust), and realized capital gains, less capital losses. It is the actual capital gain or loss that is recognized for the purposes of the refundable tax. There is no tax-free portion of capital gains, and capital losses are deductible against other income earned by the trust.

Continuing the previous example, if the RCA trust earns $5,000 of interest, dividends and realized capital gains net of capital losses, the refundable tax liability for the year would be $2,500 (50 percent of $5,000).

Under subsection 207.7(3) of the Act, the filing of the RCA trust tax return and remittance of the refundable tax liability is due 90 days following the year end of the RCA trust, which is December 31 in accordance with the rules for *inter vivos* trusts.

The refundable tax is refunded to the RCA trust at the rate of $1 for every $2 paid out in benefits to the beneficiary. This is provided for under paragraph (c) of the definition of "refundable tax" in subsection 207.5(1). For example, an $80,000 payment of retirement benefits from the RCA trust would generate a refund of refundable tax to the RCA trust of $40,000 (50 percent of $80,000).

The payment to the executive is subject to withholding at source under paragraph 153(1)(q) of the Act. The gross payment is included in the executive's income in the year of receipt under paragraphs 56(1)(x) or (z) of the Act, and is taxed accordingly.

If the SERP obligation is fully satisfied, for example in the event of the death of the executive, and there are assets remaining in the RCA trust and/or a refundable tax balance, the remaining RCA assets may be distributed to the employer as residual beneficiary of the trust, the refundable tax balance can be recovered by way of election under subsection 207.5(2) of the Act, and the RCA trust wound up in favour of the employer. Any amounts distributed to the employer are taxable under paragraph 12(1)(n.3) of the Act in the year received.

In short, (i) contributions to an RCA and income earned by an RCA are subject to a 50 percent tax that is refundable as benefits are paid from the RCA, (ii) contributions are deductible by the employer, and (iii) there are no tax consequences to the executive until retirement payments are received from the RCA trust.

While the contributions are deductible for income tax purposes, the corporate tax rate typically will be less than 50 percent, causing a net cost to the employer above what would be incurred for contributions to an unfunded SERP. The key, then, is to ensure that one or both parties receive a benefit which offsets or outweighs the additional cost associated with funding the SERP.

From the perspective of the executive, the benefit is the financial guarantee of having the funds available for retirement. The employer benefits because the obligation is funded from current cash flow while the executive is contributing to profits and, hopefully, there is the added benefit of ensuring the executive's commitment to the organization throughout his or her career.

Measures initially announced with the 2012 federal budget and implemented in Bill C-45, which received Royal Assent on December 14, 2012, introduce a penalty tax regime on "prohibited investments" and "advantages" for RCAs. These new measures are modeled after similar provisions currently applicable to RRSPs, RRIFs and TFSAs. A 50 percent tax (section 207.61) on the fair market value of a "prohibited investment" and a 100 percent tax (section 207.62) on the fair market value of an "advantage" are levied on RCA custodians. This penalty tax regime for RCAs is effective after March 28, 2012.

A "specified beneficiary" is defined as a person who has an interest or right in relation to an RCA and has or had a "significant interest" in the employer in respect of the RCA. A "significant interest" in the employer is a 10 percent or more interest (held directly or indirectly, either alone or with non-arm's length persons) in a corporation, partnership or trust. RCA specified beneficiaries are jointly and severally liable for such taxes to the extent they "participated in, assented to or acquiesced in the making of" transactions or events resulting in the liability.

A "prohibited investment" generally includes a debt of a specified beneficiary and debt or shares or rights to debt or shares of a corporation or entity that a specified beneficiary has a significant interest in. The term also encompasses shares or debt of a person or partnership that does not deal at arm's length with, or is affiliated with, the specified beneficiary.

An "advantage" includes:

- any benefit, loan or debt that is conditional on the existence of the RCA unless on arm's length terms and conditions;
- any increase in the fair market value of property under the arrangement if attributable to a transaction or event that would not have occurred in a normal commercial or investment context between arm's length parties;
- income and capital gains in respect of prohibited investments;
- any "RCA strip" — defined as a reduction in the fair market value of RCA property, one of the main purposes of which is to enable a specified beneficiary (or person or partnership who does not deal at arm's length with the specified beneficiary) to obtain a benefit in respect of RCA property.

RCAs for employees with more than a 10 percent interest in the employer (or related to someone with such an interest) are affected. Custodians of these RCAs should examine if they hold any prohibited investments or have any transactions that constitute advantages. Front-end leveraged RCAs (see section 7.7.E.iv below) are directly impacted by these new measures, essentially eliminating planning opportunities with these structures.

D. — SERP investment options

Once the decision is made to establish a funded SERP for one or more key executives, the next decision is how to invest the SERP assets. Provided that provincial pension legislation is not applicable, there are no statutory limitations on the type of investments that may be made under a SERP, although the trust document should provide a description of the investment powers of the custodian. The investments may include, for example, conventional investments such as money market instruments, stocks, bonds, mutual funds and insurance company segregated funds. Refundable tax is payable in respect of income or realized capital gains resulting from these investments. There is no preferential tax treatment on dividends or capital gains at the RCA trust level. The level of investment returns each year and the taxation of these returns can impact the required level of future contributions to the SERP. Where there are fewer years to retirement, such investments may be the most effective method of funding an RCA promise.

Since income earned in the RCA trust is subject to the 50 percent refundable tax each year and where there is a significant amount of time until retirement, it is often desirable to consider nontraditional investments that produce attractive investment returns but that are tax-deferred. One such investment is exempt life insurance. A number of strategies have developed using exempt life insurance as the investment vehicle for funded SERPs.

One note of caution when dealing with RCAs that have a significant beneficiary. Such RCAs are subject to the "prohibited investment" and "advantage" rules. In the context of an RCA subject to these rules holding life insurance, the CRA made the following comment at the 2013 CLHIA CRA Roundtable (technical interpretation 2013-0481421C6, dated May 17, 2013):

> It is not clear under what circumstances an RCA would be holding a life insurance policy that provides for more than a nominal death benefit. The holding of such a life insurance policy would appear to have little to do with providing for benefits under the RCA in relation to retirement, a loss of an office or employment, or a substantial change in services rendered. The holding of such a life insurance policy by the RCA could give rise to an advantage, and therefore, advantage tax under section 207.62 of the Act.

Perhaps the use of the split dollar concept discussed at section 7.7.E.iii below may work to avoid this problem? A note of caution should be raised in respect of this too. Comments in the 2012 federal budget documents made a reference to "arrangements (that) use insurance products to allocate costs to the arrangement for benefits that arise outside the arrangement." The Department of Finance has stated that this refers to split dollar arrangements where the RCA owns the cash surrender value of the policy and another party owns the death benefit where the death benefit owner is not properly funding the related mortality costs. Where this occurs in respect of an RCA with a specified beneficiary there could be an "advantage" to which the 100 percent special tax would apply.

Unfortunately, there is no definitive commentary or guidance on what is a fair market value sharing of costs and benefits under split dollar arrangements generally. See section 8.3 for a more detailed discussion.

Any of the below discussions should be considered in light of the "prohibited investment" and "advantage" rules where the RCA has a specified beneficiary.

E. — Life insurance funded SERP strategies

i. — Life insured SERP strategy

Investing the SERP assets in an exempt life insurance policy provides a significant advantage over traditional investments. Under the life insured SERP strategy, an exempt life insurance policy is purchased by the RCA trust on the life of the executive (or on the joint lives of the executive and his or her spouse). The insurance policy is funded using the contributions made to the RCA trust by the employer.

At the time of retirement, the RCA trust funds the retirement benefits for the executive using a combination of cash withdrawals from the insurance policy and refunds from the refundable tax account. Generally, as cash withdrawals are made, the death benefit of the policy is reduced and eventually the policy will lapse.

Following the death of the executive (and the executive's spouse in the case of a joint life policy), any life insurance proceeds payable are received tax-free by the RCA trust and may be used to fund survivor benefits or, if there is no further funding obligation, the trust may be wound up and the RCA trust assets distributed to the employer as residual beneficiary, providing a means of partial cost recovery for the employer.

The key advantage of this strategy is the opportunity for tax-sheltered wealth accumulation within the exempt life insurance policy. Assuming the arrangement is established a number of years prior to the executive's retirement, the accumulation within the insurance policy can outstrip alternative investment vehicles earning similar returns even though the cost of insurance is borne by the RCA trust. As a result, the contributions made by the employer may be less than would otherwise be the case if the RCA assets are invested solely in traditional investments.

The tax effectiveness of this strategy is, however, reduced because a partial cash withdrawal from the insurance policy results in a partial disposition for tax purposes (see section 3.2.G.ii). The resulting policy gain is included in the income of the RCA trust and is subject to the 50 percent refundable tax liability.

Any proceeds from life insurance received by the RCA trust as a consequence of death are tax-free. However, the distribution of the proceeds from the RCA trust are taxable to the recipient. In effect, this strategy converts what would otherwise be tax-free income (insurance proceeds) into taxable income (a distribution from an RCA), which is not particularly efficient from a tax planning perspective.

ii. — Leveraged life insured SERP strategy

As a partial solution to the tax inefficiencies noted above under the life insured SERP strategy, a variation has developed using leveraging techniques to access the accumulated values within the exempt life insurance policy.

Under the leveraged life insured SERP strategy, an exempt life insurance policy is purchased by the RCA trust on the life of the executive (or on the joint lives of the executive and his or her spouse).

The insurance policy is funded using the contributions made to the RCA trust by the employer. At the time of retirement, the RCA trust funds the retirement benefits for the executive using a combination of tax-free bank loans (obtained from a lending institution using the life insurance policy as collateral security) and refunds from the refundable tax account.

Following the death of the executive (and the executive's spouse in the case of a joint life policy), the life insurance proceeds are received tax-free by the RCA trust and may be used to repay the bank loan and to fund survivor benefits or, if there is no further funding obligation, the trust may be wound up and the RCA trust assets distributed to the employer as residual beneficiary, providing a means of partial cost recovery for the employer.

Typically, the RCA trust would prefer to capitalize the interest costs to the loan because the interest expense would generally be non-deductible. Interest on funds borrowed by the RCA trust under this strategy would not meet the criteria for deductibility under paragraph 20(1)(c) of the Act even if paid because the interest would not relate to funds borrowed for the purpose of earning income from business or property. If this cannot be arranged with the lending institution, it will be necessary to increase the borrowing to fund the retirement payments and the interest expense.

The key advantage of this strategy is the opportunity for tax-sheltered wealth accumulation within the exempt life insurance policy: the investment portion of the insurance policy remains intact and continues to accumulate on a tax-sheltered basis until the policy matures at the time of death of the life insured. Also, bank loans do not result in income in the RCA trust subject to the 50 percent refundable tax. As a result, the contributions made by the employer may be less than would otherwise be required if the RCA assets are invested in traditional investments. However, due to margins required by lenders, one significant downside when compared to utilizing partial surrenders (withdrawals) is that only a portion of the cash value can be accessed to provide retirement benefits impacting the amount of retirement income which may be produced under the leveraged life insured SERP strategy. In general, a life insured SERP strategy utilizing withdrawals will result in higher retirement income benefits, while a leveraged life insured SERP strategy will result in a higher net value at death.

Leveraging involves a number of financial and tax risks (see Chapter 4). The financial risks relate to the assumptions used in preparing an illustration of the leveraged life insured SERP strategy and how closely the actual long-term results correspond to the assumptions used in preparing the illustration. For example, the future investment performance of the life insurance policy is not guaranteed, the spread in interest rates between the credited rate within the insurance policy and the rate charged on the bank loan is not guaranteed, the executive may live longer than assumed and lending institutions may already be fully committed at the time the RCA trust approaches the lender for the bank loans.

In addition, if the insurance policy is surrendered prior to the death of the life insured, for example, to repay the bank if the loan is ever called by the bank, it is possible that most if not all of the cash surrender proceeds would be paid to the bank, leaving the RCA trust with a significant tax liability (albeit a refundable tax liability), no assets to continue funding the retirement income obligation (aside from the balance in the refundable tax account), and no death benefit with which to provide any similar benefits or partial cost recovery to the employer. This emphasizes the need to be conservative in the setting of the assumptions when illustrating this particular strategy and managing the structure following implementation.

From a tax perspective, the risks include possible future changes to the current income tax laws which could eliminate the benefits generally associated with leveraged life insurance strategies (including the leveraged life insured SERP strategy), a determination that the bank loan is in fact a policy loan (resulting in a partial disposition for tax purposes and causing a policy gain subject to the 50 percent refundable tax), because of the possible application of the general anti-avoidance rule under subsection 245(2) of the Act. For a discussion of these issues see section 4.2.B.

It is unlikely the bank loan would be determined to be a policy loan because the loan is not being made by the insurer and the loan undergoes normal bank underwriting. Paragraph (f) of the definition of "disposition" in subsection 148(9) of the Act specifically excludes a collateral assignment of a life insurance policy to a lending institution from the definition of a disposition, and a bank loan may be called by the lender whereas a policy loan has no terms of repayment.

If the structure were challenged under the general anti-avoidance rule because leveraging results in a tax benefit compared with a partial withdrawal from the insurance policy, many of the arguments mentioned in the preceding paragraph would apply.

As with any leveraging strategy using any financial instrument, the financial and tax risks can be reduced or eliminated through proper structure and conservative assumptions.

The proceeds from the life insurance policy under this strategy as a consequence of death are tax-free to the RCA trust, but the proceeds distributed from the RCA trust to other beneficiaries or to the employer as a residual beneficiary are taxable.

iii. — Split-dollar life insured SERP strategy

A further enhancement to either the leveraged or non-leveraged life insured SERP strategies involves the use of split-dollar insurance to maximize the overall performance associated with the use of exempt life insurance for SERPs. For a detailed discussion of split-dollar insurance, see Chapter 8.

Under the split-dollar leveraged life insured SERP strategy, an exempt life insurance policy is initially purchased by the employer on the life of the executive (or on the joint lives of the executive and his or her spouse). The cash value interest in the policy is then transferred to the RCA trust subject to a split-dollar agreement between the employer and the trust. Alternatively the policy may be purchased jointly by the employer and the RCA trust from inception.

Under the terms of the split-dollar agreement, the employer would own the pure insurance coverage and pay a reasonable share of the premium deposits for this coverage, and the RCA trust would own and fund the investment portion of the policy. The portion of the premium deposits paid by the employer would not represent a contribution to the RCA trust and would not be deductible for tax purposes. The investment portion of the policy is funded using the contributions made to the RCA trust by the employer.

At the time of retirement, the RCA trust funds the retirement benefits for the executive by using a combination of withdrawals or tax-free bank loans (obtained from a lending institution using the life insurance policy as collateral security) and refunds from the refundable tax account.

An interesting variation is for the employer to fund the retirement benefits with a bank loan using the RCA trust assets (i.e., the insurance policy cash value owned by the RCA trust) as security. In this case, the retirement payments made by the employer to the executive and the interest expense on the loan should be deductible for income tax purposes if the employer has sufficient net income for tax purposes.

Following the death of the executive (and the executive's spouse in the case of a joint life policy), the face amount of the life insurance death benefit is received tax-free by the employer and the remaining life insurance proceeds, representing the investment portion of the policy, are received tax-free by the RCA trust.

If the leveraging occurs within the RCA trust, the life insurance proceeds received by the RCA trust may be used to repay the bank loan and to fund survivor benefits or, if there is no further funding obligation, the trust may be wound up and the RCA trust assets distributed to the employer as residual beneficiary, again providing a means of partial cost recovery for the employer.

Alternatively, if the leveraging occurs at the employer level, the life insurance proceeds received by the employer may be used to repay the bank loan, and the life insurance proceeds received by the RCA trust may be used to fund survivor benefits or, if there is no further funding obligation, the trust may be wound up and the RCA trust assets distributed to the employer as residual beneficiary. A drawback to having the employer leverage the policy is that all of the RCA trust assets will be subject to tax on distribution. If instead the leveraging occurs within the RCA trust, some of the life insurance proceeds will be used to repay the bank loan and therefore only the life insurance proceeds received by the RCA trust in excess of the bank loan will be subject to tax on distribution.

The key advantages of this strategy are the opportunity for tax-sheltered wealth accumulation within the exempt life insurance policy and tax efficient access to the values accumulated within the exempt insurance policy. In addition, however, this strategy ensures that the pure insurance death benefit retains its tax-free nature as it is received directly by the employer and does not pass through the RCA trust. Further, to the extent the employer funds the retirement obligation, the employer may deduct the amount of the payment.

As discussed in section 6.2, life insurance proceeds received by a private corporation as a consequence of death are credited to the corporation's capital dividend account to the extent the proceeds exceed the adjusted cost basis to the corporation of its interest in the insurance policy immediately before death (see paragraph (d) of the definition of "capital dividend account" in subsection 89(1)). Tax-free capital dividends may be elected to be paid to the shareholders of the corporation pursuant to subsection 83(2). This is an additional benefit related to corporate-owned life insurance in private corporation situations but is not available to public corporations.

In addition to the financial and tax risks described under the leveraged life insured SERP strategy above, there is a further tax risk associated with the split-dollar arrangement. Under subsection 207.6(2), a life insurance policy purchased by an employer may be deemed to be subject property of an RCA trust under subsection 207.6(1) if the employer is obliged to provide retirement benefits to the executive and the employer acquires an interest in a life insurance policy that may reasonably be considered to be acquired to fund, in whole or in part, those benefits. These deeming rules are discussed in section 7.7.F.

Under a split-dollar arrangement, the employer and the RCA trust acquire an interest in an insurance policy. The interest in the insurance policy purchased by the RCA trust is intended to fund SERP retirement benefits to the executive. The issue is whether the pure insurance portion of the insurance policy owned by the employer will be deemed to be subject property of an RCA under the deeming rules.

If the pure insurance portion of the insurance policy owned by the employer is deemed to be subject property of an RCA, the employer's share of the premiums would be subject to the 50 percent refundable tax. As a result, an amount equal to the employer's share of the premium deposits would have to be remitted as refundable tax. While the total payment would be deductible as a contribution to an RCA under paragraph 20(1)(r), the proceeds received by the employer at the time of death would be treated as a taxable distribution from the RCA trust, which defeats the additional benefits associated with this strategy.

It is arguable that the pure insurance coverage owned by the employer under a split-dollar arrangement should not be considered subject property of an RCA. Under this strategy, a formal RCA trust is established for the purpose of accumulating assets for funding the retirement income obligation of the employer to the executive. The pure insurance portion of the life insurance policy purchased by the employer should not be construed as the funding vehicle for these benefits. In addition, note that the deeming provision which creates the RCA trust, subsection 207.6(1), refers to subject property not otherwise held by a formal trust. As a formal trust is created under this strategy, this would seem to exclude the portion of the insurance policy held by the employer from being subject property of an RCA. However, this risk must be considered when evaluating this strategy.

As a result of the benefits provided under this strategy, the contributions made by the employer may be less than would otherwise be required if the RCA assets are invested in traditional investments or in either of the life insured SERP strategies outlined above.

iv. — Front end leveraged RCA (FELRCA)

FELRCAs were the main target of the "prohibited investment" and "advantage" penalty tax regime applicable after March 28, 2012 (discussed at section 7.7.C). The FELRCA was designed to accomplish two objectives: to provide for retirement income of an owner-manager, as well as to provide financing for the business. Since any owner-manager is by definition a "specified beneficiary" of an RCA set up on the owner-manager's behalf, loans from such an RCA to the business are "prohibited investments" and thereby subject to the 50 percent penalty tax. This penalty regime essentially eliminates planning opportunities using FELRCAs.

Limited grandfathering provisions for existing FELRCAs were included in the penalty tax measures. A prohibited investment already held by an RCA before March 29, 2012 will not be subject to the 50 percent tax on prohibited investments. Amendments to the terms of a promissory note or similar debt obligation to provide for commercially reasonable payments of principal or interest are deemed not to be a disposition or acquisition of that note or obligation and therefore not the acquisition of a prohibited investment after March 28, 2012.

The advantage rules will not apply in relation to property of an RCA acquired before March 29, 2012 if the amount of the advantage is included in the income of a beneficiary or if commercially reasonable payments of principal and interest are made at least annually after 2012 on a promissory note or similar debt obligation provided that no RCA strip occurs thereafter. Amendments to the terms of a promissory note or similar debt to provide for commercially reasonable payments of principal and interest are deemed not to give rise to a disposition of the note or obligation.

Since FELRCAs are directly impacted by the "prohibited investment" and "advantage" rules, the following discussion is included for historical reference only.

A FELRCA typically had the following structure:

1. Opco would carry out a compensation review for the owner-manager and, with the assistance of an independent actuarial firm, determine a reasonable retirement income expectation and the funding level required today to provide such a benefit via an RCA (in combination with any other registered pension plan that may be in place through the employer). Opco would contribute to the RCA the lesser of the actuarially determined amount and the amount that would have been bonused to the executive to keep corporate earnings below the small business limit. The contributions and formula are detailed in a supplemental executive retirement pension agreement (SERP) entered into between Opco and the owner-manager.

2. Opco withholds and remits to the CRA 50 percent of the contribution in respect of refundable tax.

3. The RCA uses the remaining contribution to purchase a life insurance policy. The policy is owned by the RCA with the RCA as beneficiary (or on a split-dollar basis with the employer corporation).

4. The RCA borrows up to 90 percent of the full original contribution (including the refundable tax portion) from a bank (the "loan amount"). Interest on the loan amount is paid monthly. The principal of the loan amount will generally remain outstanding for a period of time but must be repaid before any retirement income payments commence from the RCA. The security for this loan will be (i) the RCA's interest in the life insurance policy, (ii) any refundable tax balance, and (iii) any other assets of the RCA (including the promissory note referred to in the following paragraph). To secure the promissory note, the lender would generally take a general security agreement ("GSA") over the assets of the trust. Additional collateral security in the form of personal or corporate guarantees may also be required.

5. The RCA lends the loan amount to Opco or to a related company of Opco in exchange for a demand promissory note. Interest on the promissory note is payable monthly. Interest is set at a rate marginally higher than the interest on the loan from the bank to the RCA. The RCA provides a GSA (which would include the demand promissory note) to the bank as collateral security for the prior loan (at step 4).

6. It is expected that the loan will be repaid prior to the time that retirement benefits will commence. The life insurance policy cash values should be sufficient to provide retirement benefits. Policy cash values will most likely be accessed by withdrawals as opposed to further leveraging.

7. If death occurs prior to repayment of the loan, the life insurance policy death benefit would be used to repay the principal and interest owing to the bank. Any excess proceeds would be used to satisfy any remaining obligations to the retiree or his/her beneficiaries. If death occurs after repayment of the loan, the proceeds would be used to satisfy the obligation to the retiree or his/her beneficiaries or be paid to the company as a residual beneficiary of the trust. Although received tax-free by the RCA trust, any life insurance proceeds distributed by the trust would be taxable to the recipient.

In addition to the financial risks associated with leveraging and the complexity of the transactions, the tax risks must be considered. The CRA has indicated in reply to Question 12 at the APFF CRA roundtable dated October 7, 2005, in technical interpretation 2005-0132401I7, both discussed above, and in technical interpretation 2005-0149321E5, dated April 27, 2006 that they may question the validity of the RCA in circumstances where amounts paid to an RCA are returned in one form or another to the employer. (Now, with the penalty tax regime targeted specifically at FELRCAs, these other tax risks seem quaint by comparison.)

F. — The RCA deeming rules

An interest in a corporate-owned life insurance policy (including annuity contracts and segregated funds) may, in certain circumstances, be deemed to be subject property of an RCA. This can result in severe and, in many cases, unintended tax implications for the employer.

Subsection 207.6(2) provides special rules where an interest in a life insurance policy, including an annuity or segregated fund, is acquired to fund retirement benefits. Where by virtue of a plan or arrangement an employer is obliged to provide benefits to any person on, after, or in contemplation of any substantial change in the services rendered by a taxpayer, the retirement of a taxpayer or the loss of an office or employment of a taxpayer, and the employer acquires an interest in a life insurance policy that may reasonably be considered to be acquired to fund, in whole or in part, those benefits, the arrangement is deemed to be an RCA and special rules apply.

Under the special rules in subsection 207.6(2), the employer is deemed to be the custodian of an RCA. (In the absence of this special rule, the life insurance company as issuer of the policy would be the custodian since the company is the person to whom the contribution, that is, the premium for the policy, is paid. CRA technical interpretation 2003-046131E5, dated January 14, 2004 confirms that the insurer would not be viewed as a custodian when it simply accepts premium payments under a policy which has been deemed to be an RCA). In addition, the life insurance policy is deemed to be subject property of an RCA, an amount equal to twice the amount of any premium paid in respect of the interest in the life insurance policy is deemed to be a contribution to the RCA, and any payment received in respect of the interest and any amount received as a refund of refundable tax is deemed to be an amount received out of or under the RCA by the recipient.

If the arrangement is deemed to be an RCA under subsection 207.6(2), the employer will be required to withhold and remit the 50 percent refundable tax based on twice the amount of the insurance premium, the employer will receive a tax deduction for twice the amount of the insurance premium, refunds from the refundable tax account will be included in the income of the recipient, and the full amount of the death benefit received by the employer will be taxable to the employer as a distribution from an RCA.

Subsection 207.6(2) provides a relieving rule under which the RCA deeming rules will only apply in respect of an arrangement which is not otherwise an RCA or is not otherwise excluded from being an RCA by virtue of paragraphs (a) to (l) and (n) in the definition of "retirement compensation arrangement" in subsection 248(1). This view is confirmed in CRA technical interpretation 9312927, dated May 10, 1993. Thus, if an interest in a life insurance policy has been purchased by an RCA trust which meets the definition of a "retirement compensation arrangement" under subsection 248(1), the RCA deeming rules under subsection 207.6(2) should not apply. This is an important exclusion if the arrangement has been structured under the split-dollar life insured SERP strategy described previously.

Corporations acquire life insurance policies on their executives and, in the case of private corporations, on their shareholders for a variety of reasons. The purpose of the insurance is typically to provide working capital (e.g., keyperson insurance protection, business loan protection, and so forth) or funding the buy/sell provisions under a shareholders' agreement in the event of death. See section 4.3.C for a specific discussion of the deemed RCA rules in the context of leveraged life insurance to pay a bonus by a corporation. In most cases, the RCA deeming rules under subsection 207.6(2) will not be a concern. However, if the insurance policy is owned and funded by the employer, the employer has an obligation to provide SERP benefits to an employee and it is reasonable to consider that the insurance policy was acquired to fund, in whole or in part, those benefits, the RCA deeming rules may apply. In these situations, the tax implications are, as described previously, severe. Further, one of the main motivations for establishing a SERP (secure creditor protected funding) will not be achieved since the policy will simply be a corporate asset available to the general creditors of the corporation.

A typical example might be where the employer purchases a keyperson insurance policy on the life of a key executive, the policy is designed to provide cash values, and the employer enters into an agreement with the executive to provide retirement benefits from the cash values in the event the executive lives to retirement. In this case, the RCA deeming rules will apply, as all of the criteria under subsection 207.6(2) are met.

If there is no obligation on the part of the employer to provide SERP benefits to an employee (or to an owner-manager of a private corporation in his/her capacity as an employee), the acquisition of an insurance policy, with or without cash values, should not trigger the RCA deeming rules.

Question 10 at the 2012 CALU CRA Roundtable (2012-0435771C6) explored the meaning of the phrase "may reasonably be considered to be acquired to fund, in whole or in part." The CRA listed the following factors it would consider in determining whether subsection 207.6(2) of the Act would apply to deem a life insurance policy held in connection with an employee retirement plan to be the subject property of an RCA:

- the identity of the employees whose lives are insured as compared to those to be provided benefits under the plan;
- the timing of the acquisition of the life insurance and the setting up of the plan;
- the extent of the monetary coverage under the insurance as contrasted with the value of the benefits under the plan; and
- reasons (other than the existence of the plan) for the employer's purchase of insurance. For example, we have previously opined that the RCA deeming rule may not necessarily apply to: (i) "key man" insurance acquired as coverage for losses or damages the employer might suffer on the death of an employee; and (ii) life insurance policies acquired solely to pay benefits in the event of death of an employee.

The test is not only applied at the time of acquisition of a policy. The CRA states that "the RCA deeming rule can apply even where the life insurance policy is acquired before the retirement benefits become provided." The context of the question was where a life insurance policy is acquired at a particular time and at a subsequent time the employer becomes legally obligated to pay retirement benefits to an employee (Question 10 2012 CALU CRA Roundtable).

Ultimately it is a question of fact in each circumstance. The CRA has stated that the policy and all relevant documentation would have to be reviewed to determine if that interest may reasonably be considered to be acquired to fund retirement benefits.

It should be noted that annuity contracts are included in the definition of a "life insurance policy" under the Act, the purchase of which can give rise to deemed RCA treatment (2007-024465, APFF Conference Q14). However, where an annuity is purchased in settlement of obligations under an existing RCA, the deemed RCA rules would not apply. The annuity purchase price would be viewed as a distribution out of the RCA and taxable to the employee.

Similarly, Question 10 at the 2012 CALU CRA Roundtable also confirmed that, a segregated fund policy is also defined as a "life insurance policy" under the Act and could be deemed to be the subject property of an RCA under subsection 207.6(2).

G. — Winding up an RCA

With continued decreases in corporate tax rates, some owner-managed businesses even before the enactment of the prohibited investment and advantage rules were discontinuing or winding-up existing RCAs set up previously. The question of whether an RCA can be wound up is a legal question requiring a review of the RCA trust agreement and RCA Plan agreement in each case. Depending upon the terms of the trust and plan, winding up the RCA prior to retirement may or may not be possible.

In technical interpretation 2004-006787, dated September 7, 2004, the CRA was asked to consider the early cessation of an RCA "due to evolving factors" and confirm if this could affect the arrangement's status as an RCA. The CRA responded as follows:

> Where a plan or arrangement is, in fact, established with a legitimate intent to fund retirement benefits, and a decision is subsequently made to terminate the plan or arrangement early, due to factors unforeseen at the outset (such as corporate takeover or unexpectedly high plan administration and funding expenses), in our view, the plan or arrangement should not generally cease to be an RCA due to the premature termination.

It was also confirmed that where it is the case that the plan was an RCA up to and at the time of termination, all the normal tax rules relating to RCA treatment would apply. This would include the ability to receive a refundable tax refund under subsection 207.7(2) of the Act.

At the 2009 APFF Conference, the CRA was asked to confirm that this was still its position. Although each case is a question of fact, the CRA did confirm that technical interpretation 2004-006787 "generally represents the position of the CRA" and stated that "several actual cases of a winding-up of a retirement compensation arrangement have been brought to the attention of the CRA and each case is studied on its own merit."

Where it is possible, and life insurance funding is in place, the following are relevant considerations and tax consequences of winding up an RCA: the trustee may wish to transfer the life insurance policy to the RCA beneficiary. Where a life insurance policy is transferred, the trust would have a disposition of the policy. Section 107.2 of the Act provides that where property of an RCA trust is distributed to a beneficiary in satisfaction of all or any part of the beneficiary's interest in the trust, this disposition would occur at fair market value. It should be noted that the provisions of subsection 148(7) would not apply to this transfer. A taxable policy gain may arise to the extent that the fair market value exceeds the adjusted cost basis of the policy. Any such income would be subject to refundable tax. However, a refund of refundable tax would also arise in respect of the distribution from the trust. This tax treatment was confirmed in technical interpretation 2013-0481421C6, dated May 17, 2013.

On the distribution of a life insurance policy to the RCA beneficiary, the beneficiary would have to include the fair market value of the policy distributed in income pursuant to paragraph 56(1)(x). This treatment was confirmed by the CRA in technical interpretations 9532467, dated February 21, 1996 and 2000-0062057, dated January 9, 2001. The fair market value of a life insurance policy is a question of fact. Such factors as: cash surrender value; policy loan value; face amount; the state of health of the life insured and his/her life expectancy; conversion privileges; other terms, such as term riders, double indemnity provisions; and the replacement value of the policy have all been cited as potential bases of valuation of a life insurance policy. (See section 3.3.A for further discussion of factors relating to the fair market value of a life insurance policy.) In this context it would be wise for the RCA trustee to seek the views of a valuation professional in determining the fair market value amount. Where an RCA holds an interest in a life insurance policy under a split-dollar arrangement, it would be the fair market value of that interest on distribution to the RCA trust beneficiary that would be relevant. Normally, the cash surrender value of the policy would be held by the RCA trust and not the death benefit portion of the policy so valuation issues may not be as big a concern on such a transfer.

As well, establishing the proper fair market value on such a transfer would also be relevant in ensuring that no “advantage” arises where these rules apply.

H. — Accounting for retirement compensation arrangements

An RCA is a funded SERP and, accordingly, may impact the corporate financial statements of the employer. Generally, a SERP is reflected in the financial statements using accounting standards applicable to pensions. Companies setting up an RCA will want to consider IAS 19 of the International Financial Reporting Standards or section 3461 of the Accounting Standards for Private Enterprises, which deals with pension obligations and future employee benefits.

8 — Split-Dollar Insurance Arrangements

Updated by John Natale, B.Comm., LL.B.

8.1 — Introduction

"Split-dollar insurance arrangements" are arrangements under which the policy values, death benefits and premium payments associated with a life insurance policy are formally allocated between two or more parties. It is neither a type of insurance contract nor a reason for purchasing life insurance. Instead, it is a method of sharing the attributes and costs of an insurance policy by having various parties share the costs and benefits associated with that policy.

Split-dollar insurance arrangements are usually employed in circumstances where more than one party requires benefits provided by a life insurance policy. One party may have a need to obtain life insurance protection while the other party to the split-dollar insurance arrangement may require a tax-deferred investment vehicle.

8.2 — Types of Split-Dollar Insurance Arrangements

There are a variety of ways in which a split-dollar insurance arrangement might be structured. Historically, non-descriptive terminology has been used for various split-dollar arrangements (such as, "Conventional", "Reverse", and "Double-Reverse"). Today, it is generally preferable to simply indicate which party is entitled to which attribute of the policy.

A. — Employee/shareholder owned death benefit

Traditionally, split-dollar insurance arrangements were designed to provide key employees or shareholders with low cost permanent insurance protection. The arrangement would be structured as follows. A life insurance policy would be jointly owned by a corporation and the employee/ shareholder. The policy cash values would be controlled by the corporation. There would be a split of the policy death benefit between the corporation and the employee/shareholder, and a sharing of the responsibility to pay premiums based upon the fair market value of the benefit receivable by each party. The premium and benefit allocation between the employee/shareholder and the corporation would typically be defined in an agreement between the employee/shareholder and the corporation. This agreement would also allocate the death benefit entitlement and rights of the parties with respect to the policy.

Under a split-dollar insurance arrangement of this type the initial face amount, which is a level death benefit established at policy issue, is owned by the employee/shareholder, who may name a beneficiary for that benefit. In the case of a universal life insurance plan, the total death benefit would include the level death benefit plus the policy's accumulated value. The accumulated value would be owned by and allocated to the corporation.

The employee/shareholder and the corporation would agree to "split" the premium in order to recognize their respective economic interests in the policy. Table 1 shows a sample illustration based on the following facts and assumptions:

- Male, age 45, non-smoker
- Projected rate of return: 3.0%
- Basic death benefit: $450,000

TABLE 1

SPLIT-DOLLAR ILLUSTRATION - SPLIT BASED ON TERM-TO-100 RATES

PREPARED FOR:	COMPANY & MR. EXECUTIVE
PREPARED BY:	FINANCIAL PLANNER
PERSONAL INFORMATION:	MALE 45 NON-SMOKER
INTEREST RATE:	3%
COVERAGE:	$450,000
ASSUMED LIFE EXPECTANCY (YEAR):	38

YEAR	AGE	TOTAL ANNUAL PREMIUM	EXECUTIVE PREMIUM	COMPANY PREMIUM	CASH SURRENDER VALUE	POLICY DEATH BENEFIT	EXECUTIVE DEATH BENEFIT	COMPANY DEATH BENEFIT
		$	$	$	$	$	$	$
1	45	10,000	5,073	4,927	3,223	459,386	450,000	9,386
2	46	10,000	5,073	4,927	6,656	468,982	450,000	18,982
3	47	10,000	5,073	4,927	16,481	478,806	450,000	28,806
4	48	10,000	5,073	4,927	26,527	488,852	450,000	38,852
5	49	10,000	5,073	4,927	41,382	499,599	450,000	49,599
6	50	10,000	5,073	4,927	53,295	510,690	450,000	60,690
7	51	10,000	5,073	4,927	65,563	522,137	450,000	72,137
8	52	10,000	5,073	4,927	83,953	533,953	450,000	83,953
9	53	10,000	5,073	4,927	96,180	546,180	450,000	96,180
10	54	10,000	5,073	4,927	108,849	558,849	450,000	108,849
11	55	10,000	5,073	4,927	121,742	571,742	450,000	121,742
12	56	10,000	5,073	4,927	135,014	585,014	450,000	135,014
13	57	10,000	5,073	4,927	148,655	598,655	450,000	148,655
14	58	10,000	5,073	4,927	162,680	612,680	450,000	162,680
15	59	10,000	5,073	4,927	177,079	627,079	450,000	177,079
16	60	10,000	5,073	4,927	191,828	641,828	450,000	191,828
17	61	10,000	5,073	4,927	206,823	656,823	450,000	206,823
18	62	10,000	5,073	4,927	222,191	672,191	450,000	222,191
19	63	10,000	5,073	4,927	237,830	687,830	450,000	237,830
20	64	10,000	5,073	4,927	255,526	705,526	450,000	255,526
21	65	10,000	5,073	4,927	273,370	723,370	450,000	273,370
22	66	10,000	5,073	4,927	291,592	741,592	450,000	291,592
23	67	10,000	5,073	4,927	310,204	760,204	450,000	310,204
24	68	10,000	5,073	4,927	329,245	779,245	450,000	329,245
25	69	10,000	5,073	4,927	348,718	798,718	450,000	348,718
26	70	10,000	5,073	4,927	368,518	818,518	450,000	368,518
27	71	10,000	5,073	4,927	388,577	838,577	450,000	388,577
28	72	10,000	5,073	4,927	408,957	858,957	450,000	408,957
29	73	10,000	5,073	4,927	429,584	879,584	450,000	429,584
30	74	10,000	5,073	4,927	450,376	900,376	450,000	450,376
31	75	10,000	5,073	4,927	471,060	921,060	450,000	471,060
32	76	10,000	5,073	4,927	491,342	941,342	450,000	491,342
33	77	10,000	5,073	4,927	511,521	961,521	450,000	511,521
34	78	10,000	5,073	4,927	531,106	981,106	450,000	531,106
35	79	10,000	5,073	4,927	549,986	999,986	450,000	549,986
36	80	10,000	5,073	4,927	568,010	1,018,010	450,000	568,010
37	81	10,000	5,073	4,927	584,694	1,034,694	450,000	584,694
38	82	10,000	5,073	4,927	599,773	1,049,773	450,000	599,773
39	83	10,000	5,073	4,927	613,432	1,063,432	450,000	613,432
40	84	10,000	5,073	4,927	625,632	1,075,632	450,000	625,632
41	85	10,000	5,073	4,927	634,425	1,084,425	450,000	634,425

B. — Corporate-owned death benefit

An alternative split-dollar insurance arrangement would involve the corporation owning the initial face amount death benefit, and the employee/shareholder owning the cash value and the death benefit portion equal to the accumulated value. Under this type of arrangement, essentially, the rights and obligations of the parties with respect to policy values, death benefits and premium payments are the mirror opposite of the previously discussed employee/shareholder owned death benefit split-dollar insurance arrangement.

Table 2 shows a sample illustration of a corporate-owned death benefit split-dollar insurance arrangement based on the following facts and assumptions:

- Male, age 45, non-smoker
- Projected rate of return: 3.0%
- Basic death benefit: $450,000

TABLE 2

SPLIT-DOLLAR ILLUSTRATION - SPLIT BASED ON TERM-TO-100 RATES

PREPARED FOR:	COMPANY & MR. EXECUTIVE
PREPARED BY:	FINANCIAL PLANNER
PERSONAL INFORMATION:	MALE 45 NON-SMOKER
INTEREST RATE:	3%
COVERAGE:	$450,000
ASSUMED LIFE EXPECTANCY (YEAR):	38

YEAR	AGE	TOTAL ANNUAL PREMIUM	COMPANY PREMIUM	EXECUTIVE PREMIUM	CASH SURRENDER VALUE	POLICY DEATH BENEFIT	COMPANY DEATH BENEFIT	EXECUTIVE DEATH BENEFIT
		$	$	$	$	$	$	$
1	45	10,000	5,073	4,927	3,223	459,386	450,000	9,386
2	46	10,000	5,073	4,927	6,656	468,982	450,000	18,982
3	47	10,000	5,073	4,927	16,481	478,806	450,000	28,806
4	48	10,000	5,073	4,927	26,527	488,852	450,000	38,852
5	49	10,000	5,073	4,927	41,382	499,599	450,000	49,599
6	50	10,000	5,073	4,927	53,295	510,690	450,000	60,690
7	51	10,000	5,073	4,927	65,563	522,137	450,000	72,137
8	52	10,000	5,073	4,927	83,953	533,953	450,000	83,953
9	53	10,000	5,073	4,927	96,180	546,180	450,000	96,180
10	54	10,000	5,073	4,927	108,849	558,849	450,000	108,849
11	55	10,000	5,073	4,927	121,742	571,742	450,000	121,742
12	56	10,000	5,073	4,927	135,014	585,014	450,000	135,014
13	57	10,000	5,073	4,927	148,655	598,655	450,000	148,655
14	58	10,000	5,073	4,927	162,680	612,680	450,000	162,680
15	59	10,000	5,073	4,927	177,079	627,079	450,000	177,079
16	60	10,000	5,073	4,927	191,828	641,828	450,000	191,828
17	61	10,000	5,073	4,927	206,823	656,823	450,000	206,823
18	62	10,000	5,073	4,927	222,191	672,191	450,000	222,191
19	63	10,000	5,073	4,927	237,830	687,830	450,000	237,830
20	64	10,000	5,073	4,927	255,526	705,526	450,000	255,526
21	65	10,000	5,073	4,927	273,370	723,370	450,000	273,370
22	66	10,000	5,073	4,927	291,592	741,592	450,000	291,592
23	67	10,000	5,073	4,927	310,204	760,204	450,000	310,204
24	68	10,000	5,073	4,927	329,245	779,245	450,000	329,245
25	69	10,000	5,073	4,927	348,718	798,718	450,000	348,718
26	70	10,000	5,073	4,927	368,518	818,518	450,000	368,518
27	71	10,000	5,073	4,927	388,577	838,577	450,000	388,577
28	72	10,000	5,073	4,927	408,957	858,957	450,000	408,957
29	73	10,000	5,073	4,927	429,584	879,584	450,000	429,584
30	74	10,000	5,073	4,927	450,376	900,376	450,000	450,376
31	75	10,000	5,073	4,927	471,060	921,060	450,000	471,060
32	76	10,000	5,073	4,927	491,342	941,342	450,000	491,342
33	77	10,000	5,073	4,927	511,521	961,521	450,000	511,521
34	78	10,000	5,073	4,927	531,106	981,106	450,000	531,106
35	79	10,000	5,073	4,927	549,986	999,986	450,000	549,986
36	80	10,000	5,073	4,927	568,010	1,018,010	450,000	568,010
37	81	10,000	5,073	4,927	584,694	1,034,694	450,000	584,694
38	82	10,000	5,073	4,927	599,773	1,049,773	450,000	599,773
39	83	10,000	5,073	4,927	613,432	1,063,432	450,000	613,432
40	84	10,000	5,073	4,927	625,632	1,075,632	450,000	625,632
41	85	10,000	5,073	4,927	634,425	1,084,425	450,000	634,425

8.3 — Financing Policy Deposits

There are a variety of methods that can be used to allocate the premium payable by the parties participating in a split-dollar insurance arrangement. However, the *Income Tax Act* contains no specific rules regarding the tax consequences of a split-dollar arrangement nor does the Act provide any guidance as to how the premium payments should be allocated. It should be noted, however, that the Act does implicitly contemplate multiple owners of insurance policies. For example, reference is repeatedly made to a policyholder disposing of "an interest in a life insurance policy" rather than simply referring to "a disposition of a life insurance policy." Nevertheless, this implicit recognition of the ability to divide ownership interests in a life insurance policy is not met with explicit rules setting out the tax consequences of multiple ownership.

While the legislation does not contain specific rules regarding split-dollar life insurance, the CRA has developed its own administrative position regarding these arrangements. The CRA's administrative views as to the reasonableness of split-dollar premium allocations have evolved over the years and are described below. The CRA's current views are that the premium allocation between the employee/shareholder and the corporation should reflect the fair market value of the various interests in the insurance contract that are being acquired by the parties participating in the split-dollar insurance arrangement.

A. — Premium split based on term insurance

In a split-dollar insurance arrangement based on term insurance, the death benefit owner pays an amount based on the cost of term insurance coverage for the amount of death benefit. The applicable term coverage could be, for example, annual renewable term, 5-year term, 10-year term, 20-year term, term-to-65, or term-to-100. In the case of a universal life policy it would be possible to use the applicable yearly renewable term or level insurance costs. The net cost of pure insurance (NCPI) for a particular policy may also be used. (The NCPI of an insurance policy is determined by multiplying the net amount of risk each year (the face amount of death benefit minus any cash value) by a prescribed factor. The prescribed factor increases with age of the insured and is determined by reference to the Canadian Institute of Actuaries 1969–1975 Standard Mortality Tables. See section 3.2.F. The August 23, 2013 draft legislation proposes a more recent table, reflection of substandard ratings and changes to the calculation of the net amount at risk for policies issued after 2015. See section 1.9.C.ii for a detailed discussion.) These insurance costs could be paid annually, or the aggregate cost could be present valued and paid over a specified period of time (although in this latter case, some of the policy's cash value may arguably rest with the death benefit owner).

B. — Premium split based on cash value

For a number of years, premium allocation based on cash value was the traditional method of allocating the costs for a split-dollar arrangement. This approach would yield an extremely low cost for the death benefit owner's portion and as a result was frequently used in the past in situations where the motivation was to provide an employee shareholder with extremely low cost insurance coverage. (This method was often referred to as a "conventional" split-dollar arrangement.)

In a split-dollar insurance arrangement based on cash values, the cash value owner pays that portion of the premium equal to the lesser of (i) the annual increase in the policy cash value and (ii) the planned annual premium. The death benefit owner pays that portion of the premium equal to the difference (if any) between the planned annual premium and the amount of premium paid by the cash value owner. For example, if the planned annual premium was $1,000 and the annual increase in cash value was $800, the cash value owner would pay $800 and the death benefit owner would pay $200. If the planned annual premium was $1,000 and the increase in cash value was $1,200, the cash value owner would pay $1,000 and the death benefit owner would pay nothing.

As a slight variation to the premium allocation being based on cash value, the allocation could be based on account value. During the early years of the policy, the cash value is generally less than the account value, the difference representing any surrender charges that decrease over time.

As described below, a premium allocation based on either the increase in cash value or account value is likely to result in the assessment of a taxable benefit to the death benefit owner.

C. — Tax treatment of split-dollar arrangements

For a number of years it has been the CRA's position that split-dollar insurance arrangements between an employer and an employee or a corporation and its shareholder may give rise to a taxable benefit in the hands of the employee or shareholder. However, the CRA has never indicated how the benefit is to be calculated. Instead, the CRA has stated that the premium should be split based on the amount a person would pay for comparable rights in an open market.

Clarification of the Canadian tax position as it relates to split-dollar arrangements requires an answer to three basic questions:

1. Does a split-dollar arrangement confer a benefit on an employee or shareholder?
2. If there is a benefit, how is it quantified?
3. Once quantified, how is that benefit characterized for tax purposes?

Although none of the answers to these questions is clearly defined, there are some indications as to how they may eventually be answered. The following provides a general discussion and historical background of several tax issues that may arise when implementing a split-dollar insurance arrangement.

i. — Assessing the benefit

As described above, one of the traditional methods of allocating premium costs for split-dollar arrangements was based on the increase in cash value of the policy.

This method, if acceptable to the CRA, would allow a corporation to confer a significant non-taxable benefit on an employee/shareholder. In the mid-1980s the CRA became concerned as to the potential abuse of split-dollar arrangements. In January of 1987 the CRA indicated that split-dollar insurance funding was under active review and that the CRA was leaning towards using NCPI as the benchmark for quantifying the benefit of the insurance face amount owned by the employee/shareholder. In March of 1987 the CRA indicated that a submission from the Life Underwriters' Association (as it was then known) would be welcome as an aid in clarifying this issue.

In June 1987 the Life Underwriters' Association made a written submission to the CRA regarding the tax consequences of split-dollar arrangements. The basic proposals in that submission were as follows:

1. It acknowledged that a split-dollar arrangement may confer a taxable benefit on the employee in an employer/employee situation.

2. It was recommended that the benefit should be calculated in relation to the NCPI of the insurance coverage being provided for the employee.

3. The NCPI should be calculated using the 1969-1975 Canadian Institute of Actuaries mortality table.

4. The taxable benefit reportable to the employee each year should be reduced by the amount of the employee's premium payment for that year. In instances where the premium paid by the employee exceeds the NCPI, the difference should be carried forward as a credit, to be applied in future years.

5. Contracts pre-existing the effective date of the split-dollar assessing practice should be "grandfathered." As a result, no taxable benefit would be assessed.

No response was received by the Life Underwriter's Association and in 1993 the submission was withdrawn.

In 1989 at the Canadian Tax Foundation Annual Conference Revenue Canada Roundtable, the issue of split-dollar insurance was raised in the context of a split-dollar arrangement where a corporate employer paid the annual increase in cash value and the employee/ shareholder paid the balance of the annual premium. The CRA stated in response that it would be a question of fact as to whether or not a taxable benefit were received and the amount paid by the employee/ shareholder and the cost of equivalent term insurance coverage would be taken into account in arriving at a determination as to the existence of a taxable benefit.

The CRA subsequently created some confusion over split-dollar arrangements when it released technical interpretation 1991-112, dated May 21, 1991. There the CRA indicated that it generally would not consider an employee/shareholder to be in receipt of a benefit under a split-dollar insurance arrangement if the annual premium, or the portion thereof that is paid by the corporation, does not exceed the increase in the cash surrender value of the policy in that year. The CRA went on to state that this position would only apply where the corporation is entitled to the cash surrender value of the policy on its termination or to a portion of the amount payable under the original policy on death equal to its cash surrender value immediately before death, as well as to any dividends that arise in connection with the policy.

Based on this position, it would be possible to structure a split-dollar insurance arrangement such that virtually all of the cost would be borne by the corporation. The result would be a significant nontaxable benefit to the individual.

The CRA then rejected this interpretation based on increased cash value and released a revised position at question 16 of the Prairie Provinces Tax Conference in May 1992. There, the CRA indicated that the 1991 technical interpretation may have been "misleading." The CRA reverted to its former position that determination of a taxable benefit is a question of fact and that the death benefit owner should pay an amount equal to that applicable for equivalent term coverage.

This position was confirmed at the 1992 Conference for Advanced Life Underwriters (CALU) and would appear to represent the CRA's current position with respect to split-dollar insurance arrangements. The question posed at the CALU conference was not in the context of a "conventional" split-dollar insurance arrangement but rather in the context of the death benefit owner's cost of a split-dollar arrangement. The CRA confirmed that no benefit would be assessed where the death benefit owner (be it the employee/shareholder or the corporation) paid a "premium for comparable rights available in the market under a separate life insurance policy."

In technical interpretation 990052, dated April 7, 1999, it appears that the taxpayer was seeking guidance on the proper allocation of costs for a split-dollar arrangement involving a universal life insurance policy. The response from the CRA suggests that the CRA does not have a clear understanding of the split-dollar concept, as it may be applied in connection with a universal life insurance policy. This interpretation expressed the view that for universal life policies it may be too difficult to split into identifiable interests and that term insurance costs may not necessarily be useful in determining any taxable benefit.

The CRA issued a follow-up technical interpretation 2000-003673, dated July 20, 2000. It stated that it "is not the case" that the CRA takes the view that "it is not possible to structure a 'split dollar' arrangement using a universal life product." The CRA indicated that the determination of a taxable benefit under a split-dollar arrangement can only be made on a case by case basis after a review of the relevant facts.

Albeit not in the life insurance context, the CRA (in technical interpretation 2004-0090181E5, dated November 30, 2004) considered whether a shareholder benefit would be conferred when premiums and benefits were shared under a critical illness insurance policy between a corporation and a shareholder. The CRA stated that a shareholder benefit would result in this context "if the corporation is impoverished as a result of these transactions. The value of the benefit could correspond to the amount that the shareholder should pay in similar circumstances to obtain the same benefit resulting from the transactions in question from a person who deals at arm's length."

In a further CRA interpretation dealing with sharing of premiums in the same context (2006-0178561E5, dated November 3, 2006), this same notion of impoverishment was reiterated with the following additional comment:

> We cannot conclude that there will be no benefit conferred on the shareholder under section 15(1) if an insurance company determines the amount of premiums payable for a policy with or without a premium refund rider, and that under a shared agreement a corporation pays the annual premiums for a critical illness insurance policy of which it is the beneficiary when its sole shareholder pays the additional annual premiums for the rider of which he is the beneficiary.

In other words, the premium for the return of premium rider is not necessarily fair market value consideration. The company may still be impoverished, in which case there could be a shareholder benefit for the amount by which the corporation was "impoverished" over what the shareholder paid. For further discussion of this notion of "impoverishment" see section 3.3.I.ii.

Returning to the life insurance context, at the 2012 CALU CRA Roundtable (technical interpretation 2012-0435661C6, dated May 8, 2012) the CRA again confirmed that "where a life insurance policy is co-owned by a corporation and a shareholder (corporation or individual) pursuant to a split dollar arrangement or other shared ownership arrangement, there is a potential for the corporation to confer a benefit through the cost sharing arrangement." As per the 1992 CALU conference, a comment about considering the premium "which would be paid for comparable rights available in the market under a separate insurance policy" was made. In this context, the CRA did not rule out the application of other benefit provisions and stated that the application of subsection 15(1), subsection 246(1), section 9 or paragraph 12(1)(x) of the Act would be considered on a case-by-case basis.

The current position of the CRA can be summarized as follows: any taxable benefit resulting from a split-dollar arrangement will generally depend on the particular fact situation and the sharing of premium among the parties must be reasonable in relation to the apportioned values.

ii. — Quantifying the benefit

Despite the uncertainty resulting from some of CRA's commentary, it appears that its views have evolved over time to a position where the quantum of the taxable benefit to the death benefit owner should be based upon the premium that would be paid if coverage of a similar nature was obtained in the open market. A fair allocation of premium will be a question of fact and arguably the determination could be based on annual renewable term costs, 5-year, 10-year, 20-year term, term-to-65 or term-to-100 rates or cost of insurance rates under a universal life policy. It is also arguable that, although NCPI is not necessarily obtainable on the open market, it does represent the pure cost of insurance and is used as a measure for this under the Act (for example see the deduction for collateral insurance in paragraph 20(1)(e.2)).

One could also argue that the net present value of the equivalent term costs (on whatever basis is chosen) may be used to determine a lump sum or shortened payment period for the death benefit cost. Additional consideration should be given to the reasonableness in this context of the discount rate used in determining the present value and whether any portion of the cash value should be allocated to the death benefit owner as representing a prepayment of the insurance premium.

The key to any premium allocation would be the reasonability of the payment from an objective perspective. In determining which method is appropriate a variety of factors need to be taken into account such as the age of the insured, the purpose of the insurance, and the impact of the employee/shareholder's death on the company.

iii. — Characterization of the taxable benefit

If a benefit is conferred on an individual by virtue of a split-dollar insurance arrangement, the characterization of the benefit must be determined. In the case of non-shareholder employees, it is the CRA's position that an amount will be included in the employee's income under paragraph 6(1)(a) of the *Income Tax Act*.

In the case of a non-employee shareholder, the CRA holds the position that the benefit is included in the income of the shareholder under subsection 15(1). When dealing with non-shareholder or employee situations, presumably, the comments made at the 2012 CALU CRA Roundtable (technical interpretation 2012-0435661C6, dated May 8, 2012) may apply to involve a potential 246(1) benefit, section 9 income from property or paragraph 12(1)(x) inclusion of reimbursed amounts.

iv. — Employee vs. shareholder

The tax treatment of the benefit is quite different, from the perspective of both the corporation and the employee/shareholder, depending on whether the benefit is assessed under paragraph 6(1)(a) or subsection 15(1) of the *Income Tax Act*.

If the individual is an employee, paragraph 6(1)(a) applies, and it would be arguable that the amount of the benefit should be deductible by the corporation as an expense (assuming the benefit constitutes part of the employee's compensation) and included in the income of the employee as "income from employment."

If the individual is a shareholder, subsection 15(1) applies. In this case the benefit would be included in the shareholder's income from property (i.e. the shares of the corporation). As such, the benefit would be a nondeductible expense to the corporation and included in the income of the shareholder as income from property (and not characterized as a dividend).

If the individual is both an employee and a shareholder it is a question of fact as to whether the benefit has been received by the individual in his/her capacity as an employee or a shareholder.

The CRA has made general statements regarding this determination (albeit not specifically in the split-dollar context) in a number of technical interpretation letters. However, the statements are not entirely consistent with each other, with the result that the CRA's position is unclear. Several technical interpretation letters contain the following general statement:

> In the case where an individual is both an employee and a shareholder, it is a question of fact whether a benefit has been conferred on the individual in the capacity of

> a shareholder or in the capacity of an employee. However, where a benefit is granted to such an individual, the benefit will be presumed to have been conferred upon him or her by reason of being a shareholder, unless the benefit is comparable in nature and quantum to benefits generally offered to employees who perform similar services and have similar responsibilities for other employers of comparable size. (2000-0055145, dated January 9, 2001)

Other letters take a more pragmatic approach. These letters accept that, in cases where the only employees are shareholder-employees, benefits will be regarded as employment benefits if they are part of a reasonable remuneration package (see, for example, technical interpretation 2005-0115691E5, dated April 28, 2005). At question 13 of the 2006 CALU Roundtable (indexed as document number 2006-0174121C6, dated May 9, 2006) the CRA indicated that in its view, the fact that an individual is the only employee and shareholder of a corporation does not mean a benefit is received qua shareholder. The CRA agreed "that a pragmatic approach to the determination is warranted and, generally, if it is reasonable to conclude that the benefit has been provided as part of a reasonable employee remuneration package we will consider it to be received qua employee."

The question of whether a particular benefit should be treated as a shareholder benefit or an employee benefit was considered in the case of *Spicy Sports Inc. v. The Queen*, [2004] 5 C.T.C. 2090 (T.C.C.) (I.P.). Although that case concerned a "cost-plus" private health services plan ("PHSP") rather than split-dollar life insurance and was decided in an informal procedure, the reasoning in the decision would also be pertinent to the life insurance context.

In the *Spicy Sports* case, the Tax Court ruled that the benefits from a cost-plus PHSP provided by Spicy Sports Inc., the employer, to an employee/shareholder owning 51 percent of the shares of the corporation were received by the individual in his capacity as a shareholder.

The Tax Court acknowledged that the issue of employee versus shareholder benefits is a question of fact. It then concluded, having regard to the generosity of the particular plan, which provided complete coverage to the employee/shareholder for a $35,996 knee surgery performed in the United States, that it would be unlikely that Spicy Sports Inc. would have entered into a contract to provide the particular cost-plus PHSP with an arm's length key employee. Accordingly, the benefit was held to be a non-deductible shareholder benefit. The CRA has subsequently commented that the Spicy Sports decision was consistent with CRA's assessing practices. See technical interpretation 2006-0204951I7, dated October 19, 2006.

v. — Deductibility of benefit

There is some risk that a benefit conferred on an employee by virtue of paragraph (6)(1)(a) will not provide a deduction to an employer. In *Green Acres Fertilizers Services Ltd. v. The Queen*, [1979] C.T.C. 431 (F.C.T.D.); affirmed [1980] C.T.C. 504 (F.C.A.) the employer was denied a deduction for the amount of an insurance premium, which it argued was part of an executive compensation package but which the Court found was paid to fund a shareholders' agreement. The employees had included the benefit in their income — however, the Court denied the corporation a corresponding deduction.

This potential problem could be addressed by including a reference to the split-dollar insurance arrangement in the employee's employment contract. By doing so, the employer would be in a stronger position to deduct any benefit that might arise.

8.4 — Adjusted Cost Basis

An additional issue that may arise in some situations concerns the adjusted cost basis of the various interests in the policy to the owners. This may become important where it is planned to transfer interests in a policy between parties to a split-dollar arrangement at a later date or for purposes of calculating the credit to a corporation's capital dividend account. For example, a split-dollar arrangement may be entered into between a shareholder and an operating company. The corporation would be entitled to a level death benefit and a shareholder would be entitled to the cash value. In some situations it may be beneficial at a later date for the company to transfer the death benefit interest in the policy to the shareholder. This transfer would be considered to be a disposition of an interest in the policy by the corporation. (See section 3.2.G.v for a general discussion of the tax implications regarding the transfer of an interest in a life insurance policy and specifically to section 3.3.I.i.) The corporation's adjusted cost basis of its interest in the policy will of course be dependent on the amount of the premiums paid by the corporation and the annual NCPI, if any, associated with the corporation's interest in the policy.

As a result, not only will the premium be required to be allocated to each party to the split-dollar insurance arrangement, each party that holds an interest in the insurance contract will have their own separate adjusted cost basis.

Further, it should be noted that the insurer would typically not be able to determine the adjusted cost basis of each owner for their interest in the policy, as this calculation would be the subject of a separate legal agreement external to the policy contract. The insurer would generally calculate the ACB at the policy level irrespective of the ownership arrangement and would report any policy gains in respect of any particular disposition without reference to the parties' separate interests and related ACBs. The aggregate adjusted cost basis of the interests owned by the split-dollar owners might not be equal to the ACB for the entire policy. This fact can be illustrated by way of a simple example. The ACB of a person's interest in an insurance policy cannot be less than zero according to section 257 of the Act. The death benefit owner's ACB will be reduced by NCPI but the cash value owner's ACB will not be reduced by NCPI, as there is no NCPI associated with the cash value. Once the ACB of the death benefit owner's interest is ground down to zero, NCPI will cease to grind ACB. If the death benefit owner owned all of the policy there would still be ACB against which NCPI could be deducted.

To avoid this issue, some planners suggest that a policy be owned wholly by one party and that the other party merely reimburse the sole owner for costs associated with the benefits "purchased" by the other party. In exchange for such payments, it is suggested that the sole owner designate the other party irrevocably as a beneficiary under the policy for the amount of death benefit being "purchased." It should be noted that an irrevocable beneficiary must consent to all policy transactions, which could affect their interest in the policy. In determining what cost the other party pays, the same types of cost structures, as discussed above, may be used.

One potential problem associated with this approach is the question of whether the cost that the other party pays to the sole owner of the policy is income to the owner. A life insurance policy is "property" and by "selling or renting" a portion of the benefit entitlement under this property, it could be argued that the sole owner derives income from that property, at least to the extent of any profit (subsection 9(1)). The counterargument is that the sole owner is merely defraying or being reimbursed for the costs of owning the entire policy.

At the 2010 CALU CRA Roundtable (2010-0359421C6, dated May 4, 2010), the CRA was asked to comment on several corporate life insurance owner and beneficiary structures. One of these was where a parent company ("Parentco") owns and pays the premiums for a life insurance policy naming its subsidiary company ("Subco") as irrevocable beneficiary and where Subco reimburses Parentco for the insurance premiums. In this situation, the CRA stated that the reimbursement of premiums paid to Parentco by Subco would be viewed as income from property to Parentco either under section 9 or paragraph 12(1)(x) of the Act. The CRA also stated that there would be no shareholder benefit under subsection 15(1) to Parentco so long as it reports the reimbursement as income. It also stated that there would be no adjusted cost basis ("ACB") adjustment to the policy owned by Parentco for the reimbursed premium because the definition of ACB in subsection 148(9) does not contemplate this. Please refer to a complete discussion of this commentary in section 6.2.D).

For purposes of the discussion in this chapter, it is assumed that the policy is jointly owned by the parties to the split-dollar arrangement and the rights and obligations of the parties are set out in a separate legal document, external to the policy contract.

8.5 — Situations Using Split-Dollar Insurance Arrangements

A. — Executive benefits

One of the most common uses of split-dollar arrangements is found in employer/employee situations where the employer is looking to attract and/or retain a key executive by means of providing desirable benefits. One such benefit could be the provision of life insurance coverage to protect the executive's dependants. This could be of particular importance to older, highly paid executives who have a need for large amounts of insurance coverage.

A split-dollar insurance arrangement could achieve the goals of both the employer and the executive. The corporation's investment in the policy could be protected in the event of either the death or the resignation of the executive and could offer the corporation an element of profit.

B. — Keyperson insurance

Keyperson insurance is normally taken out on the life of an employee or shareholder of a corporation whose contribution to the corporation is integral to its success. The insurance is owned and paid for by the corporation and the corporation is also the beneficiary. In the event of the death of the keyperson, the policy proceeds are used to compensate the corporation for resultant losses and to assist the corporation in replacing the keyperson. See section 7.3 for a more detailed discussion of keyperson insurance.

Because keyperson insurance is required for a finite period (until the keyperson quits or retires) term insurance is often purchased.

However, if the keyperson is in need of life insurance coverage and a tax-preferred investment vehicle, a permanent life insurance policy, purchased under a split-dollar arrangement, may be appropriate. Under such an arrangement the employee or shareholder would control the cash values of the policy and could pay the savings portion of the insurance premiums. This would allow the individual to access an attractive investment opportunity that might not otherwise be available (if no personal life insurance were required).

The keyperson could take advantage of the tax-deferred growth of policy values in an exempt life insurance policy. The corporation would control the death benefit required to fund its keyperson requirements. The corporation's premium commitments would be tied to equivalent term costs, reasonable in the circumstances. The corporation would meet its primary objective of insuring the keyperson and would gain the added advantage of offering an attractive, tax-free benefit to the keyperson/employee or shareholder at no additional cost to itself.

Upon retirement or termination of employment, the corporation would no longer require the death benefit portion of the policy and this interest could be transferred to the employee. Depending on the fair market value of the policy (see discussion in section 3.3.I) the transfer may result in a taxable benefit to the employee. Consideration of the deemed RCA rules should be made. See section 7.7.F for further details. If, instead, the policy were surrendered, the life insurance company would report a policy gain to the extent that the cash surrender value exceeds the entire ACB of the policy. However, in this situation, the employee should report a policy gain for the difference between the cash value portion of the policy and the employee's ACB of their interest in the policy.

C. — Buy/sell agreements

In many instances, the shareholders of closely held private corporations will enter into agreements whereby provision is made for the purchase and sale of the shareholder's interest in the company in the event of death. Typically, life insurance policies are acquired on the lives of the shareholders to provide the funding necessary to execute the agreements. These policies are usually owned either by the corporation or the individual shareholders. See section 7.4 for more information on funding buy/sell agreements using insurance.

Circumstances may arise, however, where split-dollar insurance arrangements will be of benefit either to the corporation or the shareholders, or both. It may be that personally-owned insurance is most appropriate in a given situation (whereby the death benefit is payable to the individual shareholders) but that the shareholders do not want to carry the full burden of the insurance premiums. This would be particularly true if the corporate tax rate were significantly lower than the marginal tax rates of the individual shareholders.

Under certain buy/sell agreements, it is the corporation that requires the death benefit to carry out its obligations under the agreement. However, if the shareholders participating in the agreement are looking for a tax-deferred investment vehicle, a split-dollar arrangement could be beneficial. The company would pay the equivalent term costs and the shareholder could make additional deposits to take advantage of the tax-deferred accumulation of values in an exempt life insurance policy. The shareholder would control the policy values, which would be returned tax-free in the event of death, or could be accessed over time for the shareholder's retirement.

D. — Retirement compensation arrangements

Split-dollar arrangements are often used to fund retirement compensation arrangements ("RCAs"). The death benefit from the policy could be split out of the RCA trust and be made payable to the sponsoring corporation. In this way, the death benefits could pass to the corporation tax-free and could (in the appropriate circumstances) also give rise to a credit to a private corporation's capital dividend account. The RCA trust would be entitled to the cash value of the policy and use the cash values in satisfying retirement income obligations to the executive under the RCA. More information regarding RCAs is found in section 7.7.E.iii.

It should also be noted that when dealing with RCAs that have a specified beneficiary (e.g. an owner-manager), the "prohibited investment" and "advantage" rules may come into play. In the split dollar context, if the split is not reasonable, an "advantage" may result. See 7.7.D for a detailed discussion of these rules.

E. — Family situations

A split-dollar insurance arrangement may be beneficial in facilitating the purchase of permanent life insurance in certain family situations. For example, it is not uncommon to have circumstances where parents have money to invest and their children have a large life insurance need, but limited cash flow. A solution is to jointly purchase a life insurance policy. The adult child could pay for and be entitled to a level death benefit amount equivalent to their term insurance need and the parent could pay for and be entitled to the cash value portion of the policy. The parent would then have an investment that accumulates on a tax-deferred basis.

F. — Holding company

Another situation where split-dollar insurance arrangements can be applied is where there is an operating company with a need for the death benefit portion of the insurance contract for buy/sell purposes. A holding company could benefit from the tax-free accumulation of the investment income associated with owning the cash value portion of the insurance policy.

G. — Charitable giving

It is also possible to structure a split-dollar arrangement between a donor and a charity. The CRA's long-standing view was that a "gift" of an interest in a split-dollar policy did not qualify as a charitable donation since some of the policy's benefits also accrued to the donor (see, for example, technical interpretation 9335905, dated June 6, 1994). However, the release of the December 20, 2002 Technical Bill and December 24, 2002 Technical News No. 26 (now archived) opened the way for charitable gifts even where the donor receives some element of benefit from the arrangement.

At the CALU Tax Policy Roundtable in May of 2003, the CRA stated (2003-0004315) that it was unable to provide guidelines regarding charitable gifts involving split-dollar policies. However, it did state that "it is possible that there may be arrangements that could result in a charitable gift" and that split-dollar gifting arrangements "appear to fit within the spirit of the proposed legislation on split receipting."

CRA technical interpretation 2003-0004115, dated June 2, 2003 considered a situation where a policy is jointly owned by a donor and a charity and where the donor pays all the policy premiums and is the beneficiary of the cash value portion of the policy and the charity is the beneficiary of the death benefit portion of the policy. While the CRA would only provide general comments, it indicated that in determining whether any portion of the premium would qualify as a charitable gift, the charity must have a premium obligation and this premium must relate exclusively to the benefits under the policy that accrue to the charity. It also commented that any cost reductions arising by virtue of having a single policy rather than two separate policies should be taken into account. Similar comments were made in another CRA technical interpretation (2003-0182165, dated April 17, 2003) involving term insurance.

The key issue in split-dollar situations where charitable giving is involved is establishing the "amount of any advantage" to the donor. Since, by definition, split-dollar arrangements contemplate a sharing of the benefits under a life insurance policy, there normally would be an advantage to the donor in relation to the portion of the policy that the donor would be entitled to receive. Normally, however, the donor would pay all of the premiums under the policy so that the costs are not shared. The question then becomes, what amount or portion of the premium should represent the portion of the policy to be received by the donor and thus discounted from the gift. Akin to the discussion above relating to employee and shareholder benefits, this would be a question of fact in the circumstances.

Technical interpretation 2009-031202, dated November 19, 2009, and Question 7 at the May 2011 CLHIA CRA Roundtable, indexed as 2011-0398461C6 addressed similar fact patterns involving life insurance donated to charity where the donor pays all the premiums but where the donor would receive a return of premiums paid on death. In the Roundtable response, the CRA confirmed that the charity would be required to discount any gift of premium by the amount of the advantage to the donor. It did not provide guidance relating to how the charity is to establish this amount but stated that if it "could not be reasonably ascertained, no charitable tax deduction or credit would be allowed." In technical interpretation 2009-031202, in similar circumstances, the CRA confirmed that the premium for the return of premium rider should not be receipted.

Refer to Chapter 12 for more information about issues specific to charitable giving and life insurance.

8.6 — Split-Dollar Agreement

The split-dollar agreement sets out the rights and responsibilities of each party to the split-dollar arrangement. It covers such issues as: entitlement to cash values, entitlement to the death benefit, premium obligations (including procedures in the event of default on such obligations), the right to assign death benefits, and the conditions and terms under which the split-dollar arrangement may be terminated. It is recommended that a formal legal agreement be drafted whenever a split-dollar insurance arrangement is implemented.

8.7 — Alternative to the Split-Dollar Insurance Arrangement

An alternative to the split-dollar arrangement is the use of a split beneficiary designation. In this structure, a single party would solely own the life insurance policy and multiple beneficiaries would be designated under the contract. While split beneficiary designations may avoid the complexity and cost of drafting a formal agreement required to effect a split-dollar arrangement, there are other issues that should be considered before adopting this strategy.

Unless the beneficiary designation is irrevocable, the policyholder can at any time alter or revoke a beneficiary designation by way of a change of beneficiary designation form delivered to the insurance carrier, or through a written instrument such as a Will in the case of an individual. The beneficiary will not be informed of the alteration or revocation by the insurance carrier and may be unaware of the change of beneficiary designation. As a planning point, a change of beneficiary designation by the policyholder under such circumstances may defeat the original planning for which the split beneficiary designation was being used. As noted previously, where the beneficiary designation is irrevocable, the policyholder must obtain the consent of the beneficiary to alter or revoke the beneficiary designation.

In the corporate context, a split beneficiary designation may be considered in a situation where one corporation owns a life insurance policy (Payor Corporation), but one or more related corporations are designated as beneficiaries. This structure may be adopted for creditor-protection purposes, for ease of administration where there is a need for life insurance in more than one corporation, or to maximize the credit to the capital dividend account of the beneficiary corporation. As noted at section 6.2.D, the CRA has consistently stated that GAAR would apply in such circumstances unless there are reasons for the structure other than to obtain the tax benefits of the full capital dividend account credit.

Consideration must be given to whether the Payor Corporation has conferred a taxable benefit to the beneficiary corporation, or to the shareholders of the beneficiary corporation, by paying all of the premiums on the policy. A taxable benefit may be conferred if the shareholders of the Payor Corporation and the beneficiary corporation were different, or if the proportionate shareholdings of a common group of shareholders was different between the Payor Corporation and the beneficiary corporation. In this situation subsection 15(1) may apply. There may also be a shareholder benefit issue even if the shareholders of the Payor Corporation and the beneficiary corporation are identical. See the discussion at sections 8.4 and 6.2.D for a full discussion of benefit issues and potential income inclusions arising from different owner/payor and beneficiary structures.

8.8 — Conclusion

Split-dollar arrangements may be considered where the various attributes — risk protection and tax-deferred cash value accumulation — are desired by two or more different parties. Particularly, in the employee/shareholder context, a taxable benefit may be conferred if the parties do not reasonably allocate the costs as between the corporation and the employee/shareholder.

9 — TRUSTS AND LIFE INSURANCE

Updated by Dianna Flannery, B.A. (Hons.), J.D. and Serge Lessard, LL.B., Fin. Pl., FLMI

9.1 — Introduction

Trusts have been a common feature of estate planning for centuries. Although trusts are often referred to as estate planning vehicles, a trust is, in fact, a term that describes a legal relationship that arises between a trustee (who holds legal title over property) and a beneficiary (for whose benefit title over property is held). The distinguishing characteristic of the trust and its principal attribute is the separation of ownership and control of trust property. It is this characteristic that makes trusts ideally suited to estate planning in general, and specifically to a number of attractive planning opportunities involving life insurance. Before analyzing some of the planning structures available, a (very) brief overview of the law of trusts and their taxation is in order.

9.2 — What is a Trust?

One of the most commonly cited definitions of a trust is found in *Underhill's Law of Trusts and Trustees* and reads as follows:

> A trust is an equitable obligation binding a person (who is called a trustee) to deal with property over which he has control (which is called the trust property) for the benefit of persons (who are called the beneficiaries or *cestuis que trust*) of whom he may himself be one, and any one of whom may enforce the obligation.

A trust results from the relationship of three parties:

a) the Settlor — the person who establishes the trust and who transfers legal ownership of property intended to be held in trust;

b) the Trustee(s) — the party or parties who hold legal title to the property pursuant to the terms expressed by the Settlor for the benefit of the beneficiaries; and

c) the Beneficiary(ies) — the party(ies) for whose benefit the property is held.

In order for a trust to exist, there must be evidence of three things:

a) certainty as to intention (i.e. it is intended that the property be held in trust);

b) certainty as to objects (i.e. it is clear for whose benefit the property is being held); and

c) certainty as to subject-matter (i.e. it is clear which property is the subject of the trust).

The trust provisions of the *Quebec Civil Code* ("QCC") are generally inspired by the common law however there are subtle differences that will be indicated in the course of this chapter. One of the major differences is the requirement for a trust to result from a written deed (1260 QCC). Under the QCC, a trust cannot be implied from the intentions of the settlor. However, a trust could result from the operation of a statute law and, in rarer cases, could be established by judgment when permitted by law.

As the trust is in fact not a legal entity, all business of the trust (including entering into contracts, incurring debts and liabilities, and the ownership of property) must be conducted in the name of the trustee in his or her capacity as trustee of the trust, and should be subject to the terms of the enabling trust instrument. Articles 1266 and 1278 QCC allow the settlor in the trust deed to name the trust after himself, the trustee, or the beneficiary providing that it is designated as a trust and allows the trust to enter into agreements under that name. The trustee would sign any such agreements on behalf of the trust as named. The CRA noted in technical interpretation 2005-0111731E5, dated July 4, 2006 that trustees of a trust (where there are multiple trustees) are the registered owners of the trust property and own all of the property held by the trust jointly.

Although the Trustee has legal ownership and control over the trust property, it is the beneficiaries who are beneficially interested in the property. To ensure that the interests of the beneficiaries are adequately protected, there are certain fiduciary duties imposed upon a trustee at common law. These include, amongst other things, the duty to take the same care as would a reasonable and prudent person administering another person's assets; the duty to act in the best interest of the beneficiaries (and to avoid situations where their own interests may be in conflict with those of the beneficiaries); and the duty to maintain an even hand as between beneficiaries so as to avoid making investment decisions or distribution decisions which favour one class of beneficiaries over another. These duties can, to a greater or lesser extent, be modified by the terms of the trust document. This often happens with respect to the duty to maintain an even hand, where the Settlor specifically intends for the trustee to make investment decisions or distributions of assets such that they favour one class of beneficiary over another (such as in a spouse trust).

There are a variety of circumstances where a Settlor might look to a trust as an appropriate estate planning mechanism by which a gift can be made in a controlled manner. These include:

1. Providing for minor, incapacitated or disabled beneficiaries who are unable to manage their own property;
2. Protecting assets from a spendthrift beneficiary;
3. Protecting entitlement to government benefits payable to a disabled beneficiary;
4. Creditor protection;
5. Protecting assets in the event of marital breakdown;
6. Providing for future benefits and successive interests; or

7. Providing for charitable purposes.

Generally, a trust is treated as a separate taxpayer for the purposes of the *Income Tax Act*. As a result, trusts have also long been recognized as an effective tax planning vehicle. In this regard, trusts have been used as a means of income splitting (for example, as part of an estate freeze a trust for the benefit of the freezor's children may acquire growth shares of a corporation), offshore investing (such as the so-called five year immigrant trusts), charitable gifting (charitable remainder trusts), probate avoidance, financing vehicles, and for a number of other strategies to reduce, defer and split taxable income.

9.3 — Taxation of Trusts

A. — General tax considerations

While at common law, the trust is a relationship and not a person, under subsection 104(2) of the Act a trust is deemed to be a separate taxpayer and is generally taxed as if it were an individual.

Subsection 104(1) states that references to a "trust" or "estate" in the *Income Tax Act* are to be read as references to the trustee, executor, legal representative or administrator, and accordingly, these persons are responsible for ensuring that taxes on account of the trust are paid out of the trust funds. In fact, where a trustee or executor distributes assets out of the trust prior to confirming (by obtaining a clearance certificate) that no unpaid taxes remain owing from the trust, that trustee becomes personally liable for the unpaid tax to the extent of the distribution.

Generally, for estate planning purposes, the type of trust most often involved is a personal trust. A personal trust is a category of trust defined in the *Income Tax Act*, and it essentially describes those trusts where beneficial interests were granted for no consideration.

For tax purposes, there are two major types of personal trusts; *inter vivos* trusts and testamentary trusts. Generally, *inter vivos* trusts are trusts established during the lifetime of the settlor while testamentary trusts are trusts established on or as a consequence of the death of an individual. *Inter vivos* trusts established after June 17, 1971 are generally taxed at the top marginal tax rate while testamentary trusts and pre-June 18, 1971 trusts qualify for the same graduated marginal tax rates as natural persons (but without the personal tax credit). The taxation year of an *inter vivos* trust must be the calendar year. The trustees of a testamentary trust may elect the trust year-end within limits. Trusts may pay or make income payable to beneficiaries to be taxed in their hands.

The 2013 federal budget announced the government's intention to consult on possible measures to eliminate the tax benefits that arise from taxing certain trusts at graduated rates. On June 3, 2013, the Department of Finance released a consultation paper containing its proposed direction.

The paper proposes to apply flat top-rate taxation to pre-June 18, 1971 Canadian resident *inter vivos* trusts; trusts created by Will; and estates after a reasonable period of administration — 36 months after the date of death.

It is proposed that a number of other income tax rules be amended to treat the trusts impacted by the proposals in the same manner as ordinary *inter vivos* trusts. Some of these other rules relate to items such as: income tax installments; alternative minimum tax; and calendar year taxation years. These measures are to apply to existing and new trusts in these categories beginning in 2016 and later taxation years. Should these measures be implemented much of the discussion relating to whether certain ownership and beneficiary designation planning would receive testamentary trust treatment may, for practical purposes, become less important.

Where a trust is resident in Canada, it is taxed on its worldwide income. The Supreme Court of Canada decision in *St. Michael Trust Corp., As Trustee of the Fundy Settlement v. The Queen*, 2012 SCC 14, [2012] 3 C.T.C. 265, 2012 D.T.C. 5063 held that the residency of a trust should be determined based on where the central management and control of the trust takes place and not merely the residence of the trustee(s). Prior to this case, typically one would look to the residency of a majority of the trustees of the trust to make this determination. Archived Interpretation Bulletin IT-447 "Residence of a Trust or Estate," dated May 30, 1980, discussed the CRA's views on this test. This test was also reflected in the case of *Thibodeau Family Trust v. R.*, [1978] C.T.C. 539, 78 D.T.C. 539 (Fed. T.D.). The CRA was asked at several tax conferences (e.g. 2012-0462841C6, dated October 30, 2012) to confirm if it intended to update IT-447. The CRA confirmed that this IT was one of the first to be updated and incorporated into the new Income Tax Folios publication. At the time of writing, this had not yet occurred.

Trusts are generally treated as conduits for tax purposes. Certain categories of trust income, such as dividends from taxable Canadian corporations, capital gains and foreign source income, retain their character for tax purposes when flowed out to the beneficiaries. However, trusts are not perfect conduits. For example, losses of a trust may not be transferred to the beneficiaries. The normal carryback and carryforward rules apply.

Trust income which is distributed to beneficiaries will be included in the beneficiaries' income and deductible by the trust. In order for such an amount to be deductible by the trust, the income must generally be either "paid or payable" to a beneficiary. Generally, under subsection 104(24) an amount is considered payable when a beneficiary is entitled in the year to have a legal right to enforce payment of that amount. Such entitlement is usually evidenced by a trust resolution and/or a demand promissory note. In technical interpretation 2003-001451 the CRA stated that "in order for a spouse to have a legal right to enforce payment of the income of a trust, any discretion in respect of the distribution of all or part of the income of the trust must be solely in the hands of the spouse."

B. — Attribution rules

Given the obvious attractiveness of using a trust to create a separate taxpayer and to income split, the Act includes a number of provisions which are aimed at reducing such planning amongst related parties. One of the major tax concerns relating to trusts is income attribution. The attribution rules are complex and careful planning is required to ensure the rules do not apply. When planning with *inter vivos* trusts, these rules must be considered before determining how the trust should be funded and choosing the settlor, trustee and beneficiaries. In very general terms, the *Income Tax Act* contains a number of attribution rules (at sections 74.1 through 74.5) which apply where funds are transferred or loaned to a trust for the benefit of a spouse or a related minor. In the case of a spouse, the attribution rules apply to both income and capital gains. In the case of a minor the attribution rule applies only to income, not capital gains. There are corporate attribution rules at section 74.4. In addition, there is a special rule at subsection 75(2) which is colloquially referred to as applying to "revocable and reversionary trusts" but the scope of which is much broader. Under subsection 75(2), where a trust holds property or substituted property on condition that:

a) the property may revert to the person who contributed the property;

b) the person who contributed the property controls who will subsequently receive it; or

c) during the contributor's lifetime the property may only be disposed of with the consent of the contributor,

any income or loss from the property or capital gains or capital losses realized from the property will be taxable in the hands of the contributor. The rules in subsection 75(2) apply regardless of whether income is paid or payable to a beneficiary or retained in the trust. Subsection 75(2) also applies irrespective of the age of the beneficiaries or the relationship of the beneficiaries to the contributor. It should also be noted that subsection 107(4.1) in conjunction with subsection 107(2.1) provides that if subsection 75(2) ever applies to the trust, then, as long as the contributor in respect of whom subsection 75(2) applies is alive, the trust loses its ability to transfer property to the beneficiaries (other than, generally, the contributor in respect of whom subsection 75(2) applies) on a rollover basis.

9.4 — Alter Ego and Joint Partner Trusts

Alter ego trusts and joint partner trusts created pursuant to paragraph 104(4)(iv) of the Act make it possible for individuals who have reached age 65 to use *inter vivos* trusts to implement certain estate plans and avoid probate on death. In an alter ego trust, the individual who gifts the property to the trust (the transferor) must be entitled to receive all the income of the trust and must be the only person to receive or otherwise obtain the use of income or capital of the trust prior to the death of the transferor. In a joint partner trust both the transferor and partner must be entitled to receive all the income of the trust and must be the only persons entitled to receive or otherwise obtain the use of the income or capital of the trust during their lifetimes. Both kinds of trusts will have contingent beneficiaries who will be entitled to the income or capital of the trust after the death of the transferor or the last to die of the transferor and partner. The transfer of capital property to the trust occurs on a rollover basis and therefore the tax liability arises in the trust but not until the death of the transferor in the case of an alter ego trust or the second to die in a joint partner trust. This tax treatment on death is similar to the treatment for a spouse trust.

Life insurance can be an asset used by these trusts to deal with this tax liability within the trust. The trust is typically both owner and the beneficiary of the policy. Life insurance is not "capital property", and will therefore not receive rollover treatment when transferred to an alter ego (joint partner) trust by the settlor. As well, the tax consequences (if any) arising from the situation where the trust is owner, premium payor and beneficiary of a life insurance policy should be considered in light of the CRA's commentary at 2006-0174041C6 and 2012-0435681C6 (described in more detail at section 9.5 below).

These trusts are treated as *inter vivos* trusts for tax purposes, and accordingly, the income retained in the trust is taxed at the highest marginal tax rate. These trusts are typically attractive to individuals wishing to reduce probate taxes otherwise payable, or to protect assets from creditors. They are also attractive structures where an individual wishes to create an alternate to a power of attorney, or to maintain privacy, generally not available with a probated Will. From a tax perspective, arguably, these trusts effectively put the settlor in no better position than he would have otherwise been. As *inter vivos* trusts, the residual beneficiaries, or remaindermen, would currently be in a worse tax position, if the funds are to remain in trust for their benefit after the death of the settlor (or last death of settlor and spouse) than if they were beneficiaries of a testamentary trust. See the discussion above at section 9.3.A regarding the government consultation on the elimination of graduated rates for testamentary trusts.

9.5 — Trusts and Life Insurance

Life insurance can be an attractive investment option for a trust. It can also be a valuable tax planning tool in certain trusts (for example, spouse trusts, alter ego trusts, and joint partner trusts) as it can provide liquidity necessary to fund the tax liability arising in the trust on the death of the spouse or contributor, as the case may be, with insurance proceeds payable on the death of the life insured.

The tax treatment of life insurance proceeds received by a trust is substantially the same as if the proceeds are received by an individual. Death benefit proceeds of a life insurance policy paid to a trust are received tax-free (receipt of proceeds in consequence of death is not a "disposition" of a life insurance policy under subsection 148(9) of the Act and therefore is not subject to tax). A payment from a trust may be made tax-free to a capital or income beneficiary in satisfaction of a capital or income interest of a trust (pursuant to subsections 107(2) or 106(2) and (3) of the Act). The trust document would identify capital and income beneficiaries. Notwithstanding that the beneficiary may receive death benefit proceeds from a life insurance policy via the trust, insurance proceeds do not retain their character when flowed through the trust (subsection 108(5) of the Act). As a result, if death benefits from a life insurance policy are distributed to a private corporation, the company will not receive a credit to its capital dividend account. For more discussion of this point see sections 6.2.C.i and 9.5.E.

There are two questions that must be considered prior to acquisition of a life insurance policy by a trust. First, is a trust legally able to acquire and fund a life insurance policy? Second, are there any tax consequences that might arise as a result of this investment?

From a legal perspective, the trust's ability to own and pay premiums on an insurance policy will depend on the wording of the trust document and the relevant provincial legislation. Absent specific authorization in the trust document, more general wording may sufficiently empower the trustees to do so. For example, wording which gives the trustees discretion to make expenditures or investments for the "benefit" of a beneficiary, might authorize trustees to purchase insurance or annuities on the lives of any person in respect of whom the beneficiaries have an insurable interest. In any event, before investing in an insurance product, the trustees must confirm that they are comfortable making the desired investment.

In the absence of specific wording in the trust document the "prudent investor" rule in provincial legislation which governs trustee investments now expands a trustee's ability to acquire insurance products. The trustee must still be mindful of his or her other obligations, whether imposed by statute or by common law fiduciary rules. Particularly, when making an investment in a life insurance policy, an annuity, or both, the trustee must be mindful of any diversification requirements set out in the relevant *Trustee Act*, as well as his or her obligation to act impartially or maintain an even hand as between classes of beneficiaries with varying interests.

The *Quebec Civil Code* has a slightly different approach. Under article 1278(2) QCC, the full administration of a trust is granted to the trustees. Under these rules (1306 QCC), the trustee has the obligation to preserve the property, make it productive, and use it for the purpose of the trust. The trustee has the power to alienate the property, mortgage it, change its use or, if applicable, invest it in any form of investments (1307 QCC). In fact, the trustee, unless the trust specifies otherwise, is not bound by the provisions of deemed sound investments set out in article 1339 QCC. This would not prevent the trustee, as administrator of the property of others, from having the obligation to act with prudence, diligence, and honestly and faithfully in the best interest of the beneficiary (1309 QCC).

A further question which must be considered is whether the income from either or each of these products should be allocated to the income or capital of the trust. That is, if an annuity is acquired with a lump sum amount originally representing capital of the trust, would that annuity income constitute capital or income to the trust for the purposes of allocating to beneficiaries. This will be an important consideration for trustees having to determine whether, and how much, income can be paid to each class (capital and income) of beneficiary. This is also important for the trustee when determining whether the investment is made for the benefit of one class of beneficiary or another.

Finally, the trustee must be satisfied that the rate of return acquired on the investment is a reasonable one, particularly in jurisdictions where there are apportionment rules. Again, when the trustee is determining reasonable rates of return, the trustee must be able to distinguish, for trust purposes, how much of the income received is to be treated as a return of capital, and how much is to be treated as income.

Up until the CRA Roundtable at the 2006 Annual CALU conference (2006-0174041C6 dated November 2, 2006), it was thought that there were no significant tax consequences, per se, to a trust acquiring, owning, or funding a life insurance policy. At the 2006 Roundtable, the CRA considered a situation involving a trust which otherwise satisfied the spousal trust rollover conditions at subsection 70(6) of the Act. The trust was authorized to acquire and hold an insurance policy on the life of the surviving spouse and to fund the policy premiums either from trust income or capital. The CRA was asked whether such a trust would continue to meet the conditions of subparagraph 70(6)(b)(ii) of the Act. The CRA stated that in its view, the conditions would not be satisfied and thus a rollover would not be available. A similar question was posed at the 2006 STEP Roundtable (2006-0185551C6 dated September 11, 2006).

The STEP and CALU responses reiterated that in CRA's view, a spouse trust would not qualify for a subsection 70(6) rollover if the trust funded an insurance policy on the life of the surviving spouse. At the 2012 CALU CRA Roundtable (reported as 2012-0435681C6) the CRA confirmed and expanded its previous position that a spouse trust would be tainted by the payment of insurance premiums by the trust. CRA's position is discussed in more detail below at section 9.5.H.

Technical interpretation 2006-0174041C6 the CRA went on to state that "whether the trust is one that seeks to satisfy the requirements of paragraph 70(6)(b) of the Act or not, and whether the premiums are paid out of trust income or trust capital, it would appear that the policy beneficiary (including, in the circumstances of the trust being named under the policy to receive the insurance proceeds, the trust's beneficiaries) would have a benefit, from the trust's payment of the policy premiums, resulting in the application of section 105 of the Act."

However, this technical interpretation was subsequently clarified by 2008-030188, dated October 19, 2009. In it, the CRA confirmed that no benefit under subsection 105(1) of the Act arises for beneficiaries of a trust when the trust owns and is the beneficiary of a life insurance policy.

A. — Avoidance of 21-year rule

Subsection 104(4) deems most personal trusts (other than partner (spouse) trusts, alter ego trusts, and joint partner trusts) to dispose of all capital property and land inventory every 21 years for fair market value. In order to avoid application of this deemed disposition, many personal trusts are effectively forced to distribute property to the capital beneficiaries on a rollover basis, as permitted by subsection 107(2). In effect, the 21-year deemed disposition rule will often necessitate the winding up of a trust prior to the 21st anniversary. This may be contrary to the wishes of the settlor, but the harsh tax results of subsection 104(4) may not allow any reasonable alternative.

In light of the 21-year deemed disposition rule, a cash value life insurance policy can be an attractive investment for personal trusts. By virtue of the combined operation of the definitions in subsection 248(1) and section 39 relating to capital property and capital gains, together with the special rules in the Act dealing with the taxation of life insurance policy gains, it is clear that an interest in a life insurance policy is not "capital property" or property of any other type listed in subsections 104(4) and (5). As such, the 21-year deemed disposition rule does not apply to such interests. Further, it should be noted that although a life insurance policy is not capital property, it nevertheless constitutes trust capital and is eligible to be rolled out to the capital beneficiaries of the trust on a tax-deferred basis where subsection 107(2) of the Act applies. There is some conflict in this regard between the provisions of subsection 107(2) and subsection 148(7) which deems the proceeds of disposition of certain non-arm's length transfers of a life insurance policy to be cash value (see section 3.2.G.v.b). The better view would be, and certainly from a policy perspective should be, that subsection 107(2) applies and the property should be eligible for a rollover. This position was confirmed by the CRA at the 1999 Conference for Advanced Life Underwriting (CALU) annual Canada Revenue Agency Roundtable (CRA file number 9908430).

As a life insurance policy is not treated as capital property, it can also be a good planning tool to help deal with those trusts approaching their 21st anniversary. Where a trustee is uncomfortable with the options regarding this tax liability (i.e. pay the tax or wind up the trust, an act which may be contrary to the settlor's wishes), the trustee could consider acquiring an insurance policy on the life of one or some of the capital beneficiaries, equal to the amount of the capital assets currently held by the trust. When the trustee is faced with the approach of the 21st anniversary of the trust, he or she could take steps to distribute the capital property from the trust to the capital beneficiaries, yet ensure that the value of the capital remains preserved within the trust for the benefit of the remaining intended beneficiaries through the receipt of insurance proceeds. Of course, it would be necessary to ensure that the trust would have sufficient funds to satisfy the premium obligation under the policy. It also means that the remaining beneficiaries are effectively forced to wait until the death of the life insured before receiving the cash proceeds. It does, however, allow the trustee to maintain the trust while avoiding the tax liability associated with the deemed disposition.

This works best in a family trust situation with shares of a privately held family business in the trust. The shares could be distributed to a beneficiary of an older generation (possibly with a reorganization of share structure to ensure that control is ultimately retained where it was intended), and the trust could acquire insurance on the life of that beneficiary representing the value (or a calculated future value) of the distributed share capital. At death, the insurance proceeds would be paid to the trust, and could be used to purchase the shares from the estate of the deceased beneficiary, or simply distributed to the next generation, as intended by the settlor. This type of planning permits the trust to avoid triggering a tax liability in respect of the shares at the 21st anniversary, while preserving the capital for the benefit of the next generation.

B. — Change of trustee and life insurance

The CRA was asked in technical interpretation 2000-0003865, dated April 7, 2000, whether there is a disposition of a life insurance policy where a life insurance policy is owned by a trust and there is a change of trustees. The CRA responded that where the terms of the trust provide or allow for the change of trustees that change in and by itself would not result in a disposition for purposes of section 148 of the Act. This is consistent with the definition of "disposition" at subsection 248(1) of the Act which provides that a change in legal ownership without a change in beneficial ownership would not constitute a disposition. However a change of trustees may result in a change of residency for the trust if the location of central management and control has in fact changed. See section 9.3.A.

CRA technical interpretation 2004-0087761E5 may change this position somewhat. In that letter, the CRA looked at a situation where a trust was the sole shareholder of a corporation. The CRA considered whether the replacement of a trustee amounts to an acquisition of control of the corporation. CRA's view was that the replacement of a single trustee would amount to a change of control with the possible exception in cases where the new trustee is related to the pre-existing trustees. An acquisition of control triggers a number of tax events including a deemed year end. The technical interpretation looked at trustee replacement in the context of an *inter vivos* trust but there is no reason to believe that the CRA would take a different approach in the testamentary trust context where an executor is replaced. This could have significant impact, for example, on insurance based redemption planning such as the 50 percent solution and other plans relying upon subsection 164(6) of the Act. Executors need to beware.

C. — Attribution planning

As a result of the various trust attribution rules, it is often desirable to invest trust assets in property that does not give rise to taxable income. Particularly in circumstances where the beneficiaries are minors (and subsection 75(2) does not apply) it is often desirable to invest trust funds in investments which either give rise to no income or give rise only to capital gains (which do not attract attribution). For these purposes, a cash value life insurance policy can again be an attractive investment option. Unless there is a disposition of the policy that produces a taxable policy gain, there is no taxable income generated by the asset and there is nothing to attribute. The death benefit will ultimately be received tax-free by the trust, or, alternatively, the trust could leverage the policy on a tax-free basis and distribute the loan proceeds tax-free to the beneficiaries. This type of planning is also attractive to trustees of alter ego and joint partner trusts which are treated as *inter vivos* trusts after the death of the settlor or spouse as the case may be.

D. — Testamentary insurance trusts

Many individuals debate whether insurance proceeds should be paid to their estate or directly to a named beneficiary. Where the proceeds are paid to a named beneficiary probate fees, where relevant, are avoided as are potential creditor claims. On the other hand, by paying the proceeds to the estate, it is possible to take advantage of the graduated tax rates available to testamentary trusts in respect of any income generated by the insurance proceeds. Ideally, in many cases the policyholder would like to have proceeds paid in a manner that avoids probate but preserves the graduated tax rates. (Note: See the discussion above at 9.3.A regarding the government consultation on the elimination of graduated rates for testamentary trusts.)

In technical interpretation 9605575, dated December 17, 1996, the CRA confirmed that it is possible to fund a trust using life insurance proceeds such that the trust will qualify as a testamentary trust for tax purposes in circumstances where the parameters of the trust have been laid out prior to death in a manner intended to avoid probate fees. In that technical interpretation the CRA first considered a situation where a trust was established in a testator's Will. The CRA confirmed that, in such circumstances, the payment of proceeds in respect of an insurance policy payable on the testator's death will not, in and by itself, jeopardize the status of a testamentary trust. The CRA then went on to consider a situation where a trust had been funded from the proceeds of a life insurance policy available on the death of an individual and the terms of the trust had been established by the individual during his lifetime, separate from his Will. Presumably the establishment of this trust during the individual's lifetime was intended to avoid the application of provincial probate fees which can be as high as 1.5 percent of the value of the "estate." Once again the CRA confirmed that it would consider such a trust to be a testamentary trust within the meaning of subsection 108(1) of the Act as it had been created on or after the insured's death or as a consequence thereof. Care must be taken in establishing such a trust to ensure that the double objective is properly met. In particular, during the lifetime of the settlor no property can be contributed to the trust. The original trust property must be the insurance proceeds such that the trust is not settled and does not legally exist until the death of the life insured at which time the insurance proceeds become payable.

The combined requirements of 1260 and 1819 QCC may make testamentary insurance trusts more difficult to accomplish in Quebec. In Quebec, a trust results in the transfer of assets and is formed when the trustee has accepted it (1264 QCC). With a testamentary trust, acceptance occurs of course after death but its effect is retroactive to the time of death. In Quebec, a testamentary trust has to be created through a donation *mortis causa*. This type of donation can be made by Will (or marriage contract) and therefore a testamentary trust could only be created through a Will. Where the insurance proceeds are received by the estate of the life insured, the proceeds would form part of the property of this testamentary trust. It is arguable that a testamentary insurance trust can be created by way of a beneficiary designation in favour of such a trust or a trustee of such a trust created in a Will resulting in the life insurance proceeds not passing through the estate but being held and administered by a trustee of a testamentary trust. Careful planning would be required and, ideally, execution of the beneficiary designation and the Will done contemporaneously. Where instead, a beneficiary designation is made in favour of a beneficiary directly (for example a minor child) and a trustee is appointed to administer the proceeds, in *Cie d'assurance-vie Manufacturers (Financière Manuvie) c. Massouh*, 2010 QCCS 2060, 2010 CarswellQue 4771 (Que. S.C.), this was not sufficient to create a trust in Quebec. In that case, a child was named as beneficiary directly and a so-called trustee was appointed "in accordance with the Will". The Will set out extended powers to the executors for the administration of property held on behalf of the child. The judge rejected the petition of the estate executors to administer the death benefit on behalf of the testator's daughter saying that a trust was not created. The administration of the death benefit was granted to the mother as legal tutrix (guardian).

A testamentary insurance trust must be created by the person whose life is insured. This is because an insurance trust is settled upon receipt of the insurance proceeds. This view was confirmed by the CRA in technical interpretation 9605575 referred to above, technical interpretation 2009-0350811E5, dated January 6, 2011, and technical interpretation 9625975, dated October 7, 1996, where the CRA stated that:

> A trust will generally come into existence when property is transferred to the trustee and legal ownership of the trust property rests with the trustee. We agree with your comment that there is no trust until the insurance proceeds are paid. In our opinion, the trust cannot exist on the sole basis that there is a designation in the insurance contract.

The person legally entitled to direct the payment of the proceeds into the trust, thereby settling the trust, is the person entitled to make the beneficiary designation, which is the policy owner. Therefore, the owner and the life insured must be the same person in order for the trust to be treated as "testamentary". The CRA stated in technical interpretation 2009-0350811E5 as follows:

> . . . a trust created pursuant to an individual's Will or other testamentary instrument will not lose its testamentary trust status solely by reason of the receipt of the proceeds of a life insurance policy on the life of that individual (who was the policyholder), where the trust is designated beneficiary under the policy and the trust was not created or settled before the death of the individual.

This technical interpretation also confirmed that where the terms of the trust allow for the change of trustees, the addition of a trustee would not by itself affect the testamentary trust status of the trust since there would be no change in beneficial ownership of the trust property.

It should also be noted that insurance trusts, although testamentary, will not qualify as testamentary spouse trusts under paragraphs 104(4)(a)(i) and (i.1) of the Act (see technical interpretation 9625975 discussed above). Even if the terms of a testamentary insurance trust are identical to those of a spouse trust, the testamentary insurance trust is not "created by the Will of a taxpayer". Rather, at least in common law jurisdictions, it is created by a beneficiary designation and not by the Will, wherever the beneficiary designation may be located (including in a Will).

As well, subsection 108(1) of the Act appears to permit a contribution to an existing testamentary trust from an individual other than the one creating the trust, as long as the contribution was as a result of death. From an insurance perspective, this should mean that an individual (who is both owner and life insured) can make a beneficiary designation causing insurance proceeds to fall into a newly created testamentary insurance trust, into that individual's estate, or into someone else's existing testamentary trust. For instance, where a mother owns a policy on her own life, and the father pre-deceased her, she could establish a stand-alone testamentary insurance trust for the benefit of her beneficiaries (for instance, her children), or alternatively, she might choose to have to proceeds payable to the father's existing testamentary trust (presumably for the benefit of the same children). This might be attractive in that it saves administrative fees associated with multiple trusts, but it results in the loss of an income-splitting opportunity, as there is now only one taxpayer. In all circumstances, the contributor has to be both owner and life insured.

It is not uncommon for an insurance policy to be held by more than one owner, and we now have clarification by the CRA as to their views on the ability to use at least one type of multi-owned policy to create an insurance trust. The form of ownership considered by the CRA was joint ownership. All owners arguably have full and equal rights under the contract, and that includes the right to make or change a beneficiary designation (subject to an irrevocable designation). Case law has confirmed that one party to a jointly-owned policy cannot unilaterally take steps that affect the rights of the other party, and that the courts will consider the rights of all owners where a policy might otherwise be subject to the claim of a third party (such as a creditor or a dependent of one of the owners). (See *Couture (Succession de) c. Breton*, 2006 QCCS 4814, 2006 CarswellQue 8097; *Madore-Ogilvie (Litigation Guardian of) v. Ogilvie Estate*, 2008 ONCA 39, 2008 CarswellOnt 195, 38 E.T.R. (3d) 13.) Practically, most insurers require that both owners consent in writing to beneficiary designations and alterations and therefore will not accept a designation made in the Will of one of the owners where a policy is jointly owned. Most insurers accept that the designation survives the death of one of the owners, unless amended by the surviving owner subsequently (subject to an irrevocable beneficiary designation and assuming the survivor has capacity to amend at the time). Note: There may be differences in how insurers recognize beneficiary designations made by joint owners, when one of the owners dies.

At the CALU CRA Roundtable on April 29, 2008 (technical interpretation 2008-0270421C6), the CRA was asked whether a trust settled with the proceeds of a jointly-owned life insurance policy (which was also a joint last-to-die policy on the owners' lives) would qualify as a testamentary trust where the beneficiary designation was made by the owners jointly and the surviving owner made no changes to the designation after the death of the first owner and life insured. The CRA stated that the trust would be testamentary provided that the original requirements set out in technical interpretation 9605575 were met, that the trust was not created or settled before death, and that the proceeds represented a final payment under the insurance policy.

At the 2012 CALU CRA Roundtable, Question 4 (reported as 2012-0435701C6) explored fact patterns involving a jointly owned joint last-to-die policy with an accumulated value on the first death benefit (see section 3.2.C.i for a discussion of the taxation of this form of death benefit) and the receipt of death benefit proceeds from such policies by a testamentary trust. Prior technical interpretation 2010-0358461E5, dated December 15, 2010, had confirmed the receipt of life insurance proceeds by the trustees of a spousal testamentary trust would not taint the trust for purposes of the rollover but might impact the trust's status as a testamentary trust. The questions at the 2012 CALU Conference explored specific fact patterns and at least one of those (the payment of a death benefit on the last death of the joint owners to the existing testamentary trust of the deceased joint owner), confirmed that it was possible not only not to taint the spousal trust but also to retain testamentary trust treatment. In relation to the payment of the accumulated value on first death benefit to a testamentary trust created on the death of the first person to die and the other joint owner under the policy was still living, it could not confirm that testamentary trust status would be retained.

A special trust to receive insurance proceeds would also be well advised in circumstances where the desired beneficiary is a minor at the time of the insured's death. In the absence of a trust the insurer may be obligated to pay the funds into court. Such a trust should be a formal trust and not simply an informal "in trust for" arrangement. These types of trusts are also attractive where settlors are wishing to provide for disabled or incapacitated beneficiaries while preserving their right to receive government benefits. Special trust terms would be considered in that case to preserve these rights. See, for example, *Ontario (Ministry of Community and Social Services) v. Henson* (1987), 28 E.T.R. 121 (Ont. Div. Ct.); affirmed (1989), 36 E.T.R. 192 (Ont. C.A).

E. — Business insurance trusts

Trusts are often used in the context of corporate buy/sell agreements. In circumstances where there is concern as to the corporation's solvency at the time of the death of a shareholder, it may be preferable for insurance policies to be held by a trust and the insurance proceeds to be paid to the trust. Trusts may also be considered where there are a number of shareholders and it is desirable to consolidate ownership of the policies. For example, if there are four shareholders wishing to put in place a crisscross buy/sell arrangement, each individual would require three life insurance policies for a total of twelve policies. By holding the policies in a trust, only four policies are required. Trusts may also be the preferred vehicle where there is concern as to policing of policy premiums or concern that the survivors may not willingly fulfill their obligations under the buy/sell agreement.

Where a trust is interposed as part of the buy/sell arrangement, the trust will own and be the beneficiary of the insurance policies on the lives of the shareholders. On the death of a shareholder the trust would receive the tax-free insurance proceeds. The proceeds could be distributed tax-free to the surviving shareholders to enable them to satisfy their buy/sell obligations. In fact, the proceeds would typically not be released to the survivors until such time as these obligations are satisfied.

As long as it is the surviving shareholders who have the obligation to purchase the shares from the deceased's estate, this mechanism is tax effective. However, the corporation must not be a beneficiary of the trust. As noted at section 9.3.A, a trust is an imperfect conduit. While insurance death benefits may be received tax-free by a trust and distributed tax-free to the trust beneficiaries, if the trust beneficiary is a private corporation there will be no credit to the recipient corporation's capital dividend account. This is the position taken by the CRA in technical interpretation RCT 5-1766 dated July 24, 1986. There, the CRA considered a situation where the insurance proceeds intended to fund a buy/sell arrangement were to be received by a trust. If, at the relevant time, the corporation was solvent, the proceeds were to be distributed by the trust to the corporation. If the corporation was not solvent, the proceeds would ultimately be distributed to the estate of the deceased shareholder. The CRA indicated that, in such circumstances, there would be no credit to the capital dividend account as the corporation was not the beneficiary of the policy. Accordingly, the corporation will not be able to distribute the proceeds tax-free by way of capital dividend to the surviving shareholders or redeem shares from the deceased's estate using capital dividends.

The definition of CDA was amended by Bill C-22 on June 14, 2001 to include the nontaxable portion of capital gains and capital dividends received by a trust and distributed to a private corporation. Although this change addresses a portion of the disparity, that is, allowing for capital dividends received by a trust (even if arising from life insurance proceeds) to be distributed from a trust to a corporate beneficiary of the trust to credit the corporate beneficiary's CDA, it does not address the situation where a trust receives life insurance proceeds and distributes these proceeds to a private corporation that is a beneficiary of the trust. Presumably this is because the amendments were drafted with the mutual fund trust context in mind. A submission made to the Department of Finance by CALU in February of 2009 seeks a technical amendment which would extend the same type of capital dividend account character to life insurance death benefits received by a trust and distributed to a private corporation as has been done in respect of non-taxable portion of capital gains and capital dividends received by a trust. No response from the Department has yet been provided.

At the CLHIA CRA Roundtable (Q 11 reported as 2011-0399771C6, dated May 20, 2011), the CRA was asked to consider if the concept of "constructive receipt" could be applied to a specific fact pattern involving a trust receiving life insurance proceeds and paying those proceeds to private company beneficiaries of the trust to satisfy the companies' obligations under a buy-sell agreement. The facts involved were as follows: ACo, BCo, and CCo each hold one third of the shares of Opco. Life insurance is acquired on the lives of the three controlling principals (Mr. A, Mr. B, and Mr. C). The proceeds of the policies are to be used for buy/sell purposes to acquire shares of Opco owned by a deceased principal's holding company. The policies are held by a trust under which ACo, BCo, and CCo are non-discretionary beneficiaries. The trust is the owner and beneficiary of the policies. Contributions to the trust are made by ACo, BCo, and CCo to enable the trust to pay premiums under the policies. On the death of Mr. A, principal shareholder of ACo, the trust agreement and shareholders' agreement provide that insurance proceeds payable to the trustee are to be held by the trustee pending the transfer of ACo's shares of Opco to BCo and CCo. Upon completion of the transfer of the shares, the trustee is to distribute the insurance proceeds to ACo in satisfaction of the purchase price payable by BCo and CCo pursuant to the agreements. The CRA was not prepared to extend the concept of constructive receipt to enable ACo to be viewed as having received life insurance proceeds and thus to credit ACo's CDA.

An important consideration regarding using a trust as part of a buy/sell structure is the funding of the premium payment. The parties must make sure that the shareholders are personally funding the trust to permit the trustees to pay the insurance premium. If the corporation funds the insurance premiums, the shareholders may be taxed under subsection 15(1) of the Act as having received a shareholder benefit.

F. — Trusts and United States estate tax

For those persons facing a potential United States estate tax liability, irrevocable life insurance trusts are a common planning feature. Irrevocable life insurance trusts are particularly attractive for US citizens who are residents of Canada (see section 10.2.B).

G. — Retirement compensation arrangements

Life insurance policies can also be an attractive investment for a trust which is subject to tax as a retirement compensation arrangement. The exempt life insurance contract provides the retirement compensation arrangement with an investment which does not give rise to a 50 percent refundable tax liability on its annual income (see section 7.7).

H. — Spouse trusts and life insurance

Generally an individual is deemed to have disposed of all his or her capital assets at their fair market value immediately before death according to paragraph 70(5)(a). An exception to these rules is provided in subsection 70(6) where the property is transferred to a spouse, common-law partner or spouse trust. Capital properties left to the deceased's spouse, common-law partner or spouse trust pass on a tax-deferred basis. The result is that tax on capital gains and recapture may be deferred until the surviving spouse or surviving common-law partner dies. In the case of a qualifying spouse trust, the deemed disposition is deferred until the end of the day on which the surviving spouse or common-law partner dies pursuant to subsection 104(4). Therefore if estate planning involves a spouse trust, the tax liability and the funding need are postponed until that time. Insurance on the spouse's life, either single life or joint last-to-die life insurance has often proven to be a cost effective method to fund the tax liability.

If the property transferred by the deceased to a spouse trust included shares of a corporation, the shares will be deemed to be disposed of at the end of the day on which the surviving spouse dies. Accordingly, the fair market value of the shares must be determined at that time. One way to fund some or all of this liability is for the corporation to purchase life insurance on the spouse's life. The value of the life insurance policy will be included in the value of the shares at the end of the day on which the surviving spouse dies. For deaths that occur prior to October 2, 1996 subsection 70(5.3) does not apply to subsection 104(4) and accordingly the death benefit of the life insurance policy must be included. However, subsection 70(5.3) will apply for deaths after October 1,1996 and the corporate-owned life insurance policy will be valued at cash surrender value for purposes of determining the fair market value of shares owned by a spouse trust at the end of the day on which the surviving spouse dies. This has been confirmed in CRA technical interpretation 2010-0390911E5, dated July 26, 2011. For a detailed discussion of subsection

70(5.3) see section 3.3.C. These insurance proceeds can be paid to the trust as proceeds of redemption using the 50 percent solution to get the cash into the trust.

Some concern relating to the use of corporate-owned life insurance in this context arises from CRA commentary at the 2012 CALU CRA Roundtable Question 2.3 (referenced as 2012-0435681C6). The question addressed the situation where a spousal trust holds shares of Opco B that holds a life insurance policy on the spouse that will be used to fund the tax liability in respect of the shares held by it arising on the death of the spouse. The question provided: "The directors of Opco B have signed a resolution requiring Opco B to maintain the insurance policy until the death of the survivor and to pay out the insurance proceeds to the testamentary trust as a capital and/or taxable dividend." The CRA responded as follows: "The CRA is unable to confirm that such a structure would not taint the status of the testamentary trust and also impact on the rollover of property under subparagraph 70(6)(b)(ii) of the Act." While this commentary is not definitive, it is worrisome. It is difficult to understand why this could be a problem. The trust would not use its income or capital to fund the policy. It would merely be in receipt of a dividend funded with life insurance proceeds. It would be beneficial if further clarification were provided.

Alternatively, it was widely believed that an insurance policy may be owned directly by a spouse trust either by having the trustees acquire a new policy, or alternatively, by having the ownership of an existing policy transferred to their names. The transfer of an insurance policy to a spouse takes place on a rollover basis pursuant to subsection 148(8.1) and (8.2), but this rollover does not apply to a transfer of an insurance policy to a spousal trust, alter ego trust or joint partner trust. Accordingly, tax consequences may arise at the time of transfer in the hands of the transferor. Subsection 148(7) would likely apply to such a transfer deeming proceeds of disposition equal to the cash surrender value of the policy.

The CRA has commented (see CALU CRA Roundtable 2006-0174041C6 and STEP CRA Roundtable 2006-0185551C6) that in its view a duty to fund a life insurance policy would be one under which a person other than the spouse may obtain the use of the trust capital or income. In the CRA's view, the premium payment is assumed to maintain the rights to receive the insurance proceeds. As a result, the trust would be tainted such that the subsection 70(6) rollover would not be available.

It is hard to understand the CRA's position in this regard. The CRA appears to take the position that investing in a way that will ultimately benefit capital beneficiaries is akin to the capital beneficiaries "obtaining the use" (a term not defined in the Act) of the capital. If this is really an issue, then trustees need to look at all long-term investments made in a trust (be it a spouse trust, alter ego trust, or joint partner trust which all have the same defined capital requirements).

In trying to understand the CRA's previous response a series of questions were raised at the 2012 CALU CRA Roundtable (referenced as 2012-0435681C6). Question 2 contained several parts. The first part asked the question: ". . . who, other than the surviving spouse, it considers may be entitled to the capital or income of the trust before the spouse's death, as a result of the duty on the trust to fund the life insurance policy?" The question was also posed: "Would placing a positive duty on the trustee of a spousal trust to retain and maintain any property (for example, a duty to retain the shares of a private corporation until the death of a survivor, or retain and maintain rental property until the death of the survivor) automatically taint an *inter vivos* or testamentary spousal trust?"

The CRA's response reiterated the earlier commentary. The response further stated: "This is because the premium payment is assumed to maintain, for the period covered by the premium, the rights to the insurance proceeds by the policy beneficiary — which will never be the surviving spouse." It is important to reiterate that the facts of this question state that the trust owns and is the beneficiary of the policy.

The CRA distinguished the retention and maintenance of other types of property like shares or real estate as follows: ". . . it is not, in our view, analogous to the payment of insurance premiums by the trustee to maintain rights to receive the proceeds by the policy beneficiary after the death of the spouse."

The second part of the question asked whether this response would change if there was no positive duty on the trustee to acquire or fund life insurance. In this instance, the trust document would provide the power to the trustee to purchase life insurance. The CRA responded by indicating "that the mere possibility of a person other than the survivor receiving or obtaining, before the spouse's death, use of the trust capital or income is sufficient to disqualify the rollover. This view is consistent whether the trust has the obligation or the mere power to encroach on the capital of the trust for the benefit of persons other than the surviving spouse . . .".

A qualifying spousal trust is prohibited from containing a power to encroach for anyone other than the spouse during the lifetime of the spouse. This commentary suggests that the CRA views the payment of life insurance premiums as an encroachment as opposed to the making of an investment by the trust. Investments at the trust level may be made on account of capital or income or both but should not represent an encroachment. Arguably, this prohibition on encroachment is not intended to speak to trust investments but rather distributions. The CRA commentary appears to leave us with the general view that any life insurance premiums paid by a spousal trust would taint the trust. 2012 CALU CRA Roundtable Question 3 (referenced as 2012-0435691C6) also confirmed that this is true of alter-ego and joint partner trusts as the same language (subparagraph 73(1.01)(c)(ii) and (iii) of the Act) is used in respect of such trusts.

As an alternative, a fully paid-up policy (i.e. requiring no further premiums) that is transferred to an existing spousal trust was confirmed to not taint the spousal trust (see 2012 APFF Q1, referenced as 2012-0453121C6). Problems with this solution are alluded to above. The transfer to the trust may give rise to a taxable policy gain on the disposition of the policy to the trust, as the rollover provisions of subsection 148(8.2) of the Act would not apply to such a transfer.

As an aside, it is even more difficult to understand the CRA's position in light of technical interpretation 2006-0189931E5, dated May 9, 2007 where the CRA stated that the renunciation of a spouse's interest in a spouse trust is not a disposition of the property nor does it taint the status of the trust as a qualified spouse trust unless and until the capital beneficiaries ask the court to amend the terms of the trust to obtain a distribution of trust property in their favour. It is clear from this technical interpretation that the capital beneficiaries do not obtain the use of the property until it is distributed to them. This technical interpretation is clearly inconsistent with the comments made in the above technical interpretations and makes the earlier commentary regarding spouse trusts and life insurance more perplexing.

In summary, the main question appears to be what is the appropriate test — is it, as the CRA appears to suggest, a benefit test? Based on the language of the relevant sections, the words "receive or otherwise obtain the use of" do not imply a benefit test. While life insurance held by a spousal trust may truly, ultimately benefit the residual capital beneficiaries of the trust, the words do not require that this be the case. The words require that these beneficiaries obtain the use of income or capital of the trust during the spouse's lifetime.

There is also a technical issue as to whether spousal trusts, alter ego trusts and joint partner trusts are entitled to acquire the favourably taxed prescribed annuity. The issue involves the description in Regulation 304 of the Act as to the measuring life needed to be used in order for the annuity to qualify as a prescribed annuity. Although upon a technical reading of the Act a question appears as to whether these types of trusts, and in particular an alter ego trust and a joint partner trust, would be able to acquire a prescribed annuity, the Department of Finance issued a comfort letter on July 29, 2002 indicating that it would be the Department's intention, from a policy perspective, that these types of trust be permitted to acquire prescribed annuities. The Department of Finance issued a further comfort letter on June 27, 2003 confirming the extension of the policy to joint last survivor annuities. These comfort letters were reflected in amendments to the Regulations as part of Bill C-48, which received Royal Assent on June 26, 2013. For a full discussion of this issue see Chapter 14.

Finally, and apart from the discussion above signifying potential other issues, trusts, and in particular spouse trusts, may receive insurance proceeds, either as beneficiary of a policy, or alternatively, as a result of a corporate redemption of shares. Where a Canadian corporation is the beneficiary of life insurance proceeds such that some or all of the proceeds result in a credit to its capital dividend account, that corporation may use the capital dividend account credit (and possibly the insurance proceeds, if they are available), to redeem shares from its shareholder(s). Where a spousal trust, as shareholder of the corporation, receives a capital dividend from the corporation it is usually treated as forming part of the trust's capital for trust accounting and tax law purposes. The CRA dealt with this question in technical interpretation 2004-0060161E5. The CRA stated that a capital dividend received by a trust may, in fact, be income for trust purposes in some circumstances. The CRA's position seems to be that cash dividends will be treated as income for trust purposes, regardless of their characterization as capital dividends for tax purposes, unless: (1) the trust indenture clearly and specifically provides that the settlor's/testator's intention was to have the proceeds of disposition or the value of these assets treated as capital; and (2) that the amount being distributed arose from the disposition of assets which have been bequeathed or transferred to a trust as capital. Subject to these circumstances, it is the CRA's position that notwithstanding the payment by the corporation of a capital dividend to the trust, the income beneficiary of the trust would be entitled to receive the amount from the trust.

It is unclear from this technical interpretation if the CRA is referring to trust capital or capital of the corporation. In either event, this gives rise to an important question where life insurance proceeds (which are credited to a corporation's capital dividend account) are used either to pay a capital dividend to a trust shareholder, or where they generate a deemed dividend to the trust as a result of a redemption of shares from the shareholder trust. For older trusts, the intention to have these proceeds treated as trust capital may not have been clearly articulated and, even where the intention is clear, query whether the insurance proceeds would be considered capital of the corporation at the time that the shares were bequeathed or transferred to the trust.

This is an important distinction when one is doing succession planning with trusts, as often arises with spouses and multiple families. Strategies such as the 50 percent solution and other insured redemption structures might need to be revisited in these circumstances, in order to ensure that the proceeds are actually held for that beneficiary which the settler/testator intended, and that they are payable to the beneficiary without any additional unintended taxes owing.

9.6 — RRSP Trusts and Life Insurance

An RRSP trust may own a life insurance policy but the types of policies are severely limited.

While a life insurance policy is not specifically identified in the definition of qualified investment at subsection 146(1) of the Act or section 4900 of the Regulations, subsection 198(6) of the Act deems the acquisition of an interest in, or the payment of an amount under, a life insurance policy not to be the acquisition of a non qualified investment. Subsection 198(6) applies at first instance to deferred profit-sharing plans. However, by virtue of subsection 146(11) its application is extended to RRSPs.

Conditions that the policy must meet in order for subsection 198(6) to apply are outlined in paragraphs 198(6)(c) to (e). These conditions require that the RRSP trust be the only person entitled to any benefits under the policy. The premium must be level. That is, there can be no provision to require increased premiums, even to pay for increased benefits. Lastly, and this is the most restrictive with respect to the policy design, the cash surrender value of the policy must at least be equal to, or greater than, the maximum amount payable under the policy (presumably this latter amount would be the death benefit). This latter restriction prevents the inclusion of certain benefits such as double indemnity (accidental death benefit). Dividends payable on the policy are excluded from this calculation so only the guaranteed values are included. These type of policies must, therefore, be endowment type policies. Additional information regarding life insurance and RRSPs is contained in archived Interpretation Bulletin IT-408R "Life Insurance Policies as

Investments of Registered Retirement Savings Plans and Deferred Profit Sharing Plans," dated February 15, 1980.

A "Lifetime Benefit Trust" is a new type of trust brought in by Bill C-48 which received Royal Assent on June 26, 2013. A lifetime benefit trust will permit a rollover of a refund of premiums in respect of registered funds where these funds are used to acquire a "Qualifying Trust Annuity". Under a Qualifying Trust Annuity the annuitant (i.e. the owner and payee of the annuity) is a trust for the benefit of the taxpayer. This is meant to deal with the problem originating from paragraph 60(l) of the Act, which on its face, prohibited the purchase of a life annuity with a refund of RRSP premiums on a rollover basis where the annuity was held by a trust.

The wording for section 60.011 permits a trust to take advantage of the rollover to the extent that: the trust is for the benefit of a person (taxpayer) who is a mentally infirm spouse, common-law spouse, child or grandchild of the deceased and was dependent on the deceased (prior to death) as a result of the infirmity; no person other than the taxpayer may receive, or obtain the use of, income or capital of the trust during the taxpayer's lifetime; and (amongst other criteria), the trustees are required to consider the needs of the taxpayer in determining whether to pay, or not to pay, an amount to that taxpayer. These criteria appear to contemplate the use of Henson-type trusts. Commonly, a Henson trust gives the trustees discretion as to when, how much, and to whom income and capital from the trust may be paid out, in order to align with benefits that the taxpayer may be receiving from provincial disability plans. To qualify for the rollover it is important that no person other than the taxpayer "receive or otherwise obtain the use of" income or capital of the trust during the taxpayer's lifetime. The discussion above in the spousal trust context may be equally as relevant here.

9.7 — Conclusion

Life insurance and annuities may be purchased by trusts as investments. Life insurance may also be used to cover liabilities arising in a trust on death. Trusts may arise in consequence of death and be funded with life insurance proceeds. Each situation will result in tax consequences that should be reviewed by a client's professional advisors. These and many other common uses of life insurance in trust contexts are canvassed in this chapter.

10 — INTERNATIONAL ISSUES

Updated by Jöel Campagna, C.M.A., CFP, TEP
and Caroline McKay, J.D.

10.1 — Introduction

In today's global village, estate planning is often impacted by international tax considerations. For example, a Canadian resident taxpayer may own property in a foreign jurisdiction which gives rise to a foreign tax liability. Alternatively, a Canadian resident may be a citizen of a foreign country that imposes tax based upon citizenship. International tax considerations add a significant level of complexity to estate planning. A fairly common domestic estate planning strategy may well have adverse implications in a foreign jurisdiction. Accordingly, in order for an estate plan to be effective it must be an integrated plan which fully contemplates the tax regimes of all relevant jurisdictions.

This chapter will consider certain of the international tax issues which may be of concern to Canadian residents in connection with estate planning using life insurance and will focus, in particular, on those issues pertaining to Canadian residents who, in addition to Canadian capital gains taxes at the time of death, face a potential United States estate tax liability. We will also consider the Canadian tax implications of the following two situations: (a) a non-resident owning a life insurance policy issued while resident in Canada and (b) a Canadian resident owning a foreign policy.

10.2 — United States Estate Taxes and Excise Tax on Foreign Insurance

There are two primary circumstances whereby a Canadian resident may face a tax liability under the United States estate and gift tax regime. First, a Canadian resident may be a United States citizen. Second, a Canadian resident, who is not a U.S. citizen, may own United States *situs* property giving rise to an estate tax liability. In either event, ownership of a Canadian life insurance policy may impact upon the quantum of estate taxes payable.

A. — Canadian residents who are United States citizens

i. — U.S. gift and estate tax

United States citizens and United States residents (referred to in this chapter as U.S. persons) are subject to U.S. gift and estate taxes on their worldwide estate. This contrasts markedly with Canada's tax system which is residency based. Accordingly, if an individual is a U.S. citizen and is a Canadian resident there is a potential for double taxation — Canadian capital gains taxes on the deemed disposition at death and U.S. estate taxes. Treaty provisions, described below, may serve to ameliorate this problem by permitting offsetting credits in certain situations.

In order to determine a deceased U.S. person's estate tax liability it is first necessary to determine the value of the deceased's worldwide estate. The worldwide estate is generally based on the fair market value of the deceased's worldwide assets on the date of death and includes all property, real and personal, tangible and intangible. This yields the gross estate. From this amount various deductions are allowed, including charitable bequests, certain estate administration and final expenses, mortgages and indebtedness in respect of property the value of which is included in the gross estate and, generally, a marital deduction, resulting in the taxable estate. To this amount is added taxable gifts made during the deceased's lifetime, to arrive at the estate tax base.

The estate tax rates are then assessed, on a marginal or progressive basis, whereby the percentage of tax increases as the taxable value of the estate increases. The gift and estate tax rates are governed by the U.S. Internal Revenue Code of 1986 (the "IRC"). For 2013, the rate ranges from 18 percent to 40 percent of the taxable estate. The highest rate applies where the taxable estate is over $1,000,000. The exact rate schedule for 2013 is set out in Table 1 below.

TABLE 1
Unified Transfer Tax Rate Schedule

Base for Tentative Tax		Tentative Tax* for Descendents Dying and for Gifts Made in 2013 and after	
Column A Taxable amount over	**Column B** Taxable amount not over	**Column C** Tax on amount in Column A	**Column D** Rate of tax on excess over amount in Column A
$ —	$ 10,000	$ —	18%
$ 10,000	$ 20,000	$ 1,800	20%
$ 20,000	$ 40,000	$ 3,800	22%
$ 40,000	$ 60,000	$ 8,200	24%
$ 60,000	$ 80,000	$ 13,000	26%
$ 80,000	$ 100,000	$ 18,200	28%
$ 100,000	$ 150,000	$ 23,800	30%
$ 150,000	$ 250,000	$ 38,800	32%
$ 250,000	$ 500,000	$ 70,800	34%
$ 500,000	$ 750,000	$ 155,800	37%
$ 750,000	$ 1,000,000	$ 248,300	39%
$ 1,000,000	$ —	$ 345,800	40%

The amount determined using Table 1 is the tentative estate tax liability. This tentative tax is then reduced by certain credits, the most important of which is a so-called "unified credit." For 2011 and after, the unified credit is equal to the amount of the tentative tax computed on the applicable exclusion amount. Under current law, the applicable exclusion amount was set at $5,000,000 but will be increased every year after 2011 based on an inflation adjustment (see table below). Additional credits also are available for federal gift taxes and foreign death taxes. Assuming no taxable gifts had been made during the deceased's lifetime, an individual making a gift or dying in 2013 can utilize the $2,045,800 credit to exempt the first $5,250,000 of estate value from gift and estate taxes.

The following table shows the unified credit amounts, the value of the credit, and the top estate tax rates for 2011–2013 based on currently enacted legislation.

Table 2

Calendar Year	Unified Credit Amount (US$)	Taxable value of estate sheltered by the unified credit (US$)	Highest Estate Tax Rate
2011	$1,730,800	$5,000,000	35%
2012	$1,772,800	$5,120,000	35%
2013 and after	$2,045,800	$5,250,000	40%*

Notes:

*adjusted for inflation.

The United States gift and estate tax regime is an integrated transfer tax system. That is, tax is imposed both on taxable *inter vivos* gifts (gift tax) as well as testamentary transfers (estate tax).

Gifts made during an individual's lifetime (*inter vivos* gifts) are subject to a gift tax using the same tax rate table as is used for the estate tax. The applicable tax rate is determined based on the cumulative total of gifts made to date. In other words, each taxable gift is added to the amount of gifts made in previous years to calculate the cumulative total, and then based on that cumulative total the rate that should apply is determined. Therefore, as the cumulative total of gifts increases, the rate of tax will increase.

There are two exemptions available under U.S. tax law for *inter vivos* gifts. The first exemption is known as the annual exclusion, which allows for the transfer of up to $14,000 (for 2013) to any one person during the calendar year. If the gift is to a spouse who is not a U.S. citizen, the annual exclusion amount increases to $143,000 (for 2013). Both of these annual exclusion amounts are indexed for inflation, in increments of $1,000, under the *Taxpayer Relief Act of 1997.*

The second gift tax exemption is the "unified credit" amount, which is designed to allow for the tax-free transfer of a specified amount either during lifetime or at death. Under current law, the unified credit for gift taxes is the same as the credit for estate taxes. When calculating the amount of remaining unified credit available at death, all post-1976 taxable gifts, and a portion of pre-1977 taxable gifts are also added to the estate tax base for estate tax purposes. Similarly, any gift taxes paid during life will be credited against the estate taxes payable. As a result, the exemption amount available to offset estate tax arising on assets held at death is effectively reduced by the amount already claimed as an exemption on gifts during life. Similarly, any gift taxes paid during life will be credited against the estate taxes payable.

ii. — Current U.S. estate and gift tax laws

In 2001, the U.S. Congress passed legislation (H.R. 1836, the *Economic Growth and Tax Relief Reconciliation Act of 2001*, herein after referred to as "EGTRRA") containing sweeping changes to the U.S. tax regime. Among the highlights of the legislation was a gradual phase-out of the estate tax. This gradual estate tax phase-out culminated in a one-year long repeal of the estate tax beginning January 1, 2010. Under the provisions of the statute, EGTRRA was scheduled to sunset on December 31, 2010 with the law reverting back to pre-EGTRRA law on January 1, 2011. In order to avoid this reversion, the *Tax Relief, Unemployment Insurance Reauthorization, and Job Creation Act of 2010* (the "2010 Act") was passed on December 17, 2010. The 2010 Act, which was a temporary measure, included provisions that postponed the scheduled sunset of EGTRRA until 2013, reunified the gift and estate tax systems, and implemented new estate tax rates and exemption amounts for 2011-2012. On January 1, 2013 following expiration of the 2010 Act, the *American Taxpayer Relief Act of 2012* (the "2012 Act") was passed, making most of the gift, estate and generation-skipping transfer tax provisions first introduced in the 2010 Act permanent effective December 31, 2012 and increasing the maximum gift and estate tax rate from 35 percent to 40 percent. The 2012 Act removes the built-in expiration of the 2001 EGTRRA legislation and the 2010 Act mentioned above. The 2012 Act also continues the repeal of the 5 percent surtax on estates over $10,000,000.

The following summary sets forth some of the more important provisions of the 2010 Act and 2012 Acts.

a. — *Overall reduction in estate and gift taxes*

One of the most notable changes in the 2010 Act, which was made permanent in the 2012 Act, was an increase in the applicable exclusion amount. Under prior law, the largest applicable exclusion amount capped off at $3,500,000, the current law sets the applicable exclusion at a minimum of $5,000,000, with an adjustment each year after 2011 for inflation. Such adjustment for inflation will be rounded to the nearest multiple of $10,000. Based on these adjustments for inflation, the applicable exclusion amount for 2012 was $5,120,000 and is currently set at $5,250,000 for 2013.

Although the increase in the applicable exclusion amount originally enacted as part of the 2010 Act was made permanent in the 2012 Act, the rate of tax associated with gift and estate transfers of $500,000 or more increased under the 2012 Act. Effective January 1, 2013, the 2012 Act provides for the following rates: 37 percent on amounts over $500,000 up to $750,000; 39 percent on amounts over $750,000 up to $1,000,000; and 40 percent on all amounts over $1,000,000. Given that individuals can gift or transfer at death up to $5,250,000 (for 2013) without incurring a transfer tax, once enough property has been transferred so as to cause a tax to be due, such transfer will be subject to the highest tax rate of 40 percent. Despite this increase in the tax rate from 35 percent to 40 percent under current tax law, an individual's overall tax liability for estate and gift taxes is significantly reduced when compared to the law that preceded the 2010 and 2012 Acts.

b. — *State death tax credit*

Prior to EGTRRA a decedent's federal estate tax liability would be reduced by the amount of state death taxes owed. This state death tax credit was repealed entirely in 2005, and was replaced with a federal estate tax deduction for state death taxes paid. The change from a credit to a federal estate tax deduction has had a negative impact on the revenues of states that rely upon a "pick-up" or "sponge" type of inheritance tax system based on the federal estate tax (which is the system for most states). Per the 2012 Act, the tax deduction for state death taxes has been made permanent and the state death tax credit will not be reinstated.

c. — Portability

The 2012 Act permanently adopted the concept known as "portability", first introduced in the 2010 Act, which applies to the unified credit amount. Portability is the ability for a surviving spouse to use any applicable exclusion amount left unused by his or her predeceased spouse. Thus, for example, under the Act if Spouse A dies in 2013 using only $2,000,000 of his $5,250,000 applicable exclusion amount then, upon the subsequent death of Spouse B, she may use her $5,250,000 plus his unused $3,250,000 and transfer a total of $8,500,000. To prevent serial credit collection, the Act allows the portability of the unused applicable exclusion amount of only the last spouse to die.

B. — Estate tax and life insurance proceeds

In calculating the deceased's gross estate, life insurance proceeds payable to the estate of the deceased are included under subsection 2042(1) of the *Internal Revenue Code* (U.S.). More significantly, under subsection 2042(2) of the *Code*, insurance policies on the life of the deceased with respect to which the deceased possessed any "incidents of ownership" are also included. In the leading case of *Commissioner of Internal Revenue v. Estate of Noel*, 380 U.S. 678 (1965) the United States Supreme Court held that the term "incidents of ownership" is dependent upon a general legal power to exercise ownership without regard to the owner's ability to exercise such power at any particular time. In the result, incidents of ownership are construed broadly and could include, *inter alia*, such items as:

- any ownership interest in the policy,
- being a beneficiary of the policy,
- the right to change the beneficiary under the policy,
- the right to borrow against the policy,
- the right to surrender or cancel the policy,
- an option to acquire the policy,
- the right to elect settlement options.

These incidents of ownership could be exercisable individually by the deceased or "in conjunction with any other person."

In circumstances where the insurance is corporate-owned, the life insured will be considered to possess incidents of ownership of the policy if on the life insured's date of death, the life insured owns more than 50 percent of the voting shares of the corporation and the proceeds are payable other than to or for the benefit of the corporation. In the normal course, where corporate-owned insurance is to be used for buy/sell funding purposes, or for any other *bona fide* business purpose, the insurance will not be included as part of the taxable estate. However, the value of the shares of the corporation owned by the deceased would be included as part of the taxable estate.

Where the corporation is the owner of a life insurance policy on the life of the deceased, in determining the value of the shares of the corporation to be included as part of the taxable estate, the life insurance proceeds received or receivable by the corporation would be included in the valuation. However, if the decedent and corporation were both parties to a buy/sell agreement that required the corporation to purchase the decedent's shares at death, the increased value of the corporation due to the receipt of insurance proceeds may be offset by the value of the corporation's liability to purchase the stock. *See Estate of Blount v. Comm'r*, 428 F.3d 1338 (11th Cir., 2005).

It should be noted that, where a life insured severs all incidents of ownership in respect of an existing life insurance policy, the insurance proceeds will still be included in the life insured's taxable estate for estate tax purposes under section 2035 of the *Code* if the individual dies within three years of such severance.

Since life insurance can constitute a significant taxable asset for United States estate tax purposes it is important to structure insurance ownership and funding such that the deceased does not possess any "incidents of ownership" that would subject the proceeds to estate tax.

In order to ensure that insurance proceeds are not included in the deceased's taxable estate it is common to establish an irrevocable life insurance trust, commonly referred to as an ILIT, to own the policy. The trust would also be the beneficiary of the policy. Where the deceased's estate lacks sufficient liquid assets to satisfy estate liabilities, including estate taxes, the ILIT would indirectly provide the funds to the estate. For example, the trust could loan money to the deceased's estate or could purchase assets from the deceased's estate and the estate would then have the cash necessary to satisfy its liabilities. In the usual case the beneficiaries of the trust would mirror the beneficiaries of the deceased's Will.

The ILIT, as with almost all other irrevocable U.S. trusts, typically includes so-called "Crummey" powers named after the case of *Crummey v. Commissioner*, 397 F.2d 82 (9th Cir., 1968). A trust with Crummey powers is, essentially, a trust that permits a person contributing property to the trust to take advantage of the $14,000 (for 2013) annual exclusion from gift tax. When a contribution is made to the Crummey trust, the trust beneficiaries are granted a temporary right to demand withdrawal. If the withdrawal right is not exercised during the limited time period (usually 30 days), the right is lost.

After the expiration of the withdrawal right period the contribution becomes the absolute property of the trust and can be used to fund insurance premium obligations. In the case of a husband and wife, each party can donate $14,000 for each person who is given a right of withdrawal (usually each primary beneficiary). This structure, which would be available for Canadian residents who are United States citizens, ensures that the premium payments (funded by contributions to the trust) do not give rise to a gift tax liability and the death benefit will not give rise to an estate tax liability.

The Crummey trust structure may give rise to Canadian income tax issues, including the 21-year deemed disposition rule. However, it should be noted that since the main (and possibly sole) asset held by this trust would be a life insurance policy (and not capital property) the 21-year deemed disposition rule will not have negative implications. Further, assuming the insurance policy is an exempt contract held until the death of the life insured, there will be no income attribution under subsection 75(2).

C. — Non-United States persons

Whereas U.S. persons are subject to U.S. gift and estate tax on their worldwide assets, non-US persons (i.e., persons who are neither U.S. citizens nor U.S. residents) are only subject to estate tax in respect of U.S. *situs* assets. United States *situs* assets include shares or debt of United States corporations (including those held in a Canadian registered plan such as an RRSP, RRIF, or TFSA), debt of certain U.S. persons, U.S. real property and tangible personal property situated in the United States. Life insurance proceeds (i.e. death benefit) will not constitute U.S. *situs* assets of the decedent even if the policy was issued by a United States insurer. Note, however, that if a Canadian resident (who is not a U.S. citizen) owns a life insurance policy issued by a U.S. insurance company on the life of another person (whether the insured is a U.S. person or a non-resident alien), the policy will be considered U.S. *situs* property, and the fair market value of the policy will be included in the Canadian person's gross estate for the purpose of calculating the Canadian person's U.S. estate tax liability.

Prior to November 9, 1995 and the introduction of the Third Protocol[1] (the "Protocol") to the *Canada-United States Income Tax Convention, 1980* (the "Treaty"), Canadian residents who were not U.S. persons faced a significant risk of double taxation with respect to U.S. *situs* assets which were owned at the time of death. The double taxation risk resulted from the fact that the United States estate tax was based on value whereas the Canadian tax was based upon the accrued gain in respect of capital property.

The then existing treaty did not provide any relief for double taxation in respect of these two differing regimes although the Canadian income tax liability was treated as a deductible claim against the estate for U.S. estate tax purposes.

[1]A Fifth Protocol to the Treaty was drafted on September 21, 2007 and was ratified by Canada on December 14, 2007 and by the United States on December 15, 2008. Most of the provisions of the Fifth Protocol are effective January 1, 2008; however, the Fifth Protocol does not substantially change any of the Articles discussed in this text.

i. — The Protocol

The Protocol added new Article XXIX B to the Treaty. The main areas of relief provided to Canadian residents by the Protocol are:

1. A prorated unified credit;
2. A marital credit;
3. Tax credit relief; and
4. Small estate relief.

These relieving provisions are available to Canadian residents who are not U.S. persons and are described below.

a. — Prorated unified credit (paragraph 2 of Article XXIX B)

Under the *Internal Revenue Code* (U.S.), for 2013 estates of U.S. persons are entitled to a unified credit of $2,045,800 whereas non-U.S. persons are generally entitled to a unified credit of just $13,000. Under the Protocol, Canadian residents are entitled to a pro-rated unified credit of up to $2,045,800 for 2013. More specifically, the deceased's estate is entitled to a unified credit equal to the greater of $13,000 and the amount determined by the formula:

$$\text{U.S. } \$2{,}045{,}800 \times \frac{\text{value of decedent's gross estate situated in the United States}}{\text{value of decedent's worldwide gross estate}}$$

Based on this formula, no U.S. estate tax will be payable provided the value of the decedent's worldwide estate does not exceed the value of the unified credit equivalent ($5,250,000 for 2013).

b. — Marital credit (paragraphs 3 and 4 of Article XXIX B)

Provided that the four conditions outlined below are satisfied the Protocol will provide for a nonrefundable credit against estate tax where property is transferred to a surviving spouse in circumstances where a marital deduction would have been available if the surviving spouse had been a U.S. citizen. The four conditions are:

(i) that the individual was at the time of death a citizen of the United States or a resident of either Canada or the United States;

(ii) that the surviving spouse was at the time of the individual's death a resident of either Canada or the United States;

(iii) that if both the individual and the surviving spouse were residents of the United States at the time of the individual's death, one or both was a citizen of Canada; and

(iv) that the executor of the deceased's estate elects the benefits of the marital credit and waives irrevocably the benefits of any estate tax marital deduction that would be allowed under the law of the United States on a United States federal estate tax return filed for the individual's estate by the date on which a qualified domestic trust election could be made under the law of the United States.

Where these conditions are satisfied the available credit will be generally the lesser of:

1. the amount of the unified credit available to the estate; and
2. the amount of the estate tax attributable to the qualified property.

Thus, in many of these cases twice the unified credit will be available.

c. — Tax credit relief (paragraphs 6 and 7 of Article XXIX B)

Where a Canadian resident or Canadian resident spousal trust is liable for U.S. federal or state estate tax, the estate tax payable may qualify for tax credit relief in Canada. Generally, the credit is allowed against the Canadian tax payable in respect of the deceased's income or profits arising in the United States, capital gains on United States real property and on certain other U.S. *situs* assets. Analogous relief is available to the estate of a U.S. deceased person who owns Canadian property subject to a deemed disposition at death.

d. — Small estate relief (paragraph 8 of Article XXIX B)

Where the value of the deceased Canadian resident's gross worldwide estate (determined under U.S. law) does not exceed the Canadian dollar equivalent of U.S. $1,200,000 special relief is available. In such circumstances, the U.S. estate tax is based only on U.S. real property or personal property forming part of the business property of a permanent establishment in the U.S.

ii. — Planning for life insurance

Prior to the enactment of the Protocol, life insurance was commonly viewed as one of the most effective methods for Canadian residents who were not U.S. citizens for dealing with U.S. estate taxes. Insuring a U.S. estate tax liability continues to be a prudent approach for Canadian residents be they U.S. citizens or not. However, as a result of the relief provided for by the Protocol and the special rules under United States estate tax law governing life insurance, described in section 10.2.B, the manner in which the insurance is held takes on new relevance.

Life insurance is not generally considered U.S. *situs* property. However, the insurance proceeds will form part of the deceased's worldwide estate if the deceased had any "incidents of ownership" of the policy within three years prior to death. Accordingly, in such circumstances the proceeds would impact upon the amount of the prorated unified credit available to Canadian residents who are not U.S. citizens (decreasing the available credit by increasing the value of the denominator in the equation set out in section 10.2.C.i.a). In addition, the proceeds could cause an otherwise "small estate" to have a gross value in excess of $1,200,000 thus precluding the availability of the small estate relief.

In order to maximize the benefits available under the Protocol the life insured must be careful not to maintain any incidents of ownership (described above in section 10.2.B) in relation to the policy. An irrevocable life insurance trust along the lines described in section 10.2.B could be used by a non-United States person to maximize the benefit of the unified credit.

D. — Excise tax on foreign insurance

The United States currently imposes an excise tax on each policy of insurance or reinsurance covering U.S. risks issued by any foreign insurer. For insurance policies covering life, sickness, accident or annuity contracts, IRC §4371 imposes such excise tax on the premiums paid to a foreign insurer at a rate of 1 percent. Liability for this tax attaches when a premium payment is transferred to the foreign insurer or reinsurer or to any nonresident agent, solicitor, or broker. Generally, the person who pays the premium to the foreign insurer is responsible for the tax and such tax must be reported and paid quarterly (see IRS Form 720 and Instructions).

A foreign insurer or reinsurer is defined under IRC §4372(a) as a nonresident alien individual, a foreign partnership, or a foreign corporation. For the tax to apply with respect to life insurance and other similar policies, the policy must insure a citizen or resident of the United States.

In the case of life insurance policies, there are generally two instances where this excise tax will not apply. First, the excise tax does not apply when such premiums are subject to United States income tax. This situation typically arises in the case of premiums paid to a foreign insurer engaged in the business of insurance within the United States. The second exemption from this excise tax results from a tax treaty between the United States and a treaty country that meets certain requirements. Currently, the tax treaty between the United States and Canada does not qualify for this exemption.

10.3 — Emigration and Immigration

A. — Deemed disposition

Canada is one of the few countries in the world that imposes an "emigration tax." Under paragraph 128.1(4)(b) of the Act, where a taxpayer emigrates from Canada the taxpayer is generally deemed to have disposed of most properties, including "taxable Canadian property" (defined below), owned by the taxpayer at that time and to have received deemed proceeds of disposition equal to the fair market value of each such property. The deemed proceeds of disposition then become the new cost of the subject property to the taxpayer upon the deemed reacquisition under paragraph 128.1(4)(c).

This has the effect of determining the emigrant's tax liability in respect of any accrued capital gains. The emigrant can either pay the tax immediately, or provide the CRA with security for paying it later (without interest charges), when the property is actually sold.

i. — Taxable Canadian property

The definition of taxable Canadian property is contained in subsection 248(1) and applies to the entire Act. Paragraph (k) of the definition includes as taxable Canadian property a "life insurance policy in Canada".

Subsection 138(12) defines a "life insurance policy in Canada" as meaning a life insurance policy issued or effected by an insurer upon the life of a person resident in Canada at the time the policy was issued or effected. This definition refers to an "insurer" which, according to the definition in subsection 248(1), means a corporation that carries on an insurance business. The definition does not specify a Canadian corporation nor that the insurance business be carried on in Canada.

Therefore, polices issued on the life of a Canadian resident (at the time of issue), whether issued by a Canadian or foreign insurer, will be considered taxable Canadian property.

ii. — Individuals

Under the current rules, if the taxpayer is an individual, the deemed disposition discussed in 10.3.A above applies to all property, including taxable Canadian property, other than:

- real property situated in Canada, Canadian resource properties, and timber resource properties;
- property of a business carried on by the taxpayer through a permanent establishment in Canada at the time of emigration, including capital property, eligible capital property, and property described in the inventory of the business;
- property that is an "excluded right or interest" of the taxpayer (see definition below);
- for a short-term resident, where the individual (other than a trust) has been resident in Canada for 60 months or less during the 10-year period prior to emigration, any property that the individual owned on last becoming a resident of Canada, or that the individual inherited after last becoming a resident of Canada; and
- certain property of a returning former resident who last emigrated after October 1, 1996, if the taxpayer so elects.

"Excluded right or interest" is defined in subsection 128.1(10). In general terms, an excluded right or interest is a right of an individual to future benefits or other payments under certain plans or arrangements. Excluded rights or interests also include an interest of an individual in a trust governed by certain plans. Though the list is extensive, the more common types of trusts include: pension plans (RPP's, RRSP's, RRIF's), retirement compensation arrangements, registered education savings plans, registered disability plans, deferred profit sharing plans, and employee profit sharing plans. In addition, an interest of an individual in a "life insurance policy in Canada", except for that part of the policy in respect of which the individual is deemed by paragraph 138.1(1)(e) to have an interest in a segregated fund, is considered an excluded right or interest. Thus life insurance policies in Canada, other than segregated funds, will not be subject to the deemed disposition on emigration.

iii. — Immigration

Similar rules deeming a fair market value disposition of property and reacquisition of such property at fair market value apply where a person immigrates to Canada (paragraph 128.1(1)(b)). The general rationale for these reciprocal rules is that a person should only be subject to tax in respect of gains which accrued while such person is resident in Canada. The act of immigration and emigration, essentially, crystallizes the taxpayer's tax position as of that time.

However, the deemed disposition on immigration rule will not apply to a "life insurance policy in Canada" owned by an individual as this rule does not apply to "taxable Canadian property" (subparagraph 128.1(1)(b)(i)).

There may be situations where a former Canadian resident returns to Canada. The rules relating to returning former residents are included in subsection 128.1(6). This provision has the affect of reversing the accrued gains realized on departure but only for individuals who last emigrated after October 1, 1996 and file an election.

In the case of persons who are not former residents immigrating to Canada owning foreign insurance policies, the deemed disposition and reacquisition rule will apply since the foreign insurance policy is not a "life insurance policy in Canada" and therefore does not meet the definition of "excluded right or interest". For more information concerning the taxation of foreign insurance policies, see section 10.5.

iv. — Corporate-owned policies

Where the policy is owned by a corporation and an immigrating or emigrating individual is deemed to have disposed of the shares of the corporation prior to immigration or emigration (as the case may be), subsection 70(5.3) will apply. Under subsection 70(5.3), where the particular individual (or an individual not dealing at arm's length with the particular individual) is a person whose life was insured under the policy, the policy will be deemed to have a value equal to its cash surrender value immediately prior to immigration or emigration for the purpose of valuing the shares of the corporation.

B. — Reporting requirements on emigration

When an individual emigrates from Canada, they may have an obligation to report assets owned at the time of departure. Pursuant to subsection 128.1(9), all individual emigrants who own "reportable properties" (as defined in subsection 128.1(10)), immediately after the time of emigration, where the reportable properties have a total value of more than $25,000, will be required to report their property holdings to the CRA. The definition of "reportable properties" excludes, among other things, any personal use property with a value of less than $10,000. A life insurance policy would be a "reportable property".

In CRA's view, for the purpose of determining whether reporting under 128.1(9) is required, an interest in a life insurance policy owned by an individual must be valued at its fair market value taking into account the factors listed in paragraphs 40 and 41 of Information Circular 89-3 *Policy Statement on Business Equity Valuations* (technical interpretation 2008-0270401C6).

This reporting requirement applies to all individuals who have left Canada after 1995 and should be reported on Form T1161 and included with their income tax return for the year they leave Canada.

10.4 — Non-Resident Owners of a "Life Insurance Policy in Canada"

As discussed above in section 10.3.B.i, a life insurance policy will only be a "life insurance policy in Canada" if the life insured is resident in Canada at the time the policy was issued or effected (pursuant to the definition in subsection 138(12) of the Act). Consider the following example. Mr. A, Mrs. B and Mr. C own all of the shares of ABC Co., a corporation resident in Canada. Mr. A and Mrs. B are residents of Canada; Mr. C is a non-resident. ABC Co. acquires life insurance policies on the lives of each of Mr. A, Mrs. B and Mr. C for buy/sell purposes. The insurance policies on the lives of Mr. A and Mrs. B are life insurance policies in Canada but the policy on Mr. C is not a life insurance policy in Canada since he was not resident in Canada at the time the policy was issued.

There are certain circumstances whereby a non-resident of Canada may own a life insurance policy in Canada. The most common situation involves a former resident of Canada who owned a life insurance policy in Canada at the time of emigration. As described below, special rules apply where a non-resident of Canada disposes of a life insurance policy in Canada.

A. — Dual-resident individuals

There may be circumstances where an individual is a resident of both Canada and another jurisdiction. Since most countries tax residents on their income from all sources, this raises the possibility of double taxation. Canada's bilateral tax treaties are designed to provide relief from this potential double taxation and contain tiebreaker rules to determine in which country the individual is resident for purposes of the treaty. Prior to the February, 1998 federal budget, Canada's income tax legislation did not take these treaty tiebreaker rules into account. Thus, for example, an individual could claim that she was a resident of both Canada and the United States but under the tiebreaker rules she was considered a resident of the United States. This individual could argue that she was resident in Canada for purposes of the *Income Tax Act* (and therefore not subject to rules governing non-residents) but at the same time resident in a treaty country (the United States) and therefore not liable for tax in Canada as a resident.

As a resident of Canada for purposes of the Act this individual could have acquired a Canadian life insurance policy on her life which would qualify as a life insurance policy in Canada within the meaning of subsection 138(12). However, under subsection 250(5), a person is deemed not to be resident in Canada where that person would otherwise be resident in Canada, but has become entitled under a tax treaty, as a resident of another country, to an exemption from or reduction in Canadian income tax. This provision generally applies to individuals who become entitled to treaty benefits after February 24, 1998.

B. — Taxable dispositions by a non-resident

Where a non-resident person disposes of an interest in a life insurance policy in Canada, any policy gain on the disposition is taxed under subparagraph 115(1)(a)(vi) as taxable income earned in Canada by a non-resident. The income is determined in accordance with subsection 148(1) or 148(1.1) as the case may be. The taxable amount is the amount which would have been taxable and would have been included in the non-resident's income had the non-resident been a resident of Canada at the time of disposition of the policy. The income is taxable under Part I of the Act at marginal rates rather than a flat rate applicable in respect of non-resident income from property taxed under Part XIII of the Act. It should also be noted that since this income is not considered to be income earned in a province, pursuant to subsection 120(1) of the Act, the tax is increased by 48 percent of the tax otherwise payable.

C. — Withholding tax and section 116 clearance requirements

As noted above, when a non-resident disposes of a life insurance policy in Canada the disposition is taxed under 115(1)(a)(vi). Furthermore, the non-resident must notify the Canadian tax authorities of the disposition. The rules, which are summarized below, associated with non-resident dispositions of taxable Canadian property are outlined in Information Circular IC 72-17R6, *Procedures concerning the disposition of taxable Canadian property by non-residents of Canada — Section 116*, dated September 29, 2011.

i. — Canadian "purchaser"

If the "purchaser" of the "life insurance policy in Canada" is a Canadian resident, there are two possible scenarios.

The first scenario is that the non-resident person reports the disposition (or proposed disposition) and pays the Canadian tax arising (or, alternatively, provides the Minister with acceptable security) in accordance with subsection 116(5.2) of the Act. When this is done, the Minister issues a certificate (often referred to as a "Clearance Certificate") in respect of the disposition or proposed disposition. In this case, there is no withholding tax requirement for the Canadian "purchaser".

The second scenario is that the policyholder does not remit the tax and does not obtain a clearance certificate. In this case, the Canadian resident "purchaser" will be liable for tax equal to 50 percent of the amount payable (or fair market value in the case of *inter vivos* gifts and non-arm's length transfers) for the property, is entitled to withhold this tax from the payment, and must remit the amount withheld to the Minister (under subsection 116(5.3) of the Act).[2] The tax must be remitted within 30 days after the end of the month in which the "purchaser" acquired the

---

[2]Under subsection 116(5.3), the purchaser acquiring the life insurance policy from the non-resident is liable to pay as tax, on behalf of the non-resident, 50 percent of the amount by which the amount payable exceeds the amount of proceeds stated in the certificate, if any, issued under subsection 116(5.2).

interest in the policy. Failure to remit the tax within the required time period will result in penalties and interest calculated under subsections 227(9) and 227(9.3), respectively.

Under subsection 116(5.4) of the Act, where a non-resident of Canada disposes of or is deemed to dispose of a life insurance policy in Canada by virtue of subsection 148(2) or any of paragraphs (a) to (c) or (e) of the definition of "disposition" in subsection 148(9), the *insurer* in respect of the policy is deemed to be the *purchaser* for purposes of subsections 116(5.2) and (5.3) of the Act.

What this means is that the insurance company is deemed to be the "purchaser" in respect of the following events:

1. policy dividends (paragraph 148(2)(a));
2. the deemed disposition of a nonexempt life insurance contract or certain annuity contracts as a result of the death of the policyholder, the annuitant or the life insured (paragraph 148(2)(b));
3. policy changes which cause an exempt policy to become nonexempt (paragraph 148(2)(d));
4. surrender (paragraph (a) of the definition of disposition at subsection 148(9));
5. policy loans (paragraph (b) of the definition of disposition at subsection 148(9));
6. dissolution of the interest by virtue of maturity of the policy (paragraph (c) of the definition of disposition at subsection 148(9))
7. a payment on death under a life annuity issued after November 16, 1978 and before November 13, 1981 (paragraph (e) of the definition of disposition at subsection 148(9))

The effect of these rules is that if a clearance certificate were not obtained then the insurer would be liable to withhold tax equal to 50 percent of the proceeds of disposition in respect of the life insurance policy (i.e. the dividend, withdrawal amount, etc.) on behalf of the non-resident. Note that the 50 percent tax is calculated on the entire payment, not just the policy gain.

To avoid this high rate of withholding tax, Canadian insurers typically facilitate the process of obtaining a clearance certificate by filing Form T2062B "Notice of dispositions of a life insurance policy in Canada by a Non-Resident of Canada". This form is completed by the life insurer to inform the Canada Revenue Agency when there is a disposition of a life insurance policy under one of the events described in points 1 to 7 above, by a non-resident policyholder who was resident in Canada at the time the policy was issued or effected.

The form must be accompanied by a letter of authorization from the non-resident policyholder that authorizes the insurer to withhold the tax arising from the disposition under section 115 of the Act. As a result, when a Canadian life insurer receives a request for a policy loan or withdrawal by a non-resident, or if the insurer intends to make a payment due to any of the events in 1 to 7 above to a non-resident, it will request this authorization letter from the non-resident policyholder in order to proceed with filing Form T2062B.

A cheque for the tax payable based on the federal non-resident tax rates must also accompany the form. For this purpose, the applicable rates are the graduated federal tax rates multiplied by 1.48 (as per subsection 120(1)) and applied as if the policy gain is the only income of the non-resident. Note that the tax payable is calculated based on the cumulative amount for all dispositions of the person for the year and not on each individual disposition.

After review of the form and receipt of the payment from the insurer, the CRA issues a certificate of compliance to the insurer and the non-resident person, i.e. the clearance certificate (Form T2064 or Form T2068 for proposed or actual dispositions respectively.) Then the insurer can proceed with the payment and withhold the corresponding amount from the policyholder (i.e. the amount the insurer paid to the CRA when it filed the form).

Essentially, this process permits the insurer to withhold tax at graduated tax rates rather than at 50 percent of the proceeds.

The final settlement of the tax liability is made when the non-resident person files a Canadian tax return reporting the disposition. A refund would be issued in the event that the tax withheld by the insurer exceeded the non-resident's ultimate tax liability or, alternatively, provision is made for the release of security once the established debt has been satisfied.

In archived Interpretation Bulletin IT-150R2 "Acquisition from a Non-Resident of Certain Property on Death or Mortgage Foreclosure or by Virtue of a Deemed Disposition," dated January 9, 1985, the CRA notes that section 116 does not apply to a deemed disposition on death or, generally, by mortgage foreclosure. Section 116 also does not apply to property that is transferred or distributed on or after death and as a consequence thereof. Similar commentary is found in IC72-17R6 at paragraphs 67 and 68. However, an executor acting on behalf of a non-resident person must file an income tax return for the year of death and pay any tax that may be necessary on the deemed disposition.

ii. — Inter vivos *gift or non-arm's length transfer*

Where a non-resident transfers a "life insurance policy in Canada" by way of an *inter vivos* gift or to a non-arm's length person, the purchaser's withholding tax obligation, where no clearance certificate is obtained, is significantly higher. That is, paragraph 116(5.1)(f) of the Act replaces the words "the amount payable by the taxpayer for the property so acquired" with "the fair market value of the property at the time it was so acquired". This treatment was confirmed by the CRA in technical interpretation 2013-0481411C6, dated May 17, 2013. This rule will apply whether the purchaser is resident in Canada or a non-resident of Canada.

Where the insurer is not deemed to be the purchaser (i.e. the transaction is not one of the transaction noted in items 1 to 7, above) the insurer typically will not facilitate the obtaining of the clearance certificate. Therefore, the party disposing of the interest in the policy will want to obtain a clearance certificate and provide this to the purchaser in order to avoid the purchaser withholding obligations discussed above.

iii. — Non-resident "purchaser"

The rules noted above with respect to a non-resident disposing of an interest in a life insurance policy in Canada also apply to non-resident purchasers. Consider, for example, a situation where a non-resident transfers a life insurance policy in Canada to a non-resident family member, foreign corporation, or Irrevocable Life Insurance Trust (discussed in section 10.2). If a clearance certificate is not obtained, the non-resident acquiring the policy will technically be required to remit 50 percent of the fair market value of the policy to the CRA (see 2013-0481411C6). If the purchaser is not paying cash for the policy, there will be nothing to withhold from and thus the purchaser will be required to use their own cash to satisfy the remittance obligation. What is not clear is how the Canadian tax authorities will enforce these rules in respect of a non-resident purchaser.

D. — Impact of tax treaties

If the life insurance policy in Canada is a whole life policy entitling the non-resident to policy dividends such dividends constitute a partial disposition of the policy and will trigger the reporting and withholding obligations under section 116. The proceeds of disposition are deemed under paragraph 148(2)(a) to be equal to the amount of the dividend in excess of that part of the dividend used to pay an eligible premium under the policy, or repay a policy loan under the policy. Policy dividends are taxable under Part I of the Act and included in the non-resident's income under subparagraph 115(1)(a)(vi). Policy dividends do not constitute "dividends" for purposes of Canada's bilateral income tax conventions and therefore do not qualify for a reduced rate of withholding tax.

Under Canada's bilateral tax treaties with foreign jurisdictions certain "gains" in respect of dispositions of taxable Canadian property may be exempt from tax in Canada. However, the CRA takes the position that the term "gains" in Canada's bilateral tax treaties is actually a reference to "capital gains." In technical interpretation 9518087, dated September 13, 1995 the CRA indicates that the term "gains" in paragraph 9 of Article XIII of the *Canada-United States Income Tax Convention* (1980) was limited to "capital gains." Since a "policy gain," in respect of a disposition of a life insurance policy is not a "capital gain," a disposition of a life insurance policy in Canada does not qualify for relief under the *Canada-United States Income Tax Convention*. In that technical interpretation the CRA also notes that the *Canada-United States Income Tax Convention* is patterned on the OECD Model Convention and Article XIII of the Model Convention indicates that the provision is only intended to apply to capital gains.

A contrary position was expressed in technical interpretation 2002-0152647, dated July 8, 2002. There the CRA considered the tax treatment of a life insurance policy owned by a Canadian resident but which had been issued in France. In discussing the tax treatment arising from a disposition of the policy the CRA indicated that the gain realized in respect of a disposition of an interest in a French life insurance policy would be subject to the provisions of Article XIII of the Canada France Tax Treaty.

10.5 — Foreign Life Insurance

Just as there are circumstances where a non-resident of Canada may acquire an interest in a Canadian life insurance policy, so too are there circumstances where a resident of Canada may own a foreign life insurance policy. For example, an individual may immigrate to Canada and at the time of immigration own a policy issued offshore. Alternatively, a Canadian resident may acquire a life insurance policy from a foreign jurisdiction. Ownership of such a foreign insurance policy by a Canadian resident may give rise to Canadian tax issues.

A. — Foreign property reporting rules

Since 1998, Canadian residents have been required to report their ownership interests in foreign property where the total cost amount of all their "specified foreign property" exceeds $100,000. For these purposes "cost amount" is defined in subsection 248(1) of the Act and, pursuant to paragraph (f) of this definition, the normal rules for determining the cost of a life insurance policy should apply. This treatment was confirmed by the CRA at the 2011 APFF Roundtable, as well as the 2012 CALU CRA Roundtable (2012-0444711C6). These reporting rules and definition of "specified foreign property" are contained in section 233.3 of the Act and apply to foreign life insurance policies.

In CRA technical interpretation 2000-0013255, dated October 30, 2000, the CRA indicates that a taxpayer's interest in a foreign life insurance policy "could be a 'specified foreign property'" and thus subject to the reporting rules in subsection 233.3(3) of the Act. This position was further clarified in CRA's response to question 12 at the October 8, 2010 APFF Conference. The CRA referred to paragraphs (a) and (h) of the definition of "specified foreign property" in section 233.3 of the Act to conclude that a foreign insurance policy "will meet the definition of 'specified foreign property'" (unofficial translation).

Where an interest in a life insurance policy issued by a non-resident insurer meets the definition of "specified foreign property", and the total cost of all the taxpayer's specified foreign property exceeds $100,000, the taxpayer would be subject to the foreign property reporting requirements. The taxpayer would have to file Form T1135 at the same time as, but filed separately from, the taxpayer's annual tax return. An exception from filing applies for individuals that became resident of Canada in the year (see section 233.7 of the Act). Where a property is jointly owned, the cost amount is attributed to the taxpayers based on their proportionate ownership. For example, a property owned 50/50 by a husband and wife with a total cost of $100,000 would imply each taxpayer's cost amount to be $50,000. Therefore, if this was the taxpayer's only foreign property there would not be a requirement to file the T1135 (see 2000-0033095).

As noted above, a taxpayer is required to file form T1135 at the same time as their annual tax return. Failure to file the return on time will result in late filing penalties pursuant to subsection 162(10). In addition, the CRA confirmed in Question 3 at the 2013 STEP CRA Roundtable that failure to properly complete the T1135 form could extend the normal reassessment period for a taxpayer's annual return by an additional three years.

B. — Canadian taxation of foreign life insurance

The rules governing the taxation of life insurance apply equally to Canadian and foreign life insurance policies. Thus, if a Canadian resident owns a foreign life insurance policy, the accrual rules at section 12.2 apply unless the policy qualifies as an "exempt" policy for purposes of the Act (see section 1.8.A.i and ii). Further, it is the responsibility of the policyholder to determine if the policy satisfies the requirements for exempt status. In technical interpretation 9923905, dated September 16, 1999, the CRA acknowledged that while it is possible for a foreign policy to satisfy the exempt test, it would be exceedingly difficult for the average taxpayer to determine the exempt status of a foreign policy.

At one time, it was expected that a mark-to-market regime of taxation was going to be enacted in respect of foreign life insurance policies held by Canadian resident taxpayers. As a result of the 2010 federal budget, these proposed measures (contained in proposals relating to Non-Resident Trusts and Foreign Investment Entities) have not been enacted. Furthermore, these mark-to-market proposals were not included in the amended Offshore Investment Fund Property Rules enacted in 2013 (Bill C-48, which received Royal Assent on June 26, 2013) contained in section 94.1 of the Act.

11 — Life Insurance and Partnerships

Updated by Dereka Thibault, FCA

11.1 — Introduction

In this chapter we will discuss specific applications of life insurance products in the partnership context and the taxation rules related to life insurance and partnerships.

11.2 — Partnership Entities

The term partnership is not defined in the Act. Guidance on determining if a particular relationship is a partnership is provided in archived Interpretation Bulletin IT-90, "What is a Partnership?" dated February 9, 1973. IT-90 states that to determine the existence of a partnership reference must be made to relevant provincial law. Generally, provincial legislation refers to a partnership as a legal relationship existing between two or more persons carrying on a business in common for the purpose of profit. The determination of whether a relationship is a partnership is a question of fact.

A partnership can take many forms and be arranged for varied business purposes such as active business partnerships, farming partnerships, investment partnerships or professional partnerships.

This chapter will only discuss professional partnerships. The term partnership in the context of this chapter will refer only to a professional partnership and the term partner will refer to a member of a professional partnership. Professional partnerships include law firms, accounting firms, architectural firms and medical practices.

11.3 — Unlimited Liability

One of the unique attributes of a partnership entity is that it does not generally have a legal existence separate and apart from the partners. Partners therefore have unlimited liability and their personal assets may be seized by creditors in order to satisfy any obligations which have arisen as a result of carrying on the partnership business. Perhaps one of the most important legal principles governing partnerships is that each partner is an agent of the partnership business. As a result, the actions of one partner can bind all the members of the partnership. Each partner is therefore personally liable with the other members of the partnership for all debts and obligations of the business incurred while he or she is a partner. A partner's liability further extends to any loss or injury caused by another partner provided the partner was acting within the apparent scope of his duties.

A partnership may have, as its partners, a number of corporations. In many provinces, provincial legislation allows partners of some professional partnerships to incorporate in order to benefit from the income tax rules applicable to corporations. The companies are generally referred to as professional corporations. This ability to hold a partnership interest through a professional corporation does not limit the legal liability of the individual shareholders. They will continue to be jointly and severally liable for the liabilities of the partnership.

In some provinces, accountants and lawyers can carry on their practice through a limited liability partnership (LLP). An LLP limits partner liability to third parties. In a client claim for negligence all partnership assets are exposed but only the assets of the specific partner are vulnerable. This means that the other LLP partners who were not involved with the client are not jointly and severally liable.

11.4 — Partnership Agreement

Although a partnership agreement is not necessary in order to form a partnership it is necessary in order to set out the terms of the partnership and the operations of the business. The partnership agreement sets out the rights, responsibilities and obligations of the partners and can be relied upon to avoid disputes and settle issues. If the partners want the partnership to continue after the death or insolvency of one of the partners, this must be provided for in the partnership agreement. In the absence of this provision in the agreement, provincial partnership law generally considers a partnership to be dissolved upon the death or insolvency of a partner. If this is the case, the CRA will also consider the partnership to be dissolved.

A partnership agreement addresses other issues including the departure of a partner on death, disability and retirement. The nature of the payments (income or capital) to the departing partner and the income tax consequences to both the departing partner and the remaining partners will be governed by the wording in the partnership agreement.

11.5 — General Taxation of Partnerships and Partners

Division B, subdivision j of the Act "Partnerships and their Members" contains many of the rules related to the taxation of partners and partnerships. This next section will briefly discuss the general taxation rules as a background for discussing partnership insurance needs.

A. — Income

The Act provides in subsection 96(1) that the income or loss of a partnership is calculated as if the partnership were a separate person. The revenue and expenses of the partnership are calculated at the partnership level in determining the net income or loss of the partnership. However this net income is not taxed at the partnership level but is allocated to the partners according to the partnership agreement and taxed in their hands. The partnership does not file an income tax return, although an information return must be filed annually. The taxable income is reported on the partner's own tax return. The income that is allocated to each partner retains the character of the source.

B. — Year end

Partnerships which include any individuals, professional corporations or other partnerships as partners generally are required to have a calendar year end pursuant to section 249.1 of the Act. Non-calendar year ends are permitted if an election is made under subsection 249.1(4) but additional income must be included for the period from the year end date to December 31 under section 34.1 of the Act. This effectively results in the partners recording the income on a December 31 year end. A prepayment of the tax is made for the period between the non-calendar year end and December 31.

Although this chapter only considers planning as related to professional partnerships, it should be noted that partnerships that do not include individuals or professional corporations as members have traditionally been permitted to choose any fiscal period that does not exceed 53 weeks. As a result, the current rules allow a corporate partnership to defer income earned in a partnership for up to one year. The income earned by a corporation that is a member of a partnership is included in the corporation's income for the taxation year in which the fiscal period of the partnership ends. If a corporation carries on a business through a partnership that has a fiscal period ending after the end of the corporation's taxation year, the taxation of the income may be deferred for up to one year. Bill C-13, which received Royal Assent on December 15, 2011, introduced rules to circumvent this type of planning by requiring corporate partners who hold a "significant interest" in a partnership to include a pro-rated amount of partnership income for the partnership's fiscal period that falls within the corporation's taxation year (a "stub" period). The new measures apply to corporate partners (other than professional corporations) for a taxation year if:

- the corporate partner is a member of a partnership at the end of the taxation year;
- the corporation's last fiscal period that began in the taxation year ends in a subsequent taxation year of the corporate partner; and
- the corporate partner, together with affiliated and related parties, was entitled to more than 10 percent of the partnership's income (or assets in the case of a wind-up) at the end of the last fiscal period of the partnership that ended in the taxation year.

C. — Partnership interest

A partnership interest is capital property and accordingly a capital gain or loss is calculated on a disposition of the interest. Items under paragraph 53(1)(e) of the Act that increase the adjusted cost base of a partner's partnership interest include the partner's contributions of capital, the partner's share of income of the partnership, the partner's share of any capital dividends and the partner's share of any death benefit proceeds in respect of life insurance policies received by the partnership in excess of the adjusted cost basis of such policy to the partnership. Items under paragraph 53(2)(c) of the Act that reduce the adjusted cost base of a partner's partnership interest include the partner's share of any loss of the partnership, the partner's share of any charitable gifts or political contributions made by the partnership and the partner's withdrawals.

D. — Income tax consequences of the retirement of a partner

When a partner retires from a partnership and all of the rights to partnership property for the partnership interest are not satisfied, subsection 98.1(1) of the Act applies to deem that there has not been a disposition of the partnership interest for tax purposes. Instead, the partnership interest becomes a residual interest with an adjusted cost base equal to the adjusted cost base of the partner's partnership interest immediately before retirement. Archived Interpretation Bulletin IT-242R "Retired Partners," dated September 6, 1991 explains the application of section 98.1. The retired partner is deemed not to dispose of the partnership interest until all of the rights to property under the residual interest are satisfied in full.

Payments received in satisfaction of the residual interest reduce the adjusted cost base of the interest under subparagraph 53(2)(c)(v). If the adjusted cost base becomes negative the retired partner must recognize a capital gain in accordance with paragraph 98.1(1)(c) and the adjusted cost base is adjusted to nil under subparagraph 53(1)(e)(vii). The final disposition of the residual interest occurs when the retired partner has received payment in full satisfaction of the interest.

The partnership agreement may provide for income to be allocated to a retired partner after he has ceased to be a member of the partnership. Subsection 96(1.1) applies if the principal activity of a partnership is the carrying on of business in Canada and all the partners agree to allocate a share of the income (or loss) of the partnership to the retired partner. Under subsection 96(1.1) the retired partner is deemed to be a member of the partnership and the allocated income will be included in the retired partner's income for the taxation year in which the fiscal period of the partnership ends. The purpose of all partners making a subsection 96(1.1) agreement is to include the payment in the retired partner's income thereby reducing the allocation and effectively producing a corresponding deduction from the remaining partners' income.

The partnership agreement normally provides the basis for determining the nature and the tax consequences, as discussed above, of the payments made to the retired partner.

E. — Death of an individual partner

Upon the death of an individual (not corporate) partner, subsection 70(5) of the Act deems the partner to have disposed of his partnership interest immediately prior to death for proceeds equal to fair market value. If the fair market value of the partnership interest exceeds the adjusted cost base, a capital gain is reported on the deceased partner's terminal return. If the partner has a negative adjusted cost base immediately before death, the negative amount generates a capital gain on the deemed disposition under subsection 100(2) of the Act. (In certain circumstances the recognition of a capital gain may be deferred (i.e. where the partnership interest is transferred to a spouse under paragraph 70(6)(d.1) of the Act). However, in the context of a professional partnership, generally, a partnership interest is not permitted to be transferred to any person not qualified to practise the profession.) The same consequences apply on the death of a retired partner who holds a residual interest in the partnership under section 98.1, as discussed in section 11.5.D above. Archived Interpretation Bulletin IT-278R2 "Death of a Partner or of a Retired Partner," dated September 26, 1994, discusses the death of an active or retired partner.

For the purpose of valuing a deceased person's partnership interest at death, subsection 70(5.3) of the Act provides a special rule for valuing a life insurance policy owned by the partnership. For this purpose, a life insurance policy under which the deceased partner was a life insured will be valued at the cash surrender value of the policy immediately before the partner died. As a result, the entire death benefit will not be included in the value of the partnership. Note, however, that this provision does not apply to policies under which the deceased (or a person related to the deceased) is not a life insured (for example policies on surviving partners). For a detailed discussion of valuation of life insurance policies for purposes of the deemed disposition upon death rules, refer to sections 3.3.C and E.

As discussed above, generally the applicable legislation governing members of a profession does not permit the transfer of a partnership interest to any person not qualified to practise in the profession. Accordingly, the partnership agreement would normally provide that the beneficiaries of the deceased partner, the deceased partner's spouse, executor or heirs, will not be permitted to acquire a partnership interest and become a member of a professional partnership. Where this is so, the beneficiary who acquires the asset is deemed, pursuant to subsection 100(3), to acquire a right to receive partnership property and not to have acquired an interest in a partnership. The beneficiary is deemed to acquire the right at an adjusted cost base equal to the deemed proceeds of disposition on the terminal return. Amounts received in satisfaction of the right will reduce the adjusted cost base under paragraph 53(2)(o) of the Act. The right to receive partnership property is disposed of when the beneficiary receives final payment and the right has been satisfied in full. The beneficiary may realize a capital gain on the disposition. Where the beneficiary is a spouse (or common-law partner, or spousal trust) and the spouse is not a member of the partnership nor becomes a member of the partnership by reason of the acquisition such that subsection 100(3) applies, paragraph 70(6)(d.1), which would generally permit a rollover of a partnership interest to a spouse, will not apply. Instead, where subsection 100(3) applies and the conditions of subsection 70(6) are met, paragraph 70(6)(d) will deem the proceeds of disposition to the deceased partner and cost to the spouse to be equal to the adjusted cost base of the partnership interest to the deceased partner immediately before death. Hence, a tax deferred rollover to the spouse may be possible. However, if the adjusted cost base of the partnership interest to the deceased partner immediately before death was negative, a deferral under paragraph 70(6)(d) is not possible. Instead, the deceased partner will be deemed to have a capital gain equal to the negative adjusted cost base pursuant to subsection 100(2), even though subsection 70(6) may have otherwise been applicable.

F. — Death of the sole shareholder of a corporate partner

Upon the death of the sole shareholder of a corporation that was a partner of a partnership, subsection 70(5) of the Act deems the sole shareholder to have disposed of his shares in the corporation immediately prior to death for proceeds equal to fair market value unless the shares are transferred to a surviving spouse. The fair market value of the corporation will include the fair market value of the partnership interest. If the fair market value of the shares in the corporation exceeds the adjusted cost base of the shares, a capital gain will be reported on the deceased shareholder's terminal return.

On the death of the sole shareholder, the corporation does not cease to exist and therefore the partnership interest will continue to be held and will not be disposed of until full payment in satisfaction of the interest is received. At that point, the corporation may have a capital gain if the payment exceeds the adjusted cost base of the partnership interest.

11.6 — Partnerships and the Proceeds of Life Insurance Policies

Death benefit proceeds from a life insurance policy are received by a partnership tax-free. In order to preserve income tax integration, so that the life insurance proceeds can be flowed to a partner without incurring tax, the Act provides for an addition to the adjusted cost base of a partnership interest for the net amount of life insurance proceeds allocated to a partner. For corporate partners, where the corporation is a private corporation, the Act further provides for an addition to the corporation's capital dividend account for the net amount of life insurance proceeds allocated.

This section describes in detail the income tax treatment distinguishing between individual partners and corporate partners.

A. — Individual partners

Subparagraph 53(1)(e)(iii) of the Act provides for an increase in the adjusted cost base of a partnership interest for the net proceeds of life insurance received by the partnership and allocated to the partner after 1971. The net proceeds are the amount of the life insurance death benefit received by the partnership in consequence of the death of any person insured under a policy less the adjusted cost basis of the policy to the partnership immediately before death. This is discussed in archived Interpretation Bulletin IT-430R3 "Life Insurance Proceeds Received by a Private Corporation or a Partnership as a Consequence of Death," dated February 10, 1997. According to subparagraph 53(2)(c)(v), a partner can withdraw an amount from the partnership equal to the adjusted cost base without incurring personal tax. In this manner, the partners receive tax-free the portion of the net life insurance proceeds allocated to them and integration is preserved.

If the partners are individuals, the increase in the adjusted cost base of the partnership interest for the net life insurance proceeds only applies to the surviving partners. In technical interpretation 9129745, dated March 9,1992, the CRA explains that the deceased partner is deemed to have disposed of his interest immediately before his death under subsection 70(5) of the Act and as a result is no longer considered a partner. The adjustment to the adjusted cost base of the partnership interest can only be added when the life insurance proceeds are received by the partnership. The life insurance proceeds can only be received by the partnership after the death of the partner and at that time the deceased is no longer considered to be a partner. Therefore, the CRA takes the position that a deceased partner, who is an individual, does not receive an adjustment to the adjusted cost base of the partnership interest for the net life insurance proceeds. This is the case even though the intention may be to use the proceeds from the life insurance death benefit to fund a payment to the deceased's estate. Accordingly, the estate of the deceased partner cannot receive the death benefit proceeds tax-free when the life insurance proceeds are passed through the partnership. If this result is going to significantly disadvantage a deceased partner, consideration should be given to structuring the ownership and/or beneficiaries of the life insurance at the partner level rather than the partnership level.

B. — Corporate partners

The treatment differs if the partners are corporations and the partnership is the beneficiary of the life insurance policy. Corporate partners do not cease to exist on the death of the shareholder, there is no deemed disposition by the corporation of the partnership interest on death and therefore the corporation continues to be a partner after the death of the principal shareholder. The adjustment for the net proceeds can be added to the adjusted cost base of the partnership interest owned by the deceased shareholder's corporation in accordance with the allocation provided in the partnership agreement. In technical interpretation 9119795, dated December 30, 1991, the CRA considered the situation where the partnership agreement provides that the entire amount of the life insurance proceeds will be allocated and paid in full to a deceased partner's professional corporation. The CRA's response is that in this case, it is only the adjusted cost base of that corporate partner that would be adjusted as the other partners were not allocated a share of the net proceeds. The CRA confirmed this interpretation in a 2002 ruling (2001-0114863). This ruling also clarified that changing an existing partnership agreement so that the entire life insurance proceeds are allocated to the deceased partner's corporation (rather than multiple partners' corporations) would not result in the application of subsection 103(1) or (1.1) of the Act (agreements to share income to reduce tax or in unreasonable proportions). This ruling is significant in light of CRA's recent reliance on subsection 103(1) to reallocate partnership income in circumstances where the CRA considers the allocation of partnership revenues to be abusive attempts to reduce the total tax payable by the partners. See for example *Stow v. The Queen*,

[2011] 1 C.T.C. 2434, 2010 D.T.C. 1275 (T.C.C. [General Procedure]); *Penn West Petroleum Ltd. v. The Queen*, [2007] 4 C.T.C. 2063, 2007 D.T.C. 715 (T.C.C.), and *XCO Investments Ltd. v. The Queen*, [2007] 2 C.T.C. 243, 2007 D.T.C. 5146 (F.C.A.).

Interpretation Bulletin IT-430R3 explains that if an adjustment for life insurance proceeds is made to the adjusted cost base of a corporate partner and the corporation is a private corporation, the net proceeds may also be added to the capital dividend account of the corporation as contemplated in paragraph (d) of the definition of capital dividend account in subsection 89(1). The corporate partner could then use the credit to the capital dividend account and elect to pay a tax-free capital dividend under subsection 83(2) to the shareholders.

This interpretation is explained using a numerical example in technical interpretation RCT 5-3164, dated June 10, 1987. In a follow-up letter, technical interpretation RCT 5-3610, dated August 21, 1987, the CRA clarified that an amount that is allocated to a corporate partner, added to the adjusted cost base of the partnership interest and credited to the capital dividend account must be the amount that is actually paid to and received by the partner. The CRA interprets the reference to the taxpayer's share in subparagraph 53(1)(e)(iii) to be the amount of the net proceeds from the life insurance to which the partner is entitled. The CRA argues that if the partner is not entitled to the net proceeds then the amount is not allocated to the partner and therefore cannot be added to the adjusted cost base of the partnership interest. Also, the amount would not be credited to the corporate partner's capital dividend account as subparagraph (d)(ii) of the definition of capital dividend account in subsection 89(1) requires that the life insurance proceeds be received by the corporation. Received means that the proceeds would have to be allocated and distributed by the partnership to the particular professional corporation.

At the CLHIA Roundtable dated May 20, 2011 (indexed as 2011-0398421C6), the following facts were presented to the CRA: Mr A. ("A") is the sole shareholder of A Co and Mr. B ("B") (unrelated to A) is the sole shareholder of B Co. A Co and B Co are equal partners of AB Partnership. The Partnership Agreement contains the following terms and conditions:

- AB Partnership is required to purchase insurance on the lives of A and B;
- On the death of A or B, AB Partnership must allocate and pay the life insurance proceeds to the deceased's corporation;
- On the death of A or B, the deceased's corporation will withdraw from the partnership and receive an amount from the partnership equal to the fair market value ("FMV") of the partnership interest less the life insurance proceeds allocated by the partnership to the deceased's corporation.

Assuming that A dies at a time where, the FVM of A Co's interest is $25,000, the adjusted cost base ("ACB") of the partnership interest is $10,000, life insurance proceeds are $25,000, and the ACB of the policy is nil, the CRA was asked to confirm the tax results. After stating that a review of all the facts, circumstances, and documents would be required, the CRA stated that the allocation of the insurance proceeds increase the ACB of A Co's partnership interest under subparagraph

53(1)(e)(iii) of the Act as well as A Co's capital dividend account and that the distribution of $25,000 to A Co reduces the ACB of A Co's partnership interest under subparagraph 53(2)(c)(v) of the Act.

However, when we look at the overall result, A Co received $25,000 - the ACB of its partnership interest is $10,000 (10,000 + 25,000 - 25,000) - and must now dispose of the interest for proceeds equal to the FMV of the partnership interest less the life insurance proceeds. This would result in a $10,000 capital loss (25,000 - 25,000 = 0, less 10,000 ACB). The CRA did not confirm this result. Its response may be summarized as follows: A "mechanical application" of subparagraphs 52(1)(e)(iii) and 53(2)(c)(v) together with the withdrawal from the partnership would seem to result in a capital loss to the exiting corporate partner. There is no effect to the ACB of the remaining corporate partner and therefore a deferral of tax would result. This deferral may be inappropriate, particularly in the context of large professional partnerships that may never cease to exist. Also, consideration should be given to the application of the at-risk and negative ACB rules to the corporate partner and whether the provisions of sections 69, 103, or GAAR would apply to this type of situation.

It should be noted that the potential for a capital loss to be generated on the disposition of the exiting corporate partner's (ACo in this example) partnership interest would only arise to the extent of its ACB prior to the transactions (assuming life insurance proceeds of a similar amount are allocated and distributed to it). When ACo in this example has a nil ACB to start with, there would be no potential for a capital loss to be generated in this situation. If a capital loss is generated, this would essentially bring about similar results to corporate redemption buy-sell planning prior to the introduction of the stop-loss rules in subsection 112(3.2) of the Act (see sections 7.4.D.iii and 7.4.E for further discussion of corporate redemption buy-sell and the stop-loss rules). However, given the CRA's hesitancy to confirm this result and its willingness to use other provisions of the Act to challenge it, certainty around planning in this area may require an advance ruling.

11.7 — Transferring a Life Insurance Policy to or from a Partnership

A. — Partnership transferring a life insurance policy to a partner

The partnership may choose to transfer ownership of an interest in a life insurance policy to the partner whose life is insured under the policy. This might occur when a partner withdraws from the partnership and wishes to take the policy, when the partnership no longer has the insurance need but the departing partner could utilize the insurance for estate planning purposes, or where the partnership ceases to exist.

A transfer of ownership of a life insurance policy is a disposition for income tax purposes under the definition of disposition in subsection 148(9) of the Act. The rules in subsection 148(1) of the Act include a policy gain in the taxable income of the transferor for the excess of the proceeds of the disposition over the adjusted cost basis of the interest to the transferor immediately before the transfer. The proceeds of the disposition are defined in subsection 148(9) of the Act.

Notwithstanding the general rules regarding the definition of the proceeds of the disposition of an interest in a life insurance policy, specific rules for transferring any type of partnership property are provided in subsections 98(2) and (3) of the Act. These specific rules should apply on a transfer of a life insurance policy out of a partnership to a partner and override the general rules in section 148. Where a partnership ceases to exist and where all the partnership property is distributed to the partners, each partner receives an undivided interest in each property and, if the partners make the appropriate election, the partnership will be deemed to dispose of the life insurance policy at its "cost amount" (paragraph 98(3)(f) of the Act). This expression, as it applies to a life insurance policy, is defined in subsection 248(1) of the Act as the adjusted cost basis. This being said, there may not be many situations where partners would want to have an undivided interest in life insurance policies.

Where the transfer of the policy to a partner does not meet the above noted conditions, subsection 98(2) deems the proceeds of the disposition to the partnership to be equal to the fair market value of the life insurance policy at the time of disposition. A taxable policy gain on the transfer of the policy will be included in computing the partnership income if the fair market value is in excess of the adjusted cost basis of the interest in the policy to the partnership. The partner will be deemed under subsection 98(2) to acquire the life insurance policy at an adjusted cost basis equal to the same fair market value.

To determine the fair market value of an interest in a life insurance policy the CRA has set out valuation procedures in Information Circular IC 89-3 "Policy Statement on Business Equity Valuations," dated August 25, 1989. The information circular lists the following factors that would be considered in determining the fair market value of a life insurance policy:

a) the cash surrender value of the policy;

b) the policy's loan value;

c) the face value of the policy;

d) the state of health of the insured and his/her life expectancy;

e) conversion privileges under the policy;

f) other policy terms, such as term riders, double indemnity provisions; and

g) the replacement value of the policy.

The result of applying the CRA's general valuation principles can produce a valuation which is materially higher than the cash surrender value of the policy and, in certain circumstances, could even approach the amount of the death benefit under the policy. For more information on valuing life insurance policies see section 3.3.

B. — Transfer of a life insurance policy to a partnership

The converse situation would involve a partner transferring a life insurance policy to a partnership. Since the life insurance policy is not capital property or other qualifying property for purposes of the rollover rules at subsection 97(2) of the Act, a rollover is not available. The CRA considered the tax consequences of such a transfer in technical interpretation 2007-0237291I7, dated June 5, 2007. The situation concerned a corporate partner transferring a life insurance policy to a partnership. According to the CRA, subsection 148(7) would apply to the transfer such that the transferor would be deemed to have received proceeds of the disposition equal to the policy's cash surrender value and the partnership would acquire the policy with an adjusted cost basis also equal to cash surrender value. Interestingly, subsection 148(7) refers to the transferee as the "person" that acquires the policy, rather than the "person or partnership" that acquires the policy. Nevertheless, the CRA is of the view that subsection 148(7) applies where a partnership acquires the policy.

11.8 — Partnership Insurance Needs

Life insurance is often the best and least expensive method of providing funding to meet certain partnership obligations. Insurance can be used as a vehicle for providing personal insurance for the individual partner or for meeting partnership needs such as key partner coverage, collateral life insurance and funding partnership agreements. This section outlines the income tax implications and structures that should be considered when designing life insurance strategies with partnerships.

A. — Personal insurance

The partnership may determine that the primary responsibility for planning for retirement, death and disability belongs to each individual partner. But, in the event of premature death, the partnership does not want to feel obligated to the family of the deceased partner that did not accept the responsibility to make any plans. Therefore, firms often arrange for group term life insurance until retirement for all partners, with the family of the partner as the beneficiary under the policy. The CRA addressed the issue of deductibility of group plans for partnerships in technical interpretation 9206365, dated May 4,1992. The CRA concluded that the life insurance premium costs would be considered to be personal or living expenses of the individual partners under paragraph 18(1)(h) of the Act and would therefore not be deductible in computing income at the partnership level or by the partners individually. The partner would generally pay for her share of the premium through her drawing account and corresponding reduction in adjusted cost base of the partnership interest. The coverage with a group term life insurance plan generally ceases upon retirement. The problem with this is that the need for life insurance coverage does not cease at this point but often is greater as the probability of death is higher after retirement.

In order to encourage the ownership of permanent life insurance protection that lasts beyond retirement to death, the partnership may set up a plan where the partners purchase individual life insurance policies with the family of the individual partner as beneficiary. The premiums could be paid by the partnership on behalf of the individual partner. As discussed above, the premiums would not be deductible when computing partnership income as the payments would be considered a personal expense of the individual partner under paragraph 18(1)(h) of the Act. Again, the partner would generally pay for his share of the premium through withdrawals and corresponding reduction in the adjusted cost base.

B. — Key partner coverage

In many partnerships, the success of the business is built around the talents, skills, expertise and vision of a few key partners. These partners are able to motivate employees, motivate the other partners and attract clients. If one of these partners were to die the workings of the partnership would be disrupted. Upon the death of a key partner the following may happen:

1. the business is disrupted as the other partners develop a plan for the future;
2. key clients may be concerned about the future of the partnership;
3. the firm may lose clients whose only relationship was with the deceased partner;
4. banks may restrict their financial assistance due to their concern about the firm's future;
5. other creditors may restrict their financial assistance due to their concern about the firm's future; and
6. the resources and skills provided by the deceased partner will be lost and may need to be replaced.

When these problems arise, the firm may suffer a significant financial impact unless a plan is in place to offset the monetary losses that may result from the death of the key partner.

The partnership can purchase partnership-owned life insurance on the lives of the key partners. In the event of death of one of the key partners the partnership would then receive a tax-free death benefit which can be used to meet the expenses arising on the death of the key partner. The income tax consequences of the partnership receiving the life insurance death benefit proceeds, as discussed in the previous section, would apply.

C. — Collateral life insurance

Financial institutions that provide loans or a line of credit to the partnership may require the partnership to purchase life insurance on the lives of the partners. The life insurance would then be assigned to the bank as collateral security. Upon the death of one of the partners the life insurance proceeds would be used to extinguish the loan.

The life insurance premiums may be deductible or partly deductible in the computation of partnership income if the requirements in paragraph 20(1)(e.2) of the Act are met. In order for all or a portion of the premiums payable on an insurance policy to be deductible the following general requirements must be met:

- policy must be assigned to the lender,
- the lender must be a "restricted financial institution,"
- the interest payable in respect of the debt must generally be tax deductible in computing income for the year, and
- the assignment must be required by the lender as collateral for the debt.

For a detailed discussion of collateral life insurance refer to section 6.4.E.

Providing the life insurance policy as collateral security to the bank may have an impact on the tax consequences at death. As discussed in section 11.6.A, subparagraph 53(1)(e)(iii) provides for an addition to the adjusted cost base of an interest in a partnership in respect of a partner's share of the net proceeds of a life insurance policy received by the partnership. If the life insurance death benefit proceeds are allocated to a partner that is a private corporation, the corporation may also add the amount allocated to its capital dividend account under subsection 89(1).

On January 7, 2003, the CRA released revised Interpretation Bulletin IT-430R3 "Life Insurance Proceeds Received by a Private Corporation or a Partnership as a Consequence of Death", dated February 10, 1997 (now archived). These revisions updated the CRA's position regarding the addition to the adjusted cost base of the partnership interest and the credit to the capital dividend account when the life insurance policy is provided as collateral security for indebtedness. The Interpretation Bulletin now indicates that if the life insurance is paid directly to the creditor as a collateral assignee for security, the entitlement of each of the partners to an addition to the adjusted cost base of their partnership interests and the addition to the capital dividend account (if the partner was a private corporation) remains with the debtor. On the other hand, if the creditor as beneficiary or absolute assignee of the policy receives the life insurance proceeds directly from the life insurer, the CRA in Interpretation Bulletin IT-430R3 takes the position that the addition to the adjusted cost base of the partnership interest and the credit to the capital dividend account is not available to the partners. This position was successfully challenged in *Innovative Installation Inc. v. The Queen*, 2010 FCA 285, [2011] 2 C.T.C. 73, 2010 D.T.C. 5175. The Federal Court of Appeal upheld and confirmed the Tax Court of Canada's finding that a capital dividend account credit was available to a debtor corporation for creditor insurance under which the debtor paid premiums to a lender and the lender was the owner and beneficiary of a life insurance policy. The CRA has stated that the Interpretation Bulletin will be updated (technical interpretation 2011-0401991E5, dated July 4th, 2011). See section 6.2.C.ii for a complete discussion of life insurance proceeds received by lenders.

At the 2006 Conference for Advanced Life Underwriting annual Roundtable (indexed as document number 2006-0175101C6, dated May 9, 2006), the CRA was asked to consider a situation where a partnership borrowed money from a restricted financial institution and the financial institution required one of the partners to assign a life insurance policy as security for the loan. The facts assumed that the interest on the loan was deductible in computing the partnership's income. The CRA was asked whether the partner would be entitled to claim deductions under paragraph 20(1)(e.2) in respect of premiums payable under the life insurance policy. In its response, the CRA noted that one of the requirements for the deduction of premiums under paragraph 20(1)(e.2) is that the interest on the borrowed money be deductible in computing the income of the taxpayer who paid the premiums. In the example described in the Roundtable question, the interest was deductible by the partnership in computing partnership income rather than in computing the income of the partner who is paying the premiums. Accordingly, the paragraph 20(1)(e.2) deduction was not available.

D. — Funding the partnership agreement

A partnership agreement specifies the obligations of the remaining partners on the death or withdrawal due to retirement or disability of a partner. The remaining partners may be obligated under the terms of the agreement to fund the payments specified in the partnership agreement. To ensure that the agreement is viable, the partners and the partnership must plan to accumulate funding for these events. Without proper funding the agreement may disintegrate because the remaining partners may not be in a financial position to meet their obligation under the terms of the agreement. Life insurance is often the best and the least expensive method to fund certain of the payment provisions of a partnership agreement.

There are many methods of structuring a life insurance funded buyout of a partnership interest on death. Each one has different legal, economic, and tax implications. The partners must decide which method is most appropriate in their particular circumstances. The sections which follow discuss some of these different methods.

i. — Funding obligations on death with partner-owned life insurance

One method of funding the buy-out of a partnership interest on death is to use life insurance owned and funded by the partners. This is often referred to as a "crisscross" structure. The mechanics and tax effects of crisscross structure vary depending on whether the partners are individuals or corporations, whose life is insured, and who is the beneficiary of the insurance.

a. — Basic crisscross method

When this structure is used the partnership agreement provides that, upon the death of a partner, the other partners will purchase a proportionate share of the deceased's interest in the partnership. Each partner is the owner and beneficiary of life insurance on the lives of the other partners. As an example, if there were six partners each partner would own and be the beneficiary of five policies on the lives of the other partners. Alternatively, each partner could own a multi-life policy with coverages for the five other partners. For more information on multi-life policies refer to section 2.9.B. The partners each pay the premiums for the life insurance policies. The premiums are not deductible from taxable income.

A deceased partner who is an individual is deemed by subsection 70(5) of the Act to have disposed of his partnership interest at fair market value immediately prior to death (assuming the spousal rollover in subsection 70(6) does not apply). To the extent that the fair market value exceeds the adjusted cost base of the partnership interest, the deceased partner will have a capital gain to report on his final tax return — the "terminal return". Assuming the estate, trust, or beneficiary is precluded from becoming an active member of the partnership, the deceased partner's estate is deemed to have acquired a "right to receive partnership property" under subsection 100(3) of the Act. This right has an adjusted cost base equal to the deemed proceeds of disposition of the partnership interest triggered at death.

The surviving partners would receive the proceeds of the life insurance policy held on the deceased partner on a tax-free basis. Using these funds, the surviving partners would purchase the partnership interest from the deceased partner's estate. The surviving partners' adjusted cost base of the partnership interest would be increased by the amount paid to the deceased partner's estate or corporation. Assuming that the partners are dealing at arm's length, and that the purchase of the partnership interest by the surviving partners takes place soon after death, the fair market value of the partnership interest at death should be equal to the purchase price. As a result, the estate would not typically realize a capital gain or loss on the disposition of the partnership interest to the surviving partners since the purchase price would equal the fair market value and consequently the adjusted cost base of the interest. If, however, the purchase price varied from the fair market value used for subsection 70(5) (and consequently the adjusted cost base of the interest) the estate of the deceased partner would realize a capital gain or loss.

b. — Basic crisscross method with corporate partners

When the partners of a partnership are corporations and the sole shareholder of a corporate partner dies, the tax results are a little different than if the partners are individuals. Upon the death of the sole shareholder of a corporate partner, the sole shareholder is deemed by subsection 70(5) of the Act to have disposed of her shares in the corporation at fair market value immediately prior to death (assuming the spousal rollover in subsection 70(6) does not apply). To the extent that the fair market value exceeds the adjusted cost base of the shares, the deceased shareholder will have a capital gain to report on her terminal return. There is no immediate disposition of the partnership interest because the corporation continues to exist upon the death of the sole shareholder and accordingly retains the partnership interest.

As is the case where the partners are individuals, the partnership agreement may provide that upon the death of the shareholder of a corporate partner the other corporate partners will purchase a proportionate share of the deceased shareholder's corporation's interest in the partnership. Each corporate partner is the owner and beneficiary of life insurance on the lives of the shareholders of the other corporate partners. The corporate partners each pay the premiums for the life insurance policies, and the premiums are not deductible from taxable income.

Upon the death of the shareholder of one of the corporate partners, the other corporate partners would receive the proceeds of the life insurance policy held on the deceased individual on a tax-free basis and would receive a capital dividend account credit equal to the excess of the life insurance proceeds over the corporation's adjusted cost basis of the policy — the "net proceeds". Using these funds, the corporate partners would purchase the interest from the deceased's corporation. The adjusted cost base of the partnership interest to the purchasing corporation would be increased by the amount paid to the deceased's corporation.

The deceased's corporation has a disposition of the partnership interest for proceeds equal to the purchase price. To the extent that the purchase price exceeds the adjusted cost base of the partnership interest, a gain will be realized by the deceased's corporation. Note that the adjusted cost base is unlikely to equal the fair market value or the purchase price in this situation because a corporation does not receive a "bump up" of its adjusted cost base of its partnership interest on the death of a shareholder. As a result, it is more likely that a corporate partner will realize a capital gain.

This structure is not the most tax efficient from the perspective of the deceased. Not only does he have a gain on his shares of the corporation (due to the deemed disposition at death), but he also has a disposition of his partnership interest inside the corporation. This may result in double taxation of any gain on the partnership interest. Although the deceased's corporation is not entitled to a CDA credit in respect of the insurance proceeds, it will receive a CDA credit in respect of any capital gain realized. This CDA credit may be used to mitigate some of the double taxation. From the perspective of the remaining partners, the tax result is very favourable. The other corporate partners will receive a CDA credit equal to the insurance proceeds received (net of the ACB of their interest in the policy) as well as adjusted cost base for the amount they pay to purchase the partnership interest from the deceased's corporation.

c. — Trustee'd crisscross method

Where the insurance policies are owned by each of the partners separately, it may be difficult for the partners to be certain that premiums are being paid and that the policies are being kept in force. To alleviate this concern, a trustee may be used with the crisscross method to simplify the ownership of insurance and the mechanics on death. A trustee may be more commonly used when there are more than two partners. The use of a trustee also allows for the policing of premium payments as a partner can inquire of the trustee if there are any outstanding amounts. Without the use of a trustee, the partners must rely on each other to ensure that the policies are kept in force. If a trustee is included in the partnership agreement, there should also be a separate trust agreement stating the duties and responsibilities of the trustee and the terms of the trust.

The ownership is simplified in that the trustee can purchase a single policy on each of the partners with the trustee as owner and beneficiary or a multi-life policy with life insurance coverage for each of the partners. (For a discussion of multi-life policies refer to section 2.9.B.) The partners would be the beneficiaries of the trust. The funding for the insurance would come from contributions to the trust by the partners. Upon the death of a partner, the life insurance proceeds would flow into the trust and then would be distributed to the surviving partners so that they could purchase the deceased's (or the deceased's corporation's) partnership interest. Alternatively, the trust could use the insurance proceeds to purchase the deceased's (or deceased's corporation's) partnership interest and then distribute the partnership interest to the remaining partners. Although subsection 75(2) of the Act may apply to such a trust, the application of the attribution rule should not be significant since the sole purpose of the trust is to hold the life insurance policies and the trust should not be in receipt of any taxable income.

Another alternative might be to designate the surviving partners as the beneficiaries of the policy directly rather than having the funds pass through the trust. It should be noted that the CRA is on record (2006-0174041C6 and 2008-0301881E5) as stating that a trust benefit under subsection 105(1) of the Act might arise for tax purposes where the insurance premiums are paid for by a trust on an insurance policy owned by the trust. See section 9.5 for a more detailed discussion of these technical interpretations.

The tax consequences to individual partners of using a trustee'd arrangement are the same as in a regular crisscross arrangement. The deceased individual has the same disposition of his/her partnership interest or shares. The contributions to the trust to cover the insurance premium costs are a non-deductible expense to the partners. Insurance proceeds retain their character when flowed through a trust to the partners and consequently are received tax-free by the partners. The purchase of the deceased partner's partnership interest continues in the same manner with the same tax consequences as a non-trustee'd arrangement.

The same is true if the partners are corporations except that corporate partners will not receive a CDA credit for life insurance proceeds flowed through a trust. (For a detailed discussion of this issue refer to section 9.5.E). As a result, a trustee'd arrangement is not very tax effective where the partners of the partnership are corporations. One alternative might be to designate the corporate partners as direct beneficiaries of the insurance rather than flowing the insurance proceeds through the trust. This would ensure the CDA credit is not lost. Other than the trust benefit issue referred to above, there is no commentary from the CRA that indicates whether this would be construed to be offensive. If this is effective, the tax results to the deceased's corporation and the remaining corporate partners would be the same as that described in the basic crisscross method with corporate partners.

d. — Crisscross beneficiary designation method

One issue with the basic crisscross method is that the cost of premiums may be felt to be inequitable where there is an age difference or difference in the state of health of the partners. The younger or healthier partner will pay higher premiums for insurance on the older or less healthy partner. This may be considered an equitable sharing of the risk but it does represent an unequal financial burden. A solution to alleviate this difficulty may be for each partner to own insurance on his or her own life with the other partners as joint beneficiaries of the life insurance proceeds. Upon receipt of the life insurance proceeds, the beneficiaries would purchase the deceased's (or deceased's corporation's) partnership interest.

Where the partners are corporations, there may be additional reasons to structure the insurance in this way. For example, the shareholders of the corporate partners may want to overfund the life insurance policy on their own life as an investment vehicle. In this case, they will want the policy on their life to be owned by their corporation so that the partnership income can be used to fund the policy in their corporation. The corporation can then be named as the beneficiary in respect of the cash value, and the death benefit can be used to fund the partnership buyout at death. Further, at retirement the shareholder can change the beneficiary designation such that the corporation is the sole beneficiary of the policy. Thus the shareholder has complete control of the policy and it is not necessary to transfer ownership of the policy to the retiree which could have adverse tax consequences.

Note that the CRA has stated (technical interpretations 2007-0257251E5 and 2010-0359421C6) that where one corporation is the owner of a life insurance policy and another corporation is the beneficiary, it may assess a taxable benefit under subsection 246(1) of the Act. For a detailed discussion of this issue, refer to section 6.2.D.

ii. — Funding obligations on death with partnership-owned life insurance

An alternative to using partner-owned insurance is to have the partnership own and be the beneficiary of the life insurance policies. The partnership as beneficiary of the life insurance policy would receive the proceeds of the life insurance on the life of the deceased partner on a tax-free basis. The partnership agreement can be structured so that the partnership purchases the deceased partner's interest (or the deceased's corporation's partnership interest) or, alternatively, can be structured so that the life insurance proceeds are flowed to the remaining partners in order that they can purchase the deceased partner's interest (or the deceased's corporation's partnership interest). In either case, the partnership would own and be the beneficiary of life insurance on the lives of each of the partners (or sole shareholders of corporate partners). Either separate policies could be purchased or a multi-life policy with coverages on the lives of each of the partners (or sole shareholders of corporate partners) could be purchased. (For a discussion of multi-life policies refer to section 2.9.B.) The premiums for the life insurance policies would not be deductible in computing the partnership income.

Regardless of the structure, the death of an individual partner will trigger a deemed disposition of the deceased's partnership interest at death at fair market value (presuming the spousal rollover in subsection 70(6) does not apply). To the extent that the fair market value of the partnership interest exceeds the adjusted cost base, a capital gain will arise. If the deceased partner's estate is precluded from becoming an active partner then the estate will be deemed to have acquired a "right to receive partnership property" under subsection 100(3). This right is a capital property and has an adjusted cost base equal to the deemed proceeds of disposition of the partnership interest triggered at death. If the deceased partner's estate or beneficiary is not precluded from becoming an active partner then the estate or beneficiary acquires a "continuing partnership interest". As with a right, this continuing partnership interest is a capital property and has an adjusted cost base equal to the deemed proceeds of disposition of the partnership interest triggered at death.

If the partners are corporations, the death of the sole shareholder will trigger a deemed disposition of the deceased's shares. To the extent that the fair market value of the shares exceeds the adjusted cost base, a capital gain will arise on the shares (presuming the spousal rollover in subsection 70(6) does not apply). There is, however, no deemed disposition of the partnership interest because the corporation continues to exist upon the death of the sole shareholder and accordingly retains the partnership interest.

The ultimate tax consequences to the estate of the deceased and the remaining partners depends on whether the partnership repurchases the partnership interest, or if the life insurance proceeds are flowed to the remaining partners to purchase the interest, and whether the partners are corporations or individuals.

a. — Partnership purchases the deceased partner's interest — individual partners

A partnership agreement may specify that the life insurance proceeds received by the partnership on the death of a partner must be used by the partnership to purchase the interest from the deceased partner's estate. As this would be a repurchase of capital, the amount would not be deductible in computing the net income of the partnership. This is confirmed by the CRA in technical interpretation NV90_197.198, dated November 1990 in which the CRA indicates that neither the remaining partners nor the partnership can deduct the lump sum payment in computing income as it is not laid out to earn income. The proportion of the partnership previously owned by the deceased partner would be spread among the surviving partners and increase the percentage interest owned by each in the partnership similar to a redemption of shares in a corporate buy-sell situation.

The nature and tax treatment of this payment to the deceased partner's estate will depend on the exact wording of the partnership agreement.

Partnership purchases interest utilizing a capital payment

The agreement may be worded so that this amount is to be considered the purchase price for the deceased's partnership interest. In this case there are two tax events. The first, as noted earlier, is the disposition triggered at death for proceeds equal to the fair market value of the partnership interest. To the extent that the fair market value exceeds the ACB of the interest, a capital gain will be reported on the deceased's terminal return. The second event is the payment to the estate for the partnership interest by the partnership as outlined in the partnership agreement.

In the case where the estate has a continuing partnership interest, this second event is characterized as a disposition of a partnership interest. Since the estate acquired the partnership interest at an ACB equal to the fair market value at death, and presuming that the fair market value at death equals the purchase price paid by the partnership, there should be no further gain to the estate on this second disposition.

In the case where the estate has a right to receive partnership property, this second event is characterized as a settlement of that right, and under paragraph 53(2)(o) that amount is deducted from the adjusted cost base of that right. Since this right is not a partnership interest, the amount of any negative adjusted cost base that may arise is taxed as a capital gain. Presuming that the amount received equals the fair market value at death, the amount received should reduce the ACB to zero. Since the right to partnership property has been extinguished, the estate will have a disposition of the right (as per subparagraph (b)(ii) of the definition of disposition in 248(1)). The ACB of the right has been reduced to zero, and there are no further proceeds, so there should be no gain on the disposition.

As noted in section 11.6.A, insurance proceeds cannot be allocated to a deceased partner for purposes of calculating the ACB (and presumably their taxable income) of their partnership interest. As a result, even though the insurance proceeds are utilized to buy out the deceased partner, for the purposes of calculating the taxable income and the ACB of the partnership interests of the various partners, none of the insurance proceeds can be allocated to the deceased partner. Accordingly, the surviving partners will receive an increase to their ACB equal to the excess of the insurance proceeds over the adjusted cost basis of the policy. The partnership agreement should outline the allocation of the insurance proceeds for the purpose of determining the legal income entitlement of each partner, but for the purpose of calculating taxable income it can only be allocated to surviving partners.

Partnership purchases interest utilizing an income allocation

Alternatively, the agreement may be worded such that payment to the deceased's partner's estate is to be treated as an allocation of income to the deceased partner. In technical interpretation NV90_197.198, referred to above, the CRA takes the view that in these circumstances subsection 96(1.1) of the Act will apply to include the lump sum payment in the income of the estate. Based on this interpretation, this structure has the effect of characterizing the proceeds as income to the estate rather than proceeds of disposition giving rise to capital gains treatment. This treatment appears to apply regardless of whether the estate has a continuing partnership interest or a right to receive partnership property.

In addition, the CRA indicated that since the total income of the partnership for the year is allocated amongst all the partners, this allocation would be expected to cause a corresponding reduction to the income allocated to the other partners. They further indicate that the life insurance proceeds would increase the adjusted cost base of the remaining partners pursuant to subparagraph 53(1)(e)(iii) of the Act. The mechanics of this are unclear, but presumably even though the insurance proceeds are allocated to the deceased partner for legal and accounting purposes, for tax purposes, the surviving partners would reduce their taxable income by the insurance proceeds as a non-taxable amount, and would receive an increase in the ACB of their partnership interest relating to the insurance proceeds allocated to them for tax purposes. Note, however, that the decrease in taxable income of the remaining partners also causes a corresponding decrease to the ACB of their partnership interest because the income added to the ACB has been reduced.

In addition to this income allocation, the estate will presumably have a disposition of the partnership interest or a settlement of the right to receive partnership property since after this payment the estate no longer has the interest or the right.

If the estate had a continuing interest in the partnership, then the income allocated to the estate will increase the ACB of the partnership interest, and the distribution will decrease the ACB by the same amount. As a result, the ACB of the partnership interest will still equal the fair market value at death. Since the estate has disposed of the partnership interest (and received no further proceeds), presumably a capital loss equal to the ACB of the partnership interest is triggered in the estate. It should be possible in most cases to use this capital loss to offset the capital gain triggered at death using the loss carryback provision contained in subsection 164(6) of the Act.

Similarly, if the estate had a right to partnership property, then the rules for calculating the ACB of a partnership interest no longer apply, and the ACB will still equal the fair market value at death. Since the right to partnership property has been extinguished, the estate will have a disposition of the right (as per subparagraph (b)(ii) of the definition of disposition in 248(1)). The ACB of the right can be written off as a capital loss which should again be available to carryback to the terminal return to offset the capital gain triggered at death.

b. — Partnership purchases the deceased partner's interest — corporate partners

A partnership agreement may specify that the life insurance proceeds received by the partnership on the death of the sole shareholder of a corporate partner are to be used by the partnership to purchase the partnership interest from the deceased's corporation. As in the case of individual partners this would be a repurchase of capital, and the amount would not be deductible in computing the net income of the partnership. The proportion of the partnership previously owned by the deceased's corporation would be spread among the remaining partners and increase the percentage interest owned by each remaining partner in the partnership.

The tax results to corporate partners are a little different than for individual partners for two main reasons. First, as previously discussed, if the sole shareholder of a corporate partner dies, there is a deemed disposition of the deceased's shares of the corporation but there is no deemed disposition of the partnership interest. Second, because the corporate partner does not cease to exist, life insurance can be allocated to the corporate partner for tax purposes even after the death of the corporation's sole shareholder.

If the partnership agreement is worded such that the partnership will purchase the partnership interest from the deceased's corporation using the life insurance proceeds, then most likely the insurance proceeds will be allocated to that corporation for legal purposes as well as for tax purposes. As a result, the deceased's corporation will receive a corresponding increase in the ACB of its partnership interest. Assuming the ACB of the policy was nil, then the payment by the partnership of the insurance proceeds to the corporation to "repurchase" the partnership interest should equal the ACB of the interest, and no gain will be realized on the disposition of the partnership interest. In addition, the deceased's corporation will receive a CDA credit which may allow the proceeds to be flowed out to the estate on a tax-free basis. The remaining partners would receive no increase in their ACB and no CDA credit.

If instead the partnership agreement indicates that an income allocation of the insurance proceeds will be made to the deceased's corporate partner, the process is a little different, but the end tax results are exactly the same. The insurance proceeds are again allocated to the deceased's corporation, the corporation can claim a deduction for the amount of the life insurance allocated as part of the partnership income. Just as before, the corporation receives an increase in its ACB of the partnership interest and a CDA credit to the extent the insurance proceeds exceed the ACB of the policy. Since all of the income is then distributed, the ACB is reduced by the same amount. There is no gain on the disposition of the partnership interest because there are no further proceeds. The remaining partners would receive no increase in their ACB and no CDA credit.

c. — Partners purchase the deceased partner's interest

Instead of having the partnership purchase the deceased partner's interest, the insurance proceeds could be allocated to the surviving partners (or the remaining corporate partners) and they could utilize the proceeds to purchase the partnership interest from the estate (or the corporate partner).

The partnership as beneficiary of the life insurance policy would receive the proceeds of the life insurance on the deceased partner (or sole shareholder of a corporate partner) on a tax-free basis. The partnership agreement would specify the allocation of the life insurance proceeds. Each surviving partner (or the remaining corporate partners) would add the allocated net proceeds (the proceeds from the life insurance policy less the adjusted cost basis of the life insurance policy to the partnership immediately before death) to the adjusted cost base of the partnership interest under subparagraph 53(1)(e)(iii) of the Act. The partner would then withdraw these funds from the partnership and reduce the adjusted cost base of their partnership interest. In this manner the allocated amount would be paid to the surviving partners (or remaining corporate partners) tax-free. Using these funds, the surviving partners (or remaining corporate partners) would purchase the interest from the deceased's estate or corporation. The surviving partners' (or remaining corporate partners') adjusted cost base of the partnership interest would be increased by the amount paid to the deceased's estate or corporation. In the case of individual partners, the tax results are exactly the same as if the partnership purchases the deceased partner's interest from the estate.

In the case of corporate partners, however, the tax results differ if the partnership purchases the partnership interest from a deceased's corporation. In a partnership purchase, the insurance proceeds would likely be allocated to the deceased's corporation thereby increasing this corporation's ACB in the partnership interest. Because the ACB has been increased by the net insurance proceeds, there should be little or no gain on the disposition of the partnership interest to the partnership. In addition, the deceased's corporation receives a CDA credit for the net insurance proceeds. If instead the remaining corporate partners must purchase the partnership interest from the deceased's corporation, the life insurance proceeds are allocated to the remaining corporate partners rather than to the deceased's corporation. The result is that when the deceased's corporation sells the partnership interest to the other corporate partners, a capital gain is triggered on the partnership interest. In addition there is no CDA credit related to the insurance proceeds to the deceased's corporation. The deceased's corporation will, however, receive a CDA credit as a result of any capital gain realized on the sale of the partnership interest. The remaining corporate partners will receive a CDA credit equal to the insurance proceeds allocated to them (net of the ACB of the policy). The remaining corporate partners will receive an increase in the ACB of their partnership interest by the amount paid for the interest.

d. — Splitting the premium

One issue that will need to be addressed if partnership ownership of insurance is used is how the premium will be split amongst the partners. As discussed previously, the premium payments represent a nondeductible expense to the individual partners. The question arises as to what is a fair and equitable allocation of the premium amongst the partners.

There is a great deal of flexibility available in determining an appropriate method of allocating premiums to the partners. Some of the methods that could be adopted would include allocating the premium based on:

The present value of expected benefits to be received

At first glance, this method would appear to result in the most equitable allocation of the premium to the partners. One problem with this method would include determining an appropriate discount rate on which to base the allocation of the premium to the partners and the fact that this method of allocating the premium does not recognize some of the intangible benefits that may be realized as a result of participating in the plan.

A significant benefit that arises is the fact that the partnership should in the future find it significantly easier to retain existing partners as well as attract new partners to the partnership thereby increasing the partnership's profit potential.

Based on income allocation

A second method that could be adopted to allocate the premium to the partners would be to base the allocation on the income allocated to the partners for the year. If premiums are paid quarterly or monthly, premium payments could be based upon the partner's draws and adjusted at year end to reflect the partner's income allocation for the year. The problem with this method of allocating the premium is that there is not a link between the premium payments and the eventual benefits that will be received.

Based on equal allocation

The premium could be split between the partners on an equal basis. Once again, the problem with this method is that it does not recognize the value of the benefits that will be received.

This represents just a few of the methods by which the premium could be allocated. It is important that, whichever method is chosen, it is not only considered reasonable by all of the partners, but also fully understood.

iii. — Choosing a structure for funding partnership buyout obligations at death

The choice of structure for a partnership buyout will depend upon a number of factors: whether the partners are corporations or individuals; whether it is desirable to have the insurance held in the partnership, or by the partners; whether the partners wish to use their policy for overfunding purposes; what the partners consider to be an equitable split of the premiums; and whether the partners want to minimize the tax to the deceased partner (or his corporation) or whether the ACB increase and CDA benefits related to the insurance proceeds should go to the survivors.

In general, where the partners are corporations, partnership-owned insurance will allow minimization of the tax burden to the deceased and his corporation. Where the partners are individuals, any of the partner-owned insurance structures are effective in minimizing the tax to the deceased partner and his estate. Partnership-owned insurance can also be effective but if the insurance proceeds are characterized as an income allocation, the deceased and his estate will have a larger tax burden.

One issue with partnership-owned insurance is that the insurance policy is exposed to creditors of the partnership (refer to section 11.8.D.v). As a result, if creditors are a significant issue, the partners may favour partner-owned structures.

It is important that whatever structure is chosen the partnership agreement is worded to ensure that the allocation of the insurance proceeds to the partners is clear and consistent with the method chosen.

iv. — Funding the withdrawal of a partner on retirement

The partnership agreement may provide for various payments to be made to a partner on retirement; examples include an amount in settlement of a capital interest, an amount based on the retired partner's share of work in progress, an amount based on the retired partner's share of accounts receivable and payment of retirement income. The nature of these payments as capital or income and the corresponding income tax treatment for the retired partner and the remaining partners is determined by the wording in the partnership agreement. Generally payments in satisfaction of the capital interest, payments based on work in progress and payment based on accounts receivable would be considered the retired partner's residual interest under section 98.1. Payment of retirement income generally is structured as a continuing right to income under subsection 96(1.1). The tax consequences of these classifications are explained in section 11.5.D.

a. — Magnitude of the obligation

The provision in the partnership agreement for providing post-retirement payments may result in the remaining partners having a significant financial obligation to retirees. The magnitude of this obligation has been increasing as professional firms evolve.

In the early 1980s many professional firms grew at a tremendous pace with a large number of new partners becoming members. Many of these partners will likely be retiring during the same time period. When this clustering of retirements takes place large annual outlays to the retired partners may be required and the partnership obligation may be staggering.

Many partnership agreements provide that retirement payments will continue annually until death. Exacerbating the financial cost, Canadians are living longer and life expectancy projections are being extended. Accordingly, the retirement payments will continue for a longer period, increasing the magnitude of the obligation.

b. — Funding the obligation

If the obligation is unfunded, the liability for the retirement arrangements become the responsibility of the younger, remaining partners. The demographics of professional firms are changing. Fewer younger partners are being admitted into membership. This means that there is a diminishing base of remaining partners with the responsibility for funding the obligations to the retired partners.

In the past, the large capital contributions required from new partners were used in part to fund the obligations when senior partners left. More recently, firms have found that initial contributions had to be reduced in order to make it easier to attract new partners. The new lower contributions are often needed to fund daily operating expenses of the partnership.

This change means that funds traditionally used will not be available for payment to departing partners.

Pay-as-you-go

The funds required to satisfy payments to retired partners are therefore often serviced out of current cash flow on a pay-as-you-go basis. As a cluster of partners retire the annual outlay reduces the profits available to the working partners. The extent of the outlay may threaten the financial stability of the partnership. Accordingly, many partnerships find it prudent to consider pre-funding the obligations.

Dealing with the retirement provisions in a partnership agreement and coming to a consensus on a funding arrangement constitute some of the most difficult problems that many professional partnerships face.

Sinking fund

One funding solution may be for the partnership to establish a sinking fund where a portion of the annual partnership cash flow is invested to create a fund to be used to pay future benefits. This fund is generated from after-tax profits as the annual net income, including the amount used to establish the sinking fund, would be allocated to the partners. The partners include the allocation in taxable income, add the amount to their capital account and their adjusted cost base. The funds are then used to purchase an investment. One drawback of this solution is that the investment is subject to annual taxation in the partners' hands. If taxed at the highest marginal tax rate, up to 50 percent of the growth of the fund will be eroded by income tax and the time period required to build the necessary funds may be extensive.

Funding with life insurance

A further method of funding partnership retirement obligations is to use life insurance as the funding vehicle. Using life insurance is often a more tax efficient and cost effective vehicle as the cash value within a life insurance policy accumulates tax-deferred and generates tax-free proceeds on death. A benefit of using life insurancc as the funding vehicle is that, as well as providing for the retirement obligations, the insurance will provide the partnership with the funds needed at the death of the partner to pay any obligations provided for in the partnership agreement.

Cost recovery

The partnership may consider using life insurance on a cost recovery basis. The partnership purchases, is the owner and beneficiary of life insurance on all of its insurable partners. The premiums would be funded out of the cash flow of the partnership. When a partner retires, the obligation is paid out of current cash flow on a pay-as-you-go basis.

On the death of a partner, the firm recovers all or part of the cash flow paid to the partner during retirement. The firm receives the death benefit proceeds tax-free and may use the funds for the obligations owing to the remaining retired partners at the time.

Leveraged life insurance

An alternative which may provide for pre-funding of the partnership retirement obligations in a more tax efficient and cost effective manner would be for the partnership to use the combination of a cash value life insurance policy with a loan from a financial institution.

The steps to structure a leveraged life insured program are the following:

1. The partnership purchases and is the beneficiary of a cash value life insurance policy on all the insurable partners. Individual policies could be purchased on each of the partners or alternatively one multi-life policy could be purchased with coverage on each of the partners lives. As well as pre-funding the retirement obligations, the insurance will provide the partnership with the funds needed at the death of the partner to pay any obligations provided for in the partnership agreement.

2. Premiums for the policies would be made out of the partnership's general funds. The premiums are not deductible in computing the partnership net income for tax purposes. The cash surrender value within the exempt life insurance policy(ies) accumulate(s) on a tax-deferred basis to create the asset which will be leveraged.

3. When funds are required to make payments to retired partners, the partnership applies to a financial institution for a loan. The life insurance policy(ies) would be used as collateral security in support of the loan.

4. If the retirement payments are considered to be capital payments (see discussion of the nature of retirement payments above) the entire payment is borrowed. If the retirement payments are considered to be included in the retired

partner's income and deductible from the determination of the net income of the partnership, only the after-tax amount would need to be borrowed. The payment of the retirement income would be partially financed by the tax savings realized by the remaining partners from the reduction in taxable income due to the payment.

5. The loan interest may be deductible from the net income of the partnership under paragraph 20(1)(c) of the Act, as the funds are being used for distributions. The loan is structured so that the lender agrees to make additional loans to the partnership equal to the after-tax cost of interest on the outstanding balance. The funds from these loans must be used to generate income from business or property for the interest to be considered deductible. These additional loans are added to the outstanding principal and secured by the assignment of the policy(ies). By capitalizing the after-tax cost of the interest, there is no impact for servicing the loan on the partnership's cash flow.

6. If the loan remains in good standing, it may be structured so that principal repayment does not occur until the death of one of the partners. Upon the death of one of the partners, the death benefit proceeds are received by the partnership tax-free. The partnership would use the proceeds from the death benefit to repay a portion of the outstanding bank loan.

7. As partners continue to die, the partnership would recover sufficient funds to repay the outstanding bank loans and to build up a fund for future obligations.

The use of cash value permanent life insurance combined with a bank loan may be an efficient vehicle to fund partnership retirement obligations. However, there are financial and tax risks that must be considered.

The financial risks (refer to Chapter 4 for a detailed discussion of these risks) that may be applicable are:

- life insurance illustrations and applicable assumptions;
- performance of the life insurance product;
- loan interest rate risk;
- leveraging indexed accounts;
- life expectancy.

The income tax risks that may be applicable are:

- application of the general anti-avoidance rule (discussed at section 4.2.B);
- interest deductibility.

Another issue that is a consideration, particularly for partnerships, is providing creditor protection for the life insurance policies.

c. — Interest deductibility

The courts have traditionally considered interest charges to be nondeductible expenditures for tax purposes since they are on account of capital. Consequently, such costs are only deductible if they meet the conditions of paragraph 20(1)(c) and related provisions of the Act.

Under paragraph 20(1)(c), interest is deductible when it is paid or payable in respect of the year (depending upon the method regularly followed by the taxpayer) pursuant to a legal obligation and the borrowed money is used for the purpose of earning income from a business or property, or to acquire property for the purpose of gaining or producing income therefrom, or for the purpose of gaining or producing income from a business. Interest on borrowed money used to earn exempt income or to acquire a life insurance policy is not deductible.

Generally, compound interest (i.e. interest on interest) will be deductible under paragraph 20(1)(d) of the Act if it is paid in the year and the simple interest meets the conditions in paragraph 20(1)(c). The compound interest must actually be paid. It will not be deductible if it is capitalized by simply adding the compound interest to the outstanding loan balance.

When a partnership purchases an insurance policy and subsequently uses the cash surrender value of the policy as collateral security for a loan, the interest on the borrowed funds may be deductible if the criteria discussed above are met. However, the compound interest will only be deductible if it is paid. If the interest is capitalized, the compound interest will only be considered paid in the year in which the death benefit is received and used to repay the loan. A strategy to ensure the annual deductibility of the compound interest is to arrange a new loan each year for the interest component. The new loan would be used for business purposes by the partnership, while the partnership's regular income would be used to pay the interest expense of the original loan. Since the new loan is used for business purposes, interest on the loan should be deductible. The same series of steps needs to be applied to all compound interest each year. Therefore, obtaining a deduction for compound interest requires careful and extensive planning. Further, consideration must always be given to the potential application of the general anti-avoidance rule at section 245 which may apply to negate the benefits associated with such planning. As well, consideration may be given to the proposed Reasonable Expectation of Profit rules. See section 4.2.A.iii for a discussion of these rules in the context of leveraged life insurance.

The CRA outlined its administrative position regarding interest on funds borrowed to make distributions of partnership capital in technical interpretation 9618550, dated July 17, 1996. If the funds are borrowed to make distributions of capital, in order for the interest to be fully deductible the borrowed funds cannot exceed the aggregate of the capital of the partnership determined immediately before distribution. If the funds are borrowed to make distributions of profits to partners, for the interest to be fully deductible, the borrowed funds cannot exceed the accumulated profits determined immediately before distribution.

On October 1, 2002 the CRA released a position paper on interest deductibility and indicated interest would be deductible on money borrowed to return capital to partners. Capital generally includes both the contributed capital and accumulated profits of the partnership.

Paragraph 24 of archived Interpretation Bulletin IT-533 *Interest Deductibility and Related Issues* dated October 31, 2003 confirming earlier CRA administrative practice, provides an exception to the direct use test in situations involving money borrowed by a partnership to return capital to a partner.

v. — Creditor protection

As discussed in section 11.3 above, the partners are jointly and severally liable for all the liabilities of the partnership. Professional partnerships have liability insurance to protect themselves from claims; however there remains a risk that a claim might be uninsured, in excess of the coverage or result from the financial mismanagement of the partnership. If a partnership owns and is the beneficiary of a life insurance policy with a cash surrender value, there is a risk that the asset might be subject to the claims of current or future creditors of the partnership.

Similarly, if retirement payments or death benefits flow to a retired partner or the partner's estate, the payments may also be subject to claims by creditors of the partnership.

Instead of the partnership being the owner and beneficiary of the life insurance policies, there are several alternative structures incorporating the involvement of a trust which may provide some protection from creditor claims to the partnership, a retired partner or the partner's estate.

11.9 — Conclusion

Life insurance can provide funding to meet certain partnership obligations. Life insurance may be partner-owned or partnership-owned, depending upon the context. The tax consequences will vary depending upon the ownership structure and character of the payments made.

12 — INSURANCE AND CHARITABLE GIVING

Updated by Hemal Balsara, C.P.A., C.A., CFP

12.1 — Introduction

In recent years there have been significant reductions in government funding for various social services. Government grants to charities have also been drastically reduced, yet the demand for services provided by the charitable sector is continually growing. As government funding is reduced, there is an increased need for private donors to provide more of the funding.

It is estimated that over the coming decades there will be a transfer of approximately one trillion dollars of assets from one generation to the next. Charities are hoping to tap into this transfer to make up for the shortfalls due to government cutbacks. However, with nearly 80,000 registered charities in Canada, accessing the funds from private donors will be highly competitive. Charities are always looking for new ways to attract donors without having to invest huge amounts of time and money in fundraising campaigns.

This chapter will describe how life insurance can be used in charitable giving arrangements. It will provide an overview of the basic rules concerning charitable donations and discuss various alternatives for using a life insurance policy to support charitable giving.

12.2 — What is a Charity?

It is important to understand the basic legal and tax environments in order to appreciate the type of charitable gifts that a particular charity would prefer.

There is no statutory definition of "charity." In determining whether an organization will qualify as a registered charity for tax purposes, Canadian courts have generally followed the classifications set out by *Lord McNaughton in Pemsel v. Special Commissioners of Income Tax*, [1891] A.C. 531 (H.L.). The four heads of charitable activities are stated to be (i) the relief of poverty, (ii) the advancement of education, (iii) the advancement of religion or (iv) other purposes that are beneficial to the community.

Under the *Income Tax Act* there are two main categories of charities: charitable organizations and charitable foundations. Generally, a charitable organization is actively involved in direct charitable activities. A charitable foundation will also undertake direct charitable activities; however, its primary role is often to build endowments (capital) and distribute funds to other charities. A charitable foundation can be either a public foundation or a private foundation. Charitable foundations in general, and private foundations in particular, have more stringent rules with respect to the type of investments which can be held by the foundation.

The definition of the terms "charitable organization", "public foundation" and "private foundation" are found in subsection 149.1(1) of the Act. The distinguishing feature as between public and private foundations used to hinge on who made contributions to the charity and their relationship with each other and the charity. Changes to the definitions of charitable organizations and public foundations were made in Bill C-48, which received Royal Assent on June 26, 2013. Because the term "private foundation" is defined as a foundation that is not a "public foundation", these changes are relevant to private foundations as well.

The former definitions used a "contribution test" whereby if a person, or group of persons not dealing with each other at arm's length, contributed more than 50 percent of the charitable organization's capital, that charitable organization could only be designated as a private foundation. The current definitions replace the "contribution test" with a "control test". Under the "control test", a charity will not be disqualified from being treated as a charitable organization or public foundation solely because a person, or a group of persons not dealing with each other at arm' length, have contributed more than 50 percent of the capital. However, such a person or group of persons are not permitted to control the charitable organization or public foundation in any way, nor may the person or member of the group represent more than 50 percent of the directors, trustees, officers, and similar officials of the charitable organization or public foundation. If these conditions are not met, the charity will be a private foundation.

The type of charity determines how the charity must operate and also the type of gifts it may prefer in order to maintain its registered status.

12.3 — Meaning of Charitable Giving

The CRA has indicated in archived Interpretation Bulletin, IT-110R3, "Gifts and Official Donation Receipts," dated June 20, 1997 that a charitable gift is a voluntary transfer of property without valuable consideration. The following conditions must be met in order to qualify as a gift:

(i) some property, usually cash, is transferred by the donor to a registered charity,

(ii) the transfer is voluntary; any legal obligation on the payor would cause the transfer to lose its status as a gift, and

(iii) the transfer is made without expectation of return; no valuable consideration or benefit of any kind can accrue to the donor or anyone designated by the donor.

A life insurance policy will be considered a charitable gift if it is donated to a registered charity or any other donee described in any of paragraphs (a) to (g) of the definition of "total charitable gifts" in subsection 118.1(1) of the Act,[1] provided that no rights, privileges or benefits of any kind accrue to the donor as a result of the gift, excluding any income tax relief resulting from the gift.

The concept of what constitutes a gift for purposes of the *Income Tax Act* has been significantly modified by the addition of subsections 248(30)–(41) of the Act by Bill C-48 discussed above. These "split receipting" provisions were originally introduced in 2001. Many of the comments over the years concerning their application were made in the years between 2002 and their final enactment in 2013. Under these provisions, the eligible amount of a gift is the amount by which the fair market value of property given exceeds the amount of any advantage in respect of the gift received by the donor or a person with whom the donor does not deal at arm's length. In computing the amount of any advantage, the value of any property, service, compensation or other benefit is computed. Where the value of property acquired by the donor is included in the computation of the advantage, the cost of the property is equal to the fair market value of the property at the time of the gift (subsection 248(33)). The provisions provide a rule-of-thumb that if the amount of the advantage does not exceed 80 percent of the fair market value of the transferred property, it will still be considered a gift. Also, if the amount of the advantage is more than that, it is still open to the donor to provide evidence (to the Minister) of the intention to make a gift.

A split-dollar life insurance policy is an arrangement where the premium and policy values are split between two or more parties (see Chapter 8 for more details). Prior to 2003, the CRA indicated in several technical interpretation letters (see for example 5-5294, dated March 17, 1988 and 9335905, dated June 6, 1994) that a gift of an interest in a split-dollar policy would not qualify as a donation since some of the benefits of the policy also accrued to the donor. As noted above, the Department of Finance introduced legislation affecting various gifting arrangements, notably split-receipting. Although "split-dollar" life insurance policies were not specifically addressed, CRA interpretations (2003-018265, dated April 17, 2003 and 2003-0004115, dated June 2, 2003) suggest that, subject to a case by case review, a split-dollar scenario could qualify as a donation. At the 2003 CALU Roundtable, the CRA even acknowledged that split-dollar gifting arrangements "appear to fit within the spirit of the proposed legislation on split receipting" (2003-0004315, dated May 6, 2003). This is the case where the donor is entitled to part of the policy, and the charity is entitled to another part.

In situations where the entire policy is donated to a charity (charity is owner of the policy) and the entire premium is paid by the donor but where the donor is designated as beneficiary for a particular benefit under the policy (i.e. a rider or layer of coverage), again, the question becomes what amount or portion of the premium should be viewed as being in respect of the benefit under the policy to be received

[1] As the context may require, any reference in this chapter to "charity" or "registered charity" includes other "qualified donees" referred to in the definition of "total charitable gifts" at subsection 118.1(1) of the Act.

by the donor and thus viewed as an "advantage" for purposes of the charitable gift? Technical interpretations 2009-031202, dated November 19, 2009 and Question 7 at the May 2011 CLHIA CRA Roundtable, indexed as 2011-0398461C6, addressed similar fact patterns involving life insurance donated to charity where the donor pays all the premiums but where the donor would receive a return of premiums paid on death. In the Roundtable response, the CRA confirmed that the charity would be required to discount any gift of premium by the amount of the advantage to the donor. It did not provide guidance relating to how the charity is to establish this amount but stated that if it "could not be reasonably ascertained, no charitable tax deduction or credit would be allowed." In technical interpretation 2009-031202, in similar circumstances, the CRA confirmed that the premium for the return of premium rider would be the advantage and therefore should not be receipted.

Where the split is not easily identifiable, establishing the value of any advantage to the donor and thus the remaining charitable gift can be more difficult. For example, a whole life policy that provides death benefits and accumulates cash values would not have an identifiable cost of insurance charge as is the case under a universal life policy. Where a specific amount of death benefit is to be received by the charity with the cash values to be received by the donor, it may be more difficult to establish what portion of the premium paid is in respect of a specific amount of death benefit (and thus what portion would relate to the cash value).

It is the donee's responsibility to properly calculate the amount of the gift and any advantage received by the donor. As matters of valuation are questions of fact, it is wise to seek guidance from valuation professionals in establishing these amounts. Charities may choose not to accept gifts of this nature due to this or require as a condition of accepting such gifts, that a professional valuation be undertaken.

A charitable donation may also exist where a donor gifts the entire policy to two or more charities. The CRA has commented on this situation in technical interpretation 9729345, dated January 15, 1998.

12.4 — Disbursement Quota and Life Insurance Policy Gifts

Section 149.1 of the Act provides that charitable organizations or foundations must disburse and amount equal to 3.5 percent of the value of all property not used in charitable activities or administration (in excess of the following amounts: $100,000 for charitable organizations and $25,000 for charitable foundations). Regulation 3702(1)(b)(vi) provides that the value of an unmatured life insurance policy that is not an annuity contract is nil for purposes of the 3.5 percent disbursement quota rule.

Bill C-47 which received Royal Assent on December 15, 2010 repealed the 80 percent disbursement quota and the concept of and rules relating to "enduring property". The purpose of the 80 percent rule was to ensure that a charity expended a certain percentage of total gifts each year on charitable activities or gifts to other charities. Gifts of enduring property were excluded from this rule. Enduring property included gifts by bequest or inheritance, gifts made by direct beneficiary designation in an RRSP, RRIF, TFSA or life insurance policy, as well as gifts made subject to a 10-year direction.

Prior to the elimination of the 80 percent rule it was common to make gifts of a life insurance policy and any subsequent premiums under the policy, subject to a 10-year direction. Generally, the direction would require the charity to hold the policy, any proceeds or any property substituted for the policy or proceeds for a period of not less than 10 years after receipt of the last premium payment. The CRA provided detailed comments and administrative practices relating to the appropriate way to do this in archived Interpretation Bulletin IT244R3, "*Gifts by Individuals of Life Insurance Policies as Charitable Donations*", dated September 6, 1991, and in several technical interpretations. Notwithstanding that there is no longer an 80 percent disbursement quota, charities that hold existing life insurance policies that were donated subject to these 10-year directions will still have to hold the policies in accordance with them. Charities would have accepted these gifts subject to these conditions at the time the gift was made.

The elimination of the 80 percent disbursement quota removed a large administrative burden from charities. It also allows for a much simpler process when making gifts of life insurance policies and subsequent premiums to charity.

12.5 — Tax Incentives and Limitations

As mentioned above, all levels of government have cut back on the direct funding to charities. However, the government does provide significant indirect tax benefits to all registered charities. The Canadian tax system encourages taxpayers to support the activities of registered charities by allowing gifts made to such charities to qualify for a non-refundable, non-transferable federal tax credit for individuals or, in the case of corporations, as a deduction in computing the corporation's taxable income. This tax relief helps bridge the charitable sector's need for funding and the desire of donors to give to charities.

An individual is entitled to a federal tax credit of 15 percent on the first $200 of charitable donations, and 29 percent on any remaining donations pursuant to subsection 118.1(3). After including the surtax and provincial tax, at top income levels a tax savings of approximately 40 to 53 cents (depending on the province of residence) is generated for each $1 donated in excess of $200.

Residents of Quebec must claim a separate non-refundable tax credit on their provincial tax return. A credit of 20 percent is granted on the first $2,000 of charitable donations and 24 percent on the balance. Therefore, the combined federal and Quebec credits, for donations in excess of $2,000 result in a tax savings of 53 cents for every dollar donated.

The 2013 federal budget also introduced a temporary "First-Time Donor's Super Credit" ("FTDSC"), which will supplement the existing charitable donations tax credit ("CDTC") with an additional 25 percent tax credit for first-time donors on up to $1,000 of donations. The donation must be money to qualify for the FTDSC and an individual will be considered a first-time donor if neither the individual nor the individual's spouse or common-law partner has claimed the CDTC or FTDSC in any taxation year after 2007. The FTDSC will be available for donations made on or after March 21, 2013 and may be claimed only once in a taxation year after 2012 and before 2018. These measures were contained in Bill C-60 *Economic Action Plan 2013 Act No. 1*, which received Royal Assent on June 26, 2013.

For corporations, charitable donations are deductible pursuant to subsection 110.1(1). As a deduction, the corporation receives tax relief based on its corporate tax rate.

Since 1996 tax incentives for charitable gifts have generally been significantly increased. Such things as increasing annual income limitations and special incentives for gifts of publicly-listed securities, to name a few, have been modified and/or introduced throughout the 1996, 1997, 2000, 2006, and 2007 federal budgets. The discussion below summarizes the current tax incentives and limitations for charitable gifts.

A. — Annual limits

The maximum allowable gift to charity is subject to a ceiling based on 75 percent of the donor's net income for the year. Corporations are also subject to the 75 percent limitation. Donations not claimed in the current year can be carried forward five years, again subject to the 75 percent limit in each year.

For gifts of capital property, an election is available under subsection 118.1(6) for individuals and 110.1(3) for corporations, which permits the taxpayer to choose the proceeds of disposition to be any amount between the adjusted cost base of the property to the donor and the fair market value of the property. The elected amount also becomes the value of the charitable donation.

Subsection 118.1(4) provides for a one-year carryback of donations in the year of death. The 75 percent limit is increased to 100 percent of income in the year of death or the preceding year for donations made in the year of death. Gifts made by Will are deemed to be made in the year of death.

B. — Gifts of capital property

For donations of appreciated capital property made after 1996, the formula in the definition of "total gifts" in subsection 118.1(1) provides that the 75 percent of net income limitation is increased by 25 percent of the taxable capital gain. For property that is depreciable capital property, the limit is further increased by 25 percent of the recaptured capital cost allowance. The effect of these provisions is to eliminate the tax that would occur on the taxable capital gain and recapture that must be included in income as a result of the donation of the capital property. As an example, consider an individual who owns a building which has a fair market value of $350,000, an adjusted cost base of $100,000, and an undepreciated capital cost balance of $85,000. If the individual gifts the property to a charity, a taxable capital gain of $125,000 will be triggered, along with recaptured capital cost allowance of

$15,000. The total eligible gift will be calculated as follows, assuming other additional income of $100,000:

75 percent of net income (75 percent of $240,000)	$180,000
25 percent of taxable capital gain (25 percent of $125,000)	31,250
25 percent of recapture (25 percent of $15,000)	3,750
Total eligible for donation tax credit	$215,000
Carryforward donation ($350,000 - $215,000)	$135,000

In this example, the individual has gifted property worth $350,000 to the charity, and will be able to offset the taxable capital gain and recapture resulting from the gift with the donation tax credit.

C. — Gifts of publicly-listed securities

Where there is a donation of publicly-listed securities, including shares or units of a mutual fund or segregated fund, the capital gains inclusion rate is reduced to zero. This originally only applied to such gifts made to public charities.

Where a corporation has made the donation, the full non-taxable portion of the capital gain would be credited to a corporation's capital dividend account.

The zero inclusion rate is also applicable to individuals who have acquired publicly-listed securities with stock option benefits or optioned securities. These individuals are eligible to reduce the taxable employment benefit for such donations to zero. In order to qualify, the employee must donate the securities within the earlier of 30 days after exercising the option and the end of the taxation year in which the option was exercised.

The zero capital gains inclusion rate was extended in respect of donations of publicly-listed securities to those made on or after March 19, 2007 to private foundations. A related amendment allows employees who receive public shares under an employee stock plan to donate them to a private foundation within 30 days of receipt without having to include anything in income.

However, private foundations are subject to a new reporting, compliance, and possible divestiture regime (referred to as "excess corporate holdings regime") in respect of all shares held by such foundations. These rules could impact holdings of publicly-listed shares donated pursuant to the above noted incentives. Briefly, the excess corporate holdings regime requires that if a 2 percent safe harbour threshold is exceeded, the private foundation will be required to report its holdings together with the holdings of non-arm's length persons. If the combined shareholdings of the private foundation and non-arm's length persons exceeds 20 percent of the shares of any class, the foundation and the non-arm's length persons will be required to reduce their combined holding to 20 percent or less or the foundation will be required to reduce its holdings to the 2 percent or less safe harbour threshold.

Transitional rules will allow foundations to comply with the 20 percent limitation where they have excess holdings present on March 18, 2007.

D. — Anti-avoidance rules

Special anti-avoidance rules exist where a donation of a "non-qualifying" security is made. A non-qualifying security is defined in subsection 118.1(18) as (i) an obligation of the individual or a person with which the individual does not deal at arm's length, (ii) a share of a corporation with which the individual does not deal at arm's length, or (iii) any other security issued by the individual or a person with which the individual does not deal at arm's length. Pursuant to subsection 118.1(13) where a gift of a non-qualifying security is made to a charity, the gift is ignored for purposes of the charitable donation tax credit. However, if the charity disposes of the gift within 60 months, the gift will be recognized as having been made at that later time. If the gift is disposed of by the charity within five years, the value of the gift will be deemed to be the lesser of the fair market value of the original gift and the amount received by the charity as consideration for the disposition (other than consideration that is itself a non-qualifying security). Subsection 118.1(15) explains that if the individual dies before the expiration of the five-year period but the charity disposes of the non-qualifying security within the five-year period, the gift will be treated as having been made in the year of death. If the non-qualifying security is not disposed of by the charity within the five-year period, the gift expires.

Some donors had avoided the above restrictions by transferring their private corporation shares into a trust in respect of which the charity is a beneficiary. The donation was recognized to the extent of the disposition of the beneficial interest by the donor, yet the property may have remained under the control of the donor through the donor's control of the trust. An additional anti-avoidance rule in subsection 118.1(14.1) provides that if the donor is affiliated with the trust, the same restrictions will apply as if the donor had donated the shares in his or her own name.

An additional anti-avoidance rule contained in subsection 118.1(16) restricts charitable donation treatment for loan back arrangements where an individual makes a gift to a charity and the charity holds a non-qualifying security of the individual within five years after the gift and the non-qualifying security was acquired by the charity no earlier than five years before the gift was made. In such a case the value of the gift will be reduced by the amount of the fair market value of the consideration given by the charity to acquire the non-qualifying security. This anti-avoidance rule applies regardless of the relationship between the charity and the donor.

There is an exception to this anti-avoidance rule with respect to donations of "excepted gifts." Under subsection 118.1(19), a gift is an excepted gift if (i) it is a share, (ii) the donee is not a private foundation, (iii) the donor taxpayer deals at arm's length with the donee and, (iv) where the donee is a charitable organization or public foundation the donor deals at arm's length with each director, trustee, officer and like official of the donee. Generally, where the gift is an excepted gift the anti-avoidance rule will not apply. From a tax perspective, generally speaking, gifts of private securities will only be viable where the security is a share, the excepted gift rules apply and the charity is not a private foundation.

Subsection 40(1.01) provides for a capital gains deferral in circumstances where there was a gift of a non-qualifying security. The gain would be recognized in the taxation year upon the earlier of (i) the donor receiving charitable recognition for the gift, and (ii) the expiration of a 60-month deferral period. If the non-qualifying security is not disposed of by the charity within the 60-month period, the donor is not required to bring the reserve into income. The reserve is not available if the donor becomes tax-exempt or non-resident during the 60-month period. Subsections 248(30)–(35) restrict the amount of the reserve so that it does not exceed the eligible amount of the gift as determined in these subsections.

With the significant exception of the anti-avoidance rules, the overall impact of the changes over the past decade will benefit many Canadian charities and will invite tax effective and creative gifting strategies including gifts using life insurance.

E. — Tax shelter donation arrangements

In response to the increasing number of aggressive donation schemes (at least in the view of the government) other anti-avoidance rules were introduced in 2003 and 2004.

In the 2003 federal budget, the Minister of Finance announced that the tax shelter reporting rules would apply to certain donation arrangements. In a Fact Sheet released on November 25, 2003, the CRA issued alerts to taxpayers about the risks associated with certain donation arrangements. Under these arrangements (commonly known as "buy-low, donate-high arrangements") a promoter would present an arrangement where a taxpayer would purchase property (software, medical supplies, etc.) at a discount price and would have the property appraised. The taxpayer would then donate the property to a registered charity. The tax receipt, based on the appraised value, would be high enough to produce a tax credit greater than the cost of the property and the tax payable on the capital gain realized on the disposition.

Subsections 248(30)–(41) state that the value of a gift of property for charitable donation purposes would be limited to the donor's cost of the property, where it is donated within three years of acquisition or is otherwise acquired through a gifting arrangement or in contemplation of donations (with some exceptions). Other changes were also introduced, including rules with respect to limited recourse debt used in donation schemes.

12.6 — Traditional Gifts of Life Insurance

A. — Life insurance as a gift

Charities having a constant need for cash on a day-to-day basis will prefer to receive money immediately, rather than wait for life insurance proceeds that might be received decades in the future. On the other hand, some charities such as foundations and charitable organizations that are seeking to build large endowment funds, (e.g. universities, hospitals and private schools) can afford to take a longer view and may be prepared to wait for the large returns from life insurance.

From the charity's point of view, a gift of life insurance will allow the charity to build up large sums of money without having to embark on major fundraising campaigns. Much of the work is done by an insurance advisor, and often the paperwork associated with the donation is handled by the insurance company. Life insurance allows a charity to obtain a gift from a donor that is significantly greater than it might otherwise receive. A gift of $50,000 in a Will might be considered significant, whereas a donor might easily consider funding an insurance policy for five times this amount.

A donor of modest means can make a gift to his or her favourite charity far beyond that which could be bequeathed from his or her estate. The donor can make the gift at death without putting a burden on his or her heirs. For a wealthy donor, insurance may be an attractive way to benefit a charity while at the same time minimizing liquidity problems for his or her estate. This is particularly true where the wealth is tied up in a family business that will not be sold at death, or in other illiquid assets, where it may take time to turn the assets into cash.

The following chart shows the impact of a gift of life insurance. The example compares investing $5,000 per year for five years in a GIC at 3 percent with investing $5,000 per year for five years in a joint last-to-die universal life insurance policy with an assumed interest rate of 3 percent. Both the husband and wife are 45 years old. At the joint life expectancy of 45 years, the accumulated investment or insurance proceeds are gifted to a charity.

After-tax deposits	$25,000
Gift to charity without insurance	$50,544
Gift to charity with insurance	$155,782

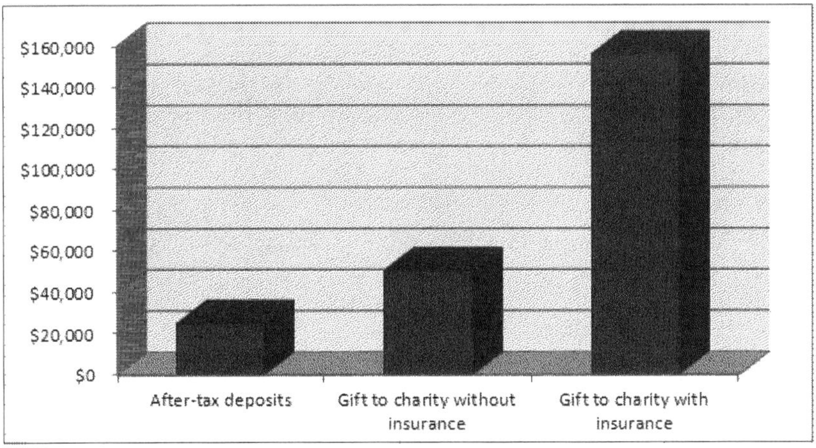

The GIC investment would result in a gift of approximately $50,000 to the charity, whereas the insurance policy would provide a gift of approximately $155,000.

B. — Types of life insurance policies

As discussed in Chapter 2, there are two main types of life insurance policies, term insurance and permanent insurance. Generally, a charity would prefer a gift of a permanent life insurance policy. Term policies are less attractive since coverage typically ends at an age less than life expectancy. If the insured lives for a long time, the policy might expire and the charity would never receive any funds. However, the lower premiums associated with term policies may make them more attractive to the donor. Group term policies are often popular for alumni groups of universities or other charities that can tap into a large pool of potential donors.

Permanent policies do not expire because of the age of the insured. These policies can build up cash values and therefore are very attractive to a charity. This type of insurance generally has higher premiums than equivalent term coverage.

Generally, an individual or a corporation purchases an exempt life insurance policy (as defined in subsection 12.2(11) and Regulation 306), rather than a non-exempt policy in order to avoid the annual taxation on the cash value growth. A charity will be indifferent as to whether the policy donated to it is exempt or non-exempt, since a registered charity is not subject to income tax by virtue of paragraph 149(1)(f).

C. — Methods of gifting life insurance

There are three main methods by which a donor can gift life insurance to a charity. First, the donor can make a bequest of life insurance proceeds through his or her Will. Second, the donor can donate the policy during his or her lifetime. Third, the charity may be named as beneficiary under a policy owned by the donor. Prior to the 2000 federal budget, where the third structure was implemented there was no tax relief. The 2000 federal budget made the tax benefit associated with this method equivalent to a gift made through the Will. Each of these options is discussed in more detail below.

i. — Bequest of policy proceeds

An individual can make a donation of life insurance proceeds through his or her Will. The policy will be owned by the individual during his or her lifetime, and the individual's estate will be the beneficiary of the policy. The individual's Will would indicate that a gift of an amount equal to the life insurance proceeds will be paid to a charity named in the Will. The charity would receive the lump sum amount equal to the insurance proceeds on the death of the insured.

The donor will not receive a tax credit for the premiums paid during his or her lifetime, but a tax credit will be available in the year of death, with a one-year carryback. Prior to 1996, when the charitable gift ceiling was 20 percent of net income, there was concern that a gift structured in this fashion could exceed the 20 percent limit. Now with the 100 percent limit for gifts in the year of death, this problem is lessened.

Where a gift of proceeds is made under an individual's Will, the insurance proceeds pass through the estate of the individual. Accordingly, the funds may be subject to probate fees and creditor claims, as well as estate litigation. Donor confidentiality may not be protected. However, the donor does retain absolute control of the policy throughout his or her life. In addition, this may offer additional planning opportunities.

With this type of charitable gift, the charity is at risk since the Will can be changed to eliminate the charity as a recipient of the insurance proceeds. Claims against the donor's estate can reduce the funds which were originally intended for the charity.

Depending on the type of policy, there may be options or riders available permitting individuals to provide for both their heirs and a favourite charity. For example, some universal life insurance products have a rider which allows the individual to recover the deposits made into the plan plus a specified growth rate. This feature allows the individual to set aside a portion of the death benefit equal to the deposits plus a chosen interest rate for his or her heirs (i.e. so that the individual's estate is not depleted by the amount of premiums paid plus interest to provide for insurance coverages), as well as provide a sizable donation to a charity.

ii. — Charity-owned policy

A charity can acquire a life insurance policy under which the donor is the life insured and the charity is the beneficiary. Since the charity does not have an insurable interest in the donor the charity must obtain the donor's consent, but this is usually a minor formality. Often, where a new policy is to be purchased for charitable giving purposes, the donor will apply for and be the initial owner of the policy (in order to facilitate the administrative process). Generally, there are two issues to consider: 1) whether the premiums paid for the policy will qualify for a charitable gift; and 2) whether the value of the policy will qualify for a charitable gift.

In general, premiums paid after transferring a policy to a charity qualify for a charitable donation credit. The donor may also get a credit for the value of the policy if an existing policy is donated. Premiums paid prior to transferring a policy to a charity will not necessarily qualify as charitable donations. This rule sometimes raises a "timing" issue where the individual is listed as the owner/insured on the application and pays the premiums to bring the policy in force prior to transferring ownership of the policy to the charity, even though the intention was to give the policy to the charity immediately.

Life insurance companies may allow donors to work through this issue by having the policy issued to the charity (as opposed to the individual) even if the individual originally applied for the policy as owner/insured. This way the charity "owns" the policy at the time of delivery while the payment of the premium is made by the donor and receipted that way. Another option may be to issue the policy to the individual followed by a reissuance, immediately, to the charity. Both of these options may also allow the individual donor to maintain privacy around medical information depending on the administrative practices of the life insurance company.

Where the policy is not issued directly to the charity or reissued immediately to the charity, a policy can be issued to the insured with the first month's premium being paid to put the policy in force. Immediately after the policy is in force, the policy can be transferred to the charity and a lump sum (or regular monthly premium) payment can be made. Generally, if the policy is transferred immediately after being put in force in this manner, there should be nominal tax consequences to transferring the policy; however, each policy should be reviewed prior to implementing this strategy to ensure that no unintended tax consequences result. The first month's premium payment would not be eligible for a charitable donation credit unless this were considered to be the fair market value of the (existing) policy transferred.

When gifting an existing policy, the lesser of cost (ACB) and fair market value otherwise determined of the policy on the transfer may also be receipted. (See the discussion below in section 12.6.C.ii.b, Value of policy, for further information.)

Under each of the alternatives described below, the donor will continue to make the premium payments on behalf of the charity owner and will be entitled to a donation tax receipt (or deduction for corporations) for the amount of the premiums. The premiums can either be paid to the charity, which forwards the funds to the insurance company, or they can be paid directly to the insurance company by the donor. If the premiums are paid directly to the insurance company, they are considered to be a constructive payment of a donation to a charity and therefore will be considered a charitable gift. As indicated by the CRA in archived Interpretation Bulletin IT-244R3, *"Gifts by Individuals of Life Insurance Policies as Charitable Donations"*, dated September 6, 1991, the fact that a donor makes a cash contribution to a charity and specifies that it be used to pay the premium on a life insurance policy does not influence the determination of whether the donation qualifies as a gift under subsection 118.1(1). One interesting strategy is where the donor gifts publicly-listed securities to the charity in order to pay the premiums on a life insurance policy. This not only provides for a sizeable gift to the charity but also the elimination of the capital gains tax realized by the donor on the disposition of the securities.

a. — Assignment of policy

Where a currently owned policy is gifted, the donor must make an absolute assignment of the policy to the registered charity and make the charity the beneficiary in order to obtain a donation tax credit. The CRA's technical interpretation 9405745, dated June 7, 1994 indicates that in order to have an absolute assignment, the donor must transfer absolutely, unconditionally and otherwise than as security, all rights, titles and interest in the policy. Therefore, according to this letter, the policy cannot be absolutely assigned to more than one registered charity. However, in technical interpretation 9729345, the CRA reversed this position and indicated that a gift of a life insurance policy to more than one charity will be treated as a charitable donation for tax purposes as long as the requirements of paragraphs 1 to 4 of IT-244R3 are satisfied.

It should be noted that more than one charity can be named as the beneficiary of a life insurance policy since a beneficiary does not have an interest in the policy. The act of naming a beneficiary is not equivalent to a gift of a proportionate part of the policy to each beneficiary.

b. — Value of policy

It is the current position of the CRA (as set out in response to Question 2 at the 2007 APFF conference, dated October 5, 2007, technical interpretation 2007-0241901C6) that where an absolute assignment of a policy is made to a charity, the donor is considered to have made a gift equal to the fair market value of the policy (less any advantage to the donor). Fair market value is a question of fact. The CRA has provided guidance relating to the factors that should be considered in valuing a life insurance policy generally, in Information Circular IC-89-3. Such factors would include: cash surrender value, policy loan value; face value; state of health and life expectancy of the life insured; conversion privileges; other policy terms such as riders, double indemnity provisions; and replacement value.

Where a gift is made immediately after issue or within certain periods of time, subsection 248(35) would apply. This was confirmed by the CRA at the 2008 APFF conference Question 11 dated October 10, 2008 (technical interpretation 2008-0284461C6). This provision would deem the donation to be the lesser of fair market value and cost amount for gifts, in this case, of life insurance, made within 3 years of purchase or within 10 years if it is reasonable to assume the policy was acquired with the intention to make a gift. For these purposes, subsection 248(35) defines "cost" of a life insurance policy as the policy's adjusted cost basis. Prior to this amendment as part of the split receipting rules discussed above, there were several CRA technical interpretations with somewhat conflicting responses.

However, fair-market value remains a question of fact. Consulting a valuation professional for assistance in establishing the fair market value of a life insurance policy is recommended.

The current position reversed the previous long-standing position of the CRA as set out in Interpretation Bulletin IT 244R3 which indicates that where an absolute assignment of a policy is made to a qualified donee, the value of the policy is the amount by which the cash surrender value at the time of assignment exceeds any policy loan outstanding, plus any accrued dividends and interest which are also assigned. This was previously confirmed by the CRA in technical interpretation 2000-0054467, dated December 19, 2000. The question posed was whether the present value of the death benefit under a policy could be receipted. The CRA responded negatively and indicated that the views set out in IT-244R3 remained unchanged. If the policy had no cash value, there was no charitable gift amount when the transfer was made, but payment of subsequent premium amounts would qualify as a charitable gift. An increase in the cash value as a result of subsequent payments of policy premiums would not effect the determination of the donation once the policy has been absolutely assigned. However, a repayment of a policy loan after an assignment entitled the donor to a tax credit in respect of the amount repaid.

At the 2006 APFF Conference (2006-0197021C6, dated October 6, 2006) the CRA confirmed that it considered the cash surrender value (that is the accumulated value less any applicable surrender charges) to be the amount receiptable for purposes of a gift of an existing policy to charity.

In technical interpretation 2006-0168591E5, dated May 17, 2006 the CRA again confirmed the administrative position that it is the cash surrender value and not the policy's fair market value (assuming that this amount would be higher than cash surrender value) in the context of a Term-to-100 policy with no cash surrender value that the policyholder had owned for many years. At that time, the CRA appeared to be open to reconsidering its position. The interpretation letter closed by stating: "We have not yet had the opportunity to reconsider our positions outlined in paragraph 3 of IT-244R3 on the value of a life insurance policy that is donated by a policyholder to a charity." The current position as discussed above, has put to rest this previous commentary and, as a result, paragraph 3 of IT-244R3 must be read taking the new position of the CRA into account.

For a handy summary, technical interpretation 2012-0432601E5, dated August 13, 2012, the CRA summarizes the tax implications of a donor making a gift of a newly acquired life insurance policy to a charity.

c. — Tax consequences of transfer

At the 2007 APFF Conference, the CRA also confirmed that in determining the policyholder tax consequences of the transfer of a life insurance policy to a charity, subsection 148(7) would govern. This subsection provides that a policy transferred by way of gift is deemed to occur at the policy's "value", which is defined in subsection 148(9) as the policy's cash surrender value and if there is no cash surrender value, then nil. To the extent that the value of the policy, as defined, exceeds the adjusted cost basis of the policy, there will be a policy gain and an income inclusion for the donor as a result of the gift pursuant to subsection 148(1). Since an insurance policy is not capital property, a gift of the policy would be subject to the 75 percent income limitation, and there would not be the extra 25 percent limit which is available for gifts of capital property.

d. — Benefits of life insurance gifts to a charity

Whether a new policy is issued to the charity with the donor as the life insured, or an existing policy is gifted to the charity, the donor will obtain a donation tax credit (or deduction for corporations) for the amount of premiums paid by the donor while the charity is the owner of the policy and a tax credit for the fair market value (or cost amount, where applicable) of the policy at the time of the gift. The donor will not receive a tax credit in respect of the death benefit. This arrangement allows donors to obtain tax relief during their lifetime rather than at death. Since the death benefit does not flow through the estate of the donor, the insurance proceeds will not be subject to probate fees and creditor claims or estate litigation. The donor gives up control of the policy and will no longer be able to change the beneficiary designation.

From the charity's point of view, the charity has a fair degree of certainty of receiving the death benefit where the policy is gifted. If the donor defaults on paying the insurance premiums, the charity has the option to continue to pay the premiums or allow the policy to lapse and take the cash surrender value, if any. Of course, the charity would prefer not to own term policies, and would favour policies which are fully paid up in a relatively short period of time. The unmatured policy itself would have a nil value for purposes of the ongoing 3.5 percent disbursement quota.

iii. — Donor-owned policy

A final choice for gifting insurance proceeds to a charity is to have the donor remain the owner of the policy, but designate the charity as beneficiary of the policy. Prior to the 2000 federal budget, the major drawback with this arrangement was that the donor would not receive a tax credit for the donation of insurance proceeds at death or during his or her lifetime. It was the CRA's view that the charity received the gift of insurance in the year of death by operation of contract as beneficiary under the policy, and not by a transfer with charitable intent. The 2000 federal budget announced that this will no longer be the case. For deaths after 1998, subsections 118.1(5.1) and 118.1(5.3) extend a donation tax credit to the individual immediately before death for direct beneficiary designations made to charities in a group or individual life insurance policy, RRIF or RRSP. Effective for 2009 and subsequent taxation years, this also applies to beneficiary designations to charities under TFSAs. The donor retains control over the policy and has the flexibility to change the policy or beneficiary designation (a drawback from the charity's point of view). This method also avoids probate fees, estate creditors and estate litigation and administration issues.

Provided the charity has not been removed as beneficiary of the insurance policy, it will receive the lump sum death benefit.

At the CALU 2003 Roundtable (2003-0004315), the CRA stated that where a charity was designated irrevocable beneficiary of a life insurance policy, no charitable gift will have been made, neither during the policyholder's lifetime nor at death. The CRA subsequently reconsidered its position. In response to question 7 at the CALU 2004 Roundtable, (2004-65451C6) the CRA confirmed that where there is an irrevocable beneficiary designation, the policyholder will be deemed to have made a gift at death.

iv. — Summary

A summary of the tax benefits arising from the various traditional gifting structures is outlined below.

Owner	**Beneficiary**	**Tax benefit during life**	**Tax benefit at death**
Taxpayer	Estate	None	Death benefit is a donation
Charity	Charity	Annual premium and value on transfer to charity is a donation	None
Taxpayer	Charity	None	Death benefit is a donation

12.7 — Other Insurance Supported Gifts

With the traditional gifts of life insurance discussed above, the donor either gets a large tax benefit in the year of death with a one-year carryback, or may obtain smaller tax credits for a number of years during life. Other gifts supported by life insurance can be used to provide large tax benefits during the donor's lifetime and to provide significant gifts to a charity sooner. The gifts can provide donors with recognition for their philanthropy during their lifetimes, and the property gifted can be replaced at death with insurance so there is no adverse financial impact for the donors' heirs.

A. — Gift of private company shares

Even with the anti-avoidance provisions (discussed at section 12.5.D, above), it is still possible to make a gift of private company shares (assuming it meets the "excepted gift" definition).

Consider the following example. Mr. Donor is the sole shareholder of a private manufacturing company (Opco) with a fair market value of $2,000,000. Mr. Donor has crystallized his capital gains exemption. He owns nominal cost base common shares and preferred shares with an aggregate redemption amount, adjusted cost base and fair market value of $800,000. Mr. Donor would like to make a significant gift to a charitable organization but most of his wealth is represented by his equity in Opco. Mr. Donor could gift his preferred shares of Opco to the charity. He could receive a charitable receipt for the full $800,000 fair market value. The charitable gift could be claimed in the year of gift or carried forward for up to five years subject to the 75 percent gift ceiling in each such year. Mr. Donor would not realize any capital gain since the adjusted cost base of the shares is equal to their fair market value. Assuming a 50 percent tax bracket the gift would result in an effective tax savings of approximately $400,000. The charity may receive dividends from Opco in respect of the shares and shares may be redeemed or retracted during Mr. Donor's lifetime. Opco will take out a life insurance policy on Mr. Donor with a face amount of at least $800,000. On the death of Mr. Donor, Opco will receive the insurance proceeds and use $800,000 of the proceeds to redeem any outstanding preferred shares from the charity. As an additional benefit to this strategy, Opco will receive a credit to its capital dividend account (CDA) in respect of the insurance proceeds equal to the amount of the proceeds in excess of the adjusted cost basis of the policy. As a tax exempt entity, the charity is indifferent as to whether it receives taxable dividends or capital dividends. When the shares are redeemed from the charity, Opco can implement the redemption using taxable dividends and can thereby trigger a refund of any available refundable dividend tax on hand and preserve the CDA for Mr. Donor's heirs. Note that this strategy would not be effective if the donee is a private foundation since the anti-avoidance rules (described at section 12.5.D) would apply where the shares are not redeemed within 60 months of the date of the gift.

B. — Capital replacement

An alternative strategy is the concept of capital replacement. An individual could donate capital property to a charity and invest the tax savings in an insurance policy. The insurance policy replaces the value of the gifted property, so that the estate is in the same (or better) position as it would have been if the gift had not been made, however, a charity has received a benefit.

Consider an example where a taxpayer gifts land to a charity. The land has a fair market value of $450,000 and an adjusted cost base of $50,000. The taxpayer would be entitled to a donation tax credit of $200,000 (75 percent of net income of:

75% × $400,000 × 50% $150,000 plus 25 percent of the taxable capital gain ($400,000 × 50% $200,000 × 25% $50,000) for the gift of land. The individual has gifted property worth $450,000 to the charity, and the taxable portion of $200,000 will be offset by the donation tax credit. The $250,000 difference, which equals the property's adjusted cost base plus the nontaxable portion of the taxable capital gain and reflects an additional benefit, would generate a tax savings of $125,000 when used as a donation tax credit in subsequent years, assuming a 50 percent marginal tax rate. This tax savings could be deposited into a life insurance contract that would provide the individual's estate with additional capital on the death of the individual. Depending on the individual's age and health, the insurance coverage would generally replace the original $450,000 worth of land, and may provide additional funds for the estate. This plan would allow the individual to eliminate the taxable capital gain that would occur on the disposition of the land, as well as provide for the individual's heirs and contribute a significant gift to a charity.

A gift to charity of publicly-listed securities can be made without capital gains tax consequences (or in the case of options, without employment income consequences). Again, the tax savings generated by the donation (whether a tax credit to an individual or deduction to a corporation) may be applied towards the purchase of an insurance policy to replace the value of the securities donated.

Another variation on the idea of capital replacement is a concept commonly called "RRSP or RRIF insurance." To illustrate this idea, consider an example where an individual has an RRSP worth $250,000 of which his non-minor children are named as beneficiaries. The individual also owns a $250,000 life insurance policy with his estate designated as beneficiary. The individual's Will contains a bequest of $250,000 for his favourite charity. Upon the death of the individual, the full $250,000 of registered funds will be included in the individual's income under subsection 146(8.8). However, the individual is entitled to claim charitable gifts of up 100 percent of net income in the year of death (and the preceding year). Therefore the $250,000 bequest to the charity will effectively eliminate the tax on the RRSP income. The individual's children will receive the full $250,000, and the charity also will receive a benefit of $250,000. This idea assumes the individual is philanthropically inclined and wants to make the donation, and not just avoid income tax at death.

This idea can be extended further to determine if the gift should be made at death by a bequest in the Will, or during life, by gifting a life insurance policy to the charity. A present value cost comparison will determine which alternative is the least expensive to the donor, and will depend on various factors, such as the donor's age and income tax bracket and the type of insurance policy purchased. To make such a comparison one could compare (i) the cost of making the donation at death, which is equal to the present value of the insurance premiums (since the tax liability at death is eliminated) to (ii) the cost of making the donation during life, which is equal to the present value of the tax liability at death, assuming no tax credit, plus the present value of the insurance premiums after considering the related tax credit.

12.8 — Conclusion

Life insurance has long been an important component of charitable giving. With the changes to the annual income limits, limits at death and added incentives for gifts of publicly-listed securities, taxpayers who have charitable intentions should be encouraged to help close the gap between the charity's need for financial support and the ever-reducing government funding levels.

13 — History of Annuities and Segregated Funds and Current Legislative Proposals

Updated by Jason Giuricich, B.B.A., C.P.A., C.A.

13.1 — Introduction

Annuities and segregated funds are two products offered by life insurance companies that do not fit within the traditional definition of life insurance. Annuities, in their various forms, have been used for centuries as a means of providing periodic income to a recipient (the "annuitant"), either for life or for a fixed number of years. On the other hand, segregated funds, or more precisely "variable insurance contracts," are a relatively recent addition to the product offerings of life insurers.

A. — Annuities

Historically, an annuity was defined as a right to receive fixed annual payments for life or for a certain number of years. Over time, the term "annuity" has been expanded to include situations where payments are made periodically, whether annually or not, and to also include variable payments.

All annuities fall into one of two types: an immediate annuity (where the annuity payments commence at the end of the first annuity frequency period) or a deferred annuity (where funds are invested to accumulate over time with the annuity payments to commence in the future). Both immediate and deferred annuities can have any number of variations. Payments out of an annuity are comprised of blended amounts of return of capital and return on investment. The insurer's liability to pay under the annuity contract can be measured against a person's life (a life annuity) or for a predetermined period of time (a term certain annuity).

Life insurance companies typically offer both life annuities and term certain annuities. Other financial institutions, such as banks and trust companies, offer term annuities but are prohibited from offering life annuities. Some charities have used the sale of annuities as a fund raising vehicle (see Chapter 16). Even the Government of Canada entered the business of offering Government Annuities ("Dominion Annuities") as a retirement income vehicle in 1908. By the 1960s, however, other social benefit plans such as Old Age Security and the Canada Pension Plan were introduced, and in 1975 an Act of Parliament formally ended the sale of Government Annuities.

It is therefore not surprising that the taxation of annuities has developed independent of the taxation of life insurance, though, as will be seen below, many of the tax policy considerations that have impacted the development of the taxation of life insurance have also affected the treatment of annuities.

B. — Segregated funds

While various institutions issue annuities, segregated funds are specific to the life insurance industry. A segregated fund is a pool of assets held by an insurer to cover its liability under corresponding variable insurance contracts. These contracts can take the form of variable life insurance or a variable annuity, but in either case the value of the contract, and therefore payments made pursuant to the contract, vary in accordance with the returns realized on the segregated assets. The term "segregated funds" requires some explanation. The assets of a segregated fund, while required to be notionally segregated from the other assets of an insurer and kept in separate accounts, still form part of the general assets of an insurer and are not held in trust by the insurer. Instead, legislative protection is given to the segregated fund policyholders through a claim on those assets that is prior to the claims of the insurer's other creditors. Through this mechanism, policyholders receive trust-like protection even though insurance companies are prohibited from acting as trustees.

Segregated funds are commonly referred to as the life insurance industry's equivalent of mutual funds. Thus, in the development of the taxation of segregated funds an attempt has been made to mirror, to the extent possible, the tax treatment of mutual funds. The most significant difference between segregated funds and mutual funds (aside from certain aspects of taxation) is that, as a result of provincial securities regulation, segregated funds provide for a minimum 75 percent guarantee on the return of premiums should the fund be held to maturity or upon the prior death of the life insured. In doing so, segregated funds fall outside the definition of securities and are not subject to the usual prospectus requirements. Mutual funds carry no such guarantee on their deposits.

13.2 — Early Taxation of Annuities from 1917 to 1971

The purchase of an annuity contract involves an exchange of capital for a right to receive periodic payments. At the time of the introduction of the *Income War Tax Act*, S.C. 1917, c. 28 in 1917, annuity payments were considered income and made subject to tax. There was, however, an exception made for life annuities. Subsection 3(1) of the *Income War Tax Act* provided that the proceeds of life insurance policies paid on the death of the insured or payments made to the insured under a life insurance annuity contract, whether upon the maturity of the contract or upon the contract's surrender, were exempt from taxation. This difference is explained by the special treatment that was afforded to life insurance generally under the legislation. Another exception was made indirectly for Dominion Annuities.

This early treatment of annuities (other than life annuities payable to the insured) ignored the fact that each annuity payment was a blend of income and a return of the capital initially expended to purchase the annuity. Some relief was provided in 1930 with the amendment of the *Income War Tax Act* adding paragraph 5(k) to provide a deduction for up to $5,000 in annuity income. The amendment was necessitated by the Exchequer Court's decision in *Kennedy v. M.N.R.*, [1928-34] C.T.C. 1 (Ex. Ct.), in which the Court found that a Dominion annuity which had been sold on the representation that it would produce tax-free income, was found to be taxable.

The deduction was limited to Dominion or "like" annuities and was subsequently reduced to $1,200 in 1932. Therefore, annuities sold by financial institutions such as insurers could, under the new rules, generate some tax-free income for the first time. However, many taxpayers found that unless the annuities they had purchased from these financial institutions exactly matched the contractual obligations under annuities offered by the government, they had great difficulty in successfully claiming the deduction. Further, annuities purchased from persons not normally engaged in selling annuities could never qualify for the deduction.

Clearly, to this point, there was little or no tax policy justification for the different tax results that fell on different annuities. The government tried to rectify this situation when a new approach, which better reflected the true nature of annuities, was adopted in 1940. Under this new system, all annuity payments, regardless of source or type, would be considered taxable and the limited deduction of $1,200 was replaced with a more general deduction for the capital portion of an annuity. In this way, only the interest portion of an annuity was considered income to the recipient. However, under this scheme the capital was only considered expended to purchase any guaranteed payments for a fixed period of time. Therefore, any payments under a life annuity that went beyond the guarantee provided in the contract were considered windfall income to the recipient and taxed accordingly. This seemed to make sense since guarantee periods were used to provide comfort to the purchasers of life annuities by promising annuitants that their heirs would at least enjoy something approximating a return of premiums paid on the contract should they die prematurely.

While this new approach introduced a measure of equity in the taxation of annuities and included grandfathering provisions for annuity contracts entered into prior to 1940, there was still enough of an outcry to cause the government to launch a Royal Commission to look into, among other things, the taxation of annuities. The Ives Commission, as it was known, accepted the approach that had been introduced in 1940 of taxing the income portion of all annuity payments. It was proposed that the capital portion of an annuity could be calculated easily by dividing the purchase price or total premiums by the term (or expected term, in the case of life annuities) of the annuity. The income portion to be taxed was therefore the excess of the annuity payments over this capital portion. The advantages of the proposal included ease of administration and even greater equity between various competing annuity products offered by banks, trusts, life insurers and the federal government.

The Ives Commission proposals were adopted in 1945. Unfortunately, or fortunately for some annuity holders, throughout the period from 1940 to beyond 1945 the rules were poorly drafted and left a number of gaps. For example, people with advance knowledge or foresight were purchasing annuities prior to the 1940 changes, making a single premium payment, and then, after the legislative changes, paying up the premiums in advance and taking immediate tax-free annuity payments thereafter. Others successfully argued that the grandfathered $1,200 exemption applied not to the entirety of the annuity payment, but rather to the income portion only, since the amended Act excluded the capital portion from the definition of income. Again, this often resulted in totally tax-free income.

The ability to exploit the drafting deficiencies of the transitional provisions was limited to those with the inclination and circumstance to take advantage of them. More widespread was the use of deferred annuities to avoid tax. The renamed *Income Tax Act* did not provide for the taxation of accrued income in an annuity, nor did it contemplate the taxation of this accrued income on the surrender of the contract prior to the commencement of annuity payments. It therefore became a widespread practice to purchase deferred annuities and surrender them for value prior to the start of payments. To put a stop to this the Act was amended in 1963 by adding subsection 7(5) specifically to include in income this accrued and realized income. However, an amount received from a deferred annuity as the result of the death of the holder of a life annuity contract was exempted under the provision as a refund of premiums or contributions.

13.3 — The Carter Commission, Tax Reform and Annuities

Prior to the 1970s, the development of the taxation of annuities was driven by the need to characterize the nature of annuities themselves. Prior to 1940, annuity payments were treated entirely as income. Changes introduced in 1940 and the subsequent review by the Ives Commission led to a more reasonable approach which recognized the true nature of annuity payments as being composed of a blend of income and a return of capital. This later approach has survived as the basis for the taxation of annuities to the present time.

With the release of the Carter Commission report in 1966, sweeping changes were introduced to Canada's system of taxation and in particular, as discussed more fully at Chapter 1, to the taxation of insurance products and life insurers. However, with one exception, the Carter report did little to immediately affect the taxation of annuities. The one area that changed was the introduction of income averaging annuity contracts (IAACs).

In the late 1960s, income averaging was seen as a requirement of an equitable tax system. Provisions existed in the Act for the averaging of farming and fishing income to reflect the tides of those vocations, but most taxpayers could not find relief from the effects of high marginal tax rates on varying incomes. This problem was discussed in some detail by the Carter Commission and as a result of its recommendations the government took the opportunity to introduce the IAAC provisions at section 61 of the post tax reform Act for 1972.

IAACs were treated like registered annuities such as RRSPs. Subsection 61(1) provided a deduction for amounts paid within the year or within 60 days of the end of the year as consideration for an IAAC. Amounts eligible for contribution to an IAAC were limited to special income receipts. These included income from arts, athletic or entertainment endeavours, lump sums received from an employer out of a pension plan, deferred-profit sharing plan, stock option plan or death benefit plan, the proceeds from the disposition of certain types of property and the taxable portion of capital gains. Essentially, an IAAC was restricted to unusual sources of income and did not extend to, for example, a salesperson who had varying commission income.

In addition to the contribution limits described above, subsection 61(4) set strict requirements, for the form of the IAACs themselves. The contract had to be made with a person licensed to carry on an annuities business in Canada, annuity payments were to commence within 10 months and the annuity payments were to be payable for life or for a maximum term of 15 years or less depending on the age of the annuitant. If the annuity was surrendered early, paragraph 56(1)(e) provided that the amount received was to be brought immediately into income.

The attraction of IAACs lay not so much in their ability to effect averaging of income, but in the opportunity to defer the payment of taxes on current receipts for a significant period of time. IAACs, like all annuities, were taxed only when the payments were actually received. There was, therefore, a tax-deferral advantage for the income generated within the annuity. IAACs, however, had the additional advantage of an up-front deduction of the purchase price of the annuity. As a result of this up-front deduction, there was no deduction for the capital element of the annuity payments. Still, the IAAC was a very attractive tax deferral vehicle. To take advantage of this tax deferral opportunity, individuals would often borrow the funds necessary to make the contribution to the IAAC. The government perceived this to be abusive and this ultimately led to the repeal of the IAAC provisions in 1981. (It is interesting to note that this is precisely what many people do with their RRSPs today.) Thus, IAACs served to focus the attention of the government on the notion of accrual taxation first introduced by the Carter Commission.

13.4 — The Introduction of the Accrual Taxation of Annuities

The early 1980s brought not only the end of IAACs, but also proposals for the introduction of a system of accrual taxation of annuities. First, in 1980, with amendments to subsections 12(3) and (4) of the Act, corporations, partnerships, unit trusts and any other trusts of which a corporation or a partnership was a beneficiary were required to report annuity income on an annual basis even though annuity payments had not commenced. The rule was applicable to annuities acquired any time after December 19, 1980 and eliminated the tax deferral opportunity formerly provided by annuities for corporations, partnerships and affected trusts.

Shortly after the change, the 1981 federal budget proposed the extension of this new system to natural persons as well, but with less stringent requirements. While corporations, partnerships and trusts would still be required to report annually, it was proposed that individuals, other than unit trusts and trusts a beneficiary of which included a corporation or partnership, would be required to report annuity income only on a triennial basis, unless the annuity was grandfathered. Under this accrual system, it was the holder of the annuity who would be taxed, rather than the recipient of the payments. This was a significant change from the way annuities were taxed prior to 1981. These proposals, contained at section 12.2 of the Act, were part of a larger package of amendments that affected not only the taxation of annuities, but of life insurance generally. After much discussion and industry representations, the new rules were introduced after the 1982 federal budget and were effective for annuities acquired after December 1, 1982.

Grandfathered annuities to which the accrual rules did not apply include:

- those acquired prior to December 2, 1982, in respect of which annuity payments had commenced before that date (paragraphs 12.2(1)(b) and 12.2(3)(b)),
- those arising from settlement options of life insurance policies acquired prior to December 2, 1982 (paragraphs 12.2(1)(d) and 12.2(3)(e), unless a prescribed premium had been paid on the policy or annuity),
- those acquired prior to December 2, 1982 (December 20, 1980 for corporations, partnerships, unit trusts and trusts a beneficiary of which included a corporation or partnership) which can never be surrendered and in respect of which the terms and conditions have not been changed (paragraphs 12.2(6)(a) and 12.2(7)(a)) (this provision was later repealed with the incorporation of these rules elsewhere in the Act), and
- those acquired prior to December 2, 1982 (December 20, 1980 for corporations, partnerships, unit trusts and trusts a beneficiary of which included a corporation or partnership) in respect of which the cash surrender value would not have exceeded the premiums paid (paragraphs 12.2(6)(b) and 12.2(7)(b)) (this provision was later repealed with the incorporation of these rules elsewhere in the Act).

Annuities which were acquired prior to December 2, 1982 that did not fit into one of the four categories described above, were not required to commence accrual reporting until 1987 (paragraph 12.2(11)(b)) unless, in the case of individuals other than unit trusts and trusts a beneficiary of which included a corporation or partnership, the annuity holder elected to report on an annual basis prior to 1987 in order to take advantage of the former $1,000 investment income deduction. Corporations, partnerships, unit trusts and trusts a beneficiary of which included a corporation or partnership which were owners of pre-December 20, 1980 annuities were required to begin accrual reporting on December 31, 1984.

The new rules put in place a scheme of accrual taxation for annuities. However, like the exception for exempt insurance policies discussed at Chapter 1, a major concession was provided. Annuities could be exempted from the new rules if they fell within the definition of a "prescribed annuity contract" (PAC) at Regulation 304. Annuities excepted from the accrual taxation rules as prescribed annuity contracts fall into two categories. The first category of prescribed annuity contracts are annuities purchased under a registered plan such as an RRSP or DPSP. These contracts are excepted from the interest accrual rules since payments out of such plans are fully subject to taxation. The second category of prescribed annuity contracts are unregistered annuities that meet certain conditions with respect to the type of holder and the pattern of payments. These conditions are described below. Provided the conditions are satisfied, the annuity payments continue to be taxed in the manner which had applied prior to the introduction of the accrual rules — that is, on receipt of payment only (included in income under paragraph 56(1)(d)) and on the basis that a portion of the payment was a return of capital (as determined under Regulation 300 and the capital amount could be deducted from income under paragraph 60(a)). PACs, therefore, still had some of the traditional deferral advantages of annuities.

When first introduced, the PAC requirements were quite restrictive. In order to qualify as a PAC, the holder was required to be at least 60 years old, or totally disabled, or someone who had inherited a qualifying PAC from a spouse. In the case of a joint and last survivor annuity, only one of the spouses had to be at least 60. The holder must have elected to have the annuity treated as a PAC and the contract was required to meet certain conditions including, among others, having been issued by a financial institution or registered charity, providing equal total payments each year, payments had to be fixed and non-participating, there could be no loans under the contract and the contract could not be disposed of, or the payments commuted, except on death. However, in 1988 the PAC rules were amended to make it easier for an individually-owned annuity to qualify so that, effective January 1, 1987 for example, any individual regardless of age could acquire a PAC.

The next significant change came in 1990 when the Act was amended to require annual accrual reporting for all annuities, not just those owned by corporations, partnerships unit trusts and trusts a beneficiary of which included a corporation or partnership, applicable for annuities acquired or materially altered after 1989. This amendment put in place the final major piece of the accrual system introduced in 1980 and having its genesis in the tax reform proposals put forward by the Carter Commission.

13.5 — Current Legislative Proposals Relating to Prescribed Annuity Contracts

On August 23, 2013, the Department of Finance released for public comment draft legislative proposals that would implement changes to modernize the exemption test and other life insurance policyholder taxation rules including the rules for the taxation of prescribed annuity contracts (see detailed discussion of the draft legislative proposals in section 1.9).

The draft legislation, and more specifically amendments to Regulation 300(2), proposes the use of the *Annuity 2000 Basic Mortality Tabl*e (instead of the *1971 Individual Annuity Mortality Table* that is currently prescribed). This change would have the effect of increasing the total expected payments and consequently increasing the taxable portion and reducing the capital element of annuity payments from a prescribed annuity. The proposed change would apply to annuities issued after 2015. The proposals include grandfathering provisions for annuities purchased prior to 2016 and for deferred annuities that will qualify for prescribed taxation once payments start as long as the annuity rates are fixed and determined before 2016.

For the purposes of determining the age of the individual to be used where the individual is determined to be a substandard risk, the draft legislative proposals add a rule that allows the use of the "rated" age or in other words the age used to determine the annuity rate. This would reduce the number of total expected payments thus increasing the capital element and reducing the taxable portion of each annuity payment. This proposal would only apply to prescribed annuities that were subject to the *Annuity 2000 Basic Mortality Table* as explained above.

13.6 — The Introduction of Segregated Funds

As noted earlier, the term "segregated fund" refers to a pool of assets held separately within the general assets of an insurer and used to cover the liabilities of the insurer under a group of variable insurance contracts. The insurer's liability (and therefore the segregated fund investors' returns) under the variable insurance contracts (whether life insurance or annuities) will vary according to the income, gains and losses realized on that pool of assets, in the same way that mutual fund investors' returns will vary with the value of a mutual fund's assets.

Segregated funds first appeared in the United States in 1952 and were introduced in Canada in 1961 through amendments to both the *Canadian and British Insurance Companies Act* and the *Foreign Insurance Companies Act*. These amendments authorized the sale of variable insurance contracts by federally registered insurance companies in Canada. By the end of the 1960s, provincial life insurance legislation had likewise been amended.

The purpose of the amendments was to give life insurance companies the ability to compete directly with the then developing mutual funds industry. However, the implementation of these legislative changes did not immediately result in a flood of segregated fund offerings by life insurers. There were issues that had to be addressed prior to any product offering. The release of the Carter Commission report in 1966 introduced the notion that investments in life insurance products and the investments of the life insurers themselves should be taxed. The details of how this would be accomplished were not resolved until amendments to the *Income Tax Act* were made in 1969 (the relevant provisions of which were not applicable until the 1970 taxation year.)

At the same time, there was concern over whether variable insurance contracts (the vehicle for investing in segregated funds) would be treated as securities. If so, their sale would require compliance with provincial securities regulation including the licensing of sellers and a prospectus requirement. This issue was not settled until 1970 when provincial securities regulators agreed to an exemption from the definition of a security for segregated fund policies provided the funds had a minimum 75 percent guarantee on the return of premiums upon maturity.

13.7 — The Taxation of Segregated Funds 1970 to 1977

The 1969 amendments to the *Income Tax Act* adopted a straightforward approach to ensuring that segregated fund policyholders were taxed annually. The insurer could allocate the income of a segregated fund to the policyholders in proportion to their share of the fund. Any income so allocated would have to be included in the income of the policyholder as required by paragraphs 6(1)(ob) and 79D(1)(b) of the Act (later paragraphs 56(1)(k) and 148(1)(b) respectively of the post tax reform Act). The insurer could then deduct from the income of the segregated fund any allocations so made. Any remaining income in the fund would be taxed in the hands of the insurer as investment income. This flow-through treatment ensured that the income of the segregated fund was taxed in the hands of the policyholders in the year that it was earned in the same way that mutual fund unit holders are taxed.

The insurer was required to report all allocations on a T5 Supplementary form, whether or not the allocations were paid or payable to the policyholders in the year. The insurer would also use the form to provide information on the source of the earnings since the income from the segregated fund would retain its character as either interest, dividends or capital gains (starting in 1972 pursuant to subsection 142(2)) in the hands of the policyholder and be taxed accordingly. Therefore, earnings from a segregated fund could be eligible for the dividend tax credit, deductions for foreign taxes, the $1,000 interest income deduction (when applicable) and favourable capital gains treatment (after 1972). However, capital losses could not be directly allocated to policyholders. Instead, losses could be netted out against gains within the fund and net gains would be allocated and reported to policyholders. Net losses could not be flowed out of the segregated fund.

Should a segregated fund policy be surrendered prior to the annual allocation date, the insurer could allocate a pro rata portion of the income representing the policyholder's partial interest for the year. Similarly, after 1972 unrealized capital gains could be allocated to the policyowner representing his or her share for the year under subsection 142(2).

Since the policyholder was taxed each year on his or her share of the segregated fund's income and gains, the Act provided that any premiums paid to acquire a segregated fund policy did not increase the adjusted cost basis (ACB) of the policy (subparagraph 79D(3)(a)(i), later 148(3)(a)(i)), the proceeds of disposition of an interest in the policy were deemed not to include the portion payable out of the segregated fund (paragraph 79D(3)(b), later 148(3)(b)) and, after 1972, there was no liability for capital gains tax on the disposition of the segregated fund policy (subparagraph 39(1)(a)(iii)).

The Act also provided technical measures to handle transfers into and out of a segregated fund. A transfer into a segregated fund policy from a non-segregated policy was treated as a disposition of part of the non-segregated policy (paragraph 79D(3)(c), later 148(3)(c)) while a transfer out of a segregated fund policy into a non-segregated policy was treated as a premium paid by the policyholder for an interest in the non-segregated policy (subparagraph 79D(3)(a)(ii), later 148(3)(a)(ii)). In the latter case, the ACB of the non-segregated policy would be increased accordingly.

In the case of segregated fund annuities, provision was also made for the annual taxation of the segregated fund during the accumulation phase. Normally payments out of an annuity are taxed as a blend of capital and interest, the capital portion being the total of all premiums paid for the annuity. In the case of segregated fund annuities, the taxable portion was the excess of the payments over the total of premiums paid and previously allocated income and gains. A new calculation was necessary each year since the annuitant could continue to receive allocations of income and gains from the segregated fund after annuity payments had commenced.

The flow-through treatment described above applied only to non-registered segregated fund life insurance policies and segregated fund annuities. If the segregated fund policy qualified as a registered plan such as a Registered Retirement Savings Plan, Deferred Profit Sharing Plan or a Registered Pension Plan, then of course it was not subject to tax until payments were made to the beneficiary.

13.8 — The Taxation of Segregated Funds 1978 to Present

The 1969 amendments to the Act were made with the intention of treating segregated fund policyholders in a manner similar to holders of mutual funds. The amendments ensured that any income from the segregated fund that was not allocated and taxed in the hands of the segregated fund holders was taxed as investment income earned by the insurer. While the 1969 amendments were effective in creating this flow-through treatment, some undesired consequences resulted from the failure of the rules to address all situations. For example, insurers were able to claim a policy reserve, thus reducing their taxable income, both at the time they allocated the income of a segregated fund to the policyholders and at the time the policyholders were actually paid.

A new approach was introduced in the 1977 budget as part of a larger package of amendments to the taxation of insurance products generally. The changes took effect for the 1978 tax year and were meant to achieve the same flow-through treatment but better fit with the operation of the Act as a whole. The relatively straightforward approach first adopted (i.e. the allocation of income to the policyholders and a corresponding deduction of income to the insurer) was replaced with an equally simple approach of deeming segregated funds to be *inter vivos* trusts. The insurer was deemed to be the trustee of the segregated fund and the policyholders were deemed to be the beneficiaries. The income of the fund was taxed in the hands of the policyholders as income from a trust in the same way that mutual fund unitholders were taxed on income from a mutual fund trust. As before, this treatment applied only to non-registered segregated funds. Where the fund qualified as a registered plan such as a Registered Retirement Savings Plan, Deferred Profit Sharing Plan or a Registered Pension Plan, the income was not subject to tax until payments were made to the beneficiary.

To effect the change, paragraphs 56(1)(k) and 148(1)(b) were repealed and section containing rules relating to segregated funds, was added. Since subsection 138.1(1) deemed a segregated fund to be an *inter vivos* trust, the rules related to trusts in section 104 came into play. For example, in order to maintain the flow-through treatment of income from the segregated fund to the policyholders, paragraph 138.1(1)(f) stated that all the income of the segregated fund was deemed to be an amount payable to the beneficiaries (the policyholders) for the purposes of section 104. In order that the income retain its character as either interest, dividends or capital gains in the hands of the policyholders, the insurer was then required to make the appropriate designations under section 104. The allocations of income were reported by the insurer to the policyholders on T3 slips each year. By doing so, the policyholder could qualify for favourable tax treatment through the use of the dividend tax credit, the then $1,000 investment income deduction and the capital gains exemption.

One significant change with the adoption of the new rules, was that under subsection 138.1(3), the insurer was required to flow through capital losses as well as capital gains. This treatment of capital losses differed from that of other trusts, and in particular mutual fund trusts, which could not allocate such losses to unit holders. Capital losses allocated to segregated fund policyholders were therefore available to offset capital gains from the disposition of other property and could be carried over to other years. There does not appear to have been any apparent tax policy reason for this difference in treatment of mutual funds and segregated funds.

Prior to the changes, both the income and the property of the segregated fund was the property of the insurer. In keeping with the scheme of a deemed trust, the property of the segregated fund was deemed to be the property of a separate segregated fund trust and not the property of the insurer (paragraph 138.1(1)(b)). However, to the extent that the segregated fund was not funded with premiums paid under a segregated fund policy, as would happen when the fund was being set up with "seed" money, the insurer was deemed to have an interest in the fund (paragraph 138.1(1)(d)). As a result, the insurer could still realize investment income from the segregated fund to the extent of its interest. By deeming the property to belong to a separate trust, the insurer was also prevented from deducting a reserve with respect to the segregated fund portion of any variable contracts.

The rules relating to segregated funds, found primarily in section 138.1, have changed little since their introduction. With one exception, any changes that have been made were for clarification purposes or in response to technical changes elsewhere in the Act. The only significant change was in the area of interest deductibility.

Normally, subject to limited exceptions, interest on money borrowed to acquire an interest in a life insurance policy (which by definition includes all variable insurance contracts) cannot be deducted for tax purposes. In 1991 subsection 20(2.2) was added, retroactive to the 1987 taxation year, making segregated fund annuity contracts an exception to the general rule. However, the restriction on interest deductibility remained in the case of segregated fund life insurance contracts.

14 — Taxation of Annuity Contracts

Updated by Barbara Cook, C.G.A., CFP

14.1 — Introduction

This chapter focuses on the taxation of non-registered annuity contracts owned by Canadian resident individuals. Registered annuity contracts include annuity contracts in or received out of deferred income plans such as registered retirement savings plans, or deferred profit sharing plans, and income averaging annuity contracts (IAACs). A detailed discussion of the taxation of these registered contracts is beyond the scope of this chapter.

There are various types of annuity contracts. They may be classified by when payments commence: (i) a deferred annuity, where single or periodic payments are made into the contract and income accumulates in the contract, and then the accumulated value of the contract is paid out in periodic payments at some later date; and (ii) an immediate annuity, where a lump sum is deposited into the contract and periodic payments begin immediately.

Annuities may also be classified by the term over which the payments continue: (i) a life annuity specifies that payments will be made over the life of the annuitant; and (ii) a term certain annuity specifies that payments will be made for a specified period of time. A life annuity may be issued on one or more lives. There can also be combinations of the term of payments such as a life annuity that guarantees a minimum term or limits payments to a maximum term.

Annuity contracts may be issued by a life insurance company or other financial institutions, or they may be payable under the terms of a Will or trust. All of these contracts are encompassed by the definition of annuity in subsection 248(1) of the *Income Tax Act* which states that an annuity *includes* an amount payable on a periodic basis at any interval, under a contract, Will, trust or otherwise.

The Act does not use the terms immediate/deferred or life/term certain to differentiate the taxation of annuities. Instead, the Act contains its own classifications of annuities and rules for their taxation. The rules for non-registered annuities are contained primarily in sections 12.2, 56, 60 and 148 of the *Income Tax Act*, and Part III of the Regulations. It is important to note that under the Act, an annuity contract is considered a life insurance policy (subsections 248(1) and 138(12)). Therefore, all references to a "life insurance policy" in the Act also apply to annuity contracts unless specifically excluded.

This chapter is divided into two major parts: first, a discussion of the taxation of annuity contracts issued after 1989, and second, an overview of the taxation of annuity contracts issued before 1990. As noted in the previous chapter, the significance of 1990 was the introduction of annual accrual taxation of individual annuities.

14.2 — Taxation of Post-1989 Contracts

A. — Taxation of annuity income

i. — Overview

In theory, each annuity payment received is composed of a portion of the original capital invested, and a portion of the investment income earned on the capital. However, the *Income Tax Act* does not necessarily tax annuities using this model. Under the Act, non-registered annuities are taxed in one of two ways: accrual taxation (subsection 12.2(1)), or taxation as payments are received (paragraphs 56(1)(d) and 60(a)). The method applied depends on the terms of the particular annuity. In general, annuities which qualify as prescribed annuity contracts are taxed as payments are received, and most other annuities are taxed on an accrual basis. The term "prescribed annuity contract" (PAC) is specifically defined in the Act, and, by definition, a deferred annuity cannot be a PAC during the deferral period (i.e. before payments have commenced). Therefore deferred annuities are always taxed on an accrual basis. However, the corollary is not always true: an immediate annuity is not necessarily a PAC; it must meet certain criteria outlined in the definition. Furthermore, under certain conditions, a deferred annuity may become a PAC when the payments under the contract commence.

ii. — Accrual taxation of annuities

Under the accrual method, annuities are taxed without regard to the amount of payments received. Instead, this method attempts to tax the income earned under the contract during the year. It is important to note that the person taxed on the income is the holder of the contract, who may or may not be the annuitant.

According to subsection 12.2(1), where a taxpayer holds an interest in a life insurance policy (which includes an annuity contract) last acquired after 1989, the income must be reported annually on an accrual basis unless it falls into the noted exceptions. The terminology "last acquired" serves to include contracts that have been disposed of and reacquired after 1990 such as in the case of an alteration to the contract. Annuity contracts excepted from this treatment are contracts which are either a prescribed annuity contract or an annuity contract that was received as the proceeds from a life insurance policy (that was not itself an annuity contract) and the policy was last acquired before December 2, 1982. It should be noted that the status of the contract (i.e. prescribed vs. non-prescribed) is determined on the anniversary day of the contract. Anniversary day is defined to mean the date which is one year less a day from the date the contract was issued, and the same date in each successive year thereafter (subsection 12.2(11)).

If the contract does not fall under one of the exceptions noted in subsection 12.2(1), then the "income" from the contract must be reported in the taxpayer's income on each anniversary day of the policy. Since individuals report their income on a calendar year basis, the amount reported on the first reporting date would be included in the individual's income for the calendar year in which the anniversary day falls.

The "income" from the contract is determined as the amount, if any, by which the accumulating fund on the anniversary day exceeds the adjusted cost basis ("ACB") of the interest in the contract. The accumulating fund is a measure of the savings accumulation within the contract. It is calculated in accordance with Regulation 307. If the contract is issued by a life insurer, the accumulating fund equals the maximum reserve that the insurer can claim for corporate tax purposes under Regulation 1401(1)(c) (i.e. MTAR). The MTAR is equal to the greater of the cash surrender value and the net present value of future benefits and obligations under the contract (i.e. the company's reserve) less the amount of policy loans outstanding. If the contract is not issued by a life insurer, the accumulating fund generally equals the cash surrender value ("CSV") minus any policy loans outstanding. The ACB of an annuity contract is defined in subsection 148(9) of the Act. The calculation is discussed in detail below, but for a non-prescribed annuity it generally includes amounts paid for the contract (premiums etc.), plus accrued income previously included in the owner's income under subsection 12.2(1), plus the mortality gain (loss) for the year, less annuity payments received during the year.

As noted in the introduction to this section, a deferred annuity will always be subject to accrual taxation during the deferral period. When a deferred annuity is annuitized, it may become a prescribed annuity if it meets the other conditions of Regulation 304 (see further discussion below). If it does not become a prescribed annuity it will continue to be taxed on an accrual basis. The calculation of "income" remains the same, but the payments received will generally decrease both the accumulating fund and the ACB. For a fixed term annuity with level payments and a level interest rate, the accumulating fund will generally decline at a faster rate than the ACB. As a result, the accrued income will generally be smaller than the amount of the payments received, and will gradually decline until it is minimal in the final year.

iii. — Taxation of annuity payments

When an annuity payment is received, if the contract is not subject to subsection 12.2(1), the payment is included in the income of the taxpayer by paragraph 56(1)(d) (unless it is included by some other provision such as the those governing RRSP, DPSP, IAAC etc.) Note that if the contract is subject to accrual taxation under subsection 12.2(1), then the receipt of an annuity payment does not trigger any tax consequences (assuming it is not a disposition), since the income is taxed annually on an accrual basis using the calculation noted in the previous section. An interest payment on an "interest only" annuity is considered a disposition (see further discussion in section 14.2.B.ii). If the payment is included in income by paragraph 56(1)(d), then the taxpayer may deduct an amount equal to the capital element of the annuity payment under paragraph 60(a). As a practical matter, the CRA only requires the net amount to be reported on the T4A slip issued by the financial institution, i.e. taxable portion = payment - capital portion. This treatment applies to prescribed annuity contracts (including deferred annuities under which payments have commenced and now qualify as prescribed annuity contracts), and annuity contracts acquired as proceeds of a life insurance policy acquired before December 2, 1982. The capital element of each payment is prescribed by Regulation 300 if the annuity is paid under a contract. If the annuity is paid under a Will or a trust, then it is up to the recipient to determine and report the capital portion.

The capital element deductible under paragraph 60(a) is calculated using the following formula from Regulation 300(1):

$$\frac{\text{adjusted purchase price}}{\text{total payments}} \times \text{annuity payment received}$$

The adjusted purchase price is a proxy for the capital element of the whole annuity contract. The term is defined in paragraph (2)(b) of Regulation 300 to be the same as the adjusted cost basis without the deduction for the amounts deducted under 60(a) (that is, adjusted cost basis as defined in 148(9), ignoring "K" in the formula: see detailed discussion of adjusted cost basis in section 14.2.B.iv). Note a different definition applies for certain contracts entered into before 1979 as outlined in Regulation 300(3) and (4). The total payments under a term certain contract is simply the total of all the payments that will be made under the contract. For a life annuity, the total payments is the total annual payments times the number of years it is expected they will be paid. For this calculation, some specific rules are outlined in Regulation 300(2)(a), (c), and (d). For example, the Regulation states the 1971 Individual Annuity Mortality Table must be used in the calculation.

The basic result of this treatment is that each payment of a prescribed annuity is considered to be a blended payment of capital and income in a ratio that does not change for the life of the contract. For this reason, this treatment is often referred to as "proportional taxation." This is more favourable than taxation on an accrual basis since it averages out the amount subject to tax and includes an element of tax deferral.

It should be noted that the August 23, 2013 draft legislation proposes the use of a more modern mortality table, the *Annuity 2000 Basic Mortality Table* instead of the *1971 Individual Annuity Mortality Table* that is currently prescribed as well as recognition of substandard risks for PACs issued after 2015. The proposed change to the mortality table would have the effect of increasing the taxable portion of each annuity payment. The proposed recognition of substandard risks would have the effect of reducing the taxable portion of each annuity payment. For a more detailed discussion see section 13.5.

The following example illustrates the tax treatment of a prescribed annuity:

> Assume a person purchases a 10-year term certain annuity with a fixed interest rate of 10 percent which pays out $15,000 per annum for a premium of $100,000. The total payment expected is $150,000 (10 years × $15,000 a year). The adjusted purchase price (or total capital of the contract) is equal to the $100,000 premium. This capital is prorated over the life of the contract, so $10,000 of each annuity payment is treated as a return of capital. In the first year the annuity earns $10,000, but only $5,000 of the $15,000 payment is taxable.

It should be remembered that a prescribed annuity provides for tax deferral — in the latter years of the contract the income that was not taxed in the early years of the contract must be brought into income.

iv. — Definition of prescribed annuity contract

Regulation 304 defines a prescribed annuity contract (PAC) to be one of three types of annuity contracts:

1. 304(1)(a): An annuity contract purchased pursuant to certain registered plans (RPP, RRSP, RRIF, TFSA, PRPP, or DPSP),
2. 304(1)(b): An annuity contract that is an income averaging annuity contract or a contract purchased with funds transferred from certain plans, or
3. 304(1)(c): An unregistered annuity contract that meets a number of conditions.

This third category of annuities is the type of annuity most often referred to as a PAC and only payments from this type of contract are subject to "proportional taxation" under paragraphs 56(1)(d) and 60(a). Payments under the first two types of PAC are included in income by other provisions specifically related to these special contracts. The remainder of this section discusses the conditions a contract must meet to qualify as a PAC under Regulation 304(1)(c).

If annuity payments under the contract have commenced after 1986, and the contract meets the criteria outlined in Regulation 304(1)(c)(i)–(v), it will automatically be a PAC unless the holder notifies the issuer in writing that the contract should not be treated as a PAC before the end of the taxation year in which the annuity payments commenced. The holder can revoke this treatment by notifying the issuer in writing. If annuity payments under the contract have commenced before 1987, and the contract meets the criteria outlined in Regulation 304(1)(c)(i)–(v), it will not be a PAC unless the holder notifies the issuer in writing that the contract should be treated as a PAC. To qualify as a PAC under Regulation 304(1)(c), the contract must meet the following conditions:

1. Annuity payments have commenced in the taxation year or a preceding taxation year (i.e. it cannot be a deferred annuity). The CRA has confirmed (2011 CLHIA Roundtable Q 8 referenced as 2011-0398471C6, dated May 2011) that where the annuity contract qualifies as a PAC, the annuity is a PAC for the entire taxation year.
2. The issuer is a qualified issuer such as a life insurance corporation, a registered charity, a bank, trust company, or credit union, an authorized issuer of investment contracts (as defined in subparagraph (b)(ii) of the definition of retirement savings plan in subsection 146(1)), or a loan corporation (other than a mutual fund corporation or mortgage investment corporation as defined in subsection 248(1)).
3. The holder (owner) of the contract:
   - is an annuitant under the contract;

- is an individual (other than a trust), a testamentary trust or a specified trust; (A specified trust for the purpose of this regulation is one described in paragraph 104(4)(a) of the Act which includes spousal trusts, alter ego trusts and joint partner trusts.)
- dealt at arm's length with the issuer throughout the year.

4. Payments out of the contract are
   - equal,
   - made at regular intervals,
   - paid not less frequently than annually, with the exception that the holder may have the right to vary the frequency and amount of payments in any year provided the present value of the total payments at the beginning of the year is unchanged.
5. Payments out of the contract are made for a fixed term or

   (a) If the holder is an individual (other than a trust), for the life of the first holder, or until the later of the death of the first holder and the death of a survivor that is a spouse, common-law partner, former spouse, former common-law partner, or sibling, or

   (b) If the holder is a trust,

   - in the case of a specified trust, for the life of an individual who is entitled to receive all of the income of the trust, or in the case of a joint partner trust, until the later of the death of the individual and the death of the beneficiary under the trust who is the individual's spouse or common-law partner
   - in the case of a testamentary trust (other than a specified trust) where the annuity is issued before October 24, 2012, for the life of an individual who is entitled to receive income from the trust
   - in the case of any other testamentary trust other than a specified trust, for the life of an individual who was entitled when the contract was first held to receive all of the income of the trust.
6. The guarantee period or fixed term cannot extend beyond the date that is (or would be if the person survived) the 91st birthday of the following individual:

   (a) If the holder is not a trust, the individual who is

   - under a joint and last survivor annuity, the younger of the first holder and the survivor,
   - where a contract is held jointly, the younger of the first holders,
   - in any other case, the first holder

   (b) If the holder is a specified trust, the individual who is

   - in the case of a joint and last survivor annuity held by a joint partner trust, the younger of the individuals who are entitled to receive all of the income of the trust

- in the case of an annuity that is not a joint and last survivor annuity, the individual who is entitled to receive all of the income of the trust

(c) If the holder is a testamentary trust, other than a specified trust, the youngest beneficiary under the trust when the contract is first held.

7. No loans exist under the contract.

8. Disposition can only take place on the death of the holder, or on the death of the spouse or common-law partner where the holder is a specified trust (i.e. the contract cannot be surrendered). The CRA has confirmed (2008 CALU Roundtable Q 10 referenced as 2008-0270471C6, dated April 29, 2008) that the collateral assignment of an annuity contract does not affect this requirement provided that the assignee is unable to enforce any disposition of the policy by the holder, but only has a right to the annuity payments.

9. No payments other than those described above can be made out of the contract.

10. No provision is made for any recourse against the issuer for failure to make payments.

Certain exceptions to these rules are provided in Regulation 304(2). Specifically, a contract will not fail to be a PAC where the contract provides that:

1. there is a decrease in the annuity payments of a joint annuity after the death of one of the annuitants;

2. on the death of the holder before 91 years of age, the contract will pay a lump sum amount provided it does not exceed the total premiums paid minus the total annuity payments received;

3. for a term certain annuity or an annuity with a guarantee period, if the holder dies during the guarantee or fixed term, the payments may be commuted into a single payment; or

4. on December 1, 1982 and at all times subsequent, the holder participates in the investment earnings, and the amount is paid out within 60 days of the year in respect of which the amount is determined.

With respect to exception 2. above, where a life annuity's contractual terms contain a provision to pay a lump sum on death equal to the excess, if any, of the premium over the total of the annuity payments made before the death of the measuring life, and this payment could occur after the holder turns 91 years of age, it will fail to meet this exception and will not qualify as a PAC. The CRA confirmed this in the 2013 CLHIA Roundtable Question 4 referenced as 2013-0481391C6, dated May 17, 2013.

For the purposes of the prescribed annuity contract rules, Regulation 304(3) deems the annuitant under an annuity contract to be the holder of the contract where: 1) the contract is held by another person in trust for the annuitant, or 2) the annuitant acquired the contract as survivor income benefits under an employee group term life insurance policy. Regulation 304(4) and (5) define an "annuitant" as the person who, at that time is entitled to receive the annuity payments under the contract (i.e. the payee); and a "spouse" and "former spouse" of a person to include someone who is married to, or who is a party to a void or voidable marriage, with the particular individual. A common-law partner is defined (subsection 248(1) of the Act) as a person of the same or opposite sex who cohabits with the taxpayer, at that time, in a conjugal relationship and who has so cohabited throughout a 12-month period ending before that time, or who is a parent of a child with the taxpayer (natural or adoptive) of whom the taxpayer is also a parent.

On October 24, 2012, a Notice of Ways and Means Motion was tabled that contained technical tax amendments that have been proposed over the past number of years. These measures, contained in Bill C-48, received Royal Assent June 26, 2013.

With Bill C-48 the Regulations relating to prescribed annuity contracts were amended to permit their purchase by certain types of trusts. This was the subject of Department of Finance comfort letters from July 29, 2002 and June 27, 2003, which confirmed that, from a policy perspective, it appears appropriate to permit an alter ego trust to hold a PAC and for a last survivor annuity contract held by a joint partner trust, and based on the lives of the settlor of the trust and their spouse or common-law partner, to be a PAC, if all of the other conditions of section 304 of the Regulations are met.

The second comfort letter also dealt with the issue that Regulation 304 appeared to only contemplate testamentary trusts, which are not specified trusts (i.e. spousal or common-law partner trusts), holding fixed term annuity contracts. Regulation 304 was silent with respect to life annuities purchased by such trusts. In this second comfort letter, the Department confirmed that: "From a policy perspective and in order to be consistent with clause 304(1)(c)(iv)(C) of the Regulations, we are prepared to recommend an amendment to the Regulations to prescribe this type of annuity contract under clause 304(1)(c)(iv)(B), where the payments continue for the life of any beneficiary entitled to receive the income of the trust."

The legislation now allows the purchase of a PAC by alter-ego and joint partner trusts, as well as allows certain testamentary trusts to purchase life annuities and receive PAC treatment. However, with respect to testamentary trusts that are not specified trusts, the new legislation is not exactly consistent with the comfort letters. For these specific testamentary trusts, the legislation limits the ability of annuities issued after October 23, 2012 to qualify as a PAC if the trust has more than one beneficiary entitled to the income of the trust when the contract is first held. No explanation is provided for this change. Annuities issued prior to October 24, 2012 relying on the comfort letters are not affected.

B. — Taxation of dispositions

i. — Overview

Gains on dispositions of insurance policies (including annuities) are included in income by subsection 148(1) and paragraph 56(1)(j) of the Act. The full gain is included in income; it is not a capital gain. The gain is equal to the amount, if any, by which the proceeds of the disposition exceed the adjusted cost basis of the contract. Note the use of the term "if any" precludes the amount from being negative.

However, subsection 20(20) permits a deduction for over-accruals on non-prescribed annuities equal to the lesser of 1) accrued amounts included in income in respect of the contract to date and 2) the excess of the adjusted cost basis of the contract, if any, over the proceeds of the disposition.

As noted earlier, the adjusted cost basis of an insurance policy (including an annuity contract) is defined in subsection 148(9). The phrase "proceeds of the disposition" is also defined in subsection 148(9). Partial dispositions are dealt with under subsection 148(4). No inclusion is required on the disposition of a policy that is or is issued pursuant to certain registered plans listed in paragraphs 148(1)(a) to (e).

ii. — What constitutes a disposition?

Disposition of an interest in a life insurance policy (including an annuity contract) generally refers to any transaction in which the interest is transferred to another party. Disposition is further defined in subsection 148(9) to specifically include and exclude certain transactions. The included transactions relevant to an annuity contract are: a surrender of the policy (commutation of the contract), a policy loan (rare on annuity contracts), a dissolution by virtue of maturity, a disposition by operation of law, and a payment in respect of certain annuity contracts entered into between November 16, 1978 and November 13, 1981. A disposition as defined in subsection 148(9) specifically excludes a collateral assignment of the contract, and an annuity payment. Note when a deferred annuity is annuitized, and annuity payments commence, there is no disposition (deemed or otherwise) of the contract. A partial surrender of a contract constitutes a disposition of the portion of the contract surrendered. Withdrawals out of an annuity such as interest payments on "interest payout annuities" are treated as partial dispositions; they are not considered annuity payments. Interest payout annuities allow the holder to periodically withdraw the interest earned in the contract.

In addition, where the holder of an interest in an annuity contract dies, paragraph 148(2)(b) deems a disposition to take place immediately before death. However, the provision does not apply to life annuity contracts entered into before November 13, 1981 or to prescribed annuity contracts. In the case of contracts to which 148(2)(b) does not apply, there will be an actual disposition on the death of the owner since the contract will either terminate or be transferred to a new owner. The purpose of the deemed disposition is to apply special rules in determining the proceeds to the deceased and adjusted cost basis to the new owner (discussed below).

iii. — Definition of proceeds of the disposition

For most purposes, the proceeds of the disposition are defined by the definition of this phrase in subsection 148(9). The general rule stated in the definition is that proceeds of the disposition equals the amount of the proceeds that the policyholder, beneficiary or assignee is entitled to receive on the disposition. In the case of a surrender or maturity, the proceeds of the disposition are specifically defined by paragraph (a) to be the cash surrender value less any amounts owing on the policy (premiums or policy loans). In the case of an annuity contract, this amount would generally be the commuted value of the contract. When paragraph 148(2)(b) applies to an annuity contract (i.e. deemed disposition on death), paragraph (d) of the definition provides that the proceeds of the disposition will equal the accumulating fund immediately after the time of death. This formula brings into income any income under the contract that has not previously been reported — such as the income since the last annual reporting on a contract subject to accrual taxation under subsection 12.2(1). Note the definition of accumulating fund is the same as discussed earlier, except that for a contract issued by a life insurer, when paragraph 148(2)(b) applies (i.e. deemed disposition on death) the accumulating fund is calculated as if the time and manner of death were known (Regulation 307(1)(b)(i)). This essentially removes the mortality gain/loss component from the reserve calculation.

For certain dispositions subsection 148(7) deems the proceeds of disposition to be equal to the value of the interest at the time of the disposition. The person acquiring the interest is also deemed to acquire the interest at an ACB equal to the value of the interest. The term "value" is defined in subsection 148(9) and is equal to the amount that the holder is entitled to receive if the policy were surrendered (essentially the cash surrender value of the policy less any policy loans, or nil if there is no cash surrender value). The provision applies where an insurance policy (including an annuity contract) is disposed of by the owner in one of four circumstances:

1. it is transferred by way of gift or bequest;
2. it is distributed from a corporation;
3. it is disposed of by operation of law only (such as a transfer to a successor owner or joint tenant); or
4. it is disposed of to any non-arm's length person;

unless paragraph 148(2)(b) applied to the disposition. Therefore it will apply to most transfers of a prescribed annuity, and to most transfers of non-prescribed annuities by reason other than the death of the owner. The provision will not apply to an arm's length sale of an annuity contract.

There are two provisions that provide for tax-free rollovers of a policy to a spouse or common-law partner (but not a spouse trust): subsection 148(8.1) applies if during the policyholder's lifetime a policy is transferred to the policyholder's spouse or common-law partner, or to a former spouse or former common-law partner of the policyholder in settlement of rights arising out of their marriage or common-law partnership; subsection 148(8.2) applies if a policy is transferred or distributed to a spouse or common-law partner as a consequence of the death of a policyholder. In order to qualify for the rollover, both the policyholder and the spouse or common-law partner (or former spouse or former common-law partner) must be resident in Canada. The provisions deem that the interest is disposed of for proceeds of the disposition equal to the adjusted cost basis to the policyholder immediately before the transfer, and the spouse, common-law partner, former spouse or former common-law partner acquires the policy at a cost equal to those proceeds. Both provisions will apply automatically unless the policyholder makes an election not to have them apply.

iv. — Definition of adjusted cost basis

The adjusted cost basis of an annuity contract is calculated using the same formula as is applied to other life insurance policies outlined in the definition of adjusted cost basis in subsection 148(9). As is the case for an insurance policy, the ACB changes over the life of the contract as the various components of the formula increase and decrease the ACB. The ACB of a post-1989 annuity contract is increased by:

1. the cost of acquiring the contract from a third party (excluding premiums paid);
2. premiums paid by or on behalf of the policyholder (for an annuity contract this will include an amount paid to "purchase" the annuity contract);
3. amounts previously included in income in respect of a disposition of an interest in the policy (i.e. gains on partial dispositions);
4. amounts previously included in income under
   - subsection 12(3) — accrued interest to a corporation, partnership, trust etc.,
   - section 12.2 — accrued income on non-prescribed annuities etc., or
   - paragraph 212(1)(o) — relating to non-residents;
5. certain policy loan repayments;
6. any gain reported on the first anniversary date of the contract; and
7. mortality gains (defined in Regulation 308(2)) on a life annuity contract (as defined in regulation 301) subject to the accrual rules in 12.2(1).

The ACB of a post-1989 annuity contract is decreased by:

1. prior proceeds of the disposition (i.e. on partial dispositions);
2. amounts previously deducted from income under paragraph 60(a) (i.e. the capital element of annuity payments included under paragraph 56(1)(d));
3. annuity payments received out of a contract subject to accrual taxation under subsection 12.2(1); and
4. mortality losses (defined in Regulation 308(3)) on a life annuity contract (as defined in regulation 301) subject to the accrual rules in subsection 12.2(1).

The adjusted cost basis cannot be negative (adjusted cost basis is determined by a formula, and pursuant to section 257, if the amount is negative it will be deemed to be nil). However, where the contract is subject to the accrual rules in subsection 12.2(1), if in any year the adjusted cost basis of the contract would have been negative, the negative amount is included in the income for that year by subsection 12.2(5).

As noted above, if an annuity contract is a life annuity contract subject to accrual taxation, the ACB must be adjusted for mortality gains and losses. A life annuity contract is defined in Regulation 301(1) to be a contract issued by an authorized issuer to one person or partnership (referred to as the annuitant) or jointly to two or more annuitants, where the terms of the contract provide for periodic payments at annual intervals (or more frequently) to commence on a specified day and continue for the life of one or more individuals. Regulation 301(2) provides clarification on contract terms that will not cause a contract to fail to be a life annuity contract: the contract may provide for

1. assignment of the annuity payments (301(2)(a));
2. payments until the sooner of death or a specified period of no less than 10 years (301(2)(b));
3. payments until the later of death or a specified period (if paid to a specified person) (301(2)(c));
4. a payment to be made on the annuitant's death (301(2)(d));
5. changes to the date of commencement of annuity payments or maturity date (301(2)(e)); or
6. proceeds payable may be received in the form of an annuity contract which is not a life annuity contract (301(2)(f)).

There are special rules which should be noted in determining the ACB of an annuity contract. In the case of a partial disposition, the adjusted cost basis of the portion is defined in subsection 148(4) to be the proportion of the total ACB that the proceeds of the disposition is of the accumulating fund for the whole contract, immediately before the disposition. Where a life insurance policy which was last acquired before December 2, 1982 is disposed of before the death of the insured, and only an annuity contract is received as proceeds, subsection 148(6) deems the purchase price of the annuity contract to be equal to the adjusted cost basis of the policy immediately before the first payment.

CRA technical interpretation 2002-0127495, dated May 7, 2002, sparked significant interest and concern with respect to the treatment of third-party life annuity contracts (i.e. annuity contracts in which the owner of the contract is not the person upon whose life the annuity is based). In this technical interpretation the CRA took the position that a corporate-owned non-prescribed annuity contract where the shareholder is the annuitant under the contract and the corporation receives the payments would not meet the requirements of Regulation 301 (as it formerly read) and, as a result, would not be a life annuity contract.

The reason for the CRA's interpretation was that the definition of "life annuity contract" in Regulation 301 stipulated, among other things, that the annuity payments are to be made to an "individual" who is referred to as the "annuitant", and such annuity payments are to continue throughout the lifetime of the annuitant. In relation to the particular question, annuity payments are received by a corporation and not an individual.

If a contract is not a "life annuity contract" that annuity's ACB, as defined by subsection 148(9) of the Act, would not be adjusted for mortality gains and losses. However, the accumulating fund (AF) of an annuity contract that is a life contingent annuity would include adjustments for mortality gains and losses. Since the taxable portion of an annuity is generally the difference between the ACB and the

AF, in addition to investment growth, the policyholder would essentially be taxed on mortality gains.

The Department of Finance subsequently provided a comfort letter, dated September 12, 2002, where it confirmed that the definition of "life annuity contract" found in Regulation 301 was overly restrictive and could result in inappropriate income inclusions.

To address this concern, Regulation 301 has been amended, effective for years after 1980, to clarify that the definition of "life annuity contract" includes life annuity contracts under which the annuitant is a partnership or a person as well as life annuity contracts under which the annuity payments are based on the life of an individual who is not the annuitant. The amendments provide that the taxation of these annuities is on the same basis as other non-prescribed annuity contracts.

C. — Taxation on death

There are three possible scenarios on the death of the original owner/ annuitant depending on the terms of the contract:

1. the contract is terminated with no further payments;
2. the contract terminates and a lump sum is paid to a beneficiary; or
3. the annuity continues or begins to pay periodic payments to the beneficiary for a guaranteed period.

In the first two cases the owner/annuitant has a disposition of the contract: an actual disposition if the contract is a PAC or a life annuity contract issued before November 13, 1981; a deemed disposition under paragraph 148(2)(b) in any other case. In the third instance, if the contract is a PAC, a strict reading of the Act would lead to the conclusion that there is an actual disposition of the contract. However, in practice, the industry and the CRA do not treat the transfer of a PAC to a beneficiary as a disposition. There have been ongoing discussions with the CRA to correct the legislation to reflect this intent, but to date no technical amendments have been released. In the case of a non-prescribed annuity transferred to a beneficiary, there would again be a deemed disposition of the contract in the hands of the deceased. The consequences to the owner and the beneficiary in each case are discussed below. Some limited commentary from the CRA has been provided in a technical interpretation (2004-010024 dated January 6, 2005). This commentary confirms that paragraph 148(2)(b) does not apply to prescribed annuities and discusses the application of paragraph 148(2)(b) to a non-prescribed term certain annuity.

i. — Contract terminates at death

If the contract simply terminates, and the contract is a PAC, there is a disposition to the owner/annuitant under the general definition of disposition in subsection 148(9). However, there should be no taxation since there are no proceeds received and therefore no gain will result. If the contract is not a PAC, there is a deemed disposition for proceeds equal to the accumulating fund immediately after the death (paragraph 148(2)(b) and paragraph (d) in the definition of proceeds of the disposition in subsection 148(9)). In the case of a contract issued by a life insurer, the accumulating fund is likely to equal the insurer's reserve (since this will generally exceed the cash surrender value). The accumulating fund is equal to the MTAR calculated as if the time and manner of death were known, so that essentially the mortality component of the reserve calculation is removed (Reg. 307(1)(b)(i)). The MTAR is equal to the greater of the cash surrender value and the insurer's reserve in respect of the contract, less any policy loans (Reg. 1401(1)(c)). Note that this calculation of the gain is the same as the accrued income calculation under 12.2(1). The result is to tax any accrued income to the date of death which has not yet been reported as a gain on disposition.

ii. — Contract terminates at death, lump sum paid to beneficiary

Where a lump sum is paid out to a beneficiary and the contract terminates, the same dispositions result as in the previous case: if the contract is a PAC, there is an actual disposition; if the contract is not a PAC, there is a deemed disposition. In the case of a PAC, the proceeds are equal to the lump sum paid (as per the definition of proceeds of the disposition in subsection 148(9)), and a gain may result. If so, the gain is reported in the terminal return of the deceased owner/annuitant. If the contract is not a PAC, the result is the same as if the contract were terminated without any payout — the proceeds are equal to the accumulating fund immediately after death. Note that the lump sum paid is not relevant in the calculation of the proceeds (however the lump sum is likely equal to the accumulating fund, and hence the proceeds, in any case.) Again, the result should be to tax any accrued income to the date of death which has not yet been reported as a gain on disposition.

A lump sum payout to a beneficiary does not have any tax implications to the beneficiary, since from the beneficiary's perspective, the beneficiary simply received cash as a bequest. If the beneficiary chooses to invest those funds in a new annuity contract, all of the tax rules outlined earlier in this chapter will apply to that new annuity, and the previous annuity has no impact on the taxation of the new contract.

iii. — Contract is transferred to beneficiary

Where the annuity is transferred to a beneficiary, assuming the spousal rollover provision does not apply, there will be a deemed disposition if it is not a PAC, and accepted practice is that there is no disposition (deemed or otherwise) if it is a PAC. In the case of a contract to which accrual taxation applies, (i.e. taxed under subsection 12.2(1)) the proceeds are again equal to the accumulating fund immediately before death, and thus the income accruing under the contract up to the date of death (since the last anniversary date) is reported as a gain to the deceased owner/annuitant. Paragraph 148(2)(c) causes the beneficiary to acquire the contract at an ACB equal to the accumulating fund immediately before death (i.e. equal to the proceeds to the deceased). This becomes the starting point for the beneficiary to compute the accrued income under the contract (assuming it is still subject to the accrual rules) and to compute any gain or loss on any subsequent dispositions. If the beneficiary immediately commutes the value of the contract, there will be a disposition, but the proceeds will equal the commuted value which is likely less than or equal to the accumulating fund, so a gain is unlikely.

In the case of a PAC, accepted practice is that taxation of the contract continues as if nothing had happened: no disposition to the deceased, and no acquisition to the beneficiary. Furthermore, the payments continuing under the contract are taxed in the same manner that they were to the original owner/annuitant: the same proportion of payments is considered to be the capital element. As noted earlier, the legislation does not specify this treatment anywhere, but both taxpayers and the CRA continue to treat PACs in this manner, and the CRA has indicated that technical amendments are forthcoming to bring the Act in line with this intent.

In the case of a spouse or common-law partner successor owner/ beneficiary, the disposition at death of any annuity contract will not result in the realization of any gains on the policy (assuming the rollover provision in subsection 148(8.2) applies, and the annuitant does not elect out of the rollover). Therefore if the spouse or common-law partner continues to receive annuity payments under the contract, the payments will continue to be taxed in the same manner as they were to the deceased: proportionate treatment in the same manner if the contract continues to qualify as a PAC; accrual taxation on the anniversary dates if the contract is subject to subsection 12.2(1). The ACB used in these calculations will be the ACB of the deceased as adjusted on an ongoing basis for increases and decreases based on events subsequent to death (as per the definition of adjusted cost basis in subsection 148(9)). If the spouse or common-law partner commutes the value of the contract immediately after the death of the original owner/annuitant, any gain will be reported by the spouse/common-law partner. The disposition will fall under the general definition of disposition and therefore the proceeds of the disposition will equal the proceeds received on commutation. The gain will be equal to the excess of these proceeds over the ACB of the contract as transferred from the original owner.

In the case of a third party contract (where the owner of the contract is different from the annuitant), when the annuitant dies, there is still a deemed disposition of the contract under paragraph 148(2)(b) for proceeds equal to the accumulating fund immediately before the death. Any gain on the disposition is reported to the owner, and the owner reacquires the contract immediately after the death at an ACB equal to the accumulating fund immediately after death. Any remaining payments will be taxed to the owner under the accrual rules using the new ACB as the starting point. Note that the definition of a PAC precludes it from being a third party contract.

14.3 — Taxation of Pre-1990 Annuity Contracts

A. — Overview

The discussion which follows is intended to highlight some of the differences in treatment from that outlined above to annuity contracts last acquired before 1990.

Individually-owned annuity contracts entered into before 1990 can be divided into two major time frames. First, contracts acquired before December 2, 1982, and secondly contracts acquired after December 1, 1982, but before 1990. The significance of December 2, 1982 is that this is the date on which triennial accrual taxation was introduced to individually-owned annuity contracts. This means that accrued income (discussed below) must be reported on every third anniversary of the contract. Former paragraph 12.2(11)(b) defines "third anniversary" to be the day that is three years after December 31 of the year of issue of the policy and December 31 of every third year thereafter.

B. — Taxation of contracts acquired before December 2, 1982

i. — Accrual taxation

A contract last acquired before December 2, 1982 is subject to triennial accrual taxation under former subsection 12.2(3) unless it meets one of the following exceptions:

1. Annuity payments have commenced before December 2, 1982 (former paragraph 12.2(3)(b));
2. It is a prescribed annuity contract (the definition is as described in section 14.2.A.iv) (former paragraph 12.2(3)(d));
3. It was received as a settlement option from a life insurance policy acquired before December 2, 1982 (former paragraph 12.2(3)(e)) and no "prescribed premium" (as defined at Regulation 309) has been paid after December 1, 1982 (former paragraph 12.2(9)(e));
4. It is a "locked-in" annuity. (That is, a contract which cannot be cancelled, surrendered or converted and in which the maturity and terms relating to payment cannot be changed after December 1, 1982.) (former paragraph 12.2(7)(a)); or
5. At any point in time after December 1, 1982, the cash surrender value is less than the total premiums paid (former paragraph 12.2(7)(b)).

If a contract acquired before December 2, 1982 does not meet one of these exceptions, at the end of every third calendar year it must report its accrued income to date. The contract is deemed to have been issued on December 31, 1984 (former paragraph 12.2(11)(b)), so the first date on which the accrued income was calculated and reported for a pre-December 2, 1982 annuity was December 31, 1987. The accrued income is then calculated and reported on December 31 of every third year thereafter (i.e. 1990, 1993, 1996, 1999 etc.). The accrued income is calculated in a similar manner as for post-1989 contracts with some additional adjustments. The accrued income is determined under former subsection 12.2(3) as the amount, if any, by which the accumulating fund on the third anniversary exceeds the ACB of the interest in the contract plus any unallocated income accrued in respect of the interest before 1982 (defined below). (Note that the ACB is increased by the amount of previously reported accrued income, so that income is only taxed once).

The definition of ACB will include any amounts reported as income under former paragraph 56(1)(d.1). The result is that annuity payments received under the contract which have been reported as income will reduce the amount of accrued income required to be reported in the third anniversary years (see also discussion below in section 14.3.B.iv).

A taxpayer can elect to report income from an annuity (other than a prescribed annuity) on an annual rather than triennial basis by virtue of former subsection 12.2(4). The accrued income is again calculated as the excess of the accumulating fund over the adjusted cost basis at the end of the year. Former subsection 12.2(4.1) allows a revocation of the election. The revocation cannot be reversed.

Where a taxpayer pays premiums after December 1, 1982 and before 1990 on a pre-1982 annuity contract, and the premiums were not fixed before December 2, 1982, former subsection 12.2(8) deemed the unfixed portion to be paid under a separate contract. Since this "separate contract" is acquired after December 2, 1982, it will be subject to triennial accrual taxation. The provision does not apply to annuities received as a settlement option on a pre-December 2, 1982 life insurance policy. Nor does it apply if the triennial accrual rules already apply to the contract.

ii. — Pre-1982 unallocated income

The amount of the unallocated income accrued in respect of the interest before 1982 is prescribed by Regulation 305. The theory is that income accruing in the contract before December 31, 1981 is not subject to accrual taxation. However, once payments commence under the contract, the income earned before December 31, 1981 and after the first anniversary date of the contract which occurs after March 31, 1977, is brought into income on a straight-line basis based on the expected number of payments under the contract. If the contract is surrendered, the full amount of the pre-1982 unallocated income will be taxed. The calculation of the amount added to income under former subsection 12.2(3) and former paragraph 56(1)(d.1) has three steps (as outlined in Regulation 305):

1. calculate the accumulating fund (AF) and the adjusted cost basis(ACB) of the contract as of December 31, 1981;
2. subtract the ACB from the AF calculated in "1.";
3. multiply the amount determined in "2." by the annuity payments received to date divided by the total expected payments.

iii. — Definition of adjusted cost basis

The definition of adjusted cost basis for pre-December 1, 1982 contracts is the same as outlined in the previous section, with the following additional adjustments. The ACB is increased by:

1. amounts previously included in income under former paragraph 56(1)(d.1);
2. the cash surrender value of the policy on its first anniversary date after March 31, 1977 (thus any income accruing before this date will never be taxed).

The ACB is decreased by:

1. the amount of any policy loan outstanding on March 31, 1978.

iv. — Taxation of annuity payments

If payments have commenced under an annuity that is subject to the triennial accrual rules, the payments received in years which are not 3rd anniversary years are included in income as they are received by former paragraph 56(1)(d.1), but the total included to date can never exceed the accrued income to date. The calculation of accrued income for this purpose is the same as noted above (i.e. AF-ACB + Pre-82 unallocated income). Thus in the years between third anniversaries, the income inclusion is equal to the lesser of 1) annuity payments received in the year and 2) accrued income to the end of the calendar year (AF-ACB) plus any pre-82 unallocated income. In the third anniversary years, the income inclusion is equal to the accrued income up to the third anniversary (AF-ACB) plus any pre-82 unallocated income. Note that ACB is always increased by the amount of previous income inclusions (accruals under section 12.2 or payments under paragraph 56(1)(d.1)). Therefore, the "accrued income" is always reduced by annuity payments which have been reported as income and accrued income reported in prior years.

If the contract falls into one of the exceptions to accrual treatment, (i.e. it is not subject to former subsection 12.2(3)) the payments will be included in income under paragraph 56(1)(d) (as it read before 1990), and a deduction for the capital portion is provided in paragraph 60(a). The effect is to tax the annuity payments out of these contracts in the same way as was previously described for PACs. That is:

$$\frac{\text{adjusted purchase price}}{\text{total payments}} \times \text{annuity payment received}$$

Note "adjusted purchase price" is defined differently for certain annuity contracts entered into before November 17, 1978 as outlined in Regulation 300(3) and (4).

v. — Taxation of dispositions

The same definition of disposition outlined for post-1989 contracts applies to contracts last acquired before December 2, 1982 with one additional case as outlined in paragraph (e) of the definition of disposition in subsection 148(9). A disposition will be considered to have occurred if an insurer makes any payment out of a life annuity contract entered into after November 16, 1978 and before November 13, 1981 other than an annuity payment, a policy loan or a policy dividend (unless the contract is in or out of an RPP, RRSP, IAAC, or DPSP). Any amount of such a payment is then included in paragraph (c) of the definition of proceeds of the disposition in subsection 148(9). The person receiving this payment must include in income the excess of the payment over the ACB of the contract to the owner by virtue of subsection 148(1.1). The implication of this provision is that if a beneficiary receives the payment, (as in a lump sum payment on death) the gain will be taxed in the hands of the beneficiary rather than in the hands of the deceased.

vi. — Taxation on death

Contracts last acquired before December 2, 1982 are subject to the same tax rules on death as contracts last acquired after 1989 except that the calculation of ACB will differ according to the rules noted earlier. There is one exception: if the contract was entered into before November 13, 1981 and it is a life annuity contract (as defined by Regulation 301(1) — see earlier discussion) the contract is excluded from the deemed disposition provision in paragraph 148(2)(b). If the contract was entered into before November 17, 1978 there is no disposition and the entire proceeds are exempt from tax. If the contract was entered into after November 16, 1978 and before November 13, 1981, there is a disposition pursuant to paragraph (e) of the definition of disposition in subsection 148(9), and the rules described in the previous paragraph will apply.

C. — Taxation of annuity contracts acquired after December 1, 1982 and before January 1, 1990

i. — Accrual taxation

A contract last acquired after December 1, 1982 and before January 1, 1990 is subject to triennial accrual taxation under former paragraph 12.2(3) unless it meets one of the following exceptions:

1. It is a prescribed annuity contract (the definition is as described in section 14.2.A.iv) (former paragraph 12.2(3)(d)).
2. It was received as a settlement option of a life insurance policy acquired before December 2, 1982 (former paragraph 12.2(3)(e)).

If a contract acquired during this time does not meet one of these exceptions, at the end of every third calendar year it must report its accrued income to date. The first date on which the accrued income was calculated and reported was December 31 of the third calendar year following the year of acquisition. The accrued income is then calculated and reported on December 31 of every third year thereafter. The accrued income is calculated under former subsection 12.2(3) in the same manner as for post-1989 contracts: it equals the amount, if any, by which the accumulating fund on the third anniversary exceeds the ACB of the interest in the contract.

The definition of ACB will include any amounts reported as income under former paragraph 56(1)(d.1). The result is that annuity payments received under the contract which have been reported as income will reduce the amount of accrued income required to be reported in the third anniversary years (see also discussion below in section 14.3.C.iii).

As with contracts acquired before December 2, 1982, a taxpayer can elect to report income from an annuity (other than a prescribed annuity) on an annual rather than triennial basis by virtue of former paragraph 12.2(4). The accrued income is again calculated as the excess of the accumulating fund over the adjusted cost basis at the end of the year. Former paragraph 12.2(4.1) allows a revocation of the election. The revocation cannot be reversed.

Where a taxpayer pays premiums after 1989 which were not fixed before 1990 on an annuity contract last acquired before 1990, subsection 12.2(8) deems the unfixed portion to be paid under a separate contract. The provision applies to contracts subject to the triennial accrual rules. Since this "separate contract" is acquired after 1989, it will be subject to the annual accrual rules. The provision does not apply to contracts taxed annually as a result of an election under subsection 12.2(4).

ii. — Definition of adjusted cost basis

The definition of adjusted cost basis for contracts acquired between December 1, 1982 and January 1, 1990 is the same as for post-1989 contracts except that the ACB is increased by amounts previously included in income under former paragraph 56(1)(d.1).

iii. — Taxation of annuity payments

If payments have commenced under an annuity subject to the triennial accrual rules, the payments received in years which are not third anniversary years are included in income as they are received by former paragraph 56(1)(d.1), but the total included to date can never exceed the accrued income to date. The calculation of accrued income for this purpose is the same as noted above (i.e. AF-ACB). Thus in the years between third anniversaries, the income inclusion is equal to the lesser of 1) annuity payments received in the year and 2) accrued income to the end of the calendar year (AF-ACB) plus any pre-1982 unallocated income. In the third anniversary years, the income inclusion is equal to the accrued income up to the third anniversary (AF-ACB) plus any pre-1982 unallocated income. Note that ACB is always increased by the amount of previous income inclusions (accruals under section 12.2 or payments under paragraph 56(1)(d.1)). Therefore, the "accrued income" is always reduced by annuity payments which have been reported as income and accrued income reported in prior years.

If the contract falls into one of the exceptions to accrual treatment, (i.e. it is not subject to subsection 12.2(3)) the payments will be included in income under paragraph 56(1)(d) (as it read before 1990), and a deduction for the capital portion is provided in paragraph 60(a). The effect is to tax the annuity payments out of these contracts in the same way as was previously described for PACs. That is:

$$\frac{\text{adjusted purchase price}}{\text{total payments}} \times \text{annuity payment received}$$

iv. — Taxation of dispositions

The disposition of annuity contracts acquired between December 1, 1982 and January 1, 1990 is taxed in the same manner as post-1989 contracts.

v. — Taxation on death

Contracts last acquired between December 1, 1982 and January 1, 1990 are taxed on death the same as contracts last acquired after 1989. An important point to note, however, is that when a contract is transferred to a beneficiary, the date of the owner's death will become the date the beneficiary last acquired the contract. As a result, the current rules will apply to the contract in the hands of the beneficiary.

14.4 — Conclusion

The taxation of non-registered annuity contracts will vary depending upon the nature of the contract, when the contract was last acquired and the particular transaction being undertaken.

15 — DEFERRED ANNUITIES

Updated by Barbara Cook, C.G.A., CFP

15.1 — Introduction

As discussed in Chapter 14, annuities are contracts that provide periodic income either for life or for a fixed number of years. A deferred annuity has an additional component in that the contract exists for a period of time prior to the commencement of the annuity payments. Thus deferred annuity contracts are a type of savings plan issued by life insurance companies. Deposits are made into these plans and interest is credited to the plans. These plans resemble Guaranteed Investment Certificates (GICs) issued by banks and trust companies. That is, interest is guaranteed until the end of a specified period with a renewal at a new interest rate for a new period of time at the end of the prior period.

In order for a life insurance company to be able to issue these savings plans they must have a "life contingency." Therefore, the plans are created to have a maturity date at which time an annuity paying a regular income becomes operable. The "life contingency" is created in a number of ways. One such life contingency would involve an annuity which becomes payable at a specified date in the future, for example at age 65, with annual payments for the life of the annuitant. Another provision is if death occurs prior to the annuity commencing, interest will be payable right up to the date of death of the annuitant. No charges will be made for cancellation prior to the end of an interest guarantee period. This is unlike a GIC type of savings plan where, at death, the options are generally either to cash in the plan with a suitable charge for early cancellation or to continue the plan under new ownership until the end of the interest period.

The legal requirements impacting upon these savings products issued by life insurers may create some conceptual difficulties and confusing terminology. For example, the maturity date of the contract is the date at which the plan is designed to commence annuity payments, not the date at which the interest guarantee period expires. There must always be an "annuitant." The annuitant is the "measuring life" and may be someone other than the owner. For example, if a corporation owns an annuity policy it must choose an annuitant upon whose life the "life contingencies" will be based.

These contracts fall under the definition of a life insurance policy for the purposes of Provincial Insurance Acts. Therefore, a beneficiary may be designated and in the event of death the proceeds will be paid directly to the named beneficiary and pass outside the estate of the deceased. Care must be exercised where the owner, annuitant and beneficiary are different people. For example, the beneficiary will receive the policy proceeds in the event of the death of the annuitant which may occur prior to the death of the owner.

Deferred annuity contracts also fall under the definition of life insurance policy under subsection 138(12) of the *Income Tax Act*. However, they do not meet the definition of exempt policy as discussed at Chapter 1.

To add further to the confusion, deferred annuities have undergone a number of changes with regard to the taxation of income from these policies. As discussed below, the taxation has evolved from a time when accrued gains were tax-free at death to the gain being taxable annually. These changes occurred over a number of years and as a consequence, the taxation of these policies will depend upon the time at which the policy was last acquired. In order to prevent retroactive taxation, allowances were made for policies which were in force at the time of the legislative change.

This discussion is arranged so that the issue date of the policy under review is the major heading with a discussion of the events which are likely to create tax as subheadings.

15.2 — Definitions

A. — Annual reporting

Income from a deferred annuity is accrued annually based upon the policy year, not a calendar year. The policy anniversary is therefore important. The first policy year is deemed to end one year after the day immediately preceding the day of issue of the policy. Each policy year thereafter is exactly one year after the end of the previous policy year. This is a convoluted way of ensuring that exactly one year is included in the first policy year.

B. — Last acquired

This definition is included to prevent substantial changes in policies that have been issued prior to a particular change. A policy will be deemed to have been last acquired prior to a particular time as long as there have been no changes that create a substantially different policy. If sufficiently substantial changes are made, the policy will be deemed to have been disposed of and a new policy acquired subsequent to the date of original issue. In other words, substantial changes to a deferred annuity policy may affect its grandfathered status for tax purposes.

C. — Disposition

Taxable dispositions include:

1. A surrender of the annuity contract;
2. A policy loan made after March 31, 1978;
3. A disposition by operation of law;
4. A deemed disposition on death under paragraph 148(2)(b) of the Act.

Non-taxable dispositions include:

1. A transfer during the lifetime of the policyholder of an interest in a life insurance policy (which includes an annuity policy under subsection 138(12)) to:

   a) the policyholder's spouse or common-law partner (but not a spouse trust), or

   b) former spouse or common-law partner, in settlement of rights arising out of their marriage or common-law partnership, and both the spouse or common-law partner, or former spouse or common-law partner, and the policyholder are resident in Canada at the time of transfer (subsection 148(8.1)).

2. A transfer of an interest in a policy following the death of the policyholder to the spouse or common-law partner of the policyholder (but not a spouse trust) and both the spouse or common-law partner and policyholder were resident in Canada immediately before the policyholder's death (subsection 148(8.2)).

The spousal or common-law partner rollover at death occurs automatically. However, the legal representative of the deceased policyholder may elect for the rollover not to apply in which case tax will be payable by the deceased.

D. — Exceptions

A disposition does not include:

1. a collateral assignment;
2. an annuity payment;
3. a payment as a consequence of death under a life annuity contract entered into before November 13, 1981.

E. — Accumulating fund

The *Income Tax Act* measures the policy gains based upon the Accumulating Fund of the policy. Unless the annuity is an old policy that is either locked in (no intermediate cash values are available during the deferral period) or is a participating policy upon which dividends are declared, the Accumulating Fund of a deferred annuity policy is its cash value less any policy loans.

15.3 — Contracts Last Acquired Prior to April 1, 1977

Prior to April 1, 1977 deferred annuities could accumulate without tax accruing until they were surrendered. This has changed. Death benefits matured without tax. This has also changed somewhat.

A. — Accrual taxation

No tax is payable on policy gains prior to the first policy anniversary after March 31, 1977, even upon surrender. This is accomplished through the addition of these gains to the adjusted cost basis of the policy under item F of the definition of adjusted cost basis at subsection 148(9).

No tax is payable during the accrual period on policy gains from the first policy anniversary after March 31, 1977 until December 31, 1981.

Policy gains from January 1, 1982 until December 31, 1987 would have been reported as income for the 1987 calendar year. This rule was to accommodate the transition from a tax deferral until surrender to the triennial reporting that was introduced in 1981 (subsequently modified to possible annual reporting).

Policy gains after December 31, 1987 are subject to the rules of post-1987 policies except some policies may still qualify for triennial reporting. Gains are taxable annually as they occur.

B. — Surrender

The basic rules on surrender are that gains that have not been taxed will become taxable at the time of surrender. This is modified by the fact that gains prior to the first policy anniversary following March 31, 1977 will not be taxable. Therefore, on surrender, the following amounts will be taxable:

a) policy gains from the first policy anniversary after March 31, 1977 until December 31, 1981

b) accrued but not reported gains under either the annual or triennial reporting requirements where surrender occurs during one of these reporting periods.

Partial surrenders are treated in a proportional manner. If a policy is partially surrendered the proportion of the surrender that is subject to tax is the same as the proportion that would be taxable in the event of a total surrender.

C. — Annuitization

If a prescribed annuity is selected the ACB of the annuity will be equal to the ACB of the deferred annuity immediately prior to the election of the income. The effect of this is to spread the following deferred tax amounts throughout the life of the prescribed annuity:

1. unreported amounts where the election to annuitize has been made during a reporting period (annual or triennial),
2. policy gains from the first policy anniversary after March 31, 1977 until December 31, 1981.

Otherwise, for a non-prescribed annuity, accrual taxation of the annuity continues throughout the life of the annuity.

It should be noted that amounts accrued prior to the first policy anniversary after March 31, 1977 will be part of the ACB of the policy and will remain tax-free throughout the period of the annuity.

D. — Death of the annuitant

As noted under "Definitions" the death of the annuitant is considered a disposition and will create the same tax consequences as surrender.

15.4 — Contracts Last Acquired After March 31, 1977 and Before January 1, 1990

Policy gains from the first policy anniversary after March 31, 1977 until December 31, 1981 were not subject to tax.

Policy gains from January 1, 1982 until December 31, 1987 would have been reported as income for the 1987 calendar year. This rule was to accommodate the transition from the former regime which permitted a tax deferral until surrender to the revised regime which provided for triennial reporting which was introduced in 1981 (subsection 12.2(3) which is now repealed but still applies to these policies). Gains were required to be reported triennially. Subsequent provisions allowed the policyholder to elect to report the income annually. Some policies may have been the subject of such an election and would have changed to annual reporting. Former subsection 12.2(4.1) allows a revocation of the election. The revocation cannot be reversed.

Policy gains after December 31, 1987 are subject to the rules of post-1987 policies except some policies may still qualify for triennial reporting.

A. — Surrender

The basic rules on surrender are that gains that have not been taxed will become taxable at the time of surrender. Therefore, on surrender, the following amounts will be taxable:

a) policy gains from the first policy anniversary after March 31, 1977 until December 31, 1981

b) accrued but not reported gains under either the annual or triennial reporting requirements where surrender occurs during one of these reporting periods.

Partial surrenders are treated in a proportional manner. If a policy is partially surrendered the proportion of the surrender that is subject to tax is the same as the proportion that would be taxable in the event of a total surrender.

B. — Annuitization

If a prescribed annuity is selected, the adjusted cost basis of the annuity will be equal to the ACB of the deferred annuity prior to the election of the income. The effect of this is to spread the following deferred tax amounts throughout the life of the prescribed annuity:

1. unreported amounts where the election to annuitize has been made during a reporting period (annual or triennial),
2. policy gains from the first policy anniversary after March 31, 1977 until December 31, 1981.

Otherwise, for a non-prescribed annuity, accrual taxation of the annuity continues throughout the life of the annuity.

C. — Death of the annuitant

As has been noted under "Definitions" the death of the annuitant is considered a disposition and will create the same tax consequences as surrender.

15.5 — Contracts Last Acquired After December 31, 1989

A. — Accrual taxation

Policy gains are reported annually based upon the policy year.

B. — Surrender

Surrenders will only give rise to taxable income for the unreported income for the current period.

Partial surrenders are treated in a proportional manner. If a policy is partially surrendered the proportion of the surrender that is subject to tax is the same as the proportion that would be taxable in the event of a total surrender.

C. — Annuitization

If a prescribed annuity is selected, the ACB of the annuity will be equal to the ACB of the deferred annuity immediately prior to the election of the income. Where the election to annuitize has been made during a reporting period the taxation of the unreported income is deferred and spread throughout the life of the prescribed annuity. On August 23, 2013, the Department of Finance released for public comment draft legislative proposals that would implement changes to modernize the exemption test and other life insurance policyholder taxation rules including the rules for the taxation of prescribed annuity contracts and deferred annuities (see detailed discussion of the draft legislative proposals in section 13.5).

Otherwise, for a non-prescribed annuity, accrual taxation of the annuity continues throughout the life of the annuity.

D. — Death of the annuitant

Death will create tax in a manner similar to surrender.

15.6 — Registered Deferred Annuities

A deferred annuity purchased as part of a registered plan such as a Registered Retirement Savings Plan, Registered Retirement Income Fund or Tax-Free Savings Account, will be treated as a qualified investment under the applicable sections of the Act. Tax consequences will be as a result of the tax rules and regulations applicable to the registered plan, not those applicable to deferred annuities.

16 — PLANNED GIVING WITH ANNUITIES

Updated by Barbara Cook, C.G.A., CFP

16.1 — Introduction

Prior to December 21, 2002, most charitable annuity arrangements were structured under the administrative guidelines laid out by the CRA in now withdrawn Interpretation Bulletin IT-111R2 "Annuities Purchased from Charitable Organizations", dated September 22, 1995. Following the release of the December 20, 2002 Technical Bill, which included new rules governing so-called split-receipting arrangements, the CRA withdrew its former administrative position set out in IT-111R2. With the passing of Bill C-48 (June 26, 2013), the contents of the Technical Bill are now reflected in the legislation, applicable for gifts made after December 20, 2002.

Split-receipting arrangements represent gifts where a person makes a donation to charity but also receives a benefit in respect of such gift. Under the former rules, tax relief was generally denied in circumstances where the donor received a benefit. As described more fully below, under the current rules, tax relief may be available in certain circumstances even if the donor receives a benefit from the charity. A discussion of the former administrative position regarding charitable annuities as well as the current rules governing charitable annuities and split-receipting follows.

16.2 — Charitable Annuities Issued Before December 21, 2002

A. — General description

For charitable annuities entered into before December 21, 2002, the following treatment still applies.

The structure for the former basic charitable gift annuity rules is outlined in CRA Interpretation Bulletin IT-111R2, "Annuities Purchased from Charitable Organizations," dated September 22, 1995 (now archived). In general terms, under a charitable annuity structure a donor acquired a life annuity from a charitable organization and received an annual income stream. To the extent the stream represented a return of capital the proceeds would be received tax-free.

Effectively, and as described in more detail below, the charitable gift annuity arrangement was often structured such that the charity received the taxable portion of the annuity (plus a portion of the capital) and the donor received the balance of the capital by way of a lifetime annual income stream. All future annuity payments to the donor would be received tax-free. Depending on the circumstances, the donor may also have received a charitable tax receipt for part of the contribution.

The charitable annuity structure represented an administrative concession from the CRA with respect to its former general position that a donor must not realize any benefit from a gift in order to be recognized as a charitable donation for tax purposes (see paragraphs 3 and 10 of Interpretation Bulletin IT-110R3 "Gifts and Official Donation Receipts," dated June 20, 1997).

B. — Example of how pre-December 21, 2002 charitable annuities work

The operation of the former charitable annuity structure is described in detail by way of an example at paragraph 6 of Interpretation Bulletin IT-111R2. The example assumes a male donor who will be 81 years old at the end of the calendar year in which the annuity payments begin. The donor wishes to receive annual annuity payments of $5,000 and gives to a charitable organization a payment of $60,000.

Attached to IT-111R2 are 1983 Individual Mortality Tables published in Volume XXXIII of the *Transactions of the Society of Actuaries* illustrating male and female life expectancy at each age. The table indicates that the 81-year-old male donor has a life expectancy of 9 years. Accordingly, his expected cumulative annuity payments will be $45,000 ($5,000 per year for 9 years.) Since the expected return is $15,000 less than the $60,000 the donor has given to the charity, the charity can issue to the donor a charitable receipt for $15,000.

In the example described in IT-111R2, no part of the annuity payment is required to be included in the individual donor's income. Each payment of $5,000 is viewed for tax purposes as a return of capital. This tax-free treatment will persist even if the donor should live for more than 9 years. This is because the sum of the annuity payments the annuitant is expected to receive is less than the amount the annuitant paid to acquire the annuity.

IT-111R2 notes that the attached mortality table may be used to determine the amount of the gift in circumstances where there is one annuitant and the annuity is an immediate life annuity. For other circumstances (such as joint and survivor annuities or annuities with a guarantee period) in order to determine the amount of the gift reference should be made to the complete 1983 Mortality Tables in Volume XXXIII of the *Transactions of the Society of Actuaries*. Alternatively, the CRA would, upon request, provide the relevant life expectancies.

When IT-111R2 was released there was an error in the attached Mortality Tables. This error was rectified by way of a Special Release dated February 10, 1997. However, the error generated some uncertainty regarding charitable annuities that had been put in place prior to the special release. In this regard, Paragraph 10 of IT-111R2 indicates that if in 1996 a charity issued a receipt based upon the erroneous table, the amount of the gift and the amount that the individual can anticipate receiving as an annuity should be recalculated and a new receipt issued along with an explanatory notation which identifies the serial number of the prior receipt.

C. — Variations of the basic structure pre-December 21, 2002 — fixed term annuities

After describing the basic structure for a charitable annuity, IT-111R2 goes on to describe the tax consequences of a variety of other examples as variations of the basic structure. Those examples include where the annuity has a fixed term such that the amount expected to be received by the donor is more/less than the $60,000 contributed. No receipt will be given if the amount anticipated to be received equals or exceeded $60,000. If the amount is expected to exceed $60,000 a portion of each payment will be included in income (the annuity payments will be included in income under paragraph 56(1)(d) of the Act, and the capital element of the payment is deducted under paragraph 60(a)).

Interestingly, where the amount expected to be received by the donor (based on the 1983 Tables) exceeded the amount given to the charity to acquire the annuity, paragraph 1 of IT-111R2 indicates that reference is to be made to the 1971 Individual Mortality Table (not the 1983 Table) published in Volume XXIII of the *Transactions of the Society of Actuaries* in order to determine the capital element of the payment for purposes of paragraph 60(a). Subparagraph 300(2)(a)(i) of the Regulations specifically requires the use of the 1971 Table for this purpose. This is interesting in that the life expectancies listed in the 1971 Table are shorter than those listed in the 1983 Table. Thus by referring to the 1971 Table the capital element will be greater and the taxable portion (if any) will be smaller.

D. — Financial realities — pre-December 21, 2002

As long as the donor paid more to the charity than the charity anticipated paying out as annuity payments, the charity would profit from the annuity arrangement. Of course, the ultimate revenue retained by the charity would depend upon the actual life span of the donor. If in the hypothetical example with the 81-year-old donor, the donor lived beyond the 9 years of life expectancy, the charity could lose money.

Certain registered charities, most notably the Salvation Army, engage in a substantial number of charitable annuities such that the risk of donor longevity is mitigated. For those charities which do not issue a sufficient number of gift annuities, the charity would typically "reinsure" its risk by acquiring an annuity from a licensed insurer. Assuming the donor only wished to receive a return of capital, the cost of the annuity to the charity would be significantly less than the amount of the contribution. For example, the cost of the $5,000 annuity for the hypothetical 81-year-old male donor may be approximately $38,000. The charity would thus be able to pocket the $22,000 difference ($60,000 - $38,000). Nevertheless, only $15,000 would be treated as a donation.

Paragraph 7 of IT-111R2 indicates that the tax treatment for the charitable annuity will be identical whether or not the charity reinsures the risk and that the favourable tax treatment will apply even where the donor requests that the charity acquire an annuity from an insurer.

E. — Benefits of the pre-December 21, 2002 charitable annuity structure

The former charitable annuity structure was attractive for a variety of reasons. First, the structure permitted individuals to receive tax-free payments. Such payments have no impact upon the various clawback and other income dependent tests for government benefits. Second, these payments alleviated the donor's concerns about outliving capital. Third, the after-tax revenues generated by the charitable annuity could be significantly greater than the after-tax return using conventional investments. If desired, a portion of the excess return could be used to invest in a life insurance contract to provide full or partial estate replacement or to provide for a larger gift to the charity. Fourth, at least part of the additional revenues received by the charity would not have fallen into the charity's 80 percent disbursement quota (repealed by Bill C-47 which received Royal Assent on December 15, 2010).

The structure was also a useful starting point for a variety of more creative structures. For example, assume a donor with $100,000 of liquid assets invested in GICs. The donor could determine the net after-tax amount generated by this investment. Assuming interest rates of 6 percent and a marginal tax rate of 50 percent the after-tax income generated by the GIC is just $3,000. The donor could personally acquire an annuity to generate that amount of after-tax income. Such an annuity would cost significantly less than $100,000. The donor could donate the difference to charity and use the resulting tax refund to acquire a life insurance contract to provide for full or partial estate replacement at the time of death. Thus the donor would be able to maintain her lifestyle, make a current gift to charity and preserve the value of the estate for her heirs.

F. — Charitable annuities and charitable foundations

Interpretation Bulletin IT-111R2 notes that the CRA does not sanction the issuance of annuities by a charity which is not authorized to undertake such an activity pursuant to its constating documents or which is prohibited from doing so by federal or provincial law. In addition, paragraph 2 of IT-111R2 notes that although for tax purposes charitable organizations may generally enter into arrangements to issue annuities without jeopardizing their registered status, charitable foundations may not. The reason for this position is that under subsections 149.1(3) and (4) charitable foundations (public foundations as well as private foundations) are generally precluded from incurring debts other than debts for operating expenses and certain other limited purposes. Violation of this provision may result in revocation of the charitable foundation's registered status.

16.3 — Charitable Annuities Issued After December 20, 2002

A. — Split-receipting — general rules

Split-receipting with respect to gifts made after December 20, 2002 are dealt with in subsections 248(30) through (41) of the Act. The rationale for these rules was to clarify the circumstances where a donor would receive tax recognition for a gift where the donor received partial consideration in respect of a transfer of property. The traditional definition of "gift" disqualified as a gift for tax purposes a transfer of property for partial consideration notwithstanding a clear gift element and donative intent. The Technical Bill overrode this traditional approach. Administrative guidelines governing split-receipting arrangements were set out by the CRA in archived Income Tax Technical News Number 26, dated December 24, 2002. These guidelines were developed in consultation with the Department of Finance. The guidelines provide examples of a number of split-receipting arrangements including charitable annuities.

Generally, under the current rules, the eligible amount of a gift is the amount by which the fair market value of property donated exceeds the amount of any advantage in respect of the gift received by the donor or a person with whom the donor does not deal at arm's length. In computing the amount of any advantage, the value of any property, service, compensation or other benefit is computed. Where the value of property acquired by the donor is included in the computation of the advantage, the cost of the property to the donor is equal to the fair market value of the property at the time of the gift (subsection 248(33)).

Accordingly, the existence of an advantage no longer precludes the donation from being treated as a gift for tax purposes. Subsection 248(30) provides a rule-of-thumb that if the amount of the advantage does not exceed 80 percent of the fair market value of the transferred property, it will still be considered a gift. Also, if the amount of the advantage is more than 80 percent, it is still open to the donor to provide evidence (to the Minister) of the intention to make a gift.

B. — Income Tax Technical News Number 26

The Guidelines set out in archived Technical News Number 26 indicate that the former administrative policy set out in IT-111R2 is withdrawn but the former policy would still apply to annuities issued prior to December 21, 2002. The Guidelines go on to outline the new rules applicable to charitable annuities in general terms followed by a specific example.

The general rule is that the amount which may be claimed as a charitable gift is equal to the excess of the amount contributed by the donor over the amount that would be paid at that time to an arm's length third party to acquire an annuity to fund the guaranteed payments. The stated example considers a donor with a life expectancy of 8 years who contributes $100,000 to a charitable organization. The donor is to receive annuity payments of $10,000 per year. The cost to provide the annuity is assumed to be $50,000. According to the CRA, under the new rules the donor will receive a charitable receipt for $50,000 (the difference between the amount paid to the charity and the cost of the annuity). Over the next 8 years the donor will receive a total of $80,000 in annuity payments of which $30,000 would be taxable.

By way of comparison, the Technical News notes that under the old rules the donor would have received a charitable receipt for $20,000 (the $100,000 transferred to the charity less the $80,000 expected cash flow from the annuity over the donor's life expectancy) and the annuity payments received by the donor would be tax free.

It should also be noted that in the example the Technical News specifically notes that the charitable annuity arrangement is being undertaken with a charitable organization. This suggests that the CRA is maintaining its historical position that while charitable organizations can generally enter into charitable annuity arrangements, charitable foundations cannot do so.

C. — Further clarifications

Unfortunately, the simplified example in Technical News Number 26 omits a number of important points. Specifically, how is the donor's life expectancy determined? Is it based on the mortality table referenced at subsection 300(2) of the Regulations used in determining the capital element of prescribed annuity payments? How is the cost of the annuity determined? Is it to be based on the best rates available in the marketplace or average market rates? How is the income component to be calculated? Is it based on a prescribed annuity or a non-prescribed annuity?

Answers to some of these questions have been provided through subsequent technical interpretations. In technical interpretation 2003-0008415, dated April 17, 2003 the CRA indicated that there was no intention to promulgate regulations upon which to base the fair market value of an annuity and that fair market value could be determined by obtaining quotations from insurance brokers or issuers of annuities.

In technical interpretation 2003-000060, dated February 17, 2003 the CRA considered how to calculate the taxable portion of the annuity contract. According to the CRA the annuity could be treated as a prescribed annuity provided that the annuity was issued by a charity and satisfied the requirements under Regulation 304(1)(c). See Chapter 14 for a discussion of the taxation of prescribed annuity contracts and non-prescribed annuity contracts. The technical interpretation went on to note that if the charity purchases an annuity from a third party in order to satisfy its payment obligation to the donor, such purchase would constitute a separate transaction which would have no bearing on the tax consequences to the donor. According to the CRA, from the donor's perspective it is the arrangement between the donor and the charity which will determine the tax implications to the donor. Thus in order to obtain prescribed annuity treatment, it would be critical for the charity to be the issuer of the annuity contract and for the other requirements of Regulation 304(1)(c) to be satisfied.

Technical interpretation 2003-000060 also notes that charitable annuity arrangements would be subject to the 80 percent rule at subsection 248(30). That is, in order for a transaction to qualify as a charitable gift, generally speaking it would be necessary to establish that the fair market value of the benefit received by the donor (i.e. the value of the annuity) is less than 80 percent of the amount paid to the charity. If the value of the annuity exceeded the 80 percent level, charitable recognition could still be available provided the donor can establish to the satisfaction of the Minister that the transfer was made with donative intent.

Technical interpretation 2003-0000605 asked for clarification of the application of the new rules in the context of an 80-year-old male donor contributing $100,000 to a charity and the charity agreeing to make annual annuity payments of $7,700 to the donor for his life with no guarantee period. The letter indicated that the cost of a commercial annuity with the same terms would be $52,300 and that the cost of a commercial annuity containing the same terms but with a guarantee period of 10 years would be $69,875.

The CRA confirmed that in the example, the amount of the donation would be $47,700 (i.e. the amount of the contribution less the cost of a commercial annuity with the same terms as the annuity between the charity and the donor).

The CRA relied upon the 1971 Individual Annuity Mortality Table referenced at paragraph 300(2)(a) of the Regulations in order to determine the taxable amount of each annuity payment to the donor and not the mortality tables used by the commercial issuer of the annuity. This would likely result in a larger capital component of each annuity payment as a result of improved mortality rates since 1971. The CRA went on to confirm that in this example, the adjusted purchase price of $52,300 and the total expected payments ($61,600) based on a life expectancy of eight years (according to the 1971 Individual Annuity Mortality Table) would result in a capital element of $6,537.50 for each payment and a taxable portion of $1,162.50.

Technical interpretation 2003-0008195, dated October 27, 2003, asked some follow-up questions involving the same facts discussed in technical interpretation 2003-000060. The response confirmed that two separate annuities are issued — one between the charity and the donor and one between the insurer and the charity where the charity purchases a commercial annuity to fulfill its obligation to provide an annuity to the donor; the former is a PAC, the latter, a non-PAC. Of course, since the charity is, itself, a tax exempt entity, the fact that its annuity is not a PAC would not be material.

Technical interpretation 2003-0008195 went on to outline an alternative scenario in which the charity did not promise to provide an annuity to the donor but, rather, acted as agent of the donor in obtaining a commercial annuity on the same terms and conditions as described in the example. The CRA reply indicated that the implications would "depend upon the terms of the relationship between the charity and the donor. If there is clearly a principal and agent relationship . . . the donor would be viewed as having purchased a commercial annuity directly from the commercial annuity provider." This would generally result in the annuity being considered a PAC (assuming that the only reason it was a non-PAC to the charity was that the holder of the contract was not an individual) and, given that the purchase price was $52,300 in this example, the charity would be permitted to issue a donation receipt for $47,700.

A third scenario was also discussed where the charity purchases a commercial annuity on its own behalf and arranges for the commercial annuity issuer to make payments and report income directly to the donor. The CRA's response was that tax results would depend on the terms of the arrangement between all the parties. The arrangement will be taxed based on which situation it is most similar to: an annuity contract between the charity and the donor or the charity acting as agent for the donor.

Technical interpretation 2003-0009195, dated November 18, 2003, contained some more specific follow-up questions relating to fair market value determinations. There the CRA confirmed that using quotations from an insurance company for the cost of the annuity stream would be reasonable. The CRA also confirmed that a quotation from the commercial insurer may be used even though there is some delay between the date of the quote and the issuance of the annuity, provided there is no significant change in market conditions during the intervening period. The CRA also addressed the situation where annuity issuers do not quote on PACs (for example, where the annuitant is over age 90). In such circumstances it would be reasonable to use a non-PAC quote. In the case of a single premium used to purchase the annuity where the single premium is below the insurer's minimum requirement, it would be reasonable to "scale down a quote for the minimum amount for which a quotation can be obtained". The letter also noted that actuarial models that "mitigate the need to obtain quotations from insurance corporations" that are "consistent with market calculations" may be used. Finally, the letter confirmed that if the value of the annuity exceeds 80 percent of the value of the property transferred to the charity, there would generally be no gift unless the donor can satisfy the Minister in each case that an intention to give a gift existed (pursuant to paragraph 248(30)(b) of the Act).

16.4 — Conclusion

While there are still some gray areas concerning the new charitable annuity rules, gifting arrangements involving annuities will continue to draw the interest of Canadian taxpayers.

17 — INSURED ANNUITIES

Updated by Jon Hreljac, B.B.A. C.M.A., CFP, and Florence Marino, B.A., LL.B., TEP

17.1 — Introduction

A. — What is an insured annuity?

An insured annuity is an attractive investment vehicle for senior citizens. With conventional interest bearing investments, a sum of capital is invested at a rate of interest for a certain length of time. At maturity, the interest earned is paid to the investor and the original capital invested is returned. The investor is then free to reinvest the capital.

An "insured annuity" invests a capital sum into an annuity which provides a regular payment stream to the investor for as long as the investor is alive. A portion of each payment to the investor is considered a return of the original capital and the remaining portion of the payment is considered a return on investment. Only the return on the investment is taxable income to the investor. At death, the annuity ceases. In order to preserve the original capital, life insurance is often obtained at the time of the annuity acquisition; hence the label "insured annuity." The life insurance premium is paid for from the annuity's stream of capital and income. At death, the life insurance death benefit is paid to the investor's estate (or named beneficiary) to replace the capital originally invested. The net after-tax and after-insurance premium amount received by the investor is usually greater than the after-tax interest income generated by the conventional investment. The net result is a larger lifetime income flow while still leaving an estate for heirs.

B. — Annuity characteristics

The annuity is often non-commutable and non-transferable, meaning it is a permanent contract for the life of the individual and cannot be cashed in or transferred to another party, either as a gift or for consideration. Further, the annuity payments need not be guaranteed for any period of time. Life annuities with no guaranteed payments are commonly referred to as "life zero" annuities.

C. — Insurance characteristics

The type of insurance that is normally used to support an insured annuity is some type of permanent insurance, since the insurance need is for life. Often, the type of insurance product supporting an annuity is a guaranteed product, so the owner is not subject to future pricing fluctuations. The insurance product need not have cash value buildup since cashing in the policy is not generally considered an option at the time of entering into an insured annuity arrangement. Since the annuity will provide funding for the individual's lifetime, life insurance premium payments can be structured to continue for life, rather than requiring the policy to become "paid-up" and self-funding at some point in time.

A term-to-100 life insurance policy normally meets these requirements, providing a level death benefit without cash values for a constant amount of annual cost. Premium payments continue until age 100 when the premiums normally cease while the insurance coverage continues. A universal life insurance policy can also be used, where only the minimum premium (representing the level cost of insurance) is paid for life. The main advantage in using this type of policy is the fact that, for a similar cost, it offers added flexibility in allowing for optional deposits which can accumulate on a tax deferred basis. Where the insured annuity uses a single deposit to the life insurance policy (some of which would be subject to annual accrual taxation until such time as the entire amount can be deposited into an "exempt" policy) in conjunction with the purchase of a life annuity, the premiums are "pre-paid" in the early years (thus creating cash value). A level cost of insurance or yearly renewable term cost universal life insurance policy may be used in this context. See Chapter 2 for a discussion of T-100 and universal life insurance policies.

D. — Insured annuities — advantages and disadvantages

An insured annuity provides a guaranteed income for life which may possibly provide an increased after-tax annual return compared to other long-term guaranteed investments. It is a conservative investment strategy requiring little or no management and a return of capital to either the estate or a beneficiary.

On the other hand, an insured annuity is locked in for life. Should investment market conditions or the owner's financial situation change dramatically, the insured annuity generally cannot be undone, except perhaps to cancel the life insurance portion. The owner has no contractual right to commute the annuity. It should be noted, however, that while the annuitant has no contractual right to cancel the annuity, extra-contractual commutation of the annuity may be possible.

E. — Owner profile

Since an insured annuity is a lifetime investment, it is generally more appropriate for those individuals who are about age 65 or over. This means that the expected length of the investment might be, say, 25 years. It would be inappropriate for a 30-year-old where the expected length of the investment could be, say, 50 years. Further, an insured annuity is particularly appropriate for individuals with non-registered funds available for investment purposes that would otherwise be taxed at high marginal tax rates as the income distributed from the insured annuity is partially comprised of a tax-free return of capital.

In order to acquire an insured annuity, individuals must be in sufficiently good health to obtain the necessary life insurance. Both the annuity and the life insurance contracts must be underwritten as separate contracts. In technical interpretations 9224315, dated October 5, 1992 and 9606425, dated April 9, 1996, the CRA stated that where the issuing of the life insurance contract is made contingent upon the purchase of the annuity contract, they may consider that the life insurance policy and the annuity contract are all one contract and hence non-exempt and subject to accrual taxation. It should be noted that if this were to occur in the corporate-owned insured annuity context this interpretation would have an impact on the capital dividend account credit available to the corporation. The adjusted cost basis under the single non-exempt policy would include the ACB of both the life insurance policy and the annuity. The CDA credit would be reduced by the combined ACB and, accordingly, would be significantly less.

17.2 — Personally-Owned Insured Annuities

A. — General comments

Under a personally-owned insured annuity strategy, the life insurance and annuity contracts are owned by an individual.

When an insured annuity is personally-owned, the annuity is generally set up as a prescribed annuity contract (see Chapter 14 on the Taxation of Annuity Income for details regarding prescribed annuities). A prescribed annuity contract which satisfies the requirements of Regulation 304 allows for levelized taxable income throughout the life of the contract.

It should be noted that the August 23, 2013 draft legislation proposes the use of a more modern mortality table, the *Annuity 2000 Basic Mortality Table* instead of the *1971 Individual Annuity Mortality Table* that is currently prescribed, as well as recognition of substandard risks for PACs issued after 2015. The proposed change to the mortality table would have the effect of increasing the taxable portion of each annuity payment. The proposed recognition of substandard risks would have the effect of reducing the taxable portion of each annuity payment. For a more detailed discussion see section 13.5.

Where a beneficiary is designated under the life insurance contract, the insurance proceeds will not be subject to probate fees, creditor claims or estate litigation. The life insurance death benefit is paid directly to the beneficiary, rather than flowing through the deceased's estate.

B. — Cash flow example

The following numerically compares $200,000 invested in an interest bearing term deposit at 4 percent, to an insured annuity, assuming:

- the individual is a female, age 70 non-smoker,
- the annual annuity income is $13,809,
- the annuity qualifies as a prescribed annuity contract whose annual taxable portion is $1,387,
- the individual's marginal tax rate is 50 percent, and
- the annual cost of life insurance is $6,980, UL, YRT 100 rates.

	Term Deposit	Insured Annuity
Initial capital	$200,000	$200,000
Income	8,000	13,809
Taxable portion	8,000	1,387
Tax payable (50% tax rate)	4,000	694
After-tax retention	4,000	13,115
Insurance premium	nil	6,980
Annual after-tax net income	4,000	6,135
Equivalent pre-tax yield	4%	6.14%

In addition to the tax regime associated with annuities and life insurance policies, contributing to the increase in after-tax cash flow from the insured annuity are the differences between the mortality tables used to determine the price of the annuity and the life insurance policy. Mortality tables generally estimate the life expectancy for individuals based on their age and gender. In pricing annuities, insurers generally use mortality rates based on the general population while, for life insurance, insurers use mortality rates based on the mortality rates of people who were healthy enough to pass the physical examinations required to obtain life insurance. Generally, the life expectancy of an annuitant from the general population will be lower than the life expectancy of a life insured of the same age. Providing that the individual is insurable, he or she will benefit from the differences in policy pricing.

C. — Treatment at death

At death, an interest-bearing investment may continue to earn interest income until its maturity. In addition a market-value adjustment is possible, although in practice these are often sufficiently small to ignore, particularly for shorter term investments. The taxpayer generally must accrue income up to the date of death (subsection 70(1) of the Act).

On the other hand, upon the death of an annuitant under an annuity contract, the contract terminates. This triggers a disposition of the contract. However, in the case of a prescribed annuity contract, there is no gain or loss realized. Non-prescribed life annuities are taxed at death (as long as they were contracts entered into after November 12, 1981) only to the extent of any income accrued but untaxed to the date of death. See Chapter 14 on the taxation of annuities for further details.

As for the life insurance policy, the death benefit proceeds of an exempt life insurance policy are tax-free to the beneficiary (subsection 148(1.1) and the definition of "disposition" in relation to an interest in a life insurance policy in subsection 148(9) of the Act).

D. — Planning considerations

Depending on the circumstances and the specific ages of the individual and his/her spouse, the annuity can be issued to be payable until the death of the last survivor, in which case the life insurance policy would also be payable on a joint last-to-die basis. Although the annuity income would be reduced (compared to a single life annuity), this would be balanced by the fact that the life insurance premium would also be reduced and that at least, statistically, the payments would potentially be made for a longer period.

While a portion of the annuity income may be taxable, that portion that is a return of capital is not taxable and will not impact entitlement to Old Age Security benefit. As shown in the above example, the taxable income is reduced by 83 percent (from $8,000 to $1,387) when compared to a 4 percent interest bearing investment.

Income from the prescribed annuity is subject to the pension income-splitting rules, to the extent the holder of the contract (owner) is at least 65 years of age. This may provide added benefits when compared to most interest bearing investments.

In order to qualify for prescribed status, the holder of the annuity contract must be the annuitant (measuring life). (See Chapter 14 for details regarding prescribed status.). This may be an issue if the holder is uninsurable or highly rated (the annuity and the life insurance must be on the same life). This may best be illustrated with an example. Assume Mr. A has $200,000 of excess liquid capital to invest in an insured annuity. He is not insurable, but his spouse Mrs. A is a standard risk and qualifies for $200,000 of life insurance coverage. If Mr. A purchases the annuity on his spouse's life, the annuity will not qualify as a prescribed annuity contract. One option would be for Mr. A to transfer the funds to Mrs. A in order for her to purchase the annuity. In technical interpretation 5-901540, dated January 14, 1991, the CRA confirmed that the income attribution rules apply to annuity income. It is interesting to note that the CRA is of the view that should the annuity income be subject to the attribution rules, it will not qualify for the pension income-splitting rules (2008 APFF Roundtable Question 2 technical interpretation 2008-0284411C6, dated October 10, 2008). Another option for Mrs. A would be for her to borrow the funds from Mr. A at the prescribed rate of interest, in which case the attribution rules would not apply (to the extent all other requirements are met).

17.3 — Insured Annuities Owned by Trusts

People often look to different trusts, (for example testamentary, spousal trusts, alter ego trusts or joint partner trusts), depending upon the circumstances, as vehicles which could acquire or hold taxable investments for the benefit of certain beneficiaries. There are certain circumstances where it might be interesting to consider implementing the insured annuity strategy through a trust. One example might be where a settlor or testator wishes to provide for a beneficiary (often a spouse) who is either spendthrift, or is uncomfortable managing investments independently. In that case, a trust could provide the necessary control, and in combination with the insured annuity strategy, the income available would be increased with limited investment risk.

Where any of these trusts are subject to the 21-year deemed disposition rule, there are advantages as well. Life insurance (including annuities) is not treated as capital property for the purposes of the *Income Tax Act*, and accordingly, would not be subject to the 21-year deemed disposition rule.

In order to increase the returns, it is more advantageous to acquire a precribed annuity contract ("PAC") as a result of its preferential tax treatment. To qualify as a PAC, specific requirements stipulate who may hold or own the contract and who the annuitant must be. In general, individuals and certain types of trusts may hold these contracts. In the trust category, Regulation 304(1)(c)(iii)(A) includes a testamentary trust and a trust described in paragraph 104(4)(a) of the Act, referred to as a "specified trust". Included in the list of specified trusts are post-1971 testamentary and inter vivos spouse or common law partner trusts and the new categories of alter ego and joint partner trusts. See section 14.2.A.iv for a discussion of testamentary and specified trusts holding prescribed annuity contracts.

Regardless of the type of annuity that is acquired, trustees considering implementing this strategy must, of course, be mindful of their fiduciary obligations. A trustee must exercise care and prudence when choosing trust investments, and has a duty to maintain an even hand between life tenant and remaindermen. Accordingly, the trustees must ensure that these types of investments are authorized investments pursuant to the terms of the trust deed, or the terms of relevant legislation in their jurisdiction. The trustees must also ensure that these investments do not affect or impair the respective entitlements of the capital and income beneficiaries of the trust. See Chapter 9 for a discussion of trusts owning insurance products.

The reader should note that the CRA has made comments which have led to some confusion concerning the ability of trusts to own life insurance policies, either because the status of the trust (e.g. spousal or alter-ego) may be tainted or because the trust may be deemed to confer a taxable benefit to the trust beneficiaries. See sections 9.5 and 9.5.H for a detailed discussion of these issues.

17.4 — Corporate-Owned Insured Annuities

A. — General comments

Under a corporate-owned insured annuity strategy, the life insurance contract and the annuity contract are owned by a corporation rather than an individual.

One of the main differences between a personally-owned and a corporate-owned insured annuity strategy is that a corporate-owned annuity cannot be a prescribed annuity. Regulation 304(1)(c)(iii) states that the holder of a prescribed annuity contract *must* be a natural person, a testamentary trust, a spouse trust or other trust listed at paragraph 104(4)(a) of the Act. Therefore a corporate-owned annuity does not receive prescribed annuity tax treatment and will have a variable amount of taxable income each year. Taxable income usually decreases each year, as the income element decreases and the capital element increases. In the first years, however, taxable income can vary somewhat due to initial administrative costs that the annuity contract incurs at its inception.

An issue was raised at the CALU Annual General Meeting on May 7, 2002 concerning the determination of the taxable portion of third party annuity contracts, including those issued to corporations. (Please refer to section 14.2.B.iv on the taxation of annuity contracts for further details). Since this issue has been resolved favourably, it has been ignored for purposes of the discussion in this chapter.

B. — Cash flow example — while living

The following is a hypothetical example of the cash flow which a corporate insured annuity might provide as compared to an alternative interest bearing investment. The assumptions are:

- individual shareholder is a 75-year-old female non-smoker,
- individual's company has $200,000 liquid investments,
- the annual annuity payment on an annuity of $1,000,000 is $88,273, the taxable portions being as shown in Table 1 below,
- the corporate tax rate on investment income is 50 percent,
- the cost of $1,000,000 insurance for a 75-year-old female (non-smoker) is $42,916, term-to-100 rates, and
- an alternative interest bearing investment would yield 4 percent pre-tax.

		Corporate Insured Annuity						Taxable Investment		
Year	Age	Annuity Payment (Before Tax)	Taxable Portion	Tax Payable @ 50%	After-Tax Amount Available	Life Insurance Premium	Net Cash Flow	Interest @ 4%	Tax Payable @ 50%	Net Cash Flow
1	75	82,273	0	0	82,273	42,916	39,357	40,000	20,000	20,000
2	76	82,273	6,645	3,323	78,951	42,916	36,034	40,000	20,000	20,000
3	77	82,273	25,617	12,809	69,465	42,916	26,548	40,000	20,000	20,000
4	78	82,273	24,449	12,225	70,049	42,916	27,132	40,000	20,000	20,000
5	79	82,273	23,320	11,660	70,613	42,916	27,697	40,000	20,000	20,000
6	80	82,273	22,207	11,104	71,170	42,916	28,253	40,000	20,000	20,000
7	81	82,273	21,102	10,551	71,722	42,916	28,806	40,000	20,000	20,000
8	82	82,273	20,010	10,005	72,268	42,916	29,352	40,000	20,000	20,000
9	83	82,273	18,931	9,466	72,808	42,916	29,891	40,000	20,000	20,000
10	84	82,273	17,865	8,933	73,341	42,916	30,424	40,000	20,000	20,000
11	85	82,273	16,815	8,408	73,866	42,916	30,949	40,000	20,000	20,000
12	86	82,273	15,820	7,910	74,363	42,916	31,447	40,000	20,000	20,000
13	87	82,273	14,898	7,449	74,824	42,916	31,908	40,000	20,000	20,000
14	88	82,273	14,008	7,004	75,269	42,916	32,353	40,000	20,000	20,000
15	89	82,273	13,152	6,576	75,697	42,916	32,781	40,000	20,000	20,000
16	90	82,273	12,331	6,166	76,108	42,916	33,191	40,000	20,000	20,000
17	91	82,273	11,588	5,794	76,479	42,916	33,563	40,000	20,000	20,000
18	92	82,273	10,943	5,472	76,802	42,916	33,885	40,000	20,000	20,000
19	93	82,273	10,344	5,172	77,101	42,916	34,185	40,000	20,000	20,000
20	94	82,273	9,786	4,893	77,380	42,916	34,464	40,000	20,000	20,000

C. — Tax implications at death

i. — To the corporation

Under a life annuity, when the annuitant dies the annuity payments cease and the annuity contract terminates. Paragraph 148(2)(b) of the Act sets out certain deemed disposition rules where the contract is a non-prescribed annuity entered into after November 12, 1981. There may be a gain on disposition equal to the excess of the accumulating fund immediately after death (paragraph (d) in the definition of "proceeds of the disposition" in subsection 148(9) of the Act) over the adjusted cost basis of the contract. The gain is income (i.e. it is not a capital gain), and is effectively a "catch-up" accrual for any unreported income arising since the last anniversary date up to the date of death. See Chapter 14 for more details on the taxation of annuity contracts.

As for the life insurance policy, the death benefit is received by the corporation tax-free (subsection 148(1.1) and the definition of "disposition" in subsection 148(9) of the Act). The amount of the death benefit proceeds received by a corporation in excess of the adjusted cost basis of the life insurance policy to the corporation immediately before the death of the life insured is credited to the corporation's CDA pursuant to the definition of the term "capital dividend account" at subsection 89(1) of the Act. Thus, a corporate-insured annuity normally will allow for most, if not all, of the death benefit proceeds to be extracted from the corporate level to the personal level without personal tax. This can be a particularly attractive tax planning point. However, as stated earlier in this chapter (see section 17.1.E) the CRA could, under certain circumstances, consider the separate annuity and life insurance contracts to constitute a single contract, resulting in a significantly reduced credit to the corporation's CDA.

ii. — To the shareholder

Subsection 70(5) of the Act deems an individual to dispose of capital property at fair market value immediately before death. This would normally include shares of a private company (Privateco). It is assumed for purposes of this example that Mr. X is the sole shareholder of Privateco and it is further assumed that at the death of Mr. X, Privateco's only assets are comprised of an insured annuity.

In order to determine Mr. X's tax liability in respect of the deemed disposition at death of his Privateco shares it is necessary to determine the fair market value of Privateco's shares immediately before death. Some assistance may be found at subsection 70(5.3) of the Act which indicates the fair market value of the shares immediately before death ". . .shall be determined as though the fair market value at that time of any life insurance policy under which the particular individual. . .was a person whose life was insured, were the cash surrender value. . .".

Thus, where the life insurance policy has no cash surrender value, which is normally the case with term-to-100 policies or minimum funded universal life policies, subsection 70(5.3) can be relied on to support the position that the life insurance contract adds no value to Privateco's shares for the purposes of the deemed disposition immediately before death. Should the life insurance policy have a cash surrender value, this must be taken into account in determining the fair market value of Privateco's shares.

The effect of the life annuity on the valuation of Privateco's shares immediately before death is not as clear. One school of thought is the life annuity adds no value to Privateco's shares. Arguments in support of this position include:

1. Subsection 138(12) of the Act indicates a "life insurance policy includes an annuity contract. . ." Thus, the annuity should be treated in the same fashion as the life insurance policy for purposes of subsection 70(5.3) of the Act. Since the annuity is generally non-commutable (i.e. it cannot be surrendered for value), subsection 70(5.3) of the Act should deem the annuity to have nil value.

2. Where the life annuity is non-commutable and non-transferable, these restrictions mean the annuity cannot be offered for sale to another party for consideration. One accepted measure of fair market value is based on the value at which non-arm's length parties would normally transact. If another person cannot purchase the asset, its fair market value can be argued to be nil.

Nonetheless, both the above arguments are subject to the risk that the CRA could attribute a value to the annuity contract and hence a value to the shares immediately before death. In technical interpretation 9321275, dated September 20, 1993 regarding the value of a corporate-owned life annuity (without any guarantee period) immediately before the death of the shareholder, the CRA was of the view that the annuity would not be a "life insurance policy under which the taxpayer was the person whose life was insured." It is interesting to note that Revenue Quebec has not adopted the same position as the CRA. Section 450.2 of the Quebec Taxation Act is similar to subsection 70(5.3) of the *Income Tax Act*. At the Provincial Roundtable held during the 2001 APFF Conference, Revenue Quebec stated at Question 16 that the annuity would be valued at its cash surrender value.

Although the wording in subsection 70(5.3) of the Act has since been changed to "any life insurance policy, under which the particular individual . . . was a person whose life was insured", this wording change does not seem to affect this particular argument.

In determining a value for the annuity, the CRA could ascribe a value based on an estimate of the individual's life expectancy immediately preceding death (without foreknowledge of such death). Such a calculation would likely be based on a present value estimate of future annuity payments. This value would decrease over time, as the estimated number of future payments is reduced with the age of the individual. While it may be imprudent to suggest a corporate-owned annuity has no value for purposes of the subsection 70(5) deemed disposition rule immediately before death, it is fair to suggest that the value of the life annuity decreases as the individual ages so that, over time, the fair market value of Privateco's shares attributable to the annuity for purposes of this deemed disposition will similarly decline.

It is interesting to note that the 2013 federal budget proposed measures would deem a value for the annuity in a leveraged insured annuity structure (see section 17.6 for more details). Proposed subsection 70(5.31) would deem the value of the annuity to essentially be its purchase price. For non-leveraged corporate insured annuities, it is unclear if the introduction of this deeming rule can be taken to confirm that the normal rule (value of the annuity otherwise is at the cash surrender value pursuant to subsection 70(5.3)) prevails, or whether the above CRA commentary must be considered when interpreting the application of the normal rule.

It should be noted that similar valuation issues arise for purposes of valuing a corporation's assets for the purpose of determining if the shares of the corporation are eligible for the capital gains exemption. Subsection 70(5.3) of the Act is very similar to paragraph 110.6(15)(a) of the Act which determines the value of a life insurance policy for purposes of valuing the assets in the determination of whether the shares would be considered "qualified small business corporation shares." In this context it is important to consider not only the implications at death but also if the shares meet the 50 percent active business asset test in the preceding 2 years. This may mean that the valuation of the annuity under a corporate-insured annuity would have to be considered yearly.

D. — Accounting for corporate-owned insured annuities

One other factor which may be important to understand is how an insured annuity will be handled on the financial statements if the arrangement is corporate-owned. Publicly accountable enterprises will be required to report using International Financial Reporting Standards (IFRS). Private enterprises will be able to choose to adopt IFRS or to use the new "Accounting Standards for Private Enterprises" (ASPE).

Under ASPE, when the company purchases the annuity, the company would record an asset on the balance sheet equal to the capital invested in the annuity. Each year, the annuity payments received from the contract would be recorded partially as income and partially as a reduction of the asset. The allocation between income and capital would be determined based on ASPE taking into account the interest rate and life expectancy of the individual at the time the contract was entered into. The insurance premiums and policy would be accounted for in a manner described in section 6.5. At death, any balance from the annuity remaining on the balance sheet would be written off (since the contract terminates at that time), and the proceeds from the life insurance net of any accounting value for the insurance asset would be recognized as income to the company.

Under IFRS, when the company purchases the annuity, it is a financial asset and the company would record an asset on the balance sheet equal to the fair value of the annuity. This fair value will usually be the fair value of the consideration given. Each year, the annuity payment would be recorded partially as a reduction of the asset. The allocation between income and capital would be based on IFRS taking into account the interest rate and life expectancy of the individual at the time the contract was entered into.

Additionally, the annuity will be required to be revalued at fair value for each reporting period. Any changes in value will be required to be recorded through income. The insurance premiums and policy would be accounted for in a manner described in section 6.5. At death, any balance from the annuity remaining on the balance sheet would be written off (since the contract terminates that that time), and the proceeds from the life insurance net of any accounting value for the insurance asset would be recognized as income to the company.

E. — Planning considerations

Where an individual holds investments both personally and through a holding company, he/she may consider a hybrid structure. The annuity can be owned personally and the life insurance policy can be corporate-owned. This provides preferential treatment for the annuity since it can qualify for prescribed status. The examples provided above show that for the same annuity (premium, age, and payout), the taxable portion of the prescribed annuity is $1,387 whereas the taxable portion of the non-prescribed annuity is still over $4,000, or more than double, after 20 years ($4,165). The life insurance policy can be funded with cheaper corporate dollars, while generating a credit to the capital dividend account.

One of the advantages of the corporate-insured annuity is a potential reduction in the value of the corporation's shares for purposes of calculating the capital gains tax on death. This advantage does not apply if the insured owns freeze shares. One may consider unfreezing some of the shares. This can reduce the capital gain on participating shares (including the unfrozen shares), but only to the extent the net cash flow generated by the corporate-insured annuity is flowed out to the shareholder.

F. — Summary

The nature of an insured annuity makes it attractive for older individuals looking for guaranteed, and long-term, rates of return. If the insured annuity can be structured in a corporation, there are the added benefits of:

1. potentially reducing the value of the corporation's shares over time as the present value of the future expected annuity payments declines, and
2. the advantage of the ultimate capital dividend account withdrawal.

17.5 — Corporate-Insured Life Annuities — With Leveraging Before March 21, 2013

A. — General comments

For leveraged insured annuities for which all borrowings were entered into before March 21, 2013, the following treatment and discussion still applies.

This section considers the corporate-owned insured annuity concept implemented in conjunction with a leveraged structure, in an attempt to obtain enhanced tax benefits. Further, assume the corporation is an investment holding company. The leveraged corporate-insured annuity generally involves liquidating the current portfolio investments to acquire a life annuity and life insurance, along with borrowing to replace the original investments. There are numerous technical complexities and risks involved in structuring these arrangements, making their tax benefits less certain.

These structures are sometimes referred to as leveraged corporate-insured annuities ("LCIAs"), corporate-insured life annuities, ("CILAs"), or "Triple Back-to-Backs." For the purpose of this discussion, the concept of a corporate-owned insured annuity with leveraging will be referred to as a "leveraged insured annuity."

Leveraged insured annuities are normally suggested as most suitable for an individual over age 65 who has portfolio investments in a Canadian-controlled private company. This is due to the tax advantages that leveraged insured annuities may offer in this situation. A leveraged insured annuity can be owned individually; however, this would be akin to arranging an insured annuity and then borrowing to reinvest.

B. — Leveraged-insured annuities — a general description

The following describes a series of transactions that typify leveraged-insured annuities:

1. A person, typically age 65 or more, owns all of the shares of a Canadian-controlled private corporation (Privateco) with significant value, which may have significant cash or near cash assets. The shareholder faces a substantial capital gain on death with respect to these shares.

2. Privateco purchases a term-to-100 or a minimum funded universal life insurance policy on the life of the shareholder naming itself as beneficiary under the contract, using available cash to pay the initial premium.

3. Privateco purchases an annuity contract to provide a lifetime stream of payments for the duration of the shareholder's life. The annuity contract would be a non-prescribed annuity (since it is corporate-owned).

4. Privateco borrows a capital sum from a bank (the Bank) to replenish the cash used to acquire the annuity. This is done to structure the borrowing so that interest on the money borrowed is deductible for income tax purposes. Interest is paid each year on the borrowed money.

5. In the process of lending money, the Bank takes as collateral an assignment of the annuity and the life insurance contract (in addition to a general security agreement with Privateco and/or a personal guarantee of the shareholder, as the Bank may require in the circumstances). Requiring this collateral may provide Privateco with a deduction for a portion of the life insurance costs pursuant to paragraph 20(1)(e.2) of the Act. Provided the conditions of this paragraph are met, the deduction would be for the lesser of: (1) the life insurance premium and, (2) the net cost of pure insurance (NCPI) for the life insurance policy.

6. On the death of the shareholder, the relevant portion of the life insurance policy's death benefit is paid to the Bank under the terms of the collateral assignment. This extinguishes Privateco's indebtedness to the Bank. Any excess proceeds over the amount of indebtedness would be paid to Privateco. Privateco would receive a CDA credit for the proceeds in excess of the adjusted cost basis of the life insurance policy. In addition, the life annuity would cease.

7. The deceased shareholder is deemed to have disposed of the Privateco shares at fair market value for tax purposes immediately before death. As a result, tax is payable on any capital gain. For purposes of determining this fair market value, the valuation of Privateco's shares would be reduced by the outstanding loan. Arguably, there would be no value attributed to the life insurance policy by virtue of the application of subsection 70(5.3) of the Act and little or no value attributed to the annuity. This could result in a significant reduction or elimination of capital gains tax from the initial position where Privateco held significant cash assets.

8. Any excess proceeds received by Privateco would flow to the shareholder's estate by way of a tax-free capital dividend (upon redemption of the shareholder's shares). Upon a redemption of shares, the Act generally deems a dividend to be paid to the extent that the proceeds of redemption exceed the paid up capital of the shares. This dividend may be paid as a capital dividend to the extent of Privateco's CDA balance and would therefore be tax-free to the estate and/or heirs.

On a current basis, the desired effect of this structure is to generate a positive after-tax cash flow (or at least an equal cash flow) to the initial position where Privateco holds significant cash assets.

Other benefits from the structure may be the reduction of capital gains tax on death, and the receipt of tax-free capital dividends.

C. — Risks involved

From the shareholder's point of view, there are significant tax and financial risks associated with this concept, including:

1. interest rate fluctuation on the bank loan with an annuity at a fixed rate;
2. potential denial of interest expense deduction;
3. potential denial of collateral insurance deduction;
4. the fair market value of the company for purposes of the deemed disposition rules on death would not be reduced as a result of the transactions; and
5. potential application of the General Anti-Avoidance Rule (GAAR).

Each of these issues is dealt with more fully below.

i. — Interest rate fluctuations

Leveraged insured annuities are not flexible planning tools and cannot easily be undone. The annuity is generally non-commutable and premium payments are required to keep the life insurance policy in force. The annuity portion of the arrangement is a fixed rate investment for the lifetime of the individual.

The bank loan, on the other hand, will likely have a fixed term or have a fluctuating interest rate. As a result, the arrangement is particularly susceptible to risks associated with changes in interest rates.

If interest rates rise, the cost of borrowing the funds will increase and negatively affect cash flow. Even if the bank loan interest rate is fixed for a specified period, such a period is likely shorter than the expected term of the annuity (i.e. the lifetime of the shareholder). The risk of losing the positive cash flow must be considered since interest rate fluctuations are an unpredictable economic reality. Of course, if interest rates fall, the cost of borrowing may be reduced and this would benefit the owner.

Another possibility is the risk of an early payment penalty if the interest rate for the loan is locked in during a decreasing interest rate environment and the shareholder dies within the loan term. Depending on the loan arrangement with the bank, a penalty may be levied for the early payment of the loan.

ii. — Interest deductibility

Interest is deductible when it meets the specific requirements contained in the Act. In particular paragraph 20(1)(c) of the Act states that, generally, interest paid or payable in the year is deductible if the borrowed money is used to produce business income or to purchase property used to produce income. The interest must be based on a legal obligation to pay and must also be reasonable in the circumstances. In short, the deductibility of interest expense is determined by the use of the borrowed funds. The funds borrowed must be directly traceable to an income-earning source in order for interest to be deductible.

If the funds borrowed in circumstances using the leveraged insured annuity concept are used directly to purchase an annuity, the funds have been borrowed to earn income, namely the interest component of the annuity. However, the Act limits the deductibility of interest expense when the borrowed funds are directly used to invest in an annuity. Subparagraph 20(1)(c)(iv) of the Act limits the deduction of interest expense to the amount of the taxable income from an annuity. The taxable income from the non-prescribed annuity declines over time, with a larger component of each annuity payment representing income in the early years and diminishing amounts representing income in the later years. Accordingly, the deduction for interest expense is greatly restricted, particularly in the later years when taxable income from the annuity is reduced.

In implementing a leveraged insured annuity structure it is often suggested that the corporation borrow funds to be used to produce income, thereby making the interest tax deductible. If current cash is used to purchase the annuity and the corporation borrows capital to replenish its investments, the corporation should arguably be entitled to deduct the interest expense incurred on the borrowed funds. Great care must be taken to maintain the connection between the interest paid and the income earning use of the borrowed funds. Where the borrowings are generally used directly to reacquire the corporation's investments (or substitute investments) which were originally liquidated to purchase the annuity and life insurance, in order to be deductible, any interest expense must be reasonable in the circumstances (paragraph 20(1)(c) of the Act) and the borrowing must be used to produce income (paragraph 18(1)(a)). Subsection 9(3) of the Act generally excludes from property income any capital gain from the disposition of that property.

Interest deductibility is dependent upon the structure and arrangement of the financing. In *Singleton v. R.*, [2001] 2 S.C.R. 1046, [2002] 1 C.T.C. 121, the taxpayer withdrew funds from his law firm capital account and used the withdrawn funds to purchase a new home. Subsequently, he borrowed funds from a bank which he used to replenish his capital account. The Tax Court had held that the fundamental purpose of the borrowing was the purchase of a residence and interest deductibility was denied. The Federal Court of Appeal overturned the decision holding that each part of the transaction had to be viewed independently and that interest was deductible. The Supreme Court of Canada upheld the Federal Court of Appeal's decision stating that 20(1)(c) of the Act was clear and unambiguous. A direct link existed between the borrowed money and an eligible use, allowing for interest deductibility. It reaffirmed the ability of taxpayers to structure their affairs in the most tax efficient manner.

On October 1, 2002 the CRA presented the preliminary results of the review of their existing interpretive and administrative positions on interest deductibility following the *Ludco (Ludco Enterprises Ltd. v. Canada*, [2002] 1 C.T.C. 95 (S.C.C.)) and *Singleton* decisions and outlined it in a paper released October 3, 2002. The interpretations outlined in the paper are consistent with CRA's administrative positions. These positions are now reflected in archived Interpretation Bulletin IT-533 "Interest Deductibility and Related Issues", dated October 31, 2003. In particular, the CRA indicated it would accept cash damming techniques that are used to ensure that borrowed money is used for specific purposes. This does provide comfort with regard to interest deductibility where a leveraged insured annuity is structured by liquidating a portfolio to acquire a life annuity and life insurance, and funds are borrowed to replace the original investments.

Other structures have been developed in order to obtain interest deductibility. For example, a subsidiary can borrow to redeem shares or to pay a dividend to a shareholder. The subsidiary would own the life insurance policy and the parent company would own the life annuity. Based on IT-533, the CRA would regard borrowing to pay dividends or to redeem shares as exceptional circumstances giving rise to interest deductibility provided that the capital replaced by the borrowing was previously used for an eligible purpose. Care should be taken when borrowed money is used to pay a large dividend to a holding company: the dividend must not be in excess of the replaced capital. In the context of borrowing to pay a dividend to a parent company that purchases an annuity, the general position of allowing deductibility of interest when borrowing to replace capital to "fill a hole" was confirmed by CRA technical interpretation 2009-0344721E5, dated July 12, 2010. However, the CRA also stated that GAAR could apply. It stated

> one of the facts of particular interest in the scenario described would be whether the corporate structure was established within a series of transactions which included Company B (subsidiary company) borrowing money and Company A (parent company) acquiring an annuity.

This letter also dealt with the consequences of a subsequent amalgamation of the companies taking the position that the interest deduction would be limited to the taxable portion of the annuity payment under subparagraph 20(1)(c)(iv) of the Act.

It should be noted that the above analysis is based on existing legislation. On October 31, 2003 the Department of Finance released draft legislation regarding the deductibility of interest and other expenses imposing a statutory "reasonable expectation of profit" test. For a more detailed discussion of this draft legislation see section 4.2.A.iii. For leveraged insured annuities, this draft legislation would mean that if there were no reasonable expectation that the income earned from the invested funds would exceed the expenses incurred in respect of the investment or business (including interest and the collateral insurance deduction), then the deductions would be limited to the income earned.

iii. — Collateral life insurance deduction

As a rule, premiums paid under a life insurance policy are not an allowable deduction for income tax purposes. There is an exception in paragraph 20(1)(e.2) of the Act for circumstances where, generally, money is borrowed to earn income and the lender requires the assignment of a life insurance policy as collateral security for the loan. See section 6.4.E for a discussion of the deduction of premiums for collateral insurance. Generally under paragraph 20(1)(e.2) of the Act the lesser of premium payments and the net cost of pure insurance under a policy used as collateral security for a loan is a legitimate business expense and may be deductible for tax purposes if a number of specific requirements are met including:

1. The policy must be assigned to the lender in the course of borrowing from the lender.
2. The lender must be a "restricted financial institution." A restricted financial institution is defined at subsection 248(1) of the Act as a bank, trust company, credit union, insurance corporation or a corporation whose principal business is the lending of money.
3. The interest payable with respect to the borrowing is, generally, deductible in computing income for tax purposes.
4. The assignment of insurance must be specifically required by the lender as collateral for the borrowing.

Provided the requirements are met, the amount deductible is the lesser of:

1. the premiums payable under the life insurance policy, and
2. the NCPI for the year for the interest in the policy that is assigned to the lender,

multiplied by that portion reasonably relating to the amount of the loan owing. The deduction for the cost of life insurance depends upon the deductibility of the interest on the borrowed money.

It is interesting to note that the CRA has indicated that even if only a portion of the interest on a loan is deductible, the entire NCPI can be deducted. In their response to Question 4 at the 2005 CALU CRA Roundtable regarding interest on a loan used to purchase an annuity contract, the CRA responded that "the condition stated in clause 20(1)(e.2)(i)(B) of the Act is met for the taxation year if part or all of the interest is deductible in the year by virtue of subparagraph 20(1)(c)(iv) of the Act" (technical interpretation 2005-0116651C6). If, however, no interest is deductible in the year, no deduction will be permitted for collateral insurance purposes.

The CRA had provided the same response to the identical question at the 2004 APFF Conference (technical interpretation 2004-0085551). The CRA has also issued an Advance Tax Ruling (2005-0143281R3) which confirms this position with reference to a particular taxpayer's situation in which money was borrowed to purchase an annuity, and the annuity and a life insurance policy were assigned as collateral security for the loan.

Of course, the collateral insurance deduction may be denied as a separate item by the CRA if it could successfully argue the requirement for collateral assignment of the life insurance policy was not justified in the circumstances.

iv. — Deemed disposition at death

With a leveraged insured annuity, the optimal desired result is that the corporation would have a fair market value of nil for purposes of subsection 70(5) of the Act and no capital gain would result on death. Since the life-zero annuity is non-commutable it would seemingly have no cash surrender value for these purposes. The term-to-100 or universal life insurance policy has no cash surrender value so it too would have no value for these purposes. The principal amount borrowed would offset the reinvestment in the corporation or the investments repurchased by the corporation (excluding any growth on those investments). Therefore, on the surface, it appears the desired result of reducing the share value for the purposes of subsection 70(5) of the Act is achieved. (See section 17.4.C.ii for further details.)

As noted above, the CRA could ascribe a value to the annuity based, for example, on an estimate of the individual's life expectancy immediately preceding death (without foreknowledge of such death). This value would decrease over time, as the estimated number of future payments is reduced with the age of the individual.

v. — The General Anti-Avoidance Rule (GAAR)

By its nature, the General Anti-Avoidance Rule (GAAR) at subsection 245(2) of the Act has extremely broad potential application. GAAR basically allows the CRA to recharacterize any transaction or step in a series of transactions and ignore its legal effect where the transaction is an "avoidance transaction." If the steps or transaction(s) are recharacterized, the income tax consequence(s) are re-determined as may be reasonable in the circumstances.

An avoidance transaction is defined as a transaction or step in a series of transactions resulting in a tax benefit. A tax benefit is defined as a reduction, avoidance or deferral of tax or an increase in a refund of tax. Having determined a tax benefit exists, GAAR may apply unless the transaction or step could reasonably be considered to have been undertaken primarily for a *bona fide* purpose, other than to obtain the tax benefit. Even where no *bona fide* purpose exists, GAAR may not apply where the transaction or step would not result directly or indirectly in a misuse of the provisions of the Act or abuse having regard to the provisions of the Act as a whole.

In order to determine whether a transaction or step results in a misuse or abuse of the Act, one must examine whether the transactions are specifically contemplated by the Act. To this end, an examination of the relevant provisions of the Act is necessary. Further, the applicability of GAAR will, of course, depend on the facts of the particular situation. As well, the form of the transaction can be quite important in determining whether the transaction can withstand scrutiny in tax cases.

It is a well-established principle in tax law that taxpayers are entitled to structure their affairs in a tax effective manner. Still, it is arguable the CRA could attempt to apply GAAR to the whole series of transactions if the CRA finds, in the particular facts of the case in question, there is a misuse or abuse of the provisions of the Act when read as a whole. For leveraged insured annuities, the following points would be relevant in this regard:

- whether an insurance need has been demonstrated;
- the economic sense of the transactions undertaken independent of any tax benefits, and
- all other facts in the particular situation.

There is a risk the CRA may argue there is little economic benefit from these series of transactions apart from the tax benefits and that the transaction does not make sound business sense. (See for example the 1996 CALU CRA Roundtable where the CRA expressed certain of its views regarding the leveraged corporate-insured annuity structure). The CRA may ignore the taxpayer's planning and determine the funds were actually borrowed to finance the annuity and life insurance purchase, as these were the only assets which were absent before the series of transactions. Accordingly, there is a risk interest deductibility may be denied or restricted to the amount of the income element of the annuity.

It should be noted that in Advance Tax Ruling 2005-0143281R3, discussed above, the CRA confirmed that it would not apply GAAR to the transactions being considered by the taxpayer. More recently, the Supreme Court of Canada considered the application of GAAR to a series of transactions designed to make interest on money borrowed to purchase a personal residence deductible (*Lipson v. The Queen*, 2009 SCC 1, [2009] 1 C.T.C. 314, 2009 D.T.C. 5528). In this case, the CRA sought to deny the interest deduction on the basis that the interest deduction provision in paragraph 20(1)(c) of the Act had been abused. They argued that the purpose and substance of the series of transactions was to make mortgage interest deductible and, therefore, even though the direct use of funds was for the purpose of producing income, the transactions frustrated the purpose of paragraph 20(1)(c). Although the Supreme Court majority decided GAAR should apply to the transactions in Lipson, it did so on the basis that the attribution rule in subsection 74.1(1) of the Act had been abused. The decision stated that ". . .the tax benefit of the interest deduction resulting from the refinancing of the shares. . . is not abusive viewed in isolation, but the ensuing tax benefit of the attribution. . .is [abusive]." Accordingly, the interest deduction was allowed to Mrs. Lipson, rather than to Mr. Lipson who had originally claimed the deduction. Many consider this case a victory for taxpayers in that the court affirmed the ability of taxpayers to structure and restructure debt to match debt with eligible uses, and equity with ineligible uses.

Regrettably, the nature of the GAAR provisions and recent case law do not allow for firm conclusions as to when the provision may apply. GAAR will always be a concern for those who are undertaking complicated tax planning. For a deeper discussion of the *Lipson* decision and GAAR see sections 4.2.A.v and 4.2.B.

vi. — Tax shelter rules

The *Income Tax Act* contains special rules relating to arrangements which fall within the definition of a "Tax Shelter". Generally these rules provide that the "promoter" of the arrangement must adhere to additional compliance and reporting requirements including a requirement to obtain a tax shelter identification number. The significance of these requirements for a person acquiring a property which is a tax shelter is that if the purchaser of a property does not report it as a tax shelter, including the tax shelter identification number, the deductions and claims for income tax purposes associated with that property can be disallowed.

A tax shelter is defined in section 237.1 of the Act. In simple terms, a property is a tax shelter if, in the first four years of acquiring the property, the total of amounts "represented to be deductible in computing income in respect of the interest in the property" equal or exceed the cost of the interest in the property. The "cost" of the property is reduced by any loan that is a "limited recourse amount" under subsections 143.2(1), (7), or (13) of the Act. Case law suggests that the CRA may be taking a more aggressive approach in applying the tax shelter rules. See for example *Baxter v. The Queen*, [2007] 3 C.T.C. 211, 2007 D.T.C. 5199 (F.C.A.); reversing [2006] 3 C.T.C. 2427, 2006 D.T.C. 2642 (T.C.C.); leave to appeal refused 2007 CarswellNat 3625 (S.C.C.); and *Maege v. The Queen*, 2006 CarswellNat 774, [2006] 3 C.T.C. 2234, 2006 D.T.C. 3193 (T.C.C.); affirmed 2007 CarswellNat 768, [2007] 5 C.T.C. 67, 2008 D.T.C. 6263 (F.C.A.).

There is a risk that a property acquired in a leveraged insured annuity arrangement may be characterized as a tax shelter under section 237.1 of the Act. To minimize this risk it is prudent to ensure that the loan terms include a requirement to repay the loan within ten years and that the interest thereon is paid annually so that the loan is not a "limited recourse amount."

In Advanced Tax Ruling 2005-014328R3, discussed above, the CRA specifically mentioned that it was not ruling on whether the annuity contract represented a tax shelter even though the taxpayer did not mention the issue nor request any clarification on the matter. The question was raised again at the 2006 APFF Conference Roundtable (Question 29 — technical interpretation 2006-0196251C6). The question related to an individual who purchased a $1.5 M insurance policy on his life, used $500,000 of his own funds, and borrowed $1.5 M to buy a $2 M life annuity. The loan was payable on demand and had a 10-year fixed interest rate. The CRA was unable to confirm whether the tax shelter rules applied to the annuity since it is a question of fact. Another ruling (2009-0340381R3) provided that the tax shelter rules did not apply to the particular scenario but, in this case, the taxpayer used not only the loan amount but also "personal capital" to purchase the annuity. Although the actual figures are not published, presumably the "personal capital" exceeded the interest and collateral insurance deductions in the first four years such that the "cost" of the annuity (after deducting the loan amount that was stipulated to be a "limited recourse amount") exceeded the deductions.

D. — Summary

Leveraged insured annuities are complex structures with risks and issues that must be considered. The main issues are:

- potential limitation or denial of interest expense (and related collateral insurance deduction) based on issues surrounding the tracing and intention of the borrowed funds, reasonableness, and the used-to-earn-income test;
- the risk of future interest rate fluctuations on the borrowings;
- that the fair market value of the company for purposes of the deemed disposition rules immediately before death may include some value in respect of the annuity; and
- the potential application of GAAR.

17.6 — Leveraged Insured Annuities on or after March 21, 2013

A. — General comments

Some warning that leveraged insured annuities were seen as "tax loopholes" came during the 2012 CALU Annual General Meeting. The Minister of Finance, Jim Flaherty, made a statement during his speech at the conference regarding the government's desire to close tax loopholes and specifically mentioned "insured leveraged annuities" in this context. There was some verbal follow up with the Department of Finance by CALU following the conference regarding this comment with the conclusion that leveraged insured annuities were "under review".

The March 21, 2013 federal budget proposed measures that would eliminate the tax benefits of leveraged insured annuities ("LIAs"). At the time of writing, draft legislative measures had not yet been released. The proposals as outlined in the Budget Notice of Ways and Means Motion and the general content of industry submissions (from CALU and CLHIA) following the budget are outlined below.

B. — What is an LIA policy?

The budget proposes to amend subsection 248(1) to include a definition for an "LIA policy". A life insurance policy issued on the life of an individual would be considered to be an "LIA policy" if:

- a person or partnership becomes obligated on or after March 21, 2013, to repay an amount to another person or partnership (the lender) at a time determined by reference to the death of the individual, and

- an annuity contract, the terms of which provide that payments are to continue for the life of the individual, and the life insurance policy on that individual, are assigned to the lender.

This definition would include corporate-insured life annuities with leveraging as described in section 17.5 above. It would also include leveraged insured annuities which are owned individually. The key component is that both the life annuity and the life insurance be assigned to a lender and that the borrowing which is repayable on death of the life insured/annuitant be made on or after March 21, 2013.

Clarification of the extent of "grandfathering" for existing arrangements that would otherwise meet the definition of an LIA where all borrowings were entered into before March 21, 2013 has been sought in industry submissions. For example, transactions involving an existing loan such as: renewal for another term with the same lender on similar terms and conditions; replacement or refinancing with another loan from a new lender on similar terms and conditions; resetting the interest rate on an existing loan at the end of a term are matters that it is hoped may be clarified either in the final legislation or explanatory notes.

Industry submissions also request clarification that changes relating to the life insurance not impact "grandfathering" from the LIA rules. Such things as replacement of the life insurance policy that is assigned to the lender or exercising policy provisions that increase or decrease coverage or modify the original policy in some manner are the subject of requests for clarification.

It should be noted that since the "LIA policy" definition requires both the annuity and the life insurance policy be used as collateral security for the borrowing, providing just the annuity or the life insurance as collateral security would not meet the definition. Also, having an annuity and a life insurance policy with no borrowing (i.e. insured annuities and corporate-insured annuities as described in sections 17.2–17.4) would also not be caught by the "LIA policy" definition.

The budget documents indicated that the government will monitor to see if structures or transactions are developed to undermine the effectiveness of the proposed measures. It stated that in respect of LIAs, that if this type of activity does occur, the government will determine if further legislative action is warranted, with possible restrospective application. Does this statement require that all structures clearly not caught by the measures be raised with the Department of Finance to confirm that this omission was intended? Industry submissions have expressed the concern that this statement is problematic since there is little guidance that allows one to determine precisely what structures and changes in tax consequences would undermine the effectiveness of the measure.

In addition, clarification was requested that the LIA rules would no longer apply to a policy which meets the definition if, for example, the loan is repaid or if the annuity or life insurance policy ceases to be used as collateral security for the loan.

C. — What are the consequences of being an LIA policy?

The budget documents state that the intention of the LIA measures is to improve the integrity and fairness of the tax system by eliminating multiple and unintended tax benefits arising from them. To this end, the following tax consequences result if a life insurance policy meets the definition of an LIA policy: no collateral life insurance deduction; no capital dividend account credit for the death benefit; valuation of the annuity at essentially its purchase price; and treatment of the life insurance policy as a non-exempt policy. Each of these will be dealt with in turn.

No collateral life insurance deduction will be allowed under paragraph 20(1)(e.2) of the Act. This is accomplished by a proposed amendment to subparagraph (i) excluding premiums under an LIA policy. The impact of this would mean that the cash flow benefits from the collateral life insurance deduction would no longer arise.

The capital dividend account of a private corporation will not be increased by the death benefit received from an LIA policy. This is accomplished by adding the words "other than an LIA policy" in the portion of paragraph (d) of the definition "capital dividend account" in subsection 89(1) of the Act at subparagraph (ii). This would appear to deny a credit to the CDA for the entire death benefit even if only a portion of a life insurance policy considered to be an LIA is used as collateral security.

For purposes of the deemed disposition on death under subsection 70(5) of the Act, the fair market value of the annuity contract assigned to the lender in connection with an LIA policy will be deemed to equal the premium paid (i.e. purchase price) of the annuity contract. Proposed subsection 70(5.31) provides as follows:

> For the purposes of subsections (5) and 104(4), the fair market value at any time of any property deemed to have been disposed of at that time as a consequence of a particular individual's death is to be determined as though the fair market value at that time of any annuity contract were the total of all amounts each of which is the amount of a premium paid on or before that time under the contract if (a) the contract is, in respect of an LIA policy, a contract referred to in subparagraph (b)(ii) of the definition "LIA policy" in subsection 248(1) [i.e. the life annuity]; and (b) the particular individual is the individual, in respect of the LIA policy, referred to in that subparagraph [i.e. the annuitant under the life annuity contract].

Industry submissions have requested that the value take into account the fact that annuity payments would have been received throughout the life of the annuitant which would have returned a portion of the original capital to the holder, and thereby should reduce the value of the annuity for these purposes. The capital returned would contribute to the value of a corporation holding the annuity. Deeming that the purchase price be used to value the annuity was viewed as double-counting if no adjustment were made. Of interest is that this subsection would only apply in relation to an LIA policy and not a life insurance policy that is part of a non-leveraged corporate insured annuity. As noted above in section 17.4.C.ii, it is unclear whether the existence of this provision would clarify the application of subsection 70(5.3) of the Act to determining the fair market value of the annuity in respect of a non-leveraged corporate insured annuity.

The life insurance policy will be treated as a non-exempt policy (*Income Tax Act* Regulation 306(1) dealing with the meaning of "exempt policy" for purposes of the accrual rules would exclude an LIA policy) and thereby subject to accrual taxation under subsection 12.2(1) of the Act. Amendments to the *Income Tax Act* Regulations relating to an insurer's obligation to make an information return are also proposed. These amendments (proposed *Income Tax Act* Regulation 201(5.1)) require that for the insurer to do the accrual reporting in respect of an LIA policy for a calendar year that the insurer be notified in writing before the end of the calendar year by, or on behalf of, the policyholder that the policy is an LIA policy. Also, there is an obligation to provide accrual tax reporting in respect of a calendar year if "it is reasonable to conclude that the insurer knew, or ought to have known, before the end of the calendar year, that the policy is an LIA policy".

Industry submissions request that this measure be removed entirely. The machinery of exempt testing and compliance is complex. It is not as easy as it sounds to actually implement and it is not anticipated that there would be significant revenue gains derived from this measure in any event.

The budget proposals do not impact interest deductibility. If the measures are enacted as proposed, this would mean that interest on borrowed money in circumstances where the definition of an LIA policy is met would continue to be deductible. See section 17.5.C.ii for a full discussion of issues relating to interest deductibility and corporate leveraged insured annuities.

D. — Summary

As a result of the 2013 federal budget measures, the main tax benefits of leveraged insured annuities have been eliminated. As a result, one would not willingly structure their affairs to meet the definition of an LIA policy. Also, care must be taken to ensure that one is not inadvertently caught by the LIA policy definition and thus in a situation where tax benefits such as the collateral life insurance deduction or a capital dividend account credit for life insurance death benefit proceeds are lost.

17.7 — Insured Annuities in the Charitable Context

As noted above, insured annuity strategies generally provide enhanced after-tax cash flows, whether individually or corporately owned. Strategies have been developed where the additional cash flow is simply gifted to charity thereby allowing the policyholder to fund a yearly charitable gift. Referring to the example shown previously in section 17.2, the individual increased the net cash flow by $2,135 by opting for an insured annuity over a 4 percent term deposit. This excess cash flow could also be used in whole or in part to fund a life insurance policy for the benefit of a charitable organization thereby providing for a sizeable gift (see Chapter 12 for comments on life insurance and charitable giving).

Another example of the use of this strategy for charitable giving is with a leveraged insured annuity before March 21, 2013 as described above at section 17.5. To the extent the corporation can generate a positive after-tax cash flow, after taking into account the annuity income, interest expense, insurance premium and income taxes, the excess cash flow can be used to fund the shareholder's own private foundation. In this example, in addition to the risks involved (as more fully described in section

17.5) care would have had to have been taken in structuring the transactions in order to provide the desired results.

17.8 — Conclusion

Insured annuities are a combination of a life annuity contract providing a stream of capital and income for life, and a life insurance policy which returns the initial capital sum invested in the annuity at death to the estate or named beneficiaries. This combination represents an attractive alternative investment vehicle for older-aged individuals when compared to interest bearing investments. This structure can be implemented in a corporate, trust, or charitable context and prior to March 21, 2013 may also have been combined with leverage.

18 — Taxation of Structured Settlements

Updated by Rita Levato, B.A., LL.B., CSSC

18.1 — Introduction

Viewed from the perspective of those outside the casualty insurance industry or legal profession, a structured settlement is merely a particular form of annuity used in the resolution of personal injury cases. All of the features of a conventional annuity are in place along with some which are special and peculiar due to the tax status of the payments contemplated by the funding annuity.

From the perspective of those involved in the process, the structured settlement is an alternative to the conventional onetime payment of compensation for personal injury or death. The scheme of periodic payments is a relatively recent innovation in the law of personal injury compensation. This is largely due to the historical position within the common law system that damages are paid on a once and for all basis. The policy reasons for the traditional position have more to do with offering the parties finality than they do with the lump sum settlement being a particularly well-adapted compensation mode taking the interest of the injured party into account. Structured settlements offer a number of advantages over lump sum payments particularly in the area of their tax treatment and the social benefits offered to the injured party.

18.2 — Taxation of the Plaintiff

By way of background, the general tax treatment accorded to personal injury damages has been to regard them as being a payment on account of capital rather than income. The leading case in this regard is *R. v. Jennings* (1966), 57 D.L.R. (2d) 644 (S.C.C.). The *Jennings* decision establishes the principle that when a person is injured, he or she does not lose income but rather the ability to earn income. This latter is then treated as a capital asset which he or she has lost. An analogy may be made between the loss of an insured chattel which would result in a payment of the insured value of that chattel which, one hopes, puts the insured party in the same position he or she would have been in before the loss. As the payment is designed to compensate the injured party, so far as money can, his or her position is neither hurt nor enhanced by the transaction and therefore no tax is payable arising out of the payment. There has been much discussion of the merits of that position but such discussion is beyond the scope of this chapter.[1]

The structured settlement as currently used in Canada, the United States, Australia, the United Kingdom and parts of Europe represents a minor extension of the tax-exempt principle of the lump sum payment. If the periodic payment scheme conforms with a series of technical requirements, then those payments will retain their character as damages and will not attract income tax in the hands of the recipient notwithstanding that there is an interest element inherent in each payment. One searches in vain in the *Income Tax Act* for statutory authority for that proposition. The only authority, apart from a great number of advance income tax rulings, is archived Interpretation Bulletin IT-365R2 "Damages, Settlements and Similar Receipts," dated May 8, 1987. Unfortunately, the bulletin deals not only with damages for personal injury or death but also other transactions so that one must be careful when reading IT-365R2 to avoid confusion with other topics. Specifically, paragraph 2 delineates the heads of damage that an injured party may receive on a tax-exempt basis. Paragraph 3, entitled "Awards Not Considered to be Annuities" is crucial in that it states that, notwithstanding that the funding vehicle for the structured settlement is an annuity, the periodic payments themselves are not to be considered annuity payments for income tax purposes provided that the contract has not been purchased by the taxpayer (injured person) or someone on the taxpayer's behalf. This represents a radical departure from the general tax treatment of annuity payments.

18.3 — Social Benefit

Lest one think that the CRA has created a massive loophole through which tens of thousands of persons may be saving vast amounts of income tax by investing in structured settlements, the definition of those who qualify for preferred tax treatment and under what circumstances is quite restrictive. First, the CRA has defined the term "personal injury" rather narrowly. It could be argued that a person sustains personal injury by virtue of being libelled or slandered. However, the CRA's position is that personal injury means a physical injury, not injury to one's feelings or reputation. Similarly, damages for breach of contract or for wrongful dismissal do not qualify as personal injuries so far as IT-365R2 is concerned.

Paragraph 5 of IT-365R2 goes on to define how an annuity qualifies as a structured settlement. In addition to the requirement that the amounts being paid must be in respect of a claim for personal injury or death, the party with the obligation to provide the payments, (normally the defendant's insurer), must acquire a single premium annuity contract which contract must be non-assignable, non-commutable, and non-transferable to provide payments on account of the agreed upon obligation. The payments are irrevocably directed to the injured party and, most signifi-

[1] See Cooper-Stephenson and Saunders, *Personal Injury Damages in Canada*, 2nd ed. (Toronto: Carswell, 1996), pp. 50 to 56.

cantly, the at-fault party or at-fault party's insurer must remain liable for the payments set out in the annuity contract.

The reason for these particular requirements is to protect the integrity of the structured settlement system. The Settlement Agreement, however configured, must provide that the wrongdoer, or the wrongdoer's insurer or the assignee of either of them, has an ongoing obligation to make periodic payments to the injured party. The Agreement simply sets out that in consideration for the injured party agreeing to terminate his or her rights against the wrongdoer or the wrongdoer's insurer or other parties, those parties agree to provide certain benefits. Almost invariably there is a requirement that cash be paid in addition to the periodic payment scheme along with costs or other expenses incurred by the plaintiff in the litigation. For purposes of securing the favourable tax treatment accorded the structured settlement, the key element is that the wrongdoer, wrongdoer's insurer or assignee agrees to make periodic payments and to fund that obligation by acquiring an annuity contract. Technically, there would not be any great difficulty in the wrongdoer agreeing simply to make payments on an agreed upon schedule. In practical terms, very few plaintiffs would be content to rely upon the covenant to pay of the wrongdoer or wrongdoer's insurer. In the result, for all practical purposes, the only long term funding vehicle for personal injury or death cases is the annuity. The annuity, so far as the scheme is concerned, is merely the asset that the wrongdoer or those representing the wrongdoer use to fund the obligation to the injured party. The owner has all of the incidents of ownership save and except that payments are directed irrevocably to the injured party.

Seen in that light, the technical requirements of the scheme make nothing but good sense. For example, a single premium annuity contract is important from the standpoint of the injured party to make sure that the obligation has been completely funded. Since the wrongdoer or the wrongdoer's representative owns the annuity contract, it is imperative that the contract not be commutable to prevent the owner from taking the cash value of the contract. Similarly, the provisions with respect to the irrevocable direction also protect the interests of the injured party. The fact that the annuity contract is non-assignable and non-transferable ensures that the obligation remains that of the party originally liable or assuming liability pursuant to an appropriate assignment of liability.

One part of the scheme which has caused certain property/casualty insurers concern is the provision contained in subparagraph 5(c)(iii) of IT-365R2 which requires the insurer or other party to remain liable for the periodic payments notwithstanding the acquisition of the annuity contract. Should the life insurance company issuing the annuity contract fail, then the owner of the contract must step in and make up any shortfall, as it remains liable to make the periodic payments. A number of property/casualty insurers have expressed concerns about assuming what may be very long-term liabilities. Indeed, traumatic injuries (which often impact younger individuals) almost invariably give rise to the use of a life annuity rather than a term certain annuity. As a result of the requirement of subparagraph 5(c)(iii) of IT-365R2, the obligation of the at-fault party's insurer may extend for 30, 40, or even 50 years or more into the future. This long-term liability raises legitimate concerns for the property/casualty insurers. As a result of these concerns, the concept of assignment has attracted a great deal of attention in recent years. Some of the implications in the process of assignment are described in detail below.

18.4 — Social Policy

Much of the foregoing deals with the technicalities and the concept of the periodic payment scheme. The practical implications of the tax-exempt scheme of payments together with the fact that the injured party may not accelerate any of the payments or call for the commutation of the contract, have some very significant benefits. There is much anecdotal evidence to suggest that persons who receive large amounts of money as settlements of personal injury cases or other sums from estates or lotteries and the like, have a high propensity to dissipate these funds. One can well imagine the young person receiving a large amount of money and treating it contemptuously since all that life can offer him or her for the loss of all of the usual expectations of life is money which anyone would acknowledge is a very poor substitute. Many people (and young people in particular) dissipate their damages in a distressingly quick fashion. Others dissipate their damages through lack of financial sophistication or bad advice. The result is unfortunate for all concerned. The injured party had been provided with capital sufficient to allow her to look after herself and live in dignity. If the compensation is dissipated she would have no way of recouping the loss and would likely become dependent upon the community. In a sense, the broader community ends up compensating twice: the first time through the loss distribution scheme, the second through social assistance. As the structured settlement provides a locked-in and guaranteed scheme of payment, the risks of investment are eliminated and the recipient is provided with a secure source of tax-free income.

Of equal importance is the fact that the structured settlement, as a financial vehicle, may have built into it a great many features which can respond to the particular circumstances and needs of the injured party. These may include, for example, special payment schemes or income streams for specific needs including replacement of capital items from time to time as well as protection from inflation. Indeed, in the hands of someone experienced in the design of structured settlement annuity contracts, there are very few anticipated future needs that cannot be responded to appropriately within an adequately funded periodic payment scheme.

The periodic payment scheme offers vital protection against mortality risk. The model customarily used in personal injury compensation involves certain assumptions with respect to the life expectancy of the injured party. The use of a discount rate to achieve a present value of that future obligation of necessity involves using life expectancy as a determining criteria. Simply put, in the conventional lump sum payment scheme, should the injured party die when statistics indicate he will, then the self-exhausting fund principal will work perfectly. However, if he or she should live on beyond life expectancy, as determined by the trier of fact, then the self-exhausting fund will have been depleted and the injured party will find him or herself, in later life, without funds. In other words, in the conventional lump sum settlement, the risk of mortality is borne by the injured party.

In the case of the structured settlement, funded as it is by a life annuity, the risk of mortality is borne by the life insurance company issuing the annuity contract. This is an enormously important benefit of structured settlements which is very poorly understood even by many of those who routinely utilize structured settlements.

Further, in the conventional case, the trier of fact is frequently left with an unenviable task of trying to make a determination as to life expectancy. Naturally, the payor will argue that the life expectancy of the injured party is very brief indeed as this will result in a reduction in the discounted present value of the future expenses. The injured party, on the other hand, or those representing the injured party, will argue strenuously that his or her life expectancy is normal or near normal. The trier of fact then must make a determination between those two positions. All that can be said with certainty about that process is that the determination will be wrong.

Clearly no one can determine the life expectancy of any particular individual. In fairness to the defendant/payor, it is not in the public interest to punish that party by ordering it to make payments on the assumption that the injured party has a normal life expectancy where that life expectancy has been dramatically reduced.

Fortunately, the life insurance industry offers impaired life annuities which, while guaranteeing payment for the life of the injured party, also recognize that many traumatically injured people have a life expectancy which is shorter than that of their peers of the same age and sex. In the result, the cost to the wrongdoer or wrongdoer's insurer and to the broader community in general is reduced while still protecting the interests of the injured party by providing a term of payment for so long as he or she lives.

18.5 — Taxation of the Owner

As noted above, the recipient of the annuity payments is exempt from taxation of structured settlement payments under the provisions of IT-365R2. However, there are tax consequences of the annuity payments to the owner of the annuity.

ATR-40, dated March 18, 1991, requires casualty insurance companies to recognize the ongoing liability implicit in the structured settlement process and to maintain a reserve. The ruling sets out the exact method of determining those amounts.

As described above, the annuity is an asset of the owner which, in the usual course, is accounted for as such. While a discussion of the taxation of property/casualty insurers is beyond the scope of this chapter, a simple overview of the owner's tax position is in order. Under factor E in the formula under Regulation 1400(3) of the *Income Tax Act*, insurers may claim a reserve for future liabilities. In this regard, insurers are different from other entities in that they can set up an amount representing their obligation in the future and shelter an equal amount for income tax purposes. Under factor E in the formula under the provisions of Regulation 1400(3), the cost of the annuity, that is, the single premium paid to acquire the annuity, is set up as a reserve for future liabilities: namely, the obligation to make the agreed upon scheme of periodic payments to the injured party. In that way, while the insurer may not writeoff the cost of the annuity as an expense in the year in which the contract is acquired, it does receive tax credit.

On the other hand, the casualty insurer is the owner of an asset that produces interest income. This interest income is taxable in the hands of the insurer which would appear to put the insurer in an adverse tax position. However, the insurer has an ongoing obligation to the injured party so that amounts paid under the annuity may be deducted from the insurer's income as an expense in the year of payment. As the annuity payment is a blend of interest and return of capital, the tax deduction in a year will exceed the amount of interest income received and therefore the amount of the reserve in the following year is reduced accordingly. The annual write-down of the reserve is not universally the case as many structured settlements involve a deferral of all or part of the income to later years. In those situations, the amount of the reserve may increase for some period of years before beginning to decrease. However, the owner is not left in a net tax payable position.

18.6 — Assignment

Reference was made earlier in the chapter to the concept of assignment. There are a number of entities which resist, for a variety of reasons, accepting liability for periodic payment schemes where those liabilities may extend far into the future. To assist those entities and, more particularly, to make the benefits of the structured settlement available to as many injured people as possible, a scheme was designed whereby the at-fault party could, under certain very restricted circumstances, assign its liability for the periodic payment, along with the ownership of the structured settlement annuity contract used to fund the obligation, to a third party. In the result, the at-fault party or at-fault party's insurer has no ongoing liability for the periodic payment scheme once the obligation has been assumed by the assignee. At that point the assignee has simply stepped into the shoes of the at-fault party or at-fault party's insurer and has all of the duties and obligations and rights that the original defendant had.

18.7 — Financial Reporting

The Office of the Superintendent of Financial Institutions (OSFI) requires disclosure in the notes to the financial statements of the structured settlement annuities owned by the property/casualty insurer in its Accounting Guideline D-5, dated April 1998. Similarly, the minimum capital test (MCT) requires a nominal capital appropriation to account for the (negligible) contingent liability of the property/casualty insurer who owns the structured settlement annuity.

The Superintendent faces conflicting objectives of attempting to ensure adequate levels of capital so that property/casualty insurers are able to meet their obligations while not burdening these companies with excessive requirements.

18.8 — Practical Application

From the standpoint of litigants, there are a number of situations which tend to favour the use of a structured settlement. The tax benefit is perhaps the most obvious advantage of a structured settlement with the greatest benefit not surprisingly being achieved in those cases where large amounts are being awarded. In many instances, the very largest cases involve substantial amounts for care of the injured party. Where the injured party is prevented from continuing employment, the lost income can also be very large. The invested proceeds of these large settlements could place the injured party in a high marginal tax bracket such that the tax benefit associated with the annuity may be substantial indeed. If one assumes a top marginal tax bracket and the need for the injured party to invest funds on a conservative basis, then the use of a structured settlement could double the after-tax income of a like amount awarded conventionally.

Security of the income is the one issue surrounding structured settlements which probably is least considered and yet for those who have been receiving structured settlement payments for an extended period of time may be the greatest reported benefit. Severely injured people face enormous challenges in their day to day lives. The very simple acts which most people take for granted present major challenges to those who are dependent upon others in every part of their daily routines. Severly injured people face more challenges than most people can imagine and they need all of their available energy to cope with the stresses of day to day living without having to worry about investment decisions for which they may be ill prepared by background or expertise to deal. The consequences of inappropriate investment patterns by the severely disabled can be catastrophic to their lifestyle. Without a doubt, the fact that the annuity provides a well planned, predictable and guaranteed income stream materially enhances the quality of life of the severely injured.

The social benefits associated with structured settlements are particularly acute for young injured people. While children and young adults enjoy a tax exemption for damage payments received up to the end of the year in which they turn 21 under paragraph 81(1)(g.1) of the *Income Tax Act*, they are entitled to demand and to receive the full principal amount of their damages at the date of their majority, putting them at a very high risk of dissipating their awards.

18.9 — Disadvantages of the Structured Settlement

While the structured settlement offers a number of important benefits, there are certain disadvantages which those receiving structured settlements or contemplating the receipt of structured settlements must recognize. Before the annuity is issued, there is a great deal of flexibility in terms of the design which, when used properly, can respond to a great range of anticipated needs. The downside is that once the annuity has been implemented, it is not possible to make any changes. Thus, the annuity is inflexible should the circumstances and needs of the plaintiff change subsequent to acquisition of the annuity.

A traditional disadvantage of the structured settlement has been the risk of inflation. That is to say annuity contracts are issued on the basis of interest assumptions current at the time of purchase. Where interest rates increase dramatically, invariably as a result of increasing levels of inflation, the recipient suffers with a corresponding reduction in purchasing power. However, the use of annuities linked to the Consumer Price Index mitigates this risk.

18.10 — Benefits to the Payor

There are significant benefits to the use of structured settlements to the injured party. However, the process requires the participation of the at-fault party, or the at-fault party's insurer, to guarantee compliance with the requirements of the CRA. Absent that participation, the provisions of IT-365R2 regarding ownership would not be complied with and the interest portion of the payments would be taxed in the usual course as annuity payments.

This, of course, creates an opportunity for sharing of benefits between the recipient and the payor. Simply put, the payor will spend less money to resolve the issues between the parties using a structured settlement due to the benefits conferred upon the plaintiff. Since there is no tax component to the injured party in the structured settlement, there need be no gross-up for the incidents of future taxation in respect of a periodic payment scheme for lost benefits in the case of a fatal accident or for future care and the like, in a personal injury situation. Since the management of large sums of money is often beyond the capability of people, many cases involve an award to provide the injured party with funds to retain investment counsel. In the case of a periodic payment scheme, the management of the investment is provided by the life insurance company, thus eliminating the need for any additional payment in this regard. As discussed above, the annuity recognizes that traumatically injured people frequently have a life expectancy which is shorter than that of their peers. The cost to provide a given level of benefit for the life of the recipient is therefore reduced.

Finally, the discount method of calculating future damages uses a statutory fixed rate. The discount rate is generally designed to reflect a true yield on funds (the nominal rate of interest less the rate of inflation). Where the true yield on an annuity is higher than the discount rate, the cost of providing benefits is lower than would be the case under the discount method. In effect, the discount rate is higher using the annuity and therefore the cost is reduced correspondingly.

In Ontario, *Roberts v. Morana* (1997), 37 O.R. (3d) 333 (Gen. Div.); affirmed (2000), 49 O.R. (3d) 157 (C.A.), the court found that the appropriate method of awarding damages consists of applying the statutory discount rate to reach a discounted present value. One then uses the amount so calculated as the funding amount for a structured settlement. However, section 116.1 of the *Courts of Justice Act*, R.S.O. 1990, c. C.43, as amended, makes substantial changes in matters involving medical malpractice. In the result, the plaintiff will either be under- or overcompensated, depending upon whether the annuity produces a net real rate of return of less than or greater than the discount rate.

18.11 — Conclusion

The structured settlement is a financial package, designed to meet the particular needs of an injured person. It responds to those needs using a variety of different income streams either in fixed terms or for the life of the injured party with various levels of indexing, guarantee periods and the like. From a tax perspective, the scheme is quite simple in that the injured party/payee receives payments on a tax-exempt basis as representing payments on account of damages that are characterized as capital rather than income. For the owner of the contract, the annuity is taxed accordingly but, as the payments being made to the injured party are an expense to the owner of the contract, there is, in effect, "a wash" entry subject to the downward adjustment in each period of the capital value of the annuity contract in the form of a reserve. In the result, neither the injured party nor the owner is left in a net tax payable position. However, section 116.1 of the *Courts of Justice Act*, R.S.O. 1990, c. C.43, as amended, makes substantial changes in matters involving medical malpractice.

The use of periodic payments appears to constitute a "win-win" solution to a complex problem. The injured party is benefited by receiving tax-exempt payments designed to meet his or her particular needs in a secure scheme which will provide benefits for so long as he or she lives. From the standpoint of the payor, generally the at-fault party's insurer, structured settlements are achieved at a more favourable cost given the elimination of the tax component, the elimination of a management fee, the recognition of impaired mortality, and real interest rates higher than the conventional discount rate.

The public interest is also advanced by virtue of the fact that the scheme reduces the cost of liability insurance by reducing the cost to the insurer which, ultimately, finds its way through the marketplace to the general public. Further, by eliminating the risk that an injured party will dissipate the damages award, the burden on the social welfare system is reduced.

19 — SEGREGATED FUNDS

Updated by Jason Giuricich, B.B.A., C.P.A., C.A.

19.1 — Introduction

A segregated fund consists of a specific group of investments managed by a life insurance company and notionally held separate and apart from its general reserves. The investments held in a segregated fund may include equities, bonds, mortgages, or any combination of these and other types of investments.

Under a segregated fund policy a portion of the premiums paid by the policyholder is invested in units of the segregated fund. The number of units that may be purchased for a given premium will depend on the current unit value of the fund which is determined by dividing the current value of the investments in the fund by the number of units outstanding. The number of units allocated to the policy will determine the allocation of fund income to the policyholder, and the value of such units will determine the amount that will be paid to the policyholder upon his or her death, or on the surrender or maturity of the policy.

19.2 — Segregated Funds versus Mutual Funds in General

While the fluctuation of fund values described above is similar to that inside a mutual fund trust, a segregated fund is not a trust and the insurer, in notionally segregating specific assets from its general reserves, is not acting as a trustee. Instead, segregated fund policyholders receive trust-like treatment through a prior claim on the segregated assets ranking above those of the insurer's general creditors and, as will be discussed below, a treatment similar to that of trusts under the *Income Tax Act*.

There are other important distinctions to be made between mutual funds and segregated funds. First, segregated fund policies invariably provide for a minimum 75 percent guarantee of the return of premiums upon maturity of the contract or the death of the life insured. In fact, there is the potential to see guarantees as high as 100 percent where certain fund-specific requirements are met. Mutual funds, however, carry no such guarantee on their deposits. Under provincial securities legislation, segregated fund policies which provide a minimum 75 percent guarantee on the return of premiums upon maturity fall outside the definition of securities and are not subject to the usual prospectus requirements. Segregated fund policies are therefore regulated under provincial insurance regulation rather than under securities legislation.

Second, since segregated fund policies are considered to be life insurance contracts for purposes of provincial insurance legislation, beneficiaries can be named. Where appropriate beneficiary designations are made, a segregated fund can enjoy the same enhanced protection from creditors during the owner's lifetime, as well as the exemption from probate fees and other estate costs upon the death of the life insured, as is available with any life insurance policy. For a discussion of creditor protection see section 5.3.A. Investments in mutual funds, on the other hand, can be seized by creditors. At death a personally-owned non-registered mutual fund investment would be included in the estate of the deceased owner and would be subject to applicable probate fees and other estate costs.

19.3 — Taxation of Segregated Funds

A segregated fund is treated as an *inter vivos* trust for tax purposes (paragraph 138.1(1)(a) of the Act). The insurer is deemed to be the trustee who has ownership or control of the related segregated fund trust (subparagraph 138.1(1)(c)(i)) and the policyholders are considered the beneficiaries of the deemed segregated fund trust. However, unlike a trust, including a mutual fund trust, a segregated fund never has any taxable income in a year as it is deemed for tax purposes to annually distribute all of its income (including capital gains and capital losses to policyholders (paragraph 138.1(1)(f) and subsection 138.1(3) of the Act). While allocations are usually done annually, they can be more frequent, for example quarterly.

The Act does not specify how a segregated fund must allocate its income, only that the allocation must be reasonable. Some segregated funds allocate their income to policyholders based on the concept of time-weighted units while others use an allocation date method similar to mutual fund trusts (see section 19.11 for a discussion of this distribution date-like method). A time-weighted unit is calculated by multiplying the number of units times the number of weeks, for example, that the units were owned during the year. A policyholder who owns units at any time during the year will, therefore, hold time-weighted units and will be entitled to receive a proportional allocation of the segregated fund's income or losses. Mutual fund trusts generally distribute income only to unitholders of record on the distribution date.

The distinction between a segregated fund's deemed allocation to policyholders and a mutual fund trust's actual distribution to unit-holders is important to the mechanics of the investment. In both cases, unit values are increased as income accumulates, such as when dividends are declared on stocks and interest accrues on debt instruments held by the fund. However, when the accumulated income is allocated to the policyholder of a segregated fund, the number of units held by the policyholder does not change, nor does the total value of the fund. In the case of a mutual fund trust, distributed income decreases the unit value; however, the distributed income is generally used to purchase additional units of the mutual fund. Therefore, since the unit value decreases but the number of units increases, the total value of the fund remains the same. In either case, however, value received by the investor will be equal.

It should be noted that while a segregated fund is required to allocate all of its income to policyholders, a mutual fund trust has the option of retaining income. However, any income retained within a mutual fund trust will be taxed at the highest marginal rate. Therefore, mutual funds normally make distributions to unitholders so that the income can be taxed at the rates applicable to the unitholders.

The property of a segregated fund is deemed to be the property of a separate segregated fund trust and not the property of the insurer (paragraph 138.1(1)(b) of the Act). However, to the extent that the segregated fund has not been funded with premiums paid under a segregated fund policy, as would happen when "seed" money is infused into the fund at its inception, the insurer is deemed to have an interest in the fund (paragraph 138.1(1)(d)). The insurer could, therefore, also realize investment income from the segregated fund due to allocations of income proportional to its own interest.

19.4 — Taxation of Income Earned in the Fund

As noted above, the income of a segregated fund is deemed to be payable to policyholders on an annual basis (but can be more frequent, such as quarterly) and is subject to tax in their hands. The amount of income payable to each policyholder will depend on the number of units allocated to the policy.

Since the segregated fund is treated as a trust for tax purposes, the insurer can make the appropriate designations under section 104 of the Act to ensure that the income earned by the fund will retain its character when allocated to the policyholders. For example, dividends received by the segregated fund from taxable Canadian corporations will, in the case of individual policyholders, qualify for the dividend gross-up and tax credit mechanism, and "eligible dividends" will retain their character. Also, 50 percent of capital gains earned by the segregated fund will be taxable capital gains of the policyholder. In the case of corporate policyholders, the ability to receive dividends without being subject to tax under Part I, is retained, although Part IV tax may apply. Non-taxable dividends received by the segregated fund can be allocated tax-free to the policyholders as well.

A segregated fund can also allocate capital losses incurred in the year to policyholders (subsection 138.1(3) of the Act). This treatment of capital losses differs from that of other trusts, and in particular mutual fund trusts, which cannot allocate such losses to unit holders. Capital losses allocated to segregated fund policyholders are, therefore, available to offset capital gains from the disposition of other property and can be carried back three years and carried forward indefinitely.

19.5 — Disposition of an Interest in a Segregated Fund Policy

Unlike other types of contracts issued by life insurance companies, a segregated fund is considered capital property under subparagraph 39(1)(a)(iii) of the Act and any gain or loss on its disposition will give rise to a capital gain or a capital loss.

A disposition of an interest in a segregated fund policy will result where a policyholder switches between funds offered under the same contract, surrenders his or her interest in the policy, exercises a maturity option under the policy, or dies.

The adjusted cost base of a policyholder's interest in a segregated fund policy is equal to the total of all premiums paid plus income and capital gains allocated to the policyholder, less acquisition fees (discussed below) and capital losses allocated to the policyholder (paragraphs 53(1)(l) and 53(2)(q) of the Act).

The adjusted cost base and fair market value of a policyholder's interest in a fund is unlikely to be the same since the fund will own assets with accrued gains or losses.

Where the fund owns assets with unrealized gains, there is the potential for double taxation. For example, if a policyholder disposes of an interest in a segregated fund he or she will realize a gain to the extent that the fair market value of the policyholder's interest in the fund (including the unrealized gain) exceeds the adjusted cost base of the interest. The potential for double taxation will arise when the fund itself disposes of the asset with the accrued gain; this gain will be allocated to the remaining policyholders, and will be taxed in their hands. In order to avoid this result, the insurer may elect under subsection 138.1(4) of the Act to treat any capital property in the fund as having been disposed of for any amount between the fair market value and the adjusted cost base of the property. The capital gain resulting from this deemed disposition is allocated to the policyholder withdrawing from the fund to the extent that the gain relates to his or her interest in the fund. In turn, the property is deemed to have been reacquired by the fund at a cost equal to its proceeds of disposition. The net result is that the policyholder includes the gain resulting from the deemed disposition in his or her income, but no gain will be realized when the policyholder withdraws from the fund. In addition, the remaining policyholders will not be taxed on the gain attributable to the withdrawing policyholder's interest in the fund, since the accrued gain has been realized and allocated to the withdrawing policyholder.

In some instances, the exchange of segregated fund units can be considered a disposition for tax purposes. In technical interpretation 2006-0174091E5, dated October 24, 2006, the CRA indicated that the exchange of segregated funds units with back-end load fees for segregated fund units without such fees would be considered a disposition for tax purposes. Any gain realized from the disposition of the interest would be treated as a capital gain under subparagraph 39(1)(a)(iii) of the Act.

19.6 — Acquisition Fees

The acquisition fee for a segregated fund policy is defined at subsection 138.1(6) of the Act to include any portion of the premium paid under the policy that is not invested in the fund, or that is used to fund a death or maturity benefit. Acquisition fees would therefore include commissions and surrender charges payable upon the early termination of the policy.

The acquisition fee for a segregated fund policy is not deductible when the policy is acquired, nor is it added to the adjusted cost base of the policy (i.e. the adjusted cost base is less than the premium paid.) The acquisition fee is instead treated as a capital loss at the time the policyholder disposes of his or her interest in the fund, and will reduce the capital gain, or increase the capital loss, realized by the policyholder on the disposition of his or her interest in the fund.

19.7 — Investment Management Fees Charged to the Fund

Annual investment management fees are charged to a segregated fund. Generally, these fees will not be deductible by the policyholders of the fund. Instead, these amounts are usually considered a fund expense and will be set off against the income of the fund before allocations of income are made to the policyholders. This puts the policyholder in the same position as if he or she had been able to deduct a *pro rata* portion of the investment management fees.

19.8 — Interest Deductibility

Paragraph 20(1)(c) of the Act generally allows a deduction for interest on money borrowed for the purpose of earning property or business income. However, this subparagraph specifically denies any deduction where the borrowed funds were used to purchase an interest in a life insurance policy. The definition of "life insurance policy" under subsection 138(12) of the Act includes segregated funds.

Subsection 20(2.2) of the Act allows an exception to the definition of a "life insurance policy" for segregated fund annuity contracts. Therefore, interest on money borrowed to purchase a segregated fund annuity contract will be subject to the usual rules governing interest deductibility.

19.9 — Segregated Funds as Registered Investments

A segregated fund policy that is registered as or owned by plans such as a registered retirement savings plan, a registered retirement income fund, or a registered pension plan is not subject to the rules discussed otherwise in this chapter. Instead, any income or gains within the segregated fund policy will accrue on a tax-deferred basis until withdrawn from the registered plan.

Starting in 2009, a segregated fund policy can also be registered as, or owned by, a tax-free savings account. As with other registered plans, any income or gains within the segregated fund policy will accrue on a tax-deferred basis; however, contributions are not deductible and withdrawals are tax-free.

Prior to the 2005 federal budget, investments held in registered plans were normally restricted to a 30 percent foreign property content, or face penalties of 1 percent per month on the foreign content in excess of that limit. Due to an anomaly in the Act segregated funds historically were not subject to the foreign property restrictions. Starting with a press release on December 19, 1996, the Department of Finance had indicated that it sought to apply foreign property limits to segregated fund registered investments. These proposals were never finalized. Now, with the elimination of the foreign property limits generally, these proposals will not be enacted. The foreign property content limits have been entirely eliminated by Bill C-43 *An Act to implement certain provisions of the budget tabled in Parliament on February 23, 2005*, which received Royal Assent on June 29, 2005. This repealed Part XI of the Act (which addressed foreign property penalties for registered plans) and is applicable to months that end after 2004.

19.10 — Residency, Segregated Funds and Withholding Taxes

An insurer is deemed by subparagraph 138.1(1)(c)(ii) of the Act to be resident in Canada in respect of any segregated fund property used or held by it in the course of carrying on a life insurance business in Canada. Where the insurer is deemed to be a resident of Canada, a non-resident purchaser of an interest in a segregated fund which in turn holds its assets in Canada, will be subject to withholding taxes on any allocations of interest or dividends from the segregated fund. Any capital gains of the segregated fund will not be subject to withholding tax.

Conversely, an insurer is deemed to be non-resident in respect of any segregated fund property not used or held by it in the course of carrying on a life insurance business in Canada and non-resident in respect of any other related segregated fund property (subparagraph 138.1(1)(c)(iii) of the Act). In this case, a non-resident purchaser of an interest in a segregated fund with its assets outside Canada will not be subject to any tax withholding in respect of allocations of interest or dividends, even though the insurer is for all other purposes a resident of Canada.

19.11 — "Fund on Fund" Segregated Funds

As noted earlier, a segregated fund consists of a specific group of investments managed by a life insurance company and notionally held separate and apart from its general reserves. The investments held in a segregated fund typically include equities, bonds, mortgages, money market deposits and so forth as determined by the manager of the segregated fund within the guidelines set out by the fund's description. The types of investments are similar to those that may be held within mutual funds.

An innovation in segregated funds has been the arrival of funds referred to as "Fund on Fund" investments or "Guaranteed Investment Funds" (GIFs). The assets of the GIF are comprised of units of a particular mutual fund. A GIF is best described as a fund of funds and is a hybrid of the traditional form of segregated funds and mutual funds, offering advantages of both.

GIFs are segregated funds and offer the same guarantees and protection from both claims of creditors and the application of probate fees and other estate costs as any other segregated fund. The policyholders of these segregated funds still receive an annual allocation of the income or losses from the funds based on the flow-through principle. However, the way in which the income is allocated can vary from that of a traditional segregated fund.

As noted earlier, the CRA has not set out the manner in which segregated fund income must be allocated, but rather requires that any allocation made must be reasonable. As described in section 19.3, in order to accommodate mid-year additions and redemptions of policyholders, some insurers have adopted a time-weighted unit principle so that allocations are made on a *pro rata* basis determined by the length of time the policyholder remains invested in the segregated fund.

Since mutual funds may distribute income annually or periodically throughout the year and net capital gains annually, a segregated fund holding units of a mutual fund will not be able to identify the nature of its income until after the distribution is made. In accordance with the CRA's requirement of reasonableness, a GIF insurer may use a unique hybrid allocation method (also known as the allocation date method), that draws from both segregated fund and mutual fund models. Under this model, the GIF policyholders of record at the allocation date (generally, year end or quarter end) will be allocated income or loss from the segregated fund since the last allocation date, regardless of when the units were purchased during the period. GIF policyholders who redeem their units during the period will not receive income allocations from the fund at the allocation date. Instead, policyholders who redeem mid-period will realize gains or losses on their investment based on any change in the unit value of the segregated fund at that time. This unit value is, of course, based on changes in the unit value of the underlying mutual fund investment. Gains or losses on redemption of units are reported on a form T3.

It should be noted that this hybrid allocation method, while reasonable under the circumstances, may not necessarily be adopted by all issuers offering this type of segregated fund. It is also possible that GIFs may be offered using the time-weighted allocation system of traditional segregated funds. Alternatively, insurers may adopt investment specific allocation and reporting methods based on the nature of the underlying mutual fund investment. For example, the allocation method described above differs for a GIF investment in a money market fund, since allocations from the money market fund are done daily, rather than annually.

19.12 — Guarantee Top-Up Payments

At the time of maturity of a segregated fund policy or on the death of the insured the policyholder or the beneficiary, respectively, is entitled to receive a top-up payment if the value of the policyholder's interest in the segregated fund is less than the guarantee amount. For example, assume an individual purchases an interest in a segregated fund for $100,000. The guarantee is 100 percent. The value of the fund declines to $90,000 at which time the policy matures or the owner, who is also the insured, dies. The policyholder or the owner's estate or a named beneficiary will receive $100,000; $90,000 being the value of the interest in the segregated fund at the time of maturity or death plus a $10,000 top-up payment. To the extent that the value of the investment falls to $90,000 at maturity or death, the owner will realize a $10,000 capital loss, 50 percent of which would be an allowable capital loss.

The tax treatment of the top-up payment is not clear under current tax legislation. Each life insurance company, therefore, applies their own interpretation to the Act in determining how they will report top-up payments. The trend for maturity and death benefit guarantee payments has been in favour of capital gains treatment.

In technical interpretations 9817165, dated February 18, 1999 and 9905255, dated June 17, 1999, the CRA was of the opinion that the payment should be treated as a capital gain. Similar conclusions were reached in technical interpretation 2001-0102235, dated May 13, 2002. The Department of Finance is reviewing this issue as part of a detailed review of all aspects of current segregated fund legislation.

19.13 — Guarantee Withdrawal Benefits

As noted above, it is generally accepted that guarantee top-up payments arising from segregated fund policies are taxable on capital account. For policies which offer guarantees on death or maturity, providing for a return of all or a portion of the originally contributed capital is a conceptually reasonable result. Upon death or maturity, the policyholder would generally expect to realize a capital loss where the value of the investment declined. The characterization of the guarantee payment as a capital gain would offset the capital losses realized on the surrender of the notional units underlying a variable annuity contract. However, recent innovations and product enhancements have introduced a type of segregated fund product to the Canadian marketplace which offers varying forms of guarantee minimum withdrawal benefits (GMWB). These guarantee withdrawal benefits differ conceptually from top-up payments. For example, these policies may provide for guarantee payments in excess of contributed capital. The taxation of such benefits is less clear than the taxation of traditional top-up payments.

These segregated fund policies are intended to provide policyholders with predictable, sustainable, and potentially increasing retirement income for a specific period of time or, for some products, for life. These policies offer all the regular benefits of segregated funds (discussed above) with the added benefit of a GMWB. The product is targeted towards individuals who want a minimum, steady retirement income without worrying about outliving their investment capital. At the same time, these investors want to have an opportunity to participate in potential investment gains which would result in an enhanced income stream or greater estate values.

The CRA's views of GMWB payments are uncertain. In response to a question posed at the CLHIA Taxation Officers Roundtable held in May, 2007 (indexed as 2007-0229731C6), the CRA stated that earlier positions taken with respect to the taxation of guarantee payments did not contemplate payments in excess of contributed capital (see, for example, technical interpretation 2001-0102235, dated May 13, 2002). As such, it is unclear how the CRA might assess guarantee payments made in excess of contributed capital. Nevertheless, industry practice has been to tax all guarantee payments which vary with respect to the value of a segregated fund on capital account by virtue of paragraph 138.1(1)(j) of the Act. Where guarantee payments continue after the value of investments in the underlying segregated fund have been fully withdrawn, it is not clear that reliance on this provision remains appropriate.

19.14 — Conclusion

With the advent of new types of segregated funds coupled with product enhancements, the advantages of segregated funds as insurance products remain and make them unique in the spectrum of investment products.

APPENDIX

Phase-out of income tax interpretation bulletins and ITTNs

The CRA has undertaken an initiative to introduce a new technical publication product, known as ***income tax folios****, to update the information currently found in the income tax interpretation bulletins and income tax technical news (ITTNs) and to introduce improved web functionality.*

On September 30, 2012, all previously archived income tax interpretation bulletins and previously archived ITTNs were cancelled and are no longer available on the CRA website. The remaining current income tax interpretation bulletins and ITTNs will continue to be available on the CRA website, but will be noted as archived, until the technical content is updated and published in an income tax folio. At that time the related interpretation bulletin(s) or ITTN(s) will be cancelled. It is expected that the update process will occur over a number of years.

Interpretation bulletins and ITTNs that have been replaced by income tax folios are identified in the Interpretation Bulletin – Income Tax Folio Table of Concordance: http://www.cra-arc.gc.ca/tx/tchncl/ncmtx/cncrdnc-eng.html.

INTERPRETATION BULLETINS

Interpretation Bulletin IT-66R6 — Capital Dividends

Date: **May 31, 1991**

Reference: ***Section 184, subsections 83(2) to (2.4), 89(1.1) and (1.2), paragraphs 89(1)(b) and (b.1)*(also section 14, subsection 212(2), paragraphs 87(2)(z.1) and 88(1)(e.2), subparagraph 40(1)(a)(iii) of the Act, and sections 2101 and 2106 of the Regulations)**

Application

This bulletin cancels and replaces Interpretation Bulletin IT-66R5 dated July 22, 1985.

Summary

This bulletin discusses the concept of capital dividends and the capital dividend account. The capital dividend account keeps track of various tax-free surpluses accumulated by a private corporation. These surpluses may be distributed as capital dividends free of tax to the corporation's Canadian-resident shareholders. A corporation paying a capital dividend must file an election in respect of the dividend when the dividend is paid or becomes payable, although, in certain circumstances, a late-filed election is acceptable. If the corporation pays a capital dividend which is in excess of the balance in its capital dividend account an additional tax may be payable on the non-qualifying portion of the dividend. However, this additional tax may be avoided by making the appropriate elections.

Discussion and Interpretation

Election under Subsection 83(2)

1. A private corporation may elect, under subsection 83(2), in prescribed manner and form (section 2101 of the Regulations and Form T2054) to pay its shareholders a dividend out of its capital dividend account. Subject to 17 to 19 below, no part of a capital dividend is included in computing Part I income of a shareholder resident in Canada. Additionally, no amount is deducted in computing the adjusted cost base of a shareholder's shares for such a dividend, provided that the election is made for the full amount of the dividend. Capital dividends paid to non-residents are subject to non-resident tax under subsection 212(2).

2. An election to pay a capital dividend should be filed on Form T2054 no later than the day on which the dividend becomes payable or the first day on which any part of the dividend is paid, whichever is earlier. For this purpose, a dividend becomes payable on the day stipulated by the resolution of the directors declaring the dividend. An election must be made on the full amount of the dividend and, accordingly, may not specify that the dividend is payable partly from its capital dividend account and partly from another source. A capital dividend may not be paid by a public corporation even though it previously had been a private corporation and there was a balance in its capital dividend account immediately before it became a public corporation.

Late-Filed Elections

3. A late-filed election that would otherwise qualify for a capital dividend is acceptable (subject to 5 below) provided that:

(a) the election is made in the prescribed manner and on the prescribed form as set forth in 1 above, and

(b) the estimated penalty for the election is paid when the election is made.

4. The estimated penalty in 3(b) above is computed as the lesser of:

(a) 1/12 of 1% of the amount of the dividend, and

(b) $41.67

multiplied by the number of months and part-months between the due date stated in 2 above and the actual filing date.

5. The late-filing provisions described in 3 above cease to be available for a particular dividend if a taxpayer does not comply with a written request from the Minister to make a late-filed election for that dividend within 90 days from the date of service of the request.

Capital Dividend Account

Components of the Capital Dividend Account

6. The rules for determining the balance in the capital dividend account are provided in paragraph 89(1)(b). The amount of each component of the capital dividend account is computed on a cumulative aggregate basis for a particular "period". This "period" begins on

- the first day of the first taxation year ending after 1971 and after the corporation last became a private corporation,

and ends

- immediately before the balance in the capital dividend account is to be determined.

For example, if a corporation that has been a private corporation with a March 31 year-end since its incorporation in 1960, pays a capital dividend on April 1, 1989, the relevant "period" for the calculation of its capital dividend account is April 1, 1971 to April 1, 1989.

The capital dividend account for a given "period" consists of:

The aggregate of:

(a) the excess of the non-taxable portion of capital gains over the non-deductible portion of capital losses (including business investment losses) incurred by the corporation (see 8 and 9 below for exclusions),

(b) the aggregate of capital dividends received by the corporation,

(c) the non-taxable portion of gains resulting from the disposition, in the period, of eligible capital property of each business of the corporation as described in subparagraph 89(1)(b)(iii) (see the related Department of Finance Explanatory Notes for S.C. 1988, c. 55 (formerly Bill C-139; Royal Assent September 13, 1988) dated June 1988 and the current version of IT-123),

(d) the net proceeds of a life insurance policy received after May 23, 1985 by the corporation as beneficiary under the policy and such proceeds received after 1971 and before May 24, 1985 where the corporation was a beneficiary under the policy prior to June 29, 1982 (see the current version of IT-430 entitled, *Life Insurance Proceeds Received by a Private Corporation or a Partnership*), and

(e) the balance, if any, in the corporation's life insurance capital dividend account immediately before May 24, 1985

less:

(f) the aggregate of all capital dividends that became payable by the corporation in the period.

7. In addition to receiving capital dividends by way of a cash, stock, specie or deemed dividend, a corporation's capital dividend account may also be increased as a result of an amalgamation of two or more corporations or a winding-up of a subsidiary. Paragraph 87(2)(z.1) provides for the transfer of the capital dividend ac-

count of a predecessor corporation to the new corporation on an amalgamation. Similarly, by a cross-reference to paragraph 87(2)(z.1), paragraph 88(1)(e.2) provides for the transfer of the capital dividend account of a subsidiary corporation to its parent on a winding-up. However, for amalgamations or windings-up occurring after 4 p.m. Eastern Daylight [Saving] Time, September 25, 1987, paragraph 87(2)(z.1) provides circumstances in which the capital dividend account of a predecessor or subsidiary corporation will not be transferred on an amalgamation or winding-up. The capital dividend account of a corporation will not be transferred in any case where, if immediately before the amalgamation or winding-up, a capital dividend were paid by it, the dividend would have been deemed to be a taxable dividend by reason of the anti-avoidance rule in subsection 83(2.1) (see 21 and 22 below). For example, if a corporation acquires all of the shares of another corporation that had a balance in its capital dividend account and winds it up, the capital dividend account of the other corporation will not be transferred if one of the main purposes of the share acquisition and wind-up was to obtain the capital dividend account.

Exclusions

8. Excluded from the amount determined in 6(a) above, for dispositions occurring after November 12, 1981, is the portion of realized capital gains or losses on property, other than designated property, which can reasonably be considered to have accrued during any period that the property was held by a corporation when it was not a private corporation, an investment corporation, a mortgage investment corporation, or a mutual fund corporation.

Under paragraph 89(1)(b.1) "designated property" of a private corporation includes:

(a) any property acquired by it before November 13, 1981, or after November 12, 1981 pursuant to a written agreement entered into on or before November 13, 1981,

(b) any property acquired by it from another private corporation with which it was not dealing at arm's length (other than pursuant to paragraph 251(5)(b)) at the time, if the property was designated property to the other private corporation,

(c) a share acquired by it in exchange for another share that was designated property of the corporation in a transaction to which section 51, 85.1, 86 or 87 or subsection 85(1) applied, or

(d) a replacement property (as described in section 44 and discussed in the current version of IT-259 entitled, *Exchanges of Property*) for a designated property that was disposed of involuntarily as described in subparagraphs 54(h)(ii), (iii) or (iv).

9. Also excluded from the amount determined in 6(a) above, for dispositions occurring after November 26, 1987, is the portion of the realized capital gains or losses on property, other than designated property, which can reasonably be considered to

have accrued during any period that the property or property for which it was substituted, was held by a corporation that was

(a) controlled, directly or indirectly in any manner whatever (see subsection 256(5.1)), by one or more non-resident persons and, after November 26, 1987, the property became the property of a Canadian-controlled private corporation, otherwise than as a consequence of the change in residence of one or more shareholders of the corporation, or

(b) exempt from tax under Part I of the Act and, after November 26, 1987, the property became the property of a private corporation that was not exempt from tax under Part I.

These exclusions apply where the status of the corporation changes after November 26, 1987 or the property is acquired, after November 26, 1987 on a rollover basis by the Canadian-controlled private corporation or the private corporation that was not exempt from tax as the case may be.

Note: If draft legislation released by the Minister of Finance on February 18, 1991 [Bill C-18, Royal Assent December 17, 1991 — ed.] is passed into law as currently proposed, the exclusions discussed in (a) and (b) above will also apply to dispositions of designated property after November 26, 1987.

Change in the Status of a Corporation

10. Subsection 89(1.1) provides that if a private corporation that was controlled, directly or indirectly in any manner whatever, by one or more non-residents becomes a Canadian-controlled private corporation after March 31, 1977 (otherwise than by a change in residence by one or more shareholders of the corporation), its capital dividend account is reduced by the full amount of the account as it stood immediately prior to the change in the corporation's status. Subsection 89(1.2) similarly applies to reduce a corporation's capital dividend account to nil, where, after November 26, 1987, the corporation ceases to be exempt from tax under Part I of the Act.

Capital Gains Reserve

11. Since the definition of "capital gain" in paragraph 39(1)(a) applies throughout the Act, the calculation of the non-taxable portion of a capital gain for the purposes of 6(a) above must take into consideration any applicable reserve under subparagraph 40(1)(a)(iii). When the balance of a corporation's capital dividend account is computed at any time during a taxation year, the amount of the reserve that will ultimately be claimed at year-end in respect of each gain realized before that time should be reflected in that calculation. Payment of a capital dividend based on a calculation which overstates the actual balance in the capital dividend account may give rise to an assessment of tax under subsection 184(2) (see 17 to 20 below).

Overstatements

12. An overstatement of the capital dividend account can arise when, subsequent to paying a capital dividend based on a capital gain reported in that year, a replace-

ment property is acquired and the provisions of section 44 are applied to retroactively reduce the previously reported capital gain. Another example would be the filing of amended returns regarding proceeds from the granting of an option under section 49.

Capital Losses

13. The non-deductible portion of capital losses reduces the balance in the capital dividend account only to the extent of the non-taxable portion of capital gains included therein as determined in 6(a) above. The full amount of those items in 6(b) to (e) above may be added to the capital dividend account although the aggregate capital losses sustained by the corporation since January 1, 1972 may have exceeded the aggregate capital gains realized since then. For example, if by the end of its 1988 taxation year a corporation that has been a private corporation since incorporation in 1971 sustained a capital loss of $15,000 in its 1982 taxation year and realized a capital gain of $10,000 in its 1985 taxation year but had received a capital dividend of $1,000 in its 1988 taxation year, the balance in the capital dividend account at the end of that 1988 year would be $1,000. The excess of the non-deductible portion of capital losses ($7,500) over the non-taxable portion of capital gains ($5,000) equalling $2,500, must be absorbed by the non-taxable portion of capital gains realized subsequent to the 1988 taxation year before any amount in respect of capital gains may be added to the capital dividend account.

Receipt of a Capital Dividend

14. The full amount of any dividend received by a corporation in respect of which the payer corporation made an election under subsection 83(2) is normally added to its capital dividend account regardless of whether or not the full amount is deemed to be a capital dividend. However, where a subsection 184(3) election is made by the payer for such a dividend, only the amount of the deemed separate capital dividend under paragraph 184(3)(a) is added (see 18 to 19 below).

Life Insurance Capital Dividend Account

15. Where a private corporation became a beneficiary under a life insurance policy after June 28, 1982 and received, before May 24, 1985, the proceeds of the policy as a consequence of the death of the person whose life was insured, the net proceeds were included in the corporation's life insurance capital dividend account (see the current version of IT-430 entitled, *Life Insurance Proceeds Received by a Corporation or Partnership*). The corporation could elect to pay tax-free life insurance capital dividends from this account which, when received by another private corporation before May 24, 1985, would be included in its life insurance capital dividend account. The balance in this account immediately before May 24, 1985 was transferred to the corporation's capital dividend account (see 6(e) above).

16. A life insurance policy is any policy of insurance where one of the risks covered is the death of the person insured but not an insurance policy which covers death only by reason of accident. This is relevant for the purposes of 6(d) and 15 above.

Excessive Elections

17. Where a corporation makes an election described in 2 or 3 above, and the full amount of the dividend does not qualify as a capital dividend, subject to 18 and 19 below, none of it will be included in computing the income of a shareholder resident in Canada but the corporation would be subject to tax under subsection 184(2). The applicable rate of tax is 75% of the non-qualifying portion of the dividend. If the non-qualifying portion of a dividend paid by a corporation in its 1988 taxation year and before June 18, 1987 resulted from the change in the portion of capital gains and losses that are included in computing the capital dividend account, subsection 184(2.1) will give relief from the tax otherwise payable under subsection 184(2) by providing that the non-qualifying portion be determined as if the corporation's taxation year ended December 31, 1987. The liability for the tax arises at the time that the election is made and (unless the tax is paid when the election is filed) interest at prescribed rates is added for the period from the date of the election to the date of payment.

Note: If draft legislation released by the Minister of Finance on February 18, 1991 [Bill C-18] is passed into law as currently proposed, every person who has received a capital dividend or capital gains dividend will, by virtue of subsection 185(4), be jointly and severally liable with the corporation for any Part III tax that becomes payable as a result of the dividend. The nature and extent of this potential liability, which will apply to dividends paid after July 13, 1990, is discussed in proposed subsections 185(4) to (6).

18. As an alternative to the payment of tax under subsection 184(2) in respect of an excessive election, a private corporation, with the concurrence of every shareholder entitled to the dividend and whose address was known to the corporation, may elect under subsection 184(3) to have the portion of the dividend that does not qualify as a capital dividend treated as a separate taxable dividend. The election must be made in the manner prescribed in section 2106 of the Regulations and within 90 days from the date of mailing of a notice of assessment in respect of the tax under subsection 184(2) that would otherwise be payable. If the dividend became payable after June 28, 1982 and before May 24, 1985, the election could specify that some or all of the excess be a separate dividend paid out of the corporation's life insurance capital dividend account and only the balance of the dividend that did not qualify as a capital dividend or a life insurance capital dividend would be a taxable dividend.

Note: If draft legislation released by the Minister of Finance on February 18, 1991 [Bill C-18] is passed into law as currently proposed, there will be a further restriction on filing the election under subsection 184(3). In addition to the current restrictions detailed above, the election will not be valid, by virtue of subsection 184(4), unless

(a) it is made within thirty months of the day on which the dividend became payable, or

(b) all the shareholders concur with the election, in which case, notwithstanding subsections 152(4) to (5), such assessment of tax, interest and penalties payable by such shareholders for any taxation year may be made as is necessary to take the corporation's election into account.

These additional restrictions will apply to elections made after July 13, 1990.

19. Where a valid election is made as described in 18 above, each shareholder resident in Canada entitled to receive a proportionate share of the actual dividend is deemed to receive, at the time that the actual dividend was paid, a share of each deemed separate dividend proportionate to the shareholder's holdings of the particular class of shares at that time. The amount of each separate dividend deemed to be received by a non-resident shareholder is computed in the same manner, but a separate capital dividend or a separate taxable dividend is deemed to have been paid on the date of the subsection 184(3) election for purposes of the non-resident tax under subsection 212(2) with the result that section 215 will apply at that time if the dividend had not been paid before that time.

20. A further alternative existed under subsection 184(3.2) for excessive elections on capital dividends that became payable after December 3, 1985 and before January 1, 1986. If the corporation had made a reasonable attempt to determine the correct amount of its capital dividend account immediately before the dividend became payable, the corporation, with the concurrence of every shareholder who received or was entitled to receive all or a portion of the dividend, could elect that all or any portion of the dividend be treated as a loan. The election was required to be made within the period set forth in paragraph 184(3.2)(a) and be accompanied by the payment for the penalty described in subsection 184(5). Provided that the amount of the dividend that was the subject of the election was repaid in full to the corporation before a date that was stipulated by the Minister the amount would be considered to be a loan to which sections 15 and 80.4 did not apply.

Anti-Avoidance Rule

21. Subsection 83(2.1) is an anti-avoidance rule which may apply to a capital dividend paid after 4 p.m. Eastern Daylight Saving Time on September 25, 1987 where one of the main purposes for which the shareholder acquired the share on which the dividend was paid was to receive the capital dividend. Where subsection 83(2.1) applies, the dividend will be received by the shareholder as a taxable dividend and consequently will be included in the shareholder's income. Further, if the dividend is received by another corporation, it will not be included in computing the recipient corporation's capital dividend account. The dividend will be a capital dividend, however, for the purposes of determining any liability of the payor corporation for tax pursuant to section 184 in respect of an excessive election and of computing its capital dividend account.

22. Subsections 83(2.2) to (2.4) provide exceptions where the anti-avoidance rule in subsection 83(2.1) will not apply. They are as follows:

(a) Subsection 83(2.2) provides that the anti-avoidance rule will not apply to a capital dividend paid to an individual where all or substantially all of the corporation's capital dividend account consisted of amounts other than those specified in paragraphs 83(2.2) (a) to (d).

(b) Subsection 83(2.3) provides that capital dividends paid by a corporation will be exempt from the anti-avoidance rule in situations where it is reasonable to consider that the purpose for paying the dividend was to distribute net life insurance proceeds which were received due to death.

(c) Subsection 83(2.4) provides that the anti-avoidance rule will not apply, in most circumstances, to a capital dividend paid to a related company where all or substantially all of the corporation's capital dividend account consisted of amounts other than those specified in paragraphs 83(2.4) (a) to (e).

For further reference see the related Department of Finance Explanatory Notes for S.C. 1988, c. 55 (formerly Bill C-139; Royal Assent September 13, 1988) dated June 1988 which introduce the above anti-avoidance provisions.

Interpretation Bulletin IT-87R2 — Policyholders' Income from Life Insurance Policies

Date: **February 15, 1996**

Reference: ***Section 12.2* (also subsections 12(3), 20(20), and 148(1), (2), (4), (8), (8.1) and (8.2), and the definitions 138(12)"life insurance policy", 148(9)"adjusted cost basis" and 148(9)"disposition"; and paragraphs 56(1)(d.1) and (j) of the *Income Tax Act*; and sections 304 to 307; subsections 201(5), 217(2), 308(1), 309(1) and (2), and the definitions of 308(1)"net cost of pure insurance" and 1404(2)"modified net premiums"; and paragraphs 1401(1)(a) and (c) of the Income Tax Regulations)**

This bulletin cancels and replaces Interpretation Bulletin IT-87R dated February 28, 1986.

This bulletin deals with the treatment of policyholders' income from certain life insurance policies and annuity contracts. It outlines the basis on which various types of taxpayers must report accrued investment income for policies last acquired before or after certain relevant dates. With some exceptions (e.g., an exempt policy), a taxpayer must report the accrued investment income on a life insurance policy or an annuity on an annual basis. However, if the policy or annuity was last acquired before 1990 and the policyholder is an individual, the accrued investment income must generally be reported every three years, unless the individual has elected to report the income on an annual basis.

The bulletin also discusses in general the tax implications arising from the disposition or deemed disposition of a life insurance policy or annuity contract.

Discussion and Interpretation

General

1. Issuers of life insurance policies are required by the rules set out in subsections 201(5) and 217(2) of the Income Tax Regulations to report on an information return (Form T4A or T5), the amount, if any, that a policyholder must include in income for a taxation year in respect of any such policy. The determination of such amounts generally requires information that is available only in the accounts of the

issuer. Accordingly, the paragraphs which follow serve only to inform taxpayers of the taxability of earnings arising from life insurance policies. Policyholders can obtain specific details about the taxability of amounts related to their policies from the issuer of the policy.

2. The term "life insurance policy" is broadly defined in subsection 138(12). In addition to a regular life insurance policy, it includes an annuity contract and a contract for which all or any part of the insurer's reserves vary in amount depending on the fair market value of a specified group of assets (i.e., a "segregated fund"). Unless otherwise stated, a reference to a "life insurance policy" in this bulletin includes an annuity contract, but not a segregated fund policy. There are special rules that apply to segregated fund policies. However, a discussion of these rules is beyond the scope of this bulletin.

3. The terms "accumulating fund" and "adjusted cost basis" are relevant to the taxation of accrual income under a life insurance policy and the taxation of income from the disposition of such a policy. These terms are explained below.

Accumulating fund

In general terms, the "accumulating fund" of a life insurance policy is a measure of the accumulated savings that have built up within the policy. To calculate the accumulating fund, it is necessary to refer to section 307 of the Regulations. Under this provision, the calculation may differ depending on the type of life insurance policy issued. For instance, the accumulating fund in respect of an interest in an annuity contract (other than a contract issued by a life insurer) is determined under paragraph 307(1)(a) of the Regulations and is essentially the greater of:

- the cash surrender value of the interest less outstanding loans made under the contract in respect of the interest; and
- the excess of the present value of future payments over the sum of outstanding loans made under the contract in respect of the interest and the present value of future premiums.

In the case of an interest in a life insurance policy (other than an annuity contract referred to above), the accumulating fund is determined under paragraph 307(1)(b) of the Regulations. Generally, it is the proportion of the taxpayer's interest in the policy of the maximum amount determined by the life insurer under paragraph 1401(1)(a) or (c) of the Regulations. Paragraph 1401(1)(a) of the Regulations determines the maximum reserve a life insurer can deduct in computing its income in respect of a deposit administration fund policy. Paragraph 1401(1)(c) of the Regulations determines the reserve for other types of life insurance policies and can generally be described as the greater of:

- the cash surrender value of the policy less outstanding policy loans in respect of the policy; and
- the excess of the present value of future benefits over the sum of outstanding policy loans and the present value of future modified net premiums (the term "modified net premiums" is defined in subsection 1404(2) of the Regulations).

Note that paragraph 307(1)(b) of the Regulations does not apply to determine the accumulating fund of an exemption test policy. Such a policy is a notional policy used to determine if a life insurance policy qualifies as an exempt policy and is therefore exempt from accrual taxation (see 4(a) below and section 306 of the Regulations).

Adjusted cost basis

The "adjusted cost basis" (ACB) to a policyholder of an interest in a life insurance policy is defined in subsection 148(9). The ACB is essentially the cost of the interest in the policy adjusted for certain items. The more common items that increase the ACB include premiums paid under the policy and any amount required to be included in income under section 12.2. Some of the more common items that reduce the ACB include:

- the proceeds of the disposition of the policyholder's interest in the policy;
- in the case of an interest in a life insurance policy (other than an annuity contract) last acquired after December 1, 1982, the "net cost of pure insurance," as defined in subsection 308(1) of the Regulations, determined immediately before the end of the calendar year ending in a taxation year commencing after May 31, 1985; and
- in the case of an interest in an annuity contract to which subsection 12.2(1) applies for the year, or would apply if the contract had an anniversary day in the year and while the policyholder held the interest, annuity payments paid out of the contract.

Policies Last Acquired After 1989

Accrual rules under subsection 12.2(1)

4. When a taxpayer holds an interest in a life insurance policy last acquired after 1989, subsection 12.2(1) generally requires the taxpayer to report accrued income (see 5 below) relevant to the policy on an annual basis. However, subsection 12.2(1) specifically excludes interests in the following types of policies from accrual taxation:

(a) an exempt policy, as prescribed by section 306 of the Regulations for the purposes of the definition in subsection 12.2(11) (An exempt policy is a policy which is issued mainly for insurance protection and not for investment purposes. Policyholders must generally rely on the issuer of a life insurance policy to determine if it is an exempt policy because the determination requires information which may not be available in life insurance contracts themselves.);

(b) a prescribed annuity contract, as defined in section 304 of the Regulations; and

(c) a contract under which the policyholder has received proceeds in the form of an annuity contract under the terms and conditions of a life insurance policy that was not an annuity contract and that was last acquired before December 2, 1982.

5. Subsection 12.2(1) applies to any taxpayer who, in a taxation year, holds an interest in a life insurance policy, other than the types of policies described in 4(a) to (c) above, on any anniversary day of the policy. Such a taxpayer is required to include in computing income for the year the excess of the accumulating fund (see 3 above) in respect of the taxpayer's interest in the policy on the anniversary day over the adjusted cost basis (see 3 above) to the taxpayer of that interest on that day. The "anniversary day" of a life insurance policy is defined in subsection 12.2(11) as:

- the day that is one year after the day immediately before the issue date of the policy; and
- the day that occurs at every successive one-year interval from the day determined above.

For example, if a policy is issued on July 1, 1994, the policy's first anniversary day is June 30, 1995. Accordingly, income accrued between July 1, 1994 and June 30, 1995 will be included in income for the policyholder's taxation year that includes June 30, 1995, unless the policy is disposed of at an earlier date.

Policies Last Acquired Before 1990

6. The provisions in section 12.2 as amended by S.C. 1990, c. 39 (formerly Bill C-28) apply only to life insurance policies last acquired after 1989. The provisions of the section prior to the amendment continue to apply to life insurance policies last acquired before 1990 and are referred to in this bulletin as "former" provisions. A summary of the accrual rules under section 12.2 as they apply to policies last acquired before 1990 and after 1989 is contained in the appendix at the end of this bulletin.

Accrual rules under former subsections 12.2(1) and (3)

7. As mentioned in 4 above, subsection 12.2(1) generally applies to an interest in a life insurance policy last acquired after 1989 by any taxpayer. In the case of policies last acquired before 1990, separate rules apply to corporate policyholders and individual policyholders.

(a) If the taxpayer is a corporation, partnership, unit trust, or a trust with a corporation or partnership as a beneficiary, former subsection 12.2(1) requires the taxpayer to report on an annual basis the accrued income relevant to the policy. The amount of accrued income that must be reported is the excess of the accumulating fund in respect of the taxpayer's interest at the end of the calendar year ending in the taxation year over the adjusted cost basis of the interest to the taxpayer at the end of that calendar year.

(b) If the taxpayer is not someone described in (a) above, but is, for example, an individual or a trust where all beneficiaries are individuals, former subsection 12.2(3) requires the taxpayer to report accrued income relevant to the policy, as determined under that subsection, every three years. A taxpayer who is subject to this rule may elect under former subsection 12.2(4) to report the policy earnings on an annual basis. To make this election in respect of a particular life insurance policy, taxpayers must notify the issuer of the policy, in writing, that they intend to report the investment income as it accrues on an annual basis.

8. Subject to 9 below, the accrual rules in former subsections 12.2(1) and (3) (set out in 7 above) apply to:

- an interest in a life insurance policy last acquired after December 1, 1982;
- in the case of former subsection 12.2(1), an interest in an annuity contract last acquired after December 19, 1980 and before December 2, 1982 under which annuity payments did not commence before December 2, 1982; and
- in the case of former subsection 12.2(3), an interest in an annuity contract last acquired before December 2, 1982 under which annuity payments did not commence before December 2, 1982.

These rules apply to taxation years commencing after 1982. Note that if former subsection 12.2(9) applies to a life insurance policy last acquired before December 2, 1982 (see 10 below), the policy will be subject to the accrual rules in former subsection 12.2(1) or (3), whichever is applicable.

9. Specifically excluded under the accrual rules in former subsection 12.2(1) or (3) are interests in the following types of policies:

- an exempt policy as described in 4(a) above [former paragraphs 12.2(1)(c) and 12.2(3)(c)];
- a prescribed annuity contract [former paragraph 12.2(3)(d)]; and
- a policy as described in 4(c) above [former paragraphs 12.2(1)(d) and 12.2(3)(e)].

Effect of former subsection 12.2(9) on pre-December 2, 1982 policies

10. Former subsection 12.2(9) provides that a life insurance policy last acquired before December 2, 1982 will be treated for tax purposes as a policy that was last acquired after December 1, 1982, if, at any time after December 1, 1982:

(a) a premium as prescribed in subsection 309(1) of the Regulations (other than a premium referred to in subsection 12.2(8)) has been paid in respect of an interest in the policy; and either

(b) the policy is not an exempt policy; or

(c) there has been an increase, as prescribed in subsection 309(2) of the Regulations, in any benefit on death under the policy.

When former subsection 12.2(9) applies, the policy will be subject to the accrual rules in former subsection 12.2(1) or (3) (see 7 to 9 above).

Unfixed premiums

11. Subsection 12.2(8) applies to an annuity contract last acquired before 1990 if the premiums paid after 1989 under the contract were not fixed before 1990. Under subsection 12.2(8), the first premium paid after 1989 under the contract which was not fixed before 1990 is deemed to have been paid to acquire an interest in a sepa-

rate annuity contract at the time it is paid to the extent that the amount of the premium was not fixed before 1990. Subsection 12.2(8) further deems any subsequent premiums paid under the original annuity contract to have been paid under that separate contract to the extent that such premiums were not fixed before 1990. The separate annuity contract will be subject to annual accrual taxation under subsection 12.2(1), unless it is a prescribed annuity contract. Subsection 12.2(8) does not apply to:

- contracts described in 4(c) above; or
- contracts already subject to annual accrual reporting pursuant to former subsection 12.2(1) or (4), or subsection 12(3).

In the case of an annuity contract (subject to certain exceptions) last acquired before December 2, 1982, any premiums paid after December 1, 1982 and before 1990 under the contract are deemed to have been paid to acquire an interest in a separate annuity contract to the extent that the premiums were not fixed before December 2, 1982. The separate contract will be subject to accrual taxation as described in 7(a) or (b), whichever is applicable.

Riders

12. A rider added at any time after 1989 to a life insurance policy (other than an annuity contract) last acquired before 1990 is subject to the provisions of subsection 12.2(10). (A rider is an attachment or addition to the policy that modifies its conditions or coverage.) This subsection is designed to prevent an individual from obtaining additional life insurance that is not subject to annual accrual reporting by adding the additional insurance to an existing policy subject to triennial accrual. When a rider providing for additional life insurance (other than an accidental death benefit) is added to a life insurance policy held by any taxpayer, subsection 12.2(10) deems the rider to be a separate life insurance policy issued at the time the rider itself was added. As a result, the separate policy will be subject to the annual accrual rules in subsection 12.2(1). In the case of a rider added at any time after December 1, 1982 and before 1990 to a policy (other than an annuity contract) last acquired before December 2, 1982, if subsection 12.2(10) applies to treat the rider as a separate life insurance policy, the separate policy will be subject to the accrual rules in former subsection 12.2(1) or (3) as described in 7(a) and (b) above.

Note: The draft legislation released by the Minister of Finance on April 26, 1995 contains a proposal to amend subsection 12.2(10) so that it does not apply to a rider added after 1994 to an exempt policy last acquired after December 1, 1982. The exclusion makes the treatment of such riders consistent with the treatment of riders added to exempt policies acquired after 1990. In both cases, if the rider causes the exempt policy to lose its exempt status, the policy will become subject to annual accrual reporting.

Other Comments Related to Accrual Taxation

Negative adjusted cost basis (ACB)

13. Subsection 12.2(5) applies when the ACB of an annuity contract is a negative amount at the end of a taxation year. This rule ensures that accrued income is brought into income even if, for example, the contract expires in the year. When a taxpayer holds an interest in an annuity contract last acquired after 1989 to which subsection 12.2(1) applies or would apply if the contract had an anniversary day in the year while the taxpayer held it, subsection 12.2(5) requires the taxpayer to include in income for the year the amount, if any, by which:

(a) the total of the amounts determined at the end of the year under any of H to L in the definition of ACB in subsection 148(9) in respect of the taxpayer's interest in the contract, exceeds

(b) the total of all amounts determined at the end of the year under any of A to G in the definition referred to in (a) above.

In the case of an interest in an annuity contract last acquired before 1990, if the ACB of the interest becomes negative at the end of the year, the negative amount is generally included in income if the contract is one to which former subsection 12.2(1), (3), or (4) applies or would apply if the contract had a third anniversary in the year.

Dispositions of Interests

14. When a policyholder disposes of an interest in a life insurance policy, the rules in paragraph 56(1)(j) and subsection 148(1) apply. These rules require the policyholder to include in income for the taxation year in which the disposition occurs the amount, if any, by which the proceeds of the disposition of the policyholder's interest that the policyholder, beneficiary or assignee is entitled to receive in the year exceed the ACB to the policyholder of that interest immediately before the disposition. When a policyholder disposes of an interest in a life insurance policy for which income has been reported in accordance with the accrual rules explained in 4 or 7 above, double taxation of such income does not occur because the amount of income that has already been reported increases the ACB of the policy.

15. Subsection 20(20) provides a deduction in respect of income accrued but not received under a life insurance policy at the time of disposition. The deduction under subsection 20(20) is limited to the lesser of:

- the total of all amounts in respect of the policyholder's interest in the policy that were included in the policyholder's income under section 12.2 or former paragraph 56(1)(d.1); and
- the excess of the ACB of the policyholder's interest over the proceeds of the disposition that the policyholder, a beneficiary or an assignee is entitled to receive.

Subsection 20(20) does not apply to dispositions on death of an interest in a life insurance policy that is not an annuity contract or dispositions of an interest in a prescribed annuity contract.

16. A "disposition" of an interest in a life insurance policy is defined in subsection 148(9) as including:

- a surrender of the interest;
- a policy loan made after March 31, 1978;
- the dissolution of the interest by virtue of the maturity of the policy; and
- a disposition of the interest by operation of law only.

Certain transactions are specifically excluded from the definition of "disposition." For example, a payment resulting from the death of the insured person under a life insurance policy (other than an annuity contract) that was last acquired before December 2, 1982, or that is an exempt policy, is not a disposition. As a result, the payment is received tax-free.

17. In addition to the definition of "disposition" in subsection 148(9), subsection 148(2) may apply to deem the policyholder to have disposed of all or part of an interest in a life insurance policy in certain circumstances. For instance, a disposition is deemed to occur:

- when a policyholder is entitled to receive a policy dividend (see 19 below); or
- when a life insurance policy is subject to the accrual taxation and the life insured or annuitant dies.

In the latter case, the policyholder is deemed by paragraph 148(2)(b) to have disposed of the policy immediately before the death. As a result, the policyholder will have to include in income any income that has accrued since the last anniversary day, but any death benefit will be received tax-free.

18. To the extent permitted by subsection 148(8), (8.1) or (8.2), a transfer of an interest in a life insurance policy to the policyholder's child or spouse may be made on a tax-deferred basis. The policyholder is deemed to have been disposed of the interest for proceeds of the disposition equal to the ACB of the interest immediately before the transfer and the child or spouse is deemed to have acquired the interest at a cost equal to those proceeds.

Policy dividends

19. Paragraph 148(2)(a) applies when a policyholder is entitled to receive a policy dividend. It deems the policyholder to have disposed of an interest in the policy for proceeds equal to the amount of such a dividend. However, when the policy dividend is received or receivable in taxation years commencing after December 20, 1991, any part of the dividend that is automatically used to pay a premium under the policy or to repay a policy loan under the policy, as provided for under the terms and conditions of the policy, is not included in the proceeds of the disposition. If the total of policy dividends that a policyholder is entitled to receive in a year exceeds the ACB of the policy, the policyholder has to include that excess amount in income for that year.

Calculation of income from partial disposition

20. Subsection 148(4) provides a special rule to calculate a policyholder's income when the policyholder disposes of part of an interest in a life insurance policy (other than an annuity contract) last acquired after December 1, 1982 or an annuity contract. In calculating the income from disposition, only the ACB of the portion of the policyholder's interest disposed of is deductible. Under subsection 148(4), the ACB of the part interest is the proportion of the ACB of the policyholder's entire interest in the policy or contract that the proceeds of the disposition is of the accumulating fund of the entire interest immediately before the disposition. Subsection 148(4) does not apply to partial dispositions resulting from a declaration of a policy dividend or the taking of a policy loan.

Other bulletins

21. In connection with the subject matter of this bulletin, the current versions of the following interpretation bulletins may be of interest to the reader:

IT-66	Capital Dividends
IT-85	Health and Welfare Trusts for Employees
IT-111	Annuities Purchased from Charitable Organizations
IT-223	Overhead Expense Insurance vs. Income Insurance
IT-227	Group Term Life Insurance Premiums
IT-244	Gifts by Individuals of Life Insurance Policies as Charitable Donations
IT-309	Premiums on Life Insurance Used as Collateral
IT-355	Interest on Loans to Buy Life Insurance Policies and Annuity Contracts, and Interest on Policy Loans
IT-408	Life Insurance Policies as Investments of Registered Retirement Savings Plans and Deferred Profit Sharing Plans
IT-416	Valuation of Shares of a Corporation Receiving Life Insurance Proceeds on Death of a Shareholder
IT-430	Life Insurance Proceeds Received by a Private Corporation or a Partnership as a Consequence of Death

If you have any comments regarding the matters discussed in this bulletin, please send them to:

Director, Technical Publications Division
Policy and Legislation Branch
Revenue Canada
875 Heron Road
Ottawa ON K1A 0L8

Appendix: Summary of the Accrual Rules Under Section 12.2

LIFE INSURANCE POLICIES LAST ACQUIRED AFTER 1989		
By any taxpayer	annual accrual reporting required under subsection 12.2(1)	see ¶ 5 and exceptions in ¶ 4
LIFE INSURANCE POLICIES LAST ACQUIRED BEFORE 1990		
By a corporation, partnership, unit trust, or a trust with a corporation or partnership as a beneficiary:		
— life insurance policy last acquired after December 1, 1982 and before 1990	— annual accrual reporting required under former subsection 12.2(1)	— see ¶s 7(a) and 8 and exceptions in ¶ 9
— annuity contract last acquired after December 19, 1980 and before December 2, 1982 under which annuity payments did not commence before December 2, 1982	— same as above	— same as above
By an individual or a trust having no corporation or a partnership as a beneficiary:		
— life insurance policy last acquired after December 1, 1982 and before 1990	— triennial accrual reporting required under former subsection 12.2(3) unless an election has been made under former subsection 12.2(4) to report on an annual accrual basis	— see ¶s 7(b) and 8 and exceptions in ¶ 9
— annuity contract last acquired before December 2, 1982 under which annuity payments did not commence before December 2, 1982	— same as above	— same as above

Explanation of Changes for Interpretation Bulletin IT-87R2
Policyholders' Income from Life Insurance Policies

Introduction

The purpose of the Explanation of Changes is to give the reasons for the revisions to an interpretation bulletin. It outlines revisions that we have made as a result of changes to the law, as well as changes reflecting new or revised departmental interpretations.

Overview

This bulletin deals with the application of the income accrual rules in section 12.2 to certain life insurance policies and annuity contracts. It also discusses in general the tax implications arising from the disposition or deemed disposition of a life insurance policy or annuity contract.

We revised the bulletin to reflect amendments to the *Income Tax Act* enacted in S.C. 1986, c. 6 (formerly Bill C-84); S.C. 1990, c. 39 (formerly Bill C-28); S.C. 1994, c. 7, Sch. II (1991, c. 49 - formerly Bill C-18); and S.C. 1994, c. 7, Sch. VIII (1993, c. 24 - formerly Bill C-92).

The draft legislation released by the Minister of Finance on April 26, 1995 contains a proposal to amend subsection 12.2(10). The proposed amendment is reflected in a note at the end of ¶ 12. The comments in this bulletin are not affected by any other draft legislation released before January 8, 1996.

Legislative and other changes

¶ 1 which currently refers to Form T5, has been revised to also refer to Form T4A.

¶ 2 has been revised to clarify that the comments in the bulletin relate to both life insurance policies and annuity contracts, unless otherwise stated. In addition, ¶ 2 notes that the bulletin does not apply to segregated fund policies.

New ¶ 3 provides an explanation of the terms "accumulating fund" and "adjusted cost basis."

New ¶ 4 explains the general rule in subsection 12.2(1), which was amended to combine the annual reporting requirements in former subsections 12.2(1) and (3). ¶ 4 also sets out the exceptions to subsection 12.2(1).

New ¶ 5 describes the calculation of the amount policyholders are required to include in income under subsection 12.2(1). It also includes the definition of "anniversary day" in subsection 12.2(11).

New ¶ 6 explains that the provisions in section 12.2 were amended by Bill C-28. However, the provisions prior to the amendment still continue to apply to a life insurance policy last acquired before 1990 and are referred to in the bulletin as "former" provisions.

The comments in former ¶ 6, which described the interaction between subsection 89(2) and the life insurance capital dividend account of a corporation, have been removed since the rules relating to the life insurance capital dividend account were repealed applicable after May 23, 1985.

New ¶ 7 (former ¶ 3) covers the income accrual rules in former subsections 12.2(1) and (3), as well as the election under former subsection 12.2(4).

New ¶ 8 comments on the application of former subsections 12.2(1) and (3). It also mentions that where former subsection 12.2(9) applies to a life insurance policy last acquired before December 2, 1982, the policy will be subject to the income accrual rules in former subsection 12.2(1) or (3), whichever is applicable.

New ¶ 9 (former ¶ 4), which describes the exceptions to former subsections 12.2(1) and (3), has been revised to add a reference to the type of policy described in former paragraphs 12.2(1)(d) and 12.2(3)(e).

New ¶ 10 (former ¶ 5) discusses subsection 12.2(9) which sets out the circumstances in which changes to a life insurance policy last acquired before December 2, 1982 will result in the policy being treated as a policy last acquired after December 1, 1982. While subsection 12.2(9) was repealed, applicable to policies last acquired after 1989, this former provision continues to apply to policies issued before December 2, 1982 in the circumstances described in ¶ 10.

New ¶ 11 explains the application of subsection 12.2(8) which provides that an annuity contract last acquired before 1990 will be subject to annual accrual taxation to the extent of any premiums paid after 1989 that were not fixed before 1990.

New ¶ 12 discusses subsection 12.2(10) which provides that certain riders added to life insurance policies are to be treated as separate life insurance policies. The note at the end of ¶ 12 describes the proposed amendment to subsection 12.2(10) contained in the draft Amendments to the Income Tax Act and Related Statutes issued by the Minister of Finance on April 26, 1995.

New ¶ 13 deals with the rule in subsection 12.2(5). Under subsection 12.2(5), when the adjusted cost basis of an annuity contract is negative at the end of a taxation year, the policyholder is required to include the negative amount in income for the year.

New ¶s 14 to 17 replace former ¶ 7. New ¶ 15 discusses subsection 20(20) which allows a deduction for income accrued but not received under certain life insurance policies at the time of disposition. New ¶ 16 has been revised to add that a life insurance policy (other than an annuity contract) that was last acquired before December 2, 1982, or that is an exempt policy, is not considered to be disposed of when the person whose life is insured under the policy dies. New ¶ 17 describes the tax consequences when the life insured or annuitant under a life insurance policy that is subject to accrual reporting dies.

New ¶ 18 refers to subsections 148(8) to (8.2) which allow transfers of interests in life insurance policies to family members on a tax-deferred basis under certain circumstances.

New ¶ 19 (former ¶ 8) reflects an amendment to paragraph 148(2)(a) to exclude from the proceeds of the disposition any part of a policy dividend that is automatically applied to pay a premium or repay a policy loan, as provided for under the terms and conditions of the policy.

New ¶ 20 deals with subsection 148(4) which provides a special rule in calculating a policyholder's income when part of an interest in a life insurance policy is disposed of.

New ¶ 21 lists other bulletins that may be of interest to the reader.

We have added an appendix which summarizes the accrual rules under section 12.2 as they apply to policies last acquired before 1990 and after 1989.

Throughout the bulletin, we have made a number of minor changes to improve the overall clarity and readability of the bulletin.

Interpretation Bulletin IT-244R3 — Gifts by Individuals of Life Insurance Policies as Charitable Donations

Date: **September 6, 1991**

Reference: ***Section 118.1*(also subsecs. 148(1) and 248(5), para. 149.1(2)(b), subpara. 149.1(12)(b)(i) and cl. 149.1(1)(e)(i)(B))**

This bulletin cancels and replaces Interpretation Bulletin IT-244R2 dated March 3, 1986.

Summary

This bulletin discusses the tax consequences arising from the donation by an individual of a life insurance policy to a charitable organization or a charitable foundation registered with the Minister of National Revenue. When an individual absolutely assigns a life insurance policy to a registered charity and makes the charity the registered beneficiary of the policy, the individual qualifies for the tax relief applicable to charitable gifts in respect of such a donation. Furthermore, if the individual continues to pay the premium on the life insurance policy, each amount so paid also qualifies as a charitable gift in the year. For 1988 and subsequent taxation years, donations made by an individual are no longer deductible in computing taxable income; tax relief is now provided to individuals in the form of a non-refundable tax credit.

Discussion and Interpretation

1. A gift by an individual of a life insurance policy (both "whole life" and "term life") to a registered charity or any other donee described in any of paragraphs (a) to (g) of the definition of "total charitable gifts" in subsection 118.1(1) of the *Income Tax Act* is considered to be a charitable gift within the context of that subsection. Therefore, such a gift entitles the donor to a tax credit (within the limits provided by the Act) in respect of the value of the gift, as discussed in 3 below, provided the policy has been absolutely assigned to the donee and the donee has become the registered beneficiary of the policy. (For 1987 and prior taxation years, the value of such a gift was deductible in computing taxable income for the year as was then provided under the Act.) In order for the gift of a life insurance policy to

represent a *bona fide* charitable gift, no right, privilege, benefit or advantage can accrue to the donor as a result of the gift (excluding, of course, any income tax relief resulting from the donation).

2. Where these conditions are met, an amount donated to a donee referred to in 1 above to enable the donee to pay the premiums of the life insurance policy is also a charitable gift. If the premiums on the policy are paid directly to the insurance company at the request of, or with the concurrence of, the donee, this action is considered to be constructive payment of a donation to the donee and therefore a charitable gift for the purposes of the Act. Furthermore, the fact that a donor makes a cash contribution to a donee and specifies that it be used to pay a premium on a life insurance policy does not influence the determination of whether or not the donation qualifies as a gift under subsection 118.1(1).

3. When a taxpayer has taken out a life insurance policy and later makes an absolute assignment of the policy to a qualified donee under subsection 118.1(1), the amount of the charitable gift is equal to the value of the policy (i.e., the amount by which the cash surrender value of the policy at the time of the absolute assignment exceeds any policy loan outstanding) and any accumulated dividends and interest which are also assigned at that time. If the policy has no value, there is no charitable gift when it is transferred, but donations of subsequent premium amounts will qualify as charitable gifts in accordance with 2 above. It should be noted that the increase in the cash surrender value of the policy as a result of the subsequent payments of policy premiums has no effect in determining the amount of the donation once the policy has been absolutely assigned to the qualified donee. However, the repayment of any outstanding policy loans by the donor after the policy has been absolutely assigned to the qualified donee will entitle the donor to a tax credit in respect of the amount repaid.

4. When a life insurance policy is absolutely assigned to a qualified donee, any consents that are required by provincial regulations to be signed to change a beneficiary must be signed before there is a valid charitable gift.

5. A donor who assigns a life insurance policy in accordance with the terms of this bulletin must consider the implications of section 148 of the Act. For the purpose of subsection 148(1), it is considered that the donor's proceeds of disposition of the life insurance policy will be the value of the policy at the time of the assignment (see 3 above). To the extent that the proceeds of disposition exceed the adjusted cost basis of the policy, there will be an income inclusion. (Any accumulated dividends assigned would have been proceeds of disposition of the policy at the time of entitlement, as discussed in the current version of IT-87, *Policyholders' Income from Life Insurance Policies*.)

Receipt by Certain Qualified Donee

6. Where a registered charity receives a gift subject to a trust or direction by a donor that the property given, or property substituted therefor, is to be held by the charity for a period of not less than 10 years, the gift is excluded from the income of the charity by virtue of subparagraph 149.1(12)(b)(i) of the Act. Clause 149.1(1)(e)(i)(B) referred to in that subparagraph provides a specific exemption of

such property from the disbursement quota of a charitable foundation and paragraph 149.1(2)(b) effectively extends the same provision to a charitable organization's spending requirements. Therefore, provided that a trust stipulates, or the donor directs, that the gift be held for at least 10 years, the value of a life insurance policy and the proceeds from the policy, whether on voluntary disposition or upon the death of the life insured, will be exempt from the disbursement quota set out in the Act. The rules respecting such directions are discussed in the current version of Information Circular 80-10 under the heading "Ten-Year Gifts".

7. By virtue of subsection 248(5), the phrase "property substituted therefor" in clause 149.1(1)(e)(i)(B) is not limited to one substitution but will apply to any subsequent substitution therefor.

8. Where a gift of a life insurance policy qualifies for exclusion from the charity's income and disbursement quota as discussed in 6 above, the amount of subsequent premiums donated relative to that life insurance policy (see 2 above) will also qualify for such exclusions. It should be noted, however, that since each payment of a premium is itself a gift, each payment must be subject to a direction that it be retained for 10 years if that gift is to be excluded from income or from the disbursement quota. One way of achieving this is for the donor, at the time the policy is given, to require the charity to keep the policy, or property substituted from the policy, for at least 10 years after the last premium is paid by the donor.

Interpretation Bulletin IT-309R2 — Premiums on Life Insurance Used as Collateral

Date: **February 28, 1995**

Reference: ***Subparagraph 20(1)(e.2)*** **(also Reg. 308)**

This bulletin cancels and replaces Interpretation Bulletin IT-309R, Expenses of Borrowing Money — Life Insurance Premiums, dated January 10, 1979.

Summary

This bulletin discusses the limited deduction that is available in calculating income from a business or property for premiums payable after 1989 under a life insurance policy when the policy has been assigned to a restricted financial institution as collateral for a loan. The amount eligible for deduction in a particular year is limited to either the premiums payable by the taxpayer under the policy for the year, or the net cost of pure insurance under the policy for the year, whichever amount is less. Furthermore, only the portion of the lesser of these amounts that can reasonably be considered to relate to the amount owing under the loan is deductible.

Discussion and Interpretation

1. Paragraph 20(1)(e.2) permits a limited deduction in calculating income from a business or property for premiums payable after 1989 under a life insurance policy (other than an annuity contract). The taxpayer seeking the deduction must also be the policyholder for the premiums to be considered to be "payable by the taxpayer

under a life insurance policy" and deductible under paragraph 20(1)(e.2). The provisions of paragraph 20(1)(e.2) will apply to permit a deduction for premiums payable under a life insurance policy if all the conditions in (a) to (c) below are satisfied:

(a) An interest in the life insurance policy is assigned to a restricted financial institution (RFI) in the course of a borrowing from the institution. An RFI is defined in subsection 248(1) and includes financial institutions such as banks, trust companies, credit unions and insurance companies.

(b) The interest payable on the borrowing is or would, but for subsections 18(2) and (3.1) and sections 21 and 28, be deductible in calculating the taxpayer's income for the year.

(c) The assignment referred to in (a) is required by the RFI as collateral for the borrowing.

2. Provided the conditions in 1 above are satisfied, the amount eligible for deduction under paragraph 20(1)(e.2) is the portion of the lesser of:

(a) the premiums payable by the taxpayer under the life insurance policy for the year, and

(b) the net cost of pure insurance under the policy for the year (see 4 below)

that can reasonably be considered to relate to the amount owing from time to time during the year under the loan for which the insurance policy has been assigned as collateral.

For example, if the life insurance coverage under an assigned policy is $500,000, and the amount owing under the loan throughout the taxation year is $200,000, the amount deductible under paragraph 20(1)(e.2) is limited to 40% of the lesser of the premiums payable and the net cost of pure insurance under the policy for the year. If the taxpayer's taxation year end does not correspond to the policy year, the premiums payable under the policy should be prorated on a reasonable basis to the taxation year. Similarly, the net cost of pure insurance, which is determined by the insurer on a calendar year basis, should be prorated on a reasonable basis to the taxation year.

Line of credit

3. An unused line of credit, even if it is subject to a standby charge or commitment fee, is not an amount owing in determining the portion that "can reasonably be considered to relate to the amount owing from time to time during the year" under the loan.

Net cost of pure insurance

4. The net cost of pure insurance under a life insurance policy is to be determined in accordance with section 308 of the *Income Tax Regulations*. The net cost of pure insurance, which may be obtained from the insurance company, is determined by referring to standard mortality assumptions and approximates the cost of the pure insurance coverage under the policy for the year. As a result, when the policy,

which has been assigned as collateral for a loan, has a savings component or some form of prefunding, the maximum deduction under paragraph 20(1)(e.2) would generally be limited by the "net cost of pure insurance" limitation in 2(b) above.

Collateral in excess of loan balance

5. It may be that an RFI, in accordance with industry practice, requires that other assets be pledged as collateral for a loan such that the total value of the collateral exceeds the loan balance. In these cases, a deduction under paragraph 20(1)(e.2) will usually not be denied unless it is clear that the lender has made the life insurance requirement simply to accommodate the taxpayer. Therefore, a deduction for the full amount of the premiums is generally available, subject to the requirements in 1 to 3 above, provided the insurance coverage does not exceed the maximum amount of the loan outstanding during the year.

Assignment of policy

6. For purposes of 1(a) above, it is not necessary that a policy be taken out at the time of borrowing. The assignment of an existing policy is acceptable. However, such an assignment must satisfy a bona fide requirement of the RFI and not be an accommodation to provide the borrower access to a deduction of otherwise non-deductible premiums.

Duplicate insurance

7. In some situations, a lender may require that the lives of more than one person be insured in respect of a particular borrowing. In such situations, the deductibility of the premiums payable by the borrower under any particular policy is determined independently of the other policies, as if each policy were the only life insurance policy assigned as collateral for the loan.

Example

8. Corporation A (December 31 year-end) borrows $400,000 from its bank on January 1, 1994. The bank (an RFI) required the following collateral:

- assignment of existing life insurance policies on two senior officers of the corporation (the policies have $500,000 and $350,000 coverage); and
- pledge of fixed assets (fair market value of assets: $100,000).

On June 30, 1994, the corporation repays $100,000 of principal on the loan.

The premiums on the life insurance policies are $1,000 and $800 a year. There is a savings component in each policy, and it has been determined that the cost of pure insurance for the year is $750 and $600 respectively for these policies. Assuming the conditions in 1(a) to (c) above are satisfied, the amount deductible under paragraph 20(1)(e.2) for 1994 for each policy is determined as follows:

	Policy I	*Policy II*
Lesser of:		
•premiums payable	$1,000	$ 800

•net cost of pure insurance	$ 750	$ 800
Lesser amount	$ 750	$ 600(A)
Portion of amount (A) that can reasonably be considered to relate to the amount owing:		
From January to June		
$750 × 6/12 × $300,000 ÷ $500,000	$ 300	
$600 × 6/12		$ 300
From July to December		
$750 × 6/12 × $300,000 ÷ $500,000	$ 225	
$600 × 6/12 × $300,000 ÷ $350,000		$ 257
Amount deductible under paragraph 20(1)(e.2) for the year:	$ 525	$ 557
Non-deductible portion of premiums:	$ 475	$ 243

If you have any comments regarding the matters discussed in this bulletin, please send them to:

Director, Technical Publications Division
Policy and Legislation Branch
Revenue Canada
875 Heron Road
Ottawa ON, K1A 0L8

Explanation of Changes for Interpretation Bulletin IT-309R2, *Premiums on Life Insurance Used as Collateral*

Introduction

The purpose of the *Explanation of Changes* is to give the reasons for the revisions to an interpretation bulletin. It outlines revisions that we have made as a result of changes to the law, as well as changes reflecting new or revised departmental interpretations.

Overview

This bulletin deals with the limited deduction that is available in calculating income from a business or property for premiums payable after 1989 under a life insurance policy, when the policy has been assigned to a restricted financial institution as collateral for a loan.

We have undertaken this revision to incorporate the amendments to the *Income Tax Act* enacted by S.C. 1994, c. 7, Sch. II (1991, c. 49 — formerly Bill C-18) to deal with the introduction of paragraph 20(1)(e.2) for premiums payable after 1989.

Legislative and other changes

We have revised ¶s 1 to 4 to reflect the Bill C-18 introduction of paragraph 20(1)(e.2). They explain the conditions that must be met for life insurance premiums to be deductible under that paragraph. Former ¶s 1 to 4 explained the limited circumstances under which life insurance premiums could be claimed, before the introduction of paragraph 20(1)(e.2), as a cost of borrowing money under subparagraph 20(1)(e)(ii). However, the decision in *Her Majesty the Queen v. Antoine Guertin*, 1988 D.T.C. 6126, [1988] 1 C.T.C. 360 overruled the position contained in former ¶s 1 to 4. Paragraph 20(1)(e.2) was enacted to counter this decision and to generally continue, with some modification, the administrative practice as set out in former ¶s 1 to 4.

Former ¶6 provided that it was not necessary for the borrower to be the policyholder to deduct the life insurance premiums as a cost of borrowing money under subparagraph 20(1)(e)(ii) as long as the borrower bore the premium cost. It also dealt with taxable benefits that may have been conferred on the policyholder in such circumstances. Under paragraph 20(1)(e.2), the life insurance premiums must be payable by the taxpayer under the life insurance policy. Since former ¶6 is not relevant for life insurance premiums deductible under paragraph 20(1)(e.2), we have deleted it.

We have revised new ¶5 (former ¶7) to explain the deductibility of life insurance premiums in situations where the lender requires collateral in excess of the loan balance.

Former ¶8 provided that in certain situations, the unused portion of a line of credit could be considered for the purpose of determining the deductible portion of the insurance premium. However, under paragraph 20(1)(e.2) only the portion of the life insurance premium that may reasonably be considered to relate to the amount owing may be deductible. As mentioned in new ¶3, any unused portion of a line of credit is not an amount owing and cannot be taken into consideration in the determination of a deduction under paragraph 20(1)(e.2). Therefore, we have deleted former 8.

The position in new ¶7 (former ¶9) was revised to eliminate the condition that there be a valid business reason for the assignment of duplicate life insurance policies. This condition is not required under paragraph 20(1)(e.2). Furthermore, under that paragraph, the deductibility of the premiums for a life insurance policy assigned as collateral for a loan is determined independently of the assignment of other life insurance policies as additional collateral for the loan. Accordingly, we have changed the position in former ¶9 that considered the face amount of only one policy and the aggregate of all the policy premiums in determining the deductible amount.

We have added new ¶8 to provide a detailed example on calculating the amount of life insurance premiums that are deductible under paragraph 20(1)(e.2), and to illustrate most of the comments made in the bulletin.

Throughout the bulletin, we have made minor changes for clarification or readability purposes.

Interpretation Bulletin [Archived] IT-355R2[1] — Interest on Loans to Buy Life Insurance Policies and Annuity Contracts, and Interest on Policy Loans

Date: **August 26, 1994**

Reference: ***Subsecs. 20(2.1) and (2.2), and para. 20(1)(c)*** **(also ss. 12.2 and 67.2, subsecs. 18(2), (3.1) and (11), the definitions 138(12)"life insurance policy", 138(12)"life insurance policy in Canada", 138(12)"policy loan" and 148(9)"adjusted cost basis", and paras. 20(1)(d) and 56(1)(d.1))**

Application

This bulletin cancels and replaces Interpretation Bulletin IT-355R dated January 12, 1981.

Summary

Interest on loans to buy life insurance policies and annuity contracts is generally not deductible in computing income for tax purposes. However, there are exceptions to this general rule and this bulletin outlines these exceptions. This bulletin also deals with the deductibility of interest on policy loans, including the conditions that a taxpayer must meet and the procedures to follow before a taxpayer can deduct the interest. A policy loan is an amount advanced by an insurer to the policyholder in accordance with the terms and conditions of a life insurance policy in Canada.

Discussion and Interpretation

Interest on loans to buy life insurance policies

1. The term "life insurance policy" is defined in subsection 138(12). It includes an annuity contract and a contract issued by an insurer where all or any part of the insurer's reserves for such a contract vary in amount depending on the fair market value of a specified group of assets (i.e., a "segregated fund").

2. Interest on borrowed money to buy a life insurance policy is not deductible under subparagraph 20(1)(c)(i). A deduction for interest on an amount payable for property that is an interest in a life insurance policy is also prohibited by subparagraph 20(1)(c)(ii). However, for the purposes of paragraphs 20(1)(c) and 20(1)(d) (compound interest), subsection 20(2.2) excludes certain policies from the definition of a life insurance policy. As a result, a deduction is allowed, to the extent permitted by paragraphs 20(1)(c) and (d) and subject to the limitation in subsection 18(11), for interest on borrowed money to buy the following types of policies:

(a) a policy that is or is issued pursuant to a registered pension plan, a registered retirement savings plan, an income-averaging annuity contract, or a deferred profit sharing plan;

---

[1] Archived by CRA in 2004.

(b) an annuity contract issued before 1978 that provided for annuity payments to commence not later than the day on which the policyholder attains 75 years of age; and

(c) for 1987 and subsequent taxation years, an annuity contract issued by an insurer where all of the insurer's reserves for the contract vary in amount depending on the fair market value of a specified group of properties (i.e., a "segregated fund").

3. Subject to certain conditions and limitations, subparagraph 20(1)(c)(iv) allows a taxpayer to deduct interest paid or payable on money borrowed to acquire an annuity contract. That is, if the annuity contract was last acquired after 1989, it must be a contract to which the annual accrual rules in section 12.2 apply or would apply if the contract had an anniversary day in the year while held by the taxpayer. In addition, if payments on such an annuity contract have commenced in a previous year, the interest expense deduction for that contract is limited in any year to the amount under that contract that is included in the taxpayer's income for the year under section 12.2. However, if the annuity contract was last acquired after June 28, 1982 and before 1990, interest is only deductible if the three year accrual rules apply or would apply to the annuity contract if it had a third anniversary in the year and, once the annuity payments have commenced, the interest expense deduction is limited to the amount under that contract that is included in the taxpayer's income for the year under section 12.2 or paragraph 56(1)(d.1).

Interest on policy loans

4. A "policy loan" is defined in subsection 138(12) as an amount advanced by an insurer to a policyholder in accordance with the terms and conditions of a life insurance policy in Canada. The phrase "life insurance policy in Canada," as defined in subsection 138(12), means a life insurance policy issued or effected by an insurer upon the life of a person resident in Canada at the time the policy was issued or effected. Accordingly, a policy loan includes amounts advanced under a life annuity contract but does not include amounts advanced under annuity certain contracts.

5. Subject to limitations in the Act on interest deductibility (such as section 67.2 and subsections 18(2) and (3.1)), interest on a policy loan is generally deductible under paragraphs 20(1)(c) and (d) if the proceeds of the loan are used for the purpose of earning income from a business or property (other than property the income from which is exempt or a life insurance policy or annuity). However, for the purposes of paragraphs 20(1)(c) and (d), subsection 20(2.1) prohibits the deduction of interest on a policy loan unless certain conditions are met. Specifically, the interest must be verified by the insurer on Form T2210, *Verification of Policy Loan Interest by the Insurer*, to be:

(a) interest paid in the year on the policy loan (interest added to a policy loan is considered to be paid at the time it is added); and

(b) interest that is not added to the adjusted cost basis, as defined in subsection 148(9), of the taxpayer's interest in the policy (since the taxpayer can either deduct the interest or add it to the adjusted cost basis, the taxpayer has to indicate on Form T2210 the amount of interest that is not to be added to the adjusted cost basis).

Both the taxpayer and the insurer have to complete Form T2210 no later than the date the taxpayer is required to file an income tax return for the taxation year in which the interest is paid. In cases where the taxpayer calculates income from the business or property on the accrual basis, the interest can be deducted in the taxation year that it was accrued if it is subsequently verified as described in (b) above. Furthermore, paragraph 20(2.1)(b) does not allow the insurer to verify interest, as described in (b) above, on a policy loan that was made before 1978 to acquire an annuity contract, or an interest therein, where the contract was issued before 1978 and provided for annuity payments to commence not later than the day on which the policyholder attains 75 years of age. As a result, interest on such policy loans is not deductible.

If you have any comments regarding the matters discussed in this bulletin, please send them to:

Director, Technical Publications Division
Policy and Legislation Branch
Revenue Canada
875 Heron Road
Ottawa, Ontario
K1A 0L8

Explanation of Changes for Interpretation Bulletin IT-355R2 — *Interest on Loans to Buy Life Insurance Policies and Annuity Contracts, and Interest on Policy Loans*

Introduction

The purpose of the *Explanation of Changes* is to give the reasons for the revisions to an interpretation bulletin. It outlines revisions that we have made as a result of changes to the law, as well as changes reflecting new or revised departmental interpretations.

Overview

Interpretation Bulletin IT-355R2 outlines the situations when interest on loans to acquire life insurance policies and annuity contracts, and interest on policy loans, can be deducted from income. This revision was undertaken to reflect certain amendments to the *Income Tax Act* enacted in 1990 by Bill C-52 and in 1991 by Bill C-18. Also, references to the *Income Tax Act* are to the *Income Tax Act* as revised by the 5th Supplement to the Revised Statutes of Canada, 1985, and by S.C. 1994, c.7 (former Bill C-15), both of which came into force on March 1, 1994.

The comments in the bulletin are not affected by the Budget Proposals of February 22, 1994 released by the Minister of Finance.

Legislative and Other Changes

We have revised para. 1 to include the definition of a "life insurance policy" in subsection 138(12).

New para. 2 (former para. 1) reflects amendments to subsection 20(2.2) under Bill C-52 and Bill C-18. The Bill C-52 amendment deleted a policy that is or is issued pursuant to a registered pension fund as an exception to the definition of a life insurance policy. The Bill C-18 amendment, however, provided an additional exception to the definition for certain annuity contracts.

New para. 3 (former para. 2) reflects amendments to subparagraph 20(1)(c)(iv) under Bill C-18. This subparagraph was amended so that it will apply to interest on money borrowed to acquire an interest in an annuity contract that would be subject to the income accrual rules if that contract had an anniversary day in the year while the taxpayer held it. It was also amended to remove a reference to paragraph 56(1)(d.1), applicable to contracts last acquired after 1989.

We have expanded new para. 4 (former para. 3) to include the definition of a "life insurance policy in Canada" in subsection 138(12).

We deleted the comments in former paras. 4 and 5 dealing with the deductibility of interest on policy loans for taxation years before 1978 since they are no longer relevant.

We revised new para. 5 (former para. 6) to clarify that paragraphs 20(1)(c) and (d) are subject to the general limitations in the Act on interest deductibility. Subsection 18(2) limits the amount that can be deducted for interest expense and property taxes relating to undeveloped land. Under subsection 18(3.1), certain real estate soft-costs have to be added to the capital cost of the building rather than deducted on a current basis. Section 67.2 restricts the amount that can be deducted for interest expense relating to the acquisition of a passenger vehicle.

A number of other changes have been made to improve the overall clarity and readability of the bulletin.

Interpretation Bulletin IT-365R2 — Damages, Settlements and Similar Receipts

Date: **May 8, 1987**

Reference: ***Section 3*** **(also section 6, subsecs. 5(1), 12.2(1) and (3), 14(1), 16(1), 56(1), and 248(1), paras. 81(1)(g.1) and (g.2) and subparas. 14(5)(a)(iv) and 56(1)(a)(ii)).**

This bulletin replaces and cancels IT-365R dated March 9, 1981 and the Special Release to IT-365R which was issued on May 25, 1984.

1. This bulletin deals with the treatment for tax purposes of amounts received

(a) out of claims for damages for personal injury or death,

(b) as compensation for the loss of property or income,

(c) as crime compensation awards, and

(d) on termination of employment.

Amounts Received as Damages in Respect of Personal Injury or Death

2. Amounts in respect of damages for personal injury or death may be received by an injured taxpayer or by a dependant of a deceased taxpayer on account of:

(a) Special damages — examples are compensation for

(i) out-of-pocket expenses such as medical and hospital expenses, and

(ii) accrued or future loss of earnings and

(b) General damages — examples are compensation for

(i) pain and suffering,

(ii) the loss of amenities of life,

(iii) the loss of earning capacity,

(iv) the shortened expectation of life and

(v) the loss of financial support caused by the death of the supporting individual.

All amounts received by a taxpayer or the taxpayer's dependant, as the case may be, that qualify as special or general damages for personal injury or death will be excluded from income regardless of the fact that the amount of such damages may have been determined with reference to the loss of earnings of the taxpayer in respect of whom the damages were awarded. However, an amount which can reasonably be considered to be income from employment rather than an award of damages will not be excluded from income. The tax treatment of an award of compensation, as adjudicated by a compensation board or commission in Canada, which is received as a result of a worker having suffered injury, disability or death while performing the duties of employment, is explained in IT-202R2.

Awards Not Considered to be Annuities

3. An award of damages for personal injury or death that decrees that it be paid in periodic payments is not, despite such periodic payments, considered to be an annuity contract for the purposes of subsections 12.2(3) and 56(1) and the periodic payments themselves are not considered to be annuity payments. However, an annuity contract purchased by a taxpayer or taxpayer's representative with proceeds of a lump sum award received for damages for personal injury or death will be an annuity contract for all purposes of the Act and will, except in the circumstances described in 6 below, give rise to income in the taxpayer's hands.

Interest Element of Awards for Personal Injury or Death

4. Where an amount in respect of damages for personal injury or death has been awarded by a Court or resolved in an out-of-court settlement, no part of such amount will be income to the recipient even though the amount includes or is augmented by an amount which, pursuant to the terms of the Court order or the settlement agreement, is referred to as interest. However, where an amount that has been awarded for damages is held on deposit, the amount of interest earned will be included in the income of the injured taxpayer unless paragraph 81(1)(g.1) or (g.2)

has application (see 6 below). Where an amount that has been awarded for damages is held in trust, any interest earned on the amount is income of the trust or of the beneficiary, depending on the circumstances.

Structured Settlement

5. A "structured settlement" is a means of paying or settling a claim for damages, usually against a casualty insurer, in such a way that amounts paid to the claimant as a result of the settlement are free from tax in the claimant's hands. To create such a structured settlement the following conditions must be complied with:

(a) a claim for damages must have been made in respect of personal injury or death,

(b) the claimant and the casualty insurer must have reached an agreement under which the latter is committed to make at least periodic payments to the claimant for either a fixed term or the life of the claimant,

(c) the casualty insurer must

(i) purchase a single premium annuity contract which must be non-assignable, non-commutable, non-transferable and designed to produce payments equal to the amounts, and at the times, specified in the agreement referred to in (b),

(ii) make an irrevocable direction to the issuer of the annuity contract to make all payments thereunder directly to the claimant, and

(iii) remain liable to make the payments as required by the settlement agreement (ie, the annuity contract payout).

As a consequence of compliance with the foregoing conditions, the casualty insurer is the owner of, and annuitant (beneficiary) under, the annuity contract and must report as income the interest element inherent in the annuity contract while the payments received by the claimant represent, in the Department's view, non-taxable payments for damages.

Income from Property that was Received by a Taxpayer Under 21 Years of Age as an Award of Damages for Personal Injury

6. For the 1984 and subsequent taxation years, paragraphs 81(1)(g.1) and (g.2) exempt from tax the income of a taxpayer from particular sources for taxation years during any part of which the taxpayer was under 21 years of age. To qualify for this exemption the income must, during the particular taxation years, be derived from one or more of the following sources:

(a) property received by or on behalf of a taxpayer who is under 21 years of age as an award of, or pursuant to an action for, damages in respect of the taxpayer's physical or mental injury,

(b) property substituted for property described in (a),

(c) a capital gain derived from the disposition of property described in (a) or (b), or

(d) invested income that was, by virtue of paragraph 81(1)(g.1) or (g.2), not required to be included in the taxpayer's income for a particular taxation year described above.

For the purposes of paragraphs 81(1)(g.1) and (g.2) income will include income received and receivable and income accrued (i.e., earned but not received) up to, but not beyond, the end of the taxation year in which the taxpayer attains the age of 21 years.

7. For taxation years ending after 1971 and before 1984, former paragraph 81(1)(g.1)

(a) caused the exempt period to end on the day immediately preceding the day on which the injured taxpayer attained the age of 21 years, and

(b) restricted exempt income to income that was actually received while the injured taxpayer was under 21 years of age.

Receipts in Respect of Non-Performance of Business Contract

8. An amount received by a taxpayer in lieu of the performance of the terms of a business contract by the other party to that contract may, depending on the facts, be either an income or capital receipt. If the receipt relates to the loss of an income-producing asset, it will be considered to be a capital receipt; on the other hand, if it is compensation for the loss of income, it will constitute business income. Again, while it is a question of fact as to whether a receipt is an income or capital amount, the following factors are important in making this distinction:

(a) if the compensation is received for the failure to receive a sum of money that would have been an income item if it had been received, the compensation will likely be an income receipt,

(b) "where for example, the structure of the recipient's business is so fashioned as to absorb the shock as one of the normal incidents to be looked for and where it appears that the compensation received is no more than a surrogatum for the future profits surrendered, the compensation received is in use to be treated as a revenue receipt and not a capital receipt", and

(c) "when the rights and advantages surrendered on cancellation are such as to destroy or materially to cripple the whole structure of the recipient's profit-making apparatus, involving the serious dislocation of the normal commercial organization and resulting perhaps in the cutting down of the staff previously required, the recipient of the compensation may properly affirm that the compensation represents the price paid for the loss or sterilization of a capital asset and is therefore a capital and not a revenue receipt."

((b) and (c) above are quotations from the judgement in *Commissioner of Inland Revenue v. Fleming and Co. (Machinery) Ltd.*, 33 T.C. 57 (H.L.))

9. Where an amount received by a taxpayer as compensation for a breach of a business contract is a capital amount according to the comments in 8 above, that amount would relate either to a particular asset of the taxpayer or to the whole structure of the taxpayer's profit-making apparatus. If, on the basis of the facts of

the case, such as the terms of a contract, settlement or judgment, the amount received relates to a particular asset (tangible or intangible) which is sold, destroyed or abandoned as a consequence of the breach of contract, it will be considered proceeds of disposition of that asset or a part thereof, as the case may be. Where the amount of compensation relates to a particular asset that was not disposed of, the amount will serve to reduce the cost of that asset to the taxpayer. On the other hand, where the amount of compensation is of a capital nature but it does not relate to a particular asset as indicated above, the amount will be considered as compensation for the destruction of, or as damages to, the whole profit-making apparatus of the taxpayer's business. Such compensation may result in an "eligible capital amount" for the purposes of subsection 14(1) and subparagraph 14(5)(a)(iv).

Compensation for Loss of Business Income or Business Properties

10. Amounts received by a taxpayer with respect to the loss of business income or business property may fall into one of the following categories:

(a) a non-taxable receipt,

(b) an income receipt,

(c) a receipt resulting from the disposition of a capital property, or

(d) an eligible capital amount.

See IT-182 for a discussion of the factors that determine the tax status of a given receipt.

Crime Compensation Awards and Similar Receipts

11. A number of provinces make crime-compensation awards pursuant to the authority of criminal-injury compensation laws. The Department considers that such crime-compensation awards are non-taxable.

12. A taxpayer who is a victim of a crime may receive compensation from a source other than the person who committed the crime or a crime-compensation board. For example, a male employee of a bank is kidnapped and upon his release the bank pays the employee an amount to compensate for "damages" inflicted on him. Where the amount of money or benefit received is compensation for damages the Department will normally consider the amount to be a non-taxable receipt even if the damages are computed with reference to the victim's salary. To qualify as a non-taxable receipt, the amount must not be in excess of a fair evaluation of the damages suffered by the employee having regard to all relevant facts of the case. The amount of the receipt will ordinarily be accepted as a fair evaluation unless there are indications (such as the employer and employee not dealing at arm's length) that the receipt includes an amount for services rendered by the employee to the employer. Any part of an amount received by a taxpayer from his employer, or former employer, that is compensation for loss of earnings (e.g., an amount paid in lieu of regular wages or benefits) resulting from a disability of short duration will be included in the income of the taxpayer.

13. Where a taxpayer, other than an employee, is in receipt of an amount that has not been awarded by a court or a crime-compensation board (a payment by a bank

to a customer, for example) for "damages" inflicted as a result of a crime, the total amount is considered to be a non-taxable receipt.

Amounts Received on Termination of Employment

14. Applicable with respect to the termination of an office or employment occurring after November 12, 1981, the defined term "termination payment" was repealed by S.C. 1980-81-82-83, c. 140. The definition of "retiring allowance" in subsection 248(1) was amended concurrently so that amounts that were previously included in the definition of a termination payment are now fully included in income as retiring allowances under subparagraph 56(1)(a)(ii). Retiring allowances are dealt with in IT-337R2.

15. Where a taxpayer receives an amount pursuant to the terms of an employment contract, the amount is to be included in computing the taxpayer's income under subsection 5(1) or section 6, whichever may be applicable, as income from an office or employment, whether or not it is received on termination of the employment. Such an amount would include, for example, salary, wages, accrued vacation pay, and an amount paid in lieu of notice of termination.

Interpretation Bulletin [Archived] IT-408R[2] — Life Insurance Policies as Investments of Registered Retirement Savings Plans and Deferred Profit Sharing Plans

Date: February 15, 1980

Reference: *Subs. 198(6)*(also subsecs. 146(11), 198(6.1) and (7))

This bulletin cancels and replaces Interpretation Bulletin IT-408 dated February 13, 1978. Current revisions are designated by vertical lines.

1. For a registered retirement savings plan (RRSP) qualified investments are described in paragraph 146(1)(g) of the Act and section 4900 of the Regulations; for a deferred profit sharing plan (DPSP) it is paragraph 204(e) of the Act and section 1502 of the Regulations. None of these identify a life insurance policy as a qualified investment of a plan under any circumstances.

2. Although a life insurance policy may not be a qualified investment of an RRSP or a DPSP, nevertheless, under certain conditions subsection 198(6) deems the acquisition of an interest in or the payment of an amount under a life insurance policy not to be the acquisition of a non-qualified investment. The conditions which must be met are those set out in paragraphs 198(6)(c), (d) and (e). Although subsection 198(6) applies in the first place to DPSPs, its application is extended as well to RRSPs through subsection 146(11).

---

[2]Archived by CRA in 2004.

3. A life insurance policy which is held by a DPSP and which meets the conditions of paragraphs 198(6)(c), (d) and (e) is subject to neither Part X nor Part XI.I tax. A similar policy held by an RRSP is not caught by the provisions of subsection 146(10) and is not subject to Part XI.I tax under subsection 207.1(1).

4. Subsection 198(6) deems a payment to acquire an interest in or an amount paid under a life insurance policy not to be the acquisition of a non-qualified investment if the following conditions are satisfied:

(a) The trust must be the only person, other than the insurer, who is entitled to any rights or benefits under the policy. In particular, the insurance element of the policy as well as its cash value (including dividends) must be payable to the trust.

(b) At some time before the 71st birthday of the person insured, the cash surrender value of the policy will be at least as great as the maximum amount payable under it. Accumulated dividends are excluded from this calculation. Subsection 198(6.1) provides that the existence of an option to take the proceeds of the form of an annuity will not disqualify a policy which would otherwise satisfy this condition.

(c) The premiums payable in respect of any 12-month period must not be greater than those payable in respect of the 12-month period following the date of issuance of the policy. Nevertheless, the Department's view is that a policy is not disqualified only because it contains a rider under which deposits in excess of the premium may be paid at the discretion of the trust in order to increase the amount payable under the policy. On the other hand such a payment must increase the cash surrender value to such an extent as to comply with (b) above.

5. Subsection 198(7), which applies only to DPSPs, provides that where not more than 25 per-cent of the employer's contributions to the plan are used to acquire interests in life insurance policies under which the trust is the only person entitled to any rights or benefits (other than the rights or benefits of the insurer), those policies are deemed not to be non-qualified investments despite the fact that they do not satisfy all the conditions of subsection 198(6). Where more than 25 per-cent of the employer's contributions are used to acquire interests in life insurance policies, only those which qualify within subsection 198(6) are not non-qualified investments and subsection 198(7) ceases to operate.

6. Paragraph 198(6)(e) disqualifies a policy which provides for a premium greater in any subsequent year than it was in the initial 12-month period. Accordingly, a rider forming part of a policy and providing for an increased premium under any circumstances would disqualify the policy. Only if the rider is issued in such a manner that it may be considered to be an investment separate from the policy would the policy not be disqualified. For this to be so it would be necessary, as a minimum, that the premiums collected, the funds accumulated, and the benefits payable under it would be accounted for by the issuer separately from the basic policy. The status as a qualified investment is determined in the usual manner.

7. The Department's view is that a double indemnity rider disqualifies the policy of which it is part, since the maximum total amount payable under the policy exceeds its cash surrender value at any time before the 71st birthday of the insured. Similarly, a policy is disqualified if it contains an option under which the holder may elect to apply policy dividends to the purchase of term insurance thereby increasing the amount payable under the policy upon death. Typically the amount of term insurance so acquired is equal to the cash surrender value of the contract from time to time.

8. Under certain conditions the Department views the prepayment of premiums of a life insurance policy, which itself is not a non-qualified investment, as being a payment under the policy within the meaning of paragraph 198(6)(a). This is so where the prepayment involves a discount so that it is in effect productively invested and the policy does not specifically bar prepayment.

Interpretation Bulletin IT-416R3 — Valuation of Shares of a Corporation Receiving Life Insurance Proceeds on Death of a Shareholder

Date: **July 10, 1987**

Reference: ***Subsections 70(5) and (5.3)***

This bulletin cancels and replaces Interpretation Bulletin IT-416R2 dated September 26, 1984. Current revisions are designated by vertical lines.

1. Paragraph 70(5)(a) deems the property of a deceased person to have been disposed of immediately before death for proceeds equal to the fair market value of the property at that time.

2. The property referred to in 1 may include shares of a corporation the value of which depends at least in part upon the value of a life insurance policy under which the decedent was the person whose life was insured. The corporation's interest in the policy may be direct or it may be through its ownership of shares of another corporation. In either case, for deaths occurring after December 1, 1982, subsection 70(5.3) provides that the value of the policy immediately before death shall be its cash surrender value at that time as determined under paragraph 148(9)(b) (see 3 below). Where the death occurred prior to December 2, 1982, the comments in paragraphs 4 and 5 below apply.

3. In determining the cash surrender value of a policy for the purposes of subsection 70(5.3), paragraph 148(9)(b) provides that policy loans outstanding, policy dividends payable and any interest payable upon such dividends shall be disregarded. In addition to those specific exclusions, the Department also considers that prepaid premiums and dividends left on deposit are not elements of the cash surrender value of a policy although their values, and the values of those elements specifically excluded, may affect the values of the shares of a corporation which is the owner and beneficiary of the policy.

Death of Shareholder before December 2, 1982

4. Where subsection 70(5.3) does not apply, the insurance policy, as a component of the assets underlying the shares, will be valued in accordance with normal valuation practices taking into consideration all facts relevant to the particular case. In this regard, the value established for the insurance policy immediately before death should be based on relevant factors relating to the deceased shortly before death, eg, the day prior to death (see 5 below).

5. Major factors that should be taken into account are:

(a) the cash surrender value, if any, of the policy,

(b) the life expectancy of the insured based on mortality tables, and

(c) the state of the health of the insured as it would be known to other persons.

For example, the value of an insurance policy could approach its face value if it were known that the insured had a terminal illness or was critically injured as a result of an accident and not expected to recover. Conversely, it would have little added value if a person in apparently excellent health were to die unexpectedly as a result of an accident or heart attack. For valuation purposes the state of health of the insured prior to death would override the effect of an unexpected death due to a cause not related to any known health problem. Therefore, if a person with terminal cancer died from an unexpected heart attack the actual cause of death would not be relevant in the valuation, but the fact that the person had terminal cancer would.

Interpretation Bulletin IT-430R3 — Life Insurance Proceeds Received by a Private Corporation or a Partnership as a Consequence of Death [Consolidated]

Date: **December 2, 2002**

Reference: **The definition 89(1)"capital dividend account" and para. 53(1)(e) (also ss. 80, 148(9)"adjusted cost basis", 148(2)(a), 212(2)(b) of the Income Tax Act)**

Latest Revision — ¶ 6

Application

This bulletin is a consolidation of the following:

- IT-430R3 dated February 10, 1997; and
- subsequent amendment thereto.

For further particulars, see the ***"Bulletin Revisions"*** **section near the end of this bulletin.**

Summary

This bulletin discusses the income tax consequences of the receipt, by a private corporation or partnership, of the proceeds of a life insurance policy as a consequence of the death of the person whose life was insured. The net proceeds of a life insurance policy (essentially the proceeds minus the adjusted cost basis of the policy), if received by a private corporation, are added to its capital dividend account. Generally, when the required election is made, a tax-free distribution of this amount can then be made to the shareholders of the corporation. The net proceeds of a life insurance policy, if received by a partnership, increase the adjusted cost base of each partner's interest in the partnership.

The capital dividend account is part of the system for integrating the corporate and shareholder income tax of private corporations and is intended to preserve the character of non-taxable receipts (such as the proceeds of certain life insurance policies) of a corporation in the hands of its shareholders.

Discussion and Interpretation

Tax Consequences to Recipients of Life Insurance Proceeds

1. Paragraph (d) of the definition of "capital dividend account" in subsection 89(1) provides the rules for the addition of the net proceeds of a life insurance policy to the capital dividend account of a private corporation.

2. Subparagraph 53(1)(e)(iii) provides for an addition to the adjusted cost base of an interest in a partnership in respect of a partner's share of the net proceeds of a life insurance policy received by the partnership.

Tax Consequences to Recipients of Dividends

3. A private corporation may elect to pay its shareholders a dividend out of its capital dividend account. These dividends do not constitute income to the shareholder resident in Canada and, in the case of capital dividends received by a private corporation, are included in the corporation's capital dividend account. If the dividend was paid from another corporation's life insurance capital dividend account, such a dividend received before May 24, 1985, is included in the recipient corporation's life insurance capital dividend account. Although a dividend paid from the life insurance capital dividend account was not included in the shareholder's income, the amount of the dividend reduced the adjusted cost base of certain shares, by virtue of paragraph 53(2)(r) as it then applied, if the shares were acquired as the result of any individual's death. The balance of the corporation's life insurance capital dividend account immediately before May 24, 1985, became a part of the corporation's capital dividend account at that time. The current version of IT-66 [IT-66R6], *Capital Dividends*, discusses the procedures required to pay a dividend from a private corporation's capital dividend account.

Non-resident shareholders are subject to a 25 per cent tax on dividends paid from a corporation's capital dividend account pursuant to paragraph 212(2)(b). However, a non-resident shareholder may qualify for relief in the form of a reduced rate of withholding tax on such dividends under a provision of a relevant tax treaty with a foreign country that has the force of law in Canada.

4. Subparagraph 53(1)(e)(ii) provides for an addition to the adjusted cost base of an interest in a partnership on the receipt of capital and life insurance capital dividends by the partnership equal to each partner's share of those dividends.

Definition of "Net Proceeds"

5. As indicated in ¶s 1 and 2 above, the "net proceeds" of a life insurance policy, if received by a private corporation, are added to its capital dividend account or, if received by a partnership, increase the adjusted cost base of a partner's interest in the partnership. The term "net proceeds" means the excess of the proceeds of the life insurance policy received as a consequence of the death of the person whose life was insured over:

(a) the amounts paid as premiums (see the definition of "premium" in subsection 148(9)) under the policy where the proceeds were received after 1971 and before April 1, 1977; or

(b) the adjusted cost basis of the policy, as defined in subsection 148(9), immediately before the death of the person insured, where the proceeds were received after March 31, 1977.

Any accumulated policy dividends and interest paid out at the time of payment of the death claim are excluded from *proceeds* described above since the right to such payments does not arise as a consequence of the death of the person whose life was insured. Any policy dividend that a policyholder has become entitled to receive reduces the *adjusted cost basis* of the policy pursuant to paragraph 148(2)(a) and the definition of "adjusted cost basis." Accordingly, all such dividends (whether or not they are left to accumulate) will be reflected in the "net proceeds" if the proceeds were received after March 31, 1977. However, that portion of policy dividends received or receivable in taxation years beginning after December 20, 1991, that are automatically applied to pay a premium under the policy or repay a policy loan under the policy, as provided for under the terms and conditions of the policy, are excluded from the proceeds of disposition. The "adjusted cost basis" (as defined in subsection 148(9)) of a life insurance policy is not increased by that portion of such dividends because they are excluded from the total of all amounts paid in respect of a premium under the policy.

Life Insurance Policy Used as Security for Indebtedness

6. A life insurance policy may be used to secure the indebtedness of a private corporation or a partnership with part or all of the proceeds arising upon the death of the person whose life was insured being paid directly to the creditor as beneficiary or as an assignee for security. In such cases, whether or not the premium cost is borne directly or indirectly by the debtor, the entitlement to the addition to the capital dividend account (or the entitlement of its partners to an addition to the adjusted cost base of each of their partnership interests) remains with that creditor (or its partners).

However, when a life insurance policy has been assigned as collateral for securing indebtedness (as opposed to an absolute assignment of the policy) or is the subject of a hypothecary claim by a creditor, and the debtor remains the beneficiary or policyholder, the proceeds in excess of the adjusted cost basis of the policy would be included in the capital dividend account of the debtor. This is so because, in such cases, the proceeds of the insurance policy would be constructively received by the debtor in its capacity as beneficiary or policyholder, even though paid directly to the creditor in accordance with the assignment or hypothec. The creditor is neither the beneficiary of the policy nor the policyholder and would not be entitled to include the proceeds in its capital dividend account because the amount it receives would not be considered to be proceeds of a life insurance policy.

Furthermore, the current version of IT-309 [IT-309R2], *Premiums on Life Insurance Used as Collateral*, contains information on the limited deduction available under paragraph 20(1)(e.2) for premiums payable under a life insurance policy when the policy has been assigned to a restricted financial institution for a loan.

7. Where an amount to which subparagraphs 53(1)(e)(ii) and (iii) apply is received by a partnership and allocated to a partner that is a private corporation, the corporation may add the amount so allocated to its capital dividend account or life insurance capital dividend account, as described in ¶ 1 above, as if the corporation had received the amount allocated to it at the time the partnership received it.

8. The increase in the capital dividend account, or the adjusted cost base of a partnership interest occurs at the time of receipt of proceeds rather than the time of entitlement to proceeds.

Application of Section 80

9. Section 80 applies to a gain realized by a taxpayer on settlement of a "commercial obligation" without payment or with insufficient payment. If the life of a debtor (or a principal shareholder or an officer of a debtor corporation or a partner of a debtor partnership) is insured and the cost is borne by the creditor without being passed directly or indirectly on to the debtor, proceeds received on death that are applied to extinguish or reduce the debtor's "commercial obligation" are not regarded as having been paid. Thus, the provisions of section 80 will apply. Similarly, if the creditor agrees to waive the repayment of the balance owing on a "commercial obligation" in the event of the death of the debtor, section 80 applies.

10. Where an individual who has issued a "commercial obligation" dies, paragraph 80(2)(p) applies when such an obligation is subsequently settled if:

- the commercial obligation is outstanding at the time of the individual's death; and
- the individual's estate was liable for that obligation before it was settled or extinguished.

Paragraph 80(2)(p) ensures that the estate is deemed to have issued the commercial debt obligation at the same time and in the same circumstances as the obligation was issued by the individual. With certain exceptions, if a commercial obligation that is issued by an individual has been settled by the estate of the individual within 6 months of the individual's death, and the estate was liable for the obligation immediately before the obligation was settled, the rules in paragraph 80(2)(q) apply. In particular, the obligation is deemed to have been settled at the beginning of the day the individual died. In effect, this means that the individual is subject to the debt forgiveness rules in section 80 at the time the obligation is deemed to be settled and if there is a "forgiven amount," as defined in subsection 80(1), it is applied to reduce the individual's tax attributes in a specified order, as required by subparagraph 80(2)(c), and subsections 80(3) to (12).

Bulletin Revisions

¶s 1 to 5 and 7 to 10 have not been revised since the issuance of IT-430R3 on February 10, 1997.

¶ 6 is revised to clarify the CCRA's position on life insurance policies assigned as collateral for securing indebtedness or subject to a hypothecary claim in Quebec and the possible impact on the debtor's capital dividend account where the debtor remains the beneficiary or policyholder. This clarification had originally been explained, in part, in *Income Tax Technical News* No. 10 of July 11, 1997. In addition, our position with respect to hypothecary claims in Quebec has been clarified. (December 2, 2002)

Interpretation Bulletin IT-529 — Flexible Employee Benefit Programs

Date: February 20, 1998

Reference: *Para. 6(1)(a)* (also subsecs. 6(3), 6(4), 15(1); the definitions 248(1)"salary deferral arrangement", 248(1)"retirement compensation arrangement", 248(1)"group term life insurance policy" and 248(1)"private health services plan"; paras. 6(1)(f), 6(1)(g), 6(1)(h), 6(1)(i), subparas. 56(1)(a)(i) and (iii))

Interpretation bulletins (ITs) provide Revenue Canada's technical interpretations of income tax law. Due to their technical nature, ITs are used primarily by departmental staff, tax specialists, and other individuals who have an interest in tax matters. For those readers who prefer a less technical explanation of the law, the Department offers other publications, such as tax guides and brochures.

While the ITs do not have the force of law, they can generally be relied upon as reflecting the Department's interpretation of the law to be applied on a consistent basis by departmental staff. In cases where an IT has not yet been revised to reflect legislative changes, readers should refer to the amended legislation and its effective date. Similarly, court decisions subsequent to the date of the IT should be considered when determining the relevancy of the comments in the IT. An interpretation described in an IT applies as of the date the IT is published, unless otherwise specified. When there is a change in a previous interpretation and the change is beneficial to taxpayers, it is usually effective for all future assessments and reassessments. If the change is not favourable to taxpayers, it will normally be effective for the current and subsequent taxation years or for transactions entered into after the date of the IT.

A change in a departmental interpretation may also be announced in the *Income Tax Technical News.*

If you have any comments regarding matters discussed in this IT, please send them to:

Director, Business and Publications Division

Income Tax Rulings and Interpretations Directorate
Policy and Legislation Branch
Revenue Canada
25 Nicholas Street
Ottawa ON K1A 0L5

Interpretation bulletins can be found on the Revenue Canada Internet site at: www.rc.gc.ca

Application

This bulletin discusses various tax consequences that may apply to flexible employee benefit programs.

Summary

This bulletin discusses the tax treatment of flexible employee benefit programs. These programs, which are sometimes referred to as "flexible benefit plans" or "cafeteria plans", are not defined in the *Income Tax Act* but can generally be described as a program of delivering company benefits where the employees are able to select the type and level of coverage from among a menu of available benefits. These programs are generally implemented to permit employees to build an individualized benefit program that most closely meets their coverage needs and budget requirements and to change their benefit elections over time as their life circumstances change.

Income tax considerations are an integral part of the design of flexible employee benefit programs and an important aspect of the selection of benefits by the employee. The design of such programs would, for example, include the choices to be made by the employee between taxable and non-taxable benefits, the conditions attached to these choices and the method of purchasing the chosen benefits. Although the Act does not contain provisions that specifically apply to these programs as a whole, the design of the program must satisfy certain conditions in order to avoid adverse tax consequences for all benefits provided under the program. These conditions are discussed in the bulletin. Provided these conditions are satisfied, the various benefit components under the program are subject to specific provisions of the Act in the same manner as if they were offered on their own outside of the program. Therefore, depending on the particular benefit and how it is paid for, it may result in a taxable benefit to the employee or a non- taxable benefit.

The bulletin discusses these tax consequences in the context of a typical flexible employee benefit program, hereafter referred to in this bulletin as a *Flex Program*. However, since the purpose of such a program is to provide flexibility in the delivery of employee benefits, a particular flexible employee benefit program will not necessarily contain all the features described below, or it may be structured in a different format.

Discussion and Interpretation

General

The subject matter of this bulletin is arranged under the following headings:

Description of a Flex Program

1. Under one type of Flex Program, the employer allocates a notional amount (commonly called flex credits) to each eligible employee. Prior to the beginning of the plan year (see paragraph 4 below), the employees participating in the Flex Program allocate their flex credits to various benefits available under the Flex Program, some of which may result in a taxable benefit to the employee and some of which may not. The employer is then obligated under the terms of the Flex Program to provide the employee with the benefits so chosen. Typically, each employee will get a booklet from the employer explaining the details of the particular Flex Program and a worksheet to assist the employee in making choices. However, regardless of the manner in which the details of the Flex Program are communicated to the employees, the tax consequences described in this bulletin will not necessarily apply unless all eligible employees are informed of their rights under the Flex Program.

2. Another type of Flex Program permits employees to select a level of coverage for each benefit available under the Flex Program, ranging from no coverage to a premium level of coverage. A standard level of coverage is established by the employer for each benefit and a dollar value is assigned to each level of coverage above or below that standard. When an employee selects a level of coverage other than the standard established by the employer, the assigned dollar value for that

level of coverage is either credited or debited to the employee's account. If an employee's selection of benefits results in a net deficiency, the additional amount required to pay for the benefits so chosen is withheld from the employee's salary. Since the tax treatment of each benefit is determined separately, a Flex Program will normally permit an employee to choose which benefit is considered to have been purchased by that employee through the use of payroll deductions. The terms and conditions of the Flex Program will determine whether any surplus can be paid to the employee as additional remuneration.

3. The allocation of flex credits annually by an employer to its employees represents the employer's contribution to benefits. In the second type of Flex Program, all benefits which are not attributable to a payment by the employee are considered to be funded by means of a contribution by the employer. A Flex Program may also allow an employee to increase the level of benefits provided under the Flex Program or acquire additional benefits by means of payroll deductions or by forfeiting some other right, such as vacation leave. In the same manner as for other payroll deductions, an employee who uses payroll deductions to purchase benefit coverage is taxed on the gross amount of salary received and not the net amount of the employee's pay cheque.

Plan Year

4. A plan year is normally defined as a twelve-month period. However, in the case of the first year of a Flex Program, the plan year may be greater or less than twelve months so that the plan year will coincide with the year end designated in the Flex Program documentation. The plan year does not have to be the calendar year and does not have to be the same for all employees. For example, in order to ease the administration of a Flex Program, employers may require employees to make their annual selections prior to the month of their birth, in which case the selection would be valid for the plan year commencing with the month of their birth. In any event, the plan year should be explained in the Flex Program documentation available to all employees.

Tax Considerations in the Design of the Overall Flex Program

5. The concept of the plan year is important to a Flex Program if the program offers employees the choice of both taxable and non-taxable benefits. As a general rule, where one part of a Flex Program could be regarded as a health and welfare trust or similar arrangement and another part could be regarded as a salary deferral arrangement, a retirement compensation arrangement, an employee benefit plan or an employee trust, the statutory rules applicable to salary deferral arrangements, retirement compensation arrangements, employee benefit plans or employee trusts, as the case may be, will apply to the entire Flex Program. However, if the employees covered by the Flex Program are required to choose which benefits will be provided under the Flex Program and how the benefit will be funded prior to the beginning of the plan year (and, subject to paragraph 6 below, the selection is irrevocable), the Flex Program can be segregated into multiple parts and the taxation of the benefits offered under the Flex Program is not altered by the fact that it is pro-

vided under the umbrella of a Flex Program. While the discussion in this bulletin concerning the tax consequences of benefits provided through a Flex Program centres on whether or not a Flex Program is an employee benefit plan, the comments are applicable with the appropriate modifications, if the Flex Program is a salary deferral arrangement, a retirement compensation arrangement or an employee trust.

6. Two exceptions to the requirement (described in paragraph 5 above) that the employee's selection of benefits be irrevocable for the duration of the plan year is the occurrence of a "life event" or a change in employment status. The term "life event" should be defined in the plan documentation if the Flex Program permits changes in the selection of benefits when such a life event occurs. A life event is typically defined to include events such as the birth or death of a dependant, a change in marital status or the loss of insurance coverage under a spouse's employer's plan. A change in an employee's place of residence which does not result in a change to the amount of flex credits allocated to the employee would not be an acceptable life event which would warrant a change to the employee's allocation of flex credits during the plan year. In certain circumstances, a Flex Program may permit an employee to make certain changes to accommodate a life event (i.e. decrease coverage in one area to provide additional coverage in another) without adversely affecting the tax treatment of benefits under the plan. This is only possible if the changes do not require a withdrawal of funds credited to that benefit option contrary to the terms of that policy or plan and the Flex Program's definition of life event is confined to events such as those described in this paragraph. Also, if the amount of flex credits allocated to an employee is altered by reason of a change in employment status (for example, a part-time employee may be entitled to less credits than a full-time employee), an employee may be required to make changes to the original selection of benefits to accommodate the increase or decrease in the amount of flex credits available. However, any such change cannot be made on a retroactive basis. For example, if an employee had selected a certain type of insurance coverage, any change to that coverage would only be effective from the date of that life event or change in employment status.

7. Assuming that flex credits have no redemptive value and that nothing of value is forfeited by the employee to acquire such credits, flex credits are considered to be notional amounts in that a flex credit has no intrinsic value by itself. A Flex Program will not be considered to be an employee benefit plan if, under the terms of such a Flex Program, flex credits are notional and the employee is required to make an irrevocable selection of benefits to be provided with the flex credits before the beginning of the plan year (subject to the exceptions described in paragraph 6 above). The allocation of flex credits by an employer does not, in and by itself, normally give rise to a taxable benefit in the hands of the employee.

8. If, after the beginning of the plan year, a Flex Program permits:

- an exchange of unallocated or newly allocated flex credits for cash (although the actual payment of cash, according to the employee's allocation of flex credits prior to the beginning of the year, may occur after the beginning of the plan year);
- a transfer of credits between benefit options; or

- a selection of benefits (other than a reselection of benefits described in paragraph 6 above or an initial selection by an employee who enters the Flex Program at any time during the plan year);

the employee will be considered to have constructively received employment income equal to the value of the allocated credits (unless the entire Flex Program is considered to be an employee benefit plan). This would result in the inclusion in the employee's income of the value of all benefits received out of the Flex Program even though some of the benefits would not have been so included if offered separately from the Flex Program. This is because a flex credit which can be saved and negotiated for cash at any time has a redemption value and is thus not considered to be a notional credit as described in the previous paragraph.

9. While a portion of the flex credits allocated to an employee may be computed as a percentage of the employee's salary, the conversion of any portion of the employee's salary to flex credits will result in an income inclusion of the amount of salary so converted. Thus, if an employee forgoes an amount to which the employee is or will become entitled, such as a negotiated salary increase, vacation or bonus, the amount of remuneration forgone is included in income in the year in which the amount is converted to flex credits as explained in paragraph 22 below. On the other hand, when a contract of employment is renegotiated upon the *expiry* of a former employment contract to incorporate a decrease in the level of salary or wages to be paid to an employee over the term of the new contract and the new contract also provides for additional flex credits, the additional credits will not be required to be included in the employee's income as part of salary and wages. However, if an employment contract is renegotiated during the term of an employment contract to decrease salary and increase the allocation of flex credits, the additional credits so allocated will be included in the employee's income as salary. Also, the benefits acquired by means of the additional credits will be considered to have been provided through employee contributions.

Setting up a Flex Program

10. All employees covered by the Flex Program must have legal access to the rights granted under the Flex Program. Generally, this means that the employees must have access to some document which outlines their entitlement under the Flex Program. As with health and welfare trusts, there is no formal registration procedure for a Flex Program and no requirement that the plan documents be submitted to Revenue Canada for approval prior to the implementation of the Flex Program. However, the advice of the local tax services office may be requested where there is any doubt as to whether the Flex Program could be considered to be an employee benefit plan, an employee trust, a retirement compensation arrangement or a salary deferral arrangement. Alternatively, an advance income tax ruling as described in the current version of Information Circular 70-6 may be requested. Full particulars of the Flex Program including a copy of all pertinent documents should accompany such a request.

Statutory Considerations

11. In determining the tax consequences arising from a Flex Program, consideration must be given to whether the Flex Program falls within the definition in subsection 248(1) of a salary deferral arrangement, a retirement compensation arrangement, an employee benefit plan or an employee trust. Flex Programs are usually designed so that both taxable and non-taxable benefits can be provided through the same plan. However, failure to be excluded from the statutory rules governing an employee benefit plan, an employee trust, a retirement compensation arrangement or a salary deferral arrangement can result in adverse tax consequences where the intention is to provide non-taxable benefits to employees. The following is a brief explanation of these terms.

Employee trust

12. This term is described in the current version of IT-502, *Employee Benefit Plans and Employee Trusts.*

Employee benefit plan

This term is described in the current version of IT-502. Virtually, all funded plans other than salary deferral arrangements and retirement compensation arrangements which provide employees with benefits (including payments by an employer under an insurance policy) could meet the definition of an employee benefit plan unless the plan fits within one of the statutory exclusions. The statutory exclusions which are common to Flex Programs are:

- private health services plans, including health care spending accounts as described in paragraph 14 below;
- group term life insurance policies; and
- group sickness or accident insurance plans.

Retirement compensation arrangement

This term is described in the *Retirement Compensation Guide*. The rules relating to retirement compensation arrangements are intended to prevent tax deferral on unregistered retirement savings plans that escape the salary deferral arrangement rules. Note that a Flex Program which permits an employee to allocate flex credits to a benefit option which is not expected to be provided until after a substantial change in services rendered by that employee (such as retirement), or the portion of the plan which relates to that choice, may be considered to be a retirement compensation arrangement.

Salary deferral arrangement

Briefly stated, a salary deferral arrangement is:

- a plan or arrangement (whether it is funded or not);
- between an employer and an employee who has a right to receive an amount under the arrangement; and

- one of the main purposes for the creation or existence of the right is to postpone the tax payable under the Act by the employee in respect of salary or wages for services rendered in the year or a preceding year.

It is important to note that the "right" mentioned in the definition includes any right that is subject to one or more conditions, unless there is a substantial risk that any one of those conditions will not be satisfied. As a result, the salary deferral arrangement rules cannot be avoided by making the employee's right to the funds subject to some condition which will likely be met anyway. For example, it is not relevant for the purpose of determining whether a Flex Program is a salary deferral arrangement whether or not the receipt of the deferred amount is contingent on:

- the employee remaining an employee for a minimum period of time;
- the employee not being dismissed for the cause or commission of a crime;
- the employee refraining from transferring or encumbering the employee's interest in the deferred amount; or
- the employee abstaining from competition or being available for consultation after retirement or termination of employment.

When all or part of a Flex Program meets the general definition of a salary deferral arrangement, the list of statutory exceptions must be examined. Those which are the most relevant to a Flex Program include:

- disability or income maintenance insurance plans;
- group sickness or accident insurance plans; and
- certain employer education and training plans.

Amounts deferred under a salary deferral arrangement are included in the employee's income in the year they are earned under paragraph 6(1)(a) by virtue of subsection 6(11). A deferred amount means an amount at the end of the year that the employee has a right to receive in the future.

Taxation of Individual Benefits

13. Except for certain statutory exclusions, employees are taxed on the value of any benefit received or enjoyed because of their employment under paragraph 6(1)(a). The tax consequences relating to some of the various benefits which may be provided under a Flex Program are described below.

Health Care

14. One option that may be found in a Flex Program is a secondary health care plan (sometimes called a "health care spending account" or a variation of that term). These plans are comprised of individual employee accounts that provide for the reimbursement of eligible medical and dental expenses as defined by the terms of the plan. A health care spending account may qualify as a private health services plan provided that it meets the criteria set out in the current version of IT-339, *Meaning of "Private Health Services Plan."* If it does not qualify as a private health services plan, the amount of any benefit received out of the plan will be taxable to the employee.

15. While some health care spending accounts are only funded to the extent of claims actually made against the account (on a pay-as-you-go basis), an employer is obligated to reimburse employees for eligible costs incurred by the employee to the extent of the balance of credits remaining in the account. A credit in a health care spending account should not be confused with a flex credit. Since a health care spending account is designed to be a plan of insurance, the amount of credits in a health care spending account (as determined by the amount of flex credits applied to this benefit option as a result of an employee allocation) sets a ceiling on the amount that can be claimed under the plan of insurance. For this purpose, there may be a distinction under the terms of the Flex Program between when the amount is allocated by the employee (prior to the beginning of the plan year) and when that allocation is applied to the health care spending account so that the employee is able to claim expenses to the extent of the limit of health care insurance in force at the time the expense is incurred. Under some Flex Programs, the full amount of the allocation is applied to the health care spending account at the beginning of the year and under others, a proportionate amount is applied each pay period. As with other plans of insurance, an employee has no inherent right to the balance of credits applied to a health care spending account.

16. One of the criteria for a private health services plan is that the plan must be a plan of insurance. In order for a health care spending account to qualify as a plan of insurance, there must be a reasonable element of risk. For example, if the plan or arrangement is such that there is little risk that the employee will not eventually be reimbursed for the full amount allocated to that employee annually, then the arrangement is not a plan of insurance and therefore, not a private health services plan. While a plan which includes a carry forward provision undoubtedly reduces the risk of loss to the employee, a plan which permits the carry forward of either the unused allocation or eligible medical expenses (but not both) up to a maximum of 12 months will not be disqualified as a private health services plan solely by reason of the carry forward provision in the plan.

17. If an employee is able to withdraw or transfer an amount from a health care spending account (other than as a premium payable in respect of another private health services plan), the health care spending account will not be a private health services plan and all amounts received out of the account, including reimbursements of eligible medical expenses, will be included in the employee's income under paragraph 6(1)(a). For example, if an employee is able to reallocate an amount which was previously applied to a health care spending account to another benefit option such as a group RRSP, the health care spending account will not qualify as a private health services plan because a contribution to an RRSP is not a qualified medical expense. However, the ability to reallocate credits to another private health services plan, such as a vision or dental plan will not affect the status of the health care spending account as a private health services plan.

18. There will generally be no advantage to an employee in using payroll deductions to contribute to a health care spending account. Since the flex credits allocated to a health care spending account will typically set a limit on the maximum reimbursement payable under the plan and the employee is taxed on the gross

amount of salary paid, including the amount withheld through payroll deductions to pay for benefits under the plan, a contribution of salary may result in the taxation of more income than the employee actually receives. While any contributions that are made by the employee to a health care spending account that is a private health services plan would qualify as a medical expense for the purpose of the medical expense tax credit, the medical expense tax credit may not fully offset the income inclusion and there is no mechanism by which an amount forfeited at the end of the year can be refunded to the employee.

Survivor Benefits

19. Flex Programs may offer choices relating to benefits to be provided to an employee's spouse or dependants after the death of the employee. The taxation of the benefit depends, to a large part, on how the benefit is funded by the employer.

20. Life insurance coverage for employees or former employees is taxable under subsection 6(4) if it is provided through a group term life insurance policy as defined in subsection 248(1). Since the definition of group term life insurance policy excludes a policy which provides coverage for anyone other than an employee or former employee, an employee's taxable benefit derived from an employer's contribution to a policy which provides coverage for a dependant or spouse is included in income under paragraph 6(1)(a). Thus, the benefit from a policy which covers both employees and their dependants is determined under paragraph 6(1)(a) but the benefit from a policy which otherwise qualifies as a group term life insurance policy which only covers employees and former employees is determined under subsection 6(4). The value of the benefit derived from life insurance coverage under a policy which is not a group term life insurance policy would ordinarily be the amount of premium paid by the employer in respect of such coverage. The rules for calculating the benefit to be included in income under subsection 6(4) are found in section 2700 of the Income Tax Regulations. Further information can be found in the Departmental publication T4130, *Employer's Guide to Payroll Deductions — Taxable Benefits.*

A payment of an uninsured amount by the employer to the surviving spouse or named beneficiary of an employee upon his or her death will ordinarily qualify as a death benefit as defined in subsection 248(1) even though the employee has allocated flex credits to ensure the payment of such amount. However, if the employer creates a fund, including an administrative services contract with an insurer, to provide for death benefits, the fund will likely be an employee benefit plan with the effect that the employer would not be entitled to a deduction for contributions to the fund until such time as the death benefit was paid. Since an administrative services contract with an insurer is not a policy of insurance, it is not a group term life insurance policy as defined in subsection 248(1).

Short-Term and Long-Term Disability Insurance

21. Even though an employee may choose to use payroll deductions to acquire coverage under a disability insurance plan, any resulting benefit received out of the plan will be taxable under paragraph 6(1)(f) unless the entire plan is funded solely

with payroll deductions. Since flex credits allocated to an employee represent the employer's obligation to provide benefits to the employee, a disability insurance plan will be considered a plan to which the employer has contributed when flex credits have been allocated by any employee to ensure coverage under that particular plan. If, however, an employer has two separate disability plans (one which is funded solely by the employees through payroll deductions and one that is funded by the employer) and the funds of the two plans are not cross-subsidized, benefits received out of the plan funded solely through payroll deductions will not be included in the employee's income and benefits derived from coverage acquired by means of an allocation of flex credits will be taxable to the extent provided by paragraph 6(1)(f). Employee-pay-all plans are discussed in the current version of IT-428, *Wage Loss Replacement Plans.*

Vacation Selling

22. Where an employee forgoes vacation or other amounts to which the employee is otherwise entitled in order to obtain or increase the amount of flex credits available under the plan, the value of the amount forgone is included in the employee's income at the time the additional flex credits are so credited. For example, assuming that an employee is entitled to a $52,000 annual salary for working 49 weeks with 3 weeks of vacation leave, the employee will be taxed on $53,000, if the employee works an extra week in exchange for additional flex credits (whether or not the flex credits are applied to benefits which would have been taxable if funded by the employer's contribution). In this situation, the employee is considered to have paid for the additional benefits by way of additional services rendered. It is the trading of vacation entitlement by the employee that triggers a taxable event and not the use of the flex credits obtained. Even when the conversion of taxable employee entitlements to flex credits is required under the terms of the Flex Program, an employee has a degree of control over the amount of salary or other entitlement forfeited by means of the choices available to the employee under the Flex Program.

Vacation Buying

23. A Flex Program may include an option under which an employee may obtain additional vacation leave. If the additional leave is funded by way of payroll deductions, the leave is effectively unpaid leave. If it is funded through an allocation of flex credits, the terms of the plan will typically require the employee to use the purchased vacation within the plan year in which it is acquired. When a Flex Program permits vacation leave so purchased to be carried forward to a subsequent plan year, the arrangement may be considered to be a salary deferral arrangement. While vacation pay trusts are excluded from the definition of a salary deferral arrangement, an arrangement to pay for the vacation leave so purchased out of a trust would not qualify as a vacation pay trust as defined in paragraph 149(1)(y). The criteria for establishing a vacation pay trust are explained in the current version of IT-389, *Vacation Pay Trusts Established under Collective Agreements.*

Cash Payments, Transfers, Diversions

24. When an employee chooses, prior to the beginning of the plan year, to receive a portion of his or her flex credits in cash or deposited into an RRSP, the amount so received or deposited is included in the employee's income as salary or wages when it is received or deposited. If the amount is placed into a registered plan such as an RRSP or an RESP, the terms of which require contributions to be made by the planholder or subscriber, the employee is considered to have received the amount of flex credits allocated to that benefit option and must include that amount in income. In the case of a contribution to an RRSP, the employee is entitled to a deduction to the extent permitted under the rules governing RRSPs. Other benefits available under a Flex Program will be included in an employee's income in the same way as they would if offered separately from the plan. For example, if one of the choices is a low interest loan from the employer, an interest benefit is calculated under section 80.4 and is included in income under subsection 6(9) of the Act.

Tax Implications to the Employer

25. For greater certainty, no deduction is available to the employer solely by reason of the allocation of flex credits to an employee. In the case of benefits which are provided through a plan of insurance, subsections 18(9) and (9.01) impose restrictions on the amount that can be deducted in the year by the employer on account of contributions to fund a plan of insurance or on account of premiums paid in respect of a policy.

Benefits to Shareholders

26. The comments in this bulletin apply only in respect of a Flex Program which is offered to a group of employees or former employees, as opposed to a group of shareholders and persons related to shareholders. When flex credits are allocated to an individual who is both an employee and a shareholder (or an employee who is related to a shareholder of the employer), the Flex Program benefits will be presumed to have been conferred upon the shareholder by reason of his or her shareholdings unless the participant is a member of a group of employees who participate in the Flex Program and the rules applicable to that Flex Program, including the allocation of flex credits and availability of benefit choices, are applied equally to all participants in the Flex Program. For comments concerning benefits provided to shareholders in their capacity as shareholders, see the current version of IT-432, *Benefits Conferred on Shareholders*. If a benefit is granted "qua shareholder," it will be taxed under subsection 15(1) without regard to any of the exceptions found in section 6. In addition, the corporation will not be entitled to a deduction for any amount paid on behalf of the shareholder.

Benefits to Former Employees

27. Where a former employee is required to include an amount in income on account of the benefits described in this bulletin, the authority for taxing the benefit is found in either subsection 6(3) or paragraph 56(1)(a) depending on whether the obligation to provide the benefit arose immediately prior to, during or immediately

after the former period of employment or at some other time. However, the amount to be included in the former employee's income will not exceed the amount that would otherwise have been included in income had the former employee been an employee at the time the benefit was conferred. For example, no amount will be included in the former employee's income on account of coverage under a private health services plan.

Related Bulletins and Guides

28. The current versions of the following bulletins and guides contain information which may be applicable to a Flex Program.

Bulletins

IT-85 *Health and Welfare Trusts for Employees*
IT-227 *Group Term Life Insurance Premiums*
IT-247 *Employer's Contribution to Pensioners' Premiums under Provincial Medical and Hospital Services Plans*
IT-339 *Meaning of "Private Health Services Plan"*
IT-389 *Vacation Pay Trusts Established under Collective Agreements*
IT-428 *Wage Loss Replacement Plans*
IT-432 *Benefits Conferred on Shareholders*
IT-470 *Employees' Fringe Benefits*
IT-502 *Employee Benefit Plans and Employee Trusts*
IT-508 *Death Benefits*
IT-519 *Medical Expense and Disability Tax Credits and Attendant Care Expense Deduction Guides*
T4130, *Employers' Guide to Payroll Deductions — Taxable Benefits*

Interpretation Bulletin IT-533 — Interest Deductibility and Related Issues

Date: **October 31, 2003**

Reference: **Para. 20(1)(c) (also ss. 9, 16, 20.1, 67.1, 67.5, 16(1), 20(2), 20(2.2), 20(3), 20.1(4), 248(1)"borrowed money", 20(1)(d), 20(1)(f), 60(d), 20(1)(c)(i), (ii), (iii) and (iv) and 20(1)(e)(iv.1))**

Application

This new bulletin discusses interest deductibility and other related matters and replaces and cancels:

- IT-80, *Interest on Money Borrowed to Redeem Shares, or to Pay Dividends*;
- IT-203, *Interest on Death Duties*;
- IT-315, *Interest Expense Incurred for the Purpose of Winding-up or Amalgamation*;
- IT-445, *The Deduction of Interest on Funds Borrowed either to be Loaned at less than a Reasonable Rate of Interest or to Honour a Guarantee Given for Inadequate Consideration in Non-arm's Length Circumstances; and*

- IT-498, *The Deductibility of Interest on Money Borrowed to Reloan to Employees or Shareholders..*

In addition, previous Canada Customs and Revenue Agency (CCRA) positions on this subject expressed in other fora may generally no longer be relied upon as the CCRA's current positions on interest deductibility.

This bulletin does not take into account proposed amendments to the law — see Appendix B.

Unless otherwise stated, all statutory references throughout the bulletin are to the Act.

Summary

This bulletin discusses the CCRA's interpretations of the deductibility of interest expense under various provisions of the Act and the judgments in numerous court decisions involving the deductibility of interest expense.

An amount is considered to be interest if it represents compensation for the use of money, if it is referable to a principal sum and if it accrues day-to-day. Generally, interest expense is considered to be a capital expenditure. Accordingly, specific provisions of the Act must be met in order for interest to be deductible.

The specific provisions of the Act include the requirement that an amount be paid in the year or payable in respect of the year, that the amount be paid pursuant to a legal obligation and that the amount be reasonable. Where money is borrowed, the use of the money must be established and the purpose of that use must be for earning income (other than exempt income or to acquire an interest in certain life insurance policies). In this context, use is the current use of the borrowed money and in certain situations may include indirect use. Where an amount is payable for property acquired, the property must be acquired for the purpose of earning income (other than exempt income or to acquire an interest in certain life insurance policies).

In certain borrowing transactions, a debt may be issued at a premium or discount. The tax treatment of these amounts is also discussed in the bulletin.

Other matters related to interest deductibility are also discussed in the bulletin. However, other tax consequences from transactions involving interest deductibility are not discussed in the bulletin.

Appendix A includes the citations for all court cases referred to in this bulletin.

Discussion and Interpretation

General

What is interest?

1. "Interest" is not defined in the Act but has been addressed in several court decisions, including *Shell*, *Sherway Centre* and *Miller*. As in *Miller*, interest for tax purposes is generally accepted to mean an amount that has met three criteria. These criteria are that the amount must be calculated on a day-to-day accrual basis, the

amount must be calculated on a principal sum (or a right to a principal sum), and the amount must be compensation for the use of the principal sum (or the right to the principal sum).

Participating payments as interest

2. Consistent with *Sherway Centre*, participating payments for amounts that are interest are deductible under paragraph 20(1)(c) where:

- the payment is limited to a stated percentage of the principal (or the facts show that the payments are intended to increase the interest rate on the loan to the prevailing market rate);
- the limiting percentage of the principal, if any, reflects prevailing arm's-length commercial interest rates; and
- no other facts indicate the presence of an equity investment.

It should be noted that participating payments are not deductible under subparagraph 20(1)(e)(iv.1) as an expense incurred in the course of borrowing money.

Deemed interest — section 16

3. Where a contract or arrangement does not explicitly identify any amount as interest but an amount can reasonably be regarded as interest, that amount is deemed to be interest under section 16. Accordingly, both parties to the contract would treat that amount as interest for income and expense purposes. See ¶37 for additional comments. In addition, refer to the current version of IT-265 [IT-265R3], *Payments of Income and Capital Combined*, for additional information on section 16.

Interest as an income or capital expenditure

4. The issue of whether interest expense is on income or capital account has been reviewed in various Supreme Court of Canada decisions including *Canada Safeway, Bronfman Trust, Tennant* and *Shell*, and was most recently analyzed by the Federal Court of Appeal in *Gifford*. In *Gifford*, the court concluded that it was bound to follow the Supreme Court of Canada decisions and that interest expense is to be considered a capital expenditure. (Note that leave to appeal this decision to the Supreme Court of Canada was granted on March 27, 2003.) Nonetheless, the CCRA has accepted that taxpayers in certain financing businesses (e.g. money-lenders) may consider interest expense for borrowed money that constitutes stock-in-trade to be on income account, and deductible under section 9. Other instances where the CCRA will accept interest expense as being on income account are discussed in ¶36.

Paragraph 20(1)(c) Pre and Post-Amble

Paid in the year or payable in respect of the year . . . pursuant to a legal obligation

5. The preamble to paragraph 20(1)(c) provides that taxpayers using the cash method deduct interest expense on a cash basis. Similarly, taxpayers using the ac-

crual method would deduct interest expense on an accrual basis. However, all taxpayers may only deduct compound interest on a cash basis pursuant to paragraph 20(1)(d). In addition, the preamble requires that all amounts must be paid or payable pursuant to a legal obligation to pay interest.

Contingent interest

6. Where an amount computed as interest expense is not payable in respect of a year because of an unsatisfied contingency, the provisions of paragraph 20(1)(c) are not met as the interest is not paid or payable since there is no legal obligation to pay (as was the case in Barbican), and accordingly, the interest is not deductible in that year.

Consistent with *Mid-West Abrasive*, when such amounts are paid in a subsequent year, the interest expense for prior years is not in respect of the year as required by paragraph 20(1)(c) and such interest is also not deductible when paid.

The fact that there may be limited recourse with respect to the security provided to obtain financing, does not, in and of itself, cause the interest paid or payable in respect of that financing to be considered contingent.

Reasonable amount

7. The deduction for interest under paragraph 20(1)(c) is the lesser of the actual amount and a reasonable amount. In considering whether or not an interest rate is reasonable, consideration will be given to prevailing market rates for debts with similar terms and credit risks, and the existence of any issue premiums — see ¶38. Further, as stated in Shell, "Where an interest rate is established in a market of lenders and borrowers acting at arm's length from each other, it is generally a reasonable rate.. . ."

Subparagraph 20(1)(c)(i)

Borrowed money

8. "Borrowed money" is defined in subsection 248(1) to include "the proceeds to a taxpayer from the sale of a post-dated bill drawn by the taxpayer on a bank" (more commonly referred to as banker's acceptances). In *McCool*, it was noted that the term borrowed money, in tax legislation, is interpreted to require "a relationship of lender and borrower between the parties." The unpaid purchase price of property is not borrowed money, but "an amount payable for property" and thus, interest expense on such amounts may only be deducted under subparagraph 20(1)(c)(ii) — see ¶s 27 to 29.

Purpose

9 Subparagraph 20(1)(c)(i) requires that the interest expense sought to be deducted be on "borrowed money used for the *purpose* of earning income from a business or property."

The finding of the purpose for the use of borrowed money will be a question of fact.

The interpretation of the term purpose was addressed in *Ludco* as follows: "...the requisite test to determine the purpose for interest deductibility under s. 20(1)(c)(i) is whether, considering all the circumstances, the taxpayer had a reasonable expectation of income at the time the investment is made." With regard to purpose, the court also stated "Absent a sham or window dressing or other vitiating circumstances, a taxpayer's ancillary purpose may be nonetheless a *bona fide*, actual, real and true objective of his or her investment, equally capable of providing the requisite purpose for interest deductibility in comparison with any more important or significant primary purpose."

Income

10. Subparagraph 20(1)(c)(i) requires that the interest sought to be deducted be on "borrowed money used for the purpose of earning *income* from a business or property." The interpretation of the term income was addressed in *Ludco* as follows: ". . . it is clear that 'income' in s. 20(1)(c)(i) refers to income generally, that is an amount that would come into income for taxation purposes, not just net income." The court also said, "The plain meaning of s. 20(1)(c)(i) does not support an interpretation of 'income' as the equivalent of 'profit' or 'net income' . . . . Therefore, absent a sham or window dressing or similar vitiating circumstances, courts should not be concerned with the sufficiency of the income expected or received." See ¶31 for additional comments.

No deduction to acquire property producing exempt income or a life insurance policy

11. No deduction is permitted for interest expense on borrowed money used to acquire property the income from which would be exempt or to acquire a life insurance policy. However, under subsection 20(2.2), certain policies are excluded from the definition of life insurance policy. Refer to the current version of IT-355 [IT-355R2], *Interest on Loans to Buy Life Insurance Policies and Annuity Contracts, and Interest on Policy Loans*, for additional information on this topic.

"Use" of borrowed money

12. Subparagraph 20(1)(c)(i) requires that the interest sought to be deducted be on "borrowed money *used* for the purpose of earning income from a business or property." The interpretation of the term "used", and in particular whether "used" means *directly used or indirectly used* and whether "used" is *first used or currently used*, is set out below.

Direct or indirect use

13. In *Bronfman Trust*, the court stated, "...the text of the Act requires tracing the use of borrowed funds to a specific eligible use..." and also stated, "The onus is on the taxpayer to trace the borrowed funds to an identifiable use which triggers the

deduction." In *Shell*, the Court described the test by saying, "If a direct link can be drawn between the borrowed money and an eligible use...", then the money was used for the purpose of earning income from a business or property. In addition, "Interest is deductible only if there is a sufficiently direct link between the borrowed money and the current eligible use...." In *Singleton*, the court said, "It is now plain from the reasoning in *Shell* that the issue to be determined is the direct use to which the borrowed funds were put." Further, in *Singleton*, the court held that "...it is an error to treat this [a sequence of transactions] as one simultaneous transaction. In order to give effect to the legal relationships, the transactions must be viewed independently."

Thus, the test to be applied is the direct use of the borrowed money. In certain circumstances, however, the courts have stated that indirect use will be accepted as an exception to the direct use test. See ¶s 22 to 26 for a further discussion of the direct use exceptions.

14. In determining what borrowed money has been used for, the onus is on the taxpayers to trace or link the borrowed money to a specific eligible use, giving effect to the existing legal relationships.

Restructuring borrowings

15. A taxpayer may restructure borrowings and the ownership of assets to meet the direct use test.

Example 1

> Ms. A owns 1,000 shares of B. Corp., a corporation listed on the TSX. Ms. A also owns a personal use condominium that was financed with borrowed money. At this point, the direct use of the borrowed money was to acquire the condominium. Ms. A may choose to sell the 1,000 shares of B. Corp., use the proceeds from the sale of the 1,000 shares of B. Corp. for any purpose, including paying down the borrowed money used to acquire the condominium, and subsequently obtain additional borrowed money to acquire another 1,000 shares of B. Corp. At this point, the additional borrowed money is directly used to acquire 1,000 shares of B. Corp.

Cash damming

16. Taxpayers may segregate (typically in separate accounts) funds received from borrowed money and funds received from other sources (e.g., funds received from operations or other sources and that are otherwise not linked to money previously borrowed). This technique, commonly referred to as cash damming, readily allows taxpayers to trace borrowed money to specific uses.

Example 2

> C Corp. establishes two accounts with its financial institution. The only deposits to account A are those consisting of borrowed money and all other deposits (from operations, etc., and that are not linked to money previously borrowed) are made to account B. C Corp. ensures that all payments from account A are for expenditures for which the conditions for interest deductibility are clearly

met. Some expenditures from account B would not give rise to a deduction for interest if borrowed money had been used to make them. Notwithstanding that some expenditures of C Corp. would be for uses that would not otherwise allow for a deduction for interest, the borrowed money is for specific eligible uses and the taxpayer has clearly demonstrated those uses.

First use or current use

17. Several decisions of the Supreme Court of Canada, notably *Canada Safeway*, *Bronfman Trust* and *Shell*, have made it clear that the relevant use is the current use and not the original use of borrowed money. In determining the current use of borrowed money, taxpayers must establish a link between the money that was borrowed and its current use.

Tracing/linking borrowed money to its current use

18. In simple situations where one property is replaced with another, such linking is straightforward. In these situations, the current use of the borrowed money is entirely with respect to the replacement property since all the proceeds of disposition from the original property are reinvested in the replacement property, as was the case in *Tennant.*

Example 3

> Mr. D acquired property E with borrowed money. Mr. D subsequently disposed of property E. All of the proceeds from that disposition were used to acquire property F. The current use of the entire amount of borrowed money is with respect to property F, as was the finding in Tennant. Accordingly, if all of the requisite deductibility tests are met with respect to property F, all of the interest would be deductible with respect to that use. However, if the current use of the borrowed money is not to earn income, the disappearing source rules (discussed in ¶19) may be applicable.

In situations where property acquired with borrowed money is replaced with more than one property, a flexible approach to linking is permitted, as applied, for example, in Ludco. Under the flexible approach to linking, taxpayers are entitled to allocate, on a dollar for dollar basis, the outstanding borrowed money to the value of the replacement properties acquired.

Example 4

> Ms. G acquired property H with $100 of borrowed money, the entire amount of which remains outstanding. Ms. G subsequently disposed of property H for $100 and used the proceeds of disposition to acquire property I for $60 and property J for $40. In linking the borrowed money to its current use, 60% ($60/$100) would be allocated to property I and 40% to property J.

Example 5

> K Corporation acquired property L with $1,000 of borrowed money, the entire amount of which remains outstanding. K Corporation subsequently disposed of property L for $1,500 and used the proceeds of disposition to acquire property M for $1,200 and property N for $300.

Under the flexible approach to linking, K Corporation may choose that the current use of the borrowed money is entirely for property M, since the value of property M exceeds the outstanding amount of borrowed money ($1,000). Alternatively, K Corporation may choose to allocate 30% ($300/$1,000) of the current use of the borrowed money to property N (and consequently the remaining 70% to property M).

Where, however, the value of the replacement properties is less than the amount of borrowed money outstanding, a pro-rata allocation of the borrowed money based on the relative value of each property would be required.

If property L was disposed of for $800 and the proceeds of disposition were used to acquire property M for $600 and property N for $200, the current use of the borrowed money would be $750 ($600/$800 × $1,000) for property M and $250 for property N.

Disappearing source rules

19. In general terms, the disappearing source rules in section 20.1 apply where borrowed money ceases to be used for the purpose of earning income (i.e., the borrowed money can no longer be traced to any income earning use). Generally, the borrowed money that is no longer linked to any income earning use is nonetheless deemed to be used for the purpose of earning income such that interest continues to be deductible for that portion of the borrowed money. Several specific conditions in section 20.1 must be met for that section to apply.

Example 6

Mr. O acquired property P with $1,000 of borrowed money, the entire amount of which remains outstanding and the interest thereon is deductible. Mr. O subsequently disposed of property P for its fair market value of $600 and used the $600 to reduce the outstanding loan. If the conditions in section 20.1 apply, the remaining $400 of borrowed money would be deemed to be used for the purpose of earning income and the interest thereon would continue to be deductible.

Tracing/linking through cash accounts, lines of credit, etc.

20. Frequently, the cash damming technique described in ¶16 is not followed or available and borrowed money is deposited to one account and commingled with other cash. In such situations, tracing/linking is problematic since cash is fungible and taxpayers are unable to trace the funds to identifiable uses. However, taxpayers are entitled to apply the flexible approach to tracing/linking described in ¶18 in such situations. Consequently, where borrowed money and other money is commingled, taxpayers may choose the uses of the borrowed money from all of the uses of the money. The same approach would also be applicable to lines of credit and other similar arrangements. The timing of transactions is relevant for this linking exercise as

this approach is only applicable for times when borrowed money and other money is commingled, and a specific use of money can never be linked to a borrowing that occurs subsequently.

Generally, however, there is no timing issue for transactions occurring on the same day.

Example 7

On a particular day, Q Corp. had an opening account balance of nil, deposited $100 of borrowed money and $200 from sales not linked to money previously borrowed, purchased a $100 property (that if acquired with borrowed money the interest thereon would otherwise be deductible) and another $200 property (that if acquired with borrowed money the interest thereon would otherwise not be deductible). In determining the use of the borrowed money, Q Corp. can allocate the $100 of borrowed money to the $100 property such that interest on that borrowed money is deductible.

Tracing/linking applied to an amalgamation or winding-up

21. Shares of another corporation may be acquired with borrowed money. Subsequently, the other corporation may be wound-up or amalgamated with the corporation that had borrowed the money to acquire the shares. Under the tracing/linking process described above, a link for the current use of the borrowed money is readily established between the shares that were initially acquired (and that have disappeared) and the assets formerly held by the acquired corporation that has been wound-up or amalgamated (and that are now held by the continuing corporation). There is no arm's-length requirement in establishing such a link.

Exceptions to the direct use test — general

22. As noted in ¶13, in certain circumstances, the courts have accepted that indirect use will be accepted as an exception to the direct use test (referred to as "exceptional circumstances" in several court decisions). In *Trans-Prairie*, the Exchequer Court concluded that interest was deductible where the taxpayer borrowed money to redeem preferred shares. The court concluded that the borrowed money returned to the shareholders "As a practical matter of business common sense, went to fill the hole left by redemption..." of the preferred shares. The indirect use concept was also addressed in *Bronfman* Trust as follows: "...there are exceptional circumstances in which, on a real appreciation of a taxpayer's transactions, it might be appropriate to allow the taxpayer to deduct interest on funds borrowed for an ineligible use because of an indirect effect on the taxpayer's income earning capacity...." Subsequent court decisions, including *Chase Manhattan*, *Canadian Helicopters*, *74712 Alberta Ltd* and *Lewisporte*, have also discussed this concept.

Exceptions to the direct use test — borrowed money used by a corporation to redeem shares, return capital or pay dividends

23. Interest expense on borrowed money used to redeem shares or return capital can be an exception to the direct use test. In connection with this use, the purpose test will be met if the borrowed money replaces capital (contributed capital or accu-

mulated profits) that was being used for purposes that would have qualified for interest deductibility had the capital been borrowed money (eligible purposes). Consistent with the concept of filling the hole, contributed capital generally means the funds provided by the shareholders to commence, or otherwise further, the carrying on of the business. While in most situations the legal or stated capital for corporate law purposes would be the best measurement of contributed capital for this purpose, other measurements may be more appropriate depending on the circumstances. In situations where some proportion of shares is being replaced with borrowed money, only the capital of those shares, computed on a pro-rata basis, would be considered to be replaced with the borrowed money. A corporation's deficit does not reduce contributed capital for purposes of this exception.

Similarly, with regard to the payment of dividends (including deemed dividends), borrowed money used to replace the accumulated profits of a corporation that have been retained and used for eligible purposes can be an exception to the direct use test. Accumulated profits would generally be the retained earnings of the corporation computed on an unconsolidated basis with investments accounted for on a cost basis. The accumulated profits of a corporation do not track any particular shareholdings.

Generally, accumulated profits can reflect transactions arising in the ordinary course of business between non-arm's length parties. The impact on accumulated profits of other non-arm's length transactions must be examined on the basis of the particular facts involved.

The key concept in this context remains that of "filling the hole" of capital withdrawn from the business.

Exceptions to the direct use test — borrowed money used by a partnership to return capital to a partner

24. The concepts described in ¶23 are equally applicable where a partnership borrows money to return capital to a partner. In such a case, the "hole that can be filled" generally consists of the capital contributed by the partner to commence or further the carrying on of the business, plus any partnership income less any partnership losses allocated to the partner, and less any previous distributions to the partner. Generally, the balance in the partner's capital account would represent this amount.

Exceptions to the direct use test — borrowed money used to make interest — free loans and contributions of capital

25. Interest expense on borrowed money used to make an interest-free loan is not generally deductible since the direct use is to acquire a property that cannot generate any income. However, where it can be shown that this direct use can nonetheless have an effect on the taxpayer's income-earning capacity, the interest may be deductible. Such was the case in *Canadian Helicopters* wherein the court found that there was a reasonable expectation on the part of the taxpayer of an income-earning capacity from the indirect use of the borrowed money directly used to make an interest-free loan. Generally, a deduction for interest would be allowed where

borrowed money is used to make an interest-free loan to a wholly-owned corporation (or in cases of multiple shareholders, where shareholders make an interest-free loan in proportion to their shareholdings) and the proceeds have an effect on the corporation's income-earning capacity, thereby increasing the potential dividends to be received. These comments are equally applicable to interest on borrowed money used to make a contribution of capital to a corporation of which the borrower is a shareholder (or to a partnership of which the borrower is a partner). A deduction for interest in other situations involving interest-free loans may also be warranted depending upon the particular facts of a given situation.

Exceptions to the direct use test — borrowed money used to make interest-free loans to employees and shareholders

26. As indicated in ¶25, a deduction for interest in certain situations involving interest-free loans may also be warranted depending upon the particular facts of a given situation. Generally, a deduction for interest would be allowed where borrowed money is used to make an interest-free loan to employees in their capacity as employees, as the value of such loans would be viewed as a form of remuneration for the services of the employees. However, interest on money borrowed to make interest-free loans to individuals in their capacity as shareholders would not generally qualify.

Subparagraph 20(1)(c)(ii)

Amount payable for property acquired

27. Subparagraph 20(1)(c)(ii) applies to interest on an amount payable for property acquired for the purpose of gaining or producing income. This would include situations where a taxpayer has assumed another person's indebtedness as part of the purchase price of an asset acquired by the taxpayer. Although (unlike subparagraph 20(1)(c)(i)) there is no "use" test in subparagraph 20(1)(c)(ii), where a property referred to in subparagraph 20(1)(c)(ii) is disposed of, the substituted property will be relevant for the continuing application of that subparagraph as well as for the disappearing source rules in section 20.1. The provisions of section 20.1 apply equally to an amount payable referred to in subparagraph 20(1)(c)(ii) by virtue of subsection 20.1(4).

Purpose of gaining or producing income

28. The phrase "purpose of gaining or producing income" in subparagraph 20(1)(c)(ii) is considered to have the same meaning as the phrase "purpose of earning income" in subparagraph 20(1)(c)(i). As is the case with borrowed money, no deduction is permitted for interest on an amount payable to acquire property the income from which would be exempt or to acquire an interest in a life insurance policy — see ¶11.

Note issued to redeem shares

29. In accordance with the decision in *Penn-Ventilator*, where a note is issued to purchase and cancel (or otherwise redeem) shares, interest expense may be deductible under subparagraph 20(1)(c)(ii) to the extent of the interest on the amount of the note issued within the limits described in ¶23 for redeeming shares. Interest on notes issued to pay dividends or to return capital would not qualify since no property is acquired in such a transaction, as required by subparagraph 20(1)(c)(ii).

Subparagraph 20(1)(c)(iii) & (iv)

Interest on an amount paid under an appropriation Act or on borrowed money to acquire an interest in an annuity contract

30. A deduction for interest may also be available in situations described in either subparagraph 20(1)(c)(iii) or (iv). These situations include interest paid or payable

- on amounts paid to the taxpayer under an appropriation Act and for the purpose of advancing or sustaining the technological capability of Canadian manufacturing or other industry,
- on certain amounts paid to the taxpayer in respect of the Northern Mineral Grants Program, or
- on borrowed money used to acquire an interest in certain annuities in respect of which section 12.2 applies.

Other Interest Deductibility and Related Issues

Borrowing for investments including common shares

31. Where an investment (e.g., interest-bearing instrument or preferred shares) carries a stated interest or dividend rate, the purpose of earning income test will be met "absent a sham or window dressing or similar vitiating circumstances" (*Ludco*). Further, assuming all of the other requisite tests are met, interest will neither be denied in full nor restricted to the amount of income from the investment where the income does not exceed the interest expense, given the meaning of the term income as discussed in ¶10.

Where an investment does not carry a stated interest or dividend rate such as some common shares, the determination of the reasonable expectation of income at the time the investment is made is less clear. Normally, however, the CCRA considers interest costs in respect of funds borrowed to purchase common shares to be deductible on the basis that there is a reasonable expectation, at the time the shares are acquired, that the common shareholder will receive dividends. Nonetheless, each situation must be dealt with on the basis of the particular facts involved.

These comments are also generally applicable to investments in mutual fund trusts and mutual fund corporations.

Example 8

R Corp. is an investment vehicle designed to provide a capital return only to the investors in its common shares. The corporate policy with respect to R

Corp. is that dividends will not be paid, that corporate earnings will be reinvested to increase the value of the shares and that shareholders are required to sell their shares to a third-party purchaser in a fixed number of years in order to realize their value. In this situation, it is not reasonable to expect income from such shareholdings and any interest expense on money borrowed to acquire R Corp. shares would not be deductible.

Example 9

S Corp. is raising capital by selling common shares. Its business plans indicate that its cash flow will be required to be reinvested for the foreseeable future and S Corp. discloses to shareholders that dividends will only be paid when operational circumstances permit (i.e., when cash flow exceeds requirements) or when it believes that shareholders could make better use of the cash. In this situation, the purpose of earning income test will generally be met and any interest on borrowed money to acquired S Corp. shares would be deductible.

Loss utilizations within an affiliated group

32. In order to transfer losses from one affiliated corporation to another, an arrangement is generally structured such that the corporation in the loss position lends money at a stated rate of interest to the profitable corporation, which in turn uses the borrowed funds to invest in preferred shares of the loss corporation, although other techniques may also be used. The direct use of the borrowed money will be the acquisition of the preferred shares. The purpose test will be applied to the acquisition of the preferred shares. For tax purposes losses are effectively transferred from the loss corporation to the profitable corporation in circumstances where the profitable corporation is entitled to deduct the interest expense and receives fully deductible inter-corporate dividends, while the loss corporation receives interest income that is offset by its accumulated losses.

Borrowed money used to honour guarantees

33. A taxpayer who provides a guarantee in respect of a debt may be called upon to honour the guarantee. In these situations, the guarantor acquires a property (by right of subrogation) that is a claim on the defaulting party for the amount paid on the guarantee. However, there is generally no income element payable in respect of this property.

Where providing guarantees is part of a taxpayer's business (i.e., for a fee), interest expense on borrowed money to honour the guarantee would generally meet the requirements of deductibility under paragraph 20(1)(c).

Where providing guarantees is not part of a taxpayer's business, the direct use of borrowed money to honour a guarantee is generally not for an income earning purpose and such interest would not be deductible. Such was the finding in *74712 Alberta Ltd.* However, where interest is charged to the defaulting party, the purpose test could be met.

In certain situations there could be exceptions to the direct use rule. Where the taxpayer can show that the guarantee was given for the purpose of increasing its income-earning capacity and must subsequently borrow money to honour the guarantee, the borrowed money may be considered to be used for the purpose of earning income. For example, there may be circumstances where the guarantor had access to the proceeds of the loan that was guaranteed. In this situation, the interest is deductible on the amount of the borrowing to honour the guarantee that can be traced to the funds that were used by the taxpayer for the purpose of earning income. There may be other situations where the taxpayer can demonstrate that the indirect use test is met. Such would be the case where a parent company guaranteed the debts of its wholly owned subsidiary (or in cases of multiple shareholders, where shareholders guarantee a loan in proportion to their shareholdings) and can show that it reasonably expected to earn income from the transaction, such as in the form of potential increased dividends to be received. A deduction for interest in other situations involving borrowings to honour a guarantee may also be warranted, such as in *Lewisporte* where the court concluded that the purpose of the borrowing to honour the guarantee was to obtain complete control over all the assets of two subsidiaries for the purpose of gaining or producing income from these assets.

Borrowing to make non-deductible expenditures

34. Certain expenditures may be restricted or non-deductible under the Act. In some situations, the wording of a particular provision will extend to any interest expense incurred in respect of a given use such that the interest expense would also be denied (e.g., section 67.5). In other situations, the wording of the provision would not, in and of itself, restrict interest deductibility (e.g., section 67.1).

Security provided for borrowed money or an amount payable

35. Lenders and other parties providing credit may require certain property to be pledged as security. The nature of the security provided in connection with borrowed money, or an amount payable for property acquired, does not impact upon the tests for interest deductibility. For example, the fact that an individual had to pledge his or her principal residence or other personal property as security to obtain a loan is not relevant in determining whether the interest on that borrowed money is deductible or not.

Interest on amounts payable where no property acquired

36. As noted in ¶4, interest expense is generally considered to be a capital expenditure, deductible only under the provisions of paragraph 20(1)(c). If the amount payable is not for property acquired, subparagraph 20(1)(c)(ii) does not apply. On an administrative basis however (and pending the outcome of the *Gifford* case — see ¶4), the deduction of interest expense on amounts payable for service costs that are currently deductible expenses is permitted under section 9.

Discounts arising on the issuance of debt obligations

37. Where money is borrowed with a stated rate of interest and in consideration for a promise to pay a larger amount, i.e., at a discount, such discount is not considered interest expense. Subsection 20(2) provides that in such cases the larger amount is

the amount borrowed (i.e., borrowed money) for the purposes of paragraph 20(1)(c). In addition, in such cases, paragraph 20(1)(f) provides for a full or partial deduction of the discount at repayment depending on the extent of the discount.

Where there is no interest stipulated to be payable, the provisions of subsection 16(1) may apply to such contracts with the result that an amount would be deemed to be interest on a debt obligation to both the investor and the issuer. Since subsection 16(1) refers to an amount under a contract as opposed to a payment, the interest expense would be deductible on a paid or payable basis. Note however, such contracts having terms greater than one year would be considered to include both simple interest (deductible on a paid or payable basis) as well as compound interest (deductible only on a paid basis).

Example 10

> T Corp. raises capital by issuing commercial paper (for which no interest is stipulated to be payable). The terms of the commercial paper contract are structured such that T Corp. receives an amount from an investor and in return promises to pay that investor a larger amount at a future date. The difference between the two amounts can reasonably be regarded as interest and T Corp. can deduct that amount subject to meeting all of the other requisite requirements for interest deductibility.

Premiums arising on the issuance of debt obligations

38. Where debts are issued with a stated interest rate greater than prevailing market rates, the debt issuer will receive greater than 100% of the principal amount of the debt issue, i.e., a premium. Where the borrowed money constitutes stock-in-trade for some taxpayers in the financing business (e.g. money-lenders), the premium amount will be included in computing income under section 9. For other taxpayers it will generally be considered a non-taxable capital receipt. Where the premium arises because the debt was deliberately priced to give rise to a premium, the interest expense otherwise deductible will not be considered reasonable and will be reduced (with reference to the amount of the premium) over the life of the debt. Since the issue premium serves to adjust the overall yield to reflect the market yield currently being offered on similar instruments, it is the CCRA's position that the stipulated interest rate on the debt is in excess of a reasonable amount as determined for the purposes of paragraph 20(1)(c).

Interest on credit card transactions

39. It is common for small business owners and proprietors to use a credit card for both business and personal use. The amounts charged for business and personal use can readily be determined. Generally, where the credit card balance is not paid in full, the payments are applied firstly to interest and secondly to the oldest charges, with the result that the outstanding balance on which interest is charged can be divided between amounts owing for business and personal use. Adequate records must be kept to verify the interest deduction in these circumstances. In situations where this cannot be done, the CCRA will allow the interest to be apportioned

according to its use (business vs. personal) based on the proportion of total business charges to total personal charges on the credit card for the period in question.

Interest on death duties

40. In certain situations, interest expense may accrue in respect of succession duties, inheritance taxes or estate taxes. Such interest accruing within the taxation year is deductible under paragraph 60(d). The person who is primarily liable for the duties or taxes (generally the executor or successor to an estate) may deduct such interest.

Refinancing transactions

41. Where borrowed money is used to repay existing borrowed money or an amount payable for property acquired, the new borrowed money is deemed to have been used for the purpose for which the money previously borrowed was used or to acquire the property upon which amounts were owing, as the case may be, by virtue of subsection 20(3).

Other provisions of the Act regarding interest deductibility

42. In addition to the legislation described above, other provisions of the Act may also have application to interest expense. Those provisions are not discussed in this bulletin, but some are noted below for reference purposes:

- sections 15.1 and 15.2, interest on small business development bonds and small business bonds;
- paragraph 18(1)(g), payments on income bonds;
- subsections 18(2) to (3.7), limit on certain interest and property tax;
- subsections 18(4) to (6), limitation re: deduction of interest by certain corporations [thin capitalization];
- subsection 18(9), limitation respecting prepaid expenses;
- subsections 18(9.1) to (9.8), penalties, bonuses and rate-reduction payments;
- subsection 18(11), limitation [on interest expense];
- paragraph 20(1)(ll), repayment of interest;
- subsection 20(14), accrued bond interest;
- subsection 20(14.1), interest on debt obligation;
- section 20.2, interest — authorized foreign bank;
- section 20.3, weak currency debt;
- section 21, cost of borrowed money;
- section 67.2, interest on money borrowed for passenger vehicle; and
- section 138(5), deductions not allowed [insurance corporations].

Appendix A — References to court cases referred to in the bulletin

74712 Alberta Ltd — *74712 Alberta Ltd. (formerly Cal-Gas & Equipment Ltd.) v. The Queen*, [1997] 2 C.T.C. 30, 1997 D.T.C. 5126 (FCA)

Barbican — *Barbican Properties Inv. v. The Queen*, [1997] 1 C.T.C. 2383, 1997 D.T.C. 5008 (FCA)

Bronfman Trust — *The Queen v. Bronfman Trust*, [1987] 1 C.T.C. 117, 1987 D.T.C. 5059 (SCC)

Canada Safeway — *Canada Safeway Ltd. v. MNR*, 57 D.T.C. 1239 (SCC)

Canadian Helicopters — *The Queen v. Canadian Helicopters Limited*, [2002] 2 C.T.C. 83, 2002 D.T.C. 6805 (FCA)

Chase Manhattan — *The Queen v. The Chase Manhattan Bank of Canada*, 2000 D.T.C. 6018 (FCA)

Gifford — *The Queen v. Thomas Gifford*, [2002] 4 C.T.C. 64, 2002 D.T.C. 7197 (FCA)[3]

Lewisporte — *Lewisporte Holdings v. The Queen*, [1999] 1 C.T.C. 2056, 1999 D.T.C. 253 (CCI)

Ludco — *Ludco Enterprises Ltd. et al. v. The Queen*, [2002] 1 C.T.C. 95, 2001 D.T.C. 5505 (SCC)

McCool — *MNR v. T. E. McCool Limited*, [1949] C.T.C. 395, 4 D.T.C. 700 (SCC)

Mid-West Abrasive — *MNR v. Mid-West Abrasive Company of Canada Limited*, [1973] C.T.C. 548, 1973 D.T.C. 5429 (FCTD)

Miller — *Miller v. The Queen*, [1985] 2 C.T.C. 139, 1985 D.T.C. 5354 (FCTD)

Penn Ventilator — *Penn Ventilator Canada Ltd. v. The Queen*, [2002] 2 C.T.C. 2636, 2002 D.T.C. 1498 (TCC)

Shell — *Shell Canada Limited v. The Queen*, [1999] 4 C.T.C. 313, 1999 D.T.C. 5669 (SCC)

Sherway Centre — *The Queen v. Sherway Centre Ltd.*, [1998] 2 C.T.C. 343, 1998 D.T.C. 6121 (FCA)

Singleton — *The Queen v. Singleton*, [2002] 1 C.T.C. 121, 2001 D.T.C. 5533 (SCC)

Tennant — *Tennant v. The Queen*, [1996] 1 C.T.C. 290, 1996 D.T.C. 6121 (SCC)

Trans-Prairie — *Trans-Prairie Pipelines Ltd. v. MNR*, [1970] C.T.C. 537, 1970 D.T.C. 6351 (Ex Ct.)

---

[3] On March 27, 2003, the Supreme Court of Canada agreed to hear the appeal of *Thomas Gifford*.

Appendix B — Draft proposals: Deductibility of interest and other expenses

On October 31, 2003, the Department of Finance released for public comment draft proposals regarding the deductibility of interest and other expenses for income tax purposes. The proposals include specific *Income Tax Act* rules to require that there be a "reasonable expectation of profit" from a business or property in order for a taxpayer to realize a loss from the business or property, and to make clear that profit in this sense does not include capital gains. In order to permit an adequate consultation period, these proposals are intended to have effect for taxation years beginning after 2004.

Information Circular 89-3 — Policy Statement on Business Equity Valuations

Date: August 25, 1989

Purpose

1. This Information Circular outlines the valuation principles, practices and policies that the Department generally considers and follows in the valuation of securities and intangible property of closely held corporations for income tax purposes.

Law

2. All valuations should be made in accordance with the provisions of the Canadian *Income Tax Act* and the *Income Tax Regulations.*

Definitions

3.

(a) Fair market value is the highest price, expressed in terms of money or money's worth, obtainable in an open and unrestricted market between knowledgeable, informed and prudent parties acting at arm's length, neither party being under any compulsion to transact.

(b) Value, as found in paragraph 7(1)(a), is generally interpreted by the Department to mean fair market value.

(c) A closely held corporation is a corporation whose shares are owned by a relatively limited number of shareholders. There is no established market for such shares, in that they are sold infrequently.

Valuation Approaches

4. The Circular discusses, in general, the approaches applicable to closely held or private corporations, recognizing that the facts and circumstances of each case will be determinative of fair market value. The valuator must use reasonable judgment and objectivity in the selection and analysis of the relevant facts of each valuation.

Factors

5. When dealing with the valuation of shares of closely held corporations and of intangible assets, the effect on value of a number of fundamental factors, such as the following, should be considered and analyzed:

(a) The nature of the business, and history of the business from its inception.

(b) The general outlook, the specific outlook and condition of the particular industry and the company's position in the industry.

(c) The balance sheet, the financial condition and the capital structure of the particular company.

(d) The company's earnings record and its earnings power.

(e) The dividend-paying capacity of the specific company.

(f) The existence of goodwill and/or other intangible assets.

(g) Sales of the company's stock.

(h) The size of the specific shareholding to be valued.

(i) The stock market prices of comparable stocks of reasonably similar corporations in the same line of business, where these shares are actively traded in an open, unrestricted and public market.

(j) The value of the corporate assets underlying the shares.

6. There are also numerous factors and issues relevant to the valuation of specific shareholdings, apart from the fundamental factors considered in valuing the enterprise as a whole. These include the existence of

(a) options, other buy-sell agreements or other contractual rights or obligations;

(b) control or minority shareholder interests;

(c) the rights and privileges of the various classes of shares under the company's letters patent, bylaws, or memorandum of association; and

(d) corporate-owned life insurance.

Weighting of Various Factors

7. Depending on the nature of the corporation's business, certain of the relevant factors may be accorded greater weight. In some businesses, earnings may be the primary determinant of value, while in others it may be asset value. The valuator must consider a different combination of factors in each case in determining fair market value.

Methods

8. The earnings and asset value methods are the two most generally accepted bases for determining value. The earnings method is of primary concern when valuing shares of operating companies that manufacture or market products or services.

9. Asset value methods are useful where:

(a) A reasonable and viable alternative to buying an existing business is to start one from scratch, such as small construction subcontractors operating on competitive bids, auto body repair shops, machine shops, some retail outlets.

(b) A business sells largely on an asset basis, that is, it derives its income largely from the assets, either tangible or intangible, rather than from the personal efforts of the owners and personnel, e.g., real estate holding companies, equipment leasing or investment companies, franchise or dealership operations.

Approaches

10. Generally speaking, the fair market value of a business is usually the greater of

(a) its liquidation value, and

(b) its going concern value.

11. The liquidation value approach is generally used where

(a) the business is not a viable ongoing operation and is consequently suitable only for liquidation;

(b) the business is a going concern, but its value is related to the liquidation value of the company's underlying assets; and

(c) it is an aid in the determination of fair market value on a going concern basis, as in determining risk.

12. The going concern value approach is normally used where the business is a continuing enterprise with the potential for earning a reasonable return on investment. Where there is adequate potential earning power in the form of economic future profits or discretionary cash flows, the determination of going concern value depends on the amount and quality of the earnings or cash flows, and the business and financial risk that these earnings or cash flows can be achieved and sustained.

Factors in Capitalization Rate Selection

13. The risk, expressed in a going concern value calculation as the capitalization rate, relates to a number of factors in the business, among which may be:

(a) The tangible asset backing.

(b) The liquidation value.

(c) The nature and history of the business operations.

(d) The general economic, money and stock market conditions and outlook.

(e) Specific industry and market comparisons.

(f) The financial condition of the specific business being valued.

(g) The quality of the business operations, including such factors as its management depth, its marketing, research and development capabilities, the composition of its labour force and product mix, and the existence of major contracts.

(h) The impact of inflation and foreign exchange fluctuations.

(i) The specific risk as related to the stability or irregularity of the maintainable level of earnings or cash flows of the particular business.

(j) The general and specific political environment.

(k) Opportunities for growth as related to the social environment of the business.

(l) The existence and importance of competitors.

(m) The cost or ease of entry into the particular industry being reviewed.

(n) The choice of and rates of return on alternate investments.

It should be noted that the foregoing list is not exhaustive.

The valuator must exercise judgment in determining the extent to which these and other potential external and internal factors are relevant in the quantification of a capitalization rate.

14. The general approach, appropriate methods and relevant factors are applicable to the determination of fair market value of any type of business interest, incorporated or unincorporated and of intangible assets, for income tax purposes.

Procedures

15. The organization of the departmental business equity valuation function is outlined in the current version of Information Circular 72-25.

16. The Regional Valuation Officer may ask for documents, statements or other information, including the following:

(a) Details and the basis of values filed, for Valuation Day or any other dates.

(b) A balance sheet with supporting statements, schedules and notes as at the date of valuation.

(c) Copies of any appraisals of the fixed assets and/or real estate.

(d) Financial statements for the five most recent fiscal periods prior to the valuation date, or since the commencement of operations, whichever represents the shorter period.

(e) If the business has been operating for five years or less, the financial statements should include an opening balance sheet.

(f) Copies of all option, buy-sell or other shareholder agreements or partnership agreements.

(g) Complete details of all acquisitions and dispositions of the taxpayer's interest in the entity, proposed or completed.

(h) Copies of any arm's length offers for substantially all of either the company's shares or its fixed assets.

(i) For small closely held companies, a list of shareholders outlining the number of shares held and any family relationships.

(j) For large closely held companies and public companies, a list of major shareholders, outlining the number of shares held and any family relationships, if applicable.

(k) For partnerships, a list of the partners outlining their profit and capital-sharing ratios.

(l) If the property is a bond or other obligation, details of the series, face value, interest rate and maturity date.

(m) Copies of extracts from the corporate letters patent, memorandum of association, or by-laws detailing the rights and privileges attaching to all classes of shares.

(n) With regard to companies, details of any recent sales of similar securities.

(o) A brief history of the business operation, including the area it serves, its relation to its competitors in the same industry, and the specific outlook and condition of the particular industry.

(p) Any pertinent facts or opinions concerning such issues as the dependence of the company on key personnel, suppliers or customers, the taxpayer's role in the company, the company's potential for growth, the adequacy of its facilities, and the existence of contracts or leases.

(q) Details of life insurance policies owned by a corporation or partnership on the lives of its key personnel.

(r) Details of and comments on the adequacy of salaries and/or other benefits paid or credited to the principal shareholders, partners or proprietor and their families.

It should be noted that the foregoing list is not exhaustive.

Policies

Options and Buy-Sell Agreements

17. Options and buy-sell agreements affect fair market value determination as required by several sections of the *Income Tax Act*, notably section 69 and subsection 70(5).

18. In a closely held corporation, fair market value must be determined by referring to share rights and restrictions, whether found in the company's articles, by-laws or valid contracts between shareholders. These rights or restrictions can have an appreciatory or a depreciatory effect on the price a willing purchaser would pay for the shares in the notional market.

19. Where these rights cannot be changed without incurring the possibility of minority shareholder court or breach of contract action, where such rights limit the amount that can be realized at the date of valuation and require the shares to be disposed of for a stipulated amount, their value must be determined according to the provisions of such agreement or article. In these circumstances, other relevant factors normally considered in valuing shares may not be relevant.

20. On the other hand, where a majority shareholder holds shares subject to rights and restrictions and can modify these same rights and restrictions without incurring the possibility of adverse minority action, the value of these shares should not be restricted to the amount prescribed by the terms of the arrangement.

21. It must be noted that an arrangement that restricts the value of the shares subject to it must be *bona fide* in nature. That is, there must be some primary legitimate business purpose, such as the orderly succession of management, control over the influx of outsiders and creation of an outside market for the shares.

22. In addition, for the provisions of any arrangement to be considered relevant to the valuation of shares, the contractual agreement must be validly constituted and binding (i.e., a legally enforceable arrangement), and there must be a reasonable estimate of fair market value made.

23. The following two types of restrictions will not render the agreement determinative of fair market value:

(a) Where a restriction on transfer is one only of consent by shareholders and/or directors, which does not stipulate a price at which shares can be transferred or does not specify events under which an obligation to transfer or option to purchase shares arises, it will not be determinative of fair market value. However, the restriction may be a depreciatory factor to consider in valuing the shares subject to the arrangement.

(b) Where a restriction is merely a right of first refusal at a stipulated price, it will not be determinative of fair market value, although it may be another depreciatory factor to consider.

24. In the situation where shares are subject to a *bona fide* commercial option at a specified or formula price at the time of valuation, the option price will likely represent the lowest (or "floor") price which a prospective and willing purchaser would pay and a willing vendor would accept. To be a *bona fide* commercial option, it must be a legally enforceable contract with a legitimate business purpose. Such an option would have a depreciatory effect on the fair market value of the shares.

25. The facts of a case would determine what amount, if any, a purchaser would pay in excess of that "floor" price and would depend on a number of factors including, when the option is exercisable; the likelihood that the option will be exercised; whether the option price is fixed, subject to periodic increases, or based on a formula which affects an increase in price as the company succeeds; and, the size of the particular shareholding.

26. An agreement may provide for a number of *inter vivos* events which will give rise to either an optional or a mandatory sale at a specific price, such as retirement, resignation, or disability. Such restrictions may have a depreciatory effect on share value. Where the terms of the agreement stipulate a mandatory sale when the shareholder wants to sell his shares, the price stipulated in the agreement should accordingly limit the value pursuant to subsection 70(5), because a prospective purchaser would not be willing to pay any more for the shares than he/she would be able to receive under the provisions of the agreement.

27. If the restrictions contained in agreements are not considered determinative of fair market value, normal valuation approaches will be used to determine the fair market value of the shares in question.

28. In order for a buy-sell agreement to be considered determinative of value pursuant to subsection 70(5), it must meet all the following requirements:

(a) The agreement must obligate the estate to sell the shares at death either under a mandatory sales and purchase agreement or at the option of a designated purchaser.

(b) The agreement must restrict the shareholder's right to dispose of his/her shares at any price during his/her lifetime.

(c) The agreement must fix a price for the shares or set out a method for determining the price on a current basis.

(d) The agreement must represent a *bona fide* business arrangement and not a device to pass the decedent's shares to his/her heirs for less than an adequate and full consideration.

29. If a buy-sell agreement, normally determinative of value, is executed between parties not acting at arm's length, its provisions should be determinative of value, as long as it meets the following criteria:

(a) It is a *bona fide* business arrangement.

(b) The stipulated price or formula price in the agreement provides full and adequate consideration, and represents the fair market value of shares determined without reference to the agreement at the time it is executed.

(c) It is a legal and binding contract.

30. In order for an agreement to be considered *bona fide*, there must be no donative intent in the agreement. In other words, while the parties to the agreement may be related, they must transact as they would at arm's length with strangers.

31. Each case will be dealt with on the basis of the related facts. These facts will determine whether a specific buy-sell or option agreement is legally enforceable and whether its provisions should be determinative of value or should be some of the many relevant factors to be considered in arriving at fair market value of the shares subject to the agreement, in accordance with generally accepted valuation principles.

Reference should also be made to the current version of IT-140.

Family and Group Control

32. The Department recognizes that in certain situations either a related group or an unrelated group of shareholders may control a corporation if they owned amongst themselves at least 50% plus 1 of the issued and outstanding voting shares of the corporation at the same time and if they have historically acted in concert as a group. It is a rebuttable presumption that a family group has acted in concert to control a corporation.

An assertion by a minority shareholder that he/she is part of a family control group must be considered in light of all relevant factors, including the rights and restrictions attributable to his/her particular shares.

In a situation where the existence of family control is recognized, the Department will employ a rateable valuation for each family group member's shares.

33. An assertion of group control by family members, such as those referred to in subsection 251(6) of the *Income Tax Act*, will be accepted, provided there is no contrary evidence that they did not act in concert. Groups of relatives other than those referred to in subsection 251(6), must provide proof that they were part of a controlling family group and acted in concert with that group.

34. With regard to control by a group of shareholders dealing at arm's length, the criteria necessary for acceptance of claims of group control will include

(a) a written agreement under which all the shareholders in the group relinquish their rights to vote and to sell their shares independently at all times; or

(b) provision in the corporate letters patent, memorandum of association or the bylaws restricting individual rights to vote and to sell their shares independently at all times; or

(c) permanent release of the individual shareholder's rights by giving of an irrevocable proxy to a designated person to vote and to sell the shares as he/she sees fit on behalf of all the shareholders in the group; or

(d) a pattern of conduct to demonstrate that the shareholders acted collusively in all matters relating to the control of the corporation.

35. In order to determine whether a certain pattern of conduct is indicative of collusive action in all matters relating to control, the following actions may be undertaken individually or in any combination:

(a) Shareholders' and directors' minutes may be examined to determine the extent of consultation among the group.

(b) A review of remuneration may be made to insure that all members of the group were treated fairly.

(c) Interviews with members of the group may be held to determine the role played by each member.

(d) Details of actual purchases and/or sales made by the claimants may be examined.

36. Where the Department is satisfied that the documentation provided indicates a consistent pattern of group control, it will apply a rateable valuation for each member's shares, and not apply a minority discount.

37. The Department also recognizes that effective control can exist in a public corporation where an individual or group has a large block of shares, where through unconditional proxies, a majority of votes at any shareholders' meeting controls management and where the remaining shares are widely dispersed. In these cases, satisfactory evidence of control must be provided.

Each case will be dealt with on its own merits.

Stock Option Benefits

38. The Department's policy concerning benefits received by employees under stock option plans pursuant to section 7 of the *Income Tax Act* revolves around a few key words contained therein.

With regard to the phrase "value of the shares" encountered in paragraph 7(1)(a), the Department generally interprets the term "value" to mean fair market value, as defined previously.

39. For purposes of determining the date upon which the corporation's shares are "acquired" pursuant to paragraph 7(1)(a), the Department considers that to be the

date at which the taxpayer acquires the rights of a shareholder with regard to the purchased shares subject to the option.

The factual circumstances of each case will determine the date at which a taxpayer obtains legal ownership or the incidence of legal ownership in and to the shares subscribed, and thereby acquires the shares.

Reference should also be made to the current version of IT-113.

Corporate-owned Life Insurance

40. According to subsection 70(5.3), in determining the subsection 70(5) value of a deceased's shares (for deaths occurring after December 1, 1982), the value of corporate-owned life insurance is its cash surrender value. This applies to the deceased, but where there are two or more shareholders and corporate-owned life insurance is required to fund a stock purchase agreement, one must determine the value of the policies held by the corporation on the other shareholders.

The factors to be considered in determining the value of such policies held on the lives of shareholders other than the deceased, should include:

(a) cash surrender value;

(b) the policy's loan value;

(c) face value;

(d) the state of health of the insured and his/her life expectancy;

(e) conversion privileges;

(f) other policy terms, such as term riders, double indemnity provisions; and

(g) replacement value.

Reference should also be made to the current version of IT-416.

41. If the death of one of the shareholders for which corporate life insurance is owned is considered "imminent" and it is proper to consider this factor in valuing a policy, the value may be greater than the policy's cash surrender value. However, one must also consider the following factors:

(a) the possibility that the insured will recover and not die;

(b) the effect that the loss of a key person would have on the business operations;

(c) whether the share interest being valued represents a majority or minority of the outstanding shares; and

(d) the importance attached to factors other than asset value in the circumstances, such as the future earnings expectations and the prospects for dividends.

No. 12 — Income Tax Technical News

Date: February 11, 1998

In This issue

- Millennium Bug Expenditures
- Meals and Beverages at Golf Clubs
- Stop-Loss Provisions — Grandfathering
- 1998 Deduction Limits and Benefit Rates for Automobiles
- Adjusted Cost Base of Partnership Interest — Subparagraph 53(1)(e)(viii)

Millennium Bug Expenditures

All businesses are concerned about the potential problems that may be caused by computer systems that may not operate properly upon the arrival of the year 2000. We have received inquiries concerning the appropriate tax treatment for the costs to be incurred to adapt a computer system for the year 2000.

Whether a particular expenditure should be expensed or treated as a capital expenditure is a question of fact that is to be determined based on an appreciation of all the surrounding circumstances. To determine whether expenditures incurred to eliminate the millennium bug are of a capital or income nature, consideration should be given to determine whether the expenditure was made with a view to bringing into existence an asset or advantage of enduring benefit.

For instance, if a particular software program is only restored to its original condition so that it performs the same applications but the problems of the millennium bug have been eliminated, the expenditures incurred to eliminate the bug would normally be considered to be of a current nature. However, any expenditure that would improve or enhance the software would usually be looked upon as being an account of capital.

Where new software or other assets are acquired to ensure the adaptation of existing software for the arrival of the year 2000, the amount of the expenditures should be added to the appropriate prescribed class, which would be eligible for capital cost allowance at prescribed rates. For computer software, other than system software, the amount of the expenditures would likely be added to class 12(o) and written off over two years.

The interpretation bulletins, in particular the current version of IT-128, *Capital Cost Allowance — Depreciable Property*, contain some discussion on whether an expenditure is capital in nature because depreciable property is acquired or improved, or whether it is currently deductible because it is in respect of the maintenance or repair of a property.

It is our view that the pronouncement of the Emerging Issues Committee (EIC) of the Canadian Institute of Chartered Accountants providing guidance on the accounting treatment for millennium bug costs is consistent with our position. Abstract EIC 80, dated April 10, 1997, states, in part, "It is a matter of professional judgement, based on all the facts, whether specific internal use software modification costs, including costs for year 2000 compliance, enhance the service potential of the software and should be accounted for as a betterment, or whether the costs merely maintain the service potential of the software and should be expensed. For example, if the software modifications merely ensure the continued effectiveness of the affected software for its originally assessed useful life, the costs would be expensed. If, however, year 2000 software compliance is effected by rewriting software applications that enhance their service potential by extending the life of the software beyond its originally assessed useful life, the costs would be accounted for as a betterment."

We will be in a position to provide more definitive guidance on the tax treatment of these costs as specific cases arise.

Meals and Beverages at Golf Clubs

The Department has reconsidered its interpretation of the word "facility" in relation to a golf course in subparagraph 18(1)(l)(i) of the *Income Tax Act*. This included consultations with officials of the Department of Finance and further consideration of the intention of Parliament with regard to the purpose of the provision. The Department's current interpretation, set out in paragraph 4 of IT-148R3, *Recreational Properties and Club Dues*, is that a facility includes "any amenities provided by a golf club". The Department will now consider that "facility", as used in subparagraph 18(1)(l)(i), should be interpreted in connection with the words "golf course" as to only include recreational amenities provided by a golf club. Accordingly, a facility will not include the dining room, banquet halls, conference rooms, beverage rooms or lounges of a golf club and, thus, the deduction of the cost of meals and beverages incurred at a golf club will not be denied under the provisions of subparagraph 18(1)(l)(i). This interpretation will be effective immediately. However, such costs will be subject to the provisions of paragraph 18(1)(a), section 67 and the limit imposed under subsection 67.1(1) of the Act.

As a result, the tax treatment of meals and beverages consumed at a golf club will be the same as that of meals and beverages consumed at other establishments. In administering this new position, the Department will require that meal and beverage expenses incurred at a golf club be clearly itemized. Therefore, an all inclusive charge that is not broken down will not be acceptable. Fees or dues for a membership or access to a golf club, including any portion attributable to golf club facilities, continue to be non-deductible pursuant to subparagraph 18(1)(l)(ii).

Stop-Loss Provisions — Grandfathering

The "stop loss" rules set out in subsections 112(3) to (3.2) of the Act may reduce the loss from the disposition of a share held as a capital property by the amount of tax-free dividends received on the share. Bill C-28 proposes to amend these provisions in several respects for share dispositions that occur after April 26, 1995, but also provides for certain dispositions to be "grandfathered" from the application of these rules. The grandfathering provisions may have application where the disposition of the share occurs pursuant to an agreement in writing made before April 27,

1995 or a life insurance policy existed on April 26, 1995 for the purpose of funding a redemption of the share.

The Department will follow the normal practice of providing rulings on these grandfathering provisions when there is a definite proposed disposition of shares. As well, the following general comments will assist taxpayers in determining whether the proposed grandfathering provisions will apply to a proposed disposition of shares or in determining whether grandfathering will apply with respect to a disposition of shares at some future but indefinite date.

(a) The proposed grandfathering provisions provided for under proposed paragraph (a) of the related coming into force (CIF) provisions will apply where the agreement in writing made before April 27, 1995 is not altered or modified in any way.

(b) The parties to an agreement in writing made before April 27, 1995 may choose to revise the terms of their relationship by concluding a separate agreement so that the existing agreement remains unchanged. Where a separate agreement is entered into by the parties to revise the terms of their relationship contained in a grandfathered agreement, the grandfathering based on the agreement made before April 27, 1995 will be lost if the separate agreement is considered to cancel, nullify or replace the grandfathered agreement.

(c) Where a disposition by the shareholder to an identified third person is contemplated in the agreement in writing made before April 27, 1995, the transitional relief under paragraph (a) of the CIF will apply to the disposition by the shareholder to the third person. However, such transitional relief will not apply to a subsequent disposition by the third person since that disposition would not be made pursuant to a grandfathered agreement (since the third person was not a party to the agreement in writing made before April 27, 1995).

(d) Where an agreement in writing made before April 27, 1995 specifically provides for "put" and/or "call" options and such options are later exercised, the disposition would be pursuant to the agreement in writing made before April 27, 1995. The third party, however, would have to be identified in this agreement.

(e) The requirement in subparagraph (b)(iii) of the CIF is that "it is reasonable to conclude on April 26, 1995 that a *main purpose* of the life insurance policy was to fund, directly or indirectly, in whole or in part, a redemption, acquisition or cancellation of the share by the corporation that issued the share, and..."

The determination of a main purpose for the acquisition of a life insurance policy can only be made based on the evaluation of the facts and circumstances of each particular case. We recognize that there can be more than one main purpose for the acquisition of a life insurance policy. In this regard, the policyholder must be able to provide documentary evidence to substantiate that a main purpose for the acquisition of a life insurance policy was to fund, directly or indirectly, in whole or in part, the redemption, acquisition or cancellation of a share. While we are not in a position to provide an exhaustive list of the documentation that should have existed prior to April 27, 1995 to substantiate a main purpose for acquiring a life insurance policy, we would expect that documents issued by the insurance company, minutes of the corporation, correspondence from the legal advisors or the accountants or any correspondence relating to the issuance of such a life insurance policy would all be relevant in making such a determination.

(f) To qualify for transitional relief under paragraph (b) of the CIF, a taxpayer must demonstrate that certain conditions related to a life insurance policy existed on April 26, 1995. It is possible that subsequent actions in respect of the policy may be relevant in determining whether the requirements (i.e. the main purpose test) set out in the proposed grandfathering provisions under paragraph (b) of the CIF relating to the life insurance policy existed on April 26, 1995. However, modifications, alterations or cancellation of such a policy subsequent to April 26, 1995 would not, in and of themselves, result in a loss of grandfathering.

(g) The determination of whether a beneficiary of "temporary coverage" would be considered a beneficiary of a life insurance policy within the meaning of paragraph (b) of the CIF is both a legal and factual determination which may also involve the review of the relevant provincial statutes.

Provided the temporary coverage, which may be referred to as a "conditional insurance agreement", is a life insurance policy for purposes of the relevant provincial insurance act, we would accept that it would be a life insurance policy for purposes of paragraph (b) of the CIF. The other requirements of paragraph (b) of the CIF would have to be satisfied.

1998 Deduction Limits and Benefit Rates for Automobiles

In *News Release* 97-112, dated December 4, 1997, the Secretary of State (International Financial Institutions) announced changes for 1998 in the ceiling on the capital cost of passenger vehicles for capital cost allowance purposes and the limit on deductible leasing costs. The changes will be of significant interest to the users of the following interpretation bulletins:

- IT-63R5, *Benefits, Including Standby Charge for an Automobile, from the Personal Use of a Motor Vehicle Supplied by an Employer — After 1992*
- IT-220R2, *Capital Cost Allowance — Proceeds of Disposition of Depreciable Property*
- IT-291R2, *Transfer of Property to a Corporation under Subsection 85(1)*
- IT-478R, *Capital Cost Allowance — Recapture and Terminal Loss*
- IT-521R, *Motor Vehicle Expenses Claimed by Self-Employed Individuals*
- IT-522R, *Vehicle, Travel and Sales Expenses of Employees*

The above bulletins will be updated in the future to reflect these changes. However, in the meantime, the following identifies the area of the relevant bulletin that is affected by each particular change.

1. The ceiling on the capital cost of passenger vehicles for capital cost allowance (CCA) purposes will be increased by $1,000 to $26,000 plus the applicable federal and provincial sales taxes on such an amount.

This change primarily affects ¶2 of IT-63R5, ¶3 of IT-220R2, ¶20 of IT-291R2, ¶10 of IT-478R, ¶10 of IT-521R and ¶9 of IT-522R.

2. The limit on deductible leasing costs will increase by $100 to $650 per month (plus the applicable federal and provincial sales taxes on such amounts), effective for leases entered into after 1997.

This change primarily affects ¶13 of IT-63R5, ¶10 of IT-521R and ¶9 of IT-522R.

In the News Release, the Secretary of State also announced that:

- The limit for deductible tax-exempt allowances paid by employers to employees will remain at 35 cents for the first 5,000 kilometres and 29 cents for each additional kilometre, except for the Yukon and Northwest Territories where the allowance will continue to be 39 cents for the first 5,000 kilometres and 33 cents for each additional kilometre.
- The maximum allowable interest deduction for amounts borrowed to purchase an automobile will remain at $250 per month.
- The general prescribed rate used to determine the taxable benefit relating to the personal portion of automobile operating expenses paid by employers will remain at 14 cents per kilometre, except in the case of taxpayers employed principally in selling or leasing automobiles where the prescribed rate will continue to be 11 cents per kilometre.

Adjusted Cost Base of Partnership Interest — Subparagraph 53(1)(e)(viii)

Subparagraph 53(1)(e)(viii) of the *Income Tax Act* provides an addition, in the calculation of the adjusted cost base (ACB) of a partner's partnership interest at a particular time, for amounts to which the deeming provisions of subsection 66.1(7), 66.2(6) or 66.4(6) has applied before that time.

We are clarifying that, for fiscal periods ending after the date of this newsletter, in calculating the ACB to a taxpayer of an interest in a partnership at a particular time, only relevant amounts which arose to a partner under subsection 66.1(7), 66.2(6) or 66.4(6) in respect of fiscal periods of the partnership ending before that particular time will be included under subparagraph 53(1)(e)(viii). In other words, amounts referred to in subparagraph 53(1)(e)(viii) will not increase the ACB of the partner's interest in the partnership until after the end of the relevant fiscal period of the partnership. This position is consistent with the provisions of paragraph 96(2.2)(b.1) which are relevant to the determination of the "at-risk amount" of a taxpayer who is a limited partner of a partnership.

We will consider advance income tax ruling requests in circumstances involving the application of the above position concerning subparagraph 53(1)(e)(viii) where there is a possibility of double taxation. It should be noted that subsection 66.4(6) and subparagraph 53(1)(e)(viii) were the subject of identical questions at two previous Revenue Canada Round Tables (question No. 18 at the Institute of Chartered Accountants of Alberta meeting on May 18, 1994, and question No. 4 at the Canadian Petroleum Tax Society meeting on June 2, 1994). The situation addressed was one where all of the assets of a partnership were to be distributed such that each partner would receive a pro-rata undivided interest in those assets immediately prior to the dissolution of the partnership. In addition, the circumstances were such that elections under subsection 98(3) would not be made and the partners would be considered to have disposed of their respective partnership interests upon dissolution of the partnership. The response provided to those questions was, essentially, that the provisions of subsection 66.4(6) would be considered to have applied such that the addition under subparagraph 53(1)(e)(viii) in computing the adjusted cost base of a partner's interest in the partnership would arise prior to its disposition upon dissolution. The response expressed in these Round Table questions remains valid, provided a fiscal period of the partnership ends after the distribution of partnership assets to the partner and prior to the partnership interest being disposed of by the partner on dissolution of the partnership.

The *Income Tax Technical News* is produced by the Policy and Legislation Branch. It is provided for information purposes only and does not replace the law. If you have any comments or suggestions about the matters discussed in this publication, please send them to:

Director, Business and Publications Division
Income Tax Rulings and Interpretations Directorate
Policy and Legislation Branch
Revenue Canada
25 Nicholas Street
Ottawa ON K1A 0L5

The *Income Tax Technical News* can be found on the Revenue Canada Internet site at: www.rc.gc.ca

No. 26 — Proposed Guidelines on Split-Receipting

Overview

The Canada Customs and Revenue Agency (CCRA) has completed its review of what constitutes a gift for purposes of the *Income Tax Act* (the Act). This review was initiated as a consequence of the decisions in various court cases that seem to call into question whether the traditional meaning of gift under common law is still the appropriate standard. Furthermore, the traditional definition of gift disqualifies as a gift a transfer of property for partial consideration, notwithstanding that there is a clear gift element and donative intent, a result with which the government and, apparently, the courts are not comfortable.

Accordingly, after consultation with representatives of the Departments of Justice and Finance, the CCRA has developed interpretational guidelines that are to be followed in determining whether a transfer of property results in the making of a gift for purposes of the Act. On December 20, 2002, the Department of Finance released proposed amendments to the Act to facilitate the interpretative approach being adopted by the CCRA. As well, existing interpretation bulletins and publications will be revised to reflect these interpretative guidelines, and to deal with a number of the more common gifting situations. While time will be allowed for interested parties to provide comments before the publications are so revised, these proposed guidelines may be followed in the interim.

Underlying the CCRA's interpretative approach to determining whether there is a gift in situations other than where there is an outright transfer of property for no consideration is that there be a clear donative intent to make a gift.

The key elements to this interpretative approach are as follows:

(a) There must be a voluntary transfer of property to the donee with a clearly ascertainable value.

(b) Any advantage[4] received or obtained by the donor or a person not dealing at arm's length with the donor in respect of the transfer must be clearly identified and its value ascertainable. If its value cannot be reasonably ascertained, no charitable tax deduction or credit will be allowed. In this regard, the donee will be required to identify the advantage and the amount thereof on any receipt provided to the donor in accordance with the proposed amendments to section 3501 of the *Income Tax Regulations*. In respect of valuations, the donee should consider obtaining a qualified independent valuation of the amount of the advantage.

(c) Consistent with the case law, in order for there to be a gift there must be a clear donative intent to enrich the donee. It is recognized that the determination of donative intent is a subjective determination which can be difficult to

[4]As defined in proposed subsection 248(31).

establish. In this regard, it is proposed that the Act be amended[5] so that a transfer of property will not necessarily be disqualified from being a gift, provided the amount of the advantage does not exceed 80% of the value of the property transferred to the donee. In exceptional circumstances where the amount of the advantage exceeds 80% of the value of the transferred property, the transfer may still nevertheless qualify as a gift under the proposed amendments, provided the donor is able to establish to the satisfaction of the Minister that there was an intention to make a gift.

(d) Generally, the proposed definition of an eligible amount of a gift[6] will be the excess of the value of the property transferred to the donee over the amount of the advantage provided to the donor. It is recognized that, whether in connection with fund raising events or direct gifts to a charity, a donor may be provided with some advantage because the donee wishes to provide the donor with a token of gratitude for making the gift. It is further recognized that the appreciation of such gifts will vary from donor to donor. Accordingly, the CCRA is prepared to administratively provide for a de minimis threshold that will simplify matters for both donors and donees where such advantages are of insignificant value. The current de minimis threshold set forth in the current version of Interpretation Bulletin IT-110R3, *Gifts and Official Donation Receipts*, will be revised to provide that the amount of the advantage received by the donor that does not exceed the lesser of 10% of the value of the property transferred to the charity and $75 will not be regarded as an advantage for purposes of determining the eligible amount as set forth in the proposed definition. Note that the revised *de minimis* threshold will not apply to cash or near cash advantages (e.g., this may include redeemable gift certificates, vouchers, coupons).

Guidelines

The following guidelines provide the CCRA's view of the manner in which the eligible amount and the amount of the advantage are to be determined with regard to various situations and fund raising events or activities, taking into account that, in many cases, there is not a readily available market value comparison of the inducement or advantage provided to the donor. In particular, the guidelines address:

- fund raising dinners
- charity auctions
- lotteries
- concerts, shows and sporting events
- golf tournaments
- membership fees

[5]Proposed subsection 248(32).

[6]As defined in proposed subsection 248(30).

- charitable annuities
- mortgaged property

Fund Raising Events or Activities

The guidelines below have general application to all fund raising events or activities:

- The attendance of celebrities at fund raising events will not be viewed as an advantage per se. Any incremental amount paid for the right to participate in an activity with a particular individual (e.g., dinner, golf) would, however, not be viewed as a gift.
- The value of any complimentary benefits provided to all participants for attending the event (e.g., pens and keychains) and the value of door and achievement prizes that all attendees are eligible for by simply attending the event will be viewed as an advantage unless the aggregate value of such items, per ticket sold, does not exceed the lesser of 10% of the ticket price and $75. For the purpose of establishing the eligible amount, and therefore the amount of the tax receipt, the value of door and achievement prizes will be aggregated and allocated on a pro rata basis to all participants.
- For the purpose of determining which items will be viewed as an advantage for purposes of applying the *de minimis* rule, the CCRA will adopt the position that the value of the activity that is the object of the fund raising event, while an advantage to be taken into account in determining the eligible amount, will not be included for this purpose (e.g., the value of a meal at a fund raising dinner, the value of a comparable ticket for a concert, the value of green fees, cart rental and meal at a golf tournament).

Fund Raising Dinners

The value of a comparable meal provided by a comparable facility will have to be ascertained. If the event is held at a restaurant, then the price the restaurant would charge a regular customer would be the comparable value. In this regard, it is acceptable to take into account group or banquet rates.

Generally, the right to participate in an auction to be held at the dinner will not be viewed as constituting an advantage.

Example

- A charity holds a fund raising dinner for which 500 tickets are sold at a cost of $200 each.
- A comparable meal could be purchased for $100, excluding GST, PST and gratuities.
- The door prizes are a trip having a value of $3,000 and jewellery having a retail value of $500 ($3,500/500 or $7 per attendee).
- Each attendee receives a logo pen and key chain with an aggregate retail value of $10.

Determination of eligible amount:

Ticket price	$ 200
Less: meal	$ 100
Eligible amount	$ 100

As a result of applying the *de minimis* threshold, the value of the door prizes and the complimentary items received by a donor will not be viewed as an advantage in determining the eligible amount, since the total value of such prizes and items is $17 per donor, which is less than the lesser of 10% of $200 ($20) and $75.

In this case, the amount of the advantage is $100, which is not more than 80% of the ticket price ($160). Accordingly, a tax receipt may be issued for the eligible amount.

Charity Auctions

Generally, it is CCRA's position that there will not be an eligible amount with respect to items obtained at charity auctions on the basis that the bid determines the value of the various items put up for auction.

However, where the value of an item is clearly otherwise ascertainable (e.g., there is a retail price for the item) and made known to all bidders in advance, an eligible amount would be present where the amount bid is in excess of the posted value. Where donative intent can be established, which may be the case where the posted value of the item does not exceed 80% of the accepted bid, a tax receipt may be issued for the eligible amount.

Example

- A corporate retailer donates a mountain bike to a charity and the charity puts it up for auction.
- The value of the bike is $400 and this amount is posted with the item.
- Any successful bid of $500 or greater would entitle the bidder to a donation receipt equal to the excess of the bid price over $400 (i.e., the eligible amount is the excess).

The retailer donating the bike will be entitled to receive a tax receipt for $400. If this represents a gift on the part of the retailer, the retailer will have revenue of $400 pursuant to section 69 and a donation deduction of $400. If the bike cost the retailer $250, the result would be a profit of $150 for tax purposes.[7]

It is the CCRA's opinion that with regard to certain personal items such as, but not limited to, the jersey of a hockey player, the right to play golf with a particular person, and the right to dine with a particular person, the value of the item will be the amount of the bid such that there will not be an eligible amount.

[7]If the retailer characterizes the transfer of the bike as a promotion or advertising expense, this will not result in any revenue or gift to the retailer, but the retailer will be entitled to include the bike cost of $250 in its cost of goods sold.

Lotteries

It is our view that participants in lotteries, while perhaps influenced in choosing which lottery they will participate in by the identity of the organizing charity, are primarily motivated by the chance to win the significant prizes that are offered. Therefore, in some cases, while there may be an element of donative intent, in our view the amount of the advantage cannot be reasonably quantified.

Accordingly, it continues to be our view that no part of the cost of a lottery ticket is a gift which may be receipted for income tax purposes.

Concerts, Shows and Sporting Events

While a particular event may be a charity fund raiser and all or a portion of the proceeds designated in favour of a charity, there will need to be clear evidence that the ticket price is in excess of the usual and current ticket price to allow a finding that there is an eligible amount. Where the amount of the advantage (including the usual and current ticket price) is 80% or less of the actual ticket price, a tax receipt may be issued for the difference. If there is no reasonably comparable event, then no portion of the ticket price can be viewed as an eligible amount.

Example

- Tickets are sold for $200 to a fund raising concert featuring Performer X.
- Each participant receives a Performer X t-shirt that normally sells for $20 and a CD that retails at $15.
- Performer X put on a similar concert in Ottawa 8 months ago as part of her regular tour and the ticket price was $100.

Determination of eligible amount:

Actual ticket price	$200
Less: Comparable non-charity ticket price	$100
Complimentary items	$35
Advantage	$135
Eligible amount	$65

The value of the complimentary items is $35, which exceeds the lesser of 10% of $200 ($20) and $75. Accordingly, the complimentary items are regarded as an advantage and must be taken into account in determining the eligible amount.

In this case, the amount of the advantage is $135. Since this amount does not exceed 80% of the actual ticket price ($160), a tax receipt may be issued for the eligible amount ($65).

Golf Tournaments

The following indicates the CCRA's view in determining the value of the various components that may be present at a fund raising golf tournament for the purpose of determining the amount of the advantage received by a participant.

1. Green fees
   - Normal green fees that would ordinarily be charged to a non-member playing the course at the time of the event.
   - No amount would be allocated to members where members are not required to pay green fees.
2. Cart rental
   - Regular cost of a cart rental.
3. Meals
   - Price that would be charged if the meal were purchased separately at the course.
4. Complimentary items
   - Amount that would have to be paid to acquire the merchandise at the donating retail outlet or the outlet from which the merchandise was obtained.
5. Door and achievement prizes
   - The retail value of all such prizes is to be aggregated and allocated pro rata to all attendees.
6. Hole-in-one prize
   - Given that the approximate odds of a hole-in-one for an average golfer on any given par-3 are over 40,000 to 1 and the fact that such prizes are not guaranteed to be given (in fact, they are rarely awarded), the CCRA accepts that for any particular participant the value of the chance to win the prize is nominal, and therefore can be ignored.
7. Raffle tickets
   - Where the raffle is conducted separately, the cost of raffle tickets is not considered a gift (this is essentially a lottery), and the value of the various prizes that will be won is not taken into account in determining the amount of the advantage.
   - Note that if participation in the raffle is included in the participation fee, the prizes will be treated as door prizes.

Example

- A charity holds a fund raising golf tournament with a participation fee of $200.
- There are 100 participants in the tournament some of whom are members of the golf course.
- The regular green fee for non-members on that day is $50.

- Members are not required to pay green fees.
- The cart rental (included in the participation fee) is normally $20.
- Each participant receives golf balls with a retail price of $15.
- The retail price of supplied food and beverage excluding GST, PST and gratuities is $30.
- The retail value of door and achievement prizes is $2,000 ($2,000/100 or $20 per participant).
- The raffle tickets for a chance to win a number of other prizes are sold separately (i.e., the purchase of such tickets is not required).
- The hole-in-one prize is the use of an automobile for one year.

Determination of eligible amount

Participation fee		$200
Less:	Green fee	$50
	Cart rental	$20
	Complimentary items/door and achievement prizes	$35
	Food and beverage	$30
	Hole-in-one prize	$0
	Advantage	$135
Eligible amount (non-members)		$65

The total value of the complimentary items and the door and achievement prizes of $35 to each participant exceeds the lesser of 10% of the participation fee of $200 ($20) and $75. Accordingly, such items constitute an advantage in determining the eligible amount.

In the case of non-members, the amount of the advantage is $135 and a tax receipt may be issued for the eligible amount of $65. If the amount of the advantage exceeded 80% of the participation fee ($160), a tax receipt could not be issued due to the absence of donative intent.

In the case of members, the eligible amount would be increased to $115 by the green fee that they would otherwise not have been required to pay.

If the golf course normally offers group rates this would be taken into account. In the above example, if the course offers a reduced green fee of $40 for tournaments where there are more than 50 participants, then $40 instead of $50 would be used for non-member green fees, which would result in an eligible amount of $75.

Membership Fees

Whether or not there is an eligible amount associated with the payment of membership fees or other amount to a registered charity of which an individual is a member will be determined on the basis of whether the membership fee or other amount exceeds the amount of the advantage. If the amount of the advantage is 80% or less of the payment to the charity, a tax receipt may be issued for the eligible amount.

Example

- The purpose of the registered charity is the promotion of Canadian theatre.
- For a contribution of $250, a contributor will receive the following:
  - recognition as a donor in the charity's newsletter;
  - a subscription to the charity's quarterly newsletter (otherwise available free of charge);
  - the right to attend annual meetings;
  - a monthly calendar of performances (otherwise available free of charge);
  - an advance invitation to certain performances;
  - an invitation to dress rehearsals (open to the general public);
  - a pewter key chain (normally sold for $10);
  - a discount for certain performances (value of $40); and
  - parking vouchers (value of $40).

Determination of eligible amount

Contribution	$250
Less: Complimentary items	
Key chain	$10
*Discount	$40
*Parking vouchers	$40
Advantage	$90
Eligible amount	160

Since the amount of the advantage ($90) received by a contributor is less than 80% of $250 ($200), donative intent may be presumed and a tax receipt may be issued in the amount of $160.

* *The onus is on the charity to provide a value for these items. The value must be reasonable, given the facts of the particular situation.*

Other Situations

Charitable Annuities

The administrative position with regard to charitable annuities is withdrawn with regard to annuities issued after December 20, 2002. The income tax treatment provided for in the current version of Interpretation Bulletin IT-111R2, *Annuities Purchased From Charitable Organizations*, will continue to apply with regard to annuities issued before December 21, 2002.

The administrative position has no basis in law and cannot be continued as a consequence of the proposed subsection 248(33), which provides for a cost for property acquired from the charity in the making of a gift.

Rather, where an amount is contributed to a charitable organization by a donor, and the advantage received by the donor is a stream of guaranteed payments for a period of time, the eligible amount will be equal to the excess of the amount contributed by the donor over the amount that would be paid at that time to an arm's length third party to acquire an annuity to fund the guaranteed payments.

Notwithstanding the withdrawal of the administrative position, charitable annuities are likely to continue as a means of fund raising, and may well be more advantageous to the donor.

Consider the following comparative example:

Facts:

- A donor makes a $100,000 contribution to a charitable organization.
- The donor's life expectancy is 8 years (assume the donor lives 8 years).
- The donor is to be provided annuity payments of $10,000 per year ($80,000).
- The cost of an annuity that will provide $80,000 over 8 years is $50,000.

Tax treatment under current administrative practice:

- The donor receives a tax receipt for $20,000 for the year of donation.
- The donor receives in total $80,000 in annuity payments tax-free.

Tax treatment — proposed:

- The donor receives a tax receipt for $50,000 for the year of donation.
- The donor receives in total $80,000 in annuity payments, of which $30,000 will be included in income over 8 years.

Mortgaged Property

Where property subject to a mortgage is transferred to a charitable organization as a donation, all relevant factors, such as encumbrances other than mortgages, will need to be taken into account in determining the value of the transferred property. With regard to determining the eligible amount, the terms and conditions of the mortgage must be taken into account in determining the amount of the advantage. In other words, the implications of a "favourable" or "unfavourable" mortgage must be reflected in the amount of the advantage received by the transferor that takes the form of being relieved of the mortgage. Accordingly, provided that the eligible amount is at least 20% of the value of the transferred property, a tax receipt may be issued for the eligible amount.

Example

- A building is transferred to a charitable organization wherein the only advantage given by the charitable organization is the assumption of a mortgage placed on the building.
- The value of the building determined without reference to the mortgage is $1,000,000.

- The amount of the outstanding mortgage to be assumed by the charitable organization is $400,000.

In order to determine the eligible amount, it will be necessary to value the mortgage. If the terms and conditions of the mortgage (e.g., interest rate, term) are representative of the current market, the eligible amount in the above example would be $600,000. If the terms and conditions of the mortgage were "unfavourable" (e.g., high interest rate) such that the mortgagor would have to pay a third party $450,000 to assume the mortgage, the eligible amount would be $550,000.

If you have any comments relating to these guidelines, please send them to:

Director, Financial Industries Division
Income Tax Rulings Directorate
Policy and Legislation Branch
Canada Customs and Revenue Agency
Ottawa ON K1A 0L5

We ask that you provide your comments before March 31, 2003. Should you require further information, please contact F. Lee Workman at (613) 957-3497 or Jenie Leigh at (613) 952-1505.

INCOME TAX EXCERPTS

Subsections 112(3)–(7) — Loss on Share ["Stop-loss" Rules]

112. (3) Loss on share that is capital property — Subject to subsections (5.5) and (5.6), the amount of any loss of a taxpayer (other than a trust) from the disposition of a share that is capital property of the taxpayer (other than a share that is property of a partnership) is deemed to be the amount of the loss determined without reference to this subsection minus,

(a) where the taxpayer is an individual, the lesser of

(i) the total of all amounts each of which is a dividend received by the taxpayer on the share in respect of which an election was made under subsection 83(2) where subsection 83(2.1) does not deem the dividend to be a taxable dividend, and

(ii) the loss determined without reference to this subsection minus all taxable dividends received by the taxpayer on the share; and

(b) where the taxpayer is a corporation, the total of all amounts received by the taxpayer on the share each of which is

(i) a taxable dividend, to the extent of the amount of the dividend that was deductible under this section or subsection 115(1) or 138(6) in computing the taxpayer's taxable income or taxable income earned in Canada for any taxation year,

(ii) a dividend in respect of which an election was made under subsection 83(2) where subsection 83(2.1) does not deem the dividend to be a taxable dividend, or

(iii) a life insurance capital dividend.

Application: Subpara. (b)(iv) of the amendment in 1998, c. 19, subsec. 131(11) (see below) amended by 2001, c. 17, s. 251, applicable to 2000 *et seq.*, and

(a) in respect of the 1998 and 1999 taxation years, where a taxpayer and a person who would have been the taxpayer's common-law partner in the 1998 or 1999 taxation year jointly elect under s. 144 of 2000, c. 12 to have ss. 130 to 142 of that Act apply, if applicable, to the 1998 or 1999 taxation year, subpara. 131(11)(b)(iv), as amended, shall be read as follows for the applicable year:

(iv) the disposition is made by

(A) the individual or the individual's spouse or common-law partner,

(B) the estate of the individual or of the individual's spouse or common-law partner within the estate's first taxation year,

(C) the particular trust where it is a trust described in paragraph 104(4)(a) or (a.1) of the *Income Tax Act* in respect of a spouse or common-law partner, the spouse or common-law partner is the beneficiary referred to in subparagraph (i) and the disposition occurs before the end of the trust's third taxation year that begins after the death of the spouse or common-law partner, or

(D) a trust described in paragraph 73(1)(c) of that Act created by the individual in respect of the individual's spouse or common-law partner, or a trust described in paragraph 70(6)(b) of that Act created by the individual's will in respect of the individual's spouse or common-law partner, before the end of the trust's third taxation year that begins after the death of the spouse or common-law partner;

(b) in respect of the 2000 taxation year, where a joint election has not been filed by the taxpayer and a person who would have been the taxpayer's common-law partner in the year 2000 to have ss. 130 to 142 of the *Modernization of Benefits and Obligations Act* apply to the year 2000, subpara. 131(11)(b)(iv), as amended, shall be read as follows for that year:

(iv) the disposition is made by

(A) the individual or the individual's spouse,

(B) the estate of the individual or of the individual's spouse within the estate's first taxation year,

(C) the particular trust where it is a post-1971 spousal or common-law partner trust or a trust described in paragraph 104(4)(a.1) of the *Income Tax Act*, the individual or the individual's spouse, as the case may be, is the beneficiary referred to in subparagraph (i) and the disposition occurs before the end of the trust's third taxation year that begins after the death of the individual or the individual's spouse, as the case may be, or

(D) a trust described in paragraph 73(1.01)(c) of that Act created by the individual, or a trust described in paragraph 70(6)(b) of that Act created by the individual's will in respect of the individual's spouse, before the end of the trust's third taxation year that begins after the death of the individual or the individual's spouse, as the case may be;

Subsec. 112(3) amended by 1998, c. 19, subsec. 131(1), applicable (by 131(11)) to dispositions that occur after April 26, 1995, other than

(a) a disposition that occurs pursuant to an agreement in writing made before April 27, 1995;

(b) a disposition of a share of the capital stock of a corporation that is made to the corporation if

(i) on April 26, 1995 the share was owned by an individual (other than a trust) or by a particular trust under which an individual (other than a trust) was a beneficiary,

(ii) on April 26, 1995 a corporation, or a partnership of which a corporation is a member, was a beneficiary of a life insurance policy that insured the life of the individual or the individual's spouse,

(iii) it was reasonable to conclude on April 26, 1995 that a main purpose of the life insurance policy was to fund, directly or indirectly, in whole or in part, a redemption, acquisition or cancellation of the share by the corporation that issued the share, and

(iv) [as amended by 2001, c. 17; see above] the disposition is made by

(A) the individual or the individual's spouse or common-law partner,

(B) the estate of the individual or of the individual's spouse or common-law partner within the estate's first taxation year,

(C) the particular trust where it is a post-1971 spousal or common-law partner trust or a trust described in para. 104(4)(a.1) of the Act, the individual's spouse or common-law partner, as the case may be, is the beneficiary referred to in subpara. (i) and the disposition occurs before the end of the trust's third taxation year that begins after the death of the individual's spouse or common-law partner, as the case may be, or

(D) a trust described in para. 73(1.01)(c) of the Act created by the individual, or a trust described in para. 70(6)(b) of the Act created by the individual's will in respect of the individual's spouse or common-law partner, before the end of the trust's third taxation year that begins after the death of the individual or the individual's spouse or common-law partner, as the case may be;

(c) a disposition of a share of the capital stock of a corporation owned by an individual on April 26, 1995 that was made by the individual's estate before 1997;

(d) a disposition of a share of the capital stock of a corporation owned by an estate on April 26, 1995, the first taxation year of which ended after that day, that was made by the estate before 1997; or

(e) a disposition of a share of the capital stock of a corporation owned by an individual on April 26, 1995 where the individual is a trust described in para. 104(4)(a) or (a.1) of the Act in respect of a spouse, that was made by the trust after the spouse's death and before 1997.

Subsec. 131(12) of the said c. 19 provides:

(12) For the purposes of paragraph [(b) above] and this subsection, a share of the capital stock of a corporation acquired in exchange for another share in a transaction to which section 51, 85, 86 or 87 of the Act applies is deemed to be the same share as the other share.

(3.01) Loss on share that is capital property — excluded dividends — A qualified dividend shall not be included in the total determined under subparagraph (3)(a)(i) or paragraph (3)(b) if the taxpayer establishes that

(a) it was received when the taxpayer and persons with whom the taxpayer was not dealing at arm's length did not own in total more than 5% of the issued shares of any class of the capital stock of the corporation from which the dividend was received; and

(b) it was received on a share that the taxpayer owned throughout the 365-day period that ended immediately before the disposition.

Application: The opening words of subsec. 112(3.01) amended by 2011, c. 24, subsec. 22(1), applicable to dispositions occurring after March 21, 2011.

Subsec. 112(3.01) added by 1998, c. 19, subsec. 131(1), applicable on the same basis as subsec. 112(3).

(3.1) Loss on share held by partnership — Subject to subsections (5.5) and (5.6), where a taxpayer (other than a partnership or a mutual fund trust) is a member of a partnership, the taxpayer's share of any loss of the partnership from the disposition of a share that is held by a particular partnership as capital property is deemed to be that share of the loss determined without reference to this subsection minus,

(a) where the taxpayer is an individual, the lesser of

(i) the total of all amounts each of which is a dividend received by the taxpayer on the share in respect of which an election was made under subsection 83(2) where subsection 83(2.1) does not deem the dividend to be a taxable dividend, and

(ii) that share of the loss determined without reference to this subsection minus all taxable dividends received by the taxpayer on the share;

(b) where the taxpayer is a corporation, the total of all amounts received by the taxpayer on the share each of which is

(i) a taxable dividend, to the extent of the amount of the dividend that was deductible under this section or subsection 115(1) or 138(6) in computing the taxpayer's taxable income or taxable income earned in Canada for any taxation year,

(ii) a dividend in respect of which an election was made under subsection 83(2) where subsection 83(2.1) does not deem the dividend to be a taxable dividend, or

(iii) a life insurance capital dividend; and

(c) where the taxpayer is a trust, the total of all amounts each of which is

(i) a taxable dividend, or

(ii) a life insurance capital dividend

received on the share and designated under subsection 104(19) or (20) by the trust in respect of a beneficiary that was a corporation, partnership or trust.

Application: Subsec. 112(3.1) amended by 1998, c. 19, subsec. 131(1), applicable on the same basis as subsec. 112(3).

(3.11) Loss on share held by partnership — excluded dividends — A qualified dividend shall not be included in the total determined under subparagraph (3.1)(a)(i) or paragraph (3.1)(b) or (c) if the taxpayer establishes that

(a) it was received when the particular partnership, the taxpayer and persons with whom the taxpayer was not dealing at arm's length did not hold in total more than 5% of the issued shares of any class of the capital stock of the corporation from which the dividend was received; and

(b) it was received on a share that the particular partnership held throughout the 365-day period that ended immediately before the disposition.

Application: The opening words of subsec. 112(3.11) amended by 2011, c. 24, subsec. 22(2), applicable to dispositions occurring after March 21, 2011.

Subsec. 112(3.11) added by 1998, c. 19, subsec. 131(1), applicable on the same basis as subsec. 112(3).

(3.12) Loss on share held by partnership — excluded dividends — A taxable dividend received on a share and designated under subsection 104(19) by a particular trust in respect of a beneficiary that was a partnership or trust shall not be included in the total determined under paragraph (3.1)(c) where the particular trust establishes that the dividend was received by an individual (other than a trust).

Application: Subsec. 112(3.12) added by 1998, c. 19, subsec. 131(1), applicable on the same basis as subsec. 112(3).

(3.2) Loss on share held by trust — Subject to subsections (5.5) and (5.6), the amount of any loss of a trust (other than a mutual fund trust) from the disposition of a share of the capital stock of a corporation that is capital property of the trust is deemed to be the amount of the loss determined without reference to this subsection minus the total of

(a) the amount, if any, by which the lesser of

(i) the total of all amounts each of which is a dividend received by the trust on the share in respect of which an election was made under subsection 83(2) where subsection 83(2.1) does not deem the dividend to be a taxable dividend, and

(ii) the loss determined without reference to this subsection minus the total of all amounts each of which is the amount of a taxable dividend

(A) received by the trust on the share,

(B) received on the share and designated under subsection 104(19) by the trust in respect of a beneficiary who is an individual (other than a trust), or

(C) that is a qualified dividend received on the share after that time and designated under subsection 104(19) by the trust in respect of a beneficiary that was a corporation, partnership or another trust where the trust establishes that

(I) it owned the share throughout the 365-day period that ended immediately before the disposition, and

(II) the dividend was received while the trust, the beneficiary and persons not dealing at arm's length with the beneficiary owned in total less than 5% of the issued shares of any class of the capital stock of the corporation from which the dividend was received

exceeds

(iii) where the trust is an individual's estate, the share was acquired as a consequence of the individual's death and the disposition occurs during the trust's first taxation year, $\frac{1}{2}$ of the lesser of

(A) the loss determined without reference to this subsection, and

(B) the individual's capital gain from the disposition of the share immediately before the individual's death, and

(b) the total of all amounts each of which is

(i) a taxable dividend, or

(ii) a life insurance capital dividend

received on the share and designated under subsection 104(19) or (20) by the trust in respect of a beneficiary that was a corporation, partnership or trust.

Application: The opening words of cl. 112(3.2)(a)(ii)(C) amended by 2011, c. 24, subsec. 22(4), applicable to dispositions occurring after March 21, 2011.

Subpara. 112(3.2)(a)(iii) amended to replace the fraction "1/4" with "1/2" by 2001, c. 17, subsec. 88(2), applicable to dispositions that occur after February 27, 2000 except that, for dispositions that occurred before October 18, 2000, the reference to "1/2" shall be read as a reference to "1/3". Subsec. 112(3.2) amended by 1998, c. 19, subsec. 131(1), applicable on the same basis as subsec. 112(3).

(3.3) Loss on share held by trust — special cases — Notwithstanding subsection (3.2), where a trust has at any time acquired a share of the capital stock of a corporation because of subsection 104(4), the amount of any loss of the trust from a disposition after that time is deemed to be the amount of the loss determined without reference to subsection (3.2) and this subsection minus the total of

(a) the amount, if any, by which the lesser of

(i) the total of all amounts each of which is a dividend received after that time by the trust on the share in respect of which an election was made under subsection 83(2) where subsection 83(2.1) does not deem the dividend to be a taxable dividend, and

(ii) the loss determined without reference to subsection (3.2) and this subsection minus the total of all amounts each of which is the amount of a taxable dividend

(A) received by the trust on the share after that time,

(B) received on the share after that time and designated under subsection 104(19) by the trust in respect of a beneficiary who is an individual (other than a trust), or

(C) that is a qualified dividend received on the share after that time and designated under subsection 104(19) by the trust in respect of a beneficiary that was a corporation, partnership or another trust where the trust establishes that

(I) it owned the share throughout the 365-day period that ended immediately before the disposition, and

(II) the dividend was received when the trust, the beneficiary and persons not dealing at arm's length with the beneficiary owned in total less than 5% of the issued shares of any class of the capital stock of the corporation from which the dividend was received

exceeds

(iii) $\frac{1}{2}$ of the lesser of

(A) the loss from the disposition, determined without reference to subsection (3.2) and this subsection, and

(B) the trust's capital gain from the disposition immediately before that time of the share because of subsection 104(4), and

(b) the total of all amounts each of which is a taxable dividend received on the share after that time and designated under subsection 104(19) by the trust in respect of a beneficiary that was a corporation, partnership or trust.

Application: The opening words of cl. 112(3.3)(a)(ii)(C) amended by 2011, c. 24, subsec. 22(4), applicable to dispositions occurring after March 21, 2011. Subpara. 112(3.3)(a)(iii) amended to replace the fraction "$\frac{1}{4}$" with "$\frac{1}{2}$" by 2001, c. 17, subsec. 88(2), applicable to dispositions that occur after February 27, 2000 except that, for dispositions that occurred before October 18, 2000, the reference to "$\frac{1}{2}$" shall be read as a reference to "$\frac{1}{3}$". Subsec. 112(3.3) added by 1998, c. 19, subsec. 131(1), applicable on the same basis as subsec. 112(3).

(3.31) Loss on share held by trust — excluded dividends — A qualified dividend received by a trust shall not be included under subparagraph (3.2)(a)(i) or (b)(ii) or (3.3)(a)(i) if the trust establishes that the dividend

(a) was received,

(i) in any case where the dividend was designated under subsection 104(19) or (20) by the trust, when the trust, the beneficiary and persons with whom the beneficiary was not dealing at arm's length did not own in total more than 5% of the issued shares of any class of the capital stock of the corporation from which the dividend was received, or

(ii) in any other case, when the trust and persons with whom the trust was not dealing at arm's length did not own in total more than 5% of the issued shares of any class of the capital stock of the corporation from which the dividend was received, and

(b) was received on a share that the trust owned throughout the 365-day period that ended immediately before the disposition.

Application: The opening words of subsec. 112(3.31) amended by 2011, c. 24, subsec. 22(5), applicable to dispositions occurring after March 21, 2011.

Subsec. 112(3.31) added by 1998, c. 19, subsec. 131(1), applicable on the same basis as subsec. 112(3).

(3.32) Loss on share held by trust — excluded dividends — A qualified dividend that is a taxable dividend received on the share and that is designated under subsection 104(19) by the trust in respect of a beneficiary that was a corporation, partnership or trust, shall not be included under paragraph (3.2)(b) or (3.3)(b) if the trust establishes that the dividend was received by an individual (other than a trust), or

(a) was received when the trust, the beneficiary and persons with whom the beneficiary was not dealing at arm's length did not own in total more than 5% of the issued shares of any class of the capital stock of the corporation from which the dividend was received; and

(b) was received on a share that the trust owned throughout the 365-day period that ended immediately before the disposition.

Application: The opening words of subsec. 112(3.32) amended by 2011, c. 24, subsec. 22(6), applicable to dispositions occurring after March 21, 2011.

Subsec. 112(3.32) added by 1998, c. 19, subsec. 131(1), applicable on the same basis as subsec. 112(3).

(4) Loss on share that is not capital property — Subject to subsections (5.5) and (5.6), the amount of any loss of a taxpayer (other than a trust) from the disposition of a share of the capital stock of a corporation that is property (other than capital property) of the taxpayer is deemed to be the amount of the loss determined without reference to this subsection minus,

(a) where the taxpayer is an individual and the corporation is resident in Canada, the total of all dividends received by the individual on the share;

(b) where the taxpayer is a partnership, the total of all dividends received by the partnership on the share; and

(c) where the taxpayer is a corporation, the total of all amounts received by the taxpayer on the share each of which is

(i) a taxable dividend, to the extent of the amount of the dividend that was deductible under this section, section 113 or subsection 115(1) or 138(6) in computing the taxpayer's taxable income or taxable income earned in Canada for any taxation year, or

(ii) a dividend (other than a taxable dividend).

Application: Subsec. 112(4) amended by 1998, c. 19, subsec. 131(1), applicable to dispositions that occur after April 26, 1995.

(4.01) Loss on share that is not capital property — excluded dividends — A qualified dividend shall not be included in the total determined under paragraph (4)(a), (b) or (c) if the taxpayer establishes that

(a) it was received when the taxpayer and persons with whom the taxpayer was not dealing at arm's length did not own in total more than 5% of the issued shares of any class of the capital stock of the corporation from which the dividend was received; and

(b) it was received on a share that the taxpayer owned throughout the 365-day period that ended immediately before the disposition.

Application: The opening words of subsec. 112(4.01) amended by 2011, c. 24, subsec. 22(7), applicable to dispositions occurring after March 21, 2011.

Subsec. 112(4) amended by 1998, c. 19, subsec. 131(1), applicable to dispositions that occur after April 26, 1995.

(4.1) Fair market value of shares held as inventory — For the purpose of section 10, the fair market value at any time of a share of the capital stock of a corporation is deemed to be equal to the fair market value of the share at that time, plus

(a) where the shareholder is a corporation, the total of all amounts received by the shareholder on the share before that time each of which is

(i) a taxable dividend, to the extent of the amount of the dividend that was deductible under this section, section 113 or subsection 115(1) or 138(6) in computing the shareholder's taxable income or taxable income earned in Canada for any taxation year, or

(ii) a dividend (other than a taxable dividend);

(b) where the shareholder is a partnership, the total of all amounts each of which is a dividend received by the shareholder on the share before that time; and

(c) where the shareholder is an individual and the corporation is resident in Canada, the total of all amounts each of which is a dividend received by the shareholder on the share before that time (or, where the shareholder is a trust, that would have been so received if this Act were read without reference to subsection 104(19)).

Application: Subsec. 112(4.1) amended by 1998, c. 19, subsec. 131(1), applicable to taxation years that end after April 26, 1995.

(4.11) Fair market value of shares held as inventory — excluded dividends — A qualified dividend shall not be included in the total determined under paragraph (4.1)(a), (b) or (c) if the shareholder establishes that

(a) it was received while the shareholder and persons with whom the shareholder was not dealing at arm's length did not hold in total more than 5% of the issued shares of any class of the capital stock of the corporation from which the dividend was received; and

(b) it was received on a share that the shareholder held throughout the 365-day period that ended at the time referred to in subsection (4.1).

Application: The opening words of subsec. 112(4.11) amended by 2011, c. 24, subsec. 22(8), applicable to dispositions occurring after March 21, 2011.

Subsec. 112(4.11) added by 1998, c. 19, subsec. 131(1), applicable to taxation years that end after April 26, 1995.

(4.2) Loss on share held by trust — Subject to subsections (5.5) and (5.6), the amount of any loss of a trust from the disposition of a share that is property (other than capital property) of the trust is deemed to be the amount of the loss determined without reference to this subsection minus

(a) the total of all amounts each of which is a dividend received by the trust on the share, to the extent that the amount was not designated under subsection 104(20) in respect of a beneficiary of the trust; and

(b) the total of all amounts each of which is a dividend received on the share that was designated under subsection 104(19) or (20) by the trust in respect of a beneficiary of the trust.

Application: Subsec. 112(4.2) amended by 1998, c. 19, subsec. 131(1), applicable to dispositions that occur after April 26, 1995.

(4.21) Loss on share held by trust — excluded dividends — A qualified dividend shall not be included in the total determined under paragraph (4.2)(a) if the taxpayer establishes that

(a) it was received when the trust and persons with whom the trust was not dealing at arm's length did not own in total more than 5% of the issued shares of any class of the capital stock of the corporation from which the dividend was received; and

(b) it was received on a share that the trust owned throughout the 365-day period that ended immediately before the disposition.

Application: The opening words of subsec. 112(4.21) amended by 2011, c. 24, subsec. 22(9), applicable to dispositions occurring after March 21, 2011.

Subsec. 112(4.21) added by 1998, c. 19, subsec. 131(1), applicable to dispositions that occur after April 26, 1995.

(4.22) Loss on share held by trust — excluded dividends — A qualified dividend shall not be included in the total determined under paragraph (4.2)(b) if the taxpayer establishes that

(a) it was received when the trust, the beneficiary and persons with whom the beneficiary was not dealing at arm's length did not own in total more than 5%

of the issued shares of any class of the capital stock of the corporation from which the dividend was received; and

(b) it was received on a share that the trust owned throughout the 365-day period that ended immediately before the disposition.

Application: The opening words of subsec. 112(4.22) amended by 2011, c. 24, subsec. 22(10), applicable to dispositions occurring after March 21, 2011.

Subsec. 112(4.22) added by 1998, c. 19, subsec. 131(1), applicable to dispositions that occur after April 26, 1995.

(4.3) [Repealed]

Application: Subsec. 112(4.3) repealed by 1998, c. 19, subsec. 131(2), applicable to dispositions that occur after April 26, 1995.

(5) Disposition of share by financial institution — Subsection (5.2) applies to the disposition of a share by a taxpayer in a taxation year where

(a) the taxpayer is a financial institution in the year;

(b) the share is a mark-to-market property for the year; and

(c) the taxpayer received

(i) a dividend on the share at a time when the taxpayer and persons with whom the taxpayer was not dealing at arm's length held in total more than 5% of the issued shares of any class of the capital stock of the corporation from which the dividend was received, or

(ii) a dividend on the share under subsection 84(3).

Application: Para. 112(5)(c) amended by 2011, c. 24, subsec. 22(11), applicable to dispositions occurring after March 21, 2011.

Subsec. 112(5) added by 1995, c. 21, subsec. 56(7), applicable to dispositions in taxation years that begin after October 1994.

(5.1) Share held for less than one year — Subsection (5.2) applies to the disposition of a share by a taxpayer in a taxation year where

(a) the disposition is an actual disposition;

(b) the taxpayer did not hold the share throughout the 365-day period that ended immediately before the disposition; and

(c) the share was a mark-to-market property of the taxpayer for a taxation year that begins after October 1994 and in which the taxpayer was a financial institution.

Application: Para. 112(5.1)(b) amended by 1998, c. 19, subsec. 131(3), applicable to dispositions that occur after April 26, 1995.

(5.2) Adjustment re dividends — Subject to subsection (5.3), where subsection (5) or (5.1) provides that this subsection applies to the disposition of a share by a taxpayer at any time, the taxpayer's proceeds of disposition shall be deemed to be the amount determined by the formula

$$A + B - (C - D)$$

where

A is the taxpayer's proceeds determined without reference to this subsection,

B is the lesser of

(a) the loss, if any, from the disposition of the share that would be determined before the application of this subsection if the cost of the share to any taxpayer were determined without reference to

(i) paragraphs 87(2)(e.2) and (e.4), 88(1)(c), 138(11.5)(e) and 142.5(2)(b),

(ii) subsection 85(1), where the provisions of that subsection are required by paragraph 138(11.5)(e) to be applied, and

(iii) paragraph 142.6(1)(d), and

(b) the total of all amounts each of which is

(i) where the taxpayer is a corporation, a taxable dividend received by the taxpayer on the share, to the extent of the amount that was deductible under this section or subsection 115(1) or 138(6) in computing the taxpayer's taxable income or taxable income earned in Canada for any taxation year,

(ii) where the taxpayer is a partnership, a taxable dividend received by the taxpayer on the share, to the extent of the amount that was deductible under this section or subsection 115(1) or 138(6) in computing the taxable income or taxable income earned in Canada for any taxation year of members of the partnership,

(iii) where the taxpayer is a trust, an amount designated under subsection 104(19) in respect of a taxable dividend on the share, or

(iv) a dividend (other than a taxable dividend) received by the taxpayer on the share,

C is the total of all amounts each of which is the amount by which

(a) the taxpayer's proceeds of disposition on a deemed disposition of the share before that time were increased because of this subsection,

(b) where the taxpayer is a corporation or trust, a loss of the taxpayer on a deemed disposition of the share before that time was reduced because of subsection (3), (3.2), (4) or (4.2), or

(c) where the taxpayer is a partnership, a loss of a member of the partnership on a deemed disposition of the share before that time was reduced because of subsection (3.1) or (4.2), and

D is the total of all amounts each of which is the amount by which the taxpayer's proceeds of disposition on a deemed disposition of the share before that time were decreased because of this subsection.

Application: Subpara. (b)(iv) of the description of B, and para. (b) of the description of C in subsec. 112(5.2), amended by 1998, c. 19, subsecs. 131(4), (5), applicable to dispositions that occur after April 26, 1995.

(5.21) Subsec. (5.2) — excluded dividends — A dividend, other than a dividend received under subsection 84(3), shall not be included in the total determined under paragraph (b) of the description of B in subsection (5.2) unless

(a) the dividend was received when the taxpayer and persons with whom the taxpayer did not deal at arm's length held in total more than 5% of the issued shares of any class of the capital stock of the corporation from which the dividend was received; or

(b) the share was not held by the taxpayer throughout the 365-day period that ended immediately before the disposition.

Application: The opening words of subsec. 112(5.21) amended by 2011, c. 24, subsec. 22(12), applicable to dispositions occurring after March 21, 2011.

Subsec. 112(5.21) added by 1998, c. 19, subsec. 131(6), applicable to dispositions that occur after April 26, 1995.

(5.3) Adjustment not applicable — For the purpose of determining the cost of a share to a taxpayer on a deemed reacquisition of the share after a deemed disposition of the share, the taxpayer's proceeds of disposition shall be determined without regard to subsection (5.2).

Application: Subsec. 112(5.3) added by 1995, c. 21, subsec. 56(7), applicable to dispositions in taxation years that begin after October 1994.

(5.4) Deemed dispositions — Where a taxpayer disposes of a share at any time,

(a) for the purpose of determining whether subsection (5.2) applies to the disposition, the conditions in subsections (5) and (5.1) shall be applied without regard to a deemed disposition and reacquisition of the share before that time; and

(b) total amounts under subsection (5.2) in respect of the disposition shall be determined from the time when the taxpayer actually acquired the share.

Application: Subsec. 112(5.4) added by 1995, c. 21, subsec. 56(7), applicable to dispositions in taxation years that begin after October 1994.

(5.5) Stop-loss rules not applicable — Subsections (3) to (4) and (4.2) do not apply to the disposition of a share by a taxpayer in a taxation year that begins after October 1994 where

(a) the share is a mark-to-market property for the year and the taxpayer is a financial institution in the year; or

(b) subsection (5.2) applies to the disposition.

Application: The opening words of subsec. 112(5.5) amended by 1998, c. 19, subsec. 131(7), applicable to dispositions that occur after April 26, 1995.

(5.6) Stop-loss rules restricted — In determining whether any of subsections (3) to (4) and (4.2) apply to reduce a loss of a taxpayer from the disposition of a share, this Act shall be read without reference to paragraphs (3.01)(b) and (3.11)(b), subclauses (3.2)(a)(ii)(C)(I) and (3.3)(a)(ii)(C)(I) and paragraphs (3.31)(b), (3.32)(b), (4.01)(b), (4.21)(b) and (4.22)(b) where

(a) the disposition occurs

(i) because of subsection 142.5(2) in a taxation year that includes October 31, 1994, or

(ii) because of paragraph 142.6(1)(b) after October 30, 1994; or

(b) the share was a mark-to-market property of the taxpayer for a taxation year that begins after October 1994 in which the taxpayer was a financial institution.

Application: The opening words of subsec. 112(5.6) amended by 1998, c. 19, subsec. 131(8), applicable to dispositions that occur after April 26, 1995.

(6) **Meaning of certain expressions** — For the purposes of this section,

(a) **["dividend", "taxable dividend"]** — "dividend" and "taxable dividend" do not include a capital gains dividend (within the meaning assigned by subsection 131(1)) or any dividend received by a taxpayer on which the taxpayer was required to pay tax under Part VII of the *Income Tax Act*, chapter 148 of the Revised Statutes of Canada, 1952, as it read on March 31, 1977;

(b) **["control"]** — one corporation is controlled by another corporation if more than 50% of its issued share capital (having full voting rights under all circumstances) belongs to the other corporation, to persons with whom the other corporation does not deal at arm's length, or to the other corporation and persons with whom the other corporation does not deal at arm's length; and

(c) **["financial institution", "mark-to-market property"]** — "financial institution" and "mark-to-market property" have the meanings assigned by subsection 142.2(1).

Application: Para. 112(6)(a) amended by 1998, c. 19, subsec. 131(9), applicable after April 26, 1995.

(6.1) **Interpretation — qualified dividend** — For the purposes of this section, a dividend on a share is a qualified dividend to the extent that

(a) it is a dividend other than a dividend received under subsection 84(3); or

(b) it is received under subsection 84(3) and,

(i) if the share is held by an individual other than a trust, the dividend is received by the individual,

(ii) if the share is held by a corporation, the dividend is received by the corporation while it is a private corporation, and is paid by another private corporation,

(iii) if the share is held by a trust,

(A) the dividend is received by the trust,

(B) the dividend is designated under subsection 104(19) by the trust in respect of a beneficiary and

(I) the beneficiary is an individual other than a trust,

(II) the beneficiary is a private corporation when the dividend is received by it and the dividend is paid by another private corporation,

(III) the beneficiary is another trust that does not designate the dividend under subsection 104(19), or

(IV) the beneficiary is a partnership all of the members of which are, when the dividend is received, a person described by any of subclauses (I) to (III), or

(C) the dividend is designated by the trust under subsection 104(19) in respect of a beneficiary that is another trust or a partnership and the trust establishes that the dividend is received by a person described by any of subclauses (B)(I) to (III), and

(iv) if the share is held by a partnership,

(A) the dividend is included in the income of a member of a partnership and

(I) the member is an individual, or

(II) the member is a private corporation when the dividend is received by it and the dividend is paid by another private corporation, or

(B) the dividend is designated under subsection 104(19) by a member of a partnership that is a trust in respect of a beneficiary described by any of subclauses (iii)(B)(I) to (IV) or is described by clause (iii)(C).

Application: Subsec. 112(6.1) added by 2011, c. 24, subsec. 22(13), applicable to dispositions occurring after March 21, 2011.

(7) Rules where shares exchanged — Where a share (in this subsection referred to as the "new share") has been acquired in exchange for another share (in this subsection referred to as the "old share") in a transaction to which section 51, 85.1, 86 or 87 applies, for the purposes of the application of any of subsections (3) to (3.32) in respect of a disposition of the new share, the new share is deemed to be the same share as the old share, except that

(a) any dividend received on the old share is deemed for those purposes to have been received on the new share only to the extent of the proportion of the dividend that

(i) the shareholder's adjusted cost base of the new share immediately after the exchange

is of

(ii) the shareholder's adjusted cost base of all new shares immediately after the exchange acquired in exchange for the old share; and

(b) the amount, if any, by which a loss from the disposition of the new share is reduced because of the application of this subsection shall not exceed the proportion of the shareholder's adjusted cost base of the old share immediately before the exchange that

(i) the shareholder's adjusted cost base of the new share immediately after the exchange

is of

(ii) the shareholder's adjusted cost base of all new shares, immediately after the exchange, acquired in exchange for the old share.

Application: Subsec. 112(7) amended by 1998, c. 19, subsec. 131(10), applicable to dispositions that occur after April 26, 1995.

(8) **Synthetic disposition — holding period** — If a synthetic disposition arrangement is entered into in respect of a property owned by a taxpayer and the synthetic disposition period of the arrangement is 30 days or more, for the purposes of paragraphs (3.01)(b) and (3.11)(b), subclauses (3.2)(a)(ii)(C)(I) and (3.3)(a)(ii)(C)(I) and paragraphs (3.31)(b), (3.32)(b), (4.01)(b), (4.11)(b), (4.21)(b), (4.22)(b), (5.1)(b) and (5.21)(b) and subsection (9), the taxpayer is deemed not to own the property during the synthetic disposition period.

Application: Subsec. 112(8) added by 2013, c. 40, s. 48, applicable to an agreement or arrangement entered into after March 20, 2013, and to an agreement or arrangement entered into before March 21, 2013, the term of which is extended after March 20, 2013, as if the agreement or arrangement were entered into at the time of the extension.

(9) **Exception** — Subsection (8) does not apply in respect of a property owned by a taxpayer in respect of a synthetic disposition arrangement if the taxpayer owned the property throughout the 365-day period (determined without reference to this subsection) that ended immediately before the synthetic disposition period of the arrangement.

Application: Subsec. 112(9) added by 2013, c. 40, s. 48, applicable to an agreement or arrangement entered into after March 20, 2013, and to an agreement or arrangement entered into before March 21, 2013, the term of which is extended after March 20, 2013, as if the agreement or arrangement were entered into at the time of the extension. In respect of an agreement or arrangement referred to above, that is entered into before September 13, 2013 and the term of which is not extended after September 12, 2013, subsection 112(9), is to be read as follows:

> (9) Subsection (8) does not apply in respect of a property owned by a taxpayer in respect of a synthetic disposition arrangement if the taxpayer owned the property throughout the 365-day period that ended immediately before the synthetic disposition period of the arrangement.

Section 148 — Life Insurance Policies

148. (1) Amounts included in computing policyholder's income — There shall be included in computing the income for a taxation year of a policyholder in respect of the disposition of an interest in a life insurance policy, other than a policy that is or is issued pursuant to

(a) a registered pension plan,

(b) a registered retirement savings plan,

(b.1) a registered retirement income fund,

(b.2) a TFSA,

(c) an income-averaging annuity contract,

(d) a deferred profit sharing plan, or

(e) an annuity contract if

(i) the payment for the annuity contract was deductible under paragraph 60(l) in computing the policyholder's income,

(i.1) the annuity contract is a qualifying trust annuity with respect to a taxpayer and the amount paid to acquire it was deductible under paragraph 60(l) in computing the taxpayer's income, or

(ii) the policyholder acquired the annuity contract in circumstances to which subsection 146(21) applied,

the amount, if any, by which the proceeds of the disposition of the policyholder's interest in the policy that the policyholder, beneficiary or assignee, as the case may be, became entitled to receive in the year exceeds the adjusted cost basis to the policyholder of that interest immediately before the disposition.

History

Para. 148(1)(e) amended by 2013, c. 34, subsec. 305(2), deemed in force on September 1, 1992.

Para. 148(1)(b.2) added by 2008, c. 28, s. 26, applicable to 2009 *et seq.*

Para. 148(1)(e) substituted by 1994, c. 21, s. 73, applicable to dispositions occurring after August 1992. That para. formerly read:

> (e) an annuity contract, the payment for which was deductible in computing the policyholder's income by virtue of paragraph 60(l),

Para. 148(1)(b.1) added by 1994, c. 7, Sch. VIII (1993, c. 24), subsec. 87(1), applicable to 1991 *et seq.*

(1.1) Amount included in computing taxpayer's income — There shall be included in computing the income for a taxation year of a taxpayer in respect of a disposition of an interest in a life insurance policy described in paragraph (e) of the definition "disposition" in subsection (9) the amount, if any, by which the amount of a payment described in paragraph (e) of that definition that the taxpayer became entitled to receive in the year exceeds the amount that would be the taxpayer's adjusted cost basis of the taxpayer's interest in the policy immediately before the disposition if, for the purposes of the definition "adjusted cost basis" in subsection (9), the taxpayer were, in respect of that interest in the policy, the policyholder.

(2) Deemed proceeds of disposition — For the purposes of subsections (1) and 20(20) and the definition "adjusted cost basis" in subsection (9),

(a) where at any time a policyholder becomes entitled to receive under a life insurance policy a particular amount as, on account of, in lieu of payment of or in satisfaction of, a policy dividend, the policyholder shall be deemed

(i) to have disposed of an interest in the policy at that time, and

(ii) to have become entitled to receive proceeds of the disposition equal to the amount, if any, by which

(A) the particular amount

exceeds

(B) the part of the particular amount applied immediately after that time to pay a premium under the policy or to repay a policy loan under the policy, as provided for under the terms and conditions of the policy;

(b) where in a taxation year a holder of an interest in, or a person whose life is insured or who is the annuitant under, a life insurance policy (other than an annuity contract or an exempt policy) last acquired after December 1, 1982 or an annuity contract (other than a life annuity contract, as defined by regulation, entered into before November 13, 1981 or a prescribed annuity contract) dies, the policyholder shall be deemed to have disposed of the policyholder's interest in the policy or the contract, as the case may be, immediately before the death;

(c) where, as a consequence of a death, a disposition of an interest in a life insurance policy is deemed to have occurred under paragraph (b), the policyholder immediately after the death shall be deemed to have acquired the interest at a cost equal to the accumulating fund in respect thereof, as determined in prescribed manner, immediately after the death; and

(d) where at any time a life insurance policy last acquired after December 1, 1982, or a life insurance policy to which subsection 12.2(9) of the *Income Tax Act*, chapter 148 of the Revised Statutes of Canada, 1952, applies by virtue of paragraph 12.2(9)(b) of that Act, ceases to be an exempt policy (otherwise than as a consequence of the death of an individual whose life is insured under the policy or at a time when that individual is totally and permanently disabled), the policyholder shall be deemed to have disposed of the policyholder's interest in the policy at that time for proceeds of disposition equal to the accumulating fund with respect to the interest, as determined in prescribed manner, at that time and to have reacquired the interest immediately after that time at a cost equal to those proceeds.

History

Para. 148(2)(a) amended by 1994, c. 7, Sch. VIII (1993, c. 24), subsec. 87(2), applicable to policy dividends received or receivable in taxation years beginning after December 20, 1991. Para. (a) formerly read:

> (a) where at a particular time a policyholder became entitled to receive under a life insurance policy an amount as, on account or in lieu of payment of, or in satisfaction of, a policy dividend, the policyholder shall be deemed to have disposed of an interest in the policy at that time and that amount shall be deemed to be proceeds of the disposition that the policyholder became entitled to receive at that time;

That portion of subsec. 148(2) preceding para. (a) amended by 1994, c. 7, Sch. II (1991, c. 49), subsec. 121(1), to add reference to subsec. 20(20), applicable to dispositions occurring after 1989.

(3) **Special rules for certain policies** — For the purposes of this section, where all or any part of an insurer's reserves for a life insurance policy vary in amount depending on the fair market value of a specified group of properties (in this subsection referred to as a "segregated fund"),

(a) in computing the adjusted cost basis of the policy,

(i) an amount paid by the policyholder or on the policyholder's behalf as or on account of premiums under the policy or to acquire an interest in the policy shall, to the extent that the amount was used by the insurer to acquire property for the purposes of the segregated fund, be deemed not to have been so paid, and

(ii) any transfer of property by the insurer from the segregated fund that resulted in an increase in the portion of its reserves for the policy that do not vary with the fair market value of the segregated fund shall be deemed to have been a premium paid under the policy by the policyholder; and

(b) the proceeds of the disposition of an interest in the policy shall be deemed not to include the portion thereof, if any, payable out of the segregated fund.

(4) **Income from disposition** — For the purpose of computing a taxpayer's income from the disposition (other than a disposition deemed to have occurred under paragraph (2)(a) or a disposition described in paragraph (b) of the definition "disposition" in subsection (9)) of a part of the taxpayer's interest in a life insurance policy (other than an annuity contract) last acquired after December 1, 1982 or an annuity contract, the adjusted cost basis to the taxpayer, immediately before the disposition, of the part is the proportion of the adjusted cost basis to the taxpayer of the taxpayer's interest immediately before the disposition that

(a) the proceeds of the disposition

are of

(b) the accumulating fund with respect to the taxpayer's interest, as determined in prescribed manner, immediately before the disposition.

(4.1) [Repealed under former Act]

(5) 10/8 policy surrender — If a policyholder has after March 20, 2013 and before April 2014 disposed of an interest in a 10/8 policy because of a partial or complete surrender of the policy, the policyholder may deduct in computing their income for the taxation year in which the disposition occurs an amount that does not exceed the least of

(a) the portion of an amount, included under subsection (1) in computing their income for the year in respect of the disposition, that is attributable to an investment account described in paragraph (b) of the definition "10/8 policy" in subsection 248(1) in respect of the policy,

(b) the total of all amounts each of which is an amount, to the extent that the amount has not otherwise been included in determining an amount under this paragraph, of a payment made after March 20, 2013 and before April 2014 that reduces the amount outstanding of a borrowing or policy loan, as the case may be, described in paragraph (a) of the definition "10/8 policy" in subsection 248(1) in respect of the policy, and

(c) the total of all amounts each of which is an amount, to the extent that the amount has not otherwise been included in determining an amount under this paragraph, that the policyholder is entitled to receive as a result of the disposition and that is paid after March 20, 2013 and before April 2014 out of an investment account described in paragraph (b) of the definition "10/8 policy" in subsection 248(1) in respect of the policy.

History

S.C. 2013, c. 40, s. 65, will add subsec. 148(5), applicable to taxation years that end after March 20, 2013.

(6) Proceeds receivable as annuity — Where, under the terms of a life insurance policy (other than an annuity contract) last acquired before December 2, 1982, a policyholder became entitled to receive from the insurer at any time before the death of the person whose life was insured thereunder, all the proceeds (other than policy dividends) payable at that time under the policy in the form of an annuity contract or annuity payments,

(a) the payments shall be regarded as annuity payments made under an annuity contract;

(b) the purchase price of the annuity contract shall be deemed to be the adjusted cost basis of the policy to the policyholder immediately before the first payment under that contract became payable; and

(c) the annuity contract or annuity payments shall be deemed not to be proceeds of the disposition of an interest in the policy.

(7) Disposition at non-arm's length and similar cases — Where, otherwise than by virtue of a deemed disposition under paragraph (2)(b), an interest of a policyholder in a life insurance policy is disposed of by way of a gift (whether during the policyholder's lifetime or by the policyholder's will), by distribution from a corporation or by operation of law only to any person, or in any manner whatever to any person with whom the policyholder was not dealing at arm's length, the policyholder shall be deemed thereupon to become entitled to receive proceeds of the disposition equal to the value of the interest at the time of the disposition, and the person who acquires the interest by virtue of the disposition shall be deemed to acquire it at a cost equal to that value.

(8) Idem — Notwithstanding any other provision in this section, where

(a) an interest of a policyholder in a life insurance policy (other than an annuity contract) has been transferred to the policyholder's child for no consideration, and

(b) a child of the policyholder or a child of the transferee is the person whose life is insured under the policy,

the interest shall be deemed to have been disposed of by the policyholder for proceeds of the disposition equal to the adjusted cost basis to the policyholder of the interest immediately before the transfer, and to have been acquired by the person who acquired the interest at a cost equal to those proceeds.

History

Paras. 148(8)(a), (b) substituted by 1994, c. 7, Sch. II (1991, c. 49), subsec. 121(2), applicable to transfers and distributions occurring after 1989. Paras. (a), (b) formerly read:

> (a) an interest of a policyholder in a life insurance policy (other than an annuity contract) has been transferred to
>
> (i) the policyholder's spouse or child, for no consideration,
>
> (ii) the spouse or a former spouse of the policyholder, in settlement of rights arising out of their marriage, or
>
> (iii) an individual, pursuant to a decree, order or judgment of a competent tribunal made in accordance with prescribed provisions of the law of a province if that individual is a person within a prescribed class of persons referred to in those provisions, and
>
> (b) the transferee or a child of the policyholder or transferee is the person whose life is insured under the policy,

(8.1) *Inter vivos* transfer to spouse [or common-law partner] — Notwithstanding any other provision of this section, where

(a) an interest of a policyholder in a life insurance policy (other than a policy that is, or is issued under, a plan or contract referred to in any of paragraphs (1)(a) to (e)) is transferred to

(i) the policyholder's spouse or common-law partner, or

(ii) a former spouse or common-law partner of the policyholder in settlement of rights arising out of their marriage or common-law partnership, and

(iii) [Repealed]

(b) both the policyholder and the transferee are resident in Canada at the time of the transfer,

unless an election is made in the policyholder's return of income under this Part for the taxation year in which the interest was transferred to have this subsection not apply, the interest shall be deemed to have been disposed of by the policyholder for proceeds of the disposition equal to the adjusted cost basis to the policyholder of the interest immediately before the transfer and to have been acquired by the transferee at a cost equal to those proceeds.

History

Subsec. 148(8.1) amended by 2000, c. 12, Sch. 2, s. 1, to replace "spouse" with "spouse or common-law partner", and by 2000, c. 12, Sch. 2, s. 9, to replace "marriage" with "marriage or common-law partnership", applicable to 2001 *et seq.*, in force July 31, 2000. See also the transitional rules reproduced in the History to 248(1)"common-law partner".

Subpara. 148(8.1)(a)(iii) repealed by 1994, c. 7, Sch. VIII (1993, c. 24), subsec. 87(3), applicable after 1992. Subpara. (a)(iii) formerly read:

> (iii) an individual of the opposite sex under an order for the support or maintenance of the individual made by a competent tribunal in accordance with the laws of a province, where the individual and the taxpayer cohabited in a conjugal relationship before the date of the order, and

Subsec. 148(8.1) added by 1994, c. 7, Sch. II (1991, c. 49), subsec. 121(3), applicable to transfers and dispositions occurring after 1989, except that, in its application with respect to transfers and distributions occurring in 1990, an election referred to in this subsec. made by a policyholder or the legal representative of a deceased policyholder by notifying the Minister of National Revenue in writing before 1992 [1994, c. 7, Sch. VIII (1993, c. 24), s. 159 provides that such an election made before December 11, 1993 shall be deemed to have been made before 1992] shall be deemed to have been made in the policyholder's return of income under Part I of the Act for the 1990 taxation year.

(8.2) Transfer to spouse [or common-law partner] at death — Notwithstanding any other provision of this section, where, as a consequence of the death of a policyholder who was resident in Canada immediately before the policyholder's death, an interest of the policyholder in a life insurance policy (other than a policy that is or is issued under a plan or contract referred to in any of paragraphs (1)(a) to (e)) is transferred or distributed to the policyholder's spouse or common-law partner who was resident in Canada immediately before the death, unless an election is made in the policyholder's return of income under this Part for the taxation year in which the policyholder died to have this subsection not apply, the interest shall be deemed to have been disposed of by the policyholder immediately before the death for proceeds of the disposition equal to the adjusted cost basis to the policyholder of the interest immediately before the transfer and to have been acquired by the spouse or common-law partner at a cost equal to those proceeds.

History

Subsec. 148(8.2) amended by 2000, c. 12, Sch. 2, s. 1, to replace "spouse" with "spouse or common-law partner", applicable to 2001 *et seq.*, in force July 31, 2000. See also the transitional rules reproduced in the History to 248(1)"common-law partner".

Subsec. 148(8.2) added by 1994, c. 7, Sch. II (1991, c. 49), subsec. 121(3), applicable to transfers and dispositions occurring after 1989, except that, in its application with respect to transfers and distributions occurring in 1990, an election referred to in this subsec. made by a policyholder or the legal representative of a deceased policyholder by notifying the Minister of National Revenue in writing before 1992 [1994, c. 7, Sch. VIII (1993, c. 24), s. 159 provides that such an election made before December 11, 1993 shall be deemed to have been made before 1992] shall be deemed to have been made in the policyholder's return of income under Part I of the Act for the 1990 taxation year.

(9) Definitions — In this section and paragraph 56(1)(d.1) of the *Income Tax Act*, chapter 148 of the Revised Statutes of Canada, 1952,

"adjusted cost basis" to a policyholder as at a particular time of the policyholder's interest in a life insurance policy means the amount determined by the formula

$$(A + B + C + D + E + F + G + G.1) - (H + I + J + K + L)$$

where

A is the total of all amounts each of which is the cost of an interest in the policy acquired by the policyholder before that time but not including an amount referred to in the description of B or E,

B is the total of all amounts each of which is an amount paid before that time by or on behalf of the policyholder in respect of a premium under the policy, other than amounts referred to in clause (2)(a)(ii)(B), in subparagraph (iii) of the description of C in paragraph (a) of the definition "proceeds of the disposition" or in subparagraph (b)(i) of that definition,

C is the total of all amounts each of which is an amount in respect of the disposition of an interest in the policy before that time that was required to be included in computing the policyholder's income or taxable income earned in Canada for a taxation year,

D is the total of all amounts each of which is an amount in respect of the policyholder's interest in the policy that was included by virtue of subsection 12(3) or section 12.2 or of paragraph 56(1)(d.1) of the *Income Tax Act*, chapter 148 of the Revised Statutes of Canada, 1952, in computing the policyholder's income for any taxation year ending before that time or the portion of an amount paid to the policyholder in respect of the policyholder's interest in the policy on which tax was imposed by virtue of paragraph 212(1)(o) before that time,

E is the total of all amounts each of which is an amount in respect of the repayment before that time and after March 31, 1978 of a policy loan not exceeding the total of the proceeds of the disposition, if any, in respect of that loan and the amount, if any, described in the description of J but not including any payment of interest thereon, any loan repayment that was deductible under paragraph 60(s) of this Act or paragraph 20(1)(hh) of the *Income Tax Act*, chapter 148 of the Revised Statutes of Canada, 1952 (as it applied in taxation years before 1985) or any loan repayment referred to in clause (2)(a)(ii)(B),

F is the amount, if any, by which the cash surrender value of the policy as at its first anniversary date after March 31, 1977 exceeds the adjusted cost basis (determined under the *Income Tax Act*, chapter 148 of the Revised Statutes of Canada, 1952, as it would have read on that date if subsection 148(8) of that Act, as it read in its application to the period ending immediately before April 1, 1978, had not been applicable) of the policyholder's interest in the policy on that date,

G is, in the case of an interest in a life annuity contract, as defined by regulation, to which subsection 12.2(1) applies for the taxation year that includes that time (or would apply if the contract had an anniversary day in the year at a time when the taxpayer held the interest), the total of all amounts each of which is a mortality gain, as defined by regulation and determined by the issuer of the contract in accordance with the regulations, in respect of the interest immediately before the end of the calendar year ending in a taxation year commencing before that time,

Proposed Amendment — Life annuity contracts

Letter from Dept. of Finance, September 12, 2002: See under Reg. 301(1).

G.1 [is,] in the case of an interest in a life insurance policy (other than an annuity contract) to which subsection (8.2) applied before that time, the total of all amounts each of which is a mortality gain, as defined by regulation and determined by the issuer of the policy in accordance with the regulations, in respect of the interest immediately before the end of the calendar year ending in a taxation year beginning before that time,

H is the total of all amounts each of which is the proceeds of the disposition of the policyholder's interest in the policy that the policyholder became entitled to receive before that time,

I is the total of all amounts each of which is an amount in respect of the policyholder's interest in the policy that was deducted by virtue of subsection 20(19) in computing the policyholder's income for any taxation year commencing before that time,

J is the amount payable on March 31, 1978 in respect of a policy loan in respect of the policy,

K is the total of all amounts each of which is an amount received before that time in respect of the policy that the policyholder was entitled to deduct under paragraph 60(a) in computing the policyholder's income for a taxation year, and

L is

(a) in the case of an interest in a life insurance policy (other than an annuity contract) that was last acquired after December 1, 1982 by the policyholder, the total of all amounts each of which is the net cost of pure insurance, as defined by regulation and determined by the issuer of the policy in accordance with the regulations, in respect of the interest immediately before the end of the calendar year ending in a taxation year commencing after May 31, 1985 and before that time,

(b) in the case of an interest in an annuity contract to which subsection 12.2(1) applies for the taxation year that includes that time (or would apply if the contract had an anniversary day in the year and while the taxpayer held the interest), the total of all annuity payments paid in respect of the interest before that time and while the policyholder held the interest, or

(c) in the case of an interest in a contract referred to in the description of G, the total of all amounts each of which is a mortality loss, as defined by regulation and determined by the issuer of the contract in accordance with the regulations, in respect of the interest before that time;

"amount payable", in respect of a policy loan, has the meaning assigned by subsection 138(12);

"cash surrender value" at a particular time of a life insurance policy means its cash surrender value at that time computed without regard to any policy loans made under the policy, any policy dividends (other than paid-up additions) payable under the policy or any interest payable on those dividends;

"child" of a policyholder includes a child as defined in subsection 70(10);

"disposition", in relation to an interest in a life insurance policy, includes

(a) a surrender thereof,

(b) a policy loan made after March 31, 1978,

(c) the dissolution of that interest by virtue of the maturity of the policy,

(d) a disposition of that interest by operation of law only, and

(e) the payment by an insurer of an amount (other than an annuity payment, a policy loan or a policy dividend) in respect of a policy (other than a policy described in paragraph (1)(a), (b), (c), (d) or (e)) that is a life annuity contract, as defined by regulation, entered into after November 16, 1978, and before November 13, 1981,

but does not include

(f) an assignment of all or any part of an interest in the policy for the purpose of securing a debt or a loan other than a policy loan,

(g) a lapse of the policy in consequence of the premiums under the policy remaining unpaid, if the policy was reinstated not later than 60 days after the end of the calendar year in which the lapse occurred,

(h) a payment under a policy as a disability benefit or as an accidental death benefit,

(i) an annuity payment,

(j) a payment under a life insurance policy (other than an annuity contract) that

(i) was last acquired before December 2, 1982, or

(ii) is an exempt policy

in consequence of the death of any person whose life was insured under the policy, or

(k) any transaction or event by which an individual becomes entitled to receive, under the terms of an exempt policy, all of the proceeds (including or excluding policy dividends) payable under the policy in the form of an annuity contract or annuity payments, if, at the time of the transaction or event, the individual whose life is insured under the policy was totally and permanently disabled;

"interest", in relation to a policy loan, has the meaning assigned by subsection 138(12);

"life insurance policy" — [Repealed under former Act]

"policy loan" means an amount advanced by an insurer to a policyholder in accordance with the terms and conditions of the life insurance policy;

"premium" under a policy includes

(a) interest paid after 1977 to a life insurer in respect of a policy loan, other than interest deductible in the 1978 or any subsequent taxation year pursuant to paragraph 20(1)(c) or (d), and

(b) a prepaid premium under the policy to the extent that it cannot be refunded otherwise than on termination or cancellation of the policy,

but does not include

(c) where the interest in the policy was last acquired after December 1, 1982, that portion of any amount paid after May 31, 1985 under the policy with respect to

(i) an accidental death benefit,

(ii) a disability benefit,

(iii) an additional risk as a result of insuring a substandard life,

(iv) an additional risk in respect of the conversion of a term policy into another policy after the end of the year,

(v) an additional risk under a settlement option,

(vi) an additional risk under a guaranteed insurability benefit, or

(vii) any other prescribed benefit that is ancillary to the policy;

"proceeds of the disposition" of an interest in a life insurance policy means the amount of the proceeds that the policyholder, beneficiary or assignee, as the case may be, is entitled to receive on a disposition of an interest in the policy and for greater certainty,

(a) in respect of a surrender or maturity thereof, means the amount determined by the formula

$$(A - B) - C$$

where

A is the cash surrender value of that interest in the policy at the time of surrender or maturity,

B is that portion of the cash surrender value represented by A that is applicable to the policyholder's interest in the related segregated fund trust as referred to in paragraph 138.1(1)(e), and

C is the total of amounts each of which is

(i) an amount payable at that time by the policyholder in respect of a policy loan in respect of the policy,

(ii) a premium under the policy that is due but unpaid at that time, or

(iii) an amount applied, immediately after the time of the surrender, to pay a premium under the policy, as provided for under the terms and conditions of the policy,

(b) in respect of a policy loan made after March 31, 1978 means the lesser of

(i) the amount of the loan, other than the part thereof applied, immediately after the loan, to pay a premium under the policy, as provided for under the terms and conditions of the policy, and

(ii) the amount, if any, by which the cash surrender value of the policy immediately before the loan was made exceeds the total of the balances outstanding at that time of any policy loans in respect of the policy,

(c) in respect of a payment described in paragraph (e) of the definition "disposition" in this subsection, means the amount of that payment, and

(d) in respect of a disposition deemed to have occurred under paragraph (2)(b), means the accumulating fund in respect of the interest, as determined in prescribed manner,

(i) immediately before the time of death in respect of a life insurance policy (other than an annuity contract) last acquired after December 1, 1982, or

(ii) immediately after the time of death in respect of an annuity contract;

"relevant authority" — [Repealed]

"tax anniversary date", in relation to a life insurance policy, means the second anniversary date of the policy to occur after October 22, 1968;

"value" at a particular time of an interest in a life insurance policy means

(a) where the interest includes an interest in the cash surrender value of the policy, the amount in respect thereof that the holder of the interest would be entitled to receive if the policy were surrendered at that time, and

(b) in any other case, nil.

History

The description of B in the definition "adjusted cost basis" in subsec. 148(9) amended by 1994, c. 7, Sch. VIII (1993, c. 24), subsec. 87(4), applicable to amounts paid in taxation years commencing after December 20, 1991. The description formerly read:

> B is the total of all amounts each of which is an amount paid before that time, by the policyholder or on the policyholder's behalf, in respect of a premium under the policy,

The description of E in "adjusted cost basis" amended by 1994, c. 7, Sch. VIII (1993, c. 24), subsec. 87(5), applicable to loan repayments occurring in taxation years beginning after December 20, 1991. The description formerly read:

> E is the total of all amounts each of which is an amount in respect of the repayment before that time and after March 31, 1978 of a policy loan not exceeding the total of the proceeds of the disposition, if any, in respect of that loan and the amount, if any, referred to in the description of J but not including any payment of interest thereon or any repayment of the loan that was deductible pursuant to paragraph 20(1)(hh) or 60(s),

G.1 and its description added to "adjusted cost basis" by 1994, c. 7, Sch. VIII (1993, c. 24), subsecs. 87(3.1), (6), applicable to transfers and distributions occurring after 1989.

The description of G in "adjusted cost basis" amended by 1994, c. 7, Sch. II (1991, c. 49), subsecs. 121(4), to substitute "subsection 12.2(1)" for "subsection 12.2(1) or (3)" and to add "(or would apply if the contract had an anniversary day in the year at a time when the taxpayer held the interest)", applicable to policies last acquired after 1989.

Para. (b) of the description of L in para. 148(9)(a) substituted by 1994, c. 7, Sch. II (1991, c. 49), subsec. 121(5), applicable to policies last acquired after 1989. Para. (b) formerly read:

> (b) in the case of an interest in an annuity contract to which subsection 12.2(1) or (3) applies, the total of all amounts each of which is an annuity payment paid in respect of the interest before that time and while the policyholder held the interest, or

(9.1) Application of subsec. 12.2(11) — The definitions in subsection 12.2(11) apply to this section.

(10) Life annuity contracts — For the purposes of this section,

(a) a reference to "insurer" or "life insurer" shall be deemed to include a reference to a person who is licensed or otherwise authorized under a law of Canada or a province to issue contracts that are annuity contracts;

(b) a reference to a "person whose life was insured" shall be deemed to include a reference to an annuitant under a life annuity contract, as defined by regulation, entered into before November 17, 1978;

(c) where a policyholder is a person who has held an interest in a life insurance policy continuously since its issue date, the interest shall be deemed to have been acquired on the later of the date on which

(i) the policy came into force, and

(ii) the application in respect of the policy signed by the policyholder was filed with the insurer;

(d) except as otherwise provided, a policyholder shall be deemed not to have disposed of or acquired an interest in a life insurance policy (other than an annuity contract) as a result only of the exercise of any provision (other than a conversion into an annuity contract) of the policy; and

(e) where an interest in a life insurance policy (other than an annuity contract) last acquired before December 2, 1982 to which subsection 12.2(9) of the *Income Tax Act*, chapter 148 of the Revised Statutes of Canada, 1952, does not apply has been acquired by a taxpayer from a person with whom the taxpayer was not dealing at arm's length, the interest shall be deemed to have been last acquired by the taxpayer before December 2, 1982.

Income Tax Regulations, Sections 300–310

Part III — Annuities and Life Insurance Policies

300. Capital element of annuity payments — **(1)** For the purposes of paragraphs 32.1(3)(b) and 60(a) of the Act, where an annuity is paid under a contract (other than an income-averaging annuity contract or an annuity contract purchased pursuant to a deferred profit sharing plan or pursuant to a plan referred to in subsection 147(15) of the Act as a "revoked plan") at a particular time, that part of the annuity payment determined in prescribed manner to be a return of capital is that proportion of a taxpayer's interest in the annuity payment that the adjusted purchase price of the taxpayer's interest in the contract at that particular time is of his interest, immediately before the commencement under the contract of payments to which paragraph 56(1)(d) of the Act applies, in the total of the payments

(a) to be made under the contract, in the case of a contract for a term of years certain; or

(b) expected to be made under the contract, in the case of a contract under which the continuation of the payments depends in whole or in part on the survival of an individual.

History

Subsec. 300(1) substituted by P.C. 1983-3530, subsec. 1(1), November 17, 1983, *Canada Gazette*, Part II, November 24, 1983, applicable to taxation years commencing after 1982.

Subsec. 300(1) substituted by P.C. 1982-1421, subsec. 1(1), May 13, 1982, *Canada Gazette*, Part II, May 26, 1982, effective with respect to annuity contracts under which annuity payments commence after 1979 except that in its application to annuity contracts under which payments commence before 1982 it shall be read as follows:

> 300. (1) For the purposes of paragraphs 32.1(3)(b) and 60(a) of the Act, if an annuity is paid under a contract, the amount deemed to be a return of capital is that proportion of each annuity payment that the consideration for, or purchase price of, the contract is of the total of the payments
>
> (a) to be made under the contract, in the case of a contract for a term of years certain; or
>
> (b) expected to be made, in the case of a contract under which the continuation of the payments depends in whole or in part on the survival of an individual.

(1.1) For the purposes of subsections (1) and (2), "annuity payment" does not include any portion of a payment under a contract the amount of which cannot be reasonably determined immediately before the commencement of payments under the contract except where the payment of such portion cannot be so determined because the continuation of the annuity payments under the contract depends in whole or in part on the survival of an individual.

History

Subsec. 300(1.1) added by P.C. 1982-1421, subsec. 1(1), May 13, 1982, *Canada Gazette*, Part II, May 26, 1982, effective with respect to annuity contracts under which annuity payments commence after 1981.

(2) For the purposes of this section

(a) where the continuance of the annuity payments under any contract depends in whole or in part on the survival of an individual, the total of the payments expected to be made under the contract

(i) shall, in the case of a contract that provides for equal payments and does not provide for a guaranteed period of payment, be equal to the product obtained by multiplying the aggregate of the annuity payments expected to be received throughout a year under the contract by the complete expectations of life using the table of mortality known as the *1971 Individual Annuity Mortality Table* as published in Volume XXIII of the *Transactions of the Society of Actuaries*, or

(ii) shall, in any other case, be calculated in accordance with subparagraph (i) with such modifications as the circumstances may require;

(b) subject to subsections 305 (3) and 305 (4), "adjusted purchase price" of a taxpayer's interest in an annuity contract at a particular time means the amount that would be determined at that time in respect of that interest under the definition "adjusted cost basis" in subsection 305 148(9) of the Act if the formula in that definition were read without reference to variable K;

(c) where the continuance of the annual payments under any contract depends on the survival of a person, the age of that person on any date as of which a calculation is being made shall be determined by subtracting the calendar year of his birth from the calendar year in which such date occurs; and

(d) where the continuance of the annual payments under any contract depends on the survival of a person, and where, in the event of the death of that person before the annual payments aggregate a stated sum, the contract provides that the unpaid balance of the stated sum shall be paid, either in a lump sum or instalments, then, for the purpose of determining the expected term of the contract, the contract shall be deemed to provide for the continuance of the payments thereunder for a minimum term certain equal to the nearest integral number of years required to complete the payment of the stated sum;

(e) [Revoked]

History

Opening words of subsec. 300(2) amended by P.C. 2011-936, subsec. 6(1), September 22, 2011, Canada Gazette, Part II, October 12, 2011, applicable with respect to annuity contracts and life insurance policies last acquired after 1989.

Para. 300(2)(b) amended by the said P.C. 2011-936, subsec. 6(2), applicable after February 1994.

All that portion of subsec. 300(2) preceding para. (a), para. 300(2)(b) substituted by P.C. 1983-3530, subsecs. 1(2), 1(3), November 17, 1983, *Canada Gazette*, Part II, November 24, 1983. All that portion of subsec. 300(2) preceding para. (a), as substituted, applicable to taxation years commencing after 1982; paragraph 300(2)(b), as substituted, effective November 12, 1981. Para. 300(2)(e) revoked by P.C. 1983-3530, subsec. 1(4), November 17, 1983, *Canada Gazette*, Part II, November 24, 1983, applicable to taxation years commencing after 1982.

Subpara. 300(2)(a)(i) substituted by P.C. 1982-2862, September 22, 1982, *Canada Gazette*, Part II, October 13, 1982, effective with respect to annuity contracts under which annuity payments commence after 1981.

Paras. 300(2)(a), (b) substituted by P.C. 1982-1421, subsec. 1(2), May 13, 1982, *Canada Gazette*, Part II, May 26, 1982, effective with respect to annuity contracts under which annuity payments commence after 1981.

(3) Where

(a) an annuity contract is a life annuity contract entered into before November 17, 1978 under which the annuity payments commence on the death of an individual,

(a.1) [Revoked]

(b) an annuity contract (other than an annuity contract described in paragraph (a)) is

(i) a life annuity contract entered into before October 23, 1968, or

(ii) any other annuity contract entered into before January 4, 1968,

under which the annuity payments commence

(iii) on the expiration of a term of years, and

(iv) before the later of January 1, 1970 or the tax anniversary date of the annuity contract,

the adjusted purchase price of a taxpayer's interest in the annuity contract shall be

(c) the lump sum, if any, that the person entitled to the annuity payments might have accepted in lieu thereof, at the date the annuity payments commence;

(d) if no lump sum described in paragraph (c) is provided for in the contract, the sum ascertainable from the contract as the present value of the annuity at the date the annuity payments commence; and

(e) if no lump sum described in paragraph (c) is provided for in the contract and no sum is ascertainable under paragraph (d),

(i) in the case of a contract issued under the *Government Annuities Act*, the premiums paid, accumulated with interest at the rate of four per cent per annum to the date the annuity payments commence, and

(ii) in the case of any other contract, the present value of the annuity payments at the date on which payments under the contract commence, computed by applying

(A) a rate of interest of four per cent per annum where the payments commence before 1972 and 5½ per cent per annum where the payments commence after 1971, and

(B) the provisions of subsection (2) where the payments depend on the survival of a person.

History

Para. 300(3)(a.1) revoked and para. 300(3)(b) substituted by P.C. 1983-3530, subsecs. 1(5) and 1(6), November 17, 1983, *Canada Gazette*, Part II, November 24, 1983, applicable to taxation years commencing after 1982.

All that portion of subsec. 300(3) preceding para. (c) substituted by P.C. 1982-1421, subsec. 1(3), May 13, 1982, *Canada Gazette*, Part II, May 25, 1982, effective January 1, 1982.

(4) Where an annuity contract would be described in paragraph (3)(b) if the reference in subparagraph (iv) thereof to "before the later of" were read as a reference to "on or after the later of", the adjusted purchase price of a taxpayer's interest in the annuity contract at a particular time shall be the greater of

(a) the aggregate of

(i) the amount that would be determined in respect of that interest under paragraph (3)(c), (d) or (e), as the case may be, if the date referred to therein was the tax anniversary date of the contract and not the date the annuity payments commence, and

(ii) the adjusted purchase price that would be determined in respect of that interest if the expression "before that time" in the descriptions of A, B, C, D and H in the definition "adjusted cost basis" in subsection 148(9) of the Act were read as "before that time and after the tax anniversary date"; and

(b) the amount determined under paragraph (2)(b) in respect of that interest.

History

Subpara. 300(4)(a)(ii) amended by P.C. 2011-936, subsec. 6(5), September 22, 2011, *Canada Gazette*, Part II, October 12, 2011, applicable after February 1994.

Subpara. 300(4)(a)(ii) substituted by P.C. 1983-3530, subsec. 1(7), November 17, 1983, *Canada Gazette*, Part II, November 24, 1983, applicable to taxation years commencing after 1982.

Subsec. 300(4) substituted by P.C. 1982-1421, subsec. 1(4), May 13, 1982, *Canada Gazette*, Part II, May 25, 1982, effective with respect to annuity contracts under which annuity payments commence after 1981.

301. Life annuity contracts — **(1)** For the purposes of this Part and section 148 of the Act, "life annuity contract" means a contract under which a person authorized under the laws of Canada or of a province to carry on in Canada an annuities business agrees to make annuity payments to one person or partnership (in this section referred to as "the annuitant") or jointly to two or more annuitants, which annuity payments are, under the terms of the contract,

(a) to be paid annually or at more frequent periodic intervals;

(b) to commence on a specified day; and

(c) to continue throughout the lifetime of one or more individuals (each of whom is referred to in this section as "the identified individual").

History

Subsec. 301(1) amended by P.C. 2011-936, subsec. 7(1), September 22, 2011, Canada Gazette, Part II, October 12, 2011, applicable to taxation years that end after 1996, and for those taxation years the adjusted cost basis of a policy holder's interest in a life insurance policy is to be determined as if the amendment also applied to taxation years that begin after 1980.

All that portion of subsec. 301(1) preceding para. (a) substituted by P.C. 1983-3530, s. 2, November 17, 1983, *Canada Gazette*, Part II, November 24, 1983, effective November 12, 1981.

Paras. 301(1)(a)–(d) revoked and substituted by 301(1)(a)–(c), (2)(a), (e) substituted, (f) added by P.C. 1982-1421, s. 2, May 13, 1982, *Canada Gazette*, Part II, May 26, 1982, effective January 1, 1982.

Subsec. 301(1) amended by P.C. 1980-1241, May 8, 1980, *Canada Gazette*, Part II, May 28, 1980, effective in respect of 1978 *et seq.*

(2) [Interpretation] — For the purposes of subsection (1), a contract shall not fail to be a life annuity contract by reason that

(a) the contract provides that the annuity payments may be assigned by the annuitant or owner;

(b) the contract provides for annuity payments to be made for a period ending on the death of the identified individual or for a specified period of not less than 10 years, whichever is the lesser;

(c) the contract provides for annuity payments to be made for a specified period or throughout the lifetime of the identified individual, whichever is longer, to the annuitant and, if the specified period is longer, to a specified person after that period;

(d) the contract provides, in addition to the annuity payments to be made throughout the lifetime of the identified individual, for a payment to be made on the death of the identified individual;

(e) the contract provides that the date

(i) on which the annuity payments commence, or

(ii) on which the contract holder becomes entitled to proceeds of the disposition,

may be changed with respect to the whole contract or any portion thereof at the option of the annuitant or owner; or

(f) the contract provides that all or a portion of the proceeds payable at any particular time under the contract may be received in the form of an annuity contract other than a life annuity contract.

302. [Revoked]

History

Paras. 301(2)(b) to (d) amended by P.C. 2011-936, subsec. 7(2), September 22, 2011, Canada Gazette, Part II, October 12, 2011, applicable to taxation years that end after 1996, and for those taxation years the adjusted cost basis of a policy holder's interest in a life insurance policy is to be determined as if the amendment also applied to taxation years that begin after 1980.

S. 302 revoked by P.C. 1983-3530, s. 3, November 17, 1983, *Canada Gazette*, Part II, November 24, 1983, applicable to taxation years commencing after 1982.

S. 302 added by P.C. 1982-1421, s. 3, May 13, 1982, *Canada Gazette*, Part II, May 26, 1982, applicable to taxation years commencing after October 28, 1980.

303. (1) Where in a taxation year the rights of a holder under an annuity contract cease upon termination or cancellation of the contract and

(a) the aggregate of all amounts, each of which is an amount in respect of the contract that was included in computing the income of the holder for the year or any previous taxation year by virtue of subsection 12(3) of the Act

exceeds the aggregate of

(b) such proportion of the amount determined under paragraph (a) that the annuity payments made under the contract before the rights of the holder have ceased is of the total of the payments expected to be made under the contract, and

(c) the aggregate of all amounts, each of which is an amount in respect of the contract that was deductible in computing the income of the holder for the year or any previous year by virtue of subsection (2), the amount of such excess may be deducted by the holder under subsection 20(19) of the Act in computing his income for the year.

History

Para. 303(1)(b) substituted by P.C. 1983-3530, s. 4, November 17, 1983, *Canada Gazette*, Part II, November 24, 1983, effective commencing November 12, 1981.

(2) For the purposes of subsection 20(19) of the Act, where an annuity contract was acquired after December 19, 1980 and annuity payments under the contract commenced before 1982, the amount that may be deducted by a holder under that subsection in respect of an annuity contract for a taxation year is that proportion of

(a) the aggregate of all amounts, each of which is an amount that was included in computing the income of the holder for any previous taxation year by virtue of subsection 12(3) of the Act in respect of the contract

that

(b) the aggregate of all annuity payments received by the holder in the year in respect of the contract

is of

(c) the total of the payments determined under paragraph 300(1)(a) or (b) in respect of the holder's interest in the contract.

History

S. 303 added by P.C. 1982-1421, s. 3, May 13, 1982, *Canada Gazette*, Part II, May 26, 1982; subsec. 303(1) applicable to taxation years commencing after October 28, 1980; subsec. 303(2) effective from December 1980.

304. Prescribed annuity contracts — **(1)** For the purposes of this Part and of subsections 12.2(1) and 20(20) and paragraph 148(2)(b) of the Act, "prescribed annuity contract", for a taxation year, means

(a) an annuity contract that is, or is issued pursuant to, an arrangement described in any of paragraphs 148(1)(a) to (b.3) and (d) of the Act;

(b) an annuity contract described in paragraph 148(1)(c) or (e) of the Act; and

(c) an annuity contract

(i) under which annuity payments have commenced in the taxation year or a preceding taxation year,

(ii) issued by any one of the following (referred to in this section as the "issuer"):

(A) a life insurance corporation,

(B) a registered charity,

(C) a corporation referred to in any of paragraphs (a) to (c) of the definition "specified financial institution" in subsection 248(1) of the Act,

(D) a corporation referred to in subparagraph (b)(ii) of the definition "retirement savings plan" in subsection 146(1) of the Act, and

(E) a corporation (other than a mutual fund corporation or a mortgage investment corporation) the principal business of which is the making of loans,

(iii) each holder of which

(A) is an individual, other than a trust that is neither a trust described in paragraph 104(4)(a) of the Act (in this paragraph referred to as a "specified trust") nor a testamentary trust,

(B) is an annuitant under the contract, and

(C) throughout the taxation year, dealt at arm's length with the issuer,

(iv) the terms and conditions of which require that, from the time the contract meets the requirements of this paragraph,

(A) all payments made out of the contract be equal annuity payments made at regular intervals but not less frequently than annually, subject to the holder's right to vary the frequency and quantum of payments to be made out of the contract in any taxation year without altering the present value at the beginning of the year of the total payments to be made in that year out of the contract,

(B) the annuity payments thereunder continue for a fixed term or

(I) if the holder is an individual (other than a trust), for the life of the first holder or until the day of the later of the death of the first holder and the death of any of the spouse, common-law partner, former spouse, former common-law partner, brothers and sisters (in this subparagraph referred to as "the survivor") of the first holder, or

(II) if the holder is a trust

1. in the case of a specified trust, for the life of an individual referred to in paragraph 104(4)(a) of the Act who is entitled to receive all of the income of the trust that arose before the individual's death, or, in the case of a joint spousal or common-law partner trust, until the day of the later of the death of the individual and the death of the beneficiary under the trust who is the individual's spouse or common-law partner,

2. in the case of a testamentary trust (other than a specified trust) where the annuity is issued before October 24, 2012, for the life of an individual who is entitled to receive income from the trust, and

3. in the case of any other testamentary trust other than a specified trust, for the life of an individual who was entitled when the contract was first held to receive all of the income of the trust that arose before the individual's death,

(C) if the annuity payments are to be made over a term that is guaranteed or fixed, the guaranteed or fixed term not exceed 91 years minus the age, when the contract was first held, in whole years of the following individual:

(I) if the holder is not a trust, the individual who is

1. in the case of a joint and last survivor annuity, the younger of the first holder and the survivor,

2. in the case of a contract that is held jointly, the younger of the first holders, and

3. in any other case, the first holder,

(II) if the holder is a specified trust, the individual who is

1. in the case of a joint and last survivor annuity held by a joint spousal or common-law partner trust, the younger of the individuals referred to in paragraph 104(4)(a) of the Act who are in combination entitled to receive all of the income of the trust that arose before the later of their deaths, and

2. in the case of an annuity that is not a joint and last survivor annuity, the individual referred to in paragraph 104(4)(a) of the Act who is entitled to receive all of the income of the trust that arose before the individual's death,

(III) if the holder is a testamentary trust other than a specified trust, the individual who was the youngest beneficiary under the trust when the contract was first held,

(D) no loans exist under the contract,

(E) the holder's rights under the contract not be disposed of otherwise than

(I) if the holder is an individual, on the holder's death,

(II) if the holder is a specified trust (other than a joint spousal or common-law partner trust), on the death of the individual referred to in paragraph 104(4)(a) of the Act who is entitled to receive all of the income of the trust that arose before the individual's death,

(III) if the holder is a specified trust that is a joint spousal or common-law partner trust, on the later of the deaths of the individuals referred to in paragraph 104(4)(a) of the Act who are in combination entitled to receive all of the income of the trust that arose before the later of their deaths, and

(IV) if the holder is a testamentary trust, other than a specified trust, and the contract was first held after October 2011, on the earlier of

1. the time at which the trust ceases to be a testamentary trust, and

2. the death of the individual referred to in subclause (B)(II) or (C)(III), as the case may be, in respect of the trust, and

(F) no payments be made out of the contract other than as permitted by this section,

(v) none of the terms and conditions of which provide for any recourse against the issuer for failure to make any payment under the contract, and

(vi) where annuity payments under the contract have commenced

(A) before 1987, in respect of which a holder thereof has notified the issuer in writing, before the end of the taxation year, that the contract is to be treated as a prescribed annuity contract,

(B) after 1986, in respect of which a holder thereof has not notified the issuer in writing, before the end of the taxation year in which the annuity payments under the contract commenced, that the contract is not to be treated as a prescribed annuity contract, or

(C) after 1986, in respect of which a holder thereof has notified the issuer in writing, before the end of the taxation year in which the annuity payments under the contract commenced, that the contract is not to be treated as a prescribed annuity contract and a holder thereof has rescinded the notification by so notifying the issuer in writing before the end of the taxation year.

(2) Notwithstanding subsection (1), an annuity contract shall not fail to be a prescribed annuity contract by reason that

(a) where the contract provides for a joint and last survivor annuity or is held jointly, the terms and conditions thereof provide that there will be a decrease in the amount of the annuity payments to be made under the contract from the time of death of one of the annuitants thereunder;

(b) the terms and conditions thereof provide that where the holder thereof dies at or before the time he attains the age of 91 years, the contract will terminate and an amount will be paid out of the contract not exceeding the amount, if any, by which the total premiums paid under the contract exceeds the total annuity payments made under the contract;

(c) where the annuity payments are to be made over a term that is guaranteed or fixed, the terms and conditions thereof provide that as a consequence of the death of the holder thereof during the guaranteed or fixed term any payments that, but for the death of the holder, would be made during the term may be commuted into a single payment; or

(d) the terms and conditions thereof, as they read on December 1, 1982 and at all subsequent times, provide that the holder participates in the investment earnings of the issuer and that the amount of such participation is to be paid within 60 days after the end of the year in respect of which it is determined.

(3) For the purposes of this section, the annuitant under an annuity contract is deemed to be the holder of the contract where

(a) the contract is held by another person in trust for the annuitant; or

(b) the contract was acquired by the annuitant under a group term life insurance policy under which life insurance was effected on the life of another person in respect of, in the course of, or by virtue of the office or employment or former office or employment of that other person.

(4) In this section, "annuitant" under an annuity contract, at any time, means a person who, at that time, is entitled to receive annuity payments under the contract.

(5) For the purpose of this section, "spouse" and "former spouse" of a particular individual include another individual who is a party to a void or voidable marriage with the particular individual.

History

Subcl. 304(1)(c)(iv)(B)(II) and cls. 304(1)(c)(iv)(C) to (E) amended by 2013, c. 34, subsecs. 378(1), (2), applicable to 2000 *et seq*., except that with regard to a contract held by a trust created by a taxpayer at a particular time in 2000 for the benefit of another individual, subcls. 304(1)(c)(iv)(B)(II) and (C)(II) are to be read without reference to "or common-law partner", unless, because of an election made under section 144 of the *Modernization of Benefits and Obligations Act* (S.C. 2000, c. 12), ss. 130 to 142 of that Act apply at the particular time to the taxpayer and the other individual.

Para. 304(1)(a) amended by 2012, c. 31, s. 60, to substitute "(b.3)" for "(b.2)", in force December 14, 2012 (proclamation of S.C. 2012, c. 16, the *Pooled Registered Pension Plans Act*, P.C. 2012-1743).

Opening words of subsec. 304(1) amended by P.C. 2011-936, s. 8, September 22, 2011, *Canada Gazette*, Part II, October 12, 2011, applicable after February 18, 2011, except that the replacement of the references to subsecs. 12.2(1), (3) and (4) with the reference to subsec. 12.2(1) that results from the amendment applies to life insurance policies last acquired after 1989.

Subpara. 304(1)(c)(ii) amended by P.C. 2009-1212, s. 1, July 30, 2009, Canada Gazette, Part II, August 19, 2009, applicable after February 22, 1994. It formerly read:

> (ii) issued by a corporation described in any of paragraphs 39(5)(b) to (d) or clause 146(1)(j)(ii)(B) [146(1)"retirement savings plan"(b)(ii)] of the Act, a life insurance corporation, a registered charity or a corporation (other than a mutual fund corpora-

tion or a mortgage investment corporation) the principal business of which is the making of loans (which corporation or charity is in this section referred to as an "issuer"),

Para. 304(1)(a) amended by 2009, c. 2, s. 90, applicable to annuity contracts issued after 2008.

Cl. 304(1)(c)(iii)(A), subcl. (c)(iv)(B)(I) and subsec. 304(4) amended and subsec. 304(5) added by P.C. 2007-849, s. 1, May 31, 2007, *Canada Gazette*, Part II, June 13, 2007, in force June 13, 2007.

Cl. 304(1)(c)(iii)(A), subcl. (c)(iv)(B)(I) and (II), (iv)(C)(II) and (III), cl. (iv)(D), and the definition "spouse" in subsec. 304(4), amended by P.C. 2001-957, s. 3, May 31, 2001, *Canada Gazette*, Part II, June 20, 2001, applicable to 2001 *et seq.*, except that if a taxpayer and a person have jointly elected pursuant to s. 144 of the *Modernization of Benefits and Obligations Act* (S.C. 2000, c. 12), in respect of the 1998, 1999 or 2000 taxation year, the amendment applies to the taxpayer and the person in respect of the applicable taxation year *et seq.*

That portion of subsec. 304(1) preceding para. (a) replaced by P.C. 1994-940, s. 1, June 2, 1994, *Canada Gazette*, Part II, June 15, 1994, applicable after 1989.

Subsec. 304(1), paras. 304(2)(a) and (c) substituted, subsecs. 304(3) and (4) added, by P.C. 1988-1115, s. 1, June 9, 1988, *Canada Gazette*, Part II, June 22, 1988, applicable to taxation years commencing after 1986.

That portion of subsec. 304(1) preceding para. (a) substituted by P.C. 1988-390, s. 2, March 3, 1988, *Canada Gazette*, Part II, March 16, 1988, effective January 1, 1983.

That portion of subsec. 304(1) preceding para. (a) substituted by P.C. 1986-1048, s. 1, May 1, 1986, *Canada Gazette*, Part II, May 14, 1986, applicable to taxation years commencing after 1982.

S. 304 substituted by P.C. 1983-3530, s. 5, November 17, 1983, *Canada Gazette*, Part II, November 24, 1983, applicable to taxation years commencing after 1982.

S. 304 added by P.C. 1982-1421, s. 3, May 13, 1982, *Canada Gazette*, Part II, May 26, 1982; subsecs. 304(1)–(4) effective with respect to annuity contracts under which annuity payments commence after 1981; subsec. 304(5) applicable to taxation years commencing after October 28, 1980.

305. [Repealed]

History

S. 305 repealed by P.C. 2011-936, s. 9, September 22, 2011, *Canada Gazette*, Part II, October 12, 2011, applicable with respect to annuity contracts and life insurance policies last acquired after 1989.

S. 305 added by P.C. 1983-3530, s. 5, November 17, 1983, *Canada Gazette*, Part II, November 24, 1983, applicable to taxation years commencing after 1982.

306. Exempt policies — **(1)** For the purposes of this Part and subsection 12.2(11) of the Act, "exempt policy" at any time means a life insurance policy (other than an annuity contract, LIA policy or a deposit administration fund policy) in respect of which the following conditions are met at that time:

(a) if that time is a policy anniversary of the policy, the accumulating fund of the policy at that time (determined without regard to any policy loan) does not exceed the total of the accumulating funds at that time of the exemption test policies issued at or before that time in respect of the policy;

(b) assuming that the terms and conditions of the policy do not change from those in effect on the last policy anniversary of the policy at or before that time and, where necessary, making reasonable assumptions about all other factors (including, in the case of a participating life insurance policy within the meaning assigned by subsection 138(12) of the Act, the assumption that the amounts of dividends paid will be as shown in the dividend scale), it is reasonable to expect that the condition in paragraph (a) will be met on each policy anniversary of the policy on which the policy could remain in force after that time and before the date determined under subparagraph (3)(d)(ii) with respect to the exemption test policies issued in respect of the policy;

(c) the condition in paragraph (a) was met on all policy anniversaries of the policy before that time; and

(d) the condition in paragraph (b) was met at all times on and after the first policy anniversary of the policy and before that time.

(2) For the purposes of subsection (1), a life insurance policy that is an exempt policy on its first policy anniversary shall be deemed to have been an exempt policy from the time of its issue until that anniversary.

(3) For the purposes of this section and section 307, a separate exemption test policy shall be deemed to have been issued to a policyholder in respect of a life insurance policy

(a) on the date of issue of the life insurance policy, and

(b) on each policy anniversary of the life insurance policy where the amount of the benefit on death thereunder exceeds 108 per cent of the amount of the benefit on death thereunder on the later of the date of its issue and the date of its preceding anniversary, if any,

and, for the purpose of determining whether the accumulating fund of the life insurance policy on any particular policy anniversary meets the condition in paragraph (1)(a), each such exemption test policy shall be deemed

(c) to have a benefit on death that is uniform throughout the term of the exemption test policy and equal to

(i) where the exemption test policy is the first such policy issued in respect of the life insurance policy, the amount on that policy anniversary of the benefit on death of the life insurance policy less the total of all amounts each of which is the amount on that policy anniversary of the benefit on death of another exemption test policy issued on or before that policy anniversary in respect of the life insurance policy, and

(ii) in any other case, the amount by which the benefit on death of the life insurance policy on the date the exemption test policy was issued exceeds 108 per cent of the amount of the benefit on death of the life insurance policy on the later of the date of issue of the life insurance policy and the date of its preceding policy anniversary, if any;

(d) to pay the amount of its benefit on death on the earlier of

(i) the date of death of the person whose life is insured under the life insurance policy, and

(ii) the later of

(A) ten years after the date of issue of the life insurance policy, and

(B) the date that the person whose life is insured would, if he survived, attain the age of 85 years; and

(e) to be a life insurance policy in Canada issued by a life insurer that carried on its life insurance business in Canada.

(4) Notwithstanding subsections (1) to (3),

(a) where at any particular time the amount of the benefit on death of a life insurance policy is reduced, an amount equal to such reduction (such amount is in this paragraph referred to as "the reduction") shall be applied at that time to reduce the amount of the benefit on death of exemption test policies issued before that time in respect of the life insurance policy (other than the exemption test policy issued in respect thereof pursuant to paragraph (3)(a)), in the order in which the dates of their issuance are proximate to the particular time, by an amount equal to the lesser of

(i) the portion, if any, of the reduction not applied to reduce the benefit on death of one or more other such exemption test policies, and

(ii) the amount, immediately before that time, of the benefit on death of the relevant exemption test policy;

(b) where on the tenth or on any subsequent policy anniversary of a life insurance policy, the accumulating fund thereof (computed without regard to any policy loan then outstanding in respect of the policy) exceeds 250 per cent of the accumulating fund thereof on its third preceding policy anniversary (computed without regard to any policy loan then outstanding in respect of the policy), each exemption test policy deemed by subsection (3) to have been issued before that time in respect of the life insurance policy shall be deemed to have been issued on the later of the date of that third preceding policy anniversary and the date on which it was deemed by subsection (3) to have been issued; and

(c) where at one or more times after December 1, 1982

(i) a prescribed premium has been paid by a taxpayer in respect of an interest in a life insurance policy (other than an annuity contract or a deposit administration fund policy) last acquired on or before that date, or

(ii) an interest in a life insurance policy (other than an annuity contract or a deposit administration fund policy) issued on or before that date has been acquired by a taxpayer from the person who held the interest continuously since that date,

the policy shall be deemed to have been an exempt policy from the date of its issue until the earliest of those times that occurred after December 1, 1982; and

(d) a life insurance policy that ceases to be an exempt policy (other than by reason of its conversion into an annuity contract) on a policy anniversary shall be deemed to be an exempt policy on that anniversary

(i) if, had that anniversary occurred 60 days after the date on which it did in fact occur, the policy would have been an exempt policy on that later date, or

(ii) if the person whose life is insured under the policy dies on that anniversary or within 60 days thereafter.

History

S.C. 2013, c. 40, s. 97, will amend the opening words of subsec. 306(1) to read as above, applicable to taxation years that end after March 20, 2013.

Subsecs. 306(1), (2) and (3) replaced by P.C. 1994-940, s. 2, June 2, 1994, *Canada Gazette*, Part II, June 15, 1994, applicable

(a) with respect to a life insurance policy issued after March 26, 1992, other than a policy for which written application was made on or before March 26, 1992; and

(b) with respect to a life insurance policy amended at any time after March 26, 1992 to increase the amount of the benefit on death.

S. 306 added by P.C. 1983-3530, s. 5, November 17, 1983, *Canada Gazette*, Part II, November 24, 1983, applicable to taxation years commencing after 1982.

307. Accumulating funds — **(1)** For the purposes of this Part and sections 12.2 and 148 of the Act, "accumulating fund", at any particular time, means,

(a) in respect of a taxpayer's interest in an annuity contract (other than a contract issued by a life insurer), the amount that is the greater of

(i) the amount, if any, by which the cash surrender value of his interest at that time exceeds the amount payable, if any, in respect of a loan outstanding at that time made under the contract in respect of the interest, and

(ii) the amount, if any, by which

(A) the present value at that time of future payments to be made out of the contract in respect of his interest

exceeds the aggregate of

(B) the present value at that time of future premiums to be paid under the contract in respect of his interest, and

(C) the amount payable, if any, in respect of a loan outstanding at that time, made under the contract in respect of his interest;

(b) in respect of a taxpayer's interest in a life insurance policy (other than an exemption test policy or an annuity contract to which paragraph (1)(a) applies), the product obtained when,

(i) where the policy is not a deposit administration fund policy and the particular time is immediately after the death of any person on whose life the life insurance policy is issued or effected, the aggregate of the maximum amounts that could be determined by the life insurer immediately before the death in respect of the policy under paragraph 1401(1)(c) and subparagraph 1401(1)(d)(i) if the mortality rates used were adjusted to reflect the assumption that the death would occur at the time and in the manner that it did occur, and

(ii) in any other case, the maximum amount that could be determined at that particular time by the life insurer under paragraph 1401(1)(a), computed as though there were only one deposit administration fund policy, or under paragraph 1401(1)(c), as the case may be, in respect of the policy

is multiplied by

(iii) the taxpayer's proportionate interest in the policy,

assuming for the purposes of this paragraph that the life insurer carried on its life insurance business in Canada, its taxation year ended at the particular time and the policy was a life insurance policy in Canada; and

(c) in respect of an exemption test policy,

(i) where the policy was issued at least 20 years before the particular time, the amount that would be determined at that particular time by the life insurer under clause 1401(1)(c)(ii)(A) in respect of the policy if the insurer's taxation year ended at that particular time, and

(ii) in any other case, the product obtained when the amount that would be determined under subparagraph (i) in respect of the policy on its twentieth policy anniversary is multiplied by the quotient obtained when the number of years since the policy was issued is divided by 20.

(2) For the purposes of subsection (1), when computing the accumulating fund of an interest described in

(a) paragraph (1)(a), the amounts determined under clauses (1)(a)(ii)(A) and (B) shall be computed using,

(i) where an interest rate for a period used by the issuer when the contract was issued in determining the terms of the contract was less than any rate so used for a subsequent period, the single rate that would, if it applied for each period, have produced the same terms, and

(ii) in any other case, the rates used by the issuer when the contract was issued in determining the terms of the contract;

(b) paragraph (1)(b), where an interest rate used for a period by a life insurer in computing the relevant amounts in paragraph 1403(1)(a) or (b) is determined under paragraph 1403(1)(c), (d) or (e), as the case may be, and that rate is less than an interest rate so determined for a subsequent period, the single rate that could, if it applied for each period, have been used in determining the premiums for the policy shall be used; and

(c) paragraph (1)(c)

(i) the rates of interest and mortality used and the age of the person whose life is insured shall be the same as those used in computing the amounts described in paragraph 1403(1)(a) or (b) in respect of the life insurance policy in respect of which the exemption test policy was issued except that

(A) where the life insurance policy is one to which paragraph 1403(1)(e) applies and the amount determined under subparagraph 1401(1)(c)(i) in respect of that policy is greater than the amount determined under subparagraph 1401(1)(c)(ii) in respect thereof, the rates of interest and mortality used may be those used in computing the cash surrender values of that policy, and

(B) where an interest rate for a period otherwise determined under this subparagraph in respect of that interest is less than an interest rate so determined for a subsequent period, the single rate that could, if it applied for each period, have been used in determining the premiums for the life insurance policy shall be used, and

(ii) notwithstanding subparagraph (i),

(A) where the rates referred to in subparagraph (i) do not exist, the minimum guaranteed rates of interest used under the life insurance policy to determine cash surrender values and the rates of mortality under the *Commissioners 1958 Standard Ordinary Mortality Table*, as published in Volume X of the *Transactions of the Society of Actuaries*, relevant to the person whose life is insured under the life insurance policy shall be used, or

(B) where, in respect of the life insurance policy in respect of which the exemption test policy was issued, the period over which the amount determined under clause 1401(1)(c)(ii)(A) does not extend to the date determined under subparagraph 306(3)(d)(ii), the weighted arithmetic mean of the interest rates used to determine such amount shall be used for the period that is after that period and before that date.

(3) Notwithstanding paragraph (2)(c),

(a) in the case of a life insurance policy issued after April 30, 1985, no rate of interest used for the purpose of determining the accumulating fund in respect of an exemption test policy issued in respect thereof shall be less than 4 per cent per annum; and

(b) in the case of a life insurance policy issued before May 1, 1985, no rate of interest used for the purpose of determining the accumulating fund in respect of an exemption test policy issued in respect thereof shall be less than 3 per cent per annum.

(4) For the purposes of paragraph (1)(c),

(a) where on the date of issue of an exemption test policy the person whose life is insured has attained the age of 75 years, the references in paragraph (1)(c) to "20" and "twentieth" shall be read as references to "10" and "tenth" respectively; and

(b) where on the date of issue of an exemption test policy the person whose life is insured has attained the age of 66 years but not the age of 75 years, the references in paragraph (1)(c) to "20" and "twentieth" shall be read as references to

(i) the number obtained when the number of years by which the age of the person whose life is insured exceeds 65 years is subtracted from 20, and

(ii) the adjectival form of the number obtained by performing the computation described in subparagraph (i),

respectively.

(5) In this section, any amount determined by reference to section 1401 shall be determined

(a) without regard to section 1402;

(b) as if each reference to "policy loan" in section 1401 were read as a reference to "policy loan, as defined in subsection 148(9) of the Act,"; and

(c) as if clauses 1401(1)(c)(i)(B) and 1401(1)(c)(ii)(C) were read without reference to the expression "or the interest thereon that has accrued to the insurer at the end of the year".

History

Opening words of subsec. 307(1) amended by P.C. 2011-936, subsec. 10(1), September 22, 2011, *Canada Gazette*, Part II, October 12, 2011, applicable with respect to annuity contracts and life insurance policies last acquired after 1989.

Para. 307(5)(b) amended by the said P.C. 2011-936, subsec. 10(3), applicable after February 1994.

Cl. 307(2)(c)(ii)(B) amended (to correct an incorrect reference) by P.C. 1991-769, s. 1, April 25, 1991, *Canada Gazette*, Part II, May 8, 1991, applicable to taxation years commencing after 1982.

Para. 307(5)(c) added by P.C. 1984-3789, s. 2, November 29, 1984, *Canada Gazette*, Part II, December 12, 1984, applicable to taxation years commencing after 1982.

S. 307 added by P.C. 1983-3530, s. 5, November 17, 1983, *Canada Gazette*, Part II, November 24, 1983, applicable to taxation years commencing after 1982.

308. Net cost of pure insurance and mortality gains and losses — **(1)** For the purposes of subparagraph 20(1)(e.2)(ii) and paragraph (a) of the description of L in the definition "adjusted cost basis" in subsection 148(9) of the Act, the net cost of pure insurance for a year in respect of a taxpayer's interest in a life insurance policy is the product obtained when the probability, computed on the basis of the rates of mortality under the 1969-75 mortality tables of the Canadian Institute of Actuaries published in Volume XVI of the Proceedings of the Canadian Institute of Actuaries or on the basis described in subsection (1.1), that a person who has the same relevant characteristics as the person whose life is insured will die in the year is multiplied by the amount by which

(a) the benefit on death in respect of the taxpayer's interest at the end of the year

exceeds

(b) the accumulating fund (determined without regard to any policy loan outstanding) in respect of the taxpayer's interest in the policy at the end of the year or the cash surrender value of such interest at the end of the year, depending on the method regularly followed by the life insurer in computing net cost of pure insurance.

(1.1) Where premiums for a particular class of life insurance policy offered by a life insurer do not depend directly on smoking or sex classification, the probability referred to in subsection (1) may be determined using rates of mortality otherwise determined provided that for each age for such class of life insurance policy, the expected value of the aggregate net cost of pure insurance, calculated using such rates of mortality, is equal to the expected value of the aggregate net cost of pure insurance, calculated using the rates of mortality under the 1969-75 mortality tables of the Canadian Institute of Actuaries published in Volume XVI of the Proceedings of the Canadian Institute of Actuaries.

(2) Subject to subsection (4), for the purposes of this section and of the description of G in the definition "adjusted cost basis" in subsection 148(9) of the Act, a "mortality gain" immediately before the end of any calendar year after 1982 in respect of a taxpayer's interest in a life annuity contract means such reasonable amount in respect of the taxpayer's interest in the life annuity contract at that time that the life insurer determines to be the increase to the accumulating fund in respect of the interest that occurred during that year as a consequence of the survival to the end of the year of one or more of the annuitants under the life annuity contract.

(3) Subject to subsection (4), for the purposes of this section and of paragraph (c) of the description of L in the definition "adjusted cost basis" in subsection 148(9) of the Act, a "mortality loss" immediately before a particular time after 1982 in respect of an interest in a life annuity contract disposed of immediately after that particular time as a consequence of the death of an annuitant under the life annuity contract means such reasonable amount that the life insurer determines to be the decrease, as a consequence of the death, in the accumulating fund in respect of the interest assuming that, in determining such decrease, the accumulating fund immediately after the death is determined in the manner described in subparagraph 307(1)(b)(i).

(4) In determining an amount for a year in respect of an interest in a life annuity contract under subsection (2) or (3), the expected value of the mortality gains in respect of the interest for the year shall be equal to the expected value of the mortality losses in respect of the interest for the year and the mortality rates for the year used in computing those expected values shall be those that would be relevant to the interest and that are specified under such of paragraphs 1403(1)(c), (d) and (e) as are applicable.

History

Subsecs. 308(2) and (3) amended by P.C. 2011-936, subsec. 11(1), September 22, 2011, *Canada Gazette*, Part II, October 12, 2011, applicable after February 1994.

That portion of subsec. 308(1) before para. (a) replaced by P.C. 1994-940, s. 3, June 2, 1994, *Canada Gazette*, Part II, June 15, 1994, applicable to years ending after 1989, except that for taxation years that ended before December 1991, the reference in subsec. 308(1) to "subparagraph 20(1)(e.2)(ii) and paragraph (a) of the description of L in the definition "adjusted cost basis" in subsection 148(9)" shall be read as "subparagraphs 20(1)(e.2)(ii) and 148(9)(a)(ix)".

That portion of subsec. 308(1) preceding para. (a) substituted and subsec. (1.1) added by P.C. 1991-769, subsecs. 2(1), (2), April 25, 1991, *Canada Gazette*, Part II, May 8, 1991, applicable to 1986 *et seq.*

S. 308 added by P.C. 1983-3530, s. 5, November 17, 1983, *Canada Gazette*, Part II, November 24, 1983, applicable to taxation years commencing May 31, 1985. S.C. 1984, c. 1, subsec. 82(4) provides that s. 308 is deemed to have been validly made on November 17, 1983, with effect as indicated above as if para. 148(9)(a) of the *Income Tax Act* as amended by 1984, c. 1, had been in force on that date.

309. Prescribed premiums and prescribed increases — **(1)** For the purposes of this section and section 306, and of subsection 89(2) of the Act, a premium at any time under a life insurance policy is a "prescribed premium" if the total amount of one or more premiums paid at that time under the policy exceeds the amount of premium that, under the policy, was scheduled to be paid at that time and that was fixed and determined on or before December 1, 1982, adjusted for such of the following transactions and events that have occurred after that date in respect of the policy:

(a) a change in underwriting class;

(b) a change in premium due to a change in frequency of premium payments within a year that does not alter the present value, at the beginning of the year, of the total premiums to be paid under the policy in the year;

(c) an addition or deletion of accidental death or guaranteed purchase option benefits or disability benefits that provide for annuity payments or waiver of premiums;

(d) a premium adjustment as a result of interest, mortality or expense considerations, or of a change in the benefit on death under the policy relating to an increase in the Consumer Price Index (as published by Statistics Canada under the authority of the *Statistics Act*) where such adjustment

(i) is made by the life insurer on a class basis pursuant to the policy's terms as they read on December 1, 1982, and

(ii) is not made as a result of the exercise of a conversion privilege under the policy;

(e) a change arising from the provision of an additional benefit on death under a participating life insurance policy, as defined in subsection 138(12) of the Act, as, on account or in lieu of payment of, or in satisfaction of

(i) policy dividends or other distributions of the life insurer's income from its participating life insurance business, or

(ii) interest earned on policy dividends that are held on deposit by the life insurer;

(f) redating lapsed policies, if the policy was reinstated not later than 60 days after the end of the calendar year in which the lapse occurred, or redating for policy loan indebtedness;

(g) a change in premium due to a correction of erroneous information contained in the application for the policy;

(h) payment of a premium after its due date, or payment of a premium no more than 30 days before its due date, as established on or before December 1, 1982; and

(i) the payment of interest described in paragraph (a) of the definition "premium" in subsection 148(9) of the Act.

(2) For the purposes of subsections 12.2(9) and 89(2) of the Act, a "prescribed increase" in a benefit on death under a life insurance policy has occurred at any time where the amount of the benefit on death under the policy at that time exceeds the amount of the benefit on death at that time under the policy that was fixed and determined on or before December 1, 1982, adjusted for such of the following transactions and events that have occurred after that date in respect of the policy:

(a) an increase resulting from a change described in paragraph (1)(e);

(b) a change as a result of interest, mortality or expense considerations, or an increase in the Consumer Price Index (as published by Statistics Canada under the authority of the *Statistics Act*) where such change is made by the life insurer on a class basis pursuant to the policy's terms as they read on December 1, 1982;

(c) an increase in consequence of the prepayment of premiums (other than prescribed premiums) under the policy where such increase does not exceed the aggregate of the premiums that would otherwise have been paid;

(d) an increase in respect of a policy for which

(i) the benefit on death was, at December 1, 1982, a specific mathematical function of the policy's cash surrender value or factors including the policy's cash surrender value, and

(ii) that function has not changed since that date,

unless any part of such increase is attributable to a prescribed premium paid in respect of a policy or to income earned on such a premium; and

(e) an increase that is granted by the life insurer on a class basis without consideration and not pursuant to any term of the contract.

(3) For the purposes of subsections (1) and (2), a life insurance policy that is issued as a result of the exercise of a renewal privilege provided under the terms of another policy as they read on December 1, 1982 shall be deemed to be a continuation of that other policy.

(4) For the purposes of subsection (2), a life insurance policy that is issued as a result of the exercise of a conversion privilege provided under the terms of another policy as they read on December 1, 1982 shall be deemed to be a continuation of that other policy except that any portion of the policy relating to the portion of the benefit on death, immediately before the conversion, that arose as a consequence of an event occurring after December 1, 1982 and described in paragraph (1)(e) shall be deemed to be a separate life insurance policy issued at the time of the conversion.

History

Subpara. 309(1)(e)(i) amended by 2013, c. 34, s. 379, applicable to taxation years that begin after October 31, 2011.

Opening words of subsec. 309(1) amended by P.C. 2011-936, subsec. 13(1), September 22, 2011, *Canada Gazette*, Part II, October 12, 2011, applicable with respect to life insurance policies last acquired after 1989.

Opening words of para. 309(1)(e) and paras. 309(1)(f) and (i) amended by the said P.C. 2011-936, subsecs. 13(2) to (4), applicable after February 1994.

S. 309 added by P.C. 1983-3530, s. 5, November 17, 1983, *Canada Gazette*, Part II, November 24, 1983, applicable to taxation years commencing after 1982.

310. Interpretation — The following definitions apply for the purposes of this section and sections 300, 301 and 304 to 309.

"amount payable" has the same meaning as in subsection 138(12) of the Act.

"benefit on death" does not include policy dividends, or any interest on a policy dividend, held on deposit by an insurer or any additional amount payable as a result of accidental death.

"cash surrender value" has the same meaning as in subsection 148(9) of the Act.

"policy anniversary" includes, in the case of a life insurance policy that is in existence throughout a calendar year and that would not otherwise have a policy anniversary for the calendar year, the end of the calendar year.

"policy loan" has the same meaning as in subsection 148(9) of the Act.

"proceeds of the disposition" has the same meaning as in subsection 148(9) of the Act.

"tax anniversary date" in relation to an annuity contract, means the second anniversary date of the contract to occur after October 22, 1968.

History

S. 310 amended by P.C. 2011-936, s. 14, September 22, 2011, Canada Gazette, Part II, October 12, 2011, applicable after February 1994.

S. 310 added by 1983-3530, s. 5, November 17, 1983, *Canada Gazette*, Part II, November 24, 1983, applicable to taxation years commencing after 1982.

Index

I

K

S